PENGUIN BOOKS

RENAISSANCE DRAMATISTS
GENERAL EDITOR: JOHN PITCHER

BEN JONSON
VOLPONE AND OTHER PLAYS

*The Renaissance Dramatists series is designed to produce a scrupulously pr...
text, with a minimum of interference, in an attempt to preserve the integrity o,
original editions. Therefore the texts of these plays follow the original spellings,
reproduce the punctuation of the early editions and manuscripts and are accompanied
by extensive explicatory Notes. Where appropriate, the volumes will also include
a Glossary and List of Historical and Mythological Names.*

BEN JONSON was born in 1572, the posthumous son of a minister, and
thanks to an unknown patron was educated at Westminster School. After
this he was for a brief time apprenticed to his stepfather as a bricklayer.
He served as a soldier in the Low Countries and married in 1594. In 1597
he was working for Henslowe's company as a player and playwright. It
was during the next two years that the groundbreaking comedies, *Every
Man in his Humour* and *Every Man out of his Humour*, were produced. These
were followed by *Cynthias Revels* (1600) and *Poetaster* (1601). Jonson's great
run of comedies consists of *Volpone, or the Foxe* (1606), *Epicoene, or the
Silent Woman* (1609), *The Alchemist* (1610) and *Bartholomew Fayre* (1614). In
addition to his comic writing Jonson also produced two powerful Roman
tragedies, *Sejanus, His Fall* (1603) and *Catiline, his Conspiracy* (1611). After
1616 Jonson abandoned the public theatre for a decade, concentrating
his efforts entirely on the court masque, a form of entertainment that
reached its highest elaboration in his hands, and his sporadic returns to
comic drama in the Caroline period met with less popular success than
his Jacobean masterpieces. In 1610 he was granted a royal pension and
made, in effect, Poet Laureate.

Jonson's life was colourful and full of incident. A quarrelsome, proud
man, he was often involved in public arguments with other writers and
sometimes used his poetry and plays to pursue these disputes. He was
twice imprisoned for his work as a ~~dramatist~~ ... mas; first for
The Isle of Dogs, a play now lost to us ... stward Ho*, when
he joined Marst... ... as a gesture of
solidarity. He also spent time incarce... ... actor in a duel
in 1598, an offen... ... pleading clerical

privilege. As far as religion was concerned he had his adventures too. While imprisoned in 1598 he converted to Roman Catholicism, despite being born to an Anglican clergyman, and then returned to his original faith twelve years later, an event he celebrated by drinking the entire chalice of communion wine. His later years were unhappy, though. Under Charles I he lost favour and was replaced as masque-writer after quarrelling with Inigo Jones, the masque-designer. He also suffered from paralysis and was unable to publish the second volume of his *Workes*. Ben Jonson died on 6 August 1637.

LORNA HUTSON is currently Reader in Renaissance Studies at Queen Mary and Westfield College, London. In September 1998 she leaves to take up a Chair in English Literature at the University of Hull. She is the author of *Thomas Nashe in Context* (1989) and *The Usurer's Daughter* (1994), as well as various articles on Renaissance literature and culture.

RICHARD ROWLAND is Lecturer in English at Jesus College, Oxford. He has edited Marlowe's *Edward II* for the New Oxford Complete Works and *A New Way to Pay Old Debts and Other Plays* by Philip Massinger for the Renaissance Dramatists series.

JOHN PITCHER is Vice President of St John's College, Oxford, and visiting Research Professor at the University of Ulster at Coleraine.

BEN JONSON
Volpone and Other Plays

Edited with an Introduction and Notes by
LORNA HUTSON

Texts prepared by RICHARD ROWLAND

PENGUIN BOOKS

PENGUIN BOOKS

Published by the Penguin Group
Penguin Books Ltd, 27 Wrights Lane, London w8 5tz, England
Penguin Putnam Inc., 375 Hudson Street, New York, New York 10014, USA
Penguin Books Australia Ltd, Ringwood, Victoria, Australia
Penguin Books Canada Ltd, 10 Alcorn Avenue, Toronto, Ontario, Canada m4v 3b2
Penguin Books (NZ) Ltd, 182–190 Wairau Road, Auckland 10, New Zealand

Penguin Books Ltd, Registered Offices: Harmondsworth, Middlesex, England

This edition first published 1998
1 3 5 7 9 10 8 6 4 2

Set in 9.5/12 pt PostScript Monotype Garamond
Typeset by Rowland Phototypesetting Ltd, Bury St Edmunds, Suffolk
Printed in England by Clays Ltd, St Ives plc

CONTENTS

SERIES STATEMENT

All editions are compromises, especially perhaps editions of drama. Dramatic speeches in verse or prose, entrances and exits of characters, stage directions, scene divisions, are communicated to us in manuscripts, typescripts and printed books. From these we receive a whole range of impressions: what the dramatist hoped to achieve, how his or her play was performed, last year or four centuries ago, and how a director and actors might present it to us again. The text of a play is a record, a memory, sometimes even a monument to what has been written and played, and adapted by actors, but it is also the ground from which that play may return to the special life of the theatre, where written or typeset words become speech, and where the book, with its conventions of silent reading, gives way to the space and sounds of the auditorium, and the spectacle of performance.

Editors of drama in English have to choose the best way of passing on play texts to modern readers, who may also be actors and audiences. One choice is to modernize or normalize the texts. With older plays (written before 1700), this involves changing the format as well as the spellings of the original texts, and the punctuation, capitals and italics, so that the words and sentences and phrases look modern. The intention is to reduce what is taken to be too difficult in these older texts for modern readers. This compromise is largely rejected in this series, as for the most part unnecessary, but also because it may impair what the past has to tell us. The punctuation and spelling we encounter in older play texts may of course come from compositors or scribes, rather than from the dramatist, but still their additions and idiosyncrasies bear the imprint of the past. Even where we judge them to be wrong in the way they printed or copied a text, a Renaissance compositor or a scribe is likely to be more interestingly and informatively wrong than a twentieth-century editor who changes the texts to make them easier for us.

For these reasons, the texts of the plays in this series reproduce, wherever possible, the spelling and punctuation of the first printed editions and manuscripts. Original readings are modified only where this is essential (type damaged during printing, turned letters, patently impossible punctuation), and there is a record of significant modifications of spelling and punctuation included in the Textual Notes at the back of each volume. Until the late seventeenth century, the modern distinctions between the letters *i* and *j*, and *u* and *v* were not observed in the printing house, and printers still used *vv* for *w*, a long *s* letter shape for our *s*, and so forth. All these forms are modernized in this series. Speech prefixes are expanded, regularized, and set in small capitals, and abbreviations are silently expanded, except those still in modern use, such as ampersands and *etc.* Where necessary, the act and scene divisions of the original texts are regularized and expanded, as are stage directions, entrances and exits, which are printed in italic, with the names of speaking parts in small capitals. Any words added to the original texts are enclosed within square brackets. Other changes, for example to the lineation of prose and verse, and to the divisions of the verse, are left to the discretion (and arguments) of the volume editors. Details of how specific plays have been edited are given in Textual Procedure. In all of this, the aim of the series is to produce a standard textual frame, within which there is a scrupulously prepared version of the text, minimally interfered with, but accompanied by adequate explicatory Notes, a Glossary and a List of Historical and Mythological Names.

John Pitcher

ACKNOWLEDGEMENTS

I would like to thank Erica Sheen, Alan Stewart, Blair Worden and my students doing the 'Text and Self' course in 1996–7 at Queen Mary and Westfield College. My bit in this book is for Nora, who once claimed that she always reads Penguin introductions.

LH

CHRONOLOGY

1572   Ben Jonson born (?11 June) posthumously. Remarriage of his mother to a master-bricklayer in Westminster.

1579   Began to attend Westminster School under William Camden.

c. 1588–94   Taken from school, and put to bricklaying. Left bricklaying (date unknown) to fight in the Low Countries. Returned to England.

1594   Married Anne Lewis.

1597   Playwright in the employ of Philip Henslowe. Imprisoned (August–October) for his part in *The Isle of Dogs*, written with Thomas Nashe. First performance of *The Case is Altered*.

1598   First performance of *Every Man in his Humour*, acted by the Lord Chamberlain's men at the Curtain in Shoreditch. Killed Gabriel Spencer in a duel in Hoxton, escaping the gallows by pleading benefit of clergy. While in prison, converted to Catholicism.

1599   Became member of Worshipful Company of Tilers and Bricklayers. Collaborated with Thomas Dekker on *Page of Plymouth* and *Robert, King of Scots* (both lost) for the Admiral's Men. *Every Man out of his Humour* acted by the Chamberlain's Men at the Globe in the winter, and at court about Christmas.

1600   *Cynthias Revels* performed by the Children of the Chapel Royal at Blackfriars.

1601   *Cynthias Revels* performed at court. *Poetaster* performed by Children of the Chapel. Paid £2 by Henslowe for additions to *The Spanish Tragedy*.

1602   Paid £10 for further additions to *The Spanish Tragedy*, and an advance for *Richard Crookback*.

1603   Death of eldest son, Benjamin, of plague. *A Particular Entertainment of the Queene and Prince . . . at Althorp* for James I on journey from Edinburgh. *Sejanus* performed by King's Men (or early 1604); Jonson called before the Privy Council to answer charges of popery and treason.

1604   *Part of the King's Entertainment in Passing to his Coronation. A Panegyre* on the King's opening of Parliament. *The Entertainment at Highgate.*

1605   *The Masque of Blacknesse. Every Man out of his Humour* and *Every Man in his Humour* revived at court by King's Men. *Eastward Ho* written with George Chapman and John Marston; acted at Blackfriars by Children of the Chapel. Chapman, Jonson and Marston imprisoned.

1606   *Hymenaei* presented for the marriage of the Countess of Essex. *Volpone, or the Foxe* acted by the King's Men at the Globe and later at Oxford and Cambridge. *The Entertainment of the Two Kings at . . . Theobalds.*

1607   *An Entertainment of King James and Queen Anne, at Theobalds.*

1608   *The Masque of Beautie. The Haddington Masque.*

1609   *The Masque of Queenes. The Key Keeper: An Entertainment at Britain's Burse. Epicoene, or the Silent Woman* acted by the Children of the Queen's Revels at the Whitefriars (or early 1610).

1610   *The Speeches at Prince Henries Barriers. The Alchemist* acted by the King's Men. James grants Jonson annual pension of 100 marks (1 mark = 13s. 14d.). Jonson reconverts to Anglicanism.

1611   *Oberon, The Faery Prince. Love Freed from Ignorance and Folly. Catiline* acted by the King's Men.

1612   *Love Restored.* Jonson travels to the Continent as tutor to Sir Walter Ralegh's son.

1613   *The Irish Masque at Court.*

1614   *A Challenge at Tilt* (for the marriage of the Earl of Somerset). *Bartholomew Fayre* acted by the Lady Elizabeth's Men at the Hope and at court.

1615   *The Golden Age Restor'd.*

1616   *Mercurie Vindicated.* Publication of *The Workes of Benjamin Jonson. The Divell is an Asse* acted by the King's Men at the Blackfriars. *Christmas his Masque.*

1617   *The Vision of Delight. Lovers Made Men.*

1618 *Pleasure Reconcil'd to Vertue. For the Honour of Wales.* Jonson travels to Edinburgh; converses with William Drummond of Hawthornden.

1619 Honorary MA at Oxford.

1620 *Newes from the New World. An Entertainment at the Blackfriars. Pans Anniversarie.*

1621 *The Gypsies Metamorphos'd.*

1622 *The Masque of Augures.*

1623 *The Alchemist* revived for court performance. *Time Vindicated.* Jonson's library destroyed in a fire.

1624 *Neptunes Triumph* (not performed). *The Masque of Owls. Volpone* revived by the King's Men at court.

1625 *The Fortunate Isles.*

1626 *The Staple of Newes* acted by the King's Men, first at the Blackfriars and then at court.

1628 Jonson suffers a stroke. Appointed City Chronologer. Interrogated over verses praising the Duke of Buckingham's assassin.

1629 *The New Inne* acted at the Blackfriars by the King's Men. Charles I increases Jonson's pension to £100.

1630 *Volpone* revived by the King's Men.

1631 *Loves Triumph through Callipolis. Chloridia. Every Man in his Humour* and *The Alchemist* revived by the King's Men at Blackfriars. Salary as City Chronologer withdrawn.

1632 *The Magnetic Lady* acted by the King's Men at Blackfriars, and possibly at court.

1633 *A Tale of a Tub* acted at the Cockpit by the Queen's Men. *The King's Entertainment at Welbeck.*

1634 *A Tale of a Tub* performed at Whitehall. *Loves Wel-come . . . at Bolsover.* Charles arranges resumption of salary as City Chronologer.

1637 Death of Jonson.

INTRODUCTION

Ben Jonson, for all our sense of his inevitability as a literary phenomenon, very nearly did not have a literary career at all. In his earliest youth it looked as though fate had selected for him a future in bricks and mortar. The death of his own father (a minister of the gospel) one month before his birth in 1572 was soon followed by his mother's second marriage to a master-bricklayer, who seems to have had no inclination to have a literate stepson. Only by the intervention of an unknown friend (sometimes said to be John Hoskyns, the author of the rhetorical treatise *Directions for Speech and Style*, *c.* 1599) did the boy Ben Jonson find himself at Westminster School, benefiting from a humanist grammar-school education under the tuition of the illustrious historian, William Camden. Here, in the course of following a basic liberal-arts curriculum designed to promote fluency in Latin composition by means of the analysis and imitation of classical authors, Jonson first made the acquaintance of the Roman comedies of Plautus and Terence, from which he learned those principles of dramatic construction which he would later adapt to create an innovative and profoundly influential dramatic form for the English stage. In the *Magnetic Lady* Jonson recalls, in the person of a front-of-house boy rebuking an ignorant and censorious dramatic critic, the time 'I learn'd *Terence*, i' the third form at *Westminster*',[1] going on to invoke the schoolboy terms of dramatic analysis that partly thanks to him still underlie modern expectations of dramatic verisimilitude. Jonson left Westminster before finishing his studies to be apprenticed (probably at the instigation of his stepfather) to the building trade. Finding it unbearable, however, he left and sought adventure in the Netherlands as a soldier before returning to London in the late 1590s to find employment as an actor and collaborator on playscripts for the theatre manager Philip Henslowe.

It has become traditional, in any introduction to the dramatic works of Ben Jonson, to invoke the contrast with Shakespeare in the terms established as early as the mid seventeenth century as an antithesis between the laboriously classical and imitative (Jonson) and the effortlessly 'native' and imaginative (Shakespeare). The contrast is invoked not exactly in order to refute it (that would be difficult; Jonson's classicism was ostentatious) but to lament its power to intimidate us and cause us to neglect to read Jonson, who, we are then assured, is theatrically exciting *in spite* of his dismaying erudition. The arguments produced to support this contention aren't always convincing, and it may even be that the terms of the traditional contrast – implying as they do an inherent incompatibility between literariness and theatre – themselves create the problem. In a study of imagery that was for many years a classic of Jonson criticism, E. B. Partridge argued that, for all its poetic qualities, drama is not ' "literature", not even when it is printed in magnificent folios, because it was not originally put down on paper in order to be read, and because, properly speaking, it can never be simply read'.[2] Many of us would, while avoiding the outright exclusion of drama from the category of literature, confess sympathy with Partridge's suspicion that 'literary' approaches to theatre are suspect, on the understandable grounds that plays are meant to be performed. But this kind of common sense actually creates an obstacle to the enjoyment and understanding of Ben Jonson. For his dramatic innovation – his virtual invention of the realistic temporality and precise physical location that we have come to associate with a long tradition of West End comedy, for example – must be considered inseparable from his attention to the literary 'technologies' – such as the rhetorical plotting of action, marked out by act and scene division – that bring into existence such innovative performance possibilities and the kinds of human experience they dramatize. Jonson, like Shakespeare, had learned such technologies partly from his *reading* of classical and neo-classical drama, and wanted to draw his own readers' attention to this fact. Unlike Shakespeare, however, he prepared his own plays for publication, most first in small quarto editions and then, in 1616, in a 'magnificent folio' entitled *The Workes of Benjamin Jonson*. The title itself was audacious in an age before copyright, when vernacular plays written for the public stage tended to be defined as the property of an acting company, rather than as 'works' in the poetic corpus of a single named author. What's more, far from suggesting that his drama was not put on paper in order to be read, Jonson frequently declared that the reader had a special access to understanding denied to the spectator. It would seem, then, less appropriate to gloss apologetically over the self-conscious literariness of Jonson's drama than to confront in it the heart of Jonson's concerns and the source of his theatrical originality and historical importance. This Penguin selection of Jonson's plays, by following the spelling, stage directions, and act and scene divisions of the folio, may help a new generation of readers to see how certain features of the physical presentation of the text are not to be ignored or apologized for as classicizing pedantry, but rather interpreted as fundamental to the extraordinary imaginative scope and sensitive emotional effects achievable by Jonson's plays in performance. The present selection of *Every Man in his Humour*, *Sejanus*, *Volpone* and *Epicoene* is representative of all that is most accomplished in Jonson's early dramatic work, and readers will accordingly find that the suggestions for further reading at the end of this introduction are more heavily weighted towards an understanding of the early years of Jonson's dramatic career.[3]

Recent shifts in the understanding of Renaissance culture in general, and of Ben Jonson's literary career in particular, have paved the way for a new appreciation of the place of his bookishness in the unique fantasy world of Jonsonian theatre. Sociologists, bibliographers and historians of the book have increasingly made literary critics aware of the way in which the physical form of a text (as a printed quarto or folio, a broadsheet, a manuscript copied for circulation, etc.) situates that text in a network of practical interests, political projects and social and familial relations. Nowadays, for example, when we think of Latin and Greek classics, we tend to imagine a venerable body of texts of historical and linguistic interest but largely irrelevant to the advance of science, technology or the arts in modern society. In the period in which Jonson came to greatness as a dramatist, however, the new editions and translations of classical texts that were pouring from printing houses all over Europe were evidently being commissioned and marketed for their *practical* relevance to everyday life. The advent of the printing press had transformed the potential of classical and modern texts – even poetry and drama – as resources in the transmission of information. Regular pagination, standardized editions, modern commentaries and the invention of the subject index all contributed to the capacity of the book as an object for the storage and retrieval of reliable knowledge, a focal point for critical discussion by different readers and a disseminator of new learning, fame and literary fashion. In terms of the cultural changes being wrought by the advent of print, it is not too much to speak of the period in which Jonson wrote as a time of revolution in information technology. Combined, the invention of printing and the related European revival of classical learning produced (among more illustrious historical consequences) the incidental effect of encouraging, among seventeenth-century English men (and even some women) a culture of bookish self-improvement, of manuals and handbooks making the techniques and topics arising from the study of classical literature relevant and informative on every practical subject, from farming to diplomatic intelligence-gathering, from courtly behaviour to innovation in military manoeuvres.

Evidence of Jonson's immersion in and fascination by this culture is everywhere in his writings. We find him, for example, pursuing a fashionable interest in the contemporary relevance of ancient warfare in his meticulous annotation of a book of Greek military tactics – 'dozens of Greek military terms are underlined and English equivalents given'[4] – while, in the chilling boudoir scene in his tragedy *Sejanus*, where a Roman matron plans the murder of her husband, Jonson footnotes realistic details on the weather hazards of Roman cosmetics with a reference to Martial, one of his favourite Latin poets. Nevertheless, routine critical dismissals of Jonson's dramatic art as the fruits of a laborious classical pedantry are beside the point, and not just because (as recent Royal Shakespeare Company productions at the Swan and the Pit have found) apparent linguistic redundancy turns out to be the resource of an extraordinary theatrical energy. They are irrelevant because they fail to recognize the focus of Jonson's dramatic imagination. In spite of repeated disavowals of dramatic interest in anything that wasn't strictly within the bounds of everyday possibility (he famously declared that, unlike Shakespeare, he was loth to fashion incredible monsters, 'to make Nature afraid in his *Playes*, like those that beget *Tales*, *Tempests* and such like Drolleries'),[5] Jonson consistently reveals a genius for finding monstrous dramatic images for the new forms of language and behaviour which he correctly perceived to be an index of the momentous historical changes being brought about by what Norbert Elias has called the 'civilizing process' affecting Europe in this period.[6]

As we become more and more aware of the ways in which technology modifies our habitual behaviour and our relationships, whether intimate or institutional (think of electronic mail or the telephone answering-machine), it becomes increasingly difficult to maintain, in a literary-critical context, the old familiar piety that the job of good literature is to present us with universal and transcendant images of human feeling. This is good for Jonson, whose reputation as a creator of dramatic character has suffered from the traditional critical preference for strong images of 'universal' passions, such as Othello's jealousy or Macbeth's ambition. By contrast with Shakespeare, Jonson's characters were traditionally said to be abstract, morality-play 'types' of virtue and vice, to lack inner being. In fact, Jonson has a complex sense of human psychology, but his interest as a dramatist lies more in the psychology of habitual behaviour than behaviour in the transitional moments of life crisis for which Shakespeare's plays are often metaphors. He is also interested in the way that human desires, anxieties and creative energies are affected by the material conditions of their communication. (Both of these interests obviously make for very good theatre, especially comedy.) Jonson is, moreover, quite exceptional in his ability to find metaphors for the historical modification, by the changing material conditions of social interaction, of what we understand to be 'human' and 'natural'. Take, for example, his image of himself as a poet and dramatist in a late play called *The Staple of Newes*. This opens with the description of the author himself, dead drunk and sweating furiously in the actors' dressing-room. '*He doth sit*', we are told, '*like an unbrac'd Drum with one of his heads beaten out: For, that you must note, a* Poet *hath two heads, as a Drum has, one for making, the other repeating, and his repeating head is all to pieces.*'[7] The poet-drum resonates in public through his '*repeating head*', a phrase which turns out to refer to the book of the play (Jonson has torn it up in a temper) without which the '*making*' head is like the loosened skin of '*an unbrac'd Drum*': redundant organic material.

Jonson's monstrous image of his authorial self as a two-headed drum, so far removed from post-Romantic ideas of poetic genius as an essence independent of the materiality of the book, is 'resonant' in more ways than one. For if Jonson's author is characterized by having a 'making' and a 'repeating' head, many of the characters of his plays appear to have only the latter, in the form of a dismaying compulsion to reproduce entire passages of memorized or transcribed reading. Whereas Shakespeare's characters speak eloquently in a literary language that appears to be natural to them, Jonson's tend to draw attention to the fact that, though we talk about 'self-expression', there is nothing natural about the self as expressed in language. People's fears and desires are, according to Jonson, shaped and articulated by phrases they have read or heard. At the end of *Every Man in his Humour*, the merchant Kitely seems to parody his own habitual posture of jealousy and suspicion by uttering a verse which he then admits, 'I ha' learned . . . out of a jealous mans part, in a play' (V.5.75) while, in *Volpone*, the deluded amateur spy, Sir Politique Would-bee, is forced to confess, with some embarrassment, that his study (headquarters of all his fantasized projects of international espionage) actually contains nothing more top-secret than 'notes,/ Drawne out of play-bookes' (V.4.41–2). Jonson's plays are full of the voices of self-conscious readers, men and women anxious to make their learning work for them in a social or political market-place where knowledge about books appears to be a commodity. As well as Sir Politique, *Volpone* features his hilariously incorrigible social-climber of a wife, the Lady Would-bee, who, during her bedside interview with the feignedly sick Volpone, succeeds in taking the latter's predictable gibe about the poet's declaring silence to be the female virtue as a handy excuse to elaborate on her knowledge of polite European letters:

> Which o' your Poets? PETRARCH? or TASSO? or DANTE?
> GUERRINI? ARIOSTO? ARETINE?
> CIECO *di Hadria*? I have read them all . . .
> DANTE is hard, and few can understand him.
> But, for a desperate wit, there's ARETINE!
> Onely, his pictures are a little obscene —
> You marke me not?   (III.4.79 – 81, 95 – 8)

Epicoene, or the Silent Woman likewise incidentally figures Sir John Daw, who prides himself on his literary talents, but declares a preference for *Corpus Juris civilis* (the textbooks of the civil law) above all other ancient and modern poets. He is humoured in his ignorance; 'Sure, *Corpus* was a *Dutch*-man', someone teases him (II.3.77).

'Reading', as Roger Chartier has reminded us, 'is not uniquely an abstract operation of the intellect: it brings the body into play, it is inscribed in a space and a relationship with oneself and others.'[8] While Jonson pokes fun at less able bibliophiles, the activity of reading can also assume the position of hero in his drama which, whether tragic or comic, offers a radical view of the human as that which is constituted by a capacity for imitation, especially literary imitation. Quintilian, one of Jonson's favourite authorities on the subject of reading, writing and speaking, advised that a persuasive and original style of speech could only be the result of a sustained programme of reading, in which 'we must be almost as thorough as if we were transcribing what we read'.[9] Thus, while the aspiration to climb the social ladder by the mechanical fulfilment of such injunctions is frequently mocked (in Sir Politique's notes from plays, or John Daw's familiarity with the spines of library books), the plays also celebrate a more complex conception of literate self-fashioning in which the productive management of one's own and others' passions is the effect of a sense of timing and judgement comparable to that attained by practice in the analysis of examples of literary composition.

Such a conception underlies Jonson's twist on the late 1590s fashion for 'humours' comedies – dramas of satiric social and linguistic observation – in his first acknowledged play, *Every Man in his Humour*. First played in 1598, the play ostensibly dramatizes a day in the city (originally Florence, then changed, in the 1616 folio, to London). Its remarkably achieved illusion of temporal realism tends, therefore, to be interpreted as part of a general concern to capture urban life in a realistic way:

> Virtually deprived of plot function, unity of time becomes in [Jonson's] hands a way of evoking, in detail, the life of a great, mercantile, Renaissance city as it moves through a typical day: from the early morning distribution of fresh water from the conduits, sordid awakenings in small lodging houses, the routine work in warehouses and offices, desultory talk in taverns and ordinaries, to supper and bed.[10]

The impression of plotlessness, however, might be better thought of as the dramatization of unrealized potential – the urban quotidian understood as a space and time replete, for those with the right kind of literary awareness, with the raw materials of comic (that is, fortunate or wealth-creating) plots. Ever since serious scholarly attention has been paid to this play, editors and critics have been exercised to account for the non-technical but nevertheless persistent undercurrent of allusion to the Galenic theory of the body as composed of four elemental 'humours', corresponding to forms of temperament (choleric, sanguine, phlegmatic and melancholic), a theory popularized in the early sixteenth century by Sir Thomas Elyot's *Castel of Health* (1539). Though the word 'humour' is evidently loosely applied, as Jonson elsewhere explains, 'By *Metaphore* . . . Vnto the generall disposition',[11] the play is full of comic moments (such as that when Cob, the water-bearer, declares that he has a 'rewme' instead of a 'humour' (III.4.13–15)) which remind us forcibly of the palpable, physical sense in which 'humour' means 'something liquid'. Such moments cumulatively build up a sense of the urban day as an entity in which time and space are realized with a precise, almost tactile, presence and inhabited by ordinary people whose emotions have an equally palpable existence as the 'humours' that flow from them verbally as they betray their day-to-day fears and aspirations. Thus, the play forges an analogy between the concept of 'humour' as the liquidly material manifestation of feeling in speech and action, and the productive connotations of other 'liquid' or negotiable assets in the prosperous city.

Jonson is good at small-time anxieties, the niggling money worries or fears of humiliation, that reduce us to moments of excruciating embarrassment or make us capable of astonishing feats of face-saving invention. Such moments are Cob's sudden hesitation over the idea that his apparently stylish lodger Bobadill can't actually pay the rent, or the marvellous scene in which Bobadill himself, waking up somewhat the worse for drink in an upstairs room in Cob's house, learns to his horror that he's in for an unexpected early morning visit from Matthew, an over-eager admirer and an aspirant poet. Hastily urging Cob's wife to take away the sick-bowl that lies next to him, Bobadill turns aside Matthew's barely concealed surprise at the sordidness of his idol's lodgings with characteristically romantic inventiveness: 'I confesse,' he declares in explanation, 'I love a cleanely and quiet privacy, above all the tumult, and roare of fortune' (I.5.43–4).

But the point here is that these moments of embarrassment or anxiety, revealed as they are in Cob's snatches of song and fragments of proverbs, or in Bobadill's pretentious play-book Senecanisms, are not merely exercises in socio-linguistic observation. To the astute, well-read listener, such utterances reveal passions that can be played upon rhetorically, just as a dramatist by his skilful use of language collaborates with and organizes the passions of the audience in producing a dramatic illusion. So while the action of *Every Man in his Humour* seems undirected – it consists in an invitation extended by the urbane Well-bred to his literature-loving friend, Edward Kno'well, to spend a day in the city, enjoying the pretentious vocabulary Bobadill and Matthew have picked up from fencing manuals, chivalric romances and play books – it actually presents the welter of social and sexual anxieties betrayed by the speech of London's wealthy citizens, would-be gallants and worried water-bearers as the 'humours' or *material resources* for Well-bred's and Kno'well's own casually undertaken comic plot, which forges an alliance between them by marriage.

Thus, Well-bred himself behaves like a dramatist, raising levels of anxiety by strategies of deferral (he delays Brayne-worme's return when he learns that old Kno'well is anxiously expecting him, saying 'Wee'le prorogue his expectation then, a little' (III.2.58)) and skill in the timely use of ambiguous language. Well-bred's recourse to an illustrative hypothesis on the subject of poison has the effect of convincing the jealous merchant Kitely that his wife has actually doctored his clothes and wine; 'will he be poyson'd with a *simile*?' asks Well-bred, innocently (IV.8.32). It is important, however, to see the social, economic and sexual anxieties experienced by these Londoners as part of a continuum: Cob's fears that Bobadill can't pay the rent lead directly to fantasies that the latter is sleeping with his wife, while Downe-right's scorn that Kitely should entrust the foundling Thomas Cash to keep his accounts reveals a traditional horror of bastardy and a double sexual standard that explains his later fury over the idea that his half-sister Bridget should associate with lascivious gallants. It's the same story for Kitely. Much has been made, by a modern and gender-blind tradition of literary criticism, of the absurdity of Kitely's sexual jealousy, as if it were a purely personal issue between himself and his wife. However, it is clear that the daily resort of fashionable gallants to Kitely's house to keep company with his wife and her sister Bridget ('Here sojourning a virgin in my house', II.1.111) would offer reason enough to any citizen householder to fear sexual scandal, with all its consequences of humiliation and loss of credit among other merchants. The sexual, and therefore economic, honour or 'credit' of a non-aristocratic household in this period depended on the chaste reputation of its women.[12] The special quality of Kitely's jealousy and the anxiety he confides to Downe-right about his house transformed into 'A *Theater* . . . a taverne, or a stewes' (II.1.60, 62), however, needs to be understood in the context of the play's larger concern with the way in which the traditional conceptions of honour were being transformed by the civilizing powers of print-culture, and by shared participation in such literary forms of entertainment as drama. Thus Downe-right, untouched by contemporary literary fashion, holds traditional views on sexual decorum and is simply outraged at the idea of Bridget's keeping company with young men. But it becomes increasingly clear that Kitely is only using the acceptable face of concern for Bridget as a cover for his own more sophisticated sexual fantasies about his wife ('Cob, which of them was't, that first kist my wife?/ (My sister, I should say)' III.6.31 – 2). It is, in fact, Kitely's familiarity with licentious Roman comedy – signalled by his fear that his trusty servant, Cash, might turn out to be like the servant in Terence's *Eunuch*, ready to welcome rapists into the house (see note to III.3.61) – that draws him into a desire to collude, like an accustomed theatre-goer, with the dramatic promise of those scenes of his own sexual disgrace that he both dreads, and longs to see. Jonson's somewhat unnerving but certainly innovative point in this comedy, then, is that the fears for sexual morality expressed by Kitely, Cob, old Kno'well, Downe-right and the others who belong to a generation or social class that associates contemporary poetry and theatre with sexual licentiousness, become the behaviour-dominating 'humours' which enable a more literate and relaxed generation – Well-bred and young Kno'well – to lead them by the nose.

Without initiating scandal, Well-bred makes strategic use of any that is to hand. His innuendo-laden references to Matthew's ability to do 'tricks' for the maiden Bridget (IV.2.81) precipitate an uproar in the Kitely household, which enables Well-bred to distract attention from his project for the marriage between Bridget and his best friend, Edward Kno'well. He improves upon the mounting chaos he has created by throwing out timely hints which excite the mutual jealousies of Kitely and his wife; in reply to Mistress Kitely's enquiry about her husband's repairing to Cob's house, he offers the entirely unjustified suggestion that Cob's house is a brothel. '[I]magine you what you thinke convenient' (IV.8.91) is his characteristically minimal, yet maximally disruptive exacerbation of her fears. So, while all the older generation scurry about, in the grip of fantasies of sexual jealousy fuelled by Well-bred's cool and detached manipulation of language, a marriage which will ally the wit of the younger Kno'well both with the wealthy Kitely household and with Well-bred himself, brews offstage.

The sexually licentious comedies of Rome and Renaissance Italy (by, for example, Plautus, Terence, Machiavelli, Ariosto) often featured parasites who owed no loyalty to a particular household and would, in return for a good meal, connive in the betrayal of a household's womenfolk to a young lover. Jonson's rewriting of the genre as a comedy of *humours* – that is, social fears and aspirations – replaces the figure of the parasite (symbolic of the scandalous leaking away of honour and wealth by the betrayal of the household) with the figure of Cob the water-bearer who productively enables the work of the city, channelling water from house to house as Well-bred channels people's anxieties, or as Kitely manages changing rates of currency on the Exchange. Metaphors of liquids and currencies abound: Kitely tells Downe-right to let his angry reprehension 'Runne in an easie current' (II.2.34) to be more effective; he names his own foster son 'Cash'; Matthew is ready to 'overflow you halfe a score, or a dozen of sonnets' (III.1.80) when he's feeling melancholy; Cash fears drowning in 'the violence of the streame' of Kitely's 'floud of passion' (III.3.142, 140); and Brayne-worme transforms a festive drink into an efficient instrument when Formall offers him 'a cup of neate grist' at the 'wind-mill' tavern (IV.6.71–2). In so far as romantic comedy endorses the myth of purity of blood, legitimizing clandestine alliances by the last-minute discovery of aristocratic parentage, Jonson's revision of such comedy in the direction of a demonstration of the potential unleashed by the civilized management of people's feelings has a socially radical sub-text. As Cob the water-bearer oxymoronically praises the noble 'fish, and bloud' of his ancestry (III.4.47), the play surreptitiously celebrates, in the final contrivance of the marriage of Bridget Well-bred and Edward Kno'well, the way in which ancient and unhelpful myths of lineal purity will be overcome by a positive sense of the contamination or confluence of commercial and poetic energies gradually transforming the social conduct and composition of Londoners.

Every Man in his Humour was thus Jonson's youthful defence of poetry; the quarto of 1601 concludes with Edward Kno'well's passionate praise of the poet's art which John Caird appropriately reinstated in the excellent RSC production of the 1616 text in Stratford in 1986. Between the success of *Every Man in his Humour* and the popular 'violence' that apparently greeted the performance of his first tragedy, *Sejanus*, in 1603, Jonson was engaged in the so-called 'War of the Theatres', actually part of a sustained attempt to dissociate himself from the conditions of professional dramatic production which demanded his collaboration with men whose work he did not entirely respect. One of the more remarkable texts to come out of this acrimonious exchange was Jonson's *Poetaster*, a play which anticipated *Sejanus* in its concern with a more sinister kind of *'repeating head'* than that which had been portrayed in Jonson's comedy of humours. This was the repeating head of Rumour, of incriminating scandal manufactured by the paid informer, or government spy, whose ability to detach the words of authors from their contexts and recirculate them as evidence of sedition was something Jonson knew and loathed from personal experience. In 1597 Jonson had, along with Thomas Nashe, been harassed by the government for his part in a 'very seditious and sclanderous' comedy called the *Isle of Dogs* (now lost),[13] after which Nashe fled London to write in dispraise of spies and in praise of red herrings, while Jonson languished under the questioning of two government informers whom he later immortalized as the most-unwanted-of-all-time party guests in *Epigrammes* 101, 'Inviting a friend to supper'.[14] Like the tragedy, *Sejanus*, Jonson's epigram hints at a resemblance between his own preferred mode of imitation – which detaches the words of classical authors from their contexts, recomposing them in a new text – and the reports of informers, which likewise endow another person's words with unintended meaning. *Sejanus*, a masterfully plotted tragedy scrutinizing the loss of political integrity in imperial Rome, forces its audience to contemplate, in the emperor Tiberius' skilful use of republican and Stoic language, and in Sejanus' manipulation of rumour, the demonic instrumentality of disembodied utterance. Often criticized for lacking a Shakespearean tragic hero, *Sejanus* is the more powerful for resisting the lure of such an ethopoetic centre. For whereas ethopoetic drama invites analysis in terms of the complexity of human individuals, Jonson's *Sejanus* rather dramatizes the complex workings of an inhuman political process; the thrilling and horrible efficiency with which words can be detached from their point of origin, and reiterated to bring about their original speaker's destruction. The uncanny vitality of quotation paralyses thought:

> our wordes,
> How innocent soever, are made crimes;
> We shall not shortly dare to tell our dreames,
> Or thinke, but 'twill be treason.   (I.67–70)

The mediation of other men's words, moreover, protects the mediator while forcing his interlocutors to incriminate themselves in acts of interpretation. Tiberius is a master of the composition of texts which displace responsibility for what they say upon readers and listeners. The terrorized and cowardly Senators expose their own abject lack of political integrity in attempting to discover, from the emperor's letters to them, which of his words offers an authentic expression of his intentions towards Sejanus:

> LACO He names him here without his titles . . .
>   No other, then SEJANUS.
> POMPONIUS   That's but haste
>   In him that writes. Here he gives large amends.
> MINUTIUS And with his owne hand written?   (IV.494–8)

In a play where much of the violent action takes place offstage and is learned about at second-hand, our very participation as an audience in the dynamics of theatrical experience becomes a process of eavesdropping, of interpretative complicity in the rumoured progression of horrors. We first *overhear* Sejanus' opponents – the Germanican party – covertly discussing the unlikelihood of the emperor's favourite having serious designs on the imperial title; immediately there follows an incident in which Sejanus suffers a blow on the face from Tiberius' son, Drusus, and we are transferred behind the scenes of Drusus' murder, to the dressing-table of his wife, who has become Sejanus' lover. Back in the company of the Germanicans, we hear them speak obliquely about their conjectures regarding recent events:

> Heare you the rumour? . . . What? . . . DRUSUS is dying . . . Dying?
> . . . That's strange! . . . what should bee his disease? . . . There was
> (late) a certaine blow/ Giv'n o' the face . . . I, to SEJANUS? . . .
> True . . . And, what of that? (II.479−88)

At the centre of this conversation, Silius, who dismisses these rumours as
'Toyes, meere toyes', nevertheless desires to know 'What wisdom's now
i'th' streets?' (II.491−2). He learns that the Senate has been unexpectedly
called. Drawn by the peculiar authority of rumour's anonymity, he walks
right into the trap set by Tiberius and Sejanus, which, in the form of his
trial for treason, unfolds with a meticulous avoidance of any but the most
neutral, procedural intervention on the part of the emperor. In the scene of
Silius' trial, Jonson returns us to the imaginative location of 'Inviting a friend
to supper'. It turns out that there were spies at the dinner table when Silius
made an unfortunate boast. 'This well agrees,' says Silius' accuser, 'with that
intemperate vaunt,/ Thou lately mad'st at AGRIPPINA's table . . . You were
he,/ That sav'd the empire' (III.272−3, 276−7). Jonson's *Sejanus* disturbs
our sense of our own autonomy by demonstrating the extent to which our
very intentions – the source, we might think, of our individuality– are defined
by the need to locate liability for meaning. Silius probably didn't intend
treason to Tiberius by his 'intemperate vaunt' – the intentions of drunken
words at the dinner table are notoriously confused – but his words fatally
acquire the effect of an intention when repeated back to him on trial. Jonson
lingers brilliantly over the cowardly violence of thus repeating back the
words of others, and over the way in which repetition defines rumour, and
lends it a special kind of political authority, in which no one guarantees the
truth of what is being said, yet the truth-effect increases with every feignedly
reluctant repetition:

> LATIARIS What sayes the *Consul*?
> COTTA (Speake it not againe,)
>   He tells me, that to day my lord SEJANUS —
> (TRIO I must entreat you COTTA, on your honour
>   Not to reveale it.
> COTTA On my life, sir.)
> LATIARIS Say.
> COTTA Is to receive the *tribuniciall* power.
>   But, as you are an honourable man,

> Let me conjure you, not to utter it ...
> MINUTIUS Lord LATIARIS, what's the newes?
> LATIARIS   I'le tell you,
> But you must sweare to keepe it secret ...   (V.406–17)

After the suicide of Silius in Act III, the accelerating violence of rumour, and of rumoured violence (we hear, almost immediately after witnessing another man's arrest, of his mangled body being thrown into the Tiber), is matched by the sense of a widening, beyond all endurance, of the inferential scope of official words, what the Germanican Arruntius calls the 'space/ Betweene the brest, and lips' (III.96–7). It is scarcely surprising that this play, which inflicts so little actual pain onstage, should be marked by such memorable expressions of violence in the desire to extract the rumoured intentions of men from precise spaces in their bodies: 'If I could gesse he had but such a thought,' says Arruntius of Sejanus,

> My sword should cleave him downe from head to heart,
> But I would finde it out: and with my hand
> I'ld hurle his panting braine about the ayre,
> In mites, as small as *atomi*, to'undoe
> The knotted bed —   (I.254–8)

If *Sejanus* has commonly been judged a failure for its lack of a central tragic figure, the eponymous hero of Jonson's dazzling satire on the English political idealization of Venice, *Volpone*, has never ceased to excite admiration and controversy. And yet a common approach to this play, focusing exclusively on the magnifico Volpone and treating the English tourists, Sir Politique and Lady Would-bee, as extraneous to the action, misleads as much as the approach which faults *Sejanus* for want of a hero. For just as the myriads of indistinguishable, whispering spies are crucial to *Sejanus'* dramatization of the violence of rumour, so, in *Volpone*, it is the bluffer's-guide Would-bees, with their bookish pretensions to intimacy with the pulse of Venetian society, who function as a satiric medium, an image of the usual English perspective on Venice as a civic ideal, the true republic. For Venice, centre of the trade in luxury goods between Europe and the Orient (the Turkey carpets, cloth of gold, velvets and damasks inventoried by Mosca being principal commodities in this commerce) was also known to the politically educated English as the most perfect modern example of the 'mixed' constitution that was supposed to have accounted for Rome's republican liberty and greatness. Gasparo Contarini's influential analysis of the Venetian constitution, translated in 1599, ascribed its greatness to its commercial freedom ('a common and general market to the whole world', he called it) and to the impartial and just execution of its laws by its *avocatori*. Whereas monarchies are subject to the mind of one man 'whom many times the inferior and brutish powers do perturbe',[15] Contarini argued, the Venetian state is subject only to laws, which are purely rational and impartial, like 'a mind without appetite, free from the infirmitie of any passion'. Inevitably enough, Contarini is an author on Sir Politique Would-bee's political reading list, and we are kept aware, throughout the play, of the way in which references to the Venetian 'state' merely bolster the illusion (after the wilfully deluded manner of the Would-bees) that there really is a wider public interest, a civilized 'commonwealth' of Venice, such as Contarini had tried to describe. 'You'have done a worthy service to the state, sir', says one of the *avocatori* to Voltore (IV.6.60), when he has, in fact, magnificently perverted the course of justice with the unwitting help of Lady Would-bee's incorrigible snobbery. As the play's action progresses, ramifying in ever more grotesque loops of deception from its centre in Volpone's luxurious bedroom, it mockingly empties out from the word 'state' any sense of a possible civic dimension to Venice, any sense of its possessing a 'common' as opposed to a private conception of 'wealth'. It is the Would-bees' perspective that constantly alerts us to this process. We watch, along with Sir Politique and his new acquaintance, Peregrine, when Volpone, dressed as Scoto of Mantua, is suddenly hounded away from the window of Corvino's house on the Piazza San Marco. Sir Politique's interpretation of the uproar – 'Some trick of state, beleeve it', he confides to Peregrine (II.3.10) – brings home to an audience just how claustrophobically, if also pervertedly, *domestic* is the focus of all this rare talent and energy expended by Volpone, who is, after all, a patrician of the Venetian state.

Contarini's confidence in the ideal rationality of the Venetian administration of justice, its freedom from ordinary passions and appetites, is acidly disposed of by Jonson in a late turning point in the action, when the *avocatori* begin to perceive the parasite Mosca – now disguised as Volpone's rich young heir – as a desirable kinsman, to be wooed accordingly – 'A proper man! and were VOLPONE dead,/ A fit match for my daughter', says one of them to himself (V.12.50–1). Yet the play expertly persuades us into a kind of pleasurable connoisseurship of these institutional and personal perversions, gradually bringing us, as it does, to be able to contemplate hitherto unimaginable extremes of greed (extremes which actually undo the logical dependence of the early-modern sense of wealth on familial ties, and family honour) as if they were perfectly natural and plausible. When the jealous merchant, Corvino, decides to volunteer to prostitute his beautiful young wife to Volpone in the hope of becoming the latter's heir, he speaks to his wife as if rationally casting his accounts:

> I' have told you reasons;
> What the physitians have set downe; how much,
> It may concerne me; what my engagements are;
> My meanes; and the necessitie of those meanes,
> For my recovery: wherefore, if you bee
> Loyall, and mine, be wonne, respect my venture.   (III.7.32–7)

When she reasonably objects that this 'venture' will actually sabotage his honour, which is inseparable from his wealth, he replies that no one will hear of it: 'as if I would goe tell it,/ Crie it, on the *piazza*! who shall know it?' he replies scornfully (III.7.48–9). Yet before the play is over he has done just that and worse; in all the publicity of a courtroom trial he bears witness on oath that his wife is 'a whore,/ Of most hot exercise', turning aside afterwards to seek reassurance of Mosca, 'There is no shame in this, now, is there?' he asks (IV.5.117–18, 127). Corvino's compulsion thus to accomplish the very aspect of sexual humiliation most dreadful to him (for, as John Creaser observes, Corvino's speech has already revealed to us a 'morbid fascination with public exposure' far outweighing his concern with 'infidelity itself'[16]) typifies the artistry with which the play as a whole imbues its most outrageous moments with an aesthetically satisfying emotional logic. The usual moral drawn from this, of course, is greed. The play is said to be a satire on avarice. However, it is possible, in view of Sir Politique's otherwise gratuitous satiric distortion of a whole contemporary literature of political analysis, that the play is saying something rather more urgent and complex. For the political literature here and elsewhere satirized by Jonson as being carried in the pockets of would-be statesmen (see *Epigrammes*, 92) was in fact contributing, in this very period, to a newly pragmatic conception of the relation between the human passions and the well-being of the political state, a conception which would (in the form of the science of 'statistics') eventually displace the idealistic civic humanism of Jonson's education with

a doctrine of support for free trade and capitalism, on the grounds that what
in an individual was a vice (avarice, social competitiveness), might become,
in aggregate, a virtue (national prosperity, civilized manners).[17] And Jonson
was, at this time, reading the writings of the great neo-Stoics, Justus Lipsius
and Michel de Montaigne, which sceptically undermined the civic humanism
of writers like Contarini. Volpone's preference for counter-intuitive forms
of gain that use 'no trade, no venter' (I.1.33) and his conception of pleasure
as a protracted anticipation of novel, witty and luxurious inversions of
customary roles and routine performances, make him a proleptically satirical
figure for our own equation of free state and free market.

A historian has suggested that Jonson's *Volpone, or the Foxe* refers obliquely
to Robert Cecil, the Earl of Salisbury and Lord Treasurer, who was frequently
linked, in popular libels, with fox imagery.[18] While this may or may not be
true, there can be no doubt that Jonson's last play in this collection, *Epicoene*,
derives its particular atmosphere of abrasive social competitiveness from
Cecil's latest investment in the gentry's passion for conspicuous consumption
– the opening of a luxury shopping centre in the Strand in London, known
as the New Exchange. While it has for some time been known that Jonson
wrote a masque for a Royal visit to open the New Exchange in April 1609,
the text of that masque has only recently been rediscovered. Its resonances
with the world of *Epicoene* – performed late in 1609 or early in 1610 – are
striking. A shopkeeper – a 'China man' – offers a fantastic array of luxury
oriental goods for sale, and then announces he is preparing for another visit
to China or Virginia for more commodities.[19] *Epicoene* itself seems to be a
reflexive dissection of the implications of developments in London of which
the New Exchange is symptomatic. The early years of James I saw the
beginnings of what came to be the London 'season', as more and more of
the gentry abandoned their country residences and travelled to London to
take up urban lodgings and enjoy the distractions and shopping opportunities
of the capital. The pressure on accommodation in the more fashionable
parts of London – particularly the Strand – was immense. Jonson captures
all of this in the irresistible portrait of Sir Amorous La-Foole, who, having
gone down to the country ('since it pleas'd my elder brother to die', I.4.54–5)
to take out more profitable leases on his land, has now returned to London,
where his conspicuous consumption is barely distinguishable from the leisure
industries it supports:

> He do' give playes, and suppers, and invites his guests to 'hem, aloud,
> out of his windore, as they ride by in coaches. He has a lodging in the
> *Strand* for the purpose. Or to watch when ladies are gone to the *China*
> houses, or to the *Exchange*, that hee may meet 'hem by chance, and
> give 'hem presents ... (I.3.32–7)

Jonson's genius for adapting classical texts to contemporary social concerns
is nowhere more in evidence than in *Epicoene*, where the play's central
character, Morose (whose name and character partly derive from a declamation by the Greek rhetorician Libanius, in which an unsociable man
complains of his talkative wife), is developed into a simultaneously sympath-
etic and repulsive figure of nervous reaction to the noise and congestion of
this new London. Cataloguing the street sounds that drive Morose to
double-line his walls and insulate his windows, and anticipating the invasion
of Morose's silent wedding by the fiddlers and trumpeters of the city ('they
have intelligence of all feasts. There's good correspondence betwixt them, and
the *London*-cookes', III.3.78–80), Jonson presciently invokes the emergent
service economy that would grow rapidly with the development of the
London season, and become a staple feature of Restoration comedy.

The action of *Epicoene*, which centres on the plot of Morose's nephew,
Dauphine, to confound his uncle's marriage plans by presenting him with
a desirably silent young woman (actually a boy in disguise) has recently
aroused the interest of critics concerned with the representation of gender
and sexuality in this period. It's clear, however, that in this comedy questions
of gender can't be separated from questions of urban social *mores*. The
identification, in sixteenth-century marriage literature, of woman's ideal
qualities as those of silence, chastity and staying quietly at home, are riven
apart in this play, where women are relentlessly and even grotesquely
associated with the new consumer culture. The play opens with an urban
gentleman, Clerimont, casually getting dressed, while discussing trivial matters – a song he has written for his mistress – with his page-boy. A visitor,
True-wit, observing this scene, remarks on what it says about Clerimont's
life-style: 'Why, here's the man that can melt away his time, and never feeles
it! what, betweene his mistris abroad, and his engle at home, high fare, soft
lodging, fine clothes ... hee thinkes the houres ha' no wings ...' (I.1.22–
5). Thereafter in the play women are always imagined as being 'abroad', like
the consumer goods and urban entertainments they pursue: 'gone to the
China houses, or to the *Exchange*'. Indeed, women become identified with

consumerism itself, as True-wit explains how the courtship of these creatures requires a man to take counsel of his *'french* taylor, barber, linnener, &c.' (IV.1.94–5), or as Mistress Otter is described as a compound of bespoke body-parts, available from shops in the West End: 'All her teeth were made i'the Blacke-*Friers*: both her eye-browes i'the *Strand*, and her haire in *Silver-street*' (IV.2.81–3). A good deal of critical energy has been expended on the question of whether Jonson's treatment of women in the play owes more to Ovid's witty instructions for urban courtship in the *Art of Love* or to Juvenal's excoriating sixth satire on modern Roman women. In fact, in Jonson's handling, the urbane Ovid and outraged Juvenal look much the same; Jonson's emphasis throughout falls on the sheer variety of wares, services and amusements – the cosmetics, the fashions, the salespeople, the instructions to servants, tailors and launderers regarding matters of dress – demanded by the London lady of fashion. Moreover, Ovidian courtship and Juvenalian revulsion seem always to be fused at any one moment in the play; it is impossible to tell, for example, whether Clerimont's song is meant to court 'his mistris abroad' (he complains that her door is shut against him) or to lampoon her (the boy says it will gain him 'ill will' at the lady's house, I.1.7). Indeed, the opening scene indicates that women may not be the primary objects of erotic interest, even while they are pretexts of wit. For, as well as deriving from Libanius' *Morose Man and his Talkative Wife*, the play *Epicoene* is much indebted to a teasing Italian comedy (1533) called *Il Marescalco* ('the stable master') by the satirist Pietro Aretino. In this comedy the homosexual stable master to an Italian Duke is tormented by the news that his master has procured a wife for him, only to be relieved to find, at last, that the bride is, in fact, his favourite page-boy, Carlo, dressed up. Aretino's play opens with a dialogue between the stable master and another boy, Giannicco, which is interrupted by an observer, who says, 'Sempre ti trovi in conclavi col tuo pivo' ('I'm always finding you closeted with your little boyfriend').[20] There's a trace of this exchange in the opening of Jonson's *Epicoene*, when True-wit's comment on Clerimont's lifestyle indicates that he is always 'closeted with his little boyfriend' (i.e. with 'his engle'). If women are identified with the noisy and gregarious world of the town – True-wit later tells Dauphine that in order to get a mistress he must 'leave to live i' your chamber' and 'come abroad' (IV.1.51, 53) – then 'engles at home', or sexually available page-boys, are perhaps a more comfortable alternative for the likes of Clerimont and Dauphine.

Whatever the implications to be drawn from this, we've clearly moved a long way from the social topography and social *mores* of the 1590s city life depicted in *Every Man in his Humour*. Moreover, as Emrys Jones remarks in relation to *Epicoene*, 'to think of Shakespeare in the midst of all these London matters is to be struck by how very far away he is from them'.[21] This volume of a selection of Jonson's early plays should demonstrate not what Jonson lacks by comparison with Shakespeare, but how unique is his achievement in finding such unforgettable dramatic images for the material, social and institutional transformations of the last decade of the sixteenth century, and the first decade of the seventeenth.

Notes

1 Induction to *Magnetic Lady*, 46–7, *Ben Jonson*, ed. C. H. Herford, Percy and Evelyn Simpson, 11 vols. (Oxford: Clarendon Press, 1925–52, VI.509 (hereafter *H&S*).

2 E. B. Partridge, *The Broken Compass: A Study of the Major Comedies of Ben Jonson* (New York: Columbia University Press, 1958), p. 9.

3 A second volume, offering a selection of the later plays in similar format, and including *The Alchemist, Bartholomew Fayre* and *The Divell is an Asse*, is planned.

4 David Macpherson, 'Ben Jonson's library and marginalia: an annotated catalogue', *Studies in Philology* 71 (1974), 23.

5 Induction, *Bartholomew Fayre*, *H&S*, VI.16.

6 See Norbert Elias, *The Civilizing Process*, tr. Edmund Jephcott, 2 vols. (New York: Pantheon Books, 1978).

7 Induction, *The Staple of Newes*, *H&S*, VI.281.

8 Roger Chartier, *The Order of Books*, tr. Lydia G. Cochrane (Stanford: Stanford University Press, 1994), p. 8.

9 Quintilian, *Institutio Oratoria*, tr. H. E. Butler, 4 vols. (London: Heinemann, 1929), IV.xi.20.

10 Anne Barton, *Ben Jonson, Dramatist* (Cambridge: Cambridge University Press, 1984), p. 46.

11 Induction, *Every Man out of his Humour*, 103–4, *H&S*, III.432.

12 Laura Gowing, *Domestic Dangers: Women, Words and Sex in Early Modern London* (Oxford: Clarendon Press, 1996), pp. 109, 94.

13 *Acts of the Privy Council*, XXXVII, 15 August 1597, p. 333.

14 *H&S*, VIII.64–5. See the excellent article by Joseph Loewenstein, 'The Jonsonian corpulence, or the poet as mouthpiece', *Journal of English Literary History* 53 (1986), 491–518.

15 Gasparo Contarini, *The Commonwealth and Government of Venice*, tr. Lewis Lewkenor (London, 1599), sig. B1v, sig. C2r–v.

16 John Creaser, introduction to Ben Jonson, *Volpone* (London: Hodder and Stoughton, 1978), p. 12.

17 See Albert O. Hirschman, *The Passions and the Interests: Political Arguments for Capitalism before its Triumph* (Princeton, N.J.: Princeton University Press, 1977); Peter Burke, 'Tacitism' in T. A. Dorey (ed.), *Tacitus* (London: Routledge and Kegan Paul, 1969), pp. 149–72; Richard Tuck, *Philosophy and Government 1572–1651* (Cambridge: Cambridge University Press, 1993), pp. 31–64.

18 Pauline Croft, 'The reputation of Robert Cecil: libels, political opinion and popular awareness in the early seventeenth century', *Transactions of the Royal Historical Society* 6 ser. (1991), 43–69.

19 James Knowles, 'Cecil's shopping centre: the rediscovery of a Ben Jonson masque in praise of trade', *The Times Literary Supplement*, 7 February 1997, pp. 14–15.

20 *Il Marescalco*, Act I, scene 2 in Pietro Aretino, *Tutte Le Commedie*, ed. G. B. De Sanctis (Milan: Mursia, 1973), p. 40 (my translation).

21 Emrys Jones, 'The first West End comedy', *Proceedings of the British Academy* 68 (1982), 252.

FURTHER READING

The standard scholarly edition of Jonson is still that edited by C. H. Herford, Percy and Evelyn Simpson, 11 vols. (Oxford: Clarendon Press, 1925–52).

Barish, Jonas A., *Ben Jonson and the Language of Prose Comedy* (Cambridge, Mass.: Harvard University Press, 1960)

Barton, Anne, *Ben Jonson, Dramatist* (Cambridge: Cambridge University Press, 1984)

Burt, Richard, *Licensed by Authority: Ben Jonson and the Discourses of Censorship* (Ithaca, N.Y.: Cornell University Press, 1993)

Dutton, Richard, *Ben Jonson: To the First Folio* (Cambridge: Cambridge University Press, 1983)

Haynes, Jonathan, *The Social Relations of Jonson's Theater* (Cambridge: Cambridge University Press, 1992)

Maus, Katherine, *Ben Jonson and the Roman Frame of Mind* (Princeton, N.J.: Princeton University Press, 1984)

Partridge, Edward B., *The Broken Compass: A Study of the Major Comedies of Ben Jonson* (New York: Columbia University Press, 1958; reprinted Westport, Conn.: Greenwood Press, 1976)

Riggs, David, *Ben Jonson: A Life* (Cambridge, Mass.: Harvard University Press, 1989)

Sackton, A. H., *Rhetoric as a Dramatic Language in Ben Jonson* (New York: Columbia University Press, 1948)

Watson, Robert N., *Ben Jonson's Parodic Strategy: Literary Imperialism in the Comedies* (Cambridge, Mass.: Harvard University Press, 1987)

Womack, Peter, *Rereading Ben Jonson* (Oxford: Basil Blackwell, 1986)

TEXTUAL PROCEDURE

Ben Jonson has a special place in the history of how plays in English have been published in Britain during the past four centuries. His folio edition of his *Workes*, published in 1616, was an enormous step forward in the physical appearance of English play texts on the printed page. Before this edition, the care Jonson took in designing the layout of each page, and the accuracy he sought in the texts, had been reserved for editions of ancient Greek and Roman dramatists. The 1616 edition was an ambitious, perhaps even an audacious, attempt to claim the attention of his contemporaries, but also the attention of posterity, the future readers of his plays. It is for this reason that the selection of plays in this volume have been based on the texts in the 1616 *Workes*.

The 1616 edition was not the first book Jonson had lavished care on. He had already published three of the plays in this volume in the smaller format of quarto editions – *Every Man in his Humour* in 1601, *Sejanus* in 1605 and *Volpone* in 1607 – and in each case he had carefully prepared the text and seen it through the press himself (which in itself was an unusual thing to do for someone writing for the popular stage). When he came to prepare the 1616 edition Jonson revised all of his plays extensively; he made countless changes to the punctuation and lexicon, but he also made major structural changes to individual plays. The punctuation in the 1607 quarto of *Volpone* was altered entirely (the pervasive dashes, used to indicate pauses in speech, were replaced by colons or semicolons), while the location of *Every Man in his Humour* was shifted from Italy to London, thus investing the 1616 text with a topographical specificity and a topicality quite absent from the 1601 quarto. In addition, the margins of the 1616 edition were embellished with stage directions; it seems certain that Jonson added such precise indications of stage business in response to his having seen his plays through rehearsal and performance. (On pp. xxxvi–xxxvii, xxxix, there are reproductions of pages from the 1607 quarto of *Volpone*, signatures N2v–N3r, and the page containing the same part of the play in the 1616 edition, p. 520: a comparison shows examples of revised punctuation, additional stage directions, and the way the 1616 text has a corrected number for the scene heading of Act V,

THE FOXE.

Corv. And credit nothing, the false spirit hath writ:
It cannot be (my *Sires*) but he is possest.

ACT.5.   SCENE.11.

Volpone. Nano. Androgyno.
Castrone.

TO make a snare, for mine owne neck! and run
My head into it, wilfully! with laughter!
When I had newly scap't, was free, and cleare!
Out of mere wantonnesse! ô, the dull Deuill
Was in this braine of mine, when I deuis'd it;
And *Mosca* gaue it second: He must now
Helpe to seare vp this veyne, or we bleed dead.
How now! who let you loose? whether go you, now?
What? to buy Ginger-bread? or to drowne Kitlings?
Nan. Sir, Maister *Mosca* call'd vs out of dores,
And bid vs all go play, and tooke the keyes. And. Yes.
Volp. Did Maister *Mosca* take the keyes? why, so!
I am farder, in. These are my fine conceipts!
I must be merry, with a mischiefe to me!
What a vile wretch was I, that could not beare
My fortune, soberly? I must ha' my *Crotchets*!
And my *Conundrums*! well, go you, and seeke him:
His meaning may be truer, then my seare.
Bid him he, streight, come to me, to the *Court*;
Thether will I; and, it 't be possible,
Vn-screw my Aduocate, vpon new hopes:
When I prouok'd him, then I lost my selfe.

ACT.5.   SCENE.10.

Avocatori, &c.

THese things can nère be reconcil'd. He, here,
Professeth, that the Gentleman was wrong'd;

And

And that the Gentlewóman was brought thether,
Forc'd by her husband: and there left. VOLT. Moſt trꝛe.
CEL. How ready is keau'n to thoſe, that pray. AVOC. 1. Bút,
    that
Volpone would haue rauiſh'd her, he holds
Vtterly falſe ; knowing his impotence.
CORV. Graue *Fathers*, he is poſſeſt ; againe, Iſay
Poſſeſt : nay, if there be *poſſeſſion*,
And *obſeſſion*, he has both. AVOC. 3. Here comes our Officer.
VOLP. The *Paraſite* will ſtreight be, here, graue *Fathers*.
AVOC. 4. You might inuent ſome other name, Sir varlet.
AVOC. 3. Did not the *Notarie* meet him ? VOLP. Not, that I
    know.
AVOC. 4. His comming will cleare all. AVOC. 2. Yet it is
    miſty.
VOLT. May't pleaſe your *Father-hoods*-- VOLP. Sir, the
    Paraſite
Will'd me to tell you, that his Maiſter liues ;
That you are ſtill the man ; your hopes the ſame ;
And this was, onely a ieſt-- VOLT. How ? VOLP. Sir, to
    trie
If you were firme, and how you ſtood affeeed.
VOLT. Art'ſure he liues ? VOLP. Do I liue, Sir ? VOLT. O
    me!
I was too violent. VOLP. Sir, you may redeeme it,
They ſaid, you were poſſeſt ; fall downe, and ſeeme ſo:
Ile helpe to make it good. God bleſſe the man !
Stop your wind hard, and ſwell: See, ſee, ſee, ſee !
He vomits crooked pinnes ! his eyes are ſet,
Like a dead hares, hung in a poulters ſhop !
His mouth's running away ! Do you ſee, Signior ?
Now, 'tis in his belly ! CORV. I, the Deuill !
VOLP. Now, in his throate. CORV. I, I perceiue it plaine.
VOLP. 'Twill out, 'twill out ; ſtand cleere. See, where it
    flyes !
In ſhape of a blew toad, with a battes wings !

Scene 12.) The meticulous care with which Jonson undertook all of these revisions, and his close supervision of the printing of the 1616 edition, has prompted the decision to use a single copy of the book (in the Bodleian Library, Oxford) as the base text for the plays in this volume.

The detail of the 1616 folio has been preserved wherever possible, in line with the general aims of the Penguin Dramatists series, to present the original spellings and punctuation of an early text to a modern readership. Stage directions, for example, often reveal a good deal about the way a dramatist conceives his stage business, and Jonson's highly unusual alignment and lineation of marginal directions have been located on the page in the present edition as closely as possible to the position they occupy in the 1616 edition. Jonson was also at pains to make the printed texts of his plays resemble typographically the sixteenth- and seventeenth-century editions of classical drama, so he heads each scene with a list of the characters who will participate in that scene, whether or not they are on stage as the scene opens; correspondingly, he scarcely ever indicates entrances or exits. The present edition aims to preserve the unusual typographical feature of this, the massed entry, but to assist the modern reader by adding entrances and exits in accordance with modern editorial convention. All additions are enclosed in square brackets

Jonson's idiosyncratic act and scene divisions are also retained, but his scene numbers have been altered from roman to arabic. Where he wished to indicate that a line should be spoken as an aside, or addressed to just one character among a group on stage, Jonson enclosed the line (and sometimes the speech prefix as well) in round brackets; these are similarly retained. One further singularity of Jonson as a writer of dramatic poetry is the extraordinary frequency with which he divides a single line of verse between two, three or even four speakers. In such instances the 1616 edition, wherever possible, prints all the speech prefixes and the verse as one line of text; the present edition, again in keeping with modern editorial tradition, assigns a separate line to each speaker.

Volpone (1616 folio, p.520)

Act v.   *Scene* XII.

AVOCATORI, &c.

These things can nere be reconcil'd. He, here,
    Professeth, that the gentleman was wrong'd;
    And that the gentlewoman was brought thither,
Forc'd by her husband: and there left. VOLT. Most true.
    CEL. How ready is heau'n to those, that pray! AVO.1. But, that
VOLPONE would haue rauish'd her, he holds
Vtterly false; knowing his impotence.
    CORV. Graue fathers, he is possest; againe, I say,
Possest: nay, if there be possession,
And obsession, he has both. AVO.3. Here comes our officer.
    VOLP. The parasite will streight be, here, graue fathers.
    AVO.4. You might inuent some other name, sir varlet.
    AVO.3. Did not the notarie meet him? VOLP. Not that I know.
    AVO.4. His comming will cleare all. AVO.2. Yet it is mistie.
    VOLT. May't please your father hoods——VOLP. Sir, the parasite

Volpone whis-pers the Aduo-cate.

Will'd me to tell you, that his master liues;
That you are still the man; your hopes the same;
And this was, onely a iest——VOLT. How? VOLP. Sir, to trie
If you were, firme, and how you stood affected.
    VOLT. Art'sure he liues? VOLP. Doe I liue, sir? VOLT. Ome!
I was to violent. VOLP. Sir, you may redeeme it,
They said, you were possest; fall downe, and seeme so:

Voltore falls.

I'le helpe to make it good. God blesse the man!
(Stop your wind hard, and swell) see, see, see, see!
He vomits crooked pinnes! his eyes are set,
Like a dead hares, hung in a poulters shop!
His mouth's running away! doe you see, signior?
Now, 'tis in his belly. (CORV. I, the deuill!)
    VOLP. Now, in his throate. (CORV. I, I perceiue it plaine.)
    VOLP. 'Twill out, t'will out; stand cleere. See, where it flies!
In shape of a blew toad, with a battes wings!
Doe not you see it, sir? CORB. What? I thinke I doe.
    CORV. 'Tis to too manifest. VOLP. Looke! he comes t'himselfe!
    VOLT. Where am I? VOLP. Take good heart, the worst is past, sir.
You are dis-possest. ATO 1 What accident is this?
    AVO. Sodaine, and full of wonder! ATO.3. If he were.
Possest, as it appeares, all this is nothing.
    CORV. He has beene, often, subbiect to these fits,
    AVO.1. Shew him that writing, do you know it, sir?
    VOLP. Deny it, sir, forsweare it, know it not.
    VOLT. Yes, I doe know it well, it is my hand:

But

Every Man in his Humour

TO THE MOST
LEARNED, AND
MY HONOR'D
FRIEND,

Mr. Cambden, CLARENTIAUX.

SIR,

There are, no doubt, a supercilious race in the world, who will esteeme all office,
done you in this kind, an injurie; so solemne a vice it is with them to use the
authoritie of their ignorance, to the crying downe of Poetry, *or the* Professors:
But, my gratitude must not leave to correct their error; since I am none of those,   10
that can suffer the benefits confer'd upon my youth, to perish with my age. It is a
fraile memorie, that remembers but present things: And, had the favour of the
times so conspir'd with my disposition, as it could have brought forth other, or
better, you had had the same proportion, & number of the fruits, the first. Now,
I pray you, to accept this, such, wherein neither the confession of my manners shall
make you blush; nor of my studies, repent you to have beene the instructer: And,
for the profession of my thanke-fulnesse, I am sure, it will, with good men, find
either praise, or excuse.

Your true lover,
BEN. JONSON.   20

The Persons of the Play.

KNO'WELL, *An old Gentleman.*

ED[WARD] KNO'WELL, *His Sonne.*

BRAYNE-WORME, *The Fathers man.*

MR. STEPHEN, *A countrey Gull.*

DOWNE-RIGHT, *A plaine Squier.*

WELL-BRED, *His halfe Brother.*

JUST[ICE] CLEMENT, *An old merry Magistrat.*

ROGER FORMALL, *His Clarke.*

KITELY, *A Merchant.*

DAME KITELY, *His wife.*

MRS. BRIDGET, *His Sister.*

MR. MATTHEW, *The towne-gull.*

CASH, KITELIES *Man.*

COB, *A Water-bearer.*

TIB, *His Wife.*

CAP[TAIN] BOBADILL, *A Paules-man.*

[SERVANTS, *etc.*]

THE SCENE
LONDON.

Every Man in his Humour.

Though neede make many *Poets*, and some such
As art, and nature have not betterd much;
Yet ours, for want, hath not so lov'd the stage,
As he dare serve th'ill customes of the age:
Or purchase your delight at such a rate,
As, for it, he himselfe must justly hate.
To make a child, now swadled, to proceede
Man, and then shoote up, in one beard, and weede,
Past threescore yeeres: or, with three rustie swords,
And helpe of some few foot-and-halfe-foote words,   10
Fight over *Yorke*, and *Lancasters* long jarres:
And in the tyring-house bring wounds, to scarres.
He rather prayes, you will be pleas'd to see
One such, to day, as other playes should be.
Where neither *Chorus* wafts you ore the seas;
Nor creaking throne comes downe, the boyes to please;
Nor nimble squibbe is seene, to make afear'd
The gentlewomen; nor roul'd bullet heard
To say, it thunders; nor tempestuous drumme
Rumbles, to tell you when the storme doth come;   20
But deedes, and language, such as men doe use:
And persons, such as *Comoedie* would chuse,
When she would shew an Image of the times,
And sport with humane follies, not with crimes.
Except, we make 'hem such by loving still
Our popular errors, when we know th'are ill.
I meane such errors, as you'll all confesse
By laughing at them, they deserve no lesse:
Which when you heartily doe, there's hope left, then,
You, that have so grac'd monsters, may like men.   30

Act I. Scene 1

KNO'WELL, BRAYNE-WORME, MR. STEPHEN.

[*Enter* KNO'WELL.]

KNO'WELL A goodly day toward! and a fresh morning!
    BRAYNE-WORME,
    [*Enter* BRAYNE-WORME.]
  Call up your yong master: bid him rise, sir.
  Tell him, I have some businesse to employ him.

BRAYNE-WORME I will sir, presently.

KNO'WELL   But heare you, sirah,
  If he be'at his booke, disturbe him not.

BRAYNE-WORME   Well sir.   [*Exit.*]

KNO'WELL How happie, yet, should I esteeme my selfe
  Could I (by any practise) weane the boy
  From one vaine course of studie, he affects.
  He is a scholler, if a man may trust
10 The liberall voice of fame, in her report
  Of good accompt, in both our *universities*,
  Either of which hath favour'd him with graces:
  But their indulgence, must not spring in me
  A fond opinion, that he cannot erre.
  My selfe was once a student; and, indeed,
  Fed with the selfe-same humour, he is now,
  Dreaming on nought but idle *poetrie*,
  That fruitlesse, and unprofitable art,
  Good unto none, but least to the professors,
20 Which, then, I thought the mistresse of all knowledge:
  But since, time, and the truth have wak'd my judgement,
  And reason taught me better to distinguish,
  The vaine, from th'usefull learnings. [*Enter* STEPHEN.] Cossin
    STEPHEN!
  What newes with you, that you are here so early?

STEPHEN Nothing, but eene come to see how you doe, uncle.

KNO'WELL That's kindly done, you are wel-come, cousse.

STEPHEN I, I know that sir, I would not ha' come else. How doe my
  cousin EDWARD, uncle?

KNO'WELL O, well cousse, goe in and see: I doubt he be scarse
   stirring yet.   30

STEPHEN Uncle, afore I goe in, can you tell me, an' he have ere a
   booke of the sciences of hawking, and hunting? I would faine
   borrow it.

KNO'WELL Why, I hope you will not a hawking now, will you?

STEPHEN No wusse; but I'll practise against next yeere uncle: I have
   bought me a hawke, and a hood, and bells, and all; I lacke nothing
   but a booke to keepe it by.

KNO'WELL O, most ridiculous.

STEPHEN Nay, looke you now, you are angrie, uncle: why you know,
   an' a man have not skill in the hawking, and hunting-languages   40
   now a dayes, I'll not give a rush for him. They are more studied
   then the *Greeke*, or the *Latine*. He is for no gallants companie
   without 'hem. And by gads lid I scorne it, I, so I doe, to be a
   consort for every *hum-drum*, hang 'hem scroyles, there's nothing
   in 'hem, i' the world. What doe you talke on it? Because I dwell
   at *Hogsden*, I shall keepe companie with none but the archers of
   Finsburie? or the citizens, that come a ducking to *Islington* ponds?
   A fine jest ifaith! Slid a gentleman mun show himselfe like a
   gentleman. Uncle, I pray you be not angrie, I know what I have
   to doe, I trow, I am no novice.   50

KNO'WELL You are a prodigall absurd cocks-combe: Goe to.
   Nay never looke at me, it's I that speake.
   Tak't as you will sir, I'll not flatter you.
   Ha' you not yet found meanes enow, to wast
   That, which your friends have left you, but you must
   Goe cast away your money on a kite,
   And know not how to keepe it, when you ha' done?
   O it's comely! this will make you a gentleman!
   Well cosen, well! I see you are eene past hope
   Of all reclaime. I, so, now you are told on it,   60
   You looke another way.

STEPHEN   What would you ha' me doe?

KNO'WELL What would I have you doe? I'll tell you kinsman,
   Learne to be wise, and practise how to thrive,
   That would I have you doe: and not to spend
   Your coyne on every bable, that you phansie,

Or every foolish braine, that humors you.
I would not have you to invade each place,
Nor thrust your selfe on all societies,
Till mens affections, or your owne desert,
70   Should worthily invite you to your ranke.
He, that is so respectlesse in his courses,
Oft sells his reputation, at cheape market.
Nor would I, you should melt away your selfe
In flashing braverie, least while you affect
To make a blaze of gentrie to the world,
A little puffe of scorne extinguish it,
And you be left, like an unsavorie snuffe,
Whose propertie is onely to offend.
I'ld ha' you sober, and containe your selfe;
80   Not, that your sayle be bigger then your boat:
But moderate your expences now (at first)
As you may keepe the same proportion still.
Nor, stand so much on your gentilitie,
Which is an aërie, and meere borrow'd thing,
From dead mens dust, and bones: and none of yours
Except you make, or hold it. Who comes here?

Act I. Scene 2

SERVANT, MR. STEPHEN, KNO'WELL, BRAYNE-WORME.

[*Enter* SERVANT.]

SERVANT Save you, gentlemen.

STEPHEN Nay, we do' not stand much on our gentilitie, friend; yet,
      you are wel-come, and I assure you, mine uncle here is a man of
      a thousand a yeare, *Middlesex* land: hee has but one sonne in all
      the world, I am his next heire (at the common law) master
      STEPHEN, as simple as I stand here, if my cossen die (as there's
      hope he will) I have a prettie living o' mine owne too, beside,
      hard-by here.

SERVANT In good time, sir.

10   STEPHEN In good time, sir? why! and in very good time, sir. You
      doe not flout, friend, doe you?

SERVANT Not I, sir.

STEPHEN Not you, sir? you were not best, sir; an' you should, here
bee them can perceive it, and that quickly to: goe to. And they
can give it againe soundly to, and neede be.

SERVANT Why, sir, let this satisfie you: good faith, I had no such
intent.

STEPHEN Sir, an' I thought you had, I would talke with you, and that
presently.

SERVANT Good master STEPHEN, so you may, sir, at your
pleasure.   20

STEPHEN And so I would sir, good my saucie companion! an' you
were out o' mine uncles ground, I can tell you; though I doe not
stand upon my gentilitie neither in't.

KNO'WELL Cossen! cossen! will this nere be left?

STEPHEN Whorson base fellow! a mechanicall serving-man! By this
cudgell, and't were not for shame, I would—

KNO'WELL What would you doe, you peremptorie gull?
If you can not be quiet, get you hence.
You see, the honest man demeanes himselfe   30
Modestly to'ards you, giving no replie
To your unseason'd, quarrelling, rude fashion:
And, still you huffe it, with a kind of cariage,
As voide of wit, as of humanitie.
Goe, get you in; fore heaven, I am asham'd
Thou hast a kinsmans interest in me.   [*Exit* STEPHEN.]

SERVANT I pray you, sir. Is this master KNO'WELL's house?

KNO'WELL Yes, marie, is it sir.

SERVANT I should enquire for a gentleman, here, one master
EDWARD KNO'WELL: doe you know any such, sir, I pray you?   40

KNO'WELL I should forget my selfe else, sir.

SERVANT Are you the gentleman? crie you mercie sir: I was requir'd
by a gentleman i' the citie, as I rode out at this end o' the towne,
to deliver you this letter, sir.

KNO'WELL To me, sir! What doe you meane? pray you remember
your court'sie. (*To his most selected friend, master* EDWARD
KNO'WELL.) What might the gentlemans name be, sir, that sent
it? nay, pray you be cover'd.

SERVANT One master WELL-BRED, sir.

50   KNO'WELL Master WELL-BRED! A yong gentleman? is he not?

SERVANT The same sir, master KITELY married his sister: the rich
merchant i' the old *Jewrie*.

KNO'WELL You say very true. BRAINE-WORME.

[*Enter* BRAYNE-WORME.]

BRAYNE-WORME Sir.

KNO'WELL Make this honest friend drinke here: pray you goe in.

[*Exeunt* BRAYNE-WORME *and* SERVANT.]

This letter is directed to my sonne:
Yet, I am EDWARD KNO'WELL too, and may
With the safe conscience of good manners, use
The fellowes error to my satisfaction.

60   Well, I will breake it ope (old men are curious)
Be it but for the stiles sake, and the phrase,
To see, if both doe answere my sonnes praises,
Who is, almost, growne the idolater
Of this yong WELL-BRED: what have we here? what's this?

The letter.   *Why,* NED, *I beseech thee; hast thou for-sworne all thy friends i' the old*
Jewrie? or dost thou think us all Jewes *that inhabit there, yet? If thou dost,*
come over, and but see our fripperie: change an olde shirt, for a whole smocke,
with us. Doe not conceive that antipathy betweene us, and Hogs-den; *as*
was betweene Jewes, *and hogs-flesh. Leave thy vigilant father, alone, to*

70   *number over his greene apricots, evening, and morning, o' the north-west wall:*
An' I had beene his sonne, I had sav'd him the labor, long since; if, taking
in all the yong wenches, that passe by, at the back-dore, and codd'ling every
kernell of the fruit for 'hem, would ha' serv'd. But, pr'y thee, come over to
me, quickly, this morning: I have such a present for thee (our Turkie *companie*
never sent the like to the Grand-SIGNIOR.) *One is a Rimer sir, o' your*
owne batch, your owne levin; but doth think himselfe Poet-major, *o' the*
towne: willing to be showne, and worthy to be seene. The other—I will not
venter his description with you, till you come, because I would ha' you make
hether with an appetite. If the worst of 'hem be not worth your jorney, draw

80   *your bill of charges, as unconscionable, as any* Guild-hall *verdict will give it*
you, and you shall be allow'd your viaticum.

From the wind-mill.

From the *Burdello*, it might come as well;
The *Spittle*: or *Pict-hatch*. Is this the man,
My sonne hath sung so, for the happiest wit,

The choysest braine, the times hath sent us forth?
I know not what he may be, in the arts;
Nor what in schooles: but surely, for his manners,
I judge him a prophane, and dissolute wretch:
Worse, by possession of such great good guifts,   90
Being the master of so loose a spirit.
Why, what unhallow'd ruffian would have writ,
In such a scurrilous manner, to a friend!
Why should he thinke, I tell my Apri-cotes?
Or play th' *Hesperian* Dragon, with my fruit,
To watch it? Well, my sonne, I'had thought
Y' had had more judgement, t'have made election
Of your companions, then t'have tane on trust,
Such petulant, geering gamsters, that can spare
No argument, or subject from their jest.   100
But I perceive, affection makes a foole
Of any man, too much the father. BRAYNE-WORME.

    [*Enter* BRAYNE-WORME.]

BRAYNE-WORME Sir.
KNO'WELL Is the fellow gone that brought this letter?
BRAYNE-WORME Yes, sir, a pretie while since.
KNO'WELL And, where's your yong master?
BRAYNE-WORME In his chamber sir.
KNO'WELL He spake not with the fellow! did he?
BRAYNE-WORME No sir, he saw him not.
KNO'WELL Take you this letter and deliver it my sonne,   110
    But with no notice, that I have open'd it, on your life.
BRAYNE-WORME O lord, sir, that were a jest, indeed!   [*Exit.*]
KNO'WELL I am resolv'd, I will not stop his journey;
    Nor practise any violent meane, to stay
    The unbridled course of youth in him: for that,
    Restrain'd, growes more impatient; and, in kind,
    Like to the eager, but the generous grey-hound,
    Who ne're so little from his game with-held,
    Turnes head, and leapes up at his holders throat.
    There is a way of winning, more by love,   120
    And urging of the modestie, then feare:
    Force workes on servile natures, not the free.

He, that's compell'd to goodnesse, may be good;
But 'tis but for that fit: where others drawne
By softnesse, and example, get a habit.
Then, if they stray, but warne 'hem: and, the same
They should for vertu'have done, they'll doe for shame.   [*Exit.*]

Act I. Scene 3

EDW. KNO'WELL, BRAYNE-WORME, MR. STEPHEN.

[*Enter* ED. KNO'WELL *and* BRAYNE-WORME.]

ED. KNO'WELL Did he open it, sayest thou?

BRAYNE-WORME Yes, o' my word sir, and read the contents.

ED. KNO'WELL That scarse contents me. What countenance (pr'y thee) made he, i' the reading of it? was he angrie, or pleas'd?

BRAYNE-WORME Nay sir, I saw him not reade it, nor open it, I assure your worship.

ED. KNO'WELL No? how know'st thou, then, that he did either?

BRAYNE-WORME Marie sir, because he charg'd me, on my life, to tell nobodie, that he open'd it: which, unlesse hee had done, hee would never feare to have it reveal'd.

ED. KNO'WELL That's true: well I thanke thee, BRAYNE-WORME.

[*Enter* STEPHEN.]

STEPHEN O, BRAYNE-WORME, did'st thou not see a fellow here in a what-sha'-call-him doublet! he brought mine uncle a letter e'en now.

BRAYNE-WORME Yes, master STEPHEN, what of him?

STEPHEN O, I ha' such a minde to beate him— Where is hee? canst thou tell?

BRAYNE-WORME Faith, he is not of that mind: he is gone, master STEPHEN.

STEPHEN Gone? which way? when went he? how long since?

BRAYNE-WORME He is rid hence. He tooke horse, at the streete dore.

STEPHEN And, I staid i' the fields! horson *scander-bag* rogue! o that I had but a horse to fetch him backe againe.

BRAYNE-WORME Why, you may ha' my mrs. gelding, to save your longing, sir.

STEPHEN But, I ha' no bootes, that's the spight on't.

BRAYNE-WORME Why, a fine wispe of hay, rould hard, master
STEPHEN.

STEPHEN No faith, it's no boote to follow him, now: let him eene   30
goe, and hang. 'Pray thee, helpe to trusse me, a little. He dos so
vexe me—

BRAYNE-WORME You'll be worse vex'd, when you are truss'd, master
STEPHEN. Best, keepe un-brac'd; and walke your selfe, till you be
cold: your choller may foundre you else.

STEPHEN By my faith, and so I will, now thou tell'st me on't: How
dost thou like my legge, BRAYNE-WORME?

BRAYNE-WORME A very good leg! master STEPHEN! but the woollen
stocking do's not commend it so well.

STEPHEN Foh, the stockings be good inough, now summer is com-   40
ming on, for the dust: Ile have a paire of silke, again' winter, that
I goe to dwell i' the towne. I thinke my legge would shew in a
silke-hose.

BRAYNE-WORME Beleeve me, master STEPHEN, rarely well.

STEPHEN In sadnesse, I thinke it would: I have a reasonable good
legge.

BRAYNE-WORME You have an excellent good legge, master
STEPHEN, but I cannot stay, to praise it longer now, and I am
very sorie for't.

STEPHEN Another time wil serve, BRAYNE-WORME. Gramercie for   50
this.   [*Exit* BRAYNE-WORME.]

ED. KNO'WELL Ha, ha, ha!

STEPHEN Slid, I hope, he laughes not at me, and he doe—

ED. KNO'WELL Here was a letter, indeede, to be intercepted by a
mans father, and doe him good with him! Hee cannot but thinke
most vertuously, both of me, and the sender, sure; that make the
carefull Costar'-monger of him in our *familiar Epistles*. Well, if he
read this with patience, Ile be gelt, and troll ballads for Mr. JOHN
TRUNDLE, yonder, the rest of my mortalitie. It is true, and likely,
my father may have as much patience as another man; for he takes   60
much physicke: and, oft taking physicke makes a man very patient.
But would your packet, master WEL-BRED, had arriv'd at him, in
such a minute of his patience; then, we had knowne the end of it,
which now is doubtfull, and threatens— What! my wise cossen!

*Kno'well laughes
having read the
letter.*

Nay, then, Ile furnish our feast with one gull more to'ard the messe. He writes to me of a brace, and here's one, that's three: O, for a fourth; Fortune, if ever thou'lt use thine eyes, I intreate thee—

STEPHEN O, now I see, who hee laught at. Hee laught at some-body
70   in that letter. By this good light, and he had laught at me—

ED. KNO'WELL How now, coussen STEPHEN, melancholy'?

STEPHEN Yes, a little. I thought, you had laught at me, cossen.

ED. KNO'WELL Why, what an' I had cousse, what would you ha' done?

STEPHEN By this light, I would ha' told mine uncle.

ED. KNO'WELL Nay, if you wold ha' told your uncle, I did laugh at you, cousse.

STEPHEN Did you, indeede?

ED. KNO'WELL Yes, indeede.

80   STEPHEN Why, then—

ED. KNO'WELL What then?

STEPHEN I am satisfied, it is sufficient.

ED. KNO'WELL Why bee so gentle cousse. And, I pray you let me intreate a courtesie of you. I am sent for, this morning, by a friend i' the old *Jewrie* to come to him; It's but crossing over the fields to *More-gate*: Will you beare me companie? I protest, it is not to draw you into bond, or any plot against the state, cousse.

STEPHEN Sir, that's all one, and 't were: you shall command me, twise so farre as *More-gate* to doe you good, in such a matter. Doe
90   you thinke I would leave you? I protest—

ED. KNO'WELL No, no, you shall not protest, cousse.

STEPHEN By my fackins, but I will, by your leave; Ile protest more to my friend, then Ile speake off, at this time.

ED. KNO'WELL You speake very well, cousse.

STEPHEN Nay, not so neither, you shall pardon me: but I speake, to serve my turne.

ED. KNO'WELL Your turne, couss? Doe you know, what you say? A gentleman of your sort, parts, carriage, and estimation, to talke o' your turne i' this companie, and to me, alone, like a tankard-bearer,
100   at a conduit! Fie. A wight, that (hetherto) his every step hath left the stampe of a great foot behind him, as every word the savour of a strong spirit! and he! this man! so grac'd, guilded, or (to use

a more fit *metaphore*) so tin-foild by nature, as not ten house-wives
pewter (again' a good time) shew's more bright to the world then
he! and he (as I said last, so I say againe, and still shall say it) this
man! to conceale such reall ornaments as these, and shaddow their
glorie, as a Millaners wife do's her wrought stomacher, with a
smokie lawne, or a black cypresse? O couss! It cannot be answer'd,
goe not about it. DRAKES old ship, at *Detford*, may sooner circle
the world againe. Come, wrong not the qualitie of your desert,   110
with looking downeward, couz; but hold up your head, so: and let
the *Idea* of what you are, be pourtray'd i' your face, that men may
reade i' your physnomie, (*Here, within this place, is to be seene the true,
rare, and accomplish'd monster, or miracle of nature,* which is all one.)
What thinke you of this, couss?

STEPHEN Why, I doe thinke of it; and I will be more prowd, and
melancholy, and gentleman-like, then I have beene: I'le ensure
you.

ED. KNO'WELL Why, that's resolute master STEPHEN! Now, if I can
but hold him up to his height, as it is happily begunne, it will doe   120
well for a suburbe-humor: we may hap have a match with the citie,
and play him for fortie pound. Come, couss.

STEPHEN I'le follow you.

ED. KNO'WELL Follow me? you must goe before.

STEPHEN Nay, an' I must, I will. Pray you, shew me, good cousin.

[*Exeunt.*]

Act I. Scene 4

MR. MATTHEW, COB.

[*Enter* MATTHEW.]

MATTHEW I thinke, this be the house: what, hough?

[*Enter* COB.]

COB Who's there? O, master MATTHEW! gi' your worship good
morrow.

MATTHEW What! COB! how do'st thou, good COB? do'st thou inhab-
ite here, COB?

COB I, sir, I and my linage ha'kept a poore house, here, in our dayes.

MATTHEW Thy linage, *Monsieur* COB, what linage? what linage?

COB Why sir, an ancient linage, and a princely. Mine ance'trie came
from a Kings belly, no worse man: and yet no man neither (by
your worships leave, I did lie in that) but *Herring* the King of fish
(from his belly, I proceed) one o' the Monarchs o' the world, I
assure you. The first red herring, that was broil'd in ADAM, and
EVE'S kitchin, doe I fetch my pedigree from, by the Harrots
bookes. His COB, was my great-great-mighty-great Grand-father.

MATTHEW Why mightie? why mightie? I pray thee.

COB O, it was a mightie while agoe, sir, and a mightie great COB.

MATTHEW How know'st thou that?

COB How know I? why, I smell his ghost, ever and anon.

MATTHEW Smell a ghost? o unsavoury jest! and the ghost of a herring
COB!

COB I sir, with favour of your worships nose, Mr. MATHEW, why
not the ghost of a herring-cob, as well as the ghost of rasher-bacon?

MATTHEW ROGER BACON, thou wouldst say?

COB I say rasher-bacon. They were both broyl'd o' the coles? and a
man may smell broyld-meate, I hope? you are a scholler, upsolve
me that, now.

MATTHEW O raw ignorance! COB, canst thou shew me of a gentleman,
one Captayne BOBADILL, where his lodging is?

COB O, my guest, sir! you meane.

MATTHEW Thy guest! Alas! ha, ha.

COB Why doe you laugh, sir? Doe you not meane Captayne
BOBADILL?

MATTHEW COB, 'pray thee, advise thyselfe well: doe not wrong the
gentleman, and thy selfe too. I dare bee sworne, hee scornes thy
house: hee! He lodge in such a base, obscure place, as thy house!
Tut, I know his disposition so well, he would not lye in thy bed,
if tho'uldst gi'it him.

COB I will not give it him, though, sir. Masse, I thought somewhat
was in't, we could not get him to bed, all night! Well, sir, though
he lye not o' my bed, he lies o' my bench: an't please you to goe
up, sir, you shall find him with two cushions under his head, and
his cloke wrapt about him, as though he had neither wun nor lost,
and yet (I warrant) he ne're cast better in his life, then he has done,
to night.

MATTHEW Why? was he drunke?

COB Drunke, sir? you heare not me say so. Perhaps, hee swallow'd
a taverne-token, or some such device, sir: I have nothing to doe
withall. I deale with water, and not with wine. Gi'me my tankard
there, hough. [*Enter* TIB, *exit.*] God b'w'you, sir. It's sixe a clocke:
I should ha' carried two turnes, by this. What hough? my stopple?   50
come.

MATTHEW Lye in a water-bearers house! A gentleman of his havings!
Well, I'le tell him my mind.

　　　[*Enter* TIB.]

COB What TIB, shew this gentleman up to the Captayne. [*Exeunt* TIB
and MATTHEW.] O, an' my house were the *Brasen-head* now! faith,
it would eene speake, *Mo fooles yet.* You should ha' some now would
take this Mr. MATTHEW to be a gentleman, at the least. His father's
an honest man, a worshipfull fish-monger, and so forth; and now
dos he creepe, and wriggle into acquaintance with all the brave
gallants about the towne, such as my guest is: (o, my guest is a   60
fine man) and they flout him invincibly. Hee useth every day to a
Merchants house (where I serve water) one master KITELY's, i'
the *old Jewry*; and here's the jest, he is in love with my masters
sister, (mistris BRIDGET) and calls her mistris: and there he will
sit you a whole after-noone some-times, reading o' these same
abominable, vile, (a poxe on 'hem, I cannot abide them) rascally
verses, *poyetrie*, *poyetrie*, and speaking of *enterludes*, 'twill make a man
burst to heare him. And the wenches, they doe so geere, and ti-he
at him—well, should they do so much to me, Ild for-sweare them
all, by the foot of PHARAOH. There's an oath! How many   70
water-bearers shall you heare sweare such an oath? o, I have a
guest (he teaches me) he dos sweare the legiblest, of any man
christned: By St. GEORGE, the foot of PHARAOH, the body of
me, as I am gentleman, and a souldier: such daintie oathes! and
withall, he dos take this same filthy roguish *tobacco*, the finest, and
cleanliest! it would doe a man good to see the fume come forth
at's tonnells! Well, he owes mee fortie shillings (my wife lent him
out of her purse, by sixe-pence a time) besides his lodging: I would
I had it. I shall ha'it, he saies, the next *Action*. *Helter skelter*, hang
sorrow, care 'll kill a cat, up-tailes all, and a louse for the hang-man.   80
　　　　　　　　　　　　　　　　　　　　　　　　　[*Exit.*]

Act I. Scene 5

BOBADILL, TIB, MATTHEW.

*Bobad. is dis-
covered lying on
his bench.*

BOBADILL   Hostesse, hostesse.

   [*Enter* TIB.]

TIB   What say you, sir?

BOBADILL   A cup o' thy small beere, sweet hostesse.

TIB   Sir, there's a gentleman, below, would speake with you.

BOBADILL   A gentleman! 'ods so, I am not within.

TIB   My husband told him you were, sir.

BOBADILL   What a plague—what meant he?

MATTHEW   Captaine BOBADILL?

BOBADILL   Who's there? (take away the bason, good hostesse) come
up, sir.

TIB   He would desire you to come up, sir. You come into a cleanly
house, here.

   [*Enter* MATTHEW.]

MATTHEW   'Save you, sir. 'Save you, Captayne.

BOBADILL   Gentle master MATTHEW! Is it you, sir? Please you sit
downe.

MATTHEW   Thanke you, good Captaine, you may see, I am some-what
audacious.

BOBADILL   Not so, sir. I was requested to supper, last night, by a sort
of gallants, where you were wish'd for, and drunke to, I assure
you.

MATTHEW   Vouchsafe me, by whom, good Captaine.

BOBADILL   Mary, by yong WELL-BRED, and others: Why, hostesse,
a stoole here, for this gentleman.

MATTHEW   No haste, sir, 'tis very well.   [*Exit* TIB.]

BOBADILL   Body of me! It was so late ere we parted last night, I can
scarse open my eyes, yet; I was but new risen, as you came: how
passes the day abroad, sir? you can tell.

MATTHEW   Faith, some halfe houre to seven: now trust mee, you
have an exceeding fine lodging here, very neat, and private!

BOBADILL   I, sir: sit downe, I pray you. Master MATTHEW (in any
case) possesse no gentlemen of our acquaintance, with notice of
my lodging.

MATTHEW Who? I sir? no.

BOBADILL Not that I need to care who know it, for the Cabbin is
convenient, but in regard I would not be too popular, and generally
visited, as some are.

MATTHEW True, Captaine, I conceive you.

BOBADILL For, doe you see, sir, by the heart of valour, in me,
(except it be to some peculiar and choice spirits, to whom I am
extraordinarily ingag'd, as your selfe, or so) I could not extend   40
thus farre.

MATTHEW O Lord, sir, I resolve so.

BOBADILL I confesse, I love a cleanely and quiet privacy, above all
the tumult, and roare of fortune. What new booke ha' you there?
What! *Goe by*, HIERONYMO!

MATTHEW I, did you ever see it acted? is't not well pend?

BOBADILL Well pend? I would faine see all the *Poets*, of these times,
pen such another play as that was! they'll prate and swagger, and
keepe a stir of arte and devices, when (as I am a gentleman) reade
'hem, they are the most shallow, pittifull, barren fellowes, that live   50
upon the face of the earth, againe!

MATTHEW Indeed, here are a number of fine speeches in this booke!
O eyes, no eyes, but fountaynes fraught with teares! There's a conceit!
fountaines fraught with teares! *O life, no life, but lively forme of death!*
Another! *O world, no world, but masse of publique wrongs!* A third!
Confus'd and fil'd with murder, and misdeeds! A fourth! O, the *Muses*!
Is't not excellent? Is't not simply the best that ever you heard,
Captayne? Ha? How doe you like it?

BOBADILL 'Tis good.

MATTHEW *To thee, the purest object to my sense,*   60
The most refined essence heaven covers,
Send I these lines, wherein I doe commence
The happy state of turtle-billing lovers.
If they prove rough, un-polish't, harsh, and rude,
Hast made the wast. Thus, mildly, I conclude.

BOBADILL Nay, proceed, proceed. Where's this?

MATTHEW This, sir? a toy o' mine owne, in my nonage: the infancy
of my *Muses*! But, when will you come and see my studie? good
faith, I can shew you some very good things, I have done of late—
That boot becomes your legge, passing well, Captayne, me thinkes!   70

*Bobadill is
making him
ready all this
while.*

BOBADILL So, so, It's the fashion, gentlemen now use.

MATTHEW Troth, Captayne, an' now you speake o' the fashion, master WELL-BRED's elder brother, and I, are fall'n out exceedingly: this other day, I hapned to enter into some discourse of a hanger, which I assure you, both for fashion, and worke-man-ship, was most peremptory-beautifull, and gentlemanlike! Yet, he condemn'd, and cry'd it downe, for the most pyed, and ridiculous that ever he saw.

BOBADILL Squire DOWNE-RIGHT? the halfe brother? was't not?

80   MATTHEW I sir, he.

BOBADILL Hang him, rooke, he! why, he has no more judgement then a malt-horse. By S. GEORGE, I wonder you'ld loose a thought upon such an animal: the most peremptory absurd clowne of *christendome*, this day, he is holden. I protest to you, as I am a gentleman, and a souldier, I ne're chang'd wordes, with his like. By his discourse, he should eate nothing but hay. He was borne for the manger, pannier, or pack-saddle! He ha's not so much as a good phrase in his belly, but all old iron, and rustie proverbes! a good commoditie for some smith, to make hob-nailes of.

90   MATTHEW I, and he thinks to carry it away with his manhood still, where he comes. He brags he will gi' me the *bastinado*, as I heare.

BOBADILL How! He the *bastinado*! how came he by that word, trow?

MATTHEW Nay, indeed, he said cudgell me; I term'd it so, for my more grace.

BOBADILL That may bee: For I was sure, it was none of his word. But, when? when said he so?

MATTHEW Faith, yesterday, they say: a young gallant, a friend of mine told me so.

BOBADILL By the foot of PHARAOH, and't were my case now, I
100   should send him a *chartel*, presently. The *bastinado*! A most proper, and sufficient *dependance*, warranted by the great CARANZA. Come hither. You shall *chartel* him. I'll shew you a trick, or two, you shall kill him with, at pleasure: the first *stoccata*, if you will, by this ayre.

MATTHEW Indeed, you have absolute knowledge i' the mysterie, I have heard, sir.

BOBADILL Of whom? Of whom ha' you heard it, I beseech you?

MATTHEW Troth, I have heard it spoken of divers, that you have very rare, and un-in-one-breath-utter-able skill, sir.

BOBADILL By heaven, no, not I; no skill i' the earth: some small
rudiments i' the science, as to know my time, distance, or so. I   110
have profest it more for noblemen, and gentlemens use, then mine
owne practise, I assure you. Hostesse, accommodate us with
another bed-staffe here, quickly: [*Enter* TIB.] Lend us another
bed-staffe. [*Exit* TIB.] The woman do's not understand the wordes
of *Action*. Looke you, sir. Exalt not your point above this state, at
any hand, and let your poynard maintayne your defence, thus:
[*Enter* TIB.] (give it the gentleman, and leave us) [*Exit* TIB.] so, sir.
Come on: O, twine your body more about, that you may fall to a
more sweet comely gentleman-like guard. So, indifferent. Hollow
your body more sir, thus. Now, stand fast o' your left leg, note   120
your distance, keepe your due proportion of time—Oh, you
disorder your point, most irregularly!

MATTHEW How is the bearing of it, now, sir?

BOBADILL O, out of measure ill! A well-experienc'd hand would
passe upon you, at pleasure.

MATTHEW How meane you, sir, passe upon me?

BOBADILL Why, thus sir (make a thrust at me) come in, upon the
answere, controll your point, and make a full carreere, at the body.
The best-practis'd gallants of the time, name it the *passada*: a most
desperate thrust, beleeve it!   130

MATTHEW Well, come, sir.

BOBADILL Why, you doe not manage your weapon with any facilitie,
or grace to invite mee: I have no spirit to play with you. Your
dearth of judgement renders you tedious.

MATTHEW But one *venue*, sir.

BOBADILL *Venue!* Fie. Most grosse denomination, as ever I heard.
O, the *stoccata*, while you live, sir. Note that. Come, put on your
cloke, and wee'll goe to some private place, where you are
acquainted, some taverne, or so—and have a bit—Ile send for
one of these Fencers, and hee shall breath you, by my direction;   140
and, then, I will teach you your tricke. You shall kill him with it,
at the first, if you please. Why, I will learne you, by the true
judgement of the eye, hand, and foot, to controll any enemies
point i' the world. Should your adversarie confront you with a
pistoll, 'twere nothing, by this hand, you should, by the same rule,

controll his bullet, in a line: except it were hayle-shot, and spred.
What money ha' you about you, Mr. MATTHEW?

MATTHEW Faith, I ha' not past a two shillings, or so.

BOBADILL 'Tis somewhat with the least: but, come. We will have a
bunch of redish, and salt, to tast our wine; and a pipe of *tobacco*,
to close the orifice of the stomach: and then, wee'll call upon yong
WEL-BRED. Perhaps wee shall meet the CORIDON, his brother,
there: and put him to the question.   [*Exeunt.*]

Act II. Scene 1

KITELY, CASH, DOWNE-RIGHT.

[*Enter* KITELY, CASH *and* DOWNE-RIGHT.]

KITELY THOMAS, Come hither.
  There lyes a note, within upon my deske,
  Here, take my key: It is no matter, neither.
  Where is the Boy?

CASH   Within, sir, i' the ware-house.

KITELY Let him tell over, straight, that *Spanish* gold,
  And weigh it, with th' pieces of eight. Doe you
  See the delivery of those silver stuffes,
  To Mr. LUCAR. Tell him, if he will,
  He shall ha' the grogran's, at the rate I told him,
  And I will meet him, on the *Exchange*, anon.

CASH Good, sir.   [*Exit.*]

KITELY Doe you see that fellow, brother DOWNE-RIGHT?

DOWNE-RIGHT I, what of him?

KITELY He is a jewell, brother.
  I tooke him of a child, up, at my dore,
  And christned him, gave him mine owne name, THOMAS,
  Since bred him at the Hospitall; where proving
  A toward impe, I call'd him home, and taught him
  So much, as I have made him my Cashier,
  And giv'n him, who had none, a surname, CASH:
  And find him, in his place so full of faith,
  That, I durst trust my life into his hands.

DOWNE-RIGHT So, would not I in any bastards, brother,

As, it is like, he is: although I knew
My selfe his father. But you said yo' had somewhat
To tell me, gentle brother, what is't? what is't?
KITELY Faith, I am very loath, to utter it,
As fearing, it may hurt your patience:
But, that I know, your judgement is of strength,
Against the neerenesse of affection——   30
DOWNE-RIGHT What need this circumstance? pray you be direct.
KITELY I will not say, how much I doe ascribe
Unto your friendship; nor, in what regard
I hold your love: but, let my past behaviour,
And usage of your sister, but confirme
How well I'ave beene affected to your——
DOWNE-RIGHT You are too tedious, come to the matter, the
matter.
KITELY Then (without further ceremonie) thus.
My brother WELL-BRED, sir, (I know not how)   40
Of late, is much declin'd in what he was,
And greatly alter'd in his disposition.
When he came first to lodge here in my house,
Ne're trust me, if I were not proud of him:
Me thought he bare himselfe in such a fashion,
So full of man, and sweetnesse in his carriage,
And (what was chiefe) it shew'd not borrowed in him,
But all he did, became him as his owne,
And seem'd as perfect, proper, and possest
As breath, with life, or colour, with the bloud.   50
But, now, his course is so irregular,
So loose, affected, and depriv'd of grace,
And he himselfe withall so farre falne off
From that first place, as scarse no note remaines,
To tell mens judgements where he lately stood.
Hee's growne a stranger to all due respect,
Forgetfull of his friends, and not content
To stale himselfe in all societies,
He makes my house here common, as a *Mart*,
A *Theater*, a publike receptacle   60
For giddie humour, and diseased riot;

And here (as in a taverne, or a stewes)
He, and his wild associates, spend their houres,
In repetition of lascivious jests,
Sweare, leape, drinke, dance, and revell night by night,
Controll my servants: and indeed what not?

DOWNE-RIGHT 'Sdeynes, I know not what I should say to him, i'
the whole world! He values me, at a crackt three-farthings, for
ought I see: It will never out o' the flesh that's bred i' the bone! I
have told him inough, one would thinke, if that would serve: But,
counsell to him, is as good, as a shoulder of mutton to a sicke
horse. Well! he knowes what to trust to, for GEORGE. Let him
spend, and spend, and domineere, till his heart ake; an' hee thinke
to bee reliev'd by me, when he is got into one o'your citie pounds,
the Counters, he has the wrong sow by the eare, ifaith: and claps
his dish at the wrong mans dore. I'le lay my hand o' my halfe-peny,
e're I part with 't, to fetch him out, I'le assure him.

KITELY Nay, good brother, let it not trouble you, thus.

DOWNE-RIGHT 'Sdeath, he mads me, I could eate my very spur-
lethers, for anger! But, why are you so tame? Why doe you not
speake to him, and tell him how he disquiets your house?

KITELY O, there are divers reasons to disswade, brother.
But, would your selfe vouchsafe to travaile in it,
(Though but with plaine, and easie circumstance)
It would, both come much better to his sense,
And savour lesse of stomack, or of passion.
You are his elder brother, and that title
Both gives, and warrants you authoritie;
Which (by your presence seconded) must breed
A kinde of dutie in him, and regard:
Whereas, if I should intimate the least,
It would but adde contempt, to his neglect,
Heape worse on ill, make up a pile of hatred
That, in the rearing, would come tottring downe,
And, in the ruine, burie all our love.
Nay, more then this, brother, if I should speake
He would be readie from his heate of humor,
And over-flowing of the vapour, in him,

To blow the eares of his familiars,
With the false breath, of telling, what disgraces,   100
And low disparadgments, I had put upon him.
Whilst they, sir, to relieve him, in the fable,
Make their loose comments, upon every word,
Gesture, or looke, I use; mocke me all over,
From my flat cap, unto my shining shooes:
And, out of their impetuous rioting phant'sies,
Beget some slander, that shall dwell with me.
And what would that be, thinke you? mary, this.
They would give out (because my wife is faire,
My selfe but lately married, and my sister   110
Here sojourning a virgin in my house)
That I were jealous! nay, as sure as death,
That they would say. And how that I had quarrell'd
My brother purposely, thereby to finde
An apt pretext, to banish them my house.

DOWNE-RIGHT Masse perhaps so: They'are like inough to doe it.

KITELY Brother, they would, beleeve it: so should I
(Like one of these penurious quack-salvers)
But set the bills up, to mine owne disgrace,
And trie experiments upon my selfe: 120
Lend scorne and envie, oportunitie,
To stab my reputation, and good name—

Act II. Scene 2

MATTHEW, BOBADIL, DOWNE-RIGHT, KITELY.

[*Enter* MATTHEW *and* BOBADILL.]

MATTHEW I will speake to him—

BOBADILL Speake to him? away, by the foot of PHARAOH, you shall
not, you shall not doe him that grace. The time of day, to you,
Gentleman o' the house. Is Mr. WELL-BRED stirring?

DOWNE-RIGHT How then? what should he doe?

BOBADILL Gentleman of the house, it is to you: is he within, sir?

KITELY He came not to his lodging to night sir, I assure you.

DOWNE-RIGHT Why, doe you heare? you.

BOBADILL The gentleman-citizen hath satisfied mee, Ile talke to no
10   scavenger.   [*Exeunt* MATTHEW *and* BOBADILL.]

DOWNE-RIGHT How, scavenger? stay sir, stay?

KITELY Nay, brother DOWNE-RIGHT.

DOWNE-RIGHT 'Heart! stand you away, and you love me.

KITELY You shall not follow him now, I pray you, brother, Good
faith you shall not: I will over-rule you.

DOWNE-RIGHT Ha? scavenger? well, goe to, I say little: but, by this
good day (god forgive me I should sweare) if I put it up so, say,
I am the rankest cow, that ever pist. 'Sdeynes, and I swallow this,
Ile ne're draw my sword in the sight of *Fleet-street* againe, while I
20   live; Ile sit in a barne, with Madge-howlet, and catch mice first.
Scavenger? 'Heart, and Ile goe neere to fill that huge tumbrell-slop
of yours, with somewhat, and I have good lucke: your GARAGAN-
TUA breech cannot carry it away so.

KITELY Oh doe not fret your selfe thus, never thinke on't.

DOWNE-RIGHT These are my brothers consorts, these! these are his
Cam'rades, his walking mates! hee's a gallant, a *Cavaliero* too, right
hang-man cut! Let me not live, and I could not finde in my heart
to swinge the whole ging of 'hem, one after another, and begin
with him first. I am griev'd, it should be said he is my brother,
30   and take these courses. Wel, as he brewes, so he shall drinke, for
GEORGE, againe. Yet, he shall heare on't, and that tightly too, and
I live, Ifaith.

KITELY But, brother, let your reprehension (then)
Runne in an easie current, not ore-high
Carried with rashnesse, or devouring choller;
But rather use the soft perswading way,
Whose powers will worke more gently, and compose
Th'imperfect thoughts you labour to reclaime:
More winning, then enforcing the consent.

40   DOWNE-RIGHT I, I, let me alone for that, I warrant you.

Bell rings.   KITELY How now? oh, the bell rings to breakefast.
Brother, I pray you goe in, and beare my wife
Companie, till I come; Ile but give order
For some dispatch of businesse, to my servants—

[*Exit* DOWNE-RIGHT.]

Act II. Scene 3

KITELY, COB, DAME KITELY.   *To them.*

[*Enter* COB.]

KITELY What, COB? our maides will have you by the back
    (Ifaith) for comming so late this morning.
COB Perhaps so, sir, take heed some body have not them by the belly,   *He passes by*
    for walking so late in the evening.   [*Exit.*]   *with his*
                                                                         tankard.
KITELY Well, yet my troubled spirit's somewhat eas'd,
    Though not repos'd in that securitie,
    As I could wish: But, I must be content.
    How e're I set a face on't to the world,
    Would I had lost this finger, at a venter,
    So WELL-BRED had ne're lodg'd within my house.   10
    Why't cannot be, where there is such resort
    Of wanton gallants, and yong revellers,
    That any woman should be honest long.
    Is't like, that factious beautie will preserve
    The publike weale of chastitie, un-shaken,
    When such strong motives muster, and make head
    Against her single peace? no, no. Beware,
    When mutuall appetite doth meet to treat,
    And spirits of one kinde, and qualitie,
    Come once to parlee, in the pride of bloud: 20
    It is no slow conspiracie, that followes.
    Well (to be plaine) if I but thought, the time
    Had answer'd their affections: all the world
    Should not perswade me, but I were a cuckold.
    Mary, I hope, they ha'not got that start:
    For oportunitie hath balkt 'hem yet,
    And shall doe still, while I have eyes, and eares
    To attend the impositions of my heart.
    My presence shall be as an iron barre,
    'Twixt the conspiring motions of desire: 30
    Yea, every looke, or glance, mine eye ejects,
    Shall checke occasion, as one doth his slave,
    When he forgets the limits of prescription.

[*Enter* DAME KITELY *and* BRIDGET.]

DAME KITELY Sister BRIDGET, pray you fetch downe the rose-water
  above in the closet. [*Exit* BRIDGET.] Sweet heart, will you come
  in, to breakefast?

KITELY An' shee have over-heard me now?

DAME KITELY I pray thee (good MUSSE) we stay for you.

KITELY By heaven I would not for a thousand angells.

40 DAME KITELY What aile you sweet heart, are you not well, speake
  good MUSSE.

KITELY Troth my head akes extremely, on a sudden.

DAME KITELY Oh, the lord!

KITELY How now? what?

DAME KITELY Alas, how it burnes? MUSSE, keepe you warme, good
  truth it is this new disease! there's a number are troubled withall!
  for loves sake, sweet heart, come in, out of the aire.

KITELY How simple, and how subtill are her answeres?
  A new disease, and many troubled with it!

50 Why, true: shee heard me, all the world to nothing.

DAME KITELY I pray thee, good sweet heart, come in; the aire will
  doe you harme, in troth.

KITELY The aire! shee has me i' the wind! sweet heart!
  Ile come to you presently: 't will away, I hope.

DAME KITELY Pray heaven it doe.   [*Exit.*]

KITELY A new disease? I know not, new, or old,
  But it may well be call'd poore mortalls plague:
  For, like a pestilence, it doth infect
  The houses of the braine. First, it begins

60 Solely to worke upon the phantasie,
  Filling her seat with such pestiferous aire,
  As soone corrupts the judgement; and from thence
  Sends like contagion to the memorie:
  Still each to other giving the infection.
  Which, as a subtle vapor, spreads it selfe,
  Confusedly, through every sensive part,
  Till not a thought, or motion, in the mind,
  Be free from the blacke poyson of suspect.
  Ah, but what miserie' is it, to know this?

70 Or, knowing it, to want the mindes erection,

In such extremes? Well, I will once more strive,
(In spight of this black cloud) my selfe to be,
And shake the feaver off, that thus shakes me.   [*Exit.*]

Act II. Scene 4

BRAYNE-WORME, ED. KNO'WELL, MR. STEPHEN.

[*Enter* BRAYNE-WORME, *disguised.*]

BRAYNE-WORME S'lid, I cannot choose but laugh, to see my selfe
translated thus, from a poore creature to a creator; for now must
I create an intolerable sort of lyes, or my present profession looses
the grace: and yet the lye to a man of my coat, is as ominous a
fruit, as the *Fico*. O sir, it holds for good politie ever, to have that
outwardly in vilest estimation, that inwardly is most deare to us.
So much, for my borrowed shape. Well, the troth is, my old master
intends to follow my yong, drie foot, over *More-fields*, to *London*,
this morning: now I, knowing, of this hunting-match, or rather
conspiracie, and to insinuate with my yong master (for so must   10
we that are blew-waiters, and men of hope and service doe, or
perhaps wee may weare motley at the yeeres end, and who weares
motley, you know) have got me afore, in this disguise, determining
here to lye in *ambuscado*, and intercept him, in the mid-way. If I
can but get his cloke, his purse, his hat, nay, any thing, to cut him
off, that is, to stay his journey, *Veni, vidi, vici*, I may say with
Captayne CAESAR, I am made for ever, ifaith. Well, now must I
practice to get the true garb of one of these *Lance-knights*, my arme
here, and my—yong master! and his cousin, Mr. STEPHEN, as I
am true counterfeit man of warre, and no souldier! [*Moves away.*]   20

[*Enter* ED. KNO'WELL *and* STEPHEN.]

ED. KNO'WELL So sir, and how then, couss?

STEPHEN 'Sfoot, I have lost my purse, I thinke.

ED. KNO'WELL How? lost your purse? where? when had you it?

STEPHEN I cannot tell, stay.

BRAYNE-WORME 'Slid, I am afeard, they will know mee, would I
could get by them.

ED. KNO'WELL What? ha' you it?

STEPHEN No, I thinke I was bewitcht, I——

ED. KNO'WELL Nay, doe not weepe the losse, hang it, let it goe.

30 STEPHEN Oh, it's here: no, and it had beene lost, I had not car'd, but for a jet ring mistris MARY sent me.

ED. KNO'WELL A jet ring? oh, the *poesie*, the *poesie*?

STEPHEN Fine, ifaith! *Though fancie sleep, my love is deepe*. Meaning that though I did not fancie her, yet shee loved me dearely.

ED. KNO'WELL Most excellent!

STEPHEN And then, I sent her another, and my *poesie* was: *The deeper, the sweeter, Ile be judg'd by* St. PETER.

ED. KNO'WELL How, by St. PETER? I doe not conceive that!

STEPHEN Mary, St. PETER, to make up the meeter.

40 ED. KNO'WELL Well, there the Saint was your good patron, hee help't you at your need: thanke him, thanke him.

He is come back. BRAYNE-WORME I cannot take leave on 'hem, so: I will venture, come what will. Gentlemen, please you change a few crownes, for a very excellent good blade, here? I am a poore gentleman, a souldier, one that (in the better state of my fortunes) scorn'd so meane a refuge, but now it is the humour of necessitie, to have it so. You seeme to be gentlemen, well affected to martiall men, else I should rather die with silence, then live with shame: how ever, vouchsafe to remember, it is my want speakes, not my selfe. This condition agrees not with my spirit—

50 ED. KNO'WELL Where hast thou serv'd?

BRAYNE-WORME May it please you, sir, in all the late warres of *Bohemia, Hungaria, Dalmatia, Poland*, where not, sir? I have beene a poore servitor, by sea and land, any time this fourteene yeeres, and follow'd the fortunes of the best Commanders in *christendome*. I was twice shot at the taking of *Alepo*, once at the reliefe of *Vienna*; I have beene at *Marseilles, Naples*, and the *Adriatique* gulfe, a gentleman-slave in the galleys, thrice, where I was most dangerously shot in the head, through both the thighs, and yet, being thus maym'd, I am void of maintenance, nothing left me but my scarres, the noted markes of my resolution.

60 STEPHEN How will you sell this rapier, friend?

BRAYNE-WORME Generous sir, I referre it to your owne judgement; you are a gentleman, give me what you please.

STEPHEN True, I am a gentleman, I know that friend: but what though? I pray you say, what would you aske?

BRAYNE-WORME I assure you, the blade may become the side, or
    thigh of the best prince, in *Europe*.

ED. KNO'WELL I, with a velvet scabberd, I thinke.

STEPHEN Nay, and't be mine, it shall have a velvet scabberd, Couss,   70
    that's flat: I'de not weare it as 'tis, and you would give me an
    angell.

BRAYNE-WORME At your worships pleasure, sir; nay, 'tis a most pure
    Toledo.

STEPHEN I had rather it were a *Spaniard*! but tell me, what shall I
    give you for it? An' it had a silver hilt——

ED. KNO'WELL Come, come, you shall not buy it; hold, there's a
    shilling fellow, take thy rapier.

STEPHEN Why, but I will buy it now, because you say so, and there's   80
    another shilling, fellow. I scorne to be out-bidden. What, shall I
    walke with a cudgell, like *Higgin-Bottom*? and may have a rapier, for
    money?

ED. KNO'WELL You may buy one in the citie.

STEPHEN Tut, Ile buy this i' the field, so I will, I have a mind to't,
    because 'tis a field rapier. Tell me your lowest price.

ED. KNO'WELL You shall not buy it, I say.

STEPHEN By this money, but I will, though I give more then 'tis
    worth.

ED. KNO'WELL Come away, you are a foole.

STEPHEN Friend, I am a foole, that's granted: but Ile have it, for that   90
    words sake. Follow me, for your money.

BRAYNE-WORME At your service, sir.   [*Exeunt.*]

Act II. Scene 5

KNO'WELL, BRAYNE-WORME.

[*Enter* KNO'WELL.]

KNO'WELL I cannot loose the thought, yet, of this letter,
    Sent to my sonne: nor leave t'admire the change
    Of manners, and the breeding of our youth,
    Within the kingdome, since my selfe was one.
    When I was yong, he liv'd not in the stewes,
    Durst have conceiv'd a scorne, and utter'd it,

On a grey head; age was authoritie
Against a buffon: and a man had, then,
A certaine reverence pai'd unto his yeeres,
10   That had none due unto his life. So much
The sanctitie of some prevail'd, for others.
But, now, we all are fall'n; youth, from their feare:
And age, from that, which bred it, good example.
Nay, would our selves were not the first, even parents,
That did destroy the hopes, in our owne children:
Or they not learn'd our vices, in their cradles,
And suck'd in our ill customes, with their milke.
Ere all their teeth be borne, or they can speake,
We make their palats cunning! The first wordes,
20   We forme their tongues with, are licentious jests!
Can it call, whore? crie, bastard? o, then, kisse it,
A wittie childe! Can't sweare? The fathers dearling!
Give it two plums. Nay, rather then 't shall learne
No bawdie song, the mother'her selfe will teach it!
But, this is in the infancie; the dayes
Of the long coate: when it puts on the breeches,
It will put off all this. I, it is like:
When it is gone into the bone alreadie.
No, no: This die goes deeper then the coate,
30   Or shirt, or skin. It staines, unto the liver,
And heart, in some. And, rather, then it should not,
Note, what we fathers doe! Looke, how we live!
What mistresses we keepe! at what expense,
In our sonnes eyes! where they may handle our gifts,
Heare our lascivious courtships, see our dalliance,
Tast of the same provoking meates, with us,
To ruine of our states! Nay, when our owne
Portion is fled, to prey on their remainder,
We call them into fellowship of vice!
40   Baite 'hem with the yong chamber-maid, to seale!
And teach 'hem all bad wayes, to buy affliction!
This is one path! but there are millions more,
In which we spoile our owne, with leading them.
Well, I thanke heaven, I never yet was he,

That travail'd with my sonne, before sixteene,
To shew him, the *Venetian cortezans*.
Nor read the grammar of cheating, I had made
To my sharpe boy, at twelve: repeating still
The rule, *Get money*; still, *Get money, Boy;*
No matter, by what meanes; Money will doe   50
More, Boy, then my Lords letter. Neither have I
Drest snailes, or mushromes curiously before him,
Perfum'd my sauces, and taught him to make 'hem;
Preceding still, with my grey gluttonie,
At all the ordinaries: and only fear'd
His palate should degenerate, not his manners.
These are the trade of fathers, now! how ever
My sonne, I hope, hath met within my threshold,
None of these houshold precedents; which are strong,
And swift, to rape youth, to their precipice.   60
But, let the house at home be nere so cleane-
Swept, or kept sweet from filth; nay, dust, and cob-webs:
If he will live, abroad, with his companions,
In dung, and leystalls; it is worth a feare.
Nor is the danger of conversing lesse,
Then all that I have mention'd of example.

> [*Enter* BRAYNE-WORME.]

BRAYNE-WORME My master? nay, faith have at you: I am flesht now,
I have sped so well. Worshipfull sir, I beseech you, respect the
estate of a poore souldier; I am asham'd of this base course of life
(god's my comfort) but extremitie provokes me to't, what remedie?   70
KNO'WELL I have not for you, now.
BRAYNE-WORME By the faith I beare unto truth, gentleman, it is no
ordinarie custome in me, but only to preserve manhood. I protest
to you, a man I have beene, a man I may be, by your sweet bountie.
KNO'WELL 'Pray thee, good friend, be satisfied.
BRAYNE-WORME Good sir, by that hand, you may doe the part of a
kind gentleman, in lending a poore souldier the price of two cannes
of beere (a matter of small value) the king of heaven shall pay you,
and I shall rest thankfull: sweet worship—
KNO'WELL Nay, and you be so importunate——   80

Hee weepes.

BRAYNE-WORME Oh, tender sir, need will have his course: I was not
made to this vile use! well, the edge of the enemie could not have
abated mee so much: It's hard when a man hath serv'd in his
Princes cause, and be thus—Honorable worship, let me derive a
small piece of silver from you, it shall not bee given in the course
of time, by this good ground, I was faine to pawne my rapier last
night for a poore supper, I had suck'd the hilts long before, I am
a pagan else: sweet honor.

KNO'WELL Beleeve me, I am taken with some wonder,

90   To thinke, a fellow of thy outward presence
Should (in the frame, and fashion of his mind)
Be so degenerate, and sordid-base!
Art thou a man? and sham'st thou not to beg?
To practise such a servile kind of life?
Why, were thy education ne're so meane,
Having thy limbs, a thousand fairer courses
Offer themselves, to thy election.
Either the warres might still supply thy wants,
Or service of some vertuous gentleman,

100   Or honest labour: nay, what can I name,
But would become thee better then to beg?
But men of thy condition feed on sloth,
As doth the beetle, on the dung shee breeds in,
Not caring how the mettall of your minds
Is eaten with the rust of idlenesse.
Now, afore me, what e're he be, that should
Relieve a person of thy qualitie,
While thou insist's in this loose desperate course,
I would esteeme the sinne, not thine, but his.

110   BRAYNE-WORME Faith sir, I would gladly finde some other course,
if so—

KNO'WELL I, you'ld gladly finde it, but you will not seeke it.

BRAYNE-WORME Alas sir, where should a man seeke? in the warres,
there's no ascent by desert in these dayes, but—and for service,
would it were as soone purchast, as wisht for (the ayre's my
comfort) I know, what I would say——

KNO'WELL What's thy name?

BRAYNE-WORME Please you, FITZ-SWORD, sir.

KNO'WELL FITZ-SWORD?

   Say, that a man should entertayne thee now,   120
   Would'st thou be honest, humble, just, and true?

BRAYNE-WORME Sir, by the place, and honor of a souldier——

KNO'WELL Nay, nay, I like not those affected othes;
   Speake plainely man: what think'st thou of my wordes?

BRAYNE-WORME Nothing, sir, but wish my fortunes were as happy,
   as my service should be honest.

KNO'WELL Well, follow me, Ile prove thee, if thy deedes
   Will carry a proportion to thy words.

BRAYNE-WORME Yes sir, straight, Ile but garter my hose. [*Exit*
   KNO'WELL.] O that my belly were hoopt now, for I am readie to   130
   burst with laughing! never was bottle, or bag-pipe fuller. S'lid, was
   there ever seene a foxe in yeeres to betray himselfe thus? now
   shall I be possest of all his counsells: and, by that conduit, my
   yong master. Well, hee is resolv'd to prove my honestie; faith, and
   I am resolv'd to prove his patience: oh I shall abuse him intollerably.
   This small piece of service, will bring him cleane out of love with
   the souldier, for ever. He will never come within the signe of it,
   the sight of a cassock, or a musket-rest againe. Hee will hate the
   musters at Mile-end for it, to his dying day. It's no matter, let the
   world thinke me a bad counterfeit, if I cannot give him the slip,   140
   at an instant: why, this is better then to have staid his journey!
   well, Ile follow him: oh, how I long to bee imployed.   [*Exit.*]

Act III. Scene 1

MATTHEW, WELL-BRED, BOBADILL, ED. KNO'WELL,
STEPHEN.

[*Enter* MATTHEW, WELL-BRED *and* BOBADILL.]

MATTHEW Yes faith, sir, we were at your lodging to seeke you, too.

WELL-BRED Oh, I came not there to night.

BOBADILL Your brother delivered us as much.

WELL-BRED Who? my brother DOWNE-RIGHT?

BOBADILL He. Mr. WELL-BRED, I know not in what kind you hold
   me, but let me say to you this: as sure as honor, I esteeme it so

much out of the sunne-shine of reputation, to through the least
beame of reguard, upon such a——

WELL-BRED Sir, I must heare no ill wordes of my brother.

10 BOBADILL I, protest to you, as I have a thing to be sav'd about me,
I never saw any gentleman-like part——

WELL-BRED Good Captayne, *faces about*, to some other discourse.

BOBADILL With your leave, sir, and there were no more men living
upon the face of the earth, I should not fancie him, by S. GEORGE.

MATTHEW Troth, nor I, he is of a rusticall cut, I know not how: he
doth not carry himselfe like a gentleman of fashion—

WELL-BRED Oh, Mr. MATTHEW, that's a grace peculiar but to a few;
quos aequus amavit JUPITER.

19 MATTHEW I understand you sir.

*Yong Kno'well
enters.* WELL-BRED No question, you doe, or you doe not, sir. [*Enter* ED.
KNO'WELL *and* STEPHEN.] NED KNO'WELL! by my soule wel-
come; how doest thou sweet spirit, my *Genius*? S'lid I shall love
APOLLO, and the mad *Thespian* girles the better, while I live, for
this; my deare *furie*: now, I see there's some love in thee! Sirra,
these bee the two I writ to thee of (nay, what a drowsie humour
is this now? why doest thou not speake?)

ED. KNO'WELL Oh, you are a fine gallant, you sent me a rare letter!

WELL-BRED Why, was't not rare?

ED. KNO'WELL Yes, Ile bee sworne, I was ne're guiltie of reading
30 the like; match it in all PLINIE, or SYMMACHUS epistles, and Ile
have my judgement burn'd in the eare for a rogue: make much of
thy vaine, for it is inimitable. But I marle what camell it was, that
had the carriage of it? for doubtlesse, he was no ordinarie beast,
that brought it!

WELL-BRED Why?

ED. KNO'WELL Why, saiest thou? why doest thou thinke that any
reasonable creature, especially in the morning (the sober time of
the day too) could have mis-tane my father for me?

WELL-BRED S'lid, you jest, I hope?

40 ED. KNO'WELL Indeed, the best use wee can turne it too, is to make
a jest on't, now: but Ile assure you, my father had the full view o'
your flourishing stile, some houre before I saw it.

WELL-BRED What a dull slave was this? But, sirrah, what said hee to
it, Ifaith?

ED. KNO'WELL Nay, I know not what he said: but I have a shrewd
  gesse what hee thought.

WELL-BRED What? what?

ED. KNO'WELL Mary, that thou art some strange dissolute yong
  fellow, and I a graine or two better, for keeping thee companie.

WELL-BRED Tut, that thought is like the moone in her last quarter,   50
  'twill change shortly: but, sirrha, I pray thee be acquainted with
  my two hang-by's, here; thou wilt take exceeding pleasure in 'hem
  if thou hear'st 'hem once goe: my wind-instruments. Ile wind 'hem
  up—but what strange piece of silence is this? the signe of the
  dumbe man?

ED. KNO'WELL Oh, sir, a kinsman of mine, one that may make your
  musique the fuller, and he please, he has his humour, sir.

WELL-BRED Oh, what ist? what ist?

ED. KNO'WELL Nay, Ile neither doe your judgement, nor his folly
  that wrong, as to prepare your apprehension: Ile leave him to the   60
  mercy o' your search, if you can take him, so.

WELL-BRED Well, Captaine BOBADILL, Mr. MATTHEW, pray you
  know this gentleman here, he is a friend of mine, and one that
  will deserve your affection. I know not your name sir, but I shall   *To Master*
  be glad of any occasion, to render me more familiar to you.   *Stephen.*

STEPHEN My name is Mr. STEPHEN, sir, I am this gentlemans owne
  cousin, sir, his father is mine unckle, sir, I am somewhat melancholy,
  but you shall command me, sir, in whatsoever is incident to a
  gentleman.   69

BOBADILL Sir, I must tell you this, I am no generall man, but for Mr.   *To Kno'well.*
  WEL-BRED's sake (you may embrace it, at what height of favour
  you please) I doe communicate with you: and conceive you, to
  bee a gentleman of some parts, I love few wordes.

ED. KNO'WELL And I fewer, sir. I have scarce inow, to thanke you.

MATTHEW But are you indeed, sir? so given to it?   *To Master*
    Stephen.

STEPHEN I, truely, sir, I am mightily given to melancholy.

MATTHEW Oh, it's your only fine humour, sir, your true melancholy
  breeds your perfect fine wit, sir: I am melancholy my selfe divers
  times, sir, and then doe I no more but take pen, and paper presently,
  and overflow you halfe a score, or a dozen of sonnets, at a sitting.   80

(ED. KNO'WELL Sure, he utters them then, by the grosse.)

STEPHEN Truely sir, and I love such things, out of measure.

ED. KNO'WELL I faith, better then in measure, Ile under-take.

MATTHEW Why, I pray you, sir, make use of my studie, it's at your
service.

STEPHEN I thanke you sir, I shall bee bold, I warrant you; have you
a stoole there, to be melancholy' upon?

MATTHEW That I have, sir, and some papers there of mine owne
doing, at idle houres, that you'le say there's some sparkes of wit
90   in 'hem, when you see them.

WELL-BRED Would the sparkes would kindle once, and become a
fire amongst 'hem, I might see selfe-love burn't for her heresie.

STEPHEN Cousin, is it well? am I melancholy inough?

ED. KNO'WELL Oh I, excellent!

WELL-BRED Captaine BOBADILL: why muse you so?

ED. KNO'WELL He is melancholy, too.

BOBADILL Faith, sir, I was thinking of a most honorable piece of
service, was perform'd to morrow, being St. MARKES day: shall
bee some ten yeeres, now?

100 ED. KNO'WELL In what place, Captaine?

BOBADILL Why, at the beleag'ring of *Strigonium*, where, in lesse then
two houres, seven hundred resolute gentlemen, as any were in
Europe, lost their lives upon the breach. Ile tell you, gentlemen, it
was the first, but the best league, that ever I beheld, with these
eies, except the taking in of—what doe you call it, last yeere, by
the *Genowayes*, but that (of all other) was the most fatall, and
dangerous exploit, that ever I was rang'd in, since I first bore
armes before the face of the enemie, as I am a gentleman, &
souldier.

110 STEPHEN 'So, I had as liefe, as an angell, I could sweare as well as
that gentleman!

ED. KNO'WELL Then, you were a servitor, at both it seemes! at
Strigonium? and what doe you call't?

BOBADILL Oh lord, sir? by S. GEORGE, I was the first man, that
entred the breach: and, had I not effected it with resolution, I had
beene slaine, if I had had a million of lives.

ED. KNO'WELL 'Twas pittie, you had not ten; a cats, and your owne,
ifaith. But, was it possible?

(MATTHEW 'Pray you, marke this discourse, sir.

120 STEPHEN So, I doe.)

BOBADILL I assure you (upon my reputation) 'tis true, and your selfe
   shall confesse.

ED. KNO'WELL You must bring me to the racke, first.

BOBADILL Observe me judicially, sweet sir, they had planted mee
   three demi-culverings, just in the mouth of the breach; now, sir
   (as we were to give on) their master gunner (a man of no meane
   skill, and marke, you must thinke) confronts me with his linstock,
   readie to give fire; I spying his intendment, discharg'd my petronel
   in his bosome, and with these single armes, my poore rapier, ranne
   violently, upon the *Moores*, that guarded the ordinance, and put   130
   'hem pell-mell to the sword.

WELL-BRED To the sword? to the rapier, Captaine?

ED. KNO'WELL Oh, it was a good figure observ'd, sir! but did you
   all this, Captaine, without hurting your blade?

BOBADILL Without any impeach, o' the earth: you shall perceive sir.
   It is the most fortunate weapon, that ever rid on poore gentlemans
   thigh: shal I tell you, sir? you talke of *Morglay*, *Excalibur*, *Durindana*,
   or so? tut, I lend no credit to that is fabled of 'hem, I know the
   vertue of mine owne, and therefore I dare, the boldlier, maintaine
   it.   140

STEPHEN I mar'le whether it be a *Toledo*, or no?

BOBADILL A most perfect *Toledo*, I assure you, sir.

STEPHEN I have a countriman of his, here.

MATTHEW Pray you, let's see, sir: yes faith, it is!

BOBADILL This a *Toledo*? pish.

STEPHEN Why doe you pish, Captaine?

BOBADILL A *Fleming*, by heaven, Ile buy them for a guilder, a piece,
   an' I would have a thousand of them.

ED. KNO'WELL How say you, cousin? I told you thus much?

WELL-BRED Where bought you it, Mr. STEPHEN?   150

STEPHEN Of a scurvie rogue souldier (a hundred of lice goe with
   him) he swore it was a *Toledo*.

BOBADILL A poore provant rapier, no better.

MATTHEW Masse, I thinke it be, indeed! now I looke on't, better.

ED. KNO'WELL Nay, the longer you looke on't, the worse. Put it up,
   put it up.

STEPHEN Well, I will put it up, but by——(I ha' forgot the Captaynes
   oath, I thought to ha' sworne by it) an' ere I meet him——

WELL-BRED O, it is past helpe now, sir, you must have patience.

160 STEPHEN Horson connie-catching raskall! I could eate the very hilts
for anger!

ED. KNO'WELL A signe of good digestion! you have an ostrich
stomack, cousin.

STEPHEN A stomack? would I had him here, you should see, an' I
had a stomack.

WELL-BRED It's better as 'tis: come, gentlemen, shall we goe?

Act III. Scene 2

E. KNO'WELL, BRAYNE-WORME, STEPHEN, WELL-BRED,
BOBADILL, MATTHEW.

[*Enter* BRAYNE-WORME.]

ED. KNO'WELL A miracle, cousin, looke here! looke here!

STEPHEN Oh, gods lid, by your leave, doe you know me, sir?

BRAYNE-WORME I sir, I know you, by sight.

STEPHEN You sold me a rapier, did you not?

BRAYNE-WORME Yes, marie, did I sir.

STEPHEN You said, it was a *Toledo*, ha?

BRAYNE-WORME True, I did so.

STEPHEN But, it is none?

BRAYNE-WORME No sir, I confesse it, it is none.

10 STEPHEN Doe you confesse it? gentlemen, beare witnesse, he has
confest it. By gods will, and you had not confest it——

ED. KNO'WELL Oh cousin, forbeare, forbeare.

STEPHEN Nay, I have done, cousin.

WELL-BRED Why you have done like a gentleman, he ha's confest
it, what would you more?

STEPHEN Yet, by his leave, he is a raskall, under his favour, doe you
see?   [*Exeunt* STEPHEN, BOBADILL *and* MATTHEW.]

ED. KNO'WELL I, by his leave, he is, and under favour: a prettie piece
of civilitie! Sirra, how doest thou like him?

20 WELL-BRED Oh, it's a most pretious foole, make much on him: I
can compare him to nothing more happily, then a drumme; for
every one may play upon him.

ED. KNO'WELL No, no, a childes whistle were farre the fitter.

BRAYNE-WORME Sir, shall I intreat a word with you?

ED. KNO'WELL With me, sir? you have not another *Toledo* to sell, ha'
you?

BRAYNE-WORME You are conceipted, sir, your name is Mr.
KNO'WELL, as I take it?

ED. KNO'WELL You are i' the right; you meane not to proceede in
the catechisme, doe you?   30

BRAYNE-WORME No sir, I am none of that coat.

ED. KNO'WELL Of as bare a coat, though; well, say sir.

BRAYNE-WORME Faith sir, I am but servant to the drum extraordinarie, and indeed (this smokie varnish being washt off, and three or
four patches remov'd) I appeare your worships in reversion, after
the decease of your good father, BRAYNE-WORME.

ED. KNO'WELL BRAYNE-WORME! S'light, what breath of a conjurer,
hath blowne thee hither in this shape?

BRAYNE-WORME The breath o' your letter, sir, this morning: the
same that blew you to the wind-mill, and your father after you.   40

ED. KNO'WELL My father?

BRAYNE-WORME Nay, never start, 'tis true, he has follow'd you over
the field's, by the foot, as you would doe a hare i' the snow.

ED. KNO'WELL Sirra, WEL-BRED, what shall we doe, sirra? my father
is come over, after me.

WELL-BRED Thy father? where is he?

BRAYNE-WORME At Justice CLEMENTS house here, in *Colman*-street,
where he but staies my returne; and then——

WELL-BRED Who's this? BRAYNE-WORME?

BRAYNE-WORME The same, sir.   50

WELL-BRED Why how, i' the name of wit, com'st thou transmuted,
thus?

BRAYNE-WORME Faith, a devise, a devise: nay, for the love of reason,
gentlemen, and avoiding the danger, stand not here, withdraw,
and Ile tell you all.

WELL-BRED But, art thou sure, he will stay thy returne?

BRAYNE-WORME Doe I live, sir? what a question is that?

WELL-BRED Wee'le prorogue his expectation then, a little: BRAYNE-
WORME, thou shalt goe with us. Come on, gentlemen, nay, I pray
thee, sweet NED, droope not: 'heart, and our wits be so wretchedly   60
dull, that one old plodding braine can out-strip us all, would we

were eene prest, to make porters of; and serve out the remnant
of our daies, in *Thames*-street, or at *Custome*-house key, in a civill
warre, against the car-men.

BRAYNE-WORME AMEN, AMEN, AMEN, say I.   [*Exeunt.*]

Act III. Scene 3

KITELY, CASH.

[*Enter* KITELY *and* CASH.]

KITELY What saies he, THOMAS? Did you speake with him?

CASH He will expect you, sir, within this halfe houre.

KITELY Has he the money readie, can you tell?

CASH Yes, sir, the money was brought in, last night.

KITELY O, that's well: fetch me my cloke, my cloke.   [*Exit* CASH.]
     Stay, let me see, an houre, to goe and come;
     I, that will be the least: and then 'twill be
     An houre, before I can dispatch with him;
     Or very neere: well, I will say two houres.
10   Two houres? ha? things, never dreamt of yet,
     May be contriv'd, I, and effected too,
     In two houres absence: well, I will not goe.
     Two houres; no, fleering oportunitie,
     I will not give your subtiltie that scope.
     Who will not judge him worthie to be rob'd,
     That sets his doores wide open to a thiefe,
     And shewes the fellon, where his treasure lies?
     Againe, what earthie spirit but will attempt
     To taste the fruit of beauties golden tree,
20   When leaden sleepe seales up the Dragons eyes?
     I will not goe. Businesse, goe by, for once.
     No beautie, no; you are of too good caract,
     To be left so, without a guard, or open!
     Your lustre too'll enflame, at any distance,
     Draw courtship to you, as a jet doth strawes,
     Put motion in a stone, strike fire from ice,
     Nay, make a porter leape you, with his burden!
     You must be then kept up, close, and well-watch'd,

For, give you oportunitie, no quick-sand
Devoures, or swallowes swifter! He that lends   30
His wife (if shee be faire) or time, or place;
Compells her to be false. I will not goe.
The dangers are to many. And, then, the dressing
Is a most mayne attractive! Our great heads,
Within the citie, never were in safetie,
Since our wives wore these little caps: Ile change 'hem,
Ile change 'hem, streight, in mine. Mine shall no more
Weare three-pild akornes, to make my hornes ake.
Nor, will I goe. I am resolv'd for that.
        [*Enter* CASH.]
Carry' in my cloke againe. Yet, stay. Yet, doe too.   40
I will deferre going, on all occasions.
CASH Sir. SNARE, your scrivener, will be there with th'bonds.
KITELY That's true! foole on me! I had cleane forgot it,
    I must goe. What's a clocke?
CASH   *Exchange* time, sir.
KITELY 'Heart, then will WELL-BRED presently be here, too,
    With one, or other of his loose consorts.
    I am a knave, if I know what to say,
    What course to take, or which way to resolve.
    My braine (me thinkes) is like an houre-glasse,
    Wherein, my' imaginations runne, like sands,   50
    Filling up time; but then are turn'd, and turn'd:
    So, that I know not what to stay upon,
    And lesse, to put in act. It shall be so.
    Nay, I dare build upon his secrecie,
    He knowes not to deceive me. THOMAS?
CASH   Sir.
KITELY Yet now, I have bethought me, too, I will not.
    THOMAS, is COB within?
CASH   I thinke he be, sir.
KITELY But hee'll prate too, there's no speech of him.
    No, there were no man o' the earth to THOMAS,
    If I durst trust him; there is all the doubt.   60
    But, should he have a chinke in him, I were gone,
    Lost i' my fame for ever: talke for th'Exchange.

    The manner he hath stood with, till this present,
    Doth promise no such change! what should I feare then?
    Well, come what will, Ile tempt my fortune, once.
    THOMAS—you may deceive me, but, I hope——
    Your love, to me, is more—

CASH   Sir, if a servants
    Duetie, with faith, may be call'd love, you are
    More then in hope, you are possess'd of it.

70 KITELY I thanke you, heartily, THOMAS; Gi' me your hand:
    With all my heart, good THOMAS. I have, THOMAS,
    A secret to impart, unto you—but
    When once you have it, I must seale your lips up:
    (So farre, I tell you, THOMAS.)

CASH   Sir, for that—

KITELY Nay, heare me, out. Thinke, I esteeme you, THOMAS,
    When, I will let you in, thus, to my private.
    It is a thing sits, neerer, to my crest,
    Then thou art ware of, THOMAS. If thou should'st
    Reveale it, but—

CASH   How? I reveale it?

KITELY   Nay,
80 I doe not thinke thou would'st; but if thou should'st:
    'Twere a great weakenesse.

CASH   A great trecherie.
    Give it no other name.

KITELY   Thou wilt not do't, then?

CASH Sir, if I doe, mankind disclaime me, ever.

KITELY He will not sweare, he has some reservation,
    Some conceal'd purpose, and close meaning, sure:
    Else (being urg'd so much) how should he choose,
    But lend an oath to all this protestation?
    H'is no precisian, that I am certaine of.
    Nor rigid *Roman*-catholike. Hee'll play,
90 At *Fayles*, and *Tick-tack*, I have heard him sweare.
    What should I thinke of it? urge him againe,
    And by some other way? I will doe so.
    Well, THOMAS, thou hast sworne not to disclose;
    Yes, you did sweare?

CASH   Not yet, sir, but I will,
    Please you—

KITELY   No, THOMAS, I dare take thy word.
    But; if thou wilt sweare, doe, as thou think'st good;
    I am resolv'd without it; at thy pleasure.

CASH By my soules safetie then, sir, I protest.
    My tongue shall ne're take knowledge of a word,
    Deliver'd me in nature of your trust.   100

KITELY It's too much, these ceremonies need not,
    I know thy faith to be as firme as rock.
    THOMAS, come hither, neere: we cannot be
    Too private, in this businesse. So it is,
    (Now, he ha's sworne, I dare the safelier venter)
    I have of late, by divers observations——
    (But, whether his oath can bind him, yea, or no;
    Being not taken lawfully? ha? say you?
    I will aske counsell, ere I doe proceed:)
    THOMAS, it will be now too long to stay,   110
    Ile spie some fitter time soone, or to morrow.

CASH Sir, at your pleasure?

KITELY   I will thinke. And, THOMAS,
    I pray you search the bookes 'gainst my returne,
    For the receipts 'twixt me, and TRAPS.

CASH   I will, sir.

KITELY And, heare you, if your mistris brother, WEL-BRED,
    Chance to bring hither any gentlemen,
    Ere I come backe; let one straight bring me word.

CASH Very well, sir.

KITELY   To the Exchange; doe you heare?
    Or here in *Colman*-street, to Justice CLEMENTS.
    Forget it not, nor be not out of the way.   120

CASH I will not, sir.

KITELY   I pray you have a care on't.
    Or whether he come, or no, if any other,
    Stranger, or else, faile not to send me word.

CASH I shall not, sir.

KITELY   Be't your speciall businesse
    Now, to remember it.

CASH   Sir. I warrant you.

KITELY But, THOMAS, this is not the secret, THOMAS,
    I told you of.

CASH   No, sir. I doe suppose it.

KITELY Beleeve me, it is not.

CASH   Sir. I doe beleeve you.

KITELY By heaven, it is not, that's enough. But, THOMAS,
130   I would not, you should utter it, doe you see?
    To any creature living, yet, I care not.
    Well, I must hence. THOMAS, conceive thus much.
    It was a tryall of you, when I meant
    So deepe a secret to you, I meane not this,
    But that I have to tell you, this is nothing, this.
    But, THOMAS, keepe this from my wife, I charge you,
    Lock'd up in silence, mid-night, buried here.
    No greater hell, then to be slave to feare.   [*Exit.*]

CASH Lock'd up in silence, mid-night, buried here.
140   Whence should this floud of passion (trow) take head? ha?
    Best, dreame no longer of this running humour,
    For feare I sinke! the violence of the streame
    Alreadie hath transported me so farre,
    That I can feele no ground at all! but soft,
    Oh, 'tis our water-bearer: somewhat ha's crost him, now.

Act III. Scene 4

COB, CASH.

[*Enter* COB.]

COB Fasting dayes? what tell you me of fasting dayes? S'lid, would
    they were all on a light fire for me: They say, the whole world
    shall bee consum'd with fire one day, but would I had these
    ember-weekes, and villanous fridayes burnt, in the meane time,
    and then——

CASH Why, how now COB, what moves thee to this choller? ha?

COB Collar, master THOMAS? I scorne your collar, I sir, I am none
    o' your cart-horse, though I carry, and draw water. An' you offer

to ride me, with your collar, or halter either, I may hap shew you
a jades trick, sir.

CASH O, you'll slip your head out of the collar? why, goodman COB,
you mistake me.

COB Nay, I have my rewme, & I can be angrie as well as another, sir.

CASH Thy rewme, COB? thy humour, thy humour? thou mistak'st.

COB Humour? mack, I thinke it be so, indeed: what is that humour?
some rare thing, I warrant.

CASH Mary, Ile tell thee, COB: It is a gentleman-like monster, bred,
in the speciall gallantrie of our time, by affectation; and fed by
folly.

COB How? must it be fed?

CASH Oh I, humour is nothing, if it bee not fed. Didst thou never
heare that? it's a common phrase, *Feed my humour.*

COB Ile none on it: Humour, avant, I know you not, be gone. Let
who will make hungrie meales for your monster-ship, it shall not
bee I. Feed you, quoth he? S'lid, I ha' much adoe, to feed my selfe;
especially, on these leane rascally dayes, too; and't had beene any
other day, but a fasting-day (a plague on them all for mee) by this
light, one might have done the common-wealth good service, and
have drown'd them all i' the floud, two or three hundred thousand
yeeres agoe. O, I doe stomack them hugely! I have a maw now,
and't were for Sr BEVIS his horse, against 'hem.

CASH I pray thee, good COB, what makes thee so out of love with
fasting-dayes?

COB Mary that, which will make any man out of love with 'hem, I
thinke: their bad conditions, and you will needs know. First, they
are of a *Flemmish* breed, I am sure on't, for they raven up more
butter, then all the dayes of the weeke, beside; next, they stinke
of fish, and leeke-porridge miserably: thirdly, they'le keepe a man
devoutly hungrie, all day, and at night send him supperlesse to
bed.

CASH Indeed, these are faults, COB.

COB Nay, and this were all, 'twere something, but they are the only
knowne enemies, to my generation. A fasting-day, no sooner
comes, but my lineage goes to racke, poore cobs they smoke for
it, they are made martyrs o' the gridiron, they melt in passion: and
your maides too know this, and yet would have me turne

10

20

30

40

He pulls out a
red herring.

HANNIBAL, and eate my owne fish, and bloud: My princely couz, fear nothing; I have not the hart to devoure you, & I might be made as rich as King COPHETUA. O, that I had roome for my

50

teares, I could weepe salt-water enough, now, to preserve the lives of ten thousand of my kin. But I may curse none but these filthie *Almanacks*, for an't were not for them, these dayes of persecution would ne're be knowne. Ile bee hang'd, an' some Fish-mongers sonne doe not make of 'hem; and puts in more fasting-dayes then he should doe, because hee would utter his fathers dryed stock-fish, and stinking conger.

CASH S'light, peace, thou'lt bee beaten like a stock-fish, else: here is Mr. MATTHEW. Now must I looke out for a messenger to my master. [*Exeunt.*]

Act III. Scene 5

WELL-BRED, ED. KNO'WELL, BRAYNE-WORME, BOBADILL, MATTHEW, STEPHEN, THOMAS, COB.

[*Enter* WELL-BRED, ED. KNO'WELL, BRAYNE-WORME, BOBADILL, MATTHEW *and* STEPHEN.]

WELL-BRED Beshrew me, but it was an absolute good jest, and exceedingly well carried!

ED. KNO'WELL I, and our ignorance maintain'd it as well, did it not?

WELL-BRED Yes faith, but was't possible thou should'st not know him? I forgive Mr. STEPHEN, for he is stupiditie it selfe!

ED. KNO'WELL 'Fore god, not I, and I might have been joyn'd patten with one of the seven wise masters, for knowing him. He had so writhen himselfe, into the habit of one of your poore *Infanterie*, your decay'd, ruinous, worme-eaten gentlemen of the round: such

10

as have vowed to sit on the skirts of the citie, let your Provost, and his halfe-dozen of halberdeirs doe what they can; and have translated begging out of the old hackney pace, to a fine easie amble, and made it runne as smooth, of the tongue, as a shove-groat shilling. Into the likenesse of one of these *Reformado's* had he moulded himselfe so perfectly, observing every tricke of their action, as varying the accent, swearing with an *emphasis*, indeed all, with so speciall, and exquisite a grace, that (hadst thou seene him) thou would'st have sworne, he might have beene Serjeant-*Major*, if not Lieutenant-*Coronell* to the regiment.

WELL-BRED Why, BRAYNE-WORME, who would have thought thou   20
hadst beene such an artificer?

ED. KNO'WELL An artificer! An architect! except a man had studied begging all his life-time, and beene a weaver of language, from his infancie, for the clothing of it! I never saw his rivall.

WELL-BRED Where got'st thou this coat, I mar'le?

BRAYNE-WORME Of a *Hounds-ditch* man, sir. One of the devil's neere kinsmen, a broker.

WELL-BRED That cannot be, if the proverbe hold; for, a craftie knave needs no broker.

BRAYNE-WORME True sir, but I did need a broker, *Ergo*.   30

WELL-BRED (Well put off) no craftie knave, you'll say.

ED. KNO'WELL Tut, he ha's more of these shifts.

BRAYNE-WORME And yet where I have one, the broker ha's ten, sir.
    [*Enter* CASH.]

CASH FRANCIS, MARTIN, ne're a one to be found, now? what a spite's this?

WELL-BRED How now, THOMAS? is my brother KITELY, within?

CASH No sir, my master went forth eene now: but master DOWNE-RIGHT is within. COB, what COB? is he gone too?

WELL-BRED Whither went your master? THOMAS, canst thou tell?

CASH I know not, to Justice CLEMENTS, I thinke, sir. COB. [*Exit.*]   40

ED. KNO'WELL Justice CLEMENT, what's he?

WELL-BRED Why, doest thou not know him? he is a citie-magistrate, a Justice here, an excellent good Lawyer, and a great scholler: but the onely mad, merrie, old fellow in *Europe!* I shew'd him you, the other day.

ED. KNO'WELL Oh, is that he? I remember him now. Good faith, and he ha's a very strange presence, mee thinkes; it shewes as if hee stood out of the ranke, from other men: I have heard many of his jests i' the *universitie*. They say, he will commit a man, for taking the wall, of his horse.   50

WELL-BRED I, or wearing his cloke of one shoulder, or serving of god: any thing indeed, if it come in the way of his humour.

Cash goes in and out calling.

CASH GASPER, MARTIN, COB: 'heart, where should they be, trow?

BOBADILL Master KITELY's man, 'pray thee vouchsafe us the lighting
of this match.

CASH Fire on your match, no time but now to vouchsafe? FRANCIS.
COB.

BOBADILL Bodie of me! here's the remainder of seven pound, since
yesterday was seven-night. 'Tis your right *Trinidado!* did you never
60   take any, master STEPHEN?

STEPHEN No truely, sir; but I'le learne to take it now, since you
commend it, so.

BOBADILL Sir, beleeve me (upon my relation) for what I tell you, the
world shal not reprove. I have been in the *Indies* (where this herb
growes) where neither my selfe, nor a dozen gentlemen more (of
my knowledge) have received the tast of any other nutriment, in
the world, for the space of one and twentie weekes, but the fume
of this simple onely. Therefore, it cannot be, but 'tis most divine!
Further, take it in the nature, in the true kind so, it makes an
70   *antidote*, that (had you taken the most deadly poysonous plant in
all *Italy*) it should expell it, and clarifie you, with as much ease, as
I speake. And, for your greene wound, your *Balsamum*, and your
St. JOHN's *woort* are all mere gulleries, and trash to it, especially
your *Trinidado*: your *Nicotian* is good too. I could say what I know
of the vertue of it, for the expulsion of rhewmes, raw humours,
crudities, obstructions, with a thousand of this kind; but I professe
my selfe no *quack-salver*. Only, thus much, by HERCULES, I doe
hold it, and will affirme it (before any Prince in *Europe*) to be the
most soveraigne, and precious weede, that ever the earth tendred
80   to the use of man.

ED. KNO'WELL This speech would ha' done decently in a *tabacco*-
traders mouth!

[*Enter* CASH *and* COB.]

CASH At Justice CLEMENTS, hee is: in the middle of *Colman*-street.

COB O, oh?

BOBADILL Where's the match I gave thee? Master KITELIES man?

CASH Would his match, and he, and pipe, and all were at SANCTO
DOMINGO! I had forgot it.   [*Exit.*]

COB By gods mee, I marle, what pleasure, or felicitie they have in
taking this roguish *tabacco*! it's good for nothing, but to choke a
90   man, and fill him full of smoke, and embers: there were foure

dyed out of one house, last weeke, with taking of it, and two more the bell went for, yester-night; one of them (they say) will ne're scape it: he voided a bushell of soot yester-day, upward, and downeward. By the stocks, an' there were no wiser men then I, I'ld have it present whipping, man, or woman, that should but deale with a *tabacco*-pipe; why, it will stifle them all in the end, as many as use it; it's little better then rats bane, or rosaker.

ALL   Oh, good Captayne, hold, hold.

BOBADILL   You base cullion, you.

    [*Enter* CASH.]

CASH   Sir, here's your match: come, thou must needs be talking, too, tho'art well inough serv'd.

COB   Nay, he will not meddle with his match, I warrant you: well it shall be a deare beating, and I live.

BOBADILL   Doe you prate? Doe you murmure?

ED. KNO'WELL   Nay, good Captayne, will you regard the humour of a foole? away, knave.

WELL-BRED   THOMAS, get him away.   [*Exeunt* CASH *and* COB.]

BOBADILL   A horson filthie slave, a dung-worme, an excrement! Body o' CAESAR, but that I scorne to let forth so meane a spirit, I'ld ha' stab'd him, to the earth.

WELL-BRED   Mary, the law forbid, sir.

BOBADILL   By PHAROAHS foot, I would have done it.

STEPHEN   Oh, he sweares admirably! (by PHAROAHS foot) (body of CAESAR) I shall never doe it, sure (upon mine honor, and by Saint GEORGE) no, I ha' not the right grace.

MATTHEW   Master STEPHEN, will you any? By this aire, the most divine *tabacco*, that ever I drunke!

STEPHEN   None, I thanke you, sir. O, this gentleman do's it, rarely too! but nothing like the other. By this aire, as I am a gentleman: by—   [*Exeunt* BOBADILL *and* MATTHEW.]

BRAYNE-WORME   Master, glance, glance! Master WELL-BRED!

STEPHEN   As I have somewhat to be saved, I protest——

WELL-BRED   You are a foole: It needes no *affidavit*.

ED. KNO'WELL   Cousin, will you any *tabacco*?

STEPHEN   I sir! upon my reputation—

ED. KNO'WELL   How now, cousin!

STEPHEN   I protest, as I am a gentleman, but no souldier, indeed——

Bobadil beates him with a cudgell.

100

110

120

Master Stephen is practising, to the post.

WELL-BRED No, Master STEPHEN? as I remember your name is
entred in the artillerie garden?

130   STEPHEN I sir, that's true: Cousin, may I swear, as I am a souldier,
by that?

ED. KNO'WELL Oh yes, that you may. It's all you have for your
money.

STEPHEN Then, as I am a gentleman, and a souldier, it is divine
tabacco!

WELL-BRED But soft, where's Mr. MATTHEW? gone?

BRAYNE-WORME No, sir, they went in here.

WELL-BRED O, let's follow them: master MATTHEW is gone to salute
his mistris, in verse. Wee shall ha' the happinesse, to heare some of
140   his poetrie, now. Hee never comes unfurnish'd. BRAYNE-WORME?

STEPHEN BRAYNE-WORME? Where? Is this BRAYNE-WORME?

ED. KNO'WELL I, cousin, no wordes of it, upon your gentilitie.

STEPHEN Not I, body of me, by this aire, S. GEORGE, and the foot
of PHAROAH.

WELL-BRED Rare! your cousins discourse is simply drawn out with
oathes.

ED. KNO'WELL 'Tis larded with 'hem. A kind of french dressing, if
you love it.   [*Exeunt.*]

Act III. Scene 6

KITELY, COB.

[*Enter* KITELY *and* COB.]

KITELY Ha? how many are there, sayest thou?

COB Mary sir, your brother, master WELL-BRED——

KITELY Tut, beside him: what strangers are there, man?

COB Strangers? let me see, one, two; masse I know not well, there
are so many.

KITELY How? so many?

COB I, there's some five, or sixe of them, at the most.

KITELY A swarme, a swarme,
Spight of the devill, how they sting my head
10   With forked stings, thus wide, and large! But, COB,
How long hast thou beene comming hither, COB?

COB A little while, sir.

KITELY Did'st thou come running?

COB No, sir.

KITELY Nay, then I am familiar with thy haste!
    Bane to my fortunes: what meant I to marry?
    I, that before was rankt in such content,
    My mind at rest too, in so soft a peace,
    Being free master of mine owne free thoughts,
    And now become a slave? What? never sigh,   20
    Be of good cheere, man: for thou art a cuckold,
    'Tis done, 'tis done! nay, when such flowing store,
    Plentie it selfe, falls in my wives lap,
    The *Cornu-copiae* will be mine, I know. But, COB,
    What entertaynement had they? I am sure
    My sister, and my wife, would bid them welcome! ha?

COB Like inough, sir, yet, I heard not a word of it.

KITELY No: their lips were seal'd with kisses, and the voyce
    Drown'd in a floud of joy, at their arrivall,
    Had lost her motion, state, and facultie.   30
    COB, which of them was't, that first kist my wife?
    (My sister, I should say) my wife, alas,
    I feare not her: ha? who was it, say'st thou?

COB By my troth, sir, will you have the truth of it?

KITELY Oh I, good COB: I pray thee, heartily.

COB Then, I am a vagabond, and fitter for *Bride-well,* then your
    worships companie, if I saw any bodie to be kist, unlesse they
    would have kist the post, in the middle of the ware-house; for
    there I left them all, at their *tabacco,* with a poxe.

KITELY How? were they not gone in, then, e're thou cam'st?   40

COB Oh no sir.

KITELY Spite of the devill! what doe I stay here, then?
    COB, follow me.   *[Exit.]*

COB Nay, soft and faire, I have egges on the spit; I cannot goe
    yet, sir. Now am I for some five and fiftie reasons hammering,
    hammering revenge: oh, for three or foure gallons of vineger, to
    sharpen my wits. Revenge: vineger revenge: vineger, and mustard
    revenge: nay, and hee had not lyen in my house, 't would never

have griev'd me, but being my guest, one, that Ile be sworne, my
wife ha's lent him her smock off her back, while his one shirt ha's
beene at washing; pawn'd her neckerchers for cleane bands for
him; sold almost all my platters, to buy him *tabacco*; and he to turne
monster of ingratitude, and strike his lawfull host! well, I hope to
raise up an host of furie for't: here comes Justice CLEMENT.

Act III. Scene 7

CLEMENT, KNO'WELL, FORMALL, COB.

[*Enter* CLEMENT, KNO'WELL *and* FORMALL.]

CLEMENT What's master KITELY gone? ROGER?

FORMALL I, sir.

CLEMENT 'Hart of me! what made him leave us so abruptly! How
now, sirra? what make you here? what would you have, ha?

COB And't please your worship, I am a poore neighbour of your
worships——

CLEMENT A poore neighbour of mine? why, speake poore neighbour.

COB I dwell, sir, at the signe of the water-tankard, hard by the greene
lattice: I have paid scot, and lot there, any time this eighteene
yeeres.

CLEMENT To the greene lattice?

COB No, sir, to the parish: mary, I have seldome scap't scot-free, at
the lattice.

CLEMENT O, well! what businesse ha's my poore neighbour with
me?

COB And't like your worship, I am come, to crave the peace of your
worship.

CLEMENT Of mee knave? peace of mee, knave? did I e're hurt thee?
or threaten thee? or wrong thee? ha?

COB No, sir, but your worships warrant, for one that ha's wrong'd
me, sir: his armes are at too much libertie, I would faine have them
bound to a treatie of peace, an' my credit could compasse it, with
your worship.

CLEMENT Thou goest farre inough about for't, I'am sure.

KNO'WELL Why, doest thou goe in danger of thy life for him? friend?

COB No sir; but I goe in danger of my death, every houre, by his meanes: an' I die, within a twelve-moneth and a day, I may sweare, by the law of the land, that he kill'd me.

CLEMENT How? how knave? sweare he kill'd thee? and by the law? what pretence? what colour hast thou for that?

COB Mary, and't please your worship, both black, and blew; colour inough, I warrant you. I have it here, to shew your worship.

CLEMENT What is he, that gave you this, sirra?

COB A gentleman, and a souldier, he saies he is, o' the citie here.

CLEMENT A souldier o' the citie? What call you him?

COB Captayne BOBADIL.

CLEMENT BOBADIL? And why did he bob, and beate you, sirrah? How began the quarrell betwixt you: ha? speake truely knave, I advise you.

COB Mary, indeed, and please your worship, onely because I spake against their vagrant *tabacco*, as I came by 'hem, when they were taking on't, for nothing else.

CLEMENT Ha? you speake against *tabacco*? FORMALL, his name.

FORMALL What's your name, sirra?

COB OLIVER, sir, OLIVER COB, sir.

CLEMENT Tell OLIVER COB, he shall goe to the jayle, FORMALL.

FORMALL OLIVER COB, my master, Justice CLEMENT, saies, you shall goe to the jayle.

COB O, I beseech your worship, for gods sake, deare master Justice.

CLEMENT Nay, gods pretious: and such drunkards, and tankards, as you are, come to dispute of *tabacco* once; I have done! away with him.

COB O, good master Justice, sweet old gentleman.

KNO'WELL Sweet OLIVER, would I could doe thee any good: Justice CLEMENT, let me intreat you, sir.

CLEMENT What? a thred-bare rascall! a begger! a slave that never drunke out of better then pisse-pot mettle in his life! and he to deprave, and abuse the vertue of an herbe, so generally receiv'd in the courts of princes, the chambers of nobles, the bowers of sweet ladies, the cabbins of souldiers! ROGER, away with him, by gods pretious—I say, goe too.

COB Deare master Justice; Let mee bee beaten againe, I have deserv'd it: but not the prison, I beseech you.

KNO'WELL Alas, poore OLIVER!

CLEMENT ROGER, make him a warrant (hee shall not goe) I but feare the knave.

FORMALL Doe not stinke, sweet OLIVER, you shall not goe, my master will give you a warrant.

COB O, the Lord maintayne his worship, his worthy worship.

CLEMENT Away, dispatch him. [*Exeunt* FORMALL *and* COB.] How
70 now, master KNO'WEL! In dumps? In dumps? Come, this becomes not.

KNO'WELL Sir, would I could not feele my cares——

CLEMENT Your cares are nothing! they are like my cap, soone put on, and as soone put off. What? your sonne is old inough, to governe himselfe: let him runne his course, it's the onely way to make him a stay'd man. If he were an unthrift, a ruffian, a drunkard, or a licentious liver, then you had reason; you had reason to take care: but, being none of these, mirth's my witnesse, an' I had twise so many cares, as you have, I'ld drowne them all in a cup of sacke.
80 Come, come, let's trie it: I muse, your parcell of a souldier returnes not all this while. [*Exeunt.*]

Act IV. Scene 1

DOWNE-RIGHT, DAME KITELY.

[*Enter* DOWNE-RIGHT *and* DAME KITELY.]

DOWNE-RIGHT Well sister, I tell you true: and you'll finde it so, in the end.

DAME KITELY Alas brother, what would you have mee to doe? I cannot helpe it: you see, my brother brings 'hem in, here, they are his friends.

DOWNE-RIGHT His friends? his fiends. S'lud, they doe nothing but hant him, up and downe, like a sort of unluckie sprites, and tempt him to all manner of villanie, that can be thought of. Well, by this light, a little thing would make me play the devill with some of
10 'hem; and 't were not more for your husbands sake, then any thing else, I'ld make the house too hot for the best on 'hem: they should say, and sweare, hell were broken loose, e're they went hence. But, by gods will, 'tis no bodies fault, but yours: for, an' you had done, as you might have done, they should have beene perboyl'd, and

bak'd too, every mothers sonne, e're they should ha' come in, e're
a one of 'hem.

DAME KITELY God's my life! did you ever heare the like? what a
strange man is this! Could I keepe out all them, thinke you? I
should put my selfe, against halfe a dozen men? should I? Good
faith, you'ld mad the patient'st body in the world, to heare you   20
talke so, without any sense, or reason!

Act IV. Scene 2

MRS. BRIDGET, MR. MATTHEW, DAME KITELY,
DOWNE-RIGHT, WEL-BRED, STEPHEN, ED. KNO'WELL,
BOBADIL, BRAYNE-WORME, CASH.

[*Enter* BRIDGET, MATTHEW *and* BOBADILL, *followed by*
WELL-BRED, STEPHEN, ED. KNO'WELL *and*
BRAYNE-WORME.]

BRIDGET Servant (in troth) you are too prodigall
  Of your wits treasure, thus to powre it forth,
  Upon so meane a subject, as my worth?

MATTHEW You say well, mistris; and I meane, as well.

DOWNE-RIGHT Hoy-day, here is stuffe!

WELL-BRED O, now stand close: pray heaven, shee can get him to
  reade: He should doe it, of his owne naturall impudencie.

BRIDGET Servant, what is this same, I pray you?

MATTHEW Mary, an *Elegie*, an *Elegie*, an odde toy——

DOWNE-RIGHT To mock an ape withall. O, I could sow up his   10
  mouth, now.

DAME KITELY Sister, I pray you let's heare it.

DOWNE-RIGHT Are you rime-given, too?

MATTHEW Mistris, Ile reade it, if you please.

BRIDGET Pray you doe, servant.

DOWNE-RIGHT O, here's no fopperie! Death, I can endure the stocks,
  better.   [*Exit.*]

ED. KNO'WELL What ayles thy brother? can he not hold his water,
  at reading of a ballad?

WELL-BRED O, no: a rime to him, is worse then cheese, or a bag-pipe.   20
  But, marke, you loose the protestation.

MATTHEW Faith, I did it in an humour; I know not how it is: but, please you come neere, sir. This gentleman ha's judgement, hee knowes how to censure of a—pray you sir, you can judge.

STEPHEN Not I, sir: upon my reputation, and, by the foot of PHAROAH.

WELL-BRED O, chide your cossen, for swearing.

ED. KNO'WELL Not I, so long as he do's not forsweare himselfe.

BOBADILL Master MATTHEW, you abuse the expectation of your
30   deare mistris, and her faire sister: Fie, while you live, avoid this prolixitie.

MATTHEW I shall, sir: well, *Incipere dulce.*

ED. KNO'WELL How! *Insipere dulce?* a sweet thing to be a foole, indeed.

WELL-BRED What, doe you take *Incipere*, in that sense?

ED. KNO'WELL You doe not? you? This was your villanie, to gull him with a *motte.*

WELL-BRED O, the Benchers phrase: *pauca verba, pauca verba.*

MATTHEW *Rare creature, let me speake without offence,*
40   *Would god my rude wordes had the influence,*
     To rule thy thoughts, as thy faire lookes doe mine,
     Then should'st thou be his prisoner, who is thine.

ED. KNO'WELL This is in HERO and LEANDER?

WELL-BRED O, I! peace, we shall have more of this.

MATTHEW *Be not unkinde, and faire, mishapen stuffe*
     Is of behaviour boysterous, and rough:

Master Stephen   WELL-BRED How like you that, sir?
answeres with
shaking his   ED. KNO'WELL S'light, he shakes his head like a bottle, to feele and
head.   there be any braine in it!
50   MATTHEW But observe the *catastrophe*, now,
     And I in dutie will exceede all other,
     As you in beautie doe excell Joves mother.

ED. KNO'WELL Well, Ile have him free of the wit-brokers, for hee utters nothing, but stolne remnants.

WELL-BRED O, forgive it him.

ED. KNO'WELL A filtching rogue? hang him. And, from the dead? it's worse then sacrilege.

WELL-BRED Sister, what ha' you here? verses? pray you, lets see. Who made these verses? they are excellent good!

MATTHEW O, master WEL-BRED, 'tis your disposition to say so, 60
sir. They were good i' the morning, I made 'hem, *extempore*, this
morning.

WELL-BRED How? *extempore?*

MATTHEW I, would I might bee hang'd else; aske Captayne BOBA-
DILL. He saw me write them, at the—(poxe on it) the starre,
yonder.

BRAYNE-WORME Can he find, in his heart, to curse the starres, so?

ED. KNO'WELL Faith, his are even with him: they ha' curst him
ynough alreadie.

STEPHEN Cosen, how doe you like this gentlemans verses? 70

ED. KNO'WELL O, admirable! the best that ever I heard, cousse!

STEPHEN Body o' CAESAR! they are admirable! The best, that ever
I heard, as I am a souldier.

[*Enter* DOWNE-RIGHT.]

DOWNE-RIGHT I am vext, I can hold ne're a bone of mee still! Heart,
I thinke, they meane to build, and breed here!

WELL-BRED Sister, you have a simple servant, here, that crownes
your beautie, with such *encomions*, and devises: you may see, what
it is to be the mistris of a wit! that can make your perfections so
transparent, that every bleare eye may looke through them, and
see him drown'd over head, and eares, in the deepe well of desire. 80
Sister KITELY, I marvaile, you get you not a servant, that can
rime, and doe tricks, too.

DOWNE-RIGHT Oh monster! impudence it selfe! tricks?

DAME KITELY Tricks, brother? what tricks?

BRIDGET Nay, speake, I pray you, what tricks?

DAME KITELY I, never spare any body here: but say, what tricks?

BRIDGET Passion of my heart! doe tricks?

WELL-BRED S'light, here's a trick vyed, and revyed! why, you munkies,
you? what a catter-waling doe you keepe? ha's hee not given you
rimes, and verses, and tricks? 90

DOWNE-RIGHT O, the fiend!

WELL-BRED Nay, you, lampe of virginitie, that take it in snuffe so!
come, and cherish this tame *poeticall furie*, in your servant, you'll be
begg'd else, shortly, for a concealement: goe to, reward his muse.
You cannot give him lesse then a shilling, in conscience, for the
booke, he had it out of, cost him a teston, at least. How now,

gallants? Mr. MATTHEW? Captayne? What? all sonnes of silence?
no spirit?

DOWNE-RIGHT   Come, you might practise your ruffian-tricks somewhere else, and not here, I wusse; this is no taverne, nor drinking-
schole, to vent your exploits in.

WELL-BRED   How now! whose cow ha's calv'd?

DOWNE-RIGHT   Mary, that ha's mine, sir. Nay, Boy, never looke
askance at me, for the matter; Ile tell you of it, I, sir, you, and your
companions, mend your selves, when I ha' done?

WELL-BRED   My companions?

DOWNE-RIGHT   Yes sir, your companions, so I say, I am not afraid
of you, nor them neither: your hang-byes here. You must have
your Poets, and your potlings, your *soldado's*, and *foolado's*, to follow
you up and downe the citie, and here they must come to domineere,
and swagger. Sirrha, you, ballad-singer, and slops, your fellow
there, get you out; get you home: or (by this steele) Ile cut off your
eares, and that, presently.

WELL-BRED   S'light, stay, let's see what he dare doe: cut off his eares?
cut a whetstone. You are an asse, doe you see? touch any man
here, and by this hand, Ile runne my rapier to the hilts in you.

DOWNE-RIGHT   Yea, that would I faine see, boy.

DAME KITELY   O Jesu! murder. THOMAS, GASPAR!

BRIDGET   Helpe, helpe, THOMAS.

[*Enter* CASH *and* SERVANTS.]

ED. KNO'WELL   Gentlemen, forbeare, I pray you.

BOBADILL   Well, sirrah, you, HOLOFERNES: by my hand, I will pinck
your flesh, full of holes, with my rapier for this; I will, by this good
heaven: Nay, let him come, let him come, gentlemen, by the body
of Saint GEORGE, Ile not kill him.

CASH   Hold, hold, good gentlemen.

DOWNE-RIGHT   You whorson, bragging coystrill!

They all draw,
and they of the
house make out
to part them.

They offer to
fight againe, and
are parted.

100

110

120

Act IV. Scene 3

KITELY.   *To them.*

[*Enter* KITELY.]

KITELY Why, how now? what's the matter? what's the stirre here?
    Whence springs the quarrell? THOMAS! where is he?
    Put up your weapons, and put off this rage.
    My wife and sister, they are cause of this,
    What, THOMAS? where is this knave?

CASH Here, sir.

WELL-BRED Come, let's goe: this is one of my brothers ancient
        humours, this.

STEPHEN I am glad, no body was hurt by his ancient humour.

     [*Exeunt* STEPHEN, WELL-BRED, ED. KNO'WELL, MATTHEW,
                BOBADILL *and* BRAYNE-WORME.]

KITELY Why, how now, brother, who enforst this brawle?   10

DOWNE-RIGHT A sort of lewd rake-hells, that care neither for god,
    nor the devill! And, they must come here to reade ballads, and
    rogery, and trash! Ile marre the knot of 'hem ere I sleepe, perhaps:
    especially BOB, there: he that's all manner of shapes! and *Songs,*
    and sonnets, his fellow.

BRIDGET Brother, indeed, you are too violent,
    To sudden, in your humour: and, you know
    My brother WEL-BREDS temper will not beare
    Anie reproofe, chiefly in such a presence,
    Where every slight disgrace, he should receive,   20
    Might wound him in opinion, and respect.

DOWNE-RIGHT Respect? what talke you of respect 'mong such,
    As ha' nor sparke of manhood, nor good manners?
    'Sdeynes I am asham'd, to heare you! respect?   [*Exit.*]

BRIDGET Yes, there was one a civill gentleman,
    And very worthily demean'd himselfe!

KITELY O, that was some love of yours, sister!

BRIDGET A love of mine? I would it were no worse, brother!
    You'lld pay my portion sooner, then you thinke for.

DAME KITELY Indeed, he seem'd to be a gentleman of an exceeding   30
    faire disposition, and of verie excellent good parts!

[*Exeunt* DAME KITELY *and* BRIDGET.]

KITELY Her love, by heaven! my wifes minion!
Faire disposition? excellent good parts?
Death, these phrases are intollerable!
Good parts? how should shee know his parts?
His parts? Well, well, well, well, well, well!
It is too plaine, too cleere: THOMAS, come hither.
What, are they gone?

CASH   I, sir, they went in.
My mistris, and your sister—

40 KITELY Are any of the gallants within?

CASH No, sir, they are all gone.

KITELY Art thou sure of it?

CASH I can assure you, sir.

KITELY What gentleman was that they prais'd so, THOMAS?

CASH One, they call him master KNO'WELL, a handsome yong
gentleman, sir.

KITELY I, I thought so: my mind gave me as much.
Ile die, but they have hid him i' the house,
Somewhere; Ile goe and search: goe with me, THOMAS.

50 Be true to me, and thou shalt find me a master.   [*Exeunt.*]

Act IV. Scene 4

COB, TIB.

[*Enter* COB.]

COB What TIB, TIB, I say.

[*Enter* TIB.]

TIB How now, what cuckold is that knocks so hard? O, husband, ist
you? what's the newes?

COB Nay, you have stonn'd me, Ifaith! you ha' giv'n me a knock o'
the forehead, will stick by me! cuckold? 'Slid, cuckold?

TIB Away, you foole, did I know it was you, that knockt? Come,
come, you may call me as bad, when you list.

COB May I? TIB, you are a whore.

TIB You lye in your throte, husband.

COB How, the lye? and in my throte too? doe you long to bee stab'd, 10
ha?

TIB Why, you are no souldier, I hope?

COB O, must you be stab'd by a souldier? Masse, that's true! when
was BOBADILL here? your Captayne? that rogue, that foist, that
fencing *Burgullian*? Ile tickle him, ifaith.

TIB Why, what's the matter? trow!

COB O, he has basted me, rarely, sumptiously! but I have it here in
black and white; for his black, and blew: shall pay him. O, the
Justice! the honestest old brave *Trojan* in *London*! I doe honour the
very flea of his dog. A plague on him though, he put me once in 20
a villanous filthy feare; mary, it vanisht away, like the smoke of
tabacco; but I was smok't soundly first. I thanke the devill, and his
good angell, my guest. Well, wife, or TIB (which you will) get you
in, and lock the doore, I charge you, let no body in to you; wife,
no body in, to you: those are my wordes. Not Captayne BOB
himselfe, nor the fiend, in his likenesse; you are a woman; you
have flesh and bloud enough in you, to be tempted: therefore,
keepe the doore, shut, upon all commers.

TIB I warrant you, there shall no body enter here, without my consent.

COB Nor, with your consent, sweet TIB, and so I leave you. 30

TIB It's more, then you know, whether you leave me so.

COB How?

TIB Why, sweet.

COB Tut, sweet, or sowre, thou art a flowre,
Keepe close thy dore, I aske no more. [*Exeunt.*]

Act IV. Scene 5

ED. KNO'WELL, WELL-BRED, STEPHEN, BRAYNE-WORME.

[*Enter* ED. KNO'WELL, WELL-BRED, STEPHEN *and*
BRAYNE-WORME.]

ED. KNO'WELL Well BRAYNE-WORME, performe this businesse, happily, and thou makest a purchase of my love, for ever.

WELL-BRED Ifaith, now let thy spirits use their best faculties. But, at
any hand, remember the message, to my brother: for, there's no
other meanes, to start him.

BRAYNE-WORME I warrant you, sir, feare nothing: I have a nimble
soule ha's wakt all forces of my phant'sie, by this time, and put
'hem in true motion. What you have possest mee withall, Ile
discharge it amply, sir. Make it no question.

10 WELL-BRED Forth, and prosper, BRAYNE-WORME. [*Exit* BRAYNE-
WORME.] Faith, NED, how dost thou approve of my abilities in
this devise?

ED. KNO'WELL Troth, well, howsoever: but, it will come excellent,
if it take.

WELL-BRED Take, man? why, it cannot choose but take, if the
circumstances miscarrie not: but, tell me, ingenuously, dost thou
affect my sister BRIDGET, as thou pretend'st?

ED. KNO'WELL Friend, am I worth beliefe?

WELL-BRED Come, doe not protest. In faith, shee is a maid of good
20 ornament, and much modestie: and, except I conceiv'd very
worthily of her, thou shouldest not have her.

ED. KNO'WELL Nay, that I am afraid will bee a question yet, whether
I shall have her, or no?

WELL-BRED Slid, thou shalt have her; by this light, thou shalt.

ED. KNO'WELL Nay, doe not sweare.

WELL-BRED By this hand, thou shalt have her: Ile goe fetch her,
presently. Point, but where to meet, and as I am an honest man,
I'll bring her.

ED. KNO'WELL Hold, hold, be temperate.

30 WELL-BRED Why, by—what shall I sweare by? thou shalt have her,
as I am—

ED. KNO'WELL 'Pray thee, be at peace, I am satisfied: and doe beleeve,
thou wilt omit no offered occasion, to make my desires compleat.

WELL-BRED Thou shalt see, and know, I will not.   [*Exeunt.*]

Act IV. Scene 6

FORMALL, KNO'WELL, BRAYNE-WORME.

[*Enter* FORMALL *and* KNO'WELL.]

FORMALL Was your man a souldier, sir?

KNO'WELL I, a knave, I tooke him begging o' the way,
This morning, as I came over *More*-fields!

O, here he is! yo' have made faire speed, beleeve me:
Where, i' the name of sloth, could you be thus—
    [*Enter* BRAYNE-WORME.]

BRAYNE-WORME Mary, peace be my comfort, where I thought I
should have had little comfort of your worships service.

KNO'WELL How so?

BRAYNE-WORME O, sir! your comming to the citie, your entertainment of me, and your sending me to watch—indeed, all the   10
circumstances either of your charge, or my imployment, are as
open to your sonne, as to your selfe!

KNO'WELL How should that be! unlesse that villaine,
    BRAYNE-WORME,
Have told him of the letter, and discover'd
All that I strictly charg'd him to conceale? 'tis so!

BRAYNE-WORME I am, partly, o' the faith, 'tis so indeed.

KNO'WELL But, how should he know thee to be my man?

BRAYNE-WORME Nay, sir, I cannot tell; unlesse it bee by the black
art! Is not your sonne a scholler, sir?

KNO'WELL Yes, but I hope his soule is not allied   20
Unto such hellish practise: if it were,
I had just cause to weepe my part in him,
And curse the time of his creation.
But, where didst thou find them, FITZ-SWORD?

BRAYNE-WORME You should rather aske, where they found me, sir,
for, Ile bee sworne I was going along in the street, thinking nothing,
when (of a suddain) a voice calls, Mr. KNO-WEL'S man; another
cries, souldier: and thus, halfe a dosen of 'hem, till they had cal'd
me within a house where I no sooner came, but they seem'd men,
and out flue al their rapiers at my bosome, with some three or   30
foure score oathes to accompanie 'hem, & al to tel me, I was but
a dead man, if I did not confesse where you were, and how I was
imployed, and about what; which, when they could not get out of
me (as I protest, they must ha' dissected, and made an *Anatomie*
o' me, first, and so I told 'hem) they lockt mee up into a roome i'
the top of a high house, whence, by great miracle (having a light
heart) I slid downe, by a bottom of pack-thred, into the street,
and so scapt. But, sir, thus much I can assure you, for I heard it,
while I was lockt up, there were a great many rich merchants, and

40 brave citizens wives with 'hem at a feast, and your sonne, Mr.
EDWARD, with-drew with one of 'hem, and has pointed to meet
her anon, at one COBS house, a water-bearer, that dwells by the
wall. Now, there, your worship shall be sure to take him, for there
he preyes, and faile he will not.

KNO'WELL Nor, will I faile, to breake his match, I doubt not.
Goe thou, along with Justice CLEMENT'S man,
And stay there for me. At one COBS house, sai'st thou?

BRAYNE-WORME I sir, there you shall have him. [*Exit* KNO'WELL.]
Yes? Invisible? Much wench, or much sonne! 'Slight, when hee
50 has staid there, three or foure houres, travelling with the expectation
of wonders, and at length be deliver'd of aire: o, the sport, that I
should then take, to looke on him, if I durst! But, now, I meane
to appeare no more afore him in this shape. I have another trick,
to act, yet. O, that I were so happy, as to light on a nupson, now,
of this Justices novice. Sir, I make you stay somewhat long.

FORMALL Not a whit, sir. 'Pray you, what doe you meane? sir?

BRAYNE-WORME I was putting up some papers——

FORMALL You ha' beene lately in the warres, sir, it seemes.

BRAYNE-WORME Mary have I, sir; to my losse: and expence of all,
60 almost—

FORMALL Troth sir, I would be glad to bestow a pottle of wine o'
you, if it please you to accept it—

BRAYNE-WORME O, sir——

FORMALL But, to heare the manner of your services, and your devices
in the warres, they say they be very strange, and not like those a
man reades in the *Romane* histories, or sees, at *Mile-end*.

BRAYNE-WORME No, I assure you, sir, why, at any time when it
please you, I shall be readie to discourse to you, all I know: and
more too, somewhat.

70 FORMALL No better time, then now, sir; wee'll goe to the wind-mill:
there we shall have a cup of neate grist, wee call it. I pray you, sir,
let mee request you, to the wind-mill.

BRAYNE-WORME Ile follow you, sir, [*Exit* FORMALL.] and make grist
o' you, if I have good lucke.   [*Exit.*]

Act IV. Scene 7

MATTHEW, ED. KNO'WELL, BOBADILL, STEPHEN,
DOWNE-RIGHT.   *To them.*

[*Enter* MATTHEW, ED. KNO'WELL, BOBADILL *and* STEPHEN.]

MATTHEW Sir, did your eyes ever tast the like clowne of him, where
we were to day, Mr. WEL-BRED'S halfe brother? I thinke, the
whole earth cannot shew his paralell, by this day-light.

ED. KNO'WELL We were now speaking of him: Captayne BOBADIL
tells me, he is fall'n foule o'you, too.

MATTHEW O, I, sir, he threatned me, with the bastinado.

BOBADILL I, but I thinke, I taught you prevention, this morning, for
that— You shall kill him, beyond question: if you be so generously
minded.

MATTHEW Indeed, it is a most excellent trick!   10

BOBADILL O, you doe not give spirit enough, to your motion,   *He practises at*
you are too tardie, too heavie! o, it must be done like lightning, *a post.*
hay?

MATTHEW Rare Captaine!

BOBADILL Tut, 'tis nothing, and 't be not done in a—*punto*!

ED. KNO'WELL Captaine, did you ever prove your selfe, upon any
of our masters of defence, here?

MATTHEW O, good sir! yes, I hope, he has.

BOBADILL I will tell you, sir. Upon my first comming to the citie,
after my long travaile, for knowledge (in that mysterie only) there   20
came three, or foure of 'hem to me, at a gentlemans house, where
it was my chance to be resident, at that time, to intreat my presence
at their scholes, and with-all so much importun'd me, that (I
protest to you as I am a gentleman) I was asham'd of their rude
demeanor, out of all measure: well, I told 'hem, that to come to a
publike schoole, they should pardon me, it was opposite (in *diameter*)
to my humour, but, if so they would give their attendance at my
lodging, I protested to doe them what right or favour I could, as
I was a gentleman, and so forth.

ED. KNO'WELL So, sir, then you tried their skill?   30

BOBADILL Alas, soone tried! you shall heare sir. Within two or three
daies after, they came; and, by honestie, faire sir, beleeve mee, I

grac't them exceedingly, shew'd them some two or three tricks of
prevention, have purchas'd 'hem, since, a credit, to admiration!
they cannot denie this: and yet now, they hate mee, and why?
because I am excellent, and for no other vile reason on the earth.

ED. KNO'WELL This is strange, and barbarous! as ever I heard!

BOBADILL Nay, for a more instance of their preposterous natures,
but note, sir. They have assaulted me some three, foure, five, sixe
of them together, as I have walkt alone, in divers skirts i' the
towne, as *Turne-bull*, *White-chappell*, *Shore-ditch*, which were then my
quarters, and since upon the *Exchange*, at my lodging, and at my
ordinarie: where I have driven them afore me, the whole length
of a street, in the open view of all our gallants, pittying to hurt
them, beleeve me. Yet, all this lenitie will not ore-come their
spleene: they will be doing with a pismier, raysing a hill, a man
may spurne abroad, with his foot, at pleasure. By my selfe, I could
have slaine them all, but I delight not in murder. I am loth to
beare any other then this bastinado for 'hem: yet, I hold it good
politie, not to goe disarm'd, for though I bee skilfull, I may bee
oppress'd with multitudes.

ED. KNO'WELL I, beleeve me, may you sir: and (in my conceit) our
whole nation should sustaine the losse by it, if it were so.

BOBADILL Alas, no: what's a peculiar man, to a nation? not seene.

ED. KNO'WELL O, but your skill, sir!

BOBADILL Indeed, that might be some losse; but, who respects it? I
will tell you, sir, by the way of private, and under seale; I am a
gentleman, and live here obscure, and to my selfe: but, were I
knowne to her Majestie, and the Lords (observe mee) I would
under-take (upon this poore head, and life) for the publique benefit
of the state, not only to spare the intire lives of her subjects in
generall, but to save the one halfe, nay, three parts of her yeerely
charge, in holding warre, and against what enemie soever. And,
how would I doe it, thinke you?

ED. KNO'WELL Nay, I know not, nor can I conceive.

BOBADILL Why thus, sir. I would select nineteene, more, to my selfe,
throughout the land; gentlemen they should bee of good spirit,
strong, and able constitution, I would choose them by an instinct,
a character, that I have: and I would teach these nineteene, the
speciall rules, as your *Punto*, your *Reverso*, your *Stoccata*, your *Imbroc-*

cata, your *Passada*, your *Montanto*: till they could all play very neare,
or altogether as well as my selfe. This done, say the enemie were
fortie thousand strong, we twentie would come into the field, the
tenth of *March*, or thereabouts; and wee would challenge twentie
of the enemie; they could not, in their honour, refuse us, well, wee
would kill them: challenge twentie more, kill them; twentie more,
kill them; twentie more, kill them too; and thus, would wee kill,
every man, his twentie a day, that's twentie score; twentie score,
that's two hundreth; two hundreth a day, five dayes a thousand;
fortie thousand; fortie times five, five times fortie, two hundreth   80
dayes kills them all up, by computation. And this, will I venture
my poore gentleman-like carcasse, to performe (provided, there
bee no treason practis'd upon us) by faire, and discreet manhood,
that is, civilly by the sword.

ED. KNO'WELL Why, are you so sure of your hand, Captaine, at all
times?

BOBADILL Tut, never misse thrust, upon my reputation with you.

ED. KNO'WELL I would not stand in DOWNE-RIGHTS state, then,
an' you meet him, for the wealth of any one street in *London*.

BOBADILL Why, sir, you mistake me! if he were here now, by this   90
welkin, I would not draw my weapon on him! let this gentleman
doe his mind: but, I will bastinado him (by the bright sunne)
where-ever I meet him.

MATTHEW Faith, and Ile have a fling at him, at my distance.

ED. KNO'WELL Gods so', looke, where he is: yonder he goes.

DOWNE-RIGHT What peevish luck have I, I cannot meet with these
bragging raskalls?   [*Exit.*]

BOBADILL It's not he? is it?

ED. KNO'WELL Yes faith, it is he.

MATTHEW Ile be hang'd, then, if that were he.   100

ED. KNO'WELL Sir, keepe your hanging good, for some greater matter,
for I assure you, that was he.

STEPHEN Upon my reputation, it was hee.

BOBADILL Had I thought it had beene he, he must not have gone
so: but I can hardly be induc'd, to beleeve, it was he, yet.

ED. KNO'WELL That I thinke, sir. [*Enter* DOWNE-RIGHT.] But see,
he is come againe!

Downe-right
walkes over the
stage.

DOWNE-RIGHT O, PHAROAHS foot, have I found you? Come, draw, to your tooles: draw, gipsie, or Ile thresh you.

110 BOBADILL Gentleman of valour, I doe beleeve in thee, heare me—

DOWNE-RIGHT Draw your weapon, then.

BOBADILL Tall man, I never thought on it, till now (body of me) I had a warrant of the peace, served on me, even now, as I came along, by a water-bearer; this gentleman saw it, Mr. MATTHEW.

DOWNE-RIGHT 'Sdeath, you will not draw, then?

He beates him,
and disarmes
him: Matthew
runnes away.

BOBADILL Hold, hold, under thy favour, forbeare.

DOWNE-RIGHT Prate againe, as you like this, you whoreson foist, you. You'le controll the point, you? Your consort is gone? had he staid, he had shar'd with you, sir.   [*Exit.*]

120 BOBADILL Well, gentlemen, beare witnesse, I was bound to the peace, by this good day.

ED. KNO'WELL No faith, it's an ill day, Captaine, never reckon it other: but, say you were bound to the peace, the law allowes you, to defend your selfe: that'll prove but a poore excuse.

BOBADILL I cannot tell, sir. I desire good construction, in faire sort. I never sustain'd the like disgrace (by heaven) sure I was strooke with a plannet thence, for I had no power to touch my weapon.

ED. KNO'WELL I, like inough, I have heard of many that have beene beaten under a plannet: goe, get you to a surgeon. 'Slid, an' these

130 be your tricks, your *passada's*, and your *mountanto's*, Ile none of them. [*Exit* BOBADILL.] O, manners! that this age should bring forth such creatures! that Nature should bee at leisure to make 'hem! Come, cousse.

STEPHEN Masse, Ile ha' this cloke.

ED. KNO'WELL Gods will, 'tis DOWNE-RIGHT'S.

STEPHEN Nay, it's mine now, another might have tane up, aswell as I: Ile weare it, so I will.

ED. KNO'WELL How, an' he see it? hee'll challenge it, assure your selfe.

140 STEPHEN I, but he shall not ha' it; Ile say, I bought it.

ED. KNO'WELL Take heed, you buy it not, too deare, cousse.

[*Exeunt.*]

Act IV. Scene 8

KITELY, WEL-BRED, DAME KIT., BRIDGET,
BRAYNE-WORME, CASH.

[*Enter* KITELY, WELL-BRED, DAME KITELY *and* BRIDGET.]

KITELY Now, trust me brother, you were much to blame,
T'incense his anger, and disturbe the peace,
Of my poore house, where there are sentinells
That every minute watch, to give alarmes,
Of civill warre, without adjection
Of your assistance, or occasion.

WELL-BRED No harme done, brother, I warrant you: since there is
no harme done. Anger costs a man nothing: and a tall man is never
his owne man, till he be angrie. To keepe his valure in obscuritie,
is to keepe himselfe, as it were, in a cloke-bag. What's a musitian,   10
unlesse he play? what's a tall man, unlesse he fight? For, indeed,
all this, my wise brother stands upon, absolutely: and, that made
me fall in with him, so resolutely.

DAME KITELY I, but what harme might have come of it, brother?

WELL-BRED Might, sister? so, might the good warme clothes, your
husband weares, be poyson'd, for any thing he knowes: or the
wholesome wine he drunke, even now, at the table——

KITELY Now, god forbid: O me. Now, I remember,
My wife drunke to me, last; and chang'd the cup:
And bade me weare this cursed sute to day.   20
See, if heav'n suffer murder undiscover'd!
I feele me ill; give me some *mithridate*,
Some *mithridate* and oile, good sister, fetch me;
O, I am sicke at heart! I burne, I burne.
If you will save my life, goe, fetch it me.

WELL-BRED O, strange humour! my verie breath ha's poyson'd
him.

BRIDGET Good brother, be content, what doe you meane?
The strength of these extreme conceits, will kill you.

DAME KITELY Beshrew your heart-bloud, brother WELL-BRED,   30
now;
For putting such a toy into his head.

WELL-BRED Is a fit *simile*, a toy? will he be poyson'd with a *simile*?
Brother KITELY, what a strange, and idle imagination is this? For
shame, bee wiser. O' my soule, there's no such matter.

KITELY Am I not sicke? how am I, then, not poyson'd?
Am I not poyson'd? how am I, then, so sicke?

DAME KITELY If you be sicke, youre owne thoughts make you
sicke.

38 WELL-BRED His jealousie is the poyson, he ha's taken.

> [*Enter* BRAYNE-WORME.]

*He comes
disguis'd like
Justice Clements
man.*

BRAYNE-WORME Mr. KITELY, my master, Justice CLEMENT, salutes
you; and desires to speake with you, with all possible speed.

KITELY No time, but now? when, I thinke, I am sicke? very sicke!
well, I will wait upon his worship. THOMAS, COB, I must seeke
them out, and set 'hem sentinells, till I returne. THOMAS, COB,
THOMAS.   [*Exit.*]

WELL-BRED This is perfectly rare, BRAYNE-WORME! but how got'st
thou this apparell, of the Justices man?

BRAYNE-WORME Mary sir, my proper fine pen-man, would needs
bestow the grist o'me, at the wind-mil, to hear some martial
discourse; where so I marshal'd him, that I made him drunke, with
50 admiration! &, because, too much heat was the cause of his
distemper, I stript him starke naked, as he lay along asleepe, and
borrowed his sute, to deliver this counterfeit message in, leaving
a rustie armor, and an old browne bill to watch him, till my returne:
which shall be, when I ha' pawn'd his apparell, and spent the better
part o' the money, perhaps.

WELL-BRED Well, thou art a successefull merry knave, BRAYNE-
WORME, his absence will be a good subject for more mirth. I pray
thee, returne to thy yong master, and will him to meet me, and
my sister BRIDGET, at the tower instantly: for, here, tell him, the
60 house is so stor'd with jealousie, there is no roome for love, to
stand upright in. We must get our fortunes committed to some
larger prison, say; and, then the tower, I know no better aire: nor
where the libertie of the house may doe us more present service.
Away.   [*Exit* BRAYNE-WORME.]

> [*Enter* KITELY *and* CASH.]

KITELY Come hether, THOMAS. Now, my secret's ripe,
And thou shalt have it: lay to both thine eares.

Harke, what I say to theé. I must goe forth, THOMAS.
Be carefull of thy promise, keepe good watch,
Note every gallant, and observe him well,
That enters in my absence, to thy mistris: 70
If shee would shew him roomes, the jest is stale,
Follow 'hem, THOMAS, or else hang on him,
And let him not goe after; marke their lookes;
Note, if shee offer but to see his band,
Or any other amorous toy, about him;
But praise his legge; or foot; or if shee say,
The day is hot, and bid him feele her hand,
How hot it is; o, that's a monstrous thing!
Note me all this, good THOMAS, marke their sighes,
And, if they doe but whisper, breake 'hem off: 80
Ile beare thee out in it. Wilt thou doe this?
Wilt thou be true, my THOMAS?

CASH   As truth's selfe, sir.

KITELY Why, I beleeve thee: where is COB, now? COB?   [*Exit.*]

DAME KITELY Hee's ever calling for COB! I wonder, how hee imploies
    COB, so!

WELL-BRED Indeed, sister, to aske how hee imploies COB, is a
    necessarie question for you, that are his wife, and a thing not very
    easie for you to be satisfied in: but this Ile assure you, COBS wife
    is an excellent bawd, sister, and, often-times, your husband hants
    her house, mary, to what end, I cannot altogether accuse him,   90
    imagine you what you thinke convenient. But, I have knowne,
    faire hides have foule hearts, e'er now, sister.

DAME KITELY Never said you truer then that, brother, so much I
    can tell you for your learning. THOMAS, fetch your cloke, and goe
    with me, Ile after him presently: [*Exit* CASH.] I would to fortune,
    I could take him there, ifaith. Il'd returne him his owne, I warrant
    him.   [*Exit.*]

WELL-BRED So, let 'hem goe: this may make sport anon. Now, my
    faire sister in-law, that you knew, but how happie a thing it were
    to be faire, and beautifull?   100

BRIDGET That touches not me, brother.

WELL-BRED That's true; that's even the fault of it: for, indeede,
    beautie stands a woman in no stead, unlesse it procure her touching.

But, sister, whether it touch you, or no, it touches your beauties;
and, I am sure, they will abide the touch; an' they doe not, a plague
of all ceruse, say I: and, it touches mee to in part, though not in
the—Well, there's a deare and respected friend of mine, sister,
stands very strongly, and worthily affected toward you, and hath
vow'd to inflame whole bone-fires of zeale, at his heart, in honor
of your perfections. I have alreadie engag'd my promise to bring
you, where you shall heare him confirme much more. NED
KNO'WELL is the man, sister. There's no exception against the
partie. You are ripe for a husband; and a minutes losse to such an
occasion, is a great trespasse in a wise beautie. What say you, sister?
On my soule hee loves you. Will you give him the meeting?

BRIDGET Faith, I had very little confidence in mine owne constancie,
brother, if I durst not meet a man: but this motion of yours,
savours of an old knight-adventurers servant, a little too much,
me thinkes.

WELL-BRED What's that, sister?

BRIDGET Mary, of the squire.

WELL-BRED No matter if it did, I would be such an one for my
friend, but see! who is return'd to hinder us?

[*Enter* KITELY.]

KITELY What villanie is this? call'd out on a false message?
This was some plot! I was not sent for. BRIDGET,
Where's your sister?

BRIDGET   I thinke shee be gone forth, sir.

KITELY How! is my wife gone forth? whether for gods sake?

BRIDGET Shee's gone abroad with THOMAS.

KITELY Abroad with THOMAS? oh, that villaine dors me.
He hath discover'd all unto my wife!

Beast that I was, to trust him: whither, I pray you,
Went shee?

BRIDGET   I know not, sir.

WELL-BRED   Ile tell you, brother,
Whither I suspect shee's gone.

KITELY   Whither, good brother?

WELL-BRED To COBS house, I beleeve: but, keepe my counsaile.

KITELY I will, I will: to COBS house? doth shee hant COBS?
Shee's gone a' purpose, now, to cuckold me,

With that lewd raskall, who, to win her favour,
Hath told her all.   [*Exit.*]

WELL-BRED   Come, hee's once more gone.

Sister, let's loose no time; th'affaire is worth it.   [*Exeunt.*]

Act IV. Scene 9

MATTHEW, BOBADIL, BRAYNE-WORME.   *To them.*

[*Enter* MATTHEW *and* BOBADILL.]

MATTHEW I wonder, Captayne, what they will say of my going away?
ha?

BOBADILL Why, what should they say? but as of a discreet gentleman?
quick, warie, respectfull of natures faire lineaments: and that's all?

MATTHEW Why, so! but what can they say of your beating?

BOBADILL A rude part, a touch with soft wood, a kind of grosse
batterie us'd, laid on strongly, borne most paciently: and that's all.

MATTHEW I, but, would any man have offered it in *Venice*? as you
say?

BOBADILL Tut, I assure you, no: you shall have there your *Nobilis*,   10
your *Gentelezza*, come in bravely upon your *reverse*, stand you close,
stand you firme, stand you faire, save your *retricato* with his left
legge, come to the *assalto* with the right, thrust with brave steele,
defie your base wood! But, wherefore doe I awake this remembrance? I was fascinated, by JUPITER: fascinated: but I will be
un-witch'd, and reveng'd, by law.

MATTHEW Doe you heare? ist not best to get a warrant, and have
him arrested, and brought before Justice CLEMENT?

BOBADILL It were not amisse, would we had it.

[*Enter* BRAYNE-WORME.]

MATTHEW Why, here comes his man, let's speake to him.   20

BOBADILL Agreed, doe you speake.

MATTHEW Save you, sir.

BRAYNE-WORME With all my heart, sir.

MATTHEW Sir, there is one DOWNE-RIGHT, hath abus'd this gentleman, and my selfe, and we determine to make our amends by law;
now, if you would doe us the favour, to procure a warrant, to

bring him afore your master, you shall bee well considered, I assure you, sir.

BRAYNE-WORME Sir, you know my service is my living, such favours as these, gotten of my master, is his only preferment, and therefore, you must consider me, as I may make benefit of my place.

MATTHEW How is that, sir?

BRAYNE-WORME Faith sir, the thing is extraordinarie, and the gentleman may be, of great accompt: yet, bee what hee will, if you will lay mee downe a brace of angells, in my hand, you shall have it, otherwise not.

MATTHEW How shall we doe, Captayne? he askes a brace of angells, you have no monie?

BOBADILL Not a crosse, by fortune.

MATTHEW Nor I, as I am a gentleman, but two pence, left of my two shillings in the morning for wine, and redish: let's find him some pawne.

BOBADILL Pawne? we have none to the value of his demand.

MATTHEW O, yes. I'll pawne this jewell in my eare, and you may pawne your silke stockings, and pull up your bootes, they will ne're be mist: It must be done, now.

BOBADILL Well, an' there be no remedie: Ile step aside, and pull 'hem off.

MATTHEW Doe you heare, sir? wee have no store of monie at this time, but you shall have good pawnes: looke you, sir, this jewell, and that gentlemans silke stockings, because we would have it dispatcht, e're we went to our chambers.

BRAYNE-WORME I am content, sir: I will get you the warrant presently, what's his name, say you? DOWNE-RIGHT?

MATTHEW I, I, GEORGE DOWNE-RIGHT.

BRAYNE-WORME What manner of man is he?

MATTHEW A tall bigge man, sir; hee goes in a cloke, most commonly, of silke russet, laid about with russet lace.

BRAYNE-WORME 'Tis very good, sir.

MATTHEW Here sir, here's my jewell.

BOBADILL And, here, are stockings.

BRAYNE-WORME Well, gentlemen, Ile procure you this warrant presently, but, who will you have to serve it?

MATTHEW That's true, Captaine: that must be consider'd.

BOBADILL Bodie o'me, I know not! 'tis service of danger!

BRAYNE-WORME Why, you were best get one o' the varlets o' the
citie, a serjeant. Ile appoint you one, if you please.

MATTHEW Will you, sir? why, we can wish no better.

BOBADILL Wee'll leave it to you, sir.

[*Exeunt* BOBADILL *and* MATTHEW.]

BRAYNE-WORME This is rare! now, will I goe pawne this cloke of   70
the Justice's mans, at the brokers, for a varlets sute, and be the
varlet my selfe; and get either more pawnes, or more monie of
DOWNE-RIGHT, for the arrest.   [*Exit.*]

Act IV. Scene 10

KNO'WEL, TIB, CASH, DAME KITELY, KITELY, COB.

[*Enter* KNO'WELL.]

KNO'WELL Oh, here it is, I am glad: I have found it now.
  Ho? who is within, here?

TIB I am within sir, what's your pleasure?

KNO'WELL To know, who is within, besides your selfe.

TIB Why, sir, you are no constable, I hope?

KNO'WELL O! feare you the constable? then, I doubt not,
  You have some guests within, deserve that feare,
  Ile fetch him straight.

    [*Enter* TIB.]

TIB   O' gods name, sir.

KNO'WELL Goe to. Come, tell me, Is not yong KNO'WEL, here?

TIB Yong KNO'WEL? I know none such, sir, o' mine honestie!   10

KNO'WELL Your honestie? dame, it flies too lightly from you:
  There is no way, but, fetch the constable.

TIB The constable? the man is mad, I thinke.   [*Exit.*]

    [*Enter* DAME KITELY *and* CASH.]

CASH Ho, who keepes house, here?

KNO'WELL O, this is the female copes-mate of my sonne?
  Now shall I meet him straight.

DAME KITELY   Knock, THOMAS, hard.

CASH Ho, good wife?

    [*Enter* TIB.]

TIB   Why, what's the matter with you?

DAME KITELY Why, woman, grieves it you to ope' your doore?
 Belike, you get something, to keepe it shut.

20 TIB What meane these questions, 'pray yee?

DAME KITELY So strange you make it? is not my husband, here?

KNO'WELL Her husband!

DAME KITELY   My tryed husband, master KITELY.

TIB I hope, he needes not to be tryed, here.

DAME KITELY No, dame: he do's it not for need, but pleasure.

TIB Neither for need, nor pleasure, is he here.

KNO'WELL This is but a device, to balke me withall.
 Soft, who is this? 'Tis not my sonne, disguisd?
 [*Enter* KITELY.]

Shee spies her DAME KITELY O, sir, have I fore-stald your honest market?
husband come: Found your close walkes? you stand amaz'd, now, doe you?
and runnes to I faith (I am glad) I have smokt you yet at last!
him. What is your jewell trow? In: come, lets see her;
31 (Fetch forth your huswife, dame) if shee be fairer,
 In any honest judgement, then my selfe,
 Ile be content with it: but, shee is change,
 Shee feedes you fat, shee soothes your appetite,
 And you are well? your wife, an honest woman,
 Is meat twice sod to you, sir? O, you trecher!

KNO'WELL Shee cannot counterfeit thus palpably.

KITELY Out on thy more then strumpets impudence!
40 Steal'st thou thus to thy haunts? and, have I taken
 Thy bawd, and thee, and thy companion,
Pointing to old This horie-headed letcher, this old goat,
Kno'well. Close at your villanie, and would'st thou 'scuse it,
 With this stale harlots jest, accusing me?
To him. O, old incontinent, do'st not thou shame,
 When all thy powers in chastitie is spent,
 To have a mind so hot? and to entice,
 And feede th'enticements of a lustfull woman?

49 DAME KITELY Out, I defie thee, I, dissembling wretch.

By Thomas. KITELY Defie me, strumpet? aske thy pandar, here,
 Can he denie it? or that wicked elder?

KNO'WELL Why, heare you, sir.

KITELY   Tut, tut, tut: never speake.
  Thy guiltie conscience will discover thee.

KNO'WELL What lunacie is this, that hants this man?

KITELY Well, good-wife BA'D, COBS wife; and you,
  That make your husband such a hoddie-doddie;
  And you, yong apple-squire; and old cuckold-maker;
  Ile ha' you every one before a Justice:
  Nay, you shall answere it, I charge you goe.

KNO'WELL Marie, with all my heart, sir: I goe willingly.   60
  Though I doe tast this as a trick, put on me,
  To punish my impertinent search; and justly:
  And halfe forgive my sonne, for the device.

KITELY Come, will you goe?

DAME KITELY   Goe? to thy shame, beleeve it.
      [*Enter* COB.]

COB Why, what's the matter, here? What's here to doe?

KITELY O, COB, art thou come? I have beene abus'd,
  And i' thy house. Never was man so, wrong'd!

COB Slid, in my house? my master KITELY? Who wrongs you in my
  house?

KITELY Marie, yong lust in old; and old in yong, here: 70
  Thy wife's their bawd, here have I taken 'hem.

COB How? bawd? Is my house come to that? Am I prefer'd thether?   *He falls upon*
  Did I charge you to keepe your dores shut, Is'BEL? and doe you   *his wife and*
  let 'hem lie open for all commers?   *beates her.*

KNO'WELL Friend, know some cause, before thou beat'st thy wife,
  This's madnesse, in thee.

COB   Why? is there no cause?

KITELY Yes, Ile shew cause before the Justice, COB:
  Come, let her goe with me.

COB   Nay, shee shall goe.

TIB Nay, I will goe. Ile see, an' you may bee allow'd to make a bundle
  o' hempe, o' your right and lawfull wife thus, at every cuckoldly   80
  knaves pleasure. Why doe you not goe?

KITELY A bitter queane. Come, wee'll ha' you tam'd.   [*Exeunt.*]

Act IV. Scene 11

BRAYNE-WORME, MATTHEW, BOBADIL, STEPHEN,

DOWNE-RIGHT.

[*Enter* BRAYNE-WORME.]

BRAYNE-WORME Well, of all my disguises, yet, now am I most like
my selfe: being in this Serjeants gowne. A man of my present
profession, never counterfeits, till hee layes hold upon a debter,
and sayes, he rests him, for then hee brings him to all manner of
unrest. A kinde of little kings wee are, bearing the diminutive of
a mace, made like a yong artichocke, that alwayes carries pepper
and salt, in it selfe. Well, I know not what danger I under-goe, by
this exploit, pray heaven, I come well of.

[*Enter* MATTHEW *and* BOBADILL.]

MATTHEW See, I thinke, yonder is the varlet, by his gowne.

BOBADILL Let's goe, in quest of him.

MATTHEW 'Save you, friend, are not you here, by appointment of
Justice CLEMENTS man?

BRAYNE-WORME Yes, an't please you, sir: he told me two gentlemen
had will'd him to procure a warrant from his master (which I have
about me) to be serv'd on one DOWNE-RIGHT.

MATTHEW It is honestly done of you both; and see, where the partie
comes, you must arrest: serve it upon him, quickly, afore hee bee
aware——

BOBADILL Beare back, master MATTHEW.

[*Enter* STEPHEN.]

BRAYNE-WORME Master DOWNE-RIGHT, I arrest you, i' the queenes
name, and must carry you afore a Justice, by vertue of this warrant.

STEPHEN Mee, friend? I am no DOWNE-RIGHT, I. I am master
STEPHEN, you doe not well, to arrest me, I tell you, truely: I am
in nobodies bonds, nor bookes, I, would you should know it. A
plague on you heartily, for making mee thus afraid afore my time.

BRAYNE-WORME Why, now are you deceived, gentlemen?

BOBADILL He weares such a cloke, and that deceived us: But see,
here a comes, indeed! this is he, officer.

[*Enter* DOWNE-RIGHT.]

DOWNE-RIGHT Why, how now, signior gull! are you turn'd filtcher
of late? come, deliver my cloke.   30

STEPHEN Your cloke, sir? I bought it, even now, in open market.

BRAYNE-WORME Master DOWNE-RIGHT, I have a warrant I must
serve upon you, procur'd by these two gentlemen.

DOWNE-RIGHT These gentlemen? these rascals?

BRAYNE-WORME Keepe the peace, I charge you, in her Majesties
name.

DOWNE-RIGHT I obey thee. What must I doe, officer?

BRAYNE-WORME Goe before master Justice CLEMENT, to answere
what they can object against you, sir. I will use you kindly, sir.

MATTHEW Come, let's before, and make the Justice, Captaine——   40

BOBADILL The varlet's a tall man! afore heaven!

> [*Exeunt* BOBADILL *and* MATTHEW.]

DOWNE-RIGHT Gull, you'll gi'me my cloke?

STEPHEN Sir, I bought it, and Ile keepe it.

DOWNE-RIGHT You will.

STEPHEN I, that I will.

DOWNE-RIGHT Officer, there's thy fee, arrest him.

BRAYNE-WORME Master STEPHEN, I must arrest you.

STEPHEN Arrest mee, I scorne it. There, take your cloke, I'le none
on't.

DOWNE-RIGHT Nay, that shall not serve your turne, now, sir. Officer,   50
I'le goe with thee, to the Justices: bring him along.

STEPHEN Why, is not here your cloke? what would you have?

DOWNE-RIGHT I'le ha' you answere it, sir.

BRAYNE-WORME Sir, Ile take your word; and this gentlemans, too:
for his apparance.

DOWNE-RIGHT I'le ha' no words taken. Bring him along.

BRAYNE-WORME Sir, I may choose, to doe that: I may take bayle.

DOWNE-RIGHT 'Tis true, you may take baile, and choose; at another
time: but you shall not, now, varlet. Bring him along, or I'le swinge
you.   60

BRAYNE-WORME Sir, I pitty the gentlemans case. Here's your money
againe.

DOWNE-RIGHT 'Sdeynes, tell not me of my money, bring him away,
I say.

BRAYNE-WORME I warrant you he will goe with you of himselfe, sir.

DOWNE-RIGHT Yet more adoe?

BRAYNE-WORME I have made a faire mash on't.

STEPHEN Must I goe?

BRAYNE-WORME I know no remedie, master STEPHEN.

70   DOWNE-RIGHT Come along, afore mee, here. I doe not love your
hanging looke behind.

STEPHEN Why, sir. I hope you cannot hang mee for it. Can hee,
fellow?

BRAYNE-WORME I thinke not, sir. It is but a whipping matter, sure!

STEPHEN Why, then, let him doe his worst, I am resolute. [*Exeunt.*]

Act V. Scene 1

CLEMENT, KNO'WEL, KITELY, DAME KITELY, TIB,
CASH, COB, SERVANTS.

[*Enter* CLEMENT, KNO'WELL, KITELY, DAME KITELY, TIB,
CASH, COB *and* SERVANTS.]

CLEMENT Nay, but stay, stay, give me leave: my chaire, sirrha. You,
master KNO'WELL, say you went thither to meet your sonne.

KNO'WELL I, sir.

CLEMENT But, who directed you, thither?

KNO'WELL That did mine owne man, sir.

CLEMENT Where is he?

KNO'WELL Nay, I know not, now; I left him with your clarke: and
appointed him, to stay here for me.

CLEMENT My clarke? about what time, was this?

10   KNO'WELL Mary, betweene one and two, as I take it.

CLEMENT And, what time came my man with the false message to
you, master KITELY?

KITELY After two, sir.

CLEMENT Very good: but, mistris KITELY, how that you were at
COBS? ha?

DAME KITELY An' please you, sir, Ile tell you: my brother, WEL-BRED,
told me, that COBS house, was a suspected place—

CLEMENT So it appeares, me thinkes: but, on.

DAME KITELY And that my husband us'd thither, daily.

20   CLEMENT No matter, so he us'd himselfe well, mistris.

DAME KITELY True sir, but you know, what growes, by such hants, often-times.

CLEMENT I see, ranke fruits of a jealous braine, mistris KITELY: but, did you find your husband there, in that case, as you suspected?

KITELY I found her there, sir.

CLEMENT Did you so? that alters the case. Who gave you knowledge, of your wives being there?

KITELY Marie, that did my brother WEL-BRED.

CLEMENT How? WEL-BRED first tell her? then tell you, after? where is WEL-BRED?   30

KITELY Gone with my sister, sir, I know not whither.

CLEMENT Why, this is a meere trick, a device; you are gull'd in this most grosly, all! alas, poore wench, wert thou beaten for this?

TIB Yes, most pitifully, and't please you.

COB And worthily, I hope: if it shall prove so.

CLEMENT I, that's like, and a piece of a sentence. [*Enter* SERVANT.] How now, sir? what's the matter?

SERVANT Sir, there's a gentleman, i'the court without, desires to speake with your worship.

CLEMENT A gentleman? what's he?   40

SERVANT A souldier, sir, he saies.

CLEMENT A souldier? take downe my armor, my sword, quickly: a souldier speake with me! why, when knaves? come on, come on, hold my cap there, so; give me my gorget, my sword: stand by, I will end your matters, anon—Let the souldier enter, [*Enter* BOBA-DILL *and* MATTHEW.] now, sir, what ha' you to say to me?

He armes himselfe.

[*Exit* SERVANT.]

Act V. Scene 2
BOBADILL, MATTHEW.

BOBADILL By your worships favour—

CLEMENT Nay, keepe out, sir, I know not your pretence, you send me word, sir, you are a souldier: why, sir, you shall bee answer'd, here, here be them have beene amongst souldiers. Sir, your pleasure.

BOBADILL Faith, sir, so it is, this gentleman, and my selfe, have beene most uncivilly wrong'd, and beaten, by one DOWNE-RIGHT, a

course fellow, about the towne, here, and for mine owne part, I
protest, being a man, in no sort, given to this filthie humour of
quarrelling, he hath assaulted mee in the way of my peace; dispoil'd

10   mee of mine honor; dis-arm'd mee of my weapons; and rudely,
laid me along, in the open streets: when, I not so much as once
offer'd to resist him.

CLEMENT O, gods precious! is this the souldier? here, take my armour
of quickly, 'twill make him swoune, I feare; hee is not fit to looke
on't, that will put up a blow.

MATTHEW An't please your worship, he was bound to the peace.

CLEMENT Why, and he were, sir, his hands were not bound, were
they?

[*Enter* SERVANT.]

SERVANT There's one of the varlets of the citie, sir, ha's brought two
20   gentlemen, here, one, upon your worships warrant.

CLEMENT My warrant?

SERVANT Yes, sir. The officer say's, procur'd by these two.

CLEMENT Bid him, come in. [*Exit* SERVANT.] Set by this picture.

[*Enter* DOWNE-RIGHT, STEPHEN *and* BRAYNE-WORME.]

What, Mr. DOWNE-RIGHT! are you brought at Mr. FRESH-WATERS
suite, here!

Act V. Scene 3

DOWNE-RIGHT, STEPHEN, BRAYNE-WORME.

DOWNE-RIGHT I faith, sir. And here's another brought at my suite.

CLEMENT What are you, sir?

STEPHEN A gentleman, sir? o, uncle!

CLEMENT Uncle? who? master KNO'WELL?

KNO'WELL I, sir! this is a wise kinsman of mine.

STEPHEN God's my witnesse, uncle, I am wrong'd here monstrously,
hee charges me with stealing of his cloke, and would I might never
stirre, if I did not find it in the street, by chance.

DOWNE-RIGHT O, did you find it, now? you said, you bought it,
10   erewhile.

STEPHEN And, you said, I stole it; nay, now my uncle is here, I'll doe
well inough, with you.

CLEMENT Well, let this breath a while; you, that have cause to
complaine, there, stand forth: had you my warrant for this gentlemans apprehension?

BOBADILL I, an't please your worship.

CLEMENT Nay, doe not speake in passion so: where had you it?

BOBADILL Of your clarke, sir.

CLEMENT That's well! an' my clarke can make warrants, and my hand
not at'hem! Where is the warrant? Officer, have you it?   20

BRAYNE-WORME No, sir, your worship's man, master FORMAL, bid
mee doe it, for these gentlemen, and he would be my discharge.

CLEMENT Why, master DOWNE-RIGHT, are you such a novice, to
bee serv'd, and never see the warrant?

DOWNE-RIGHT Sir. He did not serve it on me.

CLEMENT No? how then?

DOWNE-RIGHT Mary, sir, hee came to mee, and said, hee must serve
it, and hee would use me kindly, and so—

CLEMENT O, gods pittie, was it so, sir? he must serve it? give me my   29
long-sword there, and helpe me of; so. Come on, sir varlet, I must   *He flourishes*
cut off your legs, sirrha: nay, stand up, Ile use you kindly; I must   *over him with*
cut off your legs, I say.   *his long-sword.*

BRAYNE-WORME O, good sir, I beseech you; nay, good master Justice.

CLEMENT I must doe it; there is no remedie. I must cut off your legs,
sirrha, I must cut off your eares, you rascall, I must doe it; I must
cut off your nose, I must cut off your head.

BRAYNE-WORME O, good your worship.

CLEMENT Well, rise, how doest thou doe, now? doest thou feele thy
selfe well? hast thou no harme?

BRAYNE-WORME No, I thanke your good worship, sir.   40

CLEMENT Why, so! I said, I must cut off thy legs, and I must cut off
thy armes, and I must cut off thy head; but, I did not doe it: so,
you said, you must serve this gentleman, with my warrant, but,
you did not serve him. You knave, you slave, you rogue, doe you
say you must? sirrha, away with him, to the jayle, Ile teach you a
trick, for your *must*, sir.

BRAYNE-WORME Good sir, I beseech you, be good to me.

CLEMENT Tell him he shall to the jayle, away with him, I say.

BRAYNE-WORME Nay, sir, if you will commit mee, it shall bee for
committing more then this: I will not loose, by my travaile, any   50

graine of my fame certaine.

CLEMENT How is this!

KNO'WELL My man, BRAYNE-WORME!

STEPHEN O yes, uncle. BRAYNE-WORME ha's beene with my cossen
EDWARD, and I, all this day.

CLEMENT I told you all, there was some device!

BRAYNE-WORME Nay, excellent Justice, since I have laid my selfe
thus open to you; now, stand strong for mee: both with your
sword, and your ballance.

60 CLEMENT Bodie o' me, a merry knave! Give me a bowle of sack:
If hee belong to you, master KNO'WELL, I bespeake your
patience.

BRAYNE-WORME That is it, I have most need of. Sir, if you'll pardon
me, only; I'll glorie in all the rest, of my exploits.

KNO'WELL Sir, you know, I love not to have my favours come hard,
from me. You have your pardon: though I suspect you shrewdly
for being of counsell with my sonne, against me.

BRAYNE-WORME Yes, faith, I have, sir; though you retain'd me doubly
this morning, for your selfe: first, as BRAYNE-WORME; after, as
70 FITZ-SWORD. I was your reform'd souldier, sir. 'Twas I sent you
to COBS, upon the errand, without end.

KNO'WELL Is it possible! or that thou should'st disguise thy language
so, as I should not know thee?

BRAYNE-WORME O, sir, this ha's beene the day of my *metamorphosis*!
It is not that shape alone, that I have runne through, to day. I
brought this gentleman, master KITELY, a message too, in the
forme of master Justices man, here, to draw him out o' the way,
as well as your worship: while master WELL-BRED might make a
conveiance of mistris BRIDGET, to my yong master.

80 KITELY How! my sister stolne away?

KNO'WELL My sonne is not married, I hope!

BRAYNE-WORME Faith, sir, they are both as sure as love, a priest,
and three thousand pound (which is her portion) can make 'hem:
and by this time are readie to bespeake their wedding supper at
the wind-mill, except some friend, here, prevent 'hem, and invite
'hem home.

CLEMENT Marie, that will I (I thanke thee, for putting me in mind

on't.) Sirrah, goe you, and fetch 'hem hither, upon my warrant.
Neithers friends have cause to be sorrie, if I know the yong couple,
aright. Here, I drinke to thee, for thy good newes. But, I pray thee,   90
what hast thou done with my man FORMALL?

BRAYNE-WORME Faith, sir, after some ceremonie past, as making
him drunke, first with storie, and then with wine (but all in
kindnesse) and stripping him to his shirt: I left him in that coole
vaine, departed, sold your worships warrant to these two, pawn'd
his liverie for that varlets gowne, to serve it in; and thus have
brought my selfe, by my activitie, to your worships consideration.

CLEMENT And I will consider thee, in another cup of sack. Here's
to thee, which having drunke of, this is my sentence. Pledge me.
Thou hast done, or assisted to nothing, in my judgement, but   100
deserves to bee pardon'd for the wit o' the offence. If thy master,
or anie man, here, be angrie with thee, I shall suspect his ingine,
while I know him for't. How now? what noise is that!

[*Enter* SERVANT.]

SERVANT Sir, it is ROGER is come home.

CLEMENT Bring him in, bring him in. [*Exit* SERVANT.] What! drunke
in armes, against me? Your reason, your reason for this.

Act V. Scene 4
FORMALL.

To them.

[*Enter* FORMALL.]

FORMALL I beseech your worship to pardon me; I happen'd into ill
companie by chance, that cast me into a sleepe, and stript me of
all my clothes —

CLEMENT Well, tell him, I am Justice CLEMENT, and doe pardon
him: but, what is this to your armour! what may that signifie?

FORLMALL And't please you, sir, it hung up i' the roome, where I
was stript; and I borrow'd it of one o' the drawers, to come home
in, because I was loth, to doe penance through the street, i' my
shirt.

CLEMENT Well, stand by a while. [*Enter* ED. KNO'WELL, WELL-BRED
and BRIDGET.] Who be these? O, the yong companie, welcome,   10
welcome. Gi' you joy. Nay, mistris BRIDGET, blush not; you are

not so fresh a bride, but the newes of it is come hither afore you.
Master Bridegroome, I ha' made your peace, give mee your hand:
so will I for all the rest, ere you forsake my roofe.

Act V. Scene 5

ED. KNO'WEL, WEL-BRED, BRIDGET.

ED. KNO'WELL We are the more bound to your humanitie, sir.

CLEMENT Only these two, have so little of man in 'hem, they are no
part of my care.

WELL-BRED Yes, sir, let mee pray you for this gentleman, hee belongs,
to my sister, the bride.

CLEMENT In what place, sir?

WELL-BRED Of her delight, sir, below the staires, and in publike: her
poet, sir.

CLEMENT A *poet*? I will challenge him my selfe, presently, at *extempore*.

10   *Mount up thy Phlegon muse, and testifie,*
            How SATURNE, *sitting in an ebon cloud,*
            Disrob'd his podex white as ivorie,
            And, through the welkin, thundred all aloud.

WELL-BRED Hee is not for *extempore*, sir. Hee is all for the pocket-*muse*,
please you command a sight of it.

CLEMENT Yes, yes, search him for a tast of his veine.

WELL-BRED You must not denie the Queenes Justice, Sir, under a
writ o' rebellion.

CLEMENT What! all this verse? Bodie o' me, he carries a whole realme,

20   a common-wealth of paper, in's hose! let's see some of his subjects!
            Unto the boundlesse Ocean of thy face,
                Runnes this poore river charg'd with streames of eyes.
How? this is stolne!

ED. KNO'WELL A *Parodie*! a *parodie*! with a kind of miraculous gift, to
make it absurder then it was.

CLEMENT Is all the rest, of this batch? Bring me a torch; lay it
together, and give fire. Clense the aire. Here was enough to have
infected, the whole citie, if it had not beene taken in time! See,
see, how our *Poets* glorie shines! brighter, and brighter! still it

increases! o, now, it's at the highest: and, now, it declines as fast.   30
You may see. *Sic transit gloria mundi.*

KNO'WELL   There's an *embleme* for you, sonne, and your studies!

CLEMENT   Nay, no speech, or act of mine be drawne against such,
as professe it worthily. They are not borne everie yeere, as an
Alderman. There goes more to the making of a good *Poet*, then a
Sheriffe, Mr. KITELY. You looke upon me! though, I live i' the
citie here, amongst you, I will doe more reverence, to him, when
I meet him, then I will to the Major, out of his yeere. But, these
paper-pedlers! these inke-dablers! They cannot expect reprehension, or reproch. They have it with the fact.   40

ED. KNO'WELL   Sir, you have sav'd me the labour of a defence.

CLEMENT   It shall be discourse for supper; betweene your father and
me, if he dare under-take me. But, to dispatch away these, you
signe o'the Souldier, and picture o' the *Poet* (but, both so false, I
will not ha' you hang'd out at my dore till midnight) while we are
at supper, you two shall penitently fast it out in my court, without;
and, if you will, you may pray there, that we may be so merrie
within, as to forgive, or forget you, when we come out. Here's a
third, because, we tender your safetie, shall watch you, he is
provided for the purpose. Looke to your charge, sir.   50

STEPHEN   And what shall I doe?

CLEMENT   O! I had lost a sheepe, an he had not bleated! Why, sir,
you shall give Mr. DOWNE-RIGHT his cloke: and I will intreat him
to take it. A trencher, and a napkin, you shall have, i' the buttrie,
and keepe COB, and his wife companie, here; whom, I will intreat
first to bee reconcil'd: and you to endevour with your wit, to keepe
'hem so.

STEPHEN   Ile doe my best.

COB   Why, now I see thou art honest, TIB, I receive thee as my deare,
and mortall wife, againe.   60

TIB   And, I you, as my loving, and obedient husband.

CLEMENT   Good complement! It will bee their bridale night too. They
are married anew. Come, I conjure the rest, to put of all discontent.
    You, Mr. DOWNE-RIGHT, your anger; you, master KNO'WELL,
your cares; master KITELY, and his wife, their jealousie.
        For, I must tell you both, while that is fed,
        Hornes i' the mind are worse then o' the head.

KITELY Sir, thus they goe from me, kisse me, sweet heart.
   See, what a drove of hornes flye, in the ayre,
70   *Wing'd with my clensed, and my credulous breath!*
   Watch 'hem, suspicious eyes, watch, where they fall.
   See, see! on heads, that thinke th'have none at all!
   O, what a plenteous world of this, will come!
   When ayre raynes hornes, all may be sure of some.
   I ha' learned so much verse out of a jealous mans part, in a play.
CLEMENT 'Tis well, 'tis well! This night wee'll dedicate to friendship,
   love, and laughter. Master bride-groome, take your bride, and
   leade; every one, a fellow. Here is my mistris. BRAYNE-WORME!
   to whom all my addresses of courtship shall have their reference.
80   Whose adventures, this day, when our grand-children shall heare
   to be made a fable, I doubt not, but it shall find both spectators,
   and applause.

THE END.

This Comoedie was first
Acted, in the yeere
1598.

By the then L. CHAMBERLAYNE
his Servants.

The principall Comoedians were.

WILL. SHAKESPEARE.	RIC. BURBADGE.
AUG. PHILIPS.	JOH. HEMINGS.
HEN. CONDEL.	THO. POPE.
WILL. SLYE.	CHR. BEESTON.
WILL. KEMPE.	JOH. DUKE.

With the allowance of the Master of REVELLS.

Sejanus, His Fall

TO THE NO LESSE
NOBLE, BY VERTUE,
THEN BLOUD:

Esme

L. AUBIGNY.

MY LORD,

If ever any ruine were so great, as to survive; I thinke this be one I send you: the
Fal *of* Sejanus. *It is a poeme, that (if I well remember) in your Lordships sight,
suffer'd no lesse violence from our people here, then the subject of it did from the
rage of the people of* Rome; *but, with a different fate, as (I hope) merit:
For this hath out-liv'd their malice, and begot it selfe a greater favour then he
lost, the love of good men. Amongst whom, if I make your Lordships the first it
thankes, it is not without a just confession of the bond your benefits have, and
ever shall hold upon me.*

Your Lordships most faithfull honorer,
BEN. JONSON.

To the Readers.

The following, and voluntary Labours of my Friends, prefixt to my
Booke, have releived me in much, whereat (without them) I should
necessarilie have touchd: Now, I will onely use three or foure short,
and needfull Notes, and so rest.

First, if it be objected, that what I publish is no true *Poëme*; in the
strict Lawes of *Time*. I confesse it: as also in the want of a proper
Chorus, whose Habite, and Moodes are such, and so difficult, as not
any, whome I have seene since the *Auntients*, (no, not they who have
most presently affected Lawes) have yet come in the way off. Nor is
10   it needful, or almost possible, in these our Times, and to such Auditors,
as commonly Things are presented, to observe the ould state, and
splendour of *Drammatick Poëmes*, with preservation of any popular
delight. But of this I shall take more seasonable cause to speake; in
my Observations upon *Horace* his *Art* of *Poetry*, which (with the Text
translated) I intend, shortly to publish. In the meane time, if in truth
of Argument, dignity of Persons, gravity and height of Elocution,
fulnesse and frequencie of Sentence, I have discharg'd the other
offices of a *Tragick* writer, let not the absence of these *Formes* be
imputed to me, wherein I shall give you occasion hereafter (and
20   without my boast) to thinke I could better prescribe, then omit the
due use, for want of a convenient knowledge.

The next is, least in some nice nostrill, the *Quotations* might savour
affected, I doe let you know, that I abhor nothing more; and have
onely done it to shew my integrity in the *Story*, and save my selfe in
those common Torturers, that bring all wit to the Rack: whose Noses
are ever like Swine spoyling, and rooting up the *Muses* Gardens, and
their whole Bodies, like Moles, as blindly working under Earth to cast
any, the least, hilles upon *Vertue*.

Whereas, they are in *Latine* and the worke in *English*, it was presup-
30   posd, none but the Learned would take the paynes to conferre them,
the Authors themselves being all in the learned *Tongues*, save one, with
whose English side I have had little to doe: To which it may be
required, since I have quoted the Page, to name what Edition I
follow'd. *Tacit. Lips.* in 4°. *Antuerp. edit. 600. Dio. Folio Hen. Step.* 92.

For the rest, as *Sueton. Seneca.* &c. the Chapter doth sufficiently direct, or the Edition is not varied.

Lastly I would informe you, that this Booke, in all numbers, is not the same with that which was acted on the publike Stage, wherein a second Pen had good share: in place of which I have rather chosen, to put weaker (and no doubt lesse pleasing) of mine own, then to defraud so happy a *Genius* of his right, by my lothed usurpation.

Fare you well. And if you read farder of me, and like, I shall not be afraid of it though you praise me out.

Neque enim mihi cornea fibra est.

But that I should plant my felicity, in your generall saying *Good*, or *Well*, &c. were a weaknesse which the better sort of you might worthily contemne, if not absolutely hate me for.

BEN. JONSON. and no such,

Quem Palma negata macrum, donata reducit opimum.

The Argument.

Aelius Sejanus, *sonne to* Seius Strabo, *a gentleman of* Rome, *and borne at* Vulsinium, *after his long service in court; first, under* Augustus, *afterward,* Tiberius: *grew into that favour with the latter, and won him by those artes, as there wanted nothing, but the name, to make him a copartner of the Empire. Which greatnesse of his,* Drusus, *the Emperors sonne not brooking, after many smother'd dislikes (it one day breaking out) the* Prince *strooke him publikely on the face. To revenge which disgrace,* Livia, *the wife of* Drusus *(being before corrupted by him to her dishonour, and the discovery of her husbands councells)* Sejanus *practiseth with, together with her Physitian, called* Eudemus, *and one*

10　　Lygdus, *an Eunuch, to poyson* Drusus. *This their inhumane act having successfull, and unsuspected passage, it emboldeneth* Sejanus *to farther, & more insolent projects, even the ambition of the Empire: where finding the lets, he must encounter, to be many, & hard, in respect of the issue of* Germanicus *(who were next in hope for the succession) he deviseth to make* Tiberius *selfe, his meanes: & instill's into his eares many doubts, and suspicions, both against the* Princes, *and their mother* Agrippina: *which* Caesar *jealously hearkning to, as covetously consenteth to their ruine, and their friends. In this time, the better to mature and strengthen his designe,* Sejanus *labors to marry* Livia, *and worketh (with all his ingine) to remove* Tiberius *from the knowledge of publike businesse,*

20　　*with allurements of a quiet and retyred life: the latter of which,* Tiberius *(out of a pronenesse to lust, and a desire to hide those unnaturall pleasures, which he could not so publikely practise) embraceth: the former inkindleth his feares, and there, gives him first cause of doubt, or suspect toward* Sejanus. *Against whom, he raiseth (in private) a new instrument, one* Sertorius Macro, *and by him underworketh, discovers the others counsells, his meanes, his ends, sounds the affections of the* Senators, *divides, distracts them: at last, when* Sejanus *least looketh, and is most secure (with pretext of doing him an un-wonted honour in the* Senate*) he traines him from his guardes, and with a long doubtfull letter, in one day, hath him suspected, accused, condemned, and torne in pieces, by the rage*

30　　*of the people.*

The Persons of the Play.

TIBERIUS.

DRUSUS *se*[*nior*].	SEJANUS.
NERO.	LATIARIS.
DRUSUS *ju*[*nior*].	VARRO.
CALIGULA.	MACRO.
ARRUNTIUS.	COTTA.
SILIUS.	AFER.
SABINUS.	HATERIUS.
LEPIDUS.	SANQUINIUS.
CORDUS.	POMPONIUS.
GALLUS.	POSTHUMUS.
REGULUS.	TRIO.
TERENTIUS.	MINUTIUS.
LACO.	SATRIUS.
EUDEMUS.	NATTA.
RUFUS.	OPSIUS.

TRIBUNI.

AGRIPPINA. }	LIVIA.
	SOSIA.

PRAECONES.	LICTORES.
FLAMEN.	MINISTRI.
TUBICINES.	TIBICINES.
NUNTIUS.	SERVUS.

[PRAETOR]	[SUITOR]
[SENATORS]	[ATTENDANTS]
	[SERVANTS]

THE SCENE.

ROME

Sejanus.

Act I.

SABINUS, SILIUS, NATTA, LATIARIS, CORDUS, SATRIUS,
ARRUNTIUS, EUDEMUS, HATERIUS, &C.

[*Enter* SABINUS *and* SILIUS.]

SABINUS Haile, CAIUS SILIUS.

SILIUS   TITIUS SABINUS, Haile.
   Yo'are rarely met in court!

SABINUS   Therefore, well met.

SILIUS 'Tis true: Indeed, this place is not our sphaere.

SABINUS No, SILIUS, wee are no good inginers;
   We want the fine arts, & their thriving use,
   Should make us grac'd, or favour'd of the times:
   We have no shift of faces, no cleft tongues,
   No soft, and glutinous bodies, that can sticke,
   Like snailes, on painted walls; or, on our brests,
   Creepe up, to fall, from that proud height, to which   10
   We did by slaverie, not by service, clime.
   We are no guilty men, and then no great;
   We have nor place in court, office in state,
   That we can say, we owe unto our crimes:
   We burne with no black secrets, which can make
   Us deare to the authors; or live fear'd
   Of their still waking jealosies, to raise
   Our selves a fortune, by subverting theirs.
   We stand not in the lines, that doe advance
   To that so courted point.

     [*Enter* SATRIUS *and* NATTA.]

SILIUS   But yonder leane   20
   A paire that doe.

     [*Enter* LATIARIS.]

(SABINUS   Good cousin LATIARIS.)

SILIUS   Satrius Secundus, and Pinnarius Natta,
     The great SEJANUS clients: There be two,
     Know more, then honest councells: whose close brests
     Were they rip'd up to light, it would be found
     A poore, and idle sinne, to which their trunkes
     Had not beene made fit organs. These can lye,
     Flatter, and sweare, forsweare, deprave, informe,
     Smile, and betray; make guilty men; then beg
30   The forfeit lives, to get the livings; cut
     Mens throates with whisprings; sell to gaping sutors
     The emptie smoake, that flyes about the Palace;
     Laugh, when their patron laughes; sweat, when he sweates;
     Be hot, and cold with him; change every moode,
     Habit, and garbe, as often as he varies;
     Observe him, as his watch observes his clocke;
     And true, as turkise in the deare lords ring,
     Looke well, or ill with him: ready to praise
     His lordship, if he spit, or but pisse faire,
40   Have an indifferent stoole, or breake winde well,
     Nothing can scape their catch.

SABINUS   Alas! these things
     Deserve no note, confer'd with other vile,
     And filthier flatteries, that corrupt the times:
     When, not alone our gentries chiefe are faine
     To make their safety from such sordide acts,
     But all our *Consuls*, and no little part
     Of such as have beene *Praetors*, yea, the most
Pedarii.   Of *Senators* (that else not use their voyces)
     Start up in publique *Senate*, and there strive
50   Who shall propound most abject things, and base,
     So much, as oft TIBERIUS hath beene heard,
     Leaving the court, to crie, o race of men,
     Prepar'd for servitude! which shew'd, that, he
     Who least the publique liberty could like,
     As loathly brook'd their flat servilitie.

SILIUS   Well, all is worthy of us, were it more,
     Who with our ryots, pride, and civill hate,

Have so provok'd the justice of the gods.
We, that (within these fourescore yeeres) were borne
Free, equall lords of the triumphed world,   60
And knew no masters, but affections,
To which betraying first our liberties,
We since became the slaves to one mans lusts;
And now to many: every ministring spie
That will accuse, and sweare, is lord of you,
Of me, of all, our fortunes, and our lives.
Our lookes are call'd to question, and our wordes,
How innocent soever, are made crimes;
We shall not shortly dare to tell our dreames,
Or thinke, but 'twill be treason.

SABINUS   "Tyrannes artes   70
Are to give flatterers, grace; accusers, power;
That those may seeme to kill whom they devoure."

    [*Enter* CORDUS *and* ARRUNTIUS.]
Now good CREMUTIUS CORDUS.

CORDUS   Haile, to your lordship.

NATTA Who's that salutes your cousin?   *They whisper.*

LATIARIS   'Tis one CORDUS,
A gentleman of *Rome*: one, that has writ
Annal's of late, they say, and very well.

NATTA Annal's? of what times?

LATIARIS   I thinke of POMPEI'S,
And CAIUS CAESARS; and so downe to these.

NATTA How stands h'affected to the present state?
Is he or *Drusian*? or *Germanican*?   80
Or ours? or neutrall?

LATIARIS   I know him not so far.

NATTA Those times are somewhat queasie to be toucht.
Have you or seene, or heard part of his worke?

LATIARIS Not I, he meanes they shall be publike shortly.

NATTA O. CORDUS do you cal him?

LATIARIS   I.

        [*Exeunt* SATRIUS, NATTA *and* LATIARIS.]

SABINUS   But these our times
Are not the same, ARRUNTIUS.

ARRUNTIUS   Times? the men,
 The men are not the same: 'tis we are base,
 Poore, and degenerate from th'exalted streine
 Of our great fathers. Where is now the soule

90 Of god-like CATO? he, that durst be good,
 When CAESAR durst be evill; and had power,
 As not to live his slave, to dye his master.
 Or where the constant BRUTUS, that (being proofe
 Against all charme of benefits) did strike
 So brave a blow into the monsters heart
 That sought unkindly to captive his countrie?
 O, they are fled the light. Those mightie spirits
 Lye rak'd up, with their ashes, in their urnes,
 And not a sparke of their eternall fire

100 Glowes in a present bosome. All's but blaze,
 Flashes, and smoke, wherewith we labour so,
 There's nothing *Romane* in us; nothing good,
 Gallant, or great: 'Tis true, that CORDUS say's,
 Brave CASSIUS *was the last of all that race.*
  [*Enter* DRUSUS *senior and* HATERIUS.]

Drusus passeth SABINUS Stand by, lord DRUSUS.
by.
HATERIUS   Th'Emp'rours son, give place.
    [*Exeunt* DRUSUS *senior and* HATERIUS.]

SILIUS I like the prince well.

ARRUNTIUS   A riotous youth,
 There's little hope of him.

SABINUS   That fault his age
 Will, as it growes, correct. Me thinkes, he beares
 Himselfe, each day, more nobly then other:

110 And wins no lesse on mens affections,
 Then doth his father lose. Beleeve me, I love him;
 And chiefly for opposing to SEJANUS.

SILIUS And I, for gracing his yong kinsmen so,
 The sonnes of Prince GERMANICUS: It shewes
 A gallant cleerenesse in him, a streight minde,
 That envies not, in them, their fathers name.

ARRUNTIUS His name was, while he liv'd, above all envie;
 And being dead, without it. O, that man!

If there were seedes of the old vertue left,
They liv'd in him.

SILIUS   He had the fruits, ARRUNTIUS,   120
More then the seedes: SABINUS, and my selfe
Had meanes to know' him, within; and can report him.
We were his followers, (he would call us friends.)
He was a man most like to vertue'; In all,
And every action, neerer to the gods,
Then men, in nature; of a body' as faire
As was his mind; and no lesse reverend
In face, then fame: He could so use his state,
Temp'ring his greatnesse, with his gravitie,
As it avoyded all selfe-love in him,   130
And spight in others. What his funeralls lack'd
In images, and pompe, they had supply'd
With honourable sorrow, souldiers sadnesse,
A kind of silent mourning, such, as men
(Who know no teares, but from their captives) use
To shew in so great losses.

CORDUS   I thought once,
Considering their formes, age, manner of deaths,
The neerenesse of the places, where they fell,
T'have paralell'd him with great ALEXANDER:
For both were of best feature, of high race,   140
Yeer'd but to thirtie, and, in forraine lands,
By their owne people, alike made away.

SABINUS I know not, for his death, how you might wrest it:
But, for his life, it did as much disdaine
Comparison, with that voluptuous, rash,
Giddy, and drunken *Macedon's*, as mine
Doth with my bond-mans. All the good, in him,
(His valour, and his fortune) he made his;
But he had other touches of late *Romanes*,
That more did speake him: POMPEI's dignitie,   150
The innocence of CATO, CAESAR's spirit,
Wise BRUTUS temperance, and every vertue,
Which, parted unto others, gave them name,
Flow'd mixt in him. He was the soule of goodnesse:

And all our praises of him are like streames
Drawn from a spring, that still rise full, and leave
The part remayning greatest.

ARRUNTIUS   I am sure
He was too great for us, and that they knew
Who did remove him hence.

SABINUS   When men grow fast
160 Honor'd, and lov'd, there is a tricke in state
(Which jealous princes never faile to use)
How to decline that growth, with faire pretext,
And honourable colours of employment,
Either by embassie, the war, or such,
To shift them forth into another aire,
Where they may purge, and lessen; so was he:
And had his seconds there, sent by TIBERIUS,
And his more subtile damme, to discontent him;
To breede, and cherish mutinies; detract
170 His greatest actions; give audacious check
To his commands; and worke to put him out
In open act of treason. All which snares
When his wise cares prevented, a fine poyson
Was thought on, to mature their practices.

CORDUS Here comes SEJANUS.

SILIUS   Now observe the stoupes,
The bendings, and the falls.

ARRUNTIUS   Most creeping base!

They passe over   SEJANUS, SATRIUS, TERENTIUS. &C.
the stage.

[*Enter* SEJANUS, SATRIUS, TERENTIUS *and attendants.*]

SEJANUS I note 'hem well: No more. Say you.

SATRIUS   My lord,
There is a gentleman of *Rome* would buy——

SEJANUS How cal you him you talk'd with?

SATRIUS   'Please your lordship,
180 It is EUDEMUS, the physitian
To LIVIA, DRUSUS' wife.

SEJANUS   On with your sute.
　　Would buy, you said—
SATRIUS   A *Tribunes* place, my lord.
SEJANUS What will he give?
SATRIUS   Fiftie *sestertia.*
SEJANUS LIVIA's physitian, say you, is that fellow?
SATRIUS It is, my lord; your lordships answere?
SEJANUS   To what?
SATRIUS The place, my lord. 'Tis for a gentleman,
　　Your lordship will well like off, when you see him;
　　And one, you may make yours, by the grant.
SEJANUS Well, let him bring his money, and his name.
SATRIUS Thanke your lordship. He shall, my lord.
SEJANUS   Come hither.   190
　　Know you this same EUDEMUS? Is he learn'd?
SATRIUS Reputed so, my lord: and of deepe practice.
SEJANUS Bring him in, to me, in the gallerie;
　　And take you cause, to leave us there, togither:
　　I would confer with him, about a griefe.—On.

　　　[*Exeunt* SEJANUS, SATRIUS *and* TERENTIUS, *leaving a few suitors*
　　　　　　　　　　　　　　　　　　　　to SEJANUS.]

ARRUNTIUS So, yet! another? yet? o desperate state
　　Of grov'ling honour! Seest thou this, o sunne,
　　And doe wee see thee after? Me thinkes, day
　　Should lose his light, when men doe lose their shames,
　　And, for the emptie circumstance of life,   200
　　Betray their cause of living.
SILIUS   Nothing so.
　　SEJANUS can repaire, if JOVE should ruine.
　　He is the now court-god; And well applyed
　　With sacrifice of knees, of crookes, and cringe,
　　He will doe more then all the house of heav'n
　　Can, for a thousand *hecatombes.* 'Tis he
　　Makes us our day, or night; Hell, and *Elysium*
　　Are in his looke: We talke of RHADAMANTH,
　　Furies, and fire-brands; But 'tis his frowne
　　That is all these, where, on the adverse part,   210
　　His smile is more, then ere (yet) *Poets* fain'd

Of blisse, and shades, *nectar*——

ARRUNTIUS   A serving boy?
I knew him, at CAIUS trencher, when for hyre,
He prostituted his abused body
To that great gourmond, fat APICIUS;
And was the noted *pathick* of the time.

SABINUS And, now, the second face of the whole world.
The partner of the empire, hath his image
Rear'd equall with TIBERIUS, borne in ensignes,
220   Command's, disposes every dignitie,
Centurions, *Tribunes*, Heads of *provinces*,
Praetors, and *Consuls*, all that heretofore
Romes generall suffrage gave, is now his sale.
The gaine, or rather spoile, of all the earth,
One, and his house, receives.

SILIUS   He hath of late
Made him a strength too, strangely, by reducing
All the *Praetorian* bands into one campe,
Which he command's: pretending, that the souldier
By living loose, and scattered, fell to ryot;
230   And that if any sodaine enterprise
Should be attempted, their united strength
Would be far more, then sever'd; and their life
More strict, if from the citie more remov'd.

SABINUS Where, now, he builds, what kind of fort's he please,
Is hard to court the souldier, by his name,
Wooes, feasts the chiefest men of action,
Whose wants, not loves, compell them to be his.
And, though he ne're were liberall by kind,
Yet, to his owne darke ends, hee's most profuse,
240   Lavish, and letting flye, he cares not what
To his ambition.

ARRUNTIUS   Yet, hath he ambition?
Is there that step in state can make him higher?
Or more? or any thing he is, but lesse?

SILIUS Nothing, but Emperour.

ARRUNTIUS   The name TIBERIUS
I hope, will keepe; how ere he hath fore-gone

The dignitie, and power.

SILIUS   Sure, while he lives.

ARRUNTIUS And dead, it comes to DRUSUS. Should he fayle,
To the brave issue of GERMANICUS;
And they are three: Too many (ha?) for him
To have a plot upon?

SABINUS   I doe not know   250
The heart of his designes; but, sure, their face
Lookes farther then the present.

ARRUNTIUS   By the gods,
If I could gesse he had but such a thought,
My sword should cleave him downe from head to heart,
But I would finde it out: and with my hand
I'ld hurle his panting braine about the ayre,
In mites, as small as *atomi*, to'undoe
The knotted bed—

SABINUS   You are observ'd, ARRUNTIUS.

ARRUNTIUS Death! I dare tell him so; and all his spies: *He turnes to*
You, sir, I would, doe you looke? and you.   *Sejanus clyents.*

SABINUS   Forbeare.   [*Exeunt.*] 260

SATRIUS, EUDEMUS, SEJANUS.

[*Enter* SATRIUS *and* EUDEMUS.]

SATRIUS Here, he will instant be; Let's walke a turne.
Yo'are in a muse, EUDEMUS?

EUDEMUS   Not I, sir.
I wonder he should marke me out so! well,
JOVE, and APOLLO forme it for the best.

SATRIUS Your fortune's made unto you now, EUDEMUS,
If you can but lay hold upon the meanes;
Doe but observe his humour, and—beleeve it—
He's the noblest *Romane*, where he takes——
    [*Enter* SEJANUS.]
Here comes his lordship.

SEJANUS   Now, good SATRIUS.

SATRIUS This is the gentleman, my lord.

270   SEJANUS   Is this?

Give me your hand, we must be more acquainted.

Report, sir, hath spoke out your art, and learning:

And I am glad I have so needfull cause,

(How ever in it selfe painefull, and hard)

To make me knowne to so great vertue. Looke,

Who's that? SATRIUS [*Exit* SATRIUS.]—I have a griefe, sir,

That will desire your helpe. Your name's EUDEMUS?

EUDEMUS Yes.

SEJANUS   Sir?

EUDEMUS   It is, my lord.

SEJANUS   I heare, you are

Physitian to LIVIA, the princesse?

280   EUDEMUS I minister unto her, my good lord.

SEJANUS You minister to a royall lady, then.

EUDEMUS She is, my lord, and fayre.

SEJANUS   That's understood

Of all their sexe, who are, or would be so;

And those, that would be, physicke soone can make 'hem:

For those that are, their beauties feare no collours.

EUDEMUS Your lordship is conceited.

SEJANUS   Sir, you know it.

And can (if need be) read a learned lecture,

On this, and other secrets. Pray you tell me,

What more of ladies, besides LIVIA,

Have you your patients?

290   EUDEMUS   Many, my good lord.

The great AUGUSTA, URGULANIA,

MUTILIA PRISCA, and PLANCINA, divers——

SEJANUS And, all these tell you the particulars

Of every severall griefe? how first it grew,

And then encreas'd, what action caused that;

What passion that: and answere to each point

That you will put 'hem.

EUDEMUS   Else, my lord, we know not

How to prescribe the remedies.

SEJANUS   Goe to,

Yo'are a subtill nation, you Physitians!

And growne the onely cabinets, in court,   300
To ladies privacies. Faith which of these
Is the most pleasant lady, in her physicke?
Come, you are modest now.

EUDEMUS   'Tis fit my lord.

SEJANUS Why, sir, I doe not aske you of their urines,
Whose smel's most violet? or whose seige is best?
Or who makes hardest faces on her stool?
Which lady sleepes with her owne face, a nights?
Which puts her teeth off, with her clothes, in court?
Or, which her hayre? which her complexion?
And, in which boxe she puts it? These were questions   310
That might, perhaps, have put your gravity
To some defence of blush. But, I enquir'd,
Which was the wittiest? meriest? wantonnest?
Harmelesse intergatories, but conceipts.
Me thinks, AUGUSTA should be most perverse,
And froward in her fit?

EUDEMUS   She's so, my lord.

SEJANUS I knew it. And MUTILIA the most jocund?

EUDEMUS 'Tis very true, my lord.

SEJANUS   And why would you
Conceale this from me, now? Come, what's LIVIA?
I know, she's quick, and quaintly spirited,   320
And will have strange thoughts, when she's at leasure;
She tells 'hem all to you?

EUDEMUS   My noblest lord,
He breaths not in the empire, or on earth,
Whom I would be ambitious to serve
(In any act, that may preserve mine honour)
Before your lordship.

SEJANUS   Sir, you can loose no honor,
By trusting ought to me. The coursest act
Done to my service, I can so requite,
As all the world shall stile it honorable:
"Your idle, vertuous *definitions*   330
Keepe honor poore, and are as scorn'd, as vaine:
Those deeds breathe honor, that do sucke in gaine."

EUDEMUS But, good my lord, if I should thus betray
  The counsels of my patient, and a ladies
  Of her high place, and worth; what might your lordship,
  (Who presently are to trust me with your owne)
  Judge of my faith?

SEJANUS   Only the best, I sweare.
  Say now, that I should utter you my griefe;
  And with it, the true cause; that it were love;
340 And love to LIVIA: you should tell her this?
  Should she suspect your faith? I would you could
  Tell me as much, from her; see, if my braine
  Could be turn'd jealous.

EUDEMUS   Happily, my lord,
  I could, in time, tell you as much, and more;
  So I might safely promise but the first,
  To her, from you.

SEJANUS   As safely, my EUDEMUS,
  (I now dare call thee so) as I have put
  The secret into thee.

EUDEMUS   My lord—

SEJANUS   Protest not.
  Thy lookes are vowes to me, use onely speed,
350 And but affect her with SEJANUS love,
  Thou art a man, made, to make *Consuls*. Goe.

EUDEMUS My lord, Ile promise you a private meeting
  This day, together.

SEJANUS   Canst thou?

EUDEMUS   Yes.

SEJANUS   The place?

EUDEMUS My gardens, whither I shall your lordship.

SEJANUS Let me adore my AESCULAPIUS.
  Why, this indeed is physick! and out-speakes
  The knowledge of cheape drugs, or any use
  Can be made out of it! more comforting
  Then all your *opiates, julebes, apozemes,*
360 Magistrall *syrrupes,* or—Be gone, my friend,
  Not barely stiled, but created so;
  Expect things, greater then thy largest hopes,

To overtake thee: Fortune, shall be taught
To know how ill she hath deserv'd thus long,
To come behinde thy wishes. Goe, and speed. [*Exit* EUDEMUS.]
"Ambition makes more trusty slaves, then need."
These fellowes, by the favour of their arte,
Have, still, the meanes to tempt, oft-times, the power.
If LIVIA will be now corrupted, then
Thou hast the way, SEJANUS, to worke out   370
His secrets, who (thou knowest) endures thee not,
Her husband DRUSUS: and to worke against them.
Prosper it, PALLAS, thou, that betterst wit;
For VENUS hath the smallest share in it.

TIBERIUS, SEJANUS, DRUSUS.

[*Enter* TIBERIUS, DRUSUS *senior,* LATIARIS, NATTA, SATRIUS,
HATERIUS, ARRUNTIUS, SABINUS, SILIUS *and* CORDUS.]

TIBERIUS Wee not endure these flatteries, let him stand;   *One kneeles to*
   Our empire, ensignes, axes, roddes, and state   *him.*
   Take not away our humane nature from us:
   Looke up, on us, and fall before the gods.
SEJANUS How like a god, speakes CAESAR!
ARRUNTIUS   There, observe!
   He can indure that second, that's no flattery.   380
   O, what is it, proud slime will not beleeve
   Of his owne worth, to heare it equall prais'd
   Thus with the gods?
CORDUS   He did not heare it, sir.
ARRUNTIUS He did not? Tut, he must not, we thinke meanely.
   'Tis your most courtly, knowne confederacy,
   To have your private parasite redeeme
   What he, in publique subtilty, will lose
   To making him a name.
HATERIUS   Right mighty lord——
TIBERIUS We must make up our eares, 'gainst these assaults
   Of charming tongues; we pray you use, no more   390
   These contumelies to us: stile not us

Or lord, or mighty, who professe our selfe
The servant of the *Senate*, and are proud
T'enjoy them our good, just, and favouring lords.

CORDUS Rarely dissembled.

ARRUNTIUS   Prince-like, to the life.

SABINUS "When power, that may command, so much descends,
Their bondage, whom it stoupes to, it intends."

TIBERIUS Whence are these letters?

HATERIUS   From the *Senate*.

TIBERIUS   So.
Whence these?

LATIARIS   From thence too.

TIBERIUS   Are they sitting, now?

LATIARIS They stay thy answere, CAESAR.

400 SILIUS   If this man
Had but a minde allied unto his words,
How blest a fate were it to us, and *Rome*?
We could not thinke that state, for which to change,
Although the ayme were our old liberty:
The ghosts of those that fell for that, would grieve
Their bodies liv'd not, now, againe to serve.
"Men are deceiv'd, who thinke there can be thrall
Beneath a vertuous prince. Wish'd liberty
Ne're lovelier lookes, then under such a crowne."

410 But, when his grace is meerely but lip-good,
And, that no longer, then he aires himselfe
Abroad in publique, there, to seeme to shun
The strokes, and stripes of flatterers, which within
Are lechery unto him, and so feed
His brutish sense with their afflicting sound,
As (dead to vertue) he permits himselfe
Be carried like a pitcher, by the eares,
To every act of vice: this is a case
Deserves our feare, and doth presage the nigh,

420 And close approach of bloud and tyranny.
"Flattery is midwife unto princes rage:
And nothing sooner, doth helpe foorth a tyranne,
Then that, and whisperers grace, who have the time,

The place, the power, to make all men offenders."
ARRUNTIUS He should be told this: and be bid dissemble
    With fooles, and blinde men: We that know the evill,
    Should hunt the Palace-rattes, or give them bane;
    Fright hence these worse then ravens, that devoure
    The quicke, where they but prey upon the dead:
    He shall be told it.
SABINUS   Stay, ARRUNTIUS,   430
    We must abide our oportunity:
    And practise what is fit, as what is needfull.
    "It is not safe t'enforce a soveraigne's eare:
    Princes heare well, if they at all will heare."
ARRUNTIUS Ha? Say you so? well. In the meane time, JOVE,
    (Say not, but I doe call upon thee now.)
    Of all wilde beasts, preserve me from a tyranne;
    And of all tame, a flatterer.
SILIUS   'Tis well pray'd.
TIBERIUS Returne the lords this voyce, we are their creature:
    And it is fit, a good, and honest prince,   440
    Whom they, out of their bounty, have instructed
    With so dilate, and absolute a power,
    Should owe the office of it, to their service;
    And good of all, and every citizen.
    Nor shall it e're repent us, to have wish'd
    The *Senate* just, and fav'ring lords unto us,
    "Since their free loves doe yeeld no lesse defence
    T' a princes state, then his owne innocence."
    Say then, there can be nothing in their thought
    Shall want to please us, that hath pleased them;   450
    Our suffrage rather shall prevent, then stay
    Behind their wills: 'tis empire, to obey
    Where such, so great, so grave, so good determine.
    Yet, for the sute of *Spaine*, t'erect a temple
    In honour of our mother, and our selfe,
    We must (with pardon of the *Senate*) not
    Assent thereto. Their lordships may object
    Our not denying the same late request

Unto the *Asian* cities: We desire
460   That our defence, for suffering that, be knowne
In these briefe reasons, with our after purpose.
Since deified AUGUSTUS hindred not
A temple to be built, at *Pergamum*,
In honour of himselfe, and sacred *Rome*,
We, that have all his deedes, and wordes observ'd
Ever, in place of lawes, the rather follow'd
That pleasing precedent, because, with ours,
The *Senates* reverence also, there, was joyn'd.
But, as, t'have once receiv'd it, may deserve
470   The gaine of pardon, so, to be ador'd
With the continew'd stile, and note of gods,
Through all the *provinces*, were wild ambition,
And no lesse pride: Yea, ev'n AUGUSTUS name
Would early vanish, should it be prophan'd
With such promiscuous flatteries. For our part,
We here protest it, and are covetous
Posteritie should know it, we are mortall;
And can but deedes of men: 'twere glory' inough,
Could we be truely a prince. And, they shall adde
480   Abounding grace, unto our memorie,
That shall report us worthy our fore-fathers,
Carefull of your affaires, constant in dangers,
And not afraid of any private frowne
For publike good. These things shall be to us
Temples, and statues, reared in your mindes,
The fairest, and most during imag'rie:
For those of stone, or brasse, if they become
Odious in judgement of posteritie,
Are more contemn'd, as dying sepulchres,
490   Then tane for living monuments. We then
Make here our suite, alike to gods, and men,
The one, untill the period of our race,
T'inspire us with a free, and quiet mind,
Discerning both divine, and humane lawes;
The other, to vouchsafe us after death,

An honourable mention, and faire praise,
T'accompanie our actions, and our name:
The rest of greatnesse princes may command,
And (therefore) may neglect, only, a long,
A lasting, high, and happy memorie   500
They should, without being satisfied, pursue.
Contempt of fame begets contempt of virtue.

NATTA Rare!

SATRIUS   Most divine!

SEJANUS   The *Oracles* are ceas'd,
That only CAESAR, with their tongue, might speake.

ARRUNTIUS Let me be gone, most felt, and open this!

CORDUS Stay.

ARRUNTIUS What? to heare more cunning, and fine wordes,
With their sound flatter'd, ere their sense be meant?

TIBERIUS Their choise of *Antium*, there to place the guift
Vow'd to the goddesse, for our mothers health,   509
We will the *Senate* know, we fairely like;   *Fortuna*
As also, of their grant to LEPIDUS,   *equestris.*
For his repayring the *Aemilian* place,
And restauration of those monuments:
Their grace too in confining of SILANUS,
To th'other Is'le *Cithera*, at the sute
Of his religious sister, much commends
Their policie, so temp'red with their mercy.
But, for the honours, which they have decreed
To our SEJANUS, to advance his statue
In POMPEI's theatre (whose ruining fire   520
His vigilance, and labour kept restrain'd
In that one losse) they have, therein, out-gone
Their owne great wisedomes, by their skilfull choise,
And placing of their bounties, on a man,
Whose merit more adornes the dignitie,
Then that can him: and gives a benefit,
In taking, greater, then it can receive.
Blush not, SEJANUS, thou great aide of *Rome*,
Associate of our labours, our chief helper,

530   Let us not force thy simple modestie
With offring at thy praise, for more we cannot,
Since there's no voice can take it. No man, here,
Receive our speeches, as *hyperbole's*;
For we are far from flattering our friend,
(Let envy know) as from the need to flatter.
Nor let them aske the causes of our praise;
Princes have still their grounds rear'd with themselves,
Above the poore low flats of common men,
And, who will search the reasons of their acts,
540   Must stand on equall bases. Lead, away.
Our loves unto the *Senate*.

[*Exeunt* TIBERIUS, SEJANUS, HATERIUS, LATIARIS, SATRIUS,
NATTA, *etc.*]

ARRUNTIUS   *Caesar.*
SABINUS   Peace.
CORDUS Great POMPEI's theatre was never ruin'd
Till now, that proud SEJANUS hath a statue
Rear'd on his ashes.
ARRUNTIUS   Place the shame of souldiers,
Above the best of generalls? cracke the world!
And bruise the name of *Romanes* into dust,
Ere we behold it!
SILIUS   Checke your passion;
Lord DRUSUS tarries.
DRUSUS   Is my father mad?
Wearie of life, and rule, lords? thus to heave
550   An idoll up with praise! make him his mate!
His rivall in the empire!
ARRUNTIUS   O, good prince!
DRUSUS Allow him statues? titles? honours? such,
As he himselfe refuseth?
ARRUNTIUS   Brave, brave, DRUSUS!
DRUSUS The first ascents to soveraigntie are hard,
But, entred once, there never wants or meanes,
Or ministers, to helpe th'aspirer on.
ARRUNTIUS True, gallant DRUSUS.

DRUSUS   We must shortly pray
    To *Modestie*, that he will rest contented——
ARRUNTIUS I, where he is, and not write emperour.

        SEJANUS, DRUSUS, ARRUNTIUS, &C.   *He enters,*
                                                          followd with
                                                          clients.
    [*Enter* SEJANUS, LATIARIS *and clients.*]
SEJANUS There is your bill, and yours; Bring you your man: 560
    I' have mov'd for you, too, LATIARIS.
DRUSUS   What?
    Is your vast greatnesse growne so blindly bold,
    That you will over us?
SEJANUS   Why, then give way.
DRUSUS Give way, *Colossus*? Doe you lift? Advance you?
    Take that.   *Drusus strikes*
ARRUNTIUS Good! brave! excellent brave prince!   *him.*
DRUSUS Nay, come, approch. What? stand you off? at gaze?
    It lookes too full of death, for thy cold spirits.
    Avoid mine eye, dull camell, or my sword
    Shall make thy brav'rie fitter for a grave,
    Then for a triumph. I'le advance a statue,   570
    O'your owne bulke; but 't shall be on the crosse:
    Where I will naile your pride, at breadth, and length,
    And cracke those sinnewes, which are yet but stretch'd
    With your swolne fortunes rage.
ARRUNTIUS   A noble prince!
ALL A CASTOR, a CASTOR, a CASTOR, a CASTOR!
                              [*Exeunt all but* SEJANUS.]

                    SEJANUS.

[SEJANUS] He that, with such wrong mov'd, can beare it through
    With patience, and an even mind, knowes how
    To turne it backe. Wrath, cover'd, carryes fate:
    Revenge is lost, if I professe my hate.

580 What was my practice late, I'le now pursue
As my fell justice. This hath stil'd it new. [*Exit.*]

CHORUS — *Of Musicians.*

Act II.

SEJANUS, LIVIA, EUDEMUS.

[*Enter* SEJANUS, LIVIA *and* EUDEMUS.]

SEJANUS Physitian, thou art worthy of a province,
For the great favours done unto our loves;
And, but that greatest LIVIA beares a part
In the requitall of thy services,
I should alone, despaire of ought, like meanes,
To give them worthy satisfaction.
LIVIA EUDEMUS, (I will see it) shall receive
A fit, and full reward, for his large merit.
But for this potion, we intend to DRUSUS,
10 (No more our husband, now) whom shall we choose
As the most apt, and abled instrument,
To minister it to him?
EUDEMUS I say, LYGDUS.
SEJANUS LYGDUS? what's he?
LIVIA An Eunuch DRUSUS loves.
EUDEMUS I, and his cup-bearer.
SEJANUS Name not a second.
If DRUSUS love him, and he have that place,
We cannot thinke a fitter.
EUDEMUS True, my lord,
For free accesse, and trust, are two maine aides.
SEJANUS Skilfull physitian!
LIVIA But he must be wrought
To th'undertaking, with some labour'd arte.
SEJANUS Is he ambitious?
LIVIA No.

SEJANUS   Or covetous?   20
LIVIA Neither.
EUDEMUS   Yet, gold is a good generall charme.
SEJANUS What is he then?
LIVIA   Faith, only wanton, light.
SEJANUS How! Is he young? and faire?
EUDEMUS   A delicate youth.
SEJANUS Send him to me, I'le worke him. Royall ladie,
    Though I have lov'd you long, and with that height
    Of zeale, and dutie, (like the fire, which more
    It mounts, it trembles) thinking nought could adde
    Unto the fervour, which your eye had kindled;
    Yet, now I see your wisedome, judgement, strength,
    Quicknesse, and will, to apprehend the meanes   30
    To your owne good, and greatnesse, I protest
    My selfe through rarefied, and turn'd all flame
    In your affection: Such a spirit as yours,
    Was not created for the idle second
    To a poore flash, as DRUSUS; but to shine
    Bright, as the Moone, among the lesser lights,
    And share the sov'raigntie of all the world.
    Then LIVIA triumphs in her proper spheare,
    When shee, and her SEJANUS shall divide
    The name of CAESAR; and AUGUSTA'S starre   40
    Be dimm'd with glorie of a brighter beame:
    When AGRIPPINA'S fires are quite extinct,
    And the scarce-seene TIBERIUS borrowes all
    His little light from us, whose folded armes
    Shall make one perfect orbe. Who's that? EUDEMUS,
    Looke, 'tis not DRUSUS? [*Exit* EUDEMUS.] Ladie, doe not feare.
LIVIA Not I, my lord. My feare, and love of him
    Left me at once.
SEJANUS   Illustrous ladie! stay——
    [*Enter* EUDEMUS.]
EUDEMUS I'le tell his lordship.
SEJANUS   Who is't, EUDEMUS?
EUDEMUS One of your lordships servants, brings you word   50
    The Emp'rour hath sent for you.

SEJANUS   O! where is he?

He goes out. With your faire leave, deare Princesse. I'le but aske
A question, and returne.

EUDEMUS   Fortunate Princesse!
How are you blessed in the fruition
Of this unequald man, this soule of *Rome*,
The empires life, and voice of CAESARS world!

LIVIA So blessed, my EUDEMUS, as to know
The blisse I have, with what I ought to owe
The meanes that wrought it. How do'I looke to day?

60 EUDEMUS Excellent cleere, beleeve it. This same *fucus*
Was well laid on.

LIVIA   Me thinkes, 'tis here not white.

EUDEMUS Lend me your scarlet, lady. 'Tis the sunne
Hath giv'n some little taint unto the *ceruse*,
You should have us'd of the white oyle I gave you.
SEJANUS, for your love! his very name
Commandeth above CUPID, or his shafts——

(LIVIA Nay, now yo'have made it worse.

EUDEMUS   I'le helpe it straight.)
And, but pronounc'd, is a sufficient charme
Against all rumour; and of absolute power

70 To satisfie for any ladies honour.

(LIVIA What doe you now, EUDEMUS?

EUDEMUS   Make a light *fucus*,
To touch you ore withall.) Honor'd SEJANUS!
What act (though ne're so strange, and insolent)
But that addition will at least beare out,
If 't doe not expiate?

LIVIA   Here, good physitian.

EUDEMUS I like this studie to preserve the love
Of such a man, that comes not every houre
To greet the world. ('Tis now well, ladie, you should
Use of the *dentifrice*, I prescrib'd you, too,

80 To cleere your teeth, and the prepar'd *pomatum*,
To smoothe the skin:) A lady cannot be
Too curious of her forme, that still would hold
The heart of such a person, made her captive,

As you have his: who, to endeare him more
In your cleere eye, hath put away his wife,
The trouble of his bed, and your delights,
Faire *Apicata*, and made spacious roome
To your new pleasures.

LIVIA   Have not we return'd
That, with our hate of DRUSUS, and discoverie
Of all his councels?

EUDEMUS   Yes, and wisely, lady,   90
The ages that succeed, and stand far off
To gaze at your high prudence, shall admire
And reckon it an act, without your sexe:
It hath that rare apparance. Some will thinke
Your fortune could not yeeld a deeper sound,
Then mixt with DRUSUS; But, when they shall heare
That, and the thunder of SEJANUS meet,
SEJANUS, whose high name doth strike the starres,
And rings about the concave, great SEJANUS,
Whose glories, stile, and titles are himselfe,   100
The often iterating of SEJANUS:
They then will lose their thoughts, and be asham'd
To take acquaintance of them.

          [*Enter* SEJANUS.]

SEJANUS   I must make
A rude departure, lady. CAESAR sends
With all his haste both of command, and prayer.
Be resolute in our plot; you have my soule,
As certayne yours, as it is my bodies.
And, wise physitian, so prepare the poyson
As you may lay the subtile operation
Upon some naturall disease of his.   110
Your eunuch send to me. I kisse your hands,
Glorie of ladies, and commend my love
To your best faith, and memorie.

LIVIA   My lord,
I shall but change your wordes. Farewell. Yet, this
Remember for your heed, he loves you not;
You know, what I have told you: His designes

Are full of grudge, and danger: we must use
More then a common speed.

SEJANUS   Excellent lady,
How you do fire my bloud!

LIVIA   Well, you must goe?

120   The thoughts be best, are least set forth to shew.

[*Exit* SEJANUS.]EUDEMUS When will you take some physick, lady?

LIVIA   When
I shall, EUDEMUS: But let DRUSUS drug
Be first prepar'd.

EUDEMUS   Were LYGDUS made, that's done;
I have it readie. And to morrow-morning,
I'le send you a perfume, first to resolve,
And procure sweat, and then prepare a bath
To clense, and cleere the *cutis*; against when,
I'le have an excellent new *fucus* made,
Resistive 'gainst the sunne, the raine, or wind,

130   Which you shall lay on with a breath, or oyle,
As you best like, and last some fourteene houres.
This change came timely, lady, for your health;
And the restoring your complexion,
Which DRUSUS choller had almost burnt up:
Wherein your fortune hath prescrib'd you better
Then arte could doe.

LIVIA   Thankes, good physitian;
I'le use my fortune (you shall see) with reverence.
Is my coach ready?

EUDEMUS   It attends your highnesse.

                                          [*Exeunt.*]

SEJANUS.

[*Enter* SEJANUS.]
[SEJANUS] If this be not revenge, when I have done

140   And made it perfect, let *Aegyptian* slaves,
Parthians, and bare-foot *Hebrewes* brand my face,
And print my body full of injuries.

Thou lost thy selfe, childe DRUSUS, when thou thought'st
Thou could'st out-skip my vengeance: or out-stand
The power I had to crush thee into ayre.
Thy follyes now shall taste what kinde of man
They have provok'd, and this thy fathers house
Cracke in the flame of my incensed rage,
Whose fury shall admit no shame, or meane.
Adultery? it is the lightest ill,   150
I will commit. A race of wicked acts
Shall flow out of my anger, and o're-spread
The worlds wide face, which no posterity
Shall e're approove, nor yet keepe silent: Things,
That for their cunning, close, and cruell marke,
Thy father would wish his; and shall (perhaps)
Carry the empty name, but we the prize.
On then, my soule, and start not in thy course;
Though heav'n drop sulphure, and hell belch out fire,
Laugh at the idle terrors: Tell proud JOVE,   160
Betweene his power, and thine, there is no oddes.
'Twas onely feare, first, in the world made gods.

TIBERIUS, SEJANUS.

[*Enter* TIBERIUS, *with* ATTENDANTS.]
TIBERIUS Is yet SEJANUS come?
SEJANUS   He's here, dread CAESAR.
TIBERIUS Let all depart that chamber, and the next:
                                        [*Exeunt* ATTENDANTS.]
    Sit downe, my comfort. When the master-prince
    Of all the world, SEJANUS, saith, he feares;
    Is it not fatall?
SEJANUS   Yes, to those are fear'd.
TIBERIUS And not to him?
SEJANUS   Not, if he wisely turne
    That part of fate he holdeth, first on them.
TIBERIUS That nature, bloud, and lawes of kinde forbid.   170
SEJANUS Doe policie, and state forbid it?

TIBERIUS   No.

SEJANUS The rest of poore respects, then, let goe by:
    State is inough to make th'act just, them guilty.

TIBERIUS Long hate pursues such acts.

SEJANUS   Whom hatred frights,
    Let him not dreame on sov'raignty.

TIBERIUS   Are rites
    Of faith, love, piety, to be trod downe?
    Forgotten? and made vaine?

SEJANUS   All for a crowne.
    The prince, who shames a tyrannes name to beare,
    Shall never dare doe any thing, but feare;
180   All the command of scepters quite doth perish
    If it beginne religious thoughts to cherish:
    Whole Empires fall, swaid by those nice respects.
    It is the licence of darke deeds protects
    Ev'n states most hated: when no lawes resist
    The sword, but that it acteth what it list.

TIBERIUS Yet so, we may doe all things cruelly,
    Not safely:

SEJANUS   Yes, and doe them thoroughly.

TIBERIUS Knowes yet, SEJANUS, whom we point at?

SEJANUS   I,
    Or else my thought, my sense, or both doe erre:
    'Tis AGRIPPINA?

190 TIBERIUS   She; and her proud race.

SEJANUS Proud? dangerous, CAESAR. For in them apace
    The fathers spirit shoots up. GERMANICUS
    Lives in their lookes, their gate, their forme, t'upbraide us
    With his close death, if not revenge the same.

TIBERIUS The act's not knowne.

SEJANUS   Not prov'd. But whispring fame
    Knowledge, and proofe doth to the jealous give,
    Who, then to faile, would their owne thought beleeve.
    It is not safe, the children draw long breath,
    That are provoked by a parents death.

200 TIBERIUS It is as dangerous, to make them hence,
    If nothing but their birth be their offence.

SEJANUS Stay, till they strike at CAESAR: then their crime
    Will be enough, but late, and out of time
    For him to punish.
TIBERIUS   Doe they purpose it?
SEJANUS You know, sir, thunder speakes not till it hit.
    Be not secure: none swiftlier are opprest,
    Then they, whom confidence betrayes to rest.
    Let not your daring make your danger such:
    All power's to be fear'd, where 'tis too much.
    The youth's are (of themselves) hote, violent,   210
    Full of great thought; and that male-spirited dame,
    Their mother, slackes no meanes to put them on,
    By large allowance, popular presentings,
    Increase of traine, and state, suing for titles,
    Hath them commended with like praiers, like vowes,
    To the same Gods, with CAESAR: daies and nights
    Shee spends in banquets, and ambitious feasts
    For the Nobilitie; where CAIUS SILIUS,
    TITIUS SABINUS, olde ARRUNTIUS,
    ASINIUS GALLUS, FURNIUS, REGULUS,   220
    And others, of that discontented list,
    Are the prime guests. There, and to these, she tels
    Whose niece she was, whose daughter, and whose wife,
    And then must they compare her with AUGUSTA,
    I, and preferre her too, commend her forme,
    Extoll her fruitfulnesse; at which a showre
    Fals for the memorie of GERMANICUS,
    Which they blow over straight, with windie praise,
    And puffing hopes of her aspiring sonnes:
    Who, with these hourely ticklings, grow so pleas'd,   230
    And wantonly conceited of themselves,
    As now, they sticke not to beleeve they're such,
    As these doe give 'hem out: and would be thought
    (More then competitors) immediate heires.
    Whilest to their thirst of rule they winne the rout
    (That's still the friend of noveltie) with hope
    Of future freedome, which on everie change,
    That greedily, though emptily, expects.

   CAESAR, 'tis age in all things breeds neglects,
240   And princes that will keepe olde dignitie,
   Must not admit too youthfull heires stand by;
   Not their owne issue: but so darkely set
   As shadowes are in picture, to give height,
   And lustre to themselves.
TIBERIUS   We will command
   Their ranke thoughts downe, and with a stricter hand
   Then we have yet put forth, their traines must bate,
   Their titles, feasts and factions.
SEJANUS   Or your state.
   But how sir, will you worke?
TIBERIUS   Confine 'hem.
SEJANUS   No.
   They are too great, and that too faint a blow,
250   To give them now: it would have serv'd at first,
   When, with the weakest touch, their knot had burst.
   But, now, your care must be, not to detect
   The smallest cord, or line of your suspect,
   For such, who know the weight of princes feare,
   Will, when they find themselves discover'd, reare
   Their forces, like seene snakes, that else would lye
   Rould in their circles, close: Nought is more high,
   Daring, or desperate, then offenders found;
   Where guilt is, rage, and courage both abound.
260   The course must be, to let 'hem still swell up,
   Riot, and surfet on blind fortunes cup;
   Give 'hem more place, more dignities, more stile,
   Call 'hem to *court*, to *senate*: in the while,
   Take from their strength some one or twaine, or more
   Of the maine Fautors; (It will fright the store)
   And, by some by-occasion. Thus, with slight
   You shall disarme them first, and they (in night
   Of their ambition) not perceive the traine,
   Till, in the ingine, they are caught, and slaine.
270 TIBERIUS We would not kill, if we knew how to save;
   Yet, then a throne, 'tis cheaper give a grave.

Is there no way to bind them by deserts?
SEJANUS Sir, wolves do change their haire, but not their harts.
While thus your thought unto a meane is tied,
You neither dare inough, nor doe provide.
All modestie is fond; and chiefly where
The subject is no lesse compeld to beare,
Then praise his sov'raignes acts.
TIBERIUS   We can no longer
Keepe on our masque to thee, our deare SEJANUS;
Thy thoughts are ours, in all, and we but proov'd   280
Their voice, in our designes, which by assenting
Hath more confirm'd us, then if heartning JOVE
Had, from his hundred statues, bid us strike,
And at the stroke clickt all his marble thumb's.
But, who shall first be strooke?
SEJANUS   First, CAIUS SILIUS;
He is the most of marke, and most of danger:
In power, and reputation equall strong,
Having commanded an imperiall armie
Seven yeeres together, vanquish'd SACROVIR
In *Germanie*, and thence obtain'd to weare   290
The ornaments triumphall. His steep fall,
By how much it doth give the weightier crack,
Will send more wounding terrour to the rest,
Command them stand aloofe, and give more way
To our surprising of the principall.
TIBERIUS But what, SABINUS?
SEJANUS   Let him grow awhile,
His fate is not yet ripe: we must not plucke
At all together, lest wee catch our selves.
And ther's ARRUNTIUS too, he only talkes.
But SOSIA, SILIUS wife, would be wound in   300
Now, for she hath a furie in her brest
More, then hell ever knew; and would be sent
Thither in time. Then, is there one CREMUTIUS
CORDUS, a writing fellow, they have got
To gather notes of the precedent times,

And make them into Annal's; a most tart
And bitter spirit (I heare) who, under colour
Of praysing those, doth taxe the present state,
Censures the men, the actions, leaves no tricke,
310   No practice un-examin'd, paralels
The times, the governments, a profest champion,
For the old libertie——

TIBERIUS   A perishing wretch.
As if there were that *chaos* bred in things,
That lawes, and libertie would not rather choose
To be quite broken, and tane hence by us,
Then have the staine to be preserv'd by such.
Have we the meanes, to make these guiltie, first?

SEJANUS Trust that to me: let CAESAR, by his power,
But cause a formall meeting of the *Senate*,
320   I will have matter, and accusers readie.

TIBERIUS But how? let us consult.

SEJANUS   Wee shall mispend
The time of action. Counsels are unfit
In businesse, where all rest is more pernicious
Then rashnesse can be. Acts of this close kind
Thrive more by execution, then advice.
There is no lingring in that worke begun,
Which cannot praised be, untill through done.

TIBERIUS Our edict shall, forthwith, command a court.
While I can live, I will prevent earths furie:
330   Ἐμοῦ θανόντος γαῖα μιχθήτω πυρί   [*Exit.*]

POSTHUMUS, SEJANUS.

[*Enter* POSTHUMUS.]

POSTHUMUS My Lord SEJANUS——

SEJANUS   JULIUS POSTHUMUS,
Come with my wish! what newes from AGRIPPINA'S?

POSTHUMUS Faith none. They all locke up themselves a'late;
Or talke in character: I have not seene

A companie so chang'd. Except they had
Intelligence by augurie' of our practice.

SEJANUS When were you there?

POSTHUMUS   Last night.

SEJANUS   And what ghests found
you?

POSTHUMUS SABINUS, SILIUS, (the olde list,) ARRUNTIUS,
FURNIUS, and GALLUS.

SEJANUS   Would not these talke?

POSTHUMUS   Little.
And yet we offered choice of argument.   340
SATRIUS was with me.

SEJANUS   Well: 'tis guilt inough
Their often meeting. You forgot t' extoll
The hospitable ladie?

POSTHUMUS   No, that tricke
Was well put home, and had succeded too,
But that SABINUS cought a caution out;
For she began to swell.

SEJANUS   And may she burst.
JULIUS, I would have you goe instantly,
Unto the palace of the great AUGUSTA,
And, (by your kindest friend,) get swift accesse;   *Mutilia Prisca.*
Acquaint her, with these meetings: Tell the words   350
You brought me, (th'other day) of SILIUS,
Adde somewhat to 'hem. Make her understand
The danger of SABINUS, and the times,
Out of his closenesse. Give ARRUNTIUS words
Of malice against CAESAR; so, to GALLUS:
But (above all) to AGRIPPINA. Say,
(As you may truely) that her infinite pride,
Propt with the hopes of her too fruitfull wombe,
With popular studies gapes for soveraigntie;
And threatens CAESAR. Pray AUGUSTA then,   360
That for her owne, great CAESARS, and the pub-
lique safetie, she be pleas'd to urge these dangers.
CAESAR is too secure (he must be told,

And best hee'll take it from a mothers tongue.)
Alas! what is 't for us to sound, t' explore,
To watch, oppose, plot, practise, or prevent,
If he, for whom it is so strongly labour'd,
Shall, out of greatnesse, and free spirit, be
Supinely negligent? Our citi's now
370 Devided as in time o'th'civill warre,
And men forbeare not to declare themselves
Of AGRIPPINA's partie. Every day,
The faction multiplies; and will doe more
If not resisted: you can best inlarge it
As you find audience. Noble POSTHUMUS,
Commend me to your PRISCA: and pray her,
Shee will solicite this great businesse
To earnest, and most present execution,
With all her utmost credit with AUGUSTA.
380 POSTHUMUS I shall not faile in my instructions.   [*Exit.*]
SEJANUS This second (from his mother) will well urge
Our late designe, and spur on CAESARS rage:
Which else might grow remisse. The way, to put
A prince in bloud, is to present the shapes
Of dangers, greater then they are (like late,
Or early shadowes) and, sometimes, to faine
Where there are none, onely, to make him feare;
His feare will make him cruell: And once entred,
He doth not easily learne to stop, or spare
390 Where he may doubt. This have I made my rule,
To thrust TIBERIUS into tyrannie,
And make him toile, to turne aside those blockes,
Which I alone, could not remoove with safetie.
DRUSUS once gone, GERMANICUS three sonnes
Would clog my way; whose guardes have too much faith
To be corrupted: and their mother knowne
Of too-too unreproov'd a chastitie,
To be attempted, as light LIVIA was.
Worke then, my art, on CAESAR's feares, as they
400 On those they feare, till all my lets be clear'd:
And he in ruines of his house, and hate

Of all his subjects, bury his owne state:
When, with my peace, and safty, I will rise,
By making him the publike sacrifice.   [*Exit.*]

SATRIUS, NATTA.

[*Enter* SATRIUS *and* NATTA.]
SATRIUS They'are growne exceeding circumspect, and wary.
NATTA They have us in the wind: And yet, ARRUNTIUS
Cannot contayne himselfe.
SATRIUS   Tut, hee's not yet
Look'd after, there are others more desir'd,
That are more silent.
NATTA   Here he comes. Away.   [*Exeunt.*]

SABINUS, ARRUNTIUS, CORDUS.

[*Enter* SABINUS, ARRUNTIUS *and* CORDUS.]
SABINUS How is it, that these beagles haunt the house   410
Of AGRIPPINA?
ARRUNTIUS   O, they hunt, they hunt.
There is some game here lodg'd, which they must rouse,
To make the great-ones sport.
CORDUS   Did you observe
How they inveigh'd 'gainst CAESAR?
ARRUNTIUS   I, baytes, baytes,
For us to bite at: would I have my flesh
Torne by the publique hooke, these qualified hang-men
Should be my company.
CORDUS   Here comes another.   *Afer passes by.*
ARRUNTIUS I, there's a man, AFER the oratour!
One, that hath phrases, figures, and fine flowres,
To strew his *rethorique* with, and doth make haste   420
To get him note, or name, by any offer
Where bloud, or gaine be objects; steepes his wordes,
When he would kill, in artificiall teares:

> The Crocodile of *Tyber*! him I love,
> That man is mine. He hath my heart, and voice,
> When I would curse, he, he.

SABINUS   Contemne the slaves,
> Their present lives will be their future graves.   [*Exeunt.*]

SILIUS, AGRIPPINA, NERO, SOSIA.

[*Enter* SILIUS, AGRIPPINA, NERO *and* SOSIA.]

SILIUS May't please your highnesse not forget your selfe,
> I dare not, with my manners, to attempt
> Your trouble farder.

430   AGRIPPINA   Farewell, noble SILIUS.

SILIUS Most royall princesse.

AGRIPPINA   SOSIA stayes with us?

SILIUS Shee is your servant, and doth owe your grace
> An honest, but unprofitable love.

AGRIPPINA How can that be, when there's no gaine, but vertu's?

SILIUS You take the morall, not the politique sense.
> I meant, as shee is bold, and free of speech,
> Earnest to utter what her zealous thought
> Travailes withall, in honour of your house;
> Which act, as it is simply borne in her,

440
> Pertakes of love, and honesty, but may,
> By th'over-often, and unseason'd use,
> Turne to your losse, and danger: For your state
> Is wayted on by envies, as by eyes;
> And every second ghest your tables take,
> Is a fee'd spie, t'observe who goes, who comes,
> What conference you have, with whom, where, when,
> What the discourse is, what the lookes, the thoughts
> Of ev'ry person there, they doe extract,
> And make into a substance.

AGRIPPINA   Heare me, SILIUS,

450
> Were all TIBERIUS body stuck with eyes,
> And ev'ry wall, and hanging in my house
> Transparent, as this lawne I weare, or ayre;

Yea, had SEJANUS both his eares as long
As to my in-most closet: I would hate
To whisper any thought, or change an act,
To be made JUNO'S rivall. Vertues forces
Shew ever noblest in conspicuous courses.

SILIUS 'Tis great, and bravely spoken, like the spirit
Of AGRIPPINA: yet, your highnesse knowes,
There is nor losse, nor shame in providence: 460
Few can, what all should doe, beware inough.
You may perceive with what officious face,
SATRIUS, and NATTA, AFER, and the rest
Visite your house, of late, t'enquire the secrets;
And with what bold, and priviledg'd arte, they raile
Against AUGUSTA: yea, and at TIBERIUS,
Tell tricks of LIVIA, and SEJANUS, all
T'excite, and call your indignation on,
That they might heare it at more libertie.

AGRIPPINA Yo'are too suspitious, SILIUS.

SILIUS   .   Pray the gods,   470
I be so AGRIPPINA: But I feare
Some subtill practice. They, that durst to strike
At so examp-lesse, and un-blam'd a life,
As, that of the renown'd GERMANICUS,
Will not sit downe, with that exploit alone:
"He threatens many, that hath injur'd one."

NERO 'Twere best rip forth their tongues, seare out their eies,
When next they come.

SOSIA   A fit reward for spies.

DRUSUS *ju*: AGRIPPINA, NERO, SILIUS.

[*Enter* DRUSUS JUNIOR.]

DRUSUS JUNIOR Heare you the rumour?

AGRIPPINA   What?

DRUSUS JUNIOR   DRUSUS is dying.

AGRIPPINA Dying?

NERO   That's strange!

480   AGRIPPINA   Yo' were with him, yesternight.

DRUSUS JUNIOR One met EUDEMUS, the Physician,
    Sent for, but now: who thinkes he cannot live.

SILIUS Thinkes? if't be arriv'd at that, he knowes,
    Or none.

AGRIPPINA This's quicke! what should bee his disease?

SILIUS Poyson. Poyson——

AGRIPPINA   How, SILIUS!

NERO   What's that?

SILIUS Nay, nothing. There was (late) a certaine blow
    Giv'n o' the face.

NERO   I, to SEJANUS?

SILIUS   True.

DRUSUS JUNIOR And, what of that?

SILIUS   I'am glad I gave it not.

NERO But, there is somewhat else?

SILIUS   Yes, private meetings,
490   With a great ladie, at a physicians,
    And, a wife turn'd away——

NERO   Ha!

SILIUS   Toyes, meere toyes:
    What wisdom's now i'th' streets? i'th' common mouth?

DRUSUS JUNIOR Feares, whisp'rings, tumults, noyse, I know not
    what:
    They say, the *Senate* sit.

SILIUS   I'le thither, straight;
    And see what's in the forge.

AGRIPPINA   Good SILIUS doe.
    SOSIA, and I will in.

SILIUS   Haste you, my lords,
    To visit the sicke prince: tender your loves,
    And sorrowes to the people. This SEJANUS
    (Trust my divining soule) hath plots on all:
500   No tree, that stops his prospect, but must fall.   [*Exeunt.*]

CHORUS——*Of Musicians.*

Act III.

THE SENATE.

SEJANUS, VARRO, LATIARIS.
COTTA, AFER.
[SABINUS,] GALLUS, LEPIDUS, ARRUNTIUS.
PRAECONES, LICTORES.

[*Enter* PRAECONES, LICTORES, VARRO, SEJANUS, LATIARIS, COTTA *and* AFER.]

SEJANUS Tis only you must urge against him, VARRO,
    Nor I, nor CAESAR may appeare therein,
    Except in your defence, who are the *Consul*:
    And, under colour of late en'mitie
    Betweene your father, and his, may better doe it,
    As free from all suspition of a practice.
    Here be your notes, what points to touch at; read:
    Bee cunning in them. AFER ha's them too.
VARRO But is he summon'd?
SEJANUS   No. It was debated
    By CAESAR, and concluded as most fit   10
    To take him unprepar'd.
AFER   And prosecute
    All under name of treason.
VARRO   I conceive.
    [*Enter* SABINUS, GALLUS, LEPIDUS *and* ARRUNTIUS.]
SABINUS DRUSUS being dead, CAESAR will not be here.
GALLUS What should the businesse of this *Senate* bee?
ARRUNTIUS That can my subtile whisperers tell you: We,
    That are the good-dull-noble lookers on,
    Are only call'd to keepe the marble warme.
    What should we doe with those deepe mysteries,
    Proper to these fine heads? let them alone.
    Our ignorance may, perchance, helpe us be sav'd   20
    From whips, and *furies*.

GALLUS   See, see, see, their action!

ARRUNTIUS I, now their heads doe travaile, now they worke;
    Their faces runne like shittles, they are weaving
    Some curious cobweb to catch flyes.

SABINUS   Observe,
    They take their places.

ARRUNTIUS   What so low?

GALLUS   O yes,
    They must be seene to flatter CAESARS griefe
    Though but in sitting.

VARRO   Bid us silence.

PRAECONES   Silence.

VARRO *Fathers Conscript, may this our present meeting*
    Turne faire, and fortunate to the Common-wealth.

[SEJANUS,] SILIUS, SENATE.

[*Enter* SILIUS *and other* SENATORS.]

SEJANUS See, SILIUS enters.

SILIUS   Haile grave *Fathers*.

30 LICTORES   Stand.
    SILIUS, forbeare thy place.

SENATORS   How!

PRAECONES   SILIUS stand forth,
    The *Consul* hath to charge thee.

LICTORES   Roome for CAESAR.

ARRUNTIUS Is he come too? nay then expect a tricke.

SABINUS SILIUS accus'd? sure he will answere nobly.

TIBERIUS, SENATE.

[*Enter* TIBERIUS, *attended.*]

TIBERIUS We stand amazed, *Fathers*, to behold
    This generall dejection. Wherefore sit
    Romes Consuls thus dissolv'd, as they had lost
    All the remembrance both of stile, and place?

It not becomes. No woes are of fit waight,
To make the honour of the empire stoope: 40
Though I, in my peculiar selfe, may meete
Just reprehension, that so suddenly,
And, in so fresh a griefe, would greet the *Senate*,
When private tongues, of kinsmen, and allies,
(Inspir'd with comforts) lothly are indur'd,
The face of men not seene, and scarce the day,
To thousands, that communicate our losse.
Nor can I argue these of weaknesse; since
They take but naturall wayes: yet I must seeke
For stronger aides, and those faire helpes draw out   50
From warme imbraces of the common-wealth.
Our mother, great AUGUSTA, 'is strooke with time,
Our selfe imprest with aged characters,
DRUSUS is gone, his children young, and babes,
Our aimes must now reflect on those, that may
Give timely succour to these present ills,
And are our only glad-surviving hopes,
The noble issue of GERMANICUS,
NERO, and DRUSUS: might it please the *Consul*
Honour them in, (they both attend without.)   60
I would present them to the *Senates* care,
And raise those sunnes of joy, that should drinke up
These flouds of sorrow, in your drowned eyes.
ARRUNTIUS By JOVE, I am not OEDIPUS inough,
To understand this SPHYNX.
SABINUS   The princes come.

TIBERIUS, NERO, DRUSUS *junior.*

[*Enter* NERO *and* DRUSUS JUNIOR.]
TIBERIUS Approch you noble NERO, noble DRUSUS,
These princes, *Fathers*, when their parent dyed,
I gave unto their uncle, with this prayer,
That, though h'had proper issue of his owne,
He would no lesse bring up, and foster these,   70

Then that selfe-bloud; and by that act confirme
Their worths to him, and to posteritie:
DRUSUS tane hence, I turne my prayers to you,
And, 'fore our countrie, and our gods, beseech
You take, and rule AUGUSTUS nephewes sonnes,
Sprung of the noblest ancestors; and so
Accomplish both my dutie, and your owne.
NERO, and DRUSUS, these shall be to you
In place of parents, these your fathers, these,

80   And not unfitly: For you are so borne,
As all your good, or ill's the common-wealths.
Receyve them, you strong guardians; and blest gods,
Make all their actions answere to their blouds:
Let their great titles find increase by them,
Not they by titles. Set them, as in place,
So in example, above all the *Romanes*:
And may they know no rivals, but themselves.
Let fortune give them nothing; but attend
Upon their vertue: and that still come forth

90   Greater then hope, and better then their fame.
Relieve me, Fathers, with your generall voyce.

SENATORS *May all the gods consent to* CAESAR'S *wish,*

*A forme of
speaking they
had.*

              And adde to any honours, that may crowne
              The hopefull issue of GERMANICUS.

TIBERIUS We thanke you, reverend Fathers, in their right.

ARRUNTIUS If this were true now! but the space, the space
    Betweene the brest, and lips—TIBERIUS heart
    Lyes a thought farder, then another mans.

TIBERIUS My comforts are so flowing in my joyes,

100   As, in them, all my streames of griefe are lost,
    No lesse then are land-waters in the sea,
    Or showres in rivers; though their cause was such,
    As might have sprinkled ev'n the gods with teares:
    Yet since the greater doth embrace the lesse,
    We covetously obey.

(ARRUNTIUS   Well acted, CAESAR.)

TIBERIUS And, now I am the happy witnesse made
    Of your so much desir'd affections,

To this great issue, I could wish, the fates
Would here set peacefull period to my dayes;
How ever, to my labours, I intreat   110
(And beg it of this *Senate*) some fit ease.

(ARRUNTIUS Laugh, Fathers, laugh: Ha' you no spleenes about
      you?)

TIBERIUS The burden is too heavy, I sustayne
On my unwilling shoulders; and I pray
It may be taken off, and re-confer'd
Upon the *Consuls*, or some other *Romane*,
More able, and more worthy.

(ARRUNTIUS   Laugh on, still.)

SABINUS Why, this doth render all the rest suspected!

GALLUS It poysons all.

ARRUNTIUS   O, do' you taste it then?

SABINUS It takes away my faith to any thing   120
He shall hereafter speake.

ARRUNTIUS   I, to pray that,
Which would be to his head as hot as thunder,
('Gainst which he weares that charme) should but the court   *A wreath of*
Receive him at his word.   *laurell.*

GALLUS   Heare.

TIBERIUS   For my selfe,
I know my weakenesse, and so little covet
(Like some gone past) the waight that will oppresse me,
As my ambition is the counter-point.

(ARRUNTIUS Finely maintain'd; good still.)

SEJANUS   But *Rome*, whose bloud,
Whose nerves, whose life, whose very frame relyes
On CAESAR's strength, no lesse then heav'n on ATLAS,   130
Cannot admit it but with generall ruine.

(ARRUNTIUS Ah! are you there, to bring him of?)

SEJANUS   Let CAESAR
No more then urge a point so contrary
To CAESARS greatnesse, the griev'd *Senates* vowes,
Or *Romes* necessitie.

(GALLUS   He comes about.

ARRUNTIUS More nimbly then VERTUMNUS.)

TIBERIUS   For the publique,
    I may be drawne, to shew, I can neglect
    All private aymes; though I affect my rest:
    But, if the *Senate* still command me serve,
140   I must be glad to practise my obedience.

(ARRUNTIUS You must, and will, sir. We doe know it.)

SENATORS   CAESAR,

Another forme.   *Live long, and happy, great, and royall* CAESAR,
    The gods preserve thee, and thy modestie,
    Thy wisedome, and thy innocence.

(ARRUNTIUS   Where is't?
    The prayer's made before the subject.)

SENATORS   *Guard*

    His meeknesse, JOVE, *his pietie, his care,*
    His bountie——

ARRUNTIUS   And his subtlety, I'le put in:
    Yet hee'll keepe that himselfe, without the gods.
    All prayers are vaine for him.

TIBERIUS   We will not hold
150   Your patience, *Fathers*, with long answere; but
    Shall still contend to be, what you desire,
    And worke to satisfie so great a hope:
    Proceed to your affaires.

ARRUNTIUS   Now, SILIUS, guard thee;
    The curtin's drawing. AFER advanceth.

PRAECONES   Silence.

AFER Cite CAIUS SILIUS.

PRAECONES   CAIUS SILIUS.

SILIUS   Here.

AFER The triumph that thou hadst in *Germanie*
    For thy late victorie on SACROVIR,
    Thou hast enjoy'd so freely, CAIUS SILIUS,
    As no man it envy'd thee; nor would CAESAR,
160   Or *Rome* admit, that thou wert then defrauded
    Of any honours, thy deserts could clayme,
    In the faire service of the common-wealth:
    But now, if, after all their loves, and graces,

(Thy actions, and their courses being discover'd)
It shall appeare to CAESAR, and this *Senate*,
Thou hast defil'd those glories, with thy crimes——

SILIUS Crimes?

AFER   Patience, SILIUS.

SILIUS   Tell thy moile of patience,
I' am a *Romane*. What are my crimes? Proclaime them.
Am I too rich? too honest for the times?
Have I or treasure, jewels, land, or houses   170
That some informer gapes for? Is my strength
Too much to be admitted? Or my knowledge?
These now are crimes.

AFER   Nay, SILIUS, if the name
Of crime so touch thee, with what impotence
Wilt thou endure the matter to be search'd?

SILIUS I tell thee, AFER, with more scorne, then feare:
Employ your mercenarie tongue, and arte.
Where's my accuser?

VARRO   Here.

ARRUNTIUS   VARRO? The *Consul*?
Is he thrust in?

VARRO   'Tis I accuse thee, SILIUS.
Against the majestie of *Rome*, and CAESAR,   180
I doe pronounce thee here a guiltie cause,
First, of beginning, and occasioning,
Next, drawing out the warre in *Gallia*,
For which thou late triumph'st; dissembling long
That SACROVIR to be an enemie,
Only to make thy entertainement more,
Whil'st thou, and thy wife SOSIA poll'd the province;
Wherein, with sordide-base desire of gaine,
Thou hast discredited thy actions worth
And beene a traytor to the state.

SILIUS   Thou lyest.   190

ARRUNTIUS I thanke thee, SILIUS, speake so still, and often.

VARRO If I not prove it, CAESAR, but injustly
Have call'd him into tryall, here I bind
My selfe to suffer, what I claime 'gainst him;

And yeeld, to have what I have spoke, confirm'd
By judgement of the court, and all good men.
SILIUS CAESAR, I crave to have my cause defer'd,
Till this mans Consulship be out.
TIBERIUS   We cannot,
Nor may we graunt it.
SILIUS   Why? shall he designe
200 My day of tryall? is he my accuser?
And must he be my judge?
TIBERIUS   It hath beene usuall,
And is a right, that custome hath allow'd
The magistrate, to call forth private men;
And to appoint their day: Which priviledge
We may not in the *Consul* see infring'd,
By whose deepe watches, and industrious care
It is so labour'd, as the common-wealth
Receive no losse, by any oblique course.
SILIUS CAESAR, thy fraud is worse then violence.
210 TIBERIUS SILIUS, mistake us not, we dare not use
The credit of the *Consul,* to thy wrong,
But only doe preserve his place, and power,
So farre as it concernes the dignitie,
And honor of the state.
ARRUNTIUS   Beleeve him, SILIUS.
COTTA Why, so he may, ARRUNTIUS.
ARRUNTIUS   I say so.
And he may choose too.
TIBERIUS   By the *capitoll,*
And all our gods, but that the deare republick,
Our sacred lawes, and just authoritie
Are interess'd therein, I should be silent.
220 AFER Please' CAESAR to give way unto his tryall.
He shall have justice.
SILIUS   Nay, I shall have law;
Shall I not AFER? speake.
AFER   Would you have more?
SILIUS No, my well-spoken man, I would no more;
Nor lesse: might I injoy it naturall,

Not taught to speake unto your present ends,
Free from thine, his, and all your unkind handling,
Furious enforcing, most unjust presuming,
Malicious, and manifold applying,
Foule wresting, and impossible construction.

AFER He raves, he raves.

SILIUS   Thou durst not tell me so,   230
Had'st thou not CAESARS warrant. I can see
Whose power condemnes me.

VARRO   This betrayes his spirit.
This doth inough declare him what he is.

SILIUS What am I? speake.

VARRO   An enemie to the state.

SILIUS Because I am an enemie to thee,
And such corrupted ministers o' the state,
That here art made a present instrument
To gratifie it with thine owne disgrace.

SEJANUS This, to the *Consul*, is most insolent!
And impious!

SILIUS   I, take part. Reveale your selves.   240
Alas, I sent not your confed'racies?
Your plots, and combinations? I not know
Minion SEJANUS hates me; and that all
This boast of law, and law, is but a forme,
A net of VULCANES filing, a meere ingine,
To take that life by a pretext of justice,
Which you pursue in malice? I want braine,
Or nostrill to perswade me, that your ends,
And purposes are made to what they are,
Before my answere? O, you equall gods,   250
Whose justice not a world of wolfe-turn'd men
Shall make me to accuse (how ere provoke)
Have I for this so oft engag'd my selfe?
Stood in the heate, and fervor of a fight,
When PHOEBUS sooner hath forsooke the day
Then I the field? Against the blue-ey'd *Gaules*?
And crisped *Germanes*? when our *Romane* Eagles
Have fann'd the fire, with their labouring wings,

And no blow dealt, that left not death behind it?
260   When I have charg'd, alone, into the troopes
Of curl'd *Sicambrians*, routed them, and came
Not off, with backward ensignes of a slave,
But forward markes, wounds on my brest, and face,
Were meant to thee, o CAESAR, and thy *Rome*?
And have I this returne? did I, for this,
Performe so noble, and so brave defeate,
On SACROVIR? (o JOVE, let it become me
To boast my deedes, when he, whom they concerne,
Shall thus forget them.)

AFER   SILIUS, SILIUS,
270   These are the common customes of thy bloud,
When it is high with wine, as now with rage:
This well agrees, with that intemperate vaunt,
Thou lately mad'st at AGRIPPINA's table,
That when all other of the troops were prone
To fall into rebellion, only yours
Remain'd in their obedience. You were he,
That sav'd the empire; which had then beene lost,
Had but your legions, there, rebell'd, or mutin'd.
Your vertue met, and fronted every perill.
280   You gave to CAESAR, and to *Rome* their surety.
Their name, their strength, their spirit, and their state,
Their being was a donative from you.

ARRUNTIUS Well worded, and most like an Orator.

TIBERIUS Is this true, SILIUS?

SILIUS   Save thy question, CAESAR.
Thy spie, of famous credit, hath affirm'd it.

ARRUNTIUS Excellent *Romane*!

SABINUS   He doth answere stoutly.

SEJANUS If this be so, there needes no farder cause
Of crime against him.

VARRO   What can more impeach
The royall dignitie, and state of CAESAR,
290   Then to be urged with a benefit
He cannot pay?

COTTA   In this, all CAESARS fortune

Is made unequall to the courtesie.

LATIARIS His meanes are cleane destroy'd, that should requite.

GALLUS Nothing is great inough for SILIUS merit.

ARRUNTIUS GALLUS on that side to?

SILIUS   Come, doe not hunt,
And labour so about for circumstance,
To make him guiltie, whom you have fore-doom'd:
Take shorter wayes, I'le meet your purposes.
The wordes were mine, and more I now will say:
Since I have done thee that great service, CAESAR,   300
Thou still hast fear'd me; and, in place of grace,
Return'd me hatred: so soone, all best turnes,
With doubtfull Princes, turne deepe injuries
In estimation, when they greater rise,
Then can be answer'd. Benefits, with you,
Are of no longer pleasure, then you can
With ease restore them; that transcended once,
Your studies are not how to thanke, but kill.
It is your nature, to have all men slaves
To you, but you acknowledging to none.   310
The meanes that makes your greatnesse, must not come
In mention of it; if it doe, it takes
So much away, you thinke: and that, which help'd,
Shall soonest perish, if it stand in eye,
Where it may front, or but upbraid the high.

COTTA Suffer him speake no more.

VARRO   Note but his spirit.

AFER This shewes him in the rest.

LATIARIS   Let him be censur'd.

SEJANUS He' hath spoke inough to prove him CAESARS foe.

COTTA His thoughts looke through his words.

SEJANUS   A censure.

SILIUS   Stay,
Stay, most officious *Senate*, I shall straight   320
Delude thy furie. SILIUS hath not plac'd
His guards within him, against fortunes spight,
So weakely, but he can escape your gripe
That are but hands of fortune: Shee her selfe

When vertue doth oppose, must lose her threats.
All that can happen in humanitie,
The frowne of CAESAR, proud SEJANUS hatred,
Base VARRO'S spleene, and AFERS bloudying tongue,
The *Senates* servile flatterie, and these
330   Mustred to kill, I'am fortified against;
And can looke downe upon: they are beneath me.
It is not life whereof I stand enamour'd:
Nor shall my ende make me accuse my fate.
The coward, and the valiant man must fall,
Only the cause, and manner how, discernes them:
Which then are gladdest, when they cost us dearest.
Romanes, if any here be in this *Senate*,
Would know to mock TIBERIUS tyrannie,
Looke upon SILIUS, and so learne to die.   [*Stabs himself.*]

VARRO O, desperate act!

340 ARRUNTIUS   An honorable hand!

TIBERIUS Looke, is he dead?

SABINUS   'Twas nobly strooke, and home.

ARRUNTIUS My thought did prompt him to it. Farewell, SILIUS.
Be famous ever for thy great example.

TIBERIUS We are not pleas'd, in this sad accident,
That thus hath stalled, and abus'd our mercy,
Intended to preserve thee, noble *Romane*:
And to prevent thy hopes.

ARRUNTIUS   Excellent wolfe!
Now he is full, he howles.

SEJANUS   CAESAR doth wrong
His dignitie, and safetie, thus to mourne
350   The deserv'd end of so profest a traytor,
And doth, by this his lenitie, instruct
Others as factious, to the like offence.

TIBERIUS The confiscation meerely of his state
Had beene inough.

ARRUNTIUS   O, that was gap'd for then?

VARRO Remove the body.

SEJANUS   Let citation
Goe out for SOSIA.

GALLUS   Let her be proscrib'd.
   And for the goods, I thinke it fit that halfe
   Goe to the treasure, halfe unto the children.

LEPIDUS   With leave of CAESAR, I would thinke, that fourth
   Part, which the law doth cast on the informers,   360
   Should be inough; the rest goe to the children:
   Wherein the Prince shall shew humanitie,
   And bountie, not to force them by their want
   (Which in their parents trespasse they deserv'd)
   To take ill courses.

TIBERIUS   It shall please us.

ARRUNTIUS   I,
   Out of necessitie. This LEPIDUS
   Is grave and honest, and I have observ'd
   A moderation still in all his censures.

SABINUS   And bending to the better—Stay, who's this?

      [*Enter* CORDUS, *guarded,* SATRIUS *and* NATTA.]
   CREMUTIUS CORDUS? what? is he brought in?   370

ARRUNTIUS   More bloud unto the banquet? Noble CORDUS,
   I wish thee good: Be as thy writings, free,
   And honest.

TIBERIUS   What is he?

SEJANUS   For th'Annal's, CAESAR.

PRAECO, CORDUS, SATRIUS, NATTA.

PRAECONES   Cremutius Cordus.

CORDUS   Here.

PRAECONES   Satrius Secundus,
   Pinnarius Natta, you are his accusers.

ARRUNTIUS   Two of SEJANUS bloud-hounds, whom he breeds
   With humane flesh, to bay at citizens.

AFER   Stand forth before the *Senate*, and confront him.

SATRIUS   I doe accuse thee here, CREMUTIUS CORDUS,
   To be a man factious, and dangerous,   380
   A sower of sedition in the state,
   A turbulent, and discontented spirit,

Which I will prove from thine owne writings, here,
The Annal's thou hast publish'd; where thou bit'st
The present age, and with a vipers tooth,
Being a member of it, dar'st that ill
Which never yet degenerous bastard did
Upon his parent.

NATTA   To this, I subscribe;
And, forth a world of more particulars,
Instance in only one: Comparing men,
And times, thou praysest BRUTUS, and affirm'st
That CASSIUS was the last of all the *Romanes*.

COTTA How! what are we then?

VARRO   What is CAESAR? nothing?

AFER My lords, this strikes at every *Romanes* private,
In whom raignes gentrie, and estate of spirit,
To have a BRUTUS brought in paralell,
A parricide, an enemie of his countrie,
Rank'd, and preferr'd to any reall worth
That *Rome* now holds. This is most strangely invective.
Most full of spight, and insolent upbraiding.
Nor is't the time alone is here dispris'd,
But the whole man of time, yea CAESAR's selfe
Brought in disvalew; and he aym'd at most
By oblique glance of his licentious pen.
CAESAR, if CASSIUS were the last of *Romanes*,
Thou hast no name.

TIBERIUS   Let's heare him answere. Silence.

CORDUS So innocent I am of fact, my lords,
As but my words are argu'd; yet those words
Not reaching eyther prince, or princes parent:
The which your law of treason comprehends.
BRUTUS, and CASSIUS, I am charg'd, t' have prays'd:
Whose deedes, when many more, besides my selfe,
Have writ, not one hath mention'd without honour.
Great TITUS LIVIUS, great for eloquence,
And faith, amongst us, in his historie,
With so great prayses POMPEY did extoll,
As oft AUGUSTUS call'd him a POMPEIAN:

Yet this not hurt their friendship. In his booke
He often names SCIPIO, AFRANIUS,
Yea, the same CASSIUS, and this BRUTUS too,   420
As worthi'st men; not theeves, and parricides,
Which notes, upon their fames, are now impos'd.
ASINIUS POLLIO's writings quite throughout
Give them a noble memorie; So MESSALLA
Renown'd his generall CASSIUS: yet both these
Liv'd with AUGUSTUS, full of wealth, and honours.
To CICERO's booke, where CATO was heav'd up
Equall with heav'n, what else did CAESAR answere,
Being then *Dictator*, but with a penn'd oration,
As if before the judges? Doe but see   430
ANTONIUS letters; read but BRUTUS pleadings:
What vile reproch they hold against AUGUSTUS,
False I confesse, but with much bitternesse.
The *Epigram's* of BIBACULUS, and CATULLUS,
Are read, full stuft with spight of both the CAESARS;
Yet deified JULIUS, and no lesse AUGUSTUS!
Both bore them, and contemn'd them: (I not know
Promptly to speake it, whether done with more
Temper, or wisdome) for such obloquies
If they despised bee, they dye supprest,   440
But, if with rage acknowledg'd, they are confest.
The *Greekes* I slip, whose licence not alone,
But also lust did scape unpunished:
Or where some one (by chance) exception tooke,
He words with words reveng'd. But, in my worke,
What could be aim'd more free, or farder of
From the times scandale, then to write of those,
Whom death from grace, or hatred had exempted?
Did I, with BRUTUS, and with CASSIUS,
Arm'd, and possess'd of the PHILIPPI fields,   450
Incense the people in the civill cause,
With dangerous speeches? or doe they, being slaine
Seventie yeeres since, as by their images
(Which not the conquerour hath defac'd) appeares,
Retaine that guiltie memorie with writers?

Posteritie payes everie man his honour.
Nor shall there want, though I condemned am,
That will not only CASSIUS well approve,
And of great BRUTUS honour mindfull be,
460   But that will, also, mention make of me.

ARRUNTIUS   Freely, and nobly spoken.

SABINUS   With good temper,
I like him, that he is not moov'd with passion.

ARRUNTIUS   He puts 'hem to their whisper.

TIBERIUS   Take him hence,
We shall determine of him at next sitting.   [*Exit* CORDUS, *guarded.*]

COTTA   Meane time, give order, that his bookes be burn't,
To the *Aediles.*

SEJANUS   You have well advis'd.

AFER   It fits not such licentious things should live
T'upbraid the age.

ARRUNTIUS   If th' age were good, they might.

LATIARIS   Let 'hem be burnt.

GALLUS   All sought, and burnt, to day.

470 PRAECONES   The court is up, *Lictors,* resume the *fasces.*

          [*Exeunt all but* ARRUNTIUS, SABINUS *and* LEPIDUS.]

ARRUNTIUS, SABINUS, LEPIDUS.

ARRUNTIUS   Let 'hem be burnt! o, how ridiculous
Appeares the *Senate's* brainlesse diligence,
Who thinke they can, with present power, extinguish
The memorie of all succeeding times!

SABINUS   'Tis true, when (contrarie) the punishment
Of wit, doth make th'authoritie increase.
Nor doe they ought, that use this crueltie
Of interdiction, and this rage of burning;
But purchase to themselves rebuke, and shame,
480   And to the writers an eternall name.

LEPIDUS   It is an argument the times are sore,
When vertue cannot safely be advanc'd;
Nor vice reproov'd.

ARRUNTIUS   I, noble LEPIDUS,
  AUGUSTUS well foresaw, what we should suffer,
  Under TIBERIUS, when he did pronounce
  The *Roman* race most wretched, that should live
  Betweene so slow jawes, and so long a bruising.   [*Exeunt.*]

TIBERIUS, SEJANUS.

[*Enter* TIBERIUS *and* SEJANUS.]

TIBERIUS This businesse hath succeeded well, SEJANUS:
  And quite remoov'd all jealousie of practice
  'Gainst AGRIPPINA, and our nephewes. Now,   490
  We must bethinke us how to plant our ingines
  For th'other paire, SABINUS, and ARRUNTIUS,
  And GALLUS too (how ere he flatter us,)
  His heart we know.

SEJANUS   Give it some respite, CAESAR.
  Time shall mature, and bring to perfect crowne,
  What we, with so good vultures, have begunne:
  SABINUS shall be next.

TIBERIUS   Rather ARRUNTIUS.

SEJANUS By any meanes, preserve him. His franke tongue
  Being lent the reines, will take away all thought
  Of malice, in your course against the rest.   500
  We must keep him to stalke with.

TIBERIUS   Dearest head,
  To thy most fortunate designe I yeeld it.

SEJANUS Sir—I' have beene so long train'd up in grace,
  First, with your father, great AUGUSTUS, since,
  With your most happie bounties so familiar,
  As I not sooner would commit my hopes
  Or wishes to the gods, then to your eares.
  Nor have I ever, yet, beene covetous
  Of over-bright, and dazling honours: rather
  To watch, and travaile in great CAESAR's safetie,   510
  With the most common souldier.

TIBERIUS   'Tis confest.

His daughter
was betroth'd to
Claudius, his
sonne.

SEJANUS The only gaine, and which I count most faire
    Of all my fortunes, is that mightie CAESAR
    Hath thought me worthie his alliance. Hence
    Beginne my hopes.
TIBERIUS   H'mh?
SEJANUS   I have heard, AUGUSTUS
    In the bestowing of his daughter, thought
    But even of gentlemen of *Rome*: If so,
    (I know not how to hope so great a favour)
    But if a husband should be sought for LIVIA,
520   And I be had in minde, as CAESARS freind,
    I would but use the glorie of the kindred.
    It should not make me slothfull, or lesse caring
    For CAESARS state; it were inough to me
    It did confirme, and strengthen my weake house,
    Against the-now-unequall opposition
    Of AGRIPPINA; and for deare reguard
    Unto my children, this I wish: my selfe
    Have no ambition farder, then to end
    My dayes in service of so deare a master.
530 TIBERIUS We cannot but commend thy pietie,
    Most-lov'd SEJANUS, in acknowledging
    Those bounties; which we, faintly, such remember.
    But to thy suit. The rest of mortall men,
    In all their drifts, and counsels, pursue profit:
    Princes, alone, are of a different sort,
    Directing their maine actions still to fame.
    We therefore will take time to thinke, and answere.
    For LIVIA, she can best, her selfe, resolve
    If she will marrie, after DRUSUS, or
540   Continue in the family; besides
    She hath a mother, and a grandame yet,
    Whose neerer counsels she may guide her by:
    But I will simply deale. That enmitie,
    Thou fear'st in AGRIPPINA, would burne more,
    If LIVIAS marriage should (as 'twere in parts)
    Devide th' imperiall house; an emulation

Betweene the women might break forth: and discord
Ruine the sonnes, and nephues, on both hands.
What if it cause some present difference?
Thou art not safe, SEJANUS, if thou proove it.   550
Canst thou beleeve, that LIVIA, first the wife
To CAIUS CAESAR, then my DRUSUS, now
Will be contented to grow old with thee,
Borne but a private gentleman of *Rome*?
And rayse thee with her losse, if not her shame?
Or say, that I should wish it, canst thou thinke
The *Senate*, or the people (who have seene
Her brother, father, and our ancestors,
In highest place of empire) will indure it?
The state thou hold'st alreadie, is in talke;   560
Men murmure at thy greatnesse; and the nobles
Sticke not, in publike, to upbraid thy climbing
Above our fathers favours, or thy scale:
And dare accuse me, from their hate to thee.
Be wise, deare friend. We would not hide these things
For friendships deare respect. Nor will we stand
Adverse to thine, or LIVIA's designements.
What we had purpos'd to thee, in our thought,
And with what neere degrees of love to bind thee,
And make thee equall to us; for the present,   570
We will forbeare to speake. Only, thus much
Beleeve, our lov'd SEJANUS, we not know
That height in bloud, or honour, which thy vertue,
And minde to us, may not aspire with merit.
And this wee'll publish, on all watch'd occasion
The *Senate*, or the people shall present.

SEJANUS I am restor'd, and to my sense againe,
Which I had lost in this so blinding suit.
CAESAR hath taught me better to refuse,
Then I knew how to aske. How pleaseth CAESAR   580
T'imbrace my late advice, for leaving *Rome*?

TIBERIUS We are resolv'd.

SEJANUS   Here are some motives more

Which I have thought on since, may more confirme.

TIBERIUS Carefull SEJANUS! we will straight peruse them:
Goe forward in our maine designe, and prosper.   [*Exit.*]

SEJANUS.

[SEJANUS] If those but take, I shall: dull, heavie CAESAR!
Would'st thou tell me, thy favours were made crimes?
And that my fortunes were esteem'd thy faults?
That thou, for me, wert hated? and not thinke
590   I would with winged haste prevent that change,
When thou might'st winne all to thy selfe againe,
By forfeiture of me? Did those fond words
Fly swifter from thy lips, then this my braine,
This sparkling forge, created me an armor
T' encounter chance, and thee? Well, read my charmes,
And may they lay that hold upon thy senses,
As thou had'st snuft up hemlocke, or tane downe
The juice of poppie, and of mandrakes. Sleepe,
Voluptuous CAESAR, and securitie
600   Seize on thy stupide powers, and leave them dead
To publique cares, awake but to thy lusts,
The strength of which makes thy libidinous soule
Itch to leave *Rome*; and I have thrust it on:
With blaming of the citie businesse,
The multitude of suites, the confluence
Of suitors, then their importunacies,
The manifold distractions he must suffer,
Besides ill rumours, envies, and reproches,
All which, a quiet and retired life,
610   (Larded with ease, and pleasure) did avoid;
And yet, for any weightie, 'and great affaire,
The fittest place to give the soundest counsels.
By this, shall I remoove him both from thought,
And knowledge of his owne most deare affaires;
Draw all dispatches through my private hands;
Know his designements, and pursue mine owne;

Make mine owne strengths, by giving suites, and places;
Conferring dignities, and offices:
And these, that hate me now, wanting accesse
To him, will make their envie none, or lesse.   620
For when they see me arbiter of all,
They must observe: or else, with CAESAR fall.   [*Exit.*]

TIBERIUS, SERVUS.

[*Enter* TIBERIUS.]

TIBERIUS To marry LIVIA? will no lesse, SEJANUS,
Content thy aimes? no lower object? well!
Thou know'st how thou art wrought into our trust;
Woven in our designe; and think'st, we must
Now use thee, whatsoere thy projects are:
'Tis true. But yet with caution, and fit care.
And, now we better thinke—who's there, within?
[*Enter* SERVUS.]
SERVUS CAESAR?
TIBERIUS   To leave our journey off, were sin   630
'Gainst our decree'd delights; and would appeare
Doubt: or (what lesse becomes a prince) low feare.
Yet, doubt hath law, and feares have their excuse,
Where princes states plead necessarie use;
As ours doth now: more in SEJANUS pride,
Then all fell AGRIPPINA'S hates beside.
Those are the dreadfull enemies, we raise
With favours, and make dangerous, with prayse;
The injur'd by us may have will alike,
But 'tis the favourite hath the power, to strike: 640
And furie ever boyles more high, and strong,
Heat' with ambition, then revenge of wrong.
'Tis then a part of supreme skill, to grace
No man too much; but hold a certaine space
Betweene th'ascenders rise, and thine owne flat,
Lest, when all rounds be reach'd, his aime be that.
'Tis thought— Is MACRO in the palace? See:

If not, goe, seeke him, to come to us— [*Exit* SERVUS.] Hee
Must be the organ, we must worke by now;
650   Though none lesse apt for trust: Need doth allow
What choise would not. I' have heard, that *aconite*
Being timely taken, hath a healing might
Against the scorpions stroke; the proofe wee'll give:
That, while two poysons wrastle, we may live.
Hee hath a spirit too working, to be us'd
But to th' encounter of his like; excus'd
Are wiser sov'raignes then, that raise one ill
Against another, and both safely kill:
The prince, that feeds great natures, they will sway him;
660   Who nourisheth a lyon, must obey him.

TIBERIUS, MACRO.

[*Enter* MACRO *and* SERVUS.]

TIBERIUS   MACRO, we sent for you.

MACRO   I heard so, CAESAR.

TIBERIUS   (Leave us awhile.) [*Exit* SERVUS.] When you shal know,
      good MACRO,
The causes of our sending, and the ends;
You then will harken neerer: and be pleas'd
You stand so high, both in our choice, and trust.

MACRO   The humblest place in CAESARS choice, or trust,
May make glad MACRO proud; without ambition:
Save to doe CAESAR service.

TIBERIUS   Leave our courtings.
We are in purpose, MACRO, to depart
670   The citie for a time, and see *Campania*;
Not for our pleasures, but to dedicate
A paire of temples, one, to JUPITER
At *Capua*, th'other at *Nola*, to AUGUSTUS:
In which great worke, perhaps, our stay will be
Beyond our will produc't. Now, since we are
Not ignorant what danger may be borne
Out of our shortest absence, in a state

So subject unto envie, and embroild
With hate, and faction; we have thought on thee,
(Amongst a field of *Romanes*,) worthiest MACRO,   680
To be our eye, and eare, to keepe strict watch
On AGRIPPINA, NERO, DRUSUS, I,
And on SEJANUS: Not, that we distrust
His loyaltie, or doe repent one grace,
Of all that heape, we have conferd on him.
(For that were to disparage our election,
And call that judgement now in doubt, which then
Seem'd as unquestion'd as an oracle,)
But, greatnesse hath his cankers. Wormes, and moaths
Breed out of too fit matter, in the things   690
Which after they consume, transferring quite
The substance of their makers, int'themselves.
MACRO is sharpe, and apprehends. Besides,
I know him subtle, close, wise, and wel-read
In man, and his large nature. He hath studied
Affections, passions, knowes their springs, their ends,
Which way, and whether they will worke: 'tis proofe
Inough, of his great merit, that we trust him.
Then, to a point; (because our conference
Cannot be long without suspition)   700
Here, MACRO, we assigne thee, both to spie,
Informe, and chastise; thinke, and use thy meanes,
Thy ministers, what, where, on whom thou wilt;
Explore, plot, practise: All thou doost in this,
Shall be, as if the *Senate*, or the Lawes
Had giv'n it priviledge, and thou thence stil'd
The Saviour both of CAESAR, and of *Rome*.
We will not take thy answere, but in act:
Whereto, as thou proceed'st, we hope to heare
By trusted messengers. If't be enquir'd,   710
Wherefore we call'd you, say, you have in charge
To see our chariots readie, and our horse:
Be still our lov'd, and (shortly) honor'd MACRO.   [*Exit.*]

MACRO.

[MACRO] I will not aske, why CAESAR bids doe this:
　　　　But joy, that he bids me. It is the blisse
　　　　Of courts, to be imploy'd; no matter, how:
　　　　A princes power makes all his actions vertue.
　　　　We, whom he workes by, are dumbe instruments,
　　　　To doe, but not enquire: His great intents
720　　　Are to be serv'd, not search'd. Yet, as that bow
　　　　Is most in hand, whose owner best doth know
　　　　T'affect his aymes, so let that states-man hope
　　　　Most use, most price, can hit his princes scope.
　　　　Nor must he looke at what, or whom to strike,
　　　　But loose at all; each marke must be alike.
　　　　Were it to plot against the fame, the life
　　　　Of one, with whom I twin'd; remove a wife
　　　　From my warme side, as lov'd, as is the ayre;
　　　　Practise away each parent; draw mine heyre
730　　　In compasse, though but one; worke all my kin
　　　　To swift perdition; leave no untrain'd engin,
　　　　For friendship, or for innocence; nay, make
　　　　The gods all guiltie: I would undertake
　　　　This, being impos'd me, both with gaine, and ease.
　　　　The way to rise, is to obey, and please.
　　　　He that will thrive in state, he must neglect
　　　　The trodden paths, that truth and right respect;
　　　　And prove new, wilder wayes: for vertue, there,
　　　　Is not that narrow thing, shee is else-where.
740　　　Mens fortune there is vertue; reason, their will:
　　　　Their licence, law; and their observance, skill.
　　　　Occasion, is their foile; conscience, their staine;
　　　　Profit, their lustre: and what else is, vaine.
　　　　If then it be the lust of CAESARS power,
　　　　T'have rais'd SEJANUS up, and in an hower
　　　　O're-turne him, tumbling, downe, from height of all;
　　　　We are his ready engine: and his fall

May be our rise. It is no uncouth thing
To see fresh buildings from old ruines spring.   [*Exit.*]

CHORUS—*Of Musicians.*

Act IV.

GALLUS, AGRIPPINA, NERO, DRUSUS, CALIGULA.

[*Enter* GALLUS *and* AGRIPPINA.]

GALLUS You must have patience, royall AGRIPPINA.

AGRIPPINA I must have vengeance, first: and that were *nectar*
Unto my famish'd spirits. O, my fortune,
Let it be sodaine thou prepar'st against me;
Strike all my powers of understanding blind,
And ignorant of destinie to come:
Let me not feare, that cannot hope.

GALLUS   Deare Princesse,
These tyrannies, on your selfe, are worse then CAESAR'S.

AGRIPPINA Is this the happinesse of being borne great?
Still to be aim'd at? still to be suspected?   10
To live the subject of all jealousies?
At least the colour made, if not the ground
To every painted danger? who would not
Choose once to fall, then thus to hang for ever?

GALLUS You might be safe, if you would—

AGRIPPINA   What, my GALLUS?
Be lewd SEJANUS strumpet? Or the baud
To CAESARS lusts, he now is gone to practise?
Not these are safe, where nothing is. Your selfe,
While thus you stand but by me, are not safe.
Was SILIUS safe? or the good SOSIA safe?   20
Or was my niece, deare CLAUDIA PULCHRA safe?
Or innocent FURNIUS? They, that latest have
(By being made guiltie) added reputation

To AFERS eloquence? O, foolish friends,
Could not so fresh example warne your loves,
But you must buy my favours, with that losse
Unto your selves: and, when you might perceive
That CAESARS cause of raging must forsake him,
Before his will? Away, good GALLUS, leave me.

30   Here to be seene, is danger; to speake, treason:
To doe me least observance, is call'd faction.
You are unhappy' in me, and I in all.
Where are my sonnes? NERO? and DRUSUS? We
Are they, be shot at; Let us fall apart:
Not, in our ruines, sepulchre our friends.
Or shall we doe some action, like offence,
To mocke their studies, that would make us faultie?
And frustrate practice, by preventing it?
The danger's like: for, what they can contrive,

40   They will make good. No innocence is safe,
When power contests. Nor can they trespasse more,
Whose only being was all crime, before.

    [*Enter* NERO, DRUSUS JUNIOR *and* CALIGULA.]

NERO You heare, SEJANUS is come backe from CAESAR?
GALLUS No. How? Disgrac'd?
DRUSUS JUNIOR   More graced now, then ever.
GALLUS By what mischance?
CALIGULA   A fortune, like inough
  Once to be bad.
DRUSUS JUNIOR   But turn'd too good, to both.
GALLUS What was't?
NERO   TIBERIUS sitting at his meat,
In a farme house, they call *Spelunca*, sited
By the sea-side, among the *Fundane* hills,

50   Within a naturall cave, part of the grot
(About the entrie) fell, and over-whelm'd
Some of the wayters; others ran away:
Only SEJANUS, with his knees, hands, face,
Ore-hanging CAESAR, did oppose himselfe
To the remayning ruines, and was found
In that so labouring posture, by the souldiers

That came to succour him. With which adventure,
He hath so fixt himselfe in CAESAR'S trust,
As thunder cannot moove him, and is come
With all the height of CAESARS praise, to *Rome*.   60
AGRIPPINA And power, to turne those ruines all on us;
And bury whole posterities beneath them.
NERO, and DRUSUS, and CALIGULA,
Your places are the next, and therefore most
In their offence. Thinke on your birth, and bloud,
Awake your spirits, meete their violence,
'Tis princely, when a tyran doth oppose;
And is a fortune sent to exercise
Your vertue, as the wind doth trie strong trees:
Who by vexation grow more sound, and firme.   70
After your fathers fall, and uncles fate,
What can you hope, but all the change of stroke
That force, or slight can give? then stand upright;
And though you doe not act, yet suffer nobly:
Be worthy of my wombe, and take strong cheare;
What we doe know will come, we should not feare.   [*Exeunt.*]

MACRO.

[*Enter* MACRO.]
[MACRO] Return'd so soone? renew'd in trust, and grace?
Is CAESAR then so weake? or hath the place
But wrought this alteration, with the aire;
And he, on next remove, will all repaire?   80
MACRO, thou art inag'd: and what before
Was publique; now, must be thy private, more.
The weale of CAESAR, fitnesse did imply;
But thine own fate confers necessity
On thy employment: and the thoughts borne nearest
Unto our selves, move swiftest still, and dearest.
If he recover, thou art lost: yea, all
The weight of preparation to his fall
Will turne on thee, and crush thee. Therefore, strike

90   Before he settle, to prevent the like
        Upon thy selfe. He doth his vantage know,
        That makes it home, and gives the foremost blow.   [*Exit.*]

                    LATIARIS, RUFUS, OPSIUS.

        [*Enter* LATIARIS, RUFUS *and* OPSIUS.]

    LATIARIS   It is a service, great SEJANUS will
        See well requited, and accept of nobly.
        Here place your selves, betweene the roofe, and seeling,
        And when I bring him to his wordes of danger,
        Reveale your selves, and take him.

    RUFUS   Is he come?

    LATIARIS   I'le now goe fetch him.   [*Exit* .]

    OPSIUS   With good speed. I long
        To merit from the state, in such an action.

100 RUFUS   I hope, it will obtayne the *Consul*-ship
        For one of us.

    OPSIUS   We cannot thinke of lesse,
        To bring in one, so dangerous as SABINUS.

    RUFUS   He was a follower of GERMANICUS,
        And still is an observer of his wife,
        And children, though they be declin'd in grace;
        A daily visitant, keepes them companie
        In private, and in publique; and is noted
        To be the only client, of the house:
        Pray JOVE, he will be free to LATIARIS.

110 OPSIUS   H'is alli'd to him, and doth trust him well.

    RUFUS   And he'll requite his trust?

    OPSIUS   To doe an office
        So gratefull to the state, I know no man
        But would straine neerer bands, then kindred—

    RUFUS   List,
        I heare them come.

    OPSIUS   Shift to our holes, with silence.

LATIARIS, SABINUS.

[*Enter* LATIARIS *and* SABINUS.]

LATIARIS It is a noble constancie you shew
 To this afflicted house: that not like others,
 (The friends of season) you doe follow fortune,
 And in the winter of their fate, forsake
 The place, whose glories warm'd you. You are just,
 And worthy such a princely patrones love,   120
 As was the worlds-renown'd GERMANICUS:
 Whose ample merit when I call to thought,
 And see his wife and issue, objects made
 To so much envie, jealousie, and hate;
 It makes me ready to accuse the gods
 Of negligence, as men of tyrannie.
SABINUS They must be patient, so must we.
LATIARIS   O JOVE.
 What will become of us, or of the times,
 When, to be high, or noble, are made crimes?
 When land, and treasure are most dangerous faults? 130
SABINUS Nay, when our table, yea our bed assaults
 Our peace, and safetie? when our writings are,
 By any envious instruments (that dare
 Apply them to the guiltie) made to speake
 What they will have, to fit their tyrannous wreake?
 When ignorance is scarcely innocence:
 And knowledge made a capitall offence?
 When not so much, but the bare emptie shade
 Of libertie, is reft us? and we made,
 The prey to greedie vultures, and vile spies,   140
 That first, transfixe us with their murdering eyes?
LATIARIS Me thinkes, the *Genius* of the *Romane* race
 Should not be so extinct, but that bright flame
 Of libertie might be reviv'd againe,
 (Which no good man but with his life, should lose)
 And we not sit like spent, and patient fooles,
 Still puffing in the darke, at one poore coale,

Held on by hope, till the last sparke is out.
The cause is publique, and the honour, name,
150 The immortalitie of every soule
That is not bastard, or a slave in *Rome*,
Therein concern'd: Whereto, if men would change
The weari'd arme, and for the waightie shield
So long sustain'd, employ the ready sword,
We might have some assurance of our vowes.
This asses fortitude doth tyre us all.
It must be active valour must redeeme
Our losse, or none. The rocke, and our hard steele
Should meete, t'enforce those glorious fires againe,
160 Whose splendor cheer'd the world, and heat gave life
No lesse then doth the sunne's.

SABINUS   'Twere better stay,
In lasting darkenesse, and despaire of day.
No ill should force the subject undertake
Against the soveraigne, more then hell should make
The gods doe wrong. A good man should, and must
Sit rather downe with losse, then rise unjust.
Though, when the *Romanes* first did yeeld themselves
To one mans power, they did not meane their lives,
Their fortunes, and their liberties, should be
170 His absolute spoile, as purchas'd by the sword.

LATIARIS Why we are worse, if to be slaves, and bond
To CAESARS slave, be such, the proud SEJANUS!
He that is all, do's all, gives CAESAR leave
To hide his ulcerous, and anointed face,
With his bald crowne at *Rhodes*, while he here stalkes
Upon the heads of *Romanes*, and their Princes,
Familiarly to empire.

SABINUS   Now you touch
A point indeed, wherein he shewes his arte,
As well as power.

LATIARIS   And villany in both.
180 Doe you observe where LIVIA lodges? How
DRUSUS came dead? What men have beene cut off?

SABINUS Yes, those are things remov'd: I neerer look't,

Into his later practice, where he stands
Declar'd a master in his mysterie.
First, ere TIBERIUS went, he wrought his feare
To thinke that AGRIPPINA sought his death.
Then put those doubts in her; sent her oft word,
Under the show of friendship, to beware
Of CAESAR, for he laid to poyson her:
Drave them to frownes, to mutuall jealousies,   190
Which, now, in visible hatred are burst out.
Since, he hath had his hyred instruments
To worke on NERO, and to heave him up;
To tell him CAESAR's old; that all the people,
Yea, all the armie have their eyes on him;
That both doe long to have him undertake
Something of worth, to give the world a hope;
Bids him to court their grace: The easie youth,
Perhaps, gives eare, which straight he writes to CAESAR;
And with this comment; See yond' dangerous boy;   200
Note but the practice of the mother, there;
Shee's tying him, for purposes at hand,
With men of sword. Here's CAESAR put in fright
'Gainst sonne, and mother. Yet, he leaves not thus.
The second brother DRUSUS (a fierce nature,
And fitter for his snares, because ambitious,
And full of envie) him he clasp's, and hugs,
Poysons with praise, tells him what hearts he weares,
How bright he stands in popular expectance;
That *Rome* doth suffer with him, in the wrong   210
His mother does him, by preferring NERO:
Thus sets he them asunder, each 'gainst other,
Projects the course, that serves him to condemne,
Keepes in opinion of a friend to all,
And all drives on to ruine.

LATIARIS   CAESAR sleepes,
     And nods at this?

SABINUS   Would he might ever sleepe,
     Bogg'd in his filthy lusts.

OPSIUS   Treason to CAESAR.

RUFUS   Lay hands upon the traytor, LATIARIS,
    Or take the name thy selfe.

LATIARIS   I am for CAESAR.

SABINUS   Am I then catch'd?

220 RUFUS   How thinke you, sir? you are.

SABINUS   Spies of this head! so white! so full of yeeres!
    Well, my most reverend monsters, you may live
    To see your selves thus snar'd.

OPSIUS   Away with him.

LATIARIS   Hale him away.

RUFUS   To be a spie for traytors,
    Is honorable vigilance.

SABINUS   You doe well,
    My most officious instruments of state;
    Men of all uses: Drag me hence, away.
    The yeere is well begun, and I fall fit,
    To be an offring to SEJANUS. Goe.

230 OPSIUS   Cover him with his garments, hide his face.

SABINUS   It shall not need. Forbeare your rude assault,
    The fault's not shamefull villanie makes a fault.   [*Exeunt.*]

MACRO, CALIGULA.

[*Enter* MACRO *and* CALIGULA.]

MACRO   Sir, but observe how thicke your dangers meete
    In his cleare drifts! Your mother, and your brothers,
    Now cited to the *Senate*! Their friend, GALLUS,
    Feasted to day by CAESAR, since committed!
    SABINUS, here we met, hurryed to fetters!
    The *Senators* all strooke with feare, and silence,
    Save those, whose hopes depend not on good meanes,
240   But force their private prey, from publique spoile!
    And you must know, if here you stay, your state
    Is sure to be the subject of his hate,
    As now the object.

CALIGULA   What would you advise me?

MACRO   To goe for *Capreae* presently: and there

Give up your selfe, entirely, to your uncle.
Tell CAESAR (since your mother is acus'd
To flie for succours to AUGUSTUS statue,
And to the armie, with your brethren) you
Have rather chose, to place your aides in him,
Then live suspected; or in hourely feare   250
To be thrust out, by bold SEJANUS' plots:
Which, you shall confidently urge, to be
Most full of perill to the state, and CAESAR,
As being laid to his peculiar ends,
And not to be let run, with common safety.
All which (upon the second) I'le make plaine,
So both shall love, and trust with CAESAR gaine.
CALIGULA Away then, let's prepare us for our journey.   [*Exeunt.*]

                              ARRUNTIUS.

[*Enter* ARRUNTIUS.]
[ARRUNTIUS] Still, do'st thou suffer heav'n? will no flame,
No heate of sinne make thy just wrath to boile   260
In thy distemp'red bosome, and ore-flow
The pitchy blazes of impietie,
Kindled beneath thy throne? Still canst thou sleepe,
Patient, while vice doth make an antique face
At thy drad power, and blow dust, and smoke
Into thy nostrils? JOVE, will nothing wake thee?
Must vile SEJANUS pull thee by the beard,
Ere thou wilt open thy black-lidded eye,
And looke him dead? Well! Snore on, dreaming gods:
And let this last of that proud Giant-race,   270
Heave mountayne upon mountayne, 'gainst your state—
      [*Enter* LEPIDUS.]
Be good unto me, fortune, and you powers,
Whom I, expostulating, have profan'd;
I see (what's equall with a prodigie)
A great, a noble *Romane*, and an honest,
Live an old man! O, MARCUS LEPIDUS,

When is our turne to bleed? Thy selfe, and I
(Without our boast) are a'most all the few
Left, to be honest, in these impious times.

LEPIDUS, ARRUNTIUS.

280   LEPIDUS What we are left to be, we will be, LUCIUS,
         Though tyrannie did stare, as wide as death,
         To fright us from it.
      ARRUNTIUS   'T hath so, on SABINUS.
      LEPIDUS I saw him now drawne from the *Gemonies*,
         And (what increas'd the direnesse of the fact)
         His faithfull dogge (upbraiding all us *Romanes*)
         Never forsooke the corp's, but, seeing it throwne
         Into the streame, leap'd in, and drown'd with it.
      ARRUNTIUS O act! to be envi'd him, of us men!
         We are the next, the hooke layes hold on, MARCUS:
290   What are thy artes (good patriot, teach them me)
         That have preserv'd thy haires, to this white die,
         And kept so reverend, and so deare a head,
         Safe, on his comely shoulders?
      LEPIDUS   Arts, ARRUNTIUS?
         None, but the plaine, and passive fortitude,
         To suffer, and be silent; never stretch
         These armes, against the torrent; live at home,
         With my owne thoughts, and innocence about me,
         Not tempting the wolves jawes: these are my artes.
      ARRUNTIUS I would begin to studie 'hem, if I thought
300   They would secure me. May I pray to JOVE,
         In secret, and be safe? I, or aloud?
         With open wishes? so I doe not mention
         TIBERIUS, or SEJANUS? yes, I must,
         If I speake out. 'Tis hard, that. May I thinke,
         And not be rackt? What danger is't to dreame?
         Talke in ones sleepe? or cough? who knowes the law?
         May' I shake my head, without a comment? say
         It raines, or it holds up, and not be throwne

Upon the *Gemonies?* These now are things,
Whereon mens fortune, yea their fate depends.   310
Nothing hath priviledge 'gainst the violent eare.
No place, no day, no houre (we see) is free
(Not our religious, and most sacred times)
From some one kind of crueltie: all matter,
Nay all occasion pleaseth. Mad-mens rage,
The idlenesse of drunkards, womens nothing,
Jesters simplicity, all, all is good
That can be catch'd at. Nor is now th'event
Of any person, or for any crime,
To be expected; for, 'tis alwayes one: 320
Death, with some little difference of place,
Or time—what's this? Prince NERO? guarded?

LACO, NERO, LEPIDUS, ARRUNTIUS.

[*Enter* LACO *and* NERO, *guarded by* LICTORES.]

LACO On, *Lictors*, keepe your way: My lords, forbeare.
    On paine of CAESARS wrath, no man attempt
    Speech with the prisoner.
NERO   Noble friends, be safe:
    To loose your selves for wordes, were as vaine hazard,
    As unto me small comfort: Fare you well.
    Would all *Rome's* suffrings in my fate did dwell.
LACO *Lictors*, away.
LEPIDUS   Where goes he, LACO?
LACO   Sir,
    H'is banish'd into *Pontia*, by the *Senate*.   330
ARRUNTIUS Do' I see? and heare? and feele? May I trust sense?
    Or doth my phant'sie forme it?
LEPIDUS   Where's his brother?
LACO DRUSUS is prisoner in the palace.
ARRUNTIUS   Ha?
    I smell it now: 'tis ranke. Where's AGRIPPINA?
LACO The princesse is confin'd, to *Pandataria*.
ARRUNTIUS Bolts, VULCAN; bolts, for JOVE! PHOEBUS thy bow;

Sterne MARS, thy sword; and *blue-ey'd Maid*, thy speare;

Thy club, ALCIDES: all the armorie

Of heaven is too little!—Ha? to guard

340 The gods, I meant. Fine, rare dispatch! This same

Was swiftly borne! confin'd? imprison'd? banish'd?

Most tripartite! The cause, sir?

LACO   Treason.

ARRUNTIUS   O?

The complement of all accusings? that

Will hit, when all else failes.

LEPIDUS   This turne is strange!

But yesterday, the people would not heare

Farre lesse objected, but cry'd, CAESARS letters

Were false, and forg'd; that all these plots were malice:

And that the ruine of the Princes house

Was practis'd 'gainst his knowledge. Where are now

350 Their voyces? now, that they behold his heires

Lock'd up, disgrac'd, led into exile?

ARRUNTIUS   Hush'd.

Drown'd in their bellies. Wild SEJANUS breath

Hath, like a whirle-wind, scatter'd that poore dust,

He turnes to With this rude blast. Wee'll talke no treason, sir,

Laco, and the If that be it you stand for? Fare you well.

rest. We have no need of horse-leeches. Good spie,

Now you are spi'd, be gone.

[Exeunt LACO, NERO and LICTORES.]

LEPIDUS   I feare, you wrong him.

He has the voyce to be an honest *Romane*.

ARRUNTIUS And trusted to this office? LEPIDUS,

360 I'ld sooner trust *Greeke*-SINON, then a man

Our state employes. Hee's gone: and being gone,

I dare tell you (whom I dare better trust)

That our night-ey'd TIBERIUS doth not see

His minions drifts; or, if he doe, h'is not

So errant subtill, as we fooles doe take him:

To breed a mungrell up, in his owne house,

With his owne bloud, and (if the good gods please)

At his owne throte, flesh him, to take a leape.

I doe not beg it, heav'n: but, if the fates
Grant it these eyes, they must not winke.

LEPIDUS   They must   370
Not see it, LUCIUS.

ARRUNTIUS   Who should let 'hem?

LEPIDUS   Zeale,
And dutie; with the thought, he is our Prince.

ARRUNTIUS He is our monster: forfeited to vice
So far, as no rack'd vertue can redeeme him.
His lothed person fouler then all crimes:
An Emp'rour, only in his lusts. Retir'd
(From all regard of his owne fame, or *Rome's*)
Into an obscure Iland; where he lives
(Acting his *tragedies* with a *comick* face)
Amid'st his rout of *Chaldee's:* spending houres,   380
Dayes, weekes, and months, in the unkind abuse
Of grave *astrologie,* to the bane of men,
Casting the scope of mens nativities,
And having found ought worthy in their fortune,
Kill, or precipitate them in the sea,
And boast, he can mocke fate. Nay, muse not: these
Are farre from ends of evill, scarse degrees.
He hath his slaughter-house, at *Capreae,*
Where he doth studie murder, as an arte:
And they are dearest in his grace, that can   390
Devise the deepest tortures. Thither, too,
He hath his boyes, and beauteous girles tane up,
Out of our noblest houses, the best form'd,
Best nurtur'd, and most modest: what's their good
Serves to provoke his bad. Some are allur'd,
Some threatned; others (by their friends detain'd)
Are ravish'd hence, like captives, and, in sight
Of their most grieved parents, dealt away
Unto his *spintries, sellaries,* and slaves,
Masters of strange, and new-commented lusts,   400
For which wise nature hath not left a name.
To this (what most strikes us, and bleeding *Rome,*)
He is, with all his craft, become the ward

To his owne vassall, a stale *catamite*:
Whom he (upon our low, and suffering necks)
Hath rais'd, from excrement, to side the gods,
And have his proper sacrifice in *Rome*:
Which JOVE beholds, and yet will sooner rive
A senslesse oke with thunder, then his trunck.

To them.   LACO, POMPONIUS, MINUTIUS, TERENTIUS.

[*Enter* LACO, POMPONIUS *and* MINUTIUS.]

410   LACO These letters make men doubtfull what t'expect,
        Whether his coming, or his death.
      POMPONIUS   Troth, both:
        And which comes soonest, thanke the gods for.
      (ARRUNTIUS   List,
        Their talke is CAESAR, I would heare all voyces.)
      MINUTIUS One day, hee's well; and will returne to *Rome*:
        The next day, sicke; and knowes not when to hope it.
      LACO True, and to day, one of SEJANUS friends
        Honour'd by speciall writ; and on the morrow
        Another punish'd——
      POMPONIUS   By more speciall writ.
      MINUTIUS This man receives his praises of SEJANUS,
420   A second, but slight mention: a third, none:
        A fourth, rebukes. And thus he leaves the *Senate*
        Divided, and suspended, all uncertayne.
      LACO These forked tricks, I understand 'hem not,
        Would he would tell us whom he loves, or hates,
        That we might follow, without feare, or doubt.
      (ARRUNTIUS Good HELIOTROPE! Is this your honest man?
        Let him be yours so still. He is my knave.)
      POMPONIUS I cannot tell, SEJANUS still goes on,
        And mounts, we see: New statues are advanc'd,
430   Fresh leaves of titles, large inscriptions read,
        His fortune sworne by, himselfe new gone out
        CAESARS colleague, in the fifth *Consulship*,

More altars smoke to him, then all the gods:
What would wee more?

(ARRUNTIUS   That the deare smoke would choke him,
That would I more.

LEPIDUS   Peace, good ARRUNTIUS.)

LACO But there are letters come (they say) ev'n now,
Which doe forbid that last.

MINUTIUS   Doe you heare so?

LACO   Yes.

POMPONIUS By POLLUX, that's the worst.

(ARRUNTIUS   By HERCULES, best.)

MINUTIUS I did not like the signe, when REGULUS,
(Whom all we know no friend unto SEJANUS)   440
Did, by TIBERIUS so precise command,
Succeed a fellow in the *Consulship*:
It boded somewhat.

POMPONIUS   Not a mote. His partner,
FULCINIUS TRIO, is his owne, and sure.
Here comes TERENTIUS. [*Enter* TERENTIUS.] He can give us
more.

LEPIDUS I'le ne're beleeve, but CAESAR hath some sent   *They whisper*
Of bold SEJANUS footing. These crosse points   *with Terentius.*
Of varying letters, and opposing *Consuls*,
Mingling his honours, and his punishments,
Fayning now ill, now well, raysing SEJANUS,   450
And then depressing him, (as now of late
In all reports we have it) cannot be
Emptie of practice: 'Tis TIBERIUS arte.
For (having found his favorite growne too great,
And, with his greatnesse, strong; that all the souldiers
Are, with their leaders, made at his devotion;
That almost all the *Senate* are his creatures,
Or hold on him their maine dependances,
Either for benefit, or hope, or feare;
And that himselfe hath lost much of his owne,   460
By parting unto him; and by th'increase
Of his ranke lusts, and rages, quite disarm'd

Himselfe of love, or other publique meanes,
To dare an open contestation)
His subtilty hath chose this doubling line,
To hold him even in: not so to feare him,
As wholly put him out, and yet give checke
Unto his farder boldnesse. In meane time,
By his employments, makes him odious
470   Unto the staggering rout, whose aide (in fine)
He hopes to use, as sure, who (when they sway)
Beare downe, ore-turne all objects in their way.

ARRUNTIUS You may be a LINCEUS, LEPIDUS: yet, I
See no such cause, but that a politique tyranne
(Who can so well disguise it) should have tane
A neerer way: fain'd honest, and come home
To cut his throte, by law.

LEPIDUS   I, but his feare
Would ne're be masqu'd, all-be his vices were.

POMPONIUS His lordship then is still in grace?

TERENTIUS   Assure you,
480   Never in more, either of grace, or power.

POMPONIUS The gods are wise, and just.

(ARRUNTIUS   The fiends they are.
To suffer thee belie 'hem?)

TERENTIUS   I have here
His last, and present letters, where he writes him
The *Partner of his cares*, and *his* SEJANUS —

LACO But is that true, it is prohibited,
To sacrifice unto him?

TERENTIUS   Some such thing
CAESAR makes scruple of, but forbids it not;
No more then to himselfe: sayes, he could wish
It were forborne to all.

LACO   Is it no other?
490   TERENTIUS No other, on my trust. For your more surety,
Here is that letter too.

(ARRUNTIUS   How easily,
Doe wretched men beleeve, what they would have!

Lookes this like plot?

LEPIDUS   Noble ARRUNTIUS, stay.)

LACO He names him here without his titles.

(LEPIDUS   Note.

ARRUNTIUS Yes, and come of your notable foole. I will.)

LACO No other, then SEJANUS.

POMPONIUS   That's but haste

In him that writes. Here he gives large amends.

MINUTIUS And with his owne hand written?

POMPONIUS   Yes.

LACO   Indeed?

TERENTIUS Beleeve it, gentlemen, SEJANUS brest

Never receiv'd more full contentments in,   500

Then at this present.

POMPONIUS   Takes he well th'escape

Of young CALIGULA, with MACRO?

TERENTIUS   Faith,

At the first aire, it somewhat troubled him.

(LEPIDUS Observe you?

ARRUNTIUS   Nothing. Riddles. Till I see

SEJANUS strooke, no sound thereof strikes me.)

                    [*Exeunt* ARRUNTIUS *and* LEPIDUS.]

POMPONIUS I like it not. I muse h'would not attempt

Somewhat against him in the *Consul*-ship,

Seeing the people 'ginne to favour him.

TERENTIUS He doth repent it, now; but h'has employ'd

PAGONIANUS after him: and he holds   510

That correspondence, there, with all that are

Neere about CAESAR, as no thought can passe

Without his knowledge, thence, in act to front him.

POMPONIUS I gratulate the newes.

LACO   But, how comes MACRO

So' in trust, and favour, with CALIGULA?

POMPONIUS O sir, he ha's a wife; and the young Prince

An appetite: he can looke up, and spie

Flies in the roofe, when there are fleas i' bed;

And hath a learned nose to'assure his sleepes.

520   Who, to be favour'd of the rising sunne,
       Would not lend little of his waning moone?
       'Tis the saf'st ambition. Noble TERENTIUS.
TERENTIUS The night growes fast upon us. At your service.

                                              [*Exeunt.*]

                CHORUS —*Of Musicians.*

                      Act V.

                    SEJANUS.

       [*Enter* SEJANUS.]
[SEJANUS] Swell, swell, my joyes: and faint not to declare
       Your selves, as ample, as your causes are.
       I did not live, till now; this my first hower:
       Wherein I see my thoughts reach'd by my power.
       But this, and gripe my wishes. Great, and high,
       The world knowes only two, that's *Rome*, and I.
       My roofe receives me not; 'tis aire I tread:
       And, at each step, I feele my' advanced head
       Knocke out a starre in heav'n! Rear'd to this height,
10   All my desires seeme modest, poore and sleight,
       That did before sound impudent: 'Tis place,
       Not bloud, discernes the noble, and the base.
       Is there not something more, then to be CAESAR?
       Must we rest there? It yrkes, t' have come so far,
       To be so neere a stay. CALIGULA,
       Would thou stood'st stiffe, and many, in our way.
       Windes lose their strength, when they doe emptie flie,
       Un-met of woods or buildings; great fires die
       That want their matter to with-stand them; so,
20   It is our griefe, and will be' our losse, to know
       Our power shall want opposites; unlesse
       The gods, by mixing in the cause, would blesse

Our fortune with their conquest. That were worth
SEJANUS strife: durst fates but bring it forth.

TERENTIUS, SEJANUS.

[*Enter* TERENTIUS *and* SERVUS.]

TERENTIUS Safety, to great SEJANUS.

SEJANUS   Now, TERENTIUS?

TERENTIUS Heares not my lord the wonder?

SEJANUS   Speake it, no.

TERENTIUS I meete it violent in the peoples mouthes,
    Who runne, in routs, to POMPEY's theatre,
    To view your statue: which, they say, sends forth
    A smoke, as from a fornace, black, and dreadfull.   30

SEJANUS Some traytor hath put fire in: (you, goe see.)
    And let the head be taken off, to looke
    What 'tis—[*Exit* SERVUS.] Some slave hath
        practis'd an imposture,
    To stirre the people. [*Enter* SATRIUS, NATTA *and* SERVUS.] How
        now? why returne you?

SATRIUS, NATTA.   *To them.*

SATRIUS The head, my lord, already is tane off,
    I saw it: and, at op'ning, there leap't out
    A great, and monstrous serpent!

SEJANUS   Monstrous! why?
    Had it a beard? and hornes? no heart? a tongue
    Forked as flatterie? look'd it of the hue,
    To such as live in great mens bosomes? was   40
    The spirit of it MACRO's?

NATTA   May it please
    The most divine SEJANUS, in my dayes,
    (And by his sacred fortune, I affirme it)
    I have not seene a more extended, growne,

Foule, spotted, venomous, ugly—

SEJANUS   O, the fates!

What a wild muster's here of attributes,

T'expresse a worme, a snake?

TERENTIUS   But how that should

Come there, my lord!

SEJANUS   What! and you too, TERENTIUS?

I thinke you meane to make't a prodigie

In your reporting?

50 TERENTIUS   Can the wise SEJANUS

Thinke heav'n hath meant it lesse?

SEJANUS   O, superstition!

Why, then the falling of our bed, that brake

This morning, burd'ned with the populous weight

Of our expecting clients, to salute us;

Or running of the cat, betwixt our legs,

As we set forth unto the *capitoll*,

Were prodigies.

TERENTIUS   I thinke them ominous!

And, would they had not hap'ned. As, to day,

The fate of some your servants! who, declining

60 Their way, not able, for the throng, to follow,

Slip't downe the *Gemonies*, and brake their necks!

Besides, in taking your last augurie,

No prosperous bird appear'd, but croking ravens

Flag'd up and downe: and from the sacrifice

Flew to the prison, where they sate, all night,

Beating the aire with their obstreperous beakes!

I dare not counsell, but I could entreat

That great SEJANUS would attempt the gods,

Once more, with sacrifice.

SEJANUS   What excellent fooles

70 Religion makes of men? Beleeves TERENTIUS,

(If these were dangers, as I shame to thinke them)

The gods could change the certayne course of fate?

Or, if they could, they would (now in a moment)

For a beeves fat, or lesse, be brib'd t' invert

Those long decrees? Then thinke the gods, like flies,

Are to be taken with the steame of flesh,
Or bloud, diffus'd about their altars: thinke
Their power as cheape, as I esteeme it small.
Of all the throng, that fill th' *Olympian* hall,
And (without pitty) lade poore ATLAS back,   80
I know not that one deity, but *Fortune*;
To whom, I would throw up, in begging smoke,
One grane of incense: or whose eare I'ld buy
With thus much oyle. Her, I, indeed, adore;
And keepe her gratefull image in my house,
Some-times belonging to a *Romane* king,
But, now call'd mine, as by the better stile:
To her, I care not, if (for satisfying
Your scrupulous phant'sies) I goe offer. Bid
Our priest prepare us honny, milke, and poppy,   90
His masculine odours, and night-vestments: say,
Our rites are instant, which perform'd, you'll see
How vaine, and worthy laughter, your feares be.   [*Exeunt.*]

COTTA, POMPONIUS.

[*Enter* COTTA *and* POMPONIUS.]
COTTA POMPONIUS! whither in such speed?
POMPONIUS   I goe
   To give my lord SEJANUS notice——
COTTA   What?
POMPONIUS Of MACRO.
COTTA   Is he come?
POMPONIUS   Entred but now
   The house of REGULUS.
COTTA   The opposite *Consul*?
POMPONIUS Some halfe houre since.
COTTA   And, by night too! stay, sir;
   I'le beare you companie.
POMPONIUS   Along, then——   [*Exeunt.*]

MACRO, REGULUS, LACO.

[*Enter* MACRO, REGULUS *and* SERVUS.]

100 MACRO Tis CAESARS will, to have a frequent *Senate*.
　　　　And therefore must your edict lay deepe mulct
　　　　On such, as shall be absent.

REGULUS　　　　　　　　　　So it doth.
　　　　Beare it my fellow *Consul* to adscribe.

MACRO And tell him it must early be proclaim'd;
　　　　The place, APOLLO'S temple.　　　　[*Exit* SERVUS.]

REGULUS　　　　　　　　　　That's remembred.

MACRO And at what howre.

REGULUS　　　　　　Yes.

MACRO　　　　　　　　　　You doe forget
　　　　To send one for the *Provost* of the watch?

REGULUS I have not: here he comes.
　　　　[*Enter* LACO.]

MACRO　　　　　　　　　GRACINUS LACO,
　　　　You' are a friend most welcome: by, and by,
110　　　I'le speake with you. (You must procure this list
　　　　Of the *Praetorian* cohorts, with the names
　　　　Of the *Centurions*, and their *Tribunes*.

REGULUS　　　　　　　　　　　　I.)

MACRO I bring you letters, and a health from CAESAR—

LACO Sir, both come well.

MACRO　　　　　　　　　(And heare you, with your note,
　　　　Which are the eminent men, and most of action.

REGULUS That shall be done you too.)

The Consul goes MACRO　　　　　　　　　　Most worthy LACO,
out.　　　CAESAR salutes you. (*Consul*! death, and furies!
　　　　Gone now?) the argument will please you, sir.
　　　　(Hough! REGULUS? The anger of the gods
120　　　Follow his diligent legs, and overtake 'hem,
Returnes:　In likenesse of the gout.) O, good my lord,
　　　　We lackt you present; I would pray you send
　　　　Another to FULCINIUS TRIO, straight,
　　　　To tell him, you will come, and speake with him:

(The matter wee'le devise) to stay him, there,
While I, with LACO, doe survay the watch.
What are your strengths, GRACINUS?

LACO   Seven cohorts.   *Goes out againe.*

MACRO You see, what CAESAR writes: and (—gone againe?
H'has sure a veine of *mercury* in his feet)
Knew you, what store of the *praetorian* souldiers   130
SEJANUS holds, about him, for his guard?

LACO I cannot the just number: but, I thinke,
Three *centuries*.

MACRO   Three? good.

LACO   At most, not foure.

MACRO And who be those *Centurions*?

LACO   That the *Consul*
Can best deliver you.

MACRO   (When h'is away:
Spight, on his nimble industrie.) GRACINUS,
You find what place you hold, there, in the trust
Of royall CAESAR?

LACO   I, and I am——

MACRO   Sir,
The honours, there propos'd, are but beginnings
Of his great favours.

LACO   They are more——

MACRO   I heard him   140
When he did studie, what to adde——

LACO   My life,
And all I hold——

MACRO   You were his owne first choise;
Which doth confirme as much, as you can speake:
And will (if we succeed) make more—— Your guardes
Are seven cohorts, you say?

LACO   Yes.

MACRO   Those we must
Hold still in readinesse, and undischarg'd.

LACO I understand so much. But how it can—

MACRO Be done without suspition, you'll object?

REGULUS What's that?   *Returnes.*

LACO   The keeping of the watch in armes,
When morning comes.

150   MACRO   The *Senate* shall be met, and set
So early, in the temple, as all marke
Of that will be avoided.

REGULUS   If we need,
We have commission, to possesse the palace,
Enlarge prince DRUSUS, and make him our chiefe.

MACRO   (That secret would have burn't his reverend mouth
Had he not spit it out, now:) by the gods,
You carry things too—let me borrow' a man.
Or two, to beare these [*Exit* REGULUS.]—That of
freeing DRUSUS,
CAESAR projected as the last, and utmost;
Not else to be remembred.
          [*Enter* REGULUS *and* SERVANTS.]

160   REGULUS   Here are servants.

MACRO   These to ARRUNTIUS, these to LEPIDUS,
This beare to COTTA, this to LATIARIS.
If they demand you' of me: say, I have tane
Fresh horse, and am departed. [*Exeunt* SERVANTS.] You (my
lord)
To your colleague, and be you sure, to hold him
With long narration, of the new fresh favours,
Meant to SEJANUS, his great patron; I,
With trusted LACO, here, are for the guards:
Then, to divide. For, night hath many eies,

170   Whereof, though most doe sleepe, yet some are spies.   [*Exeunt.*]

                    PRAECONES,
              FLAMEN, MINISTRI,
         SEJANUS, TERENTIUS, SATRIUS, &C.

     [*Enter* TUBICINES, TIBICINES, PRAECONES, FLAMEN,
     MINISTRI, SEJANUS, TERENTIUS, SATRIUS, NATTA, *etc.*]

PRAECONES   *Be all profane farre hence; Flie, flie farre off:*
          Be absent farre. Farre hence be all profane.

FLAMEN We have beene faultie, but repent us now,
 And bring *pure hands, pure vestments,* and *pure minds.*

1ST MINISTER *Pure vessells.*

2ND MINISTER   And *pure offrings.*

3RD MINISTER   *Garlands pure.*

FLAMEN Bestow your *garlands*: and (with reverence) place
 The *vervin* on the altar.

PRAECONES   *Favour your tongues.*

FLAMEN *Great mother* FORTUNE, *Queene of humane state,*
 Rectresse of action, Arbitresse of fate,
 To whom all sway, all power, all empire bowes,
 Be present, and propitious to our vowes.

PRAECONES *Favour it with your tongues.*

MINISTRI *Be present, and propitious to our vowes.*
 Accept our offring, and be pleas'd, great goddesse.

TERENTIUS See, see, the image stirres!

SATRIUS   And turnes away!

NATTA *Fortune* averts her face!

FLAMEN   Avert, you gods,
 The prodigie. Still! still! Some pious rite
 We have neglected. Yet! heav'n, be appeas'd.
 And be all tokens false, or void, that speake
 Thy present wrath.

SEJANUS   Be thou dumbe, scrupulous priest:
 And gather up thy selfe, with these thy wares,
 Which I, in spight of thy blind mistris, or
 Thy juggling mysterie, religion, throw
 Thus, scorned on the earth. Nay, hold thy looke
 Averted, till I woo thee, turne againe;
 And thou shalt stand, to all posteritie,
 Th'eternall game, and laughter, with thy neck
 Writh'd to thy taile, like a ridiculous cat.
 Avoid these fumes, these superstitious lights,
 And all these coos'ning ceremonies: you,
 Your pure, and spiced conscience. [*Exeunt all but* SEJANUS,
  TERENTIUS, SATRIUS *and* NATTA.] I, the slave,
 And mock of fooles, (scorne on my worthy head)
 That have beene titled, and ador'd a god,

Tub. Tib.
Sound, while
the *Flamen*
washeth.

180

While they
sound againe,
the *Flamen*
takes of the
hony, with his
finger, &
tasts, then
ministers to
all the rest: so
of the milk, in
an earthen
vessel, he
deals about;
which done,
he sprinkleth,
upon the
altar, milke;
then
imposeth the
hony, and
kindleth his
gummes, and
after censing
about the
altar placeth
his censer
thereon, into
which they
put severall
branches of

poppy, and
the musique
ceasing,
proceed.

Yea, sacrific'd unto, my selfe, in *Rome*,
No lesse then JOVE: and I be brought, to doe
A peevish gigglot rites? Perhaps, the thought,
And shame of that made *Fortune* turne her face,
Knowing her selfe the lesser deitie,
And but my servant. Bashfull queene, if so,

210   SEJANUS thankes thy modestie. Who's that?

POMPONIUS, SEJANUS, MINUTIUS, &c.

[*Enter* POMPONIUS *and* MINUTIUS.]
POMPONIUS His fortune suffers, till he heares my newes:
   I' have waited here too long. MACRO, my lord—
SEJANUS Speake lower, & with-draw.
TERENTIUS   Are these things true?
MINUTIUS Thousands are gazing at it, in the streets.
SEJANUS What's that?
TERENTIUS   MINUTIUS tells us here, my lord,
   That, a new head being set upon your statue,
   A rope is since found wreath'd about it! and,
   But now, a fierie meteor, in the forme
   Of a great ball, was seene to rowle along

220   The troubled ayre, where yet it hangs, unperfect,
   The' amazing wonder of the multitude!
SEJANUS No more. That MACRO'S come, is more then all!
TERENTIUS Is MACRO come?
POMPONIUS   I saw him.
TERENTIUS   Where? with whom?
POMPONIUS With REGULUS.
SEJANUS   TERENTIUS—
TERENTIUS   My lord?
SEJANUS Send for the *Tribunes*, we will straight have up
   More of the souldiers, for our guard. [*Exit* TERENTIUS.] —
      MINUTIUS,
   We pray you, goe for COTTA, LATIARIS,
   TRIO the *Consul*, or what *Senators*

You know are sure, and ours. [*Exit* MINUTIUS.] You, my
    good NATTA,
For LACO, *Provost* of the watch. [*Exit* NATTA.] Now, SATRIUS,   230
The time of proofe comes on. Arme all our servants,
And without tumult. [*Exit* SATRIUS.] You, POMPONIUS,
Hold some good correspondence, with the *Consul,*
Attempt him, noble friend. [*Exit* POMPONIUS.] These things —
    begin
To looke like dangers, now, worthy my fates.
Fortune, I see thy worst: Let doubtfull states,
And things uncertaine hang upon thy will:
Me surest death shall render certaine still.
Yet, why is, now, my thought turn'd toward death,
Whom fates have let goe on, so farre, in breath,   240
Uncheck'd, or unreprov'd? I, that did helpe
To fell the loftie Cedar of the world,
GERMANICUS; that, at one stroke, cut downe
DRUSUS, that upright Elme; wither'd his vine;
Laid SILIUS, and SABINUS, two strong Okes,
Flat on the earth; besides, those other shrubs,
CORDUS, and SOSIA, CLAUDIA PULCHRA,
FURNIUS, and GALLUS, which I have grub'd up;
And since, have set my axe so strong, and deepe
Into the roote of spreading AGRIPPINE;   250
Lopt off, and scatter'd her proud branches, NERO,
DRUSUS, and CAIUS too, although re-planted;
If you will, destinies, that, after all,
I faint, now, ere I touch my period;
You are but cruell: and I alreadie' have done
Things great inough. All *Rome* hath beene my slave;
The *Senate* sate an idle looker on,
And witnesse of my power; when I have blush'd,
More, to command, then it to suffer; all
The *Fathers* have sate readie, and prepar'd,   260
To give me empire, temples, or their throtes,
When I would aske 'hem; and (what crownes the top)
Rome, Senate, people, all the world have seene

  JOVE, but my equall: CAESAR, but my second.
  'Tis then your malice, fates, who (but your owne)
  Envy, and feare, t'have any power long knowne.   [*Exit.*]

      TERENTIUS, TRIBUNES.

  [*Enter* TERENTIUS *and* TRIBUNES.]
 TERENTIUS Stay here: I'le give his lordship, you are come.

     MINUTIUS, COTTA, LATIARIS.

  [*Enter* MINUTIUS, COTTA *and* LATIARIS.]
 MINUTIUS MARCUS TERENTIUS, pray you tell my lord,

They confer their Here's COTTA, and LATIARIS.
letters. TERENTIUS   Sir, I shall.   [*Exit.*]
270 COTTA My letter is the very same with yours;
  Onely requires mee to bee present there,
  And give my voyce, to strengthen his designe.
 LATIARIS Names he not what it is?
 COTTA   No, nor to you.
 LATIARIS 'Tis strange, and singular doubtfull!
 COTTA   So it is?
  It may be all is left to lord SEJANUS.

To them.   NATTA, LACO.

  [*Enter* NATTA *and* LACO.]
 NATTA Gentlemen, where's my lord?
 TRIBUNES   Wee wait him here.
 COTTA The *Provost* LACO? what's the newes?
 LATIARIS   My lord—

SEJANUS.   *To them.*

[*Enter* SEJANUS *and* TERENTIUS.]

SEJANUS Now, my right deare, noble, and trusted friends;
  How much I am a captive to your kindnesse!
  Most worthy COTTA, LATIARIS; LACO,   280
  Your valiant hand; and gentlemen, your loves.
  I wish I could divide my selfe unto you;
  Or that it lay, within our narrow powers,
  To satisfie for so enlarged bountie.
  GRACINUS, we must pray you, hold your guardes
  Unquit, when morning comes. Saw you the *Consul*?
MINUTIUS TRIO will presently be here, my lord.
COTTA They are but giving order for the edict,
  To warne the *Senate*.
SEJANUS   How! the *Senate*?
LATIARIS   Yes.
  This morning, in APOLLO's temple.
COTTA   We   290
  Are charg'd, by letter, to be there, my lord.
SEJANUS By letter? pray you let's see!
LATIARIS   Knowes not his lordship!
COTTA It seemes so!
SEJANUS   A *Senate* warn'd? without my knowledge?
  And on this sodaine? *Senators* by letters
  Required to be there! who brought these?
COTTA   MACRO.
SEJANUS Mine enemie! And when?
COTTA   This mid-night.
SEJANUS   Time,
  With ev'ry other circumstance, doth give
  It hath some streine of engin in't! How now?

SATRIUS, SEJANUS, &c.

[*Enter* SATRIUS.]

SATRIUS My lord, SERTORIUS MACRO is without,

300   Alone, and prayes t'have private conference

     In businesse, of high nature, with your lordship,

     (He say's to me) and which reguards you much.

SEJANUS Let him come here.

SATRIUS   Better, my lord, with-draw,

     You will betray what store, and strength of friends

     Are now about you; which he comes to spie.

SEJANUS Is he not arm'd?

SATRIUS   Wee'll search him.

SEJANUS   No, but take,

     And lead him to some roome, where you, conceal'd,

     May keepe a guard upon us. [*Exit* SATRIUS.] Noble LACO,

     You are our trust: and, till our owne cohorts

310   Can be brought up, your strengths must be our guard.

He salutes them   Now, good MINUTIUS, honour'd LATIARIS,

humbly.   Most worthy, and my most unwearied friends:

     I returne instantly.   [*Exit.*]

LATIARIS   Most worthy lord!

COTTA His lordship is turn'd instant kind, me thinkes,

     I'have not observ'd it in him, heretofore.

1ST TRIBUNE 'Tis true, and it becomes him nobly.

MINUTIUS   I

     Am rap't withall.

2ND TRIBUNE   By MARS, he has my lives,

     (Were they a million) for this onely grace.

LACO I, and to name a man!

LATIARIS   As he did me!

MINUTIUS And me!

320 LATIARIS   Who would not spend his life and fortunes,

     To purchase but the looke of such a lord?

LACO He, that would nor be lords foole, nor the worlds. [*Exeunt.*]

SEJANUS, MACRO.

[*Enter* SEJANUS, MACRO *and* SATRIUS.]

SEJANUS MACRO! most welcome, as most coveted friend!
   Let me enjoy my longings. When arriv'd you?
MACRO About the noone of night.
SEJANUS   SATRIUS, give leave.
                              [*Exit* SATRIUS.]
MACRO I have beene, since I came, with both the *Consuls*,
   On a particular designe from CAESAR.
SEJANUS How fares it with our great, and royall master?
MACRO Right plentifully well; as, with a prince,
   That still holds out the great proportion   330
   Of his large favours, where his judgement hath
   Made once divine election: like the god,
   That wants not, nor is wearied to bestow
   Where merit meets his bountie, as it doth
   In you, alreadie the most happy', and ere
   The sunne shall climbe the south, most high SEJANUS.
   Let not my lord be'amus'd. For, to this end
   Was I by CAESAR sent for, to the isle,
   With speciall caution to conceale my journey;
   And, thence, had my dispatch as privately   340
   Againe to *Rome*; charg'd to come here by night;
   And, onely to the *Consuls*, make narration,
   Of his great purpose: that the benefit
   Might come more full, and striking, by how much
   It was lesse look'd for, or aspir'd by you,
   Or least informed to the common thought.
SEJANUS What may this be? part of my selfe, dear MACRO!
   If good, speake out: and share with your SEJANUS.
MACRO If bad, I should for ever lothe my selfe,
   To be the messenger to so good a lord.   350
   I doe exceed m' instructions, to acquaint
   Your lordship with thus much; but 'tis my venture
   On your retentive wisedome: and, because
   I would no jealous scruple should molest

        Or racke your peace of thought. For, I assure
        My noble lord, no *Senator* yet knowes
        The businesse meant: though all, by severall letters,
        Are warned to be there, and give their voyces,
        Onely to adde unto the state, and grace
        Of what is purpos'd.

360   SEJANUS   You take pleasure, MACRO,
        Like a coy wench, in torturing your lover.
        What can be worth this suffering?

    MACRO   That which followes,
        The *tribuniciall* dignitie, and power:
        Both which SEJANUS is to have this day
        Confer'd upon him, and by publique *Senate*.

    SEJANUS Fortune, be mine againe; thou' hast satisfied
        For thy suspected loyaltie.

    MACRO   My lord,
        I have no longer time, the day approcheth,
        And I must backe to CAESAR.

    SEJANUS   Where's CALIGULA?

370   MACRO That I forgot to tell your lordship. Why,
        He lingers yonder, about *Capreae*,
        Disgrac'd; TIBERIUS hath not seene him yet:
        He needs would thrust himselfe to goe with me,
        Against my wish, or will, but I have quitted
        His forward trouble, with as tardie note
        As my neglect, or silence could afford him.
        Your lordship cannot now command me ought,
        Because, I take no knowledge that I saw you,
        But I shall boast to live to serve your lordship:
        And so take leave.

380   SEJANUS   Honest, and worthy MACRO,
        Your love, and friendship. Who's there? [*Enter* SATRIUS.]
            SATRIUS,
        Attend my honourable friend forth. [*Exeunt* SATRIUS
            and MACRO.] O!
        How vaine, and vile a passion is this feare?
        What base, uncomely things it makes men doe?
        Suspect their noblest friends, (as I did this)

Flatter poore enemies, intreat their servants,
Stoupe, court, and catch at the benevolence
Of creatures, unto whom (within this houre)
I would not have vouchsaf'd a quarter-looke,
Or piece of face? By you, that fooles call gods,   390
Hang all the skie with your prodigious signes,
Fill earth with monsters, drop the *scorpion* downe,
Out of the *zodiack*, or the fiercer *lyon*,
Shake off the loos'ned globe from her long henge,
Rowle all the world in darknesse, and let loose
Th'inraged windes to turne up groves and townes;
When I doe feare againe, let me be strooke
With forked fire, and unpittyed die:
Who feares, is worthy of calamitie.   [*Exit.*]

POMPONIUS, REGULUS, TRIO.   *To the rest.*

[*Enter* TERENTIUS, MINUTIUS, LACO, COTTA, LATIARIS,
  TRIBUNES, POMPONIUS, REGULUS *and* TRIO.]

POMPONIUS Is not my lord here?
TERENTIUS   Sir, he will be straight.   400
COTTA What newes, FULCINIUS TRIO?
TRIO   Good, good tidings.
  (But, keepe it to your selfe) My lord SEJANUS
  Is to receive this day, in open *Senate*,
  The *tribuniciall* dignitie.
COTTA   Is't true?
TRIO No wordes; not to your thought: but, sir, beleeve it.
LATIARIS What sayes the *Consul*?
COTTA   (Speake it not againe,)
  He tells me, that to day my lord SEJANUS——
(TRIO I must entreat you COTTA, on your honour
  Not to reveale it.
COTTA   On my life, sir.)
LATIARIS   Say.
COTTA Is to receive the *tribuniciall* power.   410
  But, as you are an honourable man,

Let me conjure you, not to utter it:
For it is trusted to me, with that bond.

LATIARIS I am HARPOCRATES.

TERENTIUS   Can you assure it?

POMPONIUS The *Consul* told it me, but keepe it close.

MINUTIUS Lord LATIARIS, what's the newes?

LATIARIS   I'le tell you,
But you must sweare to keepe it secret——

To them.   SEJANUS.

[*Enter* SEJANUS.]

SEJANUS I knew the fates had on their distaffe left
More of our thread, then so.

REGULUS   Haile, great SEJANUS.

TRIO Haile, the most honor'd.

COTTA   Happy.

420 LATIARIS   High SEJANUS.

SEJANUS Doe you bring prodigies too?

TRIO   May all presage
Turne to those faire effects, whereof we bring
Your lordship newes.

REGULUS   May't please my lord with-draw.

To some that SEJANUS Yes (I will speake with you, anon.)
stand by.

TERENTIUS   My lord,
What is your pleasure for the *Tribunes*?

SEJANUS   Why,
Let 'hem be thank't, and sent away.

MINUTIUS   My lord——

LACO Wil't please your lordship to command me——

SEJANUS   No.
You' are troublesome.   [*Exit.*]

MINUTIUS   The mood is chang'd.

1ST TRIBUNE   Not speake?

2ND TRIBUNE Nor looke?

LACO   I. He is wise, will make him friends

430 Of such, who never love, but for their ends.   [*Exeunt.*]

ARRUNTIUS, LEPIDUS.

*Divers other
Senators passing
by them.*

[*Enter* ARRUNTIUS *and* LEPIDUS.]

ARRUNTIUS I, goe, make haste; take heed you be not last
      To tender your *All haile*, in the wide hall
      Of huge SEJANUS: runne, a *Lictors* pace;
      Stay not to put your robes on; but, away,
      With the pale troubled ensignes of great friendship
      Stamp't i' your face! Now, MARCUS LEPIDUS,
      You still beleeve your former augurie?
      SEJANUS must goe downe-ward? you perceive
      His wane approching fast?

LEPIDUS   Beleeve me, LUCIUS,
      I wonder at this rising!

ARRUNTIUS   I, and that we   440
      Must give our suffrage to it? you will say,
      It is to make his fall more steepe, and grievous?
      It may be so. But thinke it, they that can
      With idle wishes 'ssay to bring backe time:
      In cases desperate, all hope is crime.
      See, see! what troups of his officious friends
      Flock to salute my lord! and start before
      My great, proud lord! to get a lord-like nod!
      Attend my lord, unto the *Senate*-house!
      Bring back my lord! like servile huishers, make   450
      Way for my lord! proclaime his idoll lord-ship,
      More then ten cryers, or sixe noise of trumpets!
      Make legs, kisse hands, and take a scatter'd haire
      From my lords eminent shoulder! See, SANQUINIUS!
      With his slow belly, and his dropsie! looke,
      What toyling haste he makes! yet, here's another,
      Retarded with the gout, will be afore him!
      Get thee *liburnian* porters, thou grosse foole,
      To beare thy' obsequious fatnesse, like thy peeres.
      They' are met! The gout returnes, and his great carriage. 460

Passe over the
stage.

LICTORS, CONSULS, SEJANUS, [SANQUINIUS,
HATERIUS,] &C.

LICTORES Give way, make place; roome for the *Consul.*

SANQUINIUS   Haile,
    Haile, great SEJANUS.

HATERIUS   Haile, my honor'd lord.

ARRUNTIUS We shall be markt anon, for our not-haile.

LEPIDUS That is already done.

ARRUNTIUS   It is a note
    Of upstart greatnesse, to observe, and watch
    For these poore trifles, which the noble mind
    Neglects, and scornes.

LEPIDUS   I, and they thinke themselves
    Deeply dishonor'd, where they are omitted,
    As if they were necessities, that helpt
470   To the perfection of their dignities:
    And hate the men, that but refraine 'hem.

ARRUNTIUS   O!
    There is a farder cause of hate. Their brests
    Are guiltie, that we know their obscure springs,
    And base beginnings: thence the anger growes. On. Follow.
                                            [*Exeunt.*]

MACRO, LACO.

[*Enter* MACRO *and* LACO.]

MACRO When all are entred, shut the temple doores;
    And bring your guardes up to the gate.

LACO   I will.

MACRO If you shall heare commotion in the *Senate,*
    Present your selfe: and charge on any man
    Shall offer to come forth.

LACO   I am instructed.   [*Exeunt.*]

THE SENATE.

HATERIUS, TRIO, SANQUINIUS, COTTA, REGULUS,
SEJANUS, POMPONIUS, LATIARIS, LEPIDUS,
ARRUNTIUS, PRAECONES, LICTORES.

[*Enter* HATERIUS, TRIO, SANQUINIUS, COTTA, REGULUS,
SEJANUS, POMPONIUS, LATIARIS, LEPIDUS, ARRUNTIUS,
SENATORS, PRAECONES, LICTORES *and* PRAETOR.]

HATERIUS How well his lordship lookes to day!

TRIO   As if   480
  He had beene borne, or made for this houres state.

COTTA Your fellow *Consul's* come about, me thinkes?

TRIO I, he is wise.

SANQUINIUS   SEJANUS trusts him well.

TRIO SEJANUS is a noble, bounteous lord.

HATERIUS He is so, and most valiant.

LATIARIS   And most wise.

1ST SENATOR Hee's every thing.

LATIARIS   Worthy of all, and more
  Then bountie can bestow.

TRIO   This dignitie
  Will make him worthy.

POMPONIUS   Above CAESAR.

SANQUINIUS   Tut,
  CAESAR is but the rector of an I'sle,
  He of the empire.

TRIO   Now he will have power   490
  More to reward, then ever.

COTTA   Let us looke
  We be not slack in giving him our voyces.

LATIARIS Not I.

SANQUINIUS   Nor I.

COTTA   The readier we seeme
  To propagate his honours, will more bind
  His thought, to ours.

HATERIUS   I thinke right, with your lordship.

It is the way to have us hold our places.

SANQUINIUS I, and get more.

LATIARIS   More office, and more titles.

POMPONIUS I will not lose the part, I hope to share
In these his fortunes, for my patrimonie.

LATIARIS See, how ARRUNTIUS sits, and LEPIDUS.

TRIO Let 'hem alone, they will be markt anon.

1ST SENATOR I'le doe with others.

2ND SENATOR   So will I.

3RD SENATOR   And I.
Men grow not in the state, but as they are planted
Warme in his favours.

COTTA   Noble SEJANUS!

HATERIUS Honor'd SEJANUS!

LATIARIS   Worthy, and great SEJANUS!

ARRUNTIUS Gods! how the spunges open, and take in!
And shut againe! looke, looke! is not he blest
That gets a seate in eye-reach of him? more,
That comes in eare, or tongue-reach? o, but most,
Can claw his subtle elbow, or with a buzze
Fly-blow his eares.

PRAETOR   Proclaime the *Senates* peace;
And give last summons by the edict.

PRAECONES   Silence:
In name of CAESAR, and the SENATE. Silence.
MEMMIUS REGULUS, *and* FULCINIUS TRIO, *Consuls, these present
kalends of June, with the first light, shall hold a senate, in the temple of*
APOLLO PALATINE, *all that are Fathers, and are registred Fathers, that
have right of entring the Senate, we warne, or command, you be frequently
present, take knowledge the businesse is the common-wealths, whosoever is
absent, his fine, or mulct, will be taken, his excuse will not be taken.*

TRIO Note, who are absent, and record their names.

REGULUS *Fathers Conscript. May, what I am to utter,
Turne good, and happy, for the common-wealth.*
And thou APOLLO, in whose holy house
We here are met, inspire us all, with truth,
And libertie of censure, to our thought.
The majestie of great TIBERIUS CAESAR

Propounds to this grave *Senate*, the bestowing
Upon the man he loves, honour'd SEJANUS,
The *tribuniciall* dignitie, and power;
Here are his letters, signed with his signet: 530
What pleaseth now the Fathers to be done?
SENATORS Reade, reade'hem, open, publiquely, reade 'hem.
COTTA CAESAR hath honour'd his owne greatnesse much,
    In thinking of this act.
TRIO   It was a thought
    Happy, and worthy CAESAR.
LATIARIS   And the lord,
    As worthy it, on whom it is directed!
HATERIUS Most worthy!
SANQUINIUS   *Rome* did never boast the vertue
    That could give envie bounds, but his: SEJANUS——
1ST SENATOR Honour'd, and noble!
2ND SENATOR   Good, and great SEJANUS!
ARRUNTIUS O, most tame slaverie, and fierce flatterie!
PRAECONES   Silence.   540

TIBERIUS CAESAR
TO THE SENATE,
GREETING.

The Epistle is
read.

If you, Conscript Fathers, with your children, bee in health, it is aboundantly
well: wee with our friends here, are so. The care of the common-wealth,
howsoever we are remoov'd in person, cannot be absent to our thought; although,
oftentimes, even to princes most present, the truth of their owne affaires is hid:
then which, nothing fals out more miserable to a state, or makes the art of
governing more difficult. But since it hath beene our ease-full happinesse to
enjoy both the aides, and industrie of so vigilant a Senate, wee professe to have   550
beene the more indulgent to our pleasures, not as being carelesse of our office,
but rather secure of the necessitie. Neyther doe these common rumors of many,
and infamous libels published against our retirement, at all afflict us; being
born more out of mens ignorance, then their malice: and will, neglected, finde
their owne grave quickly; whereas too sensibly acknowledg'd, it would make
their obloquie ours. Nor doe we desire their authors (though found) bee

censur'd, since in a free state (as ours) all men ought to enjoy their mindes,
and tongues free.

(ARRUNTIUS The lapwing, the lapwing.)

560   *Yet, in things, which shall worthily, and more neere concerne the majestie of*
a prince, we shall feare to be so unnaturally cruell to our owne fame, as to
neglect them. True it is, Conscript Fathers, that wee have raysed SEJANUS,
from obscure, and almost unknown gentrie, (SENATORS How! how!)
to the highest, and most conspicuous point of greatnesse, and (wee hope)
deservingly; yet, not without danger: it being a most bold hazard in that
sov'raigne, who, by his particular love to one, dares adventure the hatred of
all his other subjects.

(ARRUNTIUS This touches, the bloud turnes.)

  But wee affie in your loves, and understandings, and doe no way suspect the
570   *merit of our* SEJANUS *to make our favours offensive to any.*

(SENATORS O! good, good.)

  Though we could have wished his zeale had runne a calmer course against
AGRIPPINA, *and our Nephewes, howsoever the opennesse of their actions,*
declared them delinquents; and, that he would have remembred, no innocence
is so safe, but it rejoyceth to stand in the sight of mercie: The use of which in
us, hee hath so quite taken away, toward them, by his loyall furie, as now
our clemencie would be thought but wearied crueltie, if we should offer to
exercise it.

(ARRUNTIUS I thanke him, there I look'd for't. A good fox!)

580   *Some there bee, that would interpret this his publique severitie to bee particular*
ambition; and that, under a pretext of service to us, hee doth but remoove his
owne lets: alleadging the strengths he hath made to himselfe, by the Praetorian
souldiers, by his faction in Court, and Senate, by the offices hee holdes himselfe,
and conferres on others, his popularitie, and dependents, his urging (and almost
driving) us to this our unwilling retirement, and lastly his aspiring to be our
sonne in-law.

(SENATORS This 's strange!

ARRUNTIUS I shall anon beleeve your vultures, MARCUS.)

  Your wisedomes, Conscript Fathers, are able to examine, and censure these
590   *suggestions. But, were they left to our absolving voyce, we durst pronounce*
them, as we thinke them, most malicious.

(SENATORS O, he has restor'd all, list.)

  Yet, are they offer'd to bee averr'd, and on the lives of the informers. What
wee should say, or rather what we should not say, Lords of the Senate, if this

bee true, our gods, and goddesses confound us if we know! Only, we must
thinke, we have plac'd our benefits ill: and conclude, that, in our choise, either
we were wanting to the gods, or the gods to us.

(ARRUNTIUS The place growes hot, they shift.) *The Senators*
shift their places.

We have not beene covetous, Honourable Fathers, to change; neither is it now,
any new lust that alters our affection, or old lothing: but those needfull jealousies 600
of state, that warne wiser princes, hourely, to provide their safetie; and doe
teach them how learned a thing it is to beware of the humblest enemy; much
more of those great ones, whom their owne employ'd favors have made fit for
their feares.

(1ST SENATOR Away.

2ND SENATOR   Sit farder.

COTTA   Let's remoove——

ARRUNTIUS Gods! how the leaves drop off, this little winde!)

We therefore desire, that the offices he holds, bee first seized by the Senate;
and himselfe suspended from all exercise of place, or power——

(SENATORS How!

SANQUINIUS   By your leave.

ARRUNTIUS   Come, *Porcpisce,* (wher's HATERIUS?
His gout keepes him most miserably constant.) 610
Your dancing shewes a tempest.)

SEJANUS   Reade no more.

REGULUS Lords of the *Senate,* hold your seates: reade on.

SEJANUS These letters, they are forg'd. *Laco enters with*
the guards.

REGULUS   A guard, sit still.

ARRUNTIUS There's change.

REGULUS   Bid silence, and reade forward.

PRAECONES Silence——and himselfe suspended from all exercise
of place, or power, but till due and mature tryall be made of his
innocency, which yet we can faintly apprehend the necessitie, to
doubt. If, Conscript Fathers, to your more searching wisedomes,
there shall appeare farther cause (*or of farder proceeding, either to seizure*
of lands, goods, or more——) *it is not our power that shall limit your authoritie,* 620
or our favour, that must corrupt your justice: either were dishonourable in you,
and both uncharitable to our selfe. We would willingly be present with your
counsailes in this businesse, but the danger of so potent a faction (if it should
prove so) forbids our attempting it: except one of the Consuls would be intreated

for our safetie, to undertake the guard of us home, then wee should most
readily adventure. In the meane time, it shall not bee fit for us to importune
so judicious a Senate, who know how much they hurt the innocent, that spare
the guiltie: and how gratefull a sacrifice, to the gods, is the life of an ingratefull
person. We reflect not, in this, on SEJANUS *(notwithstanding, if you keepe*
630   *an eye upon him—and there is* LATIARIS *a Senator, and* PINNARIUS
NATTA, two of his most trusted ministers, and so profest, whom we desire
not to have apprended) but as the necessitie of the cause exacts it.

REGULUS A guard on LATIARIS.

ARRUNTIUS   O, the spie!
The reverend spie is caught, who pitties him?
Reward, sir, for your service: now, you ha' done
Your propertie, you see what use is made?
                              [*Exeunt* LATIARIS *and* NATTA, *guarded.*]
Hang up the instrument.

SEJANUS   Give leave.

LACO   Stand, stand,
He comes upon his death, that doth advance
An inch toward my point.

SEJANUS   Have we no friends here?

ARRUNTIUS Hush't. Where now are all the hailes, and
640   acclamations?

MACRO, SENATE.

[*Enter* MACRO.]
MACRO Haile, to the *Consuls*, and this noble *Senate.*
SEJANUS Is MACRO here? O, thou art lost SEJANUS.
MACRO Sit still, and un-affrighted, *reverend Fathers.*
MACRO, by CAESARS grace, the new-made *Provost,*
And now possest of the *praetorian* bands,
An honour late belong'd to that proud man,
Bids you, be safe: and to your constant doome
Of his deservings, offers you the surety
Of all the souldiers, *tribunes*, and *centurions,*
Receiv'd in our command.
650   REGULUS   SEJANUS, SEJANUS,

Stand forth, SEJANUS.

SEJANUS   Am I call'd?

MACRO   I, thou,
    Thou insolent monster, art bid stand.

SEJANUS   Why, MACRO,
    It hath beene otherwise, betweene you, and I?
    This court that knowes us both, hath seene a difference,
    And can (if it be pleas'd to speake) confirme,
    Whose insolence is most.

MACRO   Come downe, *Typhoeus*,
    If mine be most, loe, thus I make it more;
    Kicke up thy heeles in ayre, teare off thy robe,
    Play with thy beard, and nostrills. Thus 'tis fit,
    (And no man take compassion of thy state)   660
    To use th'ingratefull viper, tread his braines
    Into the earth.

REGULUS   Forbeare.

MACRO   If I could lose
    All my humanitie now, 'twere well to torture
    So meriting a traytor. Wherefore, *Fathers*,
    Sit you amaz'd, and silent? and not censure
    This wretch, who in the houre he first rebell'd
    'Gainst CAESARS bountie, did condemne himselfe?
    Phlegra, the field, where all the sonnes of earth
    Muster'd against the gods, did ne're acknowledge
    So proud, and huge a monster.

REGULUS   Take him hence.   670
    And all the gods guard CAESAR.

TRIO   Take him hence.

HATERIUS Hence.

COTTA   To the dungeon with him.

SANQUINIUS   He deserves it.

SENATORS Crowne all our doores with bayes.

SANQUINIUS   And let an oxe
    With gilded hornes, and garlands, straight be led
    Unto the *capitoll*.

HATERIUS   And sacrific'd

      To JOVE, for CAESARS safety.

TRIO   All our gods
      Be present still to CAESAR.

COTTA   PHOEBUS.

SANQUINIUS   MARS.

HATERIUS DIANA.

SANQUINIUS   PALLAS.

SENATORS   JUNO, MERCURIE,
      All guard him.

MACRO   Forth, thou prodigie of men.

                                [*Exit* SEJANUS, *guarded.*]

680   COTTA Let all the traytors titles be defac'd.

      TRIO His images, and statues be pull'd downe.

      HATERIUS His chariot-wheeles be broken.

      ARRUNTIUS   And the legs
      Of the poore horses, that deserved naught,
      Let them be broken too.

      LEPIDUS   O, violent change,
      And whirle of mens affections!

      ARRUNTIUS   Like, as both
      Their bulkes and soules were bound on fortunes wheele,
      And must act onely with her motion!

            [*Exeunt all but* LEPIDUS, ARRUNTIUS *and a few* SENATORS.]

LEPIDUS, ARRUNTIUS.

LEPIDUS Who would depend upon the popular ayre,
      Or voyce of men, that have to day beheld
690   (That which if all the gods had fore-declar'd,
      Would not have beene beleev'd) SEJANUS fall?
      He, that this morne rose proudly, as the sunne?
      And, breaking through a mist of clients breath,
      Came on as gaz'd at, and admir'd, as he
      When superstitious *Moores* salute his light
      That had our servile nobles waiting him
      As common groomes; and hanging on his looke,
      No lesse then humane life on destinie!

That had mens knees as frequent, as the gods;
And sacrifices, more, then *Rome* had altars: 700
And this man fall! fall? I, without a looke,
That durst appeare his friend; or lend so much
Of vaine reliefe, to his chang'd state, as pitty!

ARRUNTIUS They, that before like gnats plaid in his beames,
And throng'd to circumscribe him, now not seene!
Nor deigne to hold a common seate with him!
Others, that wayted him unto the *Senate*,
Now, inhumanely ravish him to prison!
Whom (but this morne) they follow'd as their lord,
Guard through the streets, bound like a fugitive!   710
In stead of wreathes, give fetters; strokes, for stoops:
Blind shame, for honours; and black taunts, for titles!
Who would trust slippery chance?

LEPIDUS   They, that would make
Themselves her spoile: and foolishly forget,
When shee doth flatter, that shee comes to prey.
Fortune, thou hadst no deitie, if men
Had wisedome: we have placed thee so high,
By fond beliefe in thy felicitie.

SENATORS The gods guard CAESAR. All the gods guard CAESAR.   *Shout within.*

MACRO, REGULUS, SENATORS.

[*Enter* MACRO, REGULUS *and more* SENATORS.]

MACRO Now great SEJANUS, you that aw'd the state,   720
And sought to bring the nobles to your whip,
That would be CAESARS tutor, and dispose
Of dignities, and offices! that had
The publique head still bare to your designes,
And made the generall voyce to eccho yours!   That look'd for
    salutations, twelve score off,
And would have pyramid's, yea, temples rear'd
To your huge greatnesse! now, you lie as flat,
As was your pride advanc'd.

REGULUS   Thanks, to the gods.

730   SENATORS   And praise to MACRO, that hath saved *Rome*.
Liberty, liberty, liberty. Lead on,
And praise to MACRO, that hath saved *Rome*.

                              [*Exeunt all but* ARRUNTIUS *and* LEPIDUS.]

ARRUNTIUS, LEPIDUS, TERENTIUS.

ARRUNTIUS   I prophesie, out of this *Senates* flatterie,
That this new fellow, MACRO, will become
A greater prodigie in *Rome*, then he
That now is falne.
      [*Enter* TERENTIUS.]
TERENTIUS   O you, whose minds are good,
And have not forc'd all mankind, from your brests;
That yet have so much stock of vertue left,
To pitty guiltie states, when they are wretched:
740   Lend your soft eares to heare, and eyes to weepe
Deeds done by men, beyond the acts of *furies*.
The eager multitude, (who never yet
Knew why to love, or hate, but onely pleas'd
T'expresse their rage of power) no sooner heard
The murmure of SEJANUS in decline,   But with that speed,
      and heate of appetite,
With which they greedily devoure the way
To some great sports, or a new theatre,
They fill'd the *capitoll*, and POMPEI's circke;
750   Where, like so many mastives, biting stones,
As if his statues now were sensive growne
Of their wild furie, first, they teare them downe:
Then fastning ropes, drag them along the streets,
Crying in scorne, this, this was that rich head
Was crown'd with gyrlands, and with odours, this
That was in *Rome* so reverenced! Now
The fornace, and the bellowes shall to worke,
The great SEJANUS crack, and piece, by piece,
Drop i' the founders pit.

LEPIDUS   O, popular rage!

TERENTIUS The whilst, the *Senate*, at the temple of *Concord*,   760
    Make haste to meete againe, and thronging cry,
    Let us condemne him, tread him downe in water,
    While he doth lie upon the banke; away:
    Where some, more tardie, cry unto their bearers,
    He will be censur'd ere we come, runne knaves;
    And use that furious diligence, for feare
    Their bond-men should informe against their slacknesse,
    And bring their quaking flesh unto the hooke:
    The rout, they follow with confused voyce,
    Crying, they'are glad, say they could ne're abide him;   770
    Enquire, what man he was? what kind of face?
    What beard he had? what nose? what lips? protest,
    They ever did presage h' would come to this:
    They never thought him wise, nor valiant: aske
    After his garments, when he dies? what death?
    And not a beast of all the herd demands,
    What was his crime? or, who were his accusers?
    Under what proofe, or testimonie, he fell?
    There came (sayes one) a huge, long, worded letter
    From *Capreae* against him. Did there so?   780
    O, they are satisfied, no more.

LEPIDUS   Alas!
    They follow fortune, and hate men condemn'd,
    Guiltie, or not.

ARRUNTIUS   But, had SEJANUS thriv'd
    In his designe, and prosperously opprest
    The old TIBERIUS, then, in that same minute,
    These very raskals, that now rage like *furies*,
    Would have proclaim'd SEJANUS emperour.

LEPIDUS But what hath follow'd?

TERENTIUS   Sentence, by the *Senate*;
    To lose his head: which was no sooner off,
    But that, and th'unfortunate trunke were seiz'd   790
    By the rude multitude; who not content
    With what the forward justice of the state,
    Officiously had done, with violent rage

Have rent it limbe, from limbe. A thousand heads,
A thousand hands, ten thousand tongues, and voyces,
Employ'd at once in severall acts of malice!
Old men not staid with age, virgins with shame,
Late wives with losse of husbands, mothers of children,
Losing all griefe in joy of his sad fall,
800　Runne quite transported with their crueltie!
These mounting at his head, these at his face,
These digging out his eyes, those with his braine,
Sprinkling themselves, their houses, and their friends;
Others are met, have ravish'd thence an arme,
And deale small pieces of the flesh for favours;
These with a thigh; this hath cut off his hands;
And this his feet; these fingers, and these toes;
That hath his liver; he his heart: there wants
Nothing but roome for wrath, and place for hatred!
810　What cannot oft be done, is now ore-done.
The whole, and all of what was great SEJANUS,
And next to CAESAR did possesse the world,
Now torne, and scatter'd, as he needs no grave,
Each little dust covers a little part:
So lyes he no where, and yet often buryed!

ARRUNTIUS, NUNTIUS, LEPIDUS, TERENTIUS.

[*Enter* NUNTIUS.]
ARRUNTIUS　More of SEJANUS?
NUNTIUS　　　　　　　　　　Yes.
LEPIDUS　　　　　　　　　　　　　What can be added?
We know him dead.
NUNTIUS　　　　　　　　Then, there begin your pitty.
There is inough behind, to melt ev'n *Rome*,
And CAESAR into teares: (since never slave
820　Could yet so highly' offend, but tyrannie,
In torturing him, would make him worth lamenting.)
A sonne, and daughter, to the dead SEJANUS,
(Of whom there is not now so much remayning

As would give fastning to the hang-mans hooke)
Have they drawne forth for farder sacrifice;
Whose tendernesse of knowledge, unripe yeares,
And childish silly innocence was such,
As scarse would lend them feeling of their danger:
The girle so simple, as shee often askt,
Where they would lead her? for what cause they drag'd her?   830
Cry'd, *shee would doe no more. That shee could take*
Warning with beating. And because our lawes
Admit no virgin immature to die,
The wittily, and strangely-cruell MACRO,
Deliver'd her to be deflowr'd, and spoil'd,
By the rude lust of the licentious hang-man,
Then, to be strangled with her harmlesse brother.

LEPIDUS   O, act, most worthy hell, and lasting night,
To hide it from the world!

NUNTIUS   Their bodies throwne
Into the *Gemonies*, (I know not how,   840
Or by what accident return'd) the mother,
Th'expulsed APICATA, finds them there;
Whom when shee saw lie spred on the degrees,
After a world of furie on her selfe,
Tearing her haire, defacing of her face,
Beating her brests, and wombe, kneeling amaz'd,
Crying to heaven, then to them; at last,
Her drowned voyce gate up above her woes:
And with such black, and bitter execrations,
(As might affright the gods, and force the sunne   850
Runne back-ward to the east, nay, make the old
Deformed CHAOS rise againe, t' ore-whelme
Them, us, and all the world) shee fills the aire;
Upbraids the heavens with their partiall doomes,
Defies their tyrannous powers, and demands,
What shee, and those poore innocents have transgress'd,
That they must suffer such a share in vengeance,
Whilst LIVIA, LYGDUS, and EUDEMUS live,
Who, (as shee say's, and firmely vowes, to prove it
To CAESAR, and the *Senate*) poyson'd DRUSUS?   860

LEPIDUS Confederates with her husband?

NUNTIUS   I.

LEPIDUS   Strange act!

ARRUNTIUS And strangely open'd: what say's now my monster,
 The multitude? they reele now? doe they not?

NUNTIUS Their gall is gone, and now they 'gin to weepe
 The mischiefe they have done.

ARRUNTIUS   I thanke 'hem, rogues!

NUNTIUS Part are so stupide, or so flexible,
 As they beleeve him innocent; all grieve:
 And some, whose hands yet reeke with his warme bloud,
 And gripe the part which they did teare of him,
870 Wish him collected, and created new.

LEPIDUS How fortune plies her sports, when shee begins
 To practise 'hem! pursues, continues, addes!
 Confounds, with varying her empassion'd moodes!

ARRUNTIUS Do'st thou hope fortune to redeeme thy crimes?
 To make amends, for thy ill placed favours,
 With these strange punishments? Forbeare, you things,
 That stand upon the pinnacles of state,
 To boast your slippery height; when you doe fall,
 You pash your selves in pieces, nere to rise:
880 And he that lends you pitty, is not wise.

TERENTIUS Let this example moove th'insolent man,
 Not to grow proud, and carelesse of the gods:
 It is an odious wisedome, to blaspheme,
 Much more to slighten, or denie their powers.
 For, whom the morning saw so great, and high,
 Thus low, and little, 'fore the 'even doth lie.   [*Exeunt.*]

THE END.

This Tragoedie was first

acted, in the yeere

1603.

By the Kings Majesties
SERVANTS.

The principall Tragoedians were,

RIC. BURBADGE. ⎫   ⎧ WILL. SHAKE-SPEARE
AUG. PHILIPS. ⎪   ⎪ JOH. HEMINGS.
WILL. SLY.   ⎬   ⎨ HEN. CONDEL.
JOH. LOWIN.   ⎭   ⎩ ALEX. COOKE.

With the allowance of the Master of REVELLS.

Volpone, or the Foxe

TO

THE MOST

NOBLE AND

MOST EQUALL

SISTERS

THE TWO FAMOUS

UNIVERSITIES

FOR THEIR LOVE

AND

ACCEPTANCE

SHEW'N TO HIS POEME IN THE

PRESENTATION

BEN. JONSON

THE GRATEFULL ACKNOWLEDGER

DEDICATES

BOTH IT AND HIMSELFE.

Never (most equall SISTERS) *had any man a wit so presently excellent, as that it could raise it selfe; but there must come both matter, occasion, commenders, and favourers to it: If this be true, and that the fortune of all writers doth daily prove it, it behoves the carefull to provide, well, toward these accidents; and, having acquir'd them, to preserve that part of reputation most tenderly, wherein the benefit of a friend is also defended. Hence is it, that I now render my selfe gratefull, and am studious to justifie the bounty of your act: to which, though your mere authority were satisfying, yet, it being an age, wherein* Poetrie, *and the Professors of it heare so ill, on all sides, there will a reason bee look'd for in the subject. It is certayne, nor*

10 *can it with any fore-head be oppos'd, that the too-much licence of* Poetasters, *in this time, hath much deform'd their Mistris; that, every day, their manifold, and manifest ignorance, doth sticke unnaturall reproches upon her: But for their petulancy, it were an act of the greatest injustice, either to let the learned suffer; or so divine a skill (which indeed should not bee attempted with uncleane hands) to fall, under the least contempt. For, if men will impartially, and not à-squint, looke toward the offices, and function of a Poet, they will easily conclude to themselves, the impossibility of any mans being the good Poet, without first being a good man. He that is said to be able to informe yong-men to all good disciplines, inflame growne-men to all great vertues, keepe old-men in their best and supreme*

20 *state, or as they decline to child-hood, recover them to their first strength; that comes forth the interpreter, and arbiter of nature, a teacher of things divine, no lesse then humane, a master in manners; and can alone (or with a few) effect the businesse of man-kind: this, I take him, is no subject for pride, and ignorance to exercise their rayling rhetorique upon. But, it will here be hastily answer'd, that the writers of these dayes are other things; that, not only their manners, but their natures are inverted; and nothing remayning with them of the dignitie of Poet, but the abused name, which every Scribe usurps: that now, especially in* dramatick, *or (as they terme it) stage-*poetrie, *nothing but ribaldry, profanation, blasphemy, all licence of offence to god, and man, is practis'd. I dare not denie a great part*

30 *of this (and am sorry, I dare not) because in some mens abortive features (and would they had never boasted the light) it is over-true: But, that all are embarqu'd in this bold adventure for hell, is a most uncharitable thought, and, utter'd, a*

more malicious slander. For my particular, I can (and from a most cleare conscience)
affirme, that I have ever trembled to thinke toward the least prophanenesse; have
lothed the use of such foule, and un-wash'd baudr'y, as is now made the foode of
the scene. *And, howsoever I cannot escape, from some, the imputation of*
sharpnesse, but that they will say, I have taken a pride, or lust, to be bitter, and
not my yongest infant but hath come into the world with all his teeth; I would
aske of these supercilious politiques, what nation, societie, or generall order, or
state I have provok'd? what publique person? whether I have not (in all   40
these) preserv'd their dignitie, as mine owne person, safe? My workes are read,
allow'd, (I speake of those that are intirely mine) looke into them: What broad
reproofes have I us'd? Where have I beene particular? Where personall? except
to a mimick, cheater, bawd, or buffon, creatures (for their insolencies) worthy to
be tax'd? Yet, to which of these so pointingly, as he might not, either ingenuously
have confest, or wisely dissembled his disease? But it is not rumour can make
men guiltie, much lesse entitle me, to other mens crimes. I know, that nothing can
bee so innocently writ, or carryed, but may be made obnoxious to construction;
mary, whil'st I beare mine innocence about mee, I feare it not. Application, is
now, growne a trade with many; and there are, that professe to have a key for the   50
decyphering of every thing: but let wise and noble persons take heed how they be
too credulous, or give leave to these invading interpreters, to bee over-familiar with
their fames, who cunningly, and often, utter their owne virulent malice, under other
mens simplest meanings. As for those, that will (by faults which charitie hath
rak'd up, or common honestie conceal'd) make themselves a name with the
multitude, or (to draw their rude, and beastly claps) care not whose living faces
they intrench, with their petulant stiles; may they doe it, without a rivall, for me:
I choose rather to live grav'd in obscuritie, then share with them, in so preposterous
a fame. Nor can I blame the wishes of those severe, and wiser patriots, who
providing the hurts these licentious spirits may doe in a state, desire rather to see   60
fooles, and devils, and those antique reliques of barbarisme retriv'd, with all other
ridiculous, and exploded follies: then behold the wounds of private men, of princes,
and nations. For, as HORACE *makes* TREBATIUS *speake, among these*

—Sibi quisq; timet, quanquam est intactus, & odit.

And men may justly impute such rages, if continu'd, to the writer, as his sports.
The increase of which lust in liberty, together with the present trade of the stage,
in all their misc'line enter-ludes, what learned or liberall soule doth not already
abhor? where nothing but the filth of the time is utter'd, and that with such

impropriety of phrase, such plenty of soloecismes, *such dearth of sense, so bold*
70 *prolepse's, so rackt* metaphor's, *with brothelry, able to violate the eare
of a pagan, and blasphemy, to turne the bloud of a christian to water. I cannot
but be serious in a cause of this nature, wherein my fame, and the reputations of
divers honest, and learned are the question; when a Name, so ful of authority,
antiquity, and all great marke, is (through their insolence) become the lowest
scorne of the age: and those men subject to the petulancy of every vernaculous
Orator, that were wont to bee the care of Kings, and happiest Monarchs. This it
is, that hath not only rap't me to present indignation, but made me studious,
heretofore; and, by all my actions, to stand off, from them: which may most appeare
in this my latest worke (which you, most learned* ARBITRESSES, *have seene,*
80 *judg'd, and to my crowne, approv'd) wherein I have labour'd, for their instruction,
and amendment, to reduce, not onely the ancient formes, but manners of the* scene,
*the easinesse, the propriety, the innocence, and last the doctrine, which is the
principall end of* poesie, *to informe men, in the best reason of living. And though
my* catastrophe *may, in the strict rigour of* comick *law, meet with censure, as
turning back to my promise; I desire the learned, and charitable critick to have
so much faith in me, to thinke it was done off industrie: For, with what ease I
could have varied it, neerer his scale (but that I feare to boast my owne faculty) I
could here insert. But my speciall ayme being to put the snaffle in their mouths,
that crie out, we never punish vice in our* enterludes, &c. *I tooke the more*
90 *liberty; though not without some lines of example, drawne even in the ancients
themselves, the goings out of whose* comoedies *are not alwaies joyfull, but
oft-times, the bawdes, the servants, the rivals, yea, and the masters are mulcted:
and fitly, it being the office of a* comick-Poet, *to imitate justice, and instruct to
life, as well as puritie of language, or stirre up gentle affections. To which, I shall
take the occasion else-where to speake. For the present (most reverenced* SISTERS)
*as I have car'd to be thankefull for your affections past, and here made the
understanding acquainted with some ground of your favours; let me not despaire
their continuance, to the maturing of some worthier fruits: wherein, if my* MUSES
be true to me, I shall raise the despis'd head of poetrie *againe, and stripping her*
100 *out of those rotten and base rags, wherwith the Times have adulterated her form,
restore her to her primitive habit, feature, and majesty, and render her worthy to
be imbraced, and kist, of all the great and master-*spirits *of our world. As for
the vile, and slothfull, who never affected an act, worthy of celebration, or are so
inward with their owne vicious natures, as they worthily feare her; and thinke it
a high point of policie, to keepe her in contempt with their declamatorie, and windy
invectives: shee shall out of just rage incite her servants (who are* genus irritable)

to spout inke in their faces, that shall eate, farder then their marrow, into their
fames; and not CINNAMUS *the barber, with his arte, shall be able to take out*
the brands, but they shall live, and bee read, till the wretches dye, as things worst
deserving of themselves in chiefe, and then of all mankind.   110

The Persons of the Play.

VOLPONE, *a Magnifico.*

MOSCA, *his Parasite.*

VOLTORE, *an Advocate.*

CORBACCIO, *an old Gentleman.*

CORVINO, *a Merchant.*

AVOCATORI, *four Magistrates.*

NOTARIO, *the Register.*

NANO, *a Dwarfe.*

CASTRONE, *an Eunuch.*

GREGE.

POLITIQUE WOULD-BEE, *a Knight.*

PEREGRINE, *a Gent[leman]-travailer.*

BONARIO, *a yong Gentleman.*

FINE MADAME WOULD-BEE, *the Knights wife.*

CELIA, *the Merchants wife.*

COMMANDADORI, *Officers.*

MERCATORI, *three Merchants.*

ANDROGYNO, *a Hermaphrodite.*

SERVITORE, *a Servant.*

WOMEN.

THE SCENE

VENICE.

Volpone, or the Foxe.

The Argument.

V OLPONE, *childlesse, rich, faines sicke, despaires,*
O *ffers his state to hopes of severall heires,*
L *ies languishing; His Parasite receeves*
P *resents of all, assures, deludes: Then weaves*
O *ther crosse-plots, which ope' themselves, are told.*
N *ew tricks for safety, are sought; they thrive: When, bold,*
E *ach tempts th'other againe, and all are sold.*

Prologue

Now, luck yet send us, and a little wit
    Will serve, to make our play hit;
(According to the palates of the season)
    Here is ri'me, not emptie of reason:
This we were bid to credit, from our *Poet*,
    Whose true scope, if you would know it,
In all his *poemes*, stil, hath been this measure,
    To mixe profit, with your pleasure;
And not as some (whose throats their envy fayling)
    Cry hoarsely, all he writes, is rayling:
And, when his playes come forth, thinke they can flout them,
    With saying, he was a yeere about them.
To these there needs no lie, but this his creature,
    Which was, two months since, no feature;
And, though he dares give them five lives to mend it,
    'Tis knowne, five weekes fully pen'd it:
From his owne hand, without a co-adjutor,
    Novice, journey-man, or tutor.

10

Yet, thus much I can give you, as a token
20   Of his Playes worth, No egges are broken;
Nor quaking custards with fierce teeth affrighted,
     Wherewith your rout are so delighted;
Nor hales he in a gull, old ends reciting,
     To stop gaps in his loose writing;
With such a deale of monstrous, and forc'd action:
     As might make *Bet'lem* a faction:
Nor made he'his Play, for jests, stolne from each table,
     But makes jests, to fit his fable.
And, so presents quick *comoedie*, refined,
30   As best Criticks have designed,
The lawes of time, place, persons he observeth,
     From no needfull rule he swerveth.
All gall, and coppresse, from his inke, he drayneth,
     Onely, a little salt remayneth;
Wherewith, he'll rub your cheeks, til (red with laughter)
     They shall looke fresh, a weeke after.

Act I. Scene 1

VOLPONE, MOSCA.

[*Enter* VOLPONE *and* MOSCA.]

VOLPONE Good morning to the day; and, next, my gold:
Open the shrine, that I may see my *saint*.
Haile the worlds soule, and mine. More glad then is
The teeming earth, to see the long'd-for Sunne
Peepe through the hornes of the celestiall *Ram*,
Am I, to view thy splendor, darkening his:
That, lying here, amongst my other hoords,
Shew'st like a flame, by night; or like the day
Strooke out of *chaos*, when all darkenesse fled
10   Unto the center. O, thou sonne of SOL,
(But brighter then thy father) let me kisse,
With adoration, thee, and every relique
Of sacred treasure, in this blessed roome.
Well did wise Poets, by thy glorious name,

Title that age, which they would have the best;
Thou being the best of things: and far transcending
All stile of joy, in children, parents, friends,
Or any other waking dreame on earth.
Thy lookes, when they to VENUS did ascribe,
They should have giv'n her twentie thousand CUPIDS;   20
Such are thy beauties, and our loves! Deare *saint*,
Riches, the dumbe god, that giv'st all men tongues:
That canst doe nought, and yet mak'st men doe all things;
The price of soules; even hell, with thee to boot,
Is made worth heaven! Thou art vertue, fame,
Honour, and all things else! Who can get thee,
He shall be noble, valiant, honest, wise—

MOSCA   And what he will, sir. Riches are in fortune
A greater good, then wisedome is in nature.

VOLPONE   True, my beloved MOSCA. Yet, I glory   30
More in the cunning purchase of my wealth,
Then in the glad possession; since I gaine
No common way: I use no trade, no venter;
I wound no earth with plow-shares; fat no beasts
To feede the shambles; have no mills for yron,
Oyle, corne, or men, to grinde 'hem into poulder;
I blow no subtill glasse; expose no ships
To threatnings of the furrow-faced sea;
I turne no moneys, in the publike banke;
Nor usure private—

MOSCA   No, sir, nor devoure   40
Soft prodigalls. You shall ha' some will swallow
A melting heire, as glibly, as your *Dutch*
Will pills of butter, and ne're purge for't;
Teare forth the fathers of poore families
Out of their beds, and coffin them, alive,
In some kind, clasping prison, where their bones
May be forth-comming, when the flesh is rotten:
But, your sweet nature doth abhorre these courses;
You lothe, the widdowes, or the oprhans teares
Should wash your pavements; or their pittious cryes   50
Ring in your roofes; and beate the aire, for vengeance.

VOLPONE   Right, MOSCA, I doe lothe it.

MOSCA   And besides, sir,
   You are not like the thresher, that doth stand
   With a huge flaile, watching a heape of corne,
   And, hungrie, dares not taste the smallest graine,
   But feeds on mallowes, and such bitter herbs;
   Nor like the marchant, who hath fill'd his vaults
   With *Romagnía*, and rich *Candian* wines,
   Yet drinkes the lees of *Lombards* vineger:
60   You will not lie in straw, whilst moths, and wormes
   Feed on your sumptuous hangings, and soft beds.
   You know the use of riches, and dare give, now,
   From that bright heape, to me, your poore observer,
   Or to your dwarfe, or your *hermaphrodite*,
   Your *eunuch*, or what other houshold-trifle
   Your pleasure allowes maint'nance.——

VOLPONE   Hold thee, MOSCA,
   Take, of my hand; thou strik'st on truth, in all:
   And they are envious, terme thee parasite.
   Call forth my dwarfe, my eunuch, and my foole,
70   And let 'hem make me sport. [*Exit* MOSCA.] What should I doe,
   But cocker up my *genius*, and live free
   To all delights, my fortune calls me to?
   I have no wife, no parent, child, allie,
   To give my substance to; but whom I make,
   Must be my heire: and this makes men observe me.
   This drawes new clients, daily, to my house,
   Women, and men, of every sexe, and age,
   That bring me presents, send me plate, coyne, jewels,
   With hope, that when I die, (which they expect
80   Each greedy minute) it shall then returne,
   Ten-fold, upon them; whil'st some, covetous
   Above the rest, seeke to engrosse me, whole,
   And counter-worke, the one, unto the other,
   Contend in gifts, as they would seeme, in love:
   All which I suffer, playing with their hopes,
   And am content to coyne 'hem into profit,
   And looke upon their kindnesse, and take more,

And looke on that; still bearing them in hand,
Letting the cherry knock against their lips,
And, draw it, by their mouths, and back againe. How now!   90

Act I. Scene 2

NANO, ANDROGYNO, CASTRONE, VOLPONE, MOSCA.

[*Enter* NANO, ANDROGYNO, CASTRONE *and* MOSCA.]
NANO   *Now, roome, for fresh gamsters, who doe will you to know,*
        They doe bring you neither play, nor Universitie *show;*
    And therefore doe intreat you, that whatsoever they reherse,
        May not fare a whit the worse, for the false pase of the verse.
    If you wonder at this, you will wonder more, ere we passe,
        For know, here is inclos'd the Soule of PYTHAGORAS,
    That juggler divine, as hereafter shall follow;
        Which Soule (fast, and loose, sir) came first from APOLLO,
    And was breath'd into AETHALIDES, MERCURIUS *his sonne,*
        Where it had the gift to remember all that ever was done.   10
    From thence it fled forth, and made quick transmigration
        To goldy-lockt EUPHORBUS, *who was kill'd, in good fashion,*
    At the siege of old Troy, *by the Cuckold of* Sparta.
        HERMOTIMUS *was next (I find it, in my* charta)
    To whom it did passe, where no sooner it was missing,
        But with one PYRRHUS, *of* Delos, *it learn'd to goe a fishing:*
    And thence, did it enter the Sophist of Greece.
        From PYTHAGORE, *shee went into a beautifull peece,*
    Hight ASPASIA, *the* meretrix; *and the next tosse of her*
        Was, againe, of a whore, shee became a Philosopher,   20
    CRATES *the Cynick: (as it selfe doth relate it)*
        Since, Kings, Knights, and Beggers, Knaves, Lords and Fooles gat it,
    Besides, oxe, and asse, cammell, mule, goat, and brock,
        In all which it hath spoke, as in the Coblers cock.
    But I come not here, to discourse of that matter,
        Or his one, two, or three, or his great oath, by quater,
    His musicks, his trigon, his golden thigh,
        Or his telling how elements shift: but I
    Would aske, how of late, thou hast suffered translation,

30   *And shifted thy coat, in these dayes of reformation?*

ANDROGYNO *Like one of the reformed, a Foole, as you see,*
   Counting all old doctrine heresie.

NANO *But not on thine owne forbid meates hast thou venter'd?*

ANDROGYNO *On fish, when first, a* carthusian *I enter'd.*

NANO *Why, then thy dogmaticall silence hath left thee?*

ANDROGYNO *Of that an obstreperous Lawyer bereft mee.*

NANO *O wonderfull change! when Sir Lawyer forsooke thee,*
   For PYTHAGORE'S *sake, what body then tooke thee?*

ANDROGYNO *A good dull moyle.*

NANO   *And how! by that meanes,*
40   *Thou wert brought to allow of the eating of beanes?*

ANDROGYNO *Yes.*

NANO   *But, from the moyle, into whom did'st thou passe?*

ANDROGYNO *Into a very strange beast, by some writers cal'd an asse;*
   By others, a precise, pure, illuminate brother,
   Of those devoure flesh, and sometimes one another:
   And will drop you forth a libell, or a sanctified lie,
   Betwixt every spoonefull of a nativitie-pie.

NANO *Now quit thee, for heaven, of that profane nation;*
   And gently, report thy next transmigration.

ANDROGYNO *To the same that I am.*

NANO   *A creature of delight?*
50   *And (what is more then a Foole) an* hermaphrodite?
   Now 'pray thee, sweet Soule, in all thy variation,
   Which body would'st thou choose, to take up thy station?

ANDROGYNO *Troth, this I am in, even here would I tarry.*

NANO *'Cause here, the delight of each sexe thou canst vary?*

ANDROGYNO *Alas, those pleasures be stale, and forsaken;*
   No, 'tis your Foole, wherewith I am so taken,
   The onely one creature, that I can call blessed:
   For all other formes I have prov'd most distressed.

NANO *Spoke true, as thou wert in* PYTHAGORAS *still.*
60   *This learned opinion we celebrate will,*
   Fellow eunuch (as behooves us) with all our wit, and art,
   To dignifie that, whereof our selves are so great, and speciall a part.

VOLPONE Now very, very pretty: MOSCA, this

Was thy invention?

MOSCA   If it please my patron,
    Not else.

VOLPONE   It doth, good MOSCA.

MOSCA   Then it was, sir.

SONG.

[NANO]   *Fooles, they are the onely nation*
            Worth mens envy, or admiration;
            Free from care, or sorrow-taking,
            Selves, and others merry-making:
            All they speake, or doe, is sterling.   70
            Your Foole, he is your great mans dearling,
            And your ladies sport, and pleasure;
            Tongue, and bable are his treasure.
            Eene his face begetteth laughter,
            And he speakes truth, free from slaughter;
            Hee's the grace of every feast,
            And, sometimes, the chiefest guest:
            Hath his trencher, and his stoole,
            When wit waites upon the foole.
                O, who would not bee   80
                Hee, hee, hee?

VOLPONE   Who's that? away, [*Exeunt* NANO *and* CASTRONE.] looke   *One knocks*
    MOSCA   *without.*

MOSCA   Foole, be gone,   [*Exit* ANDROGYNO.]
    'Tis signior VOLTORE, the Advocate,
    I know him, by his knock.

VOLPONE   Fetch me my gowne,
    My furres, and night-caps; say, my couch is changing:
    And let him entertayne himselfe, awhile,
    Without i' th' gallerie. [*Exit* MOSCA.] Now, now, my clients
    Beginne their visitation! vulture, kite,
    Raven, and gor-crow, all my birds of prey,
    That thinke me turning carcasse, now they come: 90
    I am not for 'hem yet. [*Enter* MOSCA.] How now? the newes?

MOSCA A piece of plate, sir.

VOLPONE   Of what bignesse?

MOSCA   Huge,
    Massie, and antique, with your name inscrib'd,
    And armes ingraven.

VOLPONE   Good! and not a foxe
    Stretch'd on the earth, with fine delusive sleights,
    Mocking a gaping crow? ha, MOSCA?

MOSCA   Sharpe, sir.

VOLPONE Give me my furres. Why dost thou laugh so, man?

MOSCA I cannot choose, sir, when I apprehend
    What thoughts he has (without) now, as he walkes:
100   That this might be the last gift, he should give;
    That this would fetch you; if you dyed to day,
    And gave him all, what he should be to morrow;
    What large returne would come of all his venters;
    How he should worship'd be, and reverenc'd;
    Ride, with his furres, and foot-clothes; waited on
    By herds of fooles, and clients; have cleere way
    Made for his moyle, as letter'd as himselfe;
    Be cald the great, and learned Advocate:
    And then concludes, there's nought impossible.

VOLPONE Yes, to be learned, MOSCA.

110 MOSCA   O, no: rich
    Implies it. Hood an asse, with reverend purple,
    So you can hide his two ambitious eares,
    And, he shall passe for a cathedrall Doctor.

VOLPONE My caps, my caps, good MOSCA, fetch him in.

MOSCA Stay, sir, your ointment for your eyes.

VOLPONE   That's true;
    Dispatch, dispatch: I long to have possession
    Of my new present.

MOSCA   That, and thousands more,
    I hope, to see you lord of.

VOLPONE   Thankes, kind MOSCA.

MOSCA And that, when I am lost in blended dust,
120   And hundred such, as I am, in succession—

VOLPONE Nay, that were too much, MOSCA.

MOSCA   You shall live,
   Still, to delude these *harpyies*.

VOLPONE   Loving MOSCA,
   'Tis well, my pillow now, and let him enter.
   Now, my fain'd cough, my phthisick, and my gout,
   My apoplexie, palsie, and catarrhes,
   Helpe, with your forced functions, this my posture,
   Wherein, this three yeere, I have milk'd their hopes.
   He comes, I heare him (uh, uh, uh, uh) o.   [*Exit* MOSCA.]

Act I. Scene 3
MOSCA, VOLTORE, VOLPONE.

[*Enter* MOSCA *and* VOLTORE.]

MOSCA You still are, what you were, sir. Onely you
   (Of all the rest) are he, commands his love:
   And you doe wisely, to preserve it, thus,
   With early visitation, and kind notes
   Of your good meaning to him, which, I know,
   Cannot but come most gratefull. Patron, sir.
   Here's signior VOLTORE is come—

VOLPONE   What say you?

MOSCA Sir, signior VOLTORE is come, this morning,
   To visit you.

VOLPONE   I thanke him.

MOSCA   And hath brought
   A piece of antique plate, bought of S. MARKE,   10
   With which he here presents you.

VOLPONE   He is welcome.
   Pray him, to come more often.

MOSCA   Yes.

VOLTORE   What sayes he?

MOSCA He thanks you, and desires you see him often.

VOLPONE MOSCA.

MOSCA   My patron?

VOLPONE   Bring him neere, where is he?
I long to feele his hand.

MOSCA   The plate is here, sir.

VOLTORE How fare you, sir?

VOLPONE   I thanke you, signior VOLTORE.
Where is the plate? mine eyes are bad.

VOLTORE   I'm sorry,
To see you still thus weake.

MOSCA   That he is not weaker.

VOLPONE You are too munificent.

VOLTORE   No, sir, would to heaven,
20   I could as well give health to you, as that plate.

VOLPONE You give, sir, what you can. I thanke you. Your love
Hath taste in this, and shall not be un-answer'd.
I pray you see me often.

VOLTORE   Yes, I shall, sir.

VOLPONE Be not far from me.

MOSCA   Doe you observe that, sir?

VOLPONE Harken unto me, still: It will concerne you.

MOSCA You are a happy man, sir, know your good.

VOLPONE I cannot now last long—

(MOSCA   You are his heire, sir.

VOLTORE Am I?)

VOLPONE   I feele me going, (uh, uh, uh, uh.)
I am sayling to my port, (uh, uh, uh, uh?)
30   And I am glad, I am so neere my haven.

MOSCA Alas, kind gentleman, well, we must all goe—

VOLTORE But, MOSCA—

MOSCA   Age wil conquer.

VOLTORE   'Pray thee heare me.
Am I inscrib'd his heire, for certayne?

MOSCA   Are you?
I doe beseech you, sir, you will vouchsafe
To write me, i' your family. All my hopes,
Depend upon your worship. I am lost,
Except the rising sunne doe shine on me.

VOLTORE It shall both shine, and warme thee, MOSCA.

MOSCA   Sir.

I am a man, that have not done your love
All the worst offices: here I weare your keyes,   40
See all your coffers, and your caskets lockt,
Keepe the poore inventorie of your jewels,
Your plate, and moneyes, am your steward, sir,
Husband your goods here.

VOLTORE   But am I sole heire?

MOSCA Without a partner, sir, confirm'd this morning;
The waxe is warme yet, and the inke scarse drie
Upon the parchment.

VOLTORE   Happy, happy, me!
By what good chance, sweet MOSCA?

MOSCA   Your desert, sir;
I know no second cause.

VOLTORE   Thy modestie
Is loth to know it; well, we shall requite it.   50

MOSCA He ever lik'd your course, sir, that first tooke him.
I, oft, have heard him say, how he admir'd
Men of your large profession, that could speake
To every cause, and things mere contraries,
Till they were hoarse againe, yet all be law;
That, with most quick agilitie, could turne,
And re-turne; make knots, and undoe them;
Give forked counsell; take provoking gold
On either hand, and put it up: these men,
He knew, would thrive, with their humilitie.   60
And (for his part) he thought, he should be blest
To have his heire of such a suffering spirit,
So wise, so grave, of so perplex'd a tongue,
And loud withall, that would not wag, nor scarce
Lie still, without a fee; when every word
Your worship but lets fall, is a *cecchine!*
Who's that? one knocks, I would not have you seene, sir.   *Another*
And yet—pretend you came, and went in haste;   *knocks.*
I'le fashion an excuse. And, gentle sir,
When you doe come to swim, in golden lard,   70
Up to the armes, in honny, that your chin
Is borne up stiffe, with fatnesse of the floud,

Thinke on your vassall; but remember me:
I ha' not beene your worst of clients.

VOLTORE   MOSCA—

MOSCA When will you have your inventorie brought, sir?
Or see a coppy of the will? (anon)
I'le bring 'hem to you, sir. Away, be gone,
Put businesse i' your face.

                                          [*Exit* VOLTORE.]

VOLPONE   Excellent, MOSCA!
Come hither, let me kisse thee.

MOSCA   Keepe you still, sir.
Here is CORBACCIO.

80   VOLPONE   Set the plate away,
The vulture's gone, and the old raven's come.

Act I. Scene 4

MOSCA, CORBACCIO, VOLPONE.

MOSCA Betake you, to your silence, and your sleepe:
Stand there, and multiply. Now, shall wee see
A wretch, who is (indeed) more impotent,
Then this can faine to be; yet hopes to hop
Over his grave. [*Enter* CORBACCIO.] Signior CORBACCIO!
Yo' are very welcome, sir.

CORBACCIO   How do's your patron?

MOSCA Troth, as he did, sir, no amends.

CORBACCIO   What? mends he?

MOSCA No, sir: he is rather worse.

CORBACCIO   That's well. Where is he?

MOSCA Upon his couch, sir, newly fall'n asleepe.

CORBACCIO Do's he sleepe well?

10   MOSCA   No winke, sir, all this night,
Nor yesterday, but slumbers.

CORBACCIO   Good! He should take
Some counsell of physicians: I have brought him
An *opiate* here, from mine owne Doctor—

MOSCA He will not heare of drugs.

CORBACCIO   Why? I my selfe
  Stood by, while 't was made; saw all th'ingredients:
  And know, it cannot but most gently worke.
  My life for his, 'tis but to make him sleepe.
VOLPONE I, his last sleepe, if he would take it.
MOSCA   Sir,
  He ha's no faith in physick.
CORBACCIO   'Say you? 'say you?
MOSCA He ha's no faith in physick: he do's thinke,   20
  Most of your Doctors are the greater danger,
  And worse disease, t'escape. I often have
  Heard him protest, that your physitian
  Should never be his heire.
CORBACCIO   Not I his heire?
MOSCA Not your physitian, sir.
CORBACCIO   O, no, no, no,
  I doe not meane it.
MOSCA   No, sir, nor their fees
  He cannot brooke: he sayes, they flay a man,
  Before they kill him.
CORBACCIO   Right, I doe conceive you.
MOSCA And then, they doe it by experiment;
  For which the law not onely doth absolve 'hem,   30
  But gives them great reward: and, he is loth
  To hire his death, so.
CORBACCIO   It is true, they kill,
  With as much licence, as a judge.
MOSCA   Nay, more;
  For he but kills, sir, where the law condemnes,
  And these can kill him, too.
CORBACCIO   I, or me:
  Or any man. How do's his apoplexe?
  Is that strong on him, still?
MOSCA   Most violent.
  His speech is broken, and his eyes are set,
  His face drawne longer, then 't was wont—
CORBACCIO   .   How? how?
  Stronger, then he was wont?

40 MOSCA   No, sir: his face
        Drawne longer, then 't was wont.
   CORBACCIO   O, good.
   MOSCA   His mouth
        Is ever gaping, and his eye-lids hang.
   CORBACCIO   Good.
   MOSCA A freezing numnesse stiffens all his joynts,
        And makes the colour of his flesh like lead.
   CORBACCIO   'Tis good.
   MOSCA His pulse beats slow, and dull.
   CORBACCIO   Good symptomes, still.
   MOSCA And, from his brain——
   CORBACCIO   Ha? how? not from his brain?
   MOSCA Yes, sir, and from his brain——
   (CORBACCIO   I conceive you, good.)
   MOSCA Flowes a cold sweat, with a continuall rhewme,
        Forth the resolved corners of his eyes.
50 CORBACCIO Is't possible? yet I am better, ha!
        How do's he, with the swimming of his head?
   MOSCA O, sir, 'tis past, the *scotomy*; he, now,
        Hath lost his feeling, and hath left to snort:
        You hardly can perceive him, that he breathes.
   CORBACCIO Excellent, excellent, sure I shall out-last him:
        This makes me yong againe, a score of yeeres.
   MOSCA I was a comming for you, sir.
   CORBACCIO   Has he made his will?
        What has he giv'n me?
   MOSCA   No, sir.
   CORBACCIO   Nothing? ha?
   MOSCA He has not made his will, sir.
   CORBACCIO   Oh, oh, oh.
60   When then did VOLTORE, the Lawyer, here?
   MOSCA He smelt a carcasse, sir, when he but heard
        My master was about his testament;
        (As I did urge him to it, for your good——)
   CORBACCIO He came unto him, did he? I thought so.
   MOSCA Yes, and presented him this piece of plate.
   CORBACCIO To be his heire?

MOSCA   I doe not know, sir.

CORBACCIO   True,
  I know it too.

MOSCA   By your owne scale, sir.

CORBACCIO   Well,
  I shall prevent him, yet. See, MOSCA, looke,
  Here, I have brought a bag of bright *cecchines*,
  Will quite weigh downe his plate.

MOSCA   Yea, mary, sir!   70
  This is true physick, this your sacred medicine,
  No talke of *opiates*, to this great *elixir*.

CORBACCIO 'Tis *aurum palpabile*, if not *potabile*.

MOSCA It shall be minister'd to him, in his bowle?

CORBACCIO I, doe, doe, doe.

MOSCA   Most blessed cordiall!
  This will recover him.

CORBACCIO   Yes, doe, doe, doe.

MOSCA I thinke, it were not best, sir.

CORBACCIO   What?

MOSCA   To recover him.

CORBACCIO O, no, no, no; by no meanes.

MOSCA   Why, sir, this
  Will worke some strange effect, if he but feele it.

CORBACCIO 'Tis true, therefore forbeare, I'le take my venter: 80
  Give me 't againe.

MOSCA   At no hand, pardon me;
  You shall not doe your selfe that wrong, sir. I
  Will so advise you, you shall have it all.

CORBACCIO How?

MOSCA   All, sir, 'tis your right, your owne; no man
  Can claime a part: 'tis yours, without a rivall,
  Decree'd by destinie.

CORBACCIO   How? how, good MOSCA?

MOSCA I'le tell you, sir. This fit he shall recover—

CORBACCIO I doe conceive you.

MOSCA   And, on first advantage
  Of his gayn'd sense, will I re-importune him
  Unto the making of his testament: 90

And shew him this.

CORBACCIO   Good, good.

MOSCA   'Tis better yet,
If you will heare, sir.

CORBACCIO   Yes, with all my heart.

MOSCA   Now, would I counsell you, make home with speed;
There, frame a will: whereto you shall inscribe
My master your sole heire.

CORBACCIO   And disinherit
My sonne?

MOSCA   O, sir, the better: for that colour
Shall make it much more taking.

CORBACCIO   O, but colour?

MOSCA   This will, sir, you shall send it unto me.
Now, when I come to inforce (as I will doe)
100   Your cares, your watchings, and your many prayers,
Your more then many gifts, your this dayes present,
And, last, produce your will; where (without thought,
Or least regard, unto your proper issue,
A sonne so brave, and highly meriting)
The streame of your diverted love hath throwne you
Upon my master, and made him your heire:
He cannot be so stupide, or stone dead,
But, out of conscience, and mere gratitude—

CORBACCIO   He must pronounce me, his?

MOSCA   'Tis true.

CORBACCIO   This plot
Did I thinke on before.

110 MOSCA   I doe beleeve it.

CORBACCIO   Doe you not beleeve it?

MOSCA   Yes, sir.

CORBACCIO   Mine owne project.

MOSCA   Which when he hath done, sir—

CORBACCIO   Publish'd me his heire?

MOSCA   And you so certayne, to survive him—

CORBACCIO   I.

MOSCA   Being so lusty a man—

CORBACCIO   'Tis true.

MOSCA   Yes, sir—

CORBACCIO I thought on that too. See, how he should be
    The very organ, to expresse my thoughts!

MOSCA You have not onely done your selfe a good—

CORBACCIO But multiplyed it on my sonne?

MOSCA   'Tis right, sir.

CORBACCIO Still, my invention.

MOSCA   'Lasse sir, heaven knowes,
    It hath beene all my studie, all my care,   120
    (I e'ene grow grey withall) how to worke things—

CORBACCIO I doe conceive, sweet MOSCA.

MOSCA   You are he,
    For whom I labour, here.

CORBACCIO   I, doe, doe, doe:
    I'le straight about it.

MOSCA   Rooke goe with you, raven.

CORBACCIO I know thee honest.

MOSCA   You doe lie, sir—

CORBACCIO   And—

MOSCA Your knowledge is no better then your eares, sir.

CORBACCIO I doe not doubt, to be a father to thee.

MOSCA Nor I, to gull my brother of his blessing.

CORBACCIO I may ha' my youth restor'd to me, why not?

MOSCA Your worship is a precious asse—

CORBACCIO   What say'st thou?   130

MOSCA I doe desire your worship, to make haste, sir.

CORBACCIO 'Tis done, 'tis done, I goe.   [*Exit.*]

VOLPONE   O, I shall burst;
    Let out my sides, let out my sides—

MOSCA   Contayne
    Your fluxe of laughter, sir: you know, this hope
    Is such a bait, it covers any hooke.

VOLPONE O, but thy working, and thy placing it!
    I cannot hold; good rascall, let me kisse thee:
    I never knew thee, in so rare a humour.

MOSCA Alas, sir, I but doe, as I am taught;

140   Follow your grave instructions; give 'hem wordes;
         Powre oyle into their eares: and send them hence.
VOLPONE 'Tis true, 'tis true. What a rare punishment
         Is avarice, to it selfe?
MOSCA   I, with our helpe, sir.
VOLPONE So many cares, so many maladies,
         So many feares attending on old age,
         Yea, death so often call'd on, as no wish
         Can be more frequent with 'hem, their limbs faint,
         Their senses dull, their seeing, hearing, going,
         All dead before them; yea, their very teeth,
150   Their instruments of eating, fayling them:
         Yet this is reckon'd life! Nay, here was one,
         Is now gone home, that wishes to live longer!
         Feeles not his gout, nor palsie, faines himselfe
         Yonger, by scores of yeeres, flatters his age,
         With confident belying it, hopes he may
         With charmes, like AESON, have his youth restor'd:
         And with these thoughts so battens, as if fate
         Would be as easily cheated on, as he,

Another And all turnes aire! Who's that, there, now? a third?
knocks. MOSCA Close, to your couch againe: I heare his voyce.
161   It is CORVINO, our spruce Merchant.
VOLPONE   Dead.
MOSCA Another bout, sir, with your eyes. Who's there?

Act I. Scene 5

MOSCA, CORVINO, VOLPONE.

[*Enter* CORVINO.]
MOSCA Signior CORVINO! come most wisht for! O,
       How happy were you, if you knew it, now!
CORVINO Why? what? wherein?
MOSCA   The tardie houre is come, sir.
CORVINO He is not dead?
MOSCA   Not dead, sir, but as good;

He knowes no man.

CORVINO   How shall I doe, then?

MOSCA   Why, sir?

CORVINO I have brought him, here, a pearle.

MOSCA   Perhaps, he has

So much remembrance left, as to know you, sir;

He still calls on you, nothing but your name

Is in his mouth: Is your pearle orient, sir?

CORVINO *Venice* was never owner of the like.   10

VOLPONE Signior CORVINO.

MOSCA   Harke.

VOLPONE   Signior CORVINO.

MOSCA He calls you, step and give it him. H'is here, sir,

And he has brought you a rich pearle.

CORVINO   How doe you, sir?

Tell him, it doubles the twelfe *caract*.

MOSCA   Sir,

He cannot understand, his hearing's gone;

And yet it comforts him, to see you—

CORVINO   Say,

I have a diamant for him, too.

MOSCA   Best shew 't, sir,

Put it into his hand; 'tis onely there

He apprehends: he has his feeling, yet.

See, how he grasps it!

CORVINO   'Lasse, good gentleman!   20

How pittifull the sight is!

MOSCA   Tut, forget, sir.

The weeping of an heire should still be laughter,

Under a visor.

CORVINO   Why? am I his heire?

MOSCA Sir, I am sworne, I may not shew the will,

Till he be dead: But, here has beene CORBACCIO,

Here has beene VOLTORE, here were others too,

I cannot number 'hem, they were so many,

All gaping here for legacies; but I,

Taking the vantage of his naming you,

30   (Signior CORVINO, Signior CORVINO) tooke
            Paper, and pen, and inke, and there I ask'd him,
            Whom he would have his heire? CORVINO. Who
            Should be executor? CORVINO. And,
            To any question, he was silent too,
            I still interpreted the nods, he made
            (Through weakenesse) for consent: and sent home th'others,
            Nothing bequeath'd them, but to crie, and curse.

They embrace.   CORVINO O, my deare MOSCA. Do's he not perceive us?

            MOSCA No more then a blind harper. He knowes no man,
40   No face of friend, nor name of any servant,
            Who 't was that fed him last, or gave him drinke:
            Not those, he hath begotten, or brought up
            Can he remember.

            CORVINO   Has he children?

            MOSCA   Bastards,
            Some dozen, or more, that he begot on beggers,
            Gipseys, and *Jewes*, and black-*moores*, when he was drunke.
            Knew you not that, sir? 'Tis the common fable.
            The Dwarfe, the Foole, the Eunuch are all his;
            H' is the true father of his family,
            In all, save me: but he has giv'n 'hem nothing.

50   CORVINO That's well, that's well. Art sure he does not heare us?

            MOSCA Sure, sir? why, looke you, credit your owne sense.
            The poxe approch, and adde to your diseases,
            If it would send you hence the sooner, sir.
            For, your incontinence, it hath deserv'd it
            Throughly, and throughly, and the plague to boot.
            (You may come neere, sir) would you would once close
            Those filthy eyes of yours, that flow with slime,
            Like two frog-pits; and those same hanging cheeks,
            Cover'd with hide, in stead of skin: (nay, helpe, sir)
60   That looke like frozen dish-clouts, set on end.

            CORVINO Or, like an old smok'd wall, on which the raine
            Ran downe in streakes.

            MOSCA   Excellent, sir, speake out;
            You may be lowder yet: a culvering,
            Discharged in his eare, would hardly bore it.

CORVINO His nose is like a common sewre, still running.

MOSCA 'Tis good! and, what his mouth?

CORVINO   A very draught.

MOSCA O, stop it up—

CORVINO   By no meanes.

MOSCA   'Pray you let me.

   Faith, I could stifle him, rarely, with a pillow,

   As well, as any woman, that should keepe him.

CORVINO Doe as you will, but I'le be gone.

MOSCA   Be so;   70

It is your presence makes him last so long.

CORVINO I pray you, use no violence.

MOSCA   No, sir? why?

   Why should you be thus scrupulous? 'pray you, sir.

CORVINO Nay, at your discretion.

MOSCA   Well, good sir, be gone.

CORVINO I will not trouble him now, to take my pearle?

MOSCA Puh, nor your diamant. What a needlesse care

   Is this afflicts you? Is not all, here, yours?

   Am not I here? whom you have made? your creature?

   That owe my being to you?

CORVINO   Gratefull MOSCA!

   Thou art my friend, my fellow, my companion,   80

   My partner, and shalt share in all my fortunes.

MOSCA Excepting one.

CORVINO   What's that?

MOSCA   Your gallant wife, sir.

                      [*Exit* CORVINO.]

   Now, is he gone: we had no other meanes,

   To shoot him hence, but this.

VOLPONE   My divine MOSCA!

   Thou hast to day out-gone thy selfe. Who's there?   *Another*

   I will be troubled with no more. Prepare   *knocks.*

   Me musicke, dances, banquets, all delights;

   The *Turke* is not more sensuall, in his pleasures,

   Then will VOLPONE. [*Exit* MOSCA.] Let mee see, a pearle?

   A diamant? plate? *cecchines*? good mornings purchase;   90

   Why, this is better then rob churches, yet:

Or fat, by eating (once a mon'th) a man.
   [*Enter* MOSCA.]
Who is't?

MOSCA   The beauteous lady WOULD-BEE, sir,
Wife, to the *English* Knight, Sir POLITIQUE WOULD-BEE,
(This is the stile, sir, is directed mee)
Hath sent to know, how you have slept to night,
And if you would be visited.

VOLPONE   Not, now.
Some three houres, hence—

MOSCA   I told the Squire, so much.

VOLPONE When I am high with mirth, and wine: then, then.
100   'Fore heaven, I wonder at the desperate valure
Of the bold *English*, that they dare let loose
Their wives, to all encounters!

MOSCA   Sir, this knight
Had not his name for nothing, he is politique,
And knowes, how ere his wife affect strange aires,
Shee hath not yet the face, to be dishonest.
But, had shee signior CORVINO's wives face—

VOLPONE Has shee so rare a face?

MOSCA   O, sir, the wonder,
The blazing starre of *Italie*! a wench
O' the first yeere! a beautie, ripe, as harvest!
110   Whose skin is whiter then a swan, all over!
Then silver, snow, or lillies! a soft lip,
Would tempt you to eternitie of kissing!
And flesh, that melteth, in the touch, to bloud!
Bright as your gold! and lovely, as your gold!

VOLPONE Why had not I knowne this, before?

MOSCA   Alas, sir.
My selfe, but yesterday, discover'd it.

VOLPONE How might I see her?

MOSCA   O, not possible;
Shee's kept as warily, as is your gold:
Never do's come abroad, never takes ayre,
120   But at a windore. All her lookes are sweet,
As the first grapes, or cherries: and are watch'd

As neere, as they are.

VOLPONE   I must see her—

MOSCA   Sir.

There is a guard, of ten spies thick, upon her;
All his whole houshold: each of which is set
Upon his fellow, and have all their charge,
When he goes out, when he comes in, examin'd.

VOLPONE I will goe see her, though but at her windore.

MOSCA In some disguise, then.

VOLPONE   That is true. I must

Maintayne mine owne shape, still, the same: wee'll thinke.

                                        [*Exeunt.*]

Act II. Scene 1

POLITIQUE WOULD-BEE, PEREGRINE.

[*Enter* SIR POLITIQUE *and* PEREGRINE.]

SIR POLITIQUE Sir, to a wise man, all the world's his soile.
It is not *Italie*, nor *France*, nor *Europe*,
That must bound me, if my fates call me forth.
Yet, I protest, it is no salt desire
Of seeing countries, shifting a religion,
Nor any dis-affection to the state
Where I was bred (and, unto which I owe
My dearest plots) hath brought me out; much lesse,
That idle, antique, stale, grey-headed project
Of knowing mens minds, and manners, with ULYSSES: 10
But, a peculiar humour of my wives,
Laid for this height of *Venice*, to observe,
To quote, to learne the language, and so forth—
I hope you travell, sir, with licence?

PEREGRINE   Yes.

SIR POLITIQUE I dare the safelier converse— How long, sir,
Since you left *England*?

PEREGRINE   Seven weekes.

SIR POLITIQUE   So lately!
You ha' not beene with my lord Ambassador?

PEREGRINE Not yet, sir.

SIR POLITIQUE 'Pray you, what newes, sir, vents our climate?
I heard, last night, a most strange thing reported
By some of my lords followers, and I long
To heare, how 't will be seconded!

PEREGRINE What was't, sir?

SIR POLITIQUE Mary, sir, of a raven, that should build
In a ship royall of the Kings.

PEREGRINE This fellow
Do's he gull me, trow? or is gull'd? your name, sir?

SIR POLITIQUE My name is POLITIQUE WOULD-BEE.

PEREGRINE O, that speaks him.
A Knight, sir?

SIR POLITIQUE A poore knight, sir.

PEREGRINE Your lady
Lies here, in *Venice*, for intelligence
Of tyres, and fashions, and behaviour,
Among the curtizans? the fine lady WOULD-BEE?

SIR POLITIQUE Yes, sir, the spider, and the bee, oft-times,
Suck from one flowre.

PEREGRINE Good sir POLITIQUE!
I cry you mercie; I have heard much of you:
'Tis true, sir, of your raven.

SIR POLITIQUE On your knowledge?

PEREGRINE Yes, and your lyons whelping, in the *Tower*.

SIR POLITIQUE Another whelpe!

PEREGRINE Another, sir.

SIR POLITIQUE Now, heaven!
What prodigies be these? The fires at *Berwike*!
And the new starre! these things concurring, strange!
And full of omen! Saw you those meteors?

PEREGRINE I did, sir.

SIR POLITIQUE Fearefull! Pray you sir, confirme me,
Were there three porcpisces seene, above the bridge,
As they give out?

PEREGRINE Sixe, and a sturgeon, sir.

SIR POLITIQUE I am astonish'd!

PEREGRINE Nay, sir, be not so;

Ile tell you a greater prodigie, then these——

SIR POLITIQUE What should these things portend!

PEREGRINE   The verie day
   (Let me be sure) that I put forth from *London*,
   There was a whale discover'd, in the river,
   As high as *Woolvich*, that had waited there
   (Few know how manie mon'ths) for the subversion
   Of the *Stode*-Fleet.

SIR POLITIQUE   Is't possible? Beleeve it,
   'Twas either sent from *Spaine*, or the *Arch-dukes*!   50
   SPINOLA's whale, upon my life, my credit!
   Will they not leave these projects? Worthie sir,
   Some other newes.

PEREGRINE   Faith, STONE, the foole, is dead;
   And they doe lacke a taverne-foole, extremely.

SIR POLITIQUE Is MASS' STONE dead!

PEREGRINE   H'is dead, sir, why? I hope
   You thought him not immortall? O, this Knight
   (Were he well knowne) would be a precious thing
   To fit our *English* stage: He that should write
   But such a fellow, should be thought to faine
   Extremely, if not maliciously.

SIR POLITIQUE   STONE dead!   60

PEREGRINE Dead. Lord! how deeply, sir, you apprehend it?
   He was no kinsman to you?

SIR POLITIQUE   That I know of.
   Well! that same fellow was an unknowne foole.

PEREGRINE And yet you knew him, it seemes?

SIR POLITIQUE   I did so. Sir,
   I knew him one of the most dangerous heads
   Living within the state, and so I held him.

PEREGRINE Indeed, sir?

SIR POLITIQUE   While he liv'd, in action.
   He has receiv'd weekely intelligence,
   Upon my knowledge, out of the *low Countries*,
   (For all parts of the world) in cabages;   70
   And those dispens'd, againe, to' Ambassadors,
   In oranges, musk-melons, apricotes,

    Limons, pome-citrons, and such like: sometimes,

    In *Colchester*-oysters, and your *Selsey*-cockles.

PEREGRINE You make me wonder!

SIR POLITIQUE   Sir, upon my knowledge.

    Nay, I have observ'd him, at your publique ordinarie,

    Take his advertisement, from a traveller

    (A conceal'd states-man) in a trencher of meat:

    And, instantly, before the meale was done,

    Convey an answere in a tooth-pick.

80   PEREGRINE   Strange!

    How could this be, sir?

SIR POLITIQUE   Why, the meat was cut

    So like his character, and so laid, as he

    Must easily reade the cypher.

PEREGRINE   I have heard,

    He could not reade, sir.

SIR POLITIQUE   So, 'twas given out,

    (In politie) by those, that did imploy him:

    But he could read, and had your languages,

    And to't, as sound a noddle——

PEREGRINE   I have heard, sir,

    That your *Bab'ouns* were spies; and that they were

    A kind of subtle nation, neere to *China*.

90   SIR POLITIQUE I, I, your *Mamuluchi*. Faith, they had

    Their hand in a *French* plot, or two; but they

    Were so extremely given to women, as

    They made discovery of all: yet I

    Had my advises here (on wensday last)

    From one of their owne coat, they were return'd,

    Made their relations (as the fashion is)

    And now stand faire, for fresh imployment.

PEREGRINE   'Hart!

    This, sir POLL. will be ignorant of nothing.

    It seemes, sir, you know all?

SIR POLITIQUE   Not all, sir. But,

100   I have some generall notions; I doe love

    To note, and to observe: though I live out,

    Free from the active torrent, yet I'ld marke

The currents, and the passages of things,
For mine owne private use; and know the ebbes,
And flowes of state.
PEREGRINE   Beleeve it, sir, I hold
My selfe, in no small tie, unto my fortunes,
For casting me thus luckily, upon you;
Whose knowledge (if your bountie equall it)
May doe me great assistance, in instruction
For my behaviour, and my bearing, which   110
Is yet so rude, and raw—
SIR POLITIQUE   Why? came you forth
Emptie of rules, for travaile?
PEREGRINE   Faith, I had
Some common ones, from out that vulgar *grammar*,
Which he, that cry'd *Italian* to me, taught me.
SIR POLITIQUE Why, this it is, that spoiles all our brave blouds;
Trusting our hopefull gentrie unto pedants:
Fellowes of out-side, and mere barke. You seeme
To be a gentleman, of ingenuous race—
I not professe it, but my fate hath beene
To be, where I have beene consulted with,   120
In this high kind, touching some great mens sonnes,
Persons of bloud, and honour—
PEREGRINE   Who be these, sir?

Act II. Scene 2

MOSCA, POLITIQUE, PEREGRINE, VOLPONE, NANO, GREGE.

[*Enter* MOSCA *and* NANO.]
MOSCA Under that windore, there 't must be. The same.
SIR POLITIQUE Fellowes, to mount a banke! Did your instructer
In the deare tongues, never discourse to you
Of the *Italian* mountebankes?
PEREGRINE   Yes, sir.
SIR POLITIQUE   Why,
Here shall you see one.
PEREGRINE   They are quack-salvers,

Fellowes, that live by venting oyles, and drugs?

SIR POLITIQUE Was that the character he gave you of them?

PEREGRINE As I remember.

SIR POLITIQUE   Pitie his ignorance.
They are the onely-knowing men of *Europe*!
10   Great generall schollers, excellent phisicians,
Most admir'd states-men, profest favourites,
And cabinet-counsellors, to the greatest princes!
The onely languag'd-men, of all the world!

PEREGRINE And, I have heard, they are most lewd impostors;
Made all of termes, and shreds; no lesse belyers
Of great-mens favours, then their owne vile med'cines;
Which they will utter, upon monstrous othes:
Selling that drug, for two pence, ere they part,
Which they have valu'd at twelve crownes, before.

20   SIR POLITIQUE Sir, calumnies are answer'd best with silence:
Your selfe shall judge. Who is it mounts, my friends?

MOSCA SCOTO of *Mantua*, sir.

SIR POLITIQUE   Is't he? nay, then
I'le proudly promise, sir, you shall behold
Another man, then has beene phant'sied to you.
I wonder, yet, that he should mount his banke
Here, in this nooke, that has beene wont t'appeare
In face of the *piazza*! Here, he comes.

[*Enter* VOLPONE *and* GREGE.]

VOLPONE Mount, *Zany*.

GREGE   Follow, follow, follow, follow, follow.

SIR POLITIQUE See how the people follow him! h'is a man
30   May write 10000 crownes, in banke, here. Note,
Marke but his gesture: I doe use to observe
The state he keeps, in getting up!

PEREGRINE   'Tis worth it, sir.

VOLPONE *Most noble gent: and my worthy patrons, it may seeme strange, that
I, your* SCOTO MANTUANO, *who was ever wont to fixe my banke in face
of the publike* piazza, *neere the shelter of the* portico, *to the* procuratìa,
should, now (after eight months absence, from this illustrous city of Venice)
humbly retire my selfe, into an obscure nooke of the piazza.

SIR POLITIQUE Did not I, now, object the same?

PEREGRINE   Peace, sir.

VOLPONE *Let me tell you: I am not (as your* Lombard *proverb saith) cold
on my feet; or content to part with my commodities at a cheaper rate, then I*   40
*accustomed: looke not for it. Nor, that the calumnious reports of that impudent
detractor, and shame to our profession,* (ALESSANDRO BUTTONE, *I
meane) who gave out, in publike, I was condemn'd a 'Sforzato to the galleys,
for poysoning the Cardinall* BEMBO'S—*Cooke, hath at all attached, much
lesse dejected me. No, no, worthy gent. (to tell you true) I cannot indure, to
see the rabble of these ground* Ciarlitani, *that spread their clokes on the
pavement, as if they meant to do feates of activitie, and then come in, lamely,
with their mouldy tales out of* BOCCACIO, *like stale* TABARINE, *the
Fabulist: some of them discoursing their travells, and of their tedious captivity
in the* Turkes *galleyes, when indeed (were the truth knowne) they*   50
*were the Christians galleyes, where very temperately, they eate bread, and
drunke water, as a wholesome penance (enjoyn'd them by their Confessors)
for base pilferies.*

SIR POLITIQUE Note but his bearing, and contempt of these.

VOLPONE *These turdy-facy-nasty-paty-lousy-farticall rogues, with one poore
groats-worth of un-prepar'd antimony, finely wrapt up in severall 'scartoccios, are able, very well, to kill their twentie a weeke, and play; yet, these
meagre starv'd spirits, who have halfe stopt the organs of their mindes with
earthy appilations, want not their favourers among your shrivel'd, sallad-eating
artizans: who are over-joy'd, that they may have their halfe-pe'rth of physick,*   60
though it purge 'hem into another world, 't makes no matter.

SIR POLITIQUE Excellent! ha' you heard better language, sir?

VOLPONE *Well, let 'hem goe. And gentlemen, honorable gentlemen, know, that
for this time, our banke, being thus remov'd from the clamours of the* canaglia,
shall be the scene *of pleasure, and delight: For, I have nothing to sell, little,
or nothing to sell.*

SIR POLITIQUE I told you, sir, his end.

PEREGRINE   You did so, sir.

VOLPONE *I protest, I, and my sixe servants, are not able to make of this
precious liquor, so fast, as it is fetch'd away from my lodging, by gentlemen of
your city; strangers of the* terra-ferma; *worshipfull merchants; I, and senators*   70
*too: who, ever since my arrivall, have detayned me to their uses, by their
splendidous liberalities. And worthily. For, what availes your rich man to*

have his magazines *stuft with* moscadelli, *or of the purest grape, when his
physitians prescribe him (on paine of death) to drinke nothing but water,
cocted with* anise-seeds? *O, health! health! the blessing of the rich! the riches
of the poore! who can buy thee at too deare a rate, since there is no enjoying
this world, without thee? Be not then so sparing of your purses, honorable
gentlemen, as to abridge the naturall course of life*—

PEREGRINE You see his end?

SIR POLITIQUE   I, is't not good?

80   VOLPONE *For, when a humide fluxe, or catarrhe, by the mutability of aire,
falls from your head, into an arme, or shoulder, or any other part; take you
a duckat, or your* cecchine *of gold, and apply to the place affected: see, what
good effect it can worke. No, no, 'tis this blessed* unguento, *this rare
extraction, that hath only power to disperse all malignant humours, that
proceed, either of hot, cold, moist, or windy causes*—

PEREGRINE I would he had put in drie to.

SIR POLITIQUE   'Pray you, observe.

VOLPONE *To fortifie the most indigest, and crude stomack, I, were it of one,
that (through extreme weakenesse) vomited bloud, applying only a warme
napkin to the place, after the unction, and fricace; for the* vertigine, *in the*
90   *head, putting but a drop into your nostrills, likewise, behind the eares; a most
soveraigne, and approved remedie: the* mal-caduco, *crampes, convulsions,*
paralysies, epilepsies, tremor-cordia, *retyred-nerves, ill vapours of the spleene,
stoppings of the liver, the stone, the strangury,* hernia ventosa, iliaca passio;
stops a disenteria, *immediately; easeth the torsion of the small guts; and
cures* melancolia hypocondriaca, *being taken and applyed, according to
my printed receipt. For, this is the physitian, this the medicine; this counsells,*

*Pointing to his
bill and his
glasse.*

*this cures; this gives the direction, this workes the effect: and (in summe) both
together may bee term'd an abstract of the theorick, and practick in the*
Aesculapian *arte. 'Twill cost you eight crownes. And,* ZAN FRITADA,
100   *'pray thee sing a verse,* extempore, *in honour of it.*

SIR POLITIQUE How doe you like him, sir?

PEREGRINE   Most strangely, I!

SIR POLITIQUE Is not his language rare?

PEREGRINE   But *Alchimy*,
    I never heard the like: or BROUGHTONS bookes.

SONG.

NANO *Had old* HIPPOCRATES, *or* GALEN,
   (That to their bookes put med'cines all in)
   But knowne this secret, they had never
   (Of which they will be guiltie ever)
   Beene murderers of so much paper,
   Or wasted many a hurtlesse taper:
   No Indian *drug had ere beene famed,* 110
   Tabacco, sassafras not named;
   Ne yet, of guacum *one small stick, sir,*
   Nor RAYMUND LULLIES *great elixir.*
   Ne, had been knowne the Danish GONSWART.
   Or PARACELSUS, *with his long-sword.*

PEREGRINE All this, yet, will not doe, eight crownes is high.

VOLPONE *No more. Gentlemen, if I had but time to discourse to you the*
miraculous effects of this my oile, surnamed oglio del SCOTO; *with the*
count-lesse catalogue of those I have cured of th'aforesaid, and many more
diseases; the pattents and priviledges of all the Princes, and common-wealths 120
of Christendome; or but the depositions of those that appear'd on my part,
before the signiory *of the* Sanitâ, *and most learned colledge of physitians;*
where I was authorized, upon notice taken of the admirable vertues of my
medicaments, and mine owne excellency, in matter of rare, and unknowne
secrets, not onely to disperse them publiquely in this famous citie, but in all
the territories, that happily joy under the governement of the most pious and
magnificent states of Italy. *But may some other gallant fellow say, O, there*
be divers, that make profession to have as good, and as experimented receipts,
as yours: Indeed, very many have assay'd, like apes in imitation of that, which
is really and essentially in mee, to make of this oyle; bestow'd great cost in 130
furnaces, stilles, alembeks, continuall fires, and preparation of the ingredients,
(as indeede there goes to it sixe hundred severall simples, besides, some quantity
of humane fat, for the conglutination, which we buy of the anatomistes) but,
when these practitioners come to the last decoction, blow, blow, puff, puff, and
all flies in fumo: *ha, ha, ha. Poore wretches! I rather pittie their folly, and*
indiscretion, then their losse of time, and money; for those may be recovered
by industrie: but to bee a foole borne, is a disease incurable. For my selfe, I
alwaies from my youth have indevour'd to get the rarest secrets, and booke
them; either in exchange, or for money: I spared nor cost, nor labour, where

140   *any thing was worthy to bee learned. And gentlemen, honourable gentlemen,*
I will undertake (by vertue of chymicall art) out of the honourable hat, that
covers your head, to extract the foure elements; that is to say, the fire, ayre,
water, and earth, and returne you your felt without burne, or staine. For,
whil'st others have beene at the balloo, *I have beene at my booke: and am*
now past the craggie pathes of studie, and come to the flowrie plaines of honour,
and reputation.

SIR POLITIQUE   I doe assure you, sir, that is his ayme.

VOLPONE *But, to our price.*

PEREGRINE   And that withall, sir POL.

VOLPONE *You all know (honourable gentlemen) I never valu'd this* ampulla,
150   *or viall, at lesse then eight crownes, but for this time, I am content, to be*
depriv'd of it for sixe; sixe crownes is the price; and lesse in courtesie, I know
you cannot offer me: take it, or leave it, howsoever, both it, and I, am at your
service. I aske you not, as the value of the thing, for then I should demand of
you a thousand crownes, so the Cardinals MONTALTO, FERNESE, *the*
great duke of Tuscany, *my gossip, with divers other princes have given me;*
but I despise money: onely to shew my affection to you, honourable gentlemen,
and your illustrous state here, I have neglected the messages of these princes,
mine owne offices, fram'd my journey hither, onely to present you with the
fruits of my travels. Tune your voices once more to the touch of your instruments,
160   *and give the honourable assembly some delightfull recreation.*

PEREGRINE What monstrous, and most painefull circumstance
Is here, to get some three, or foure *gazets*!
Some three-pence, i'th' whole, for that 'twill come to.

SONG.

NANO   *You that would last long, list to my song,*
                  Make no more coyle, but buy of this oyle.
                  Would you be ever faire? and yong?
                  Stout of teeth? and strong of tongue?
                  Tart of palat? quick of eare?
                  Sharpe of sight? of nostrill cleare?
170   *Moist of hand? and light of foot?*
                  (Or I will come neerer to't)
                  Would you live free from all diseases?

> *Doe the act, your mistris pleases;*
> *Yet fright all aches from your bones?*
> *Here's a med'cine, for the nones.*

VOLPONE   Well, I am in a humour (at this time) to make a present of the
small quantitie my coffer containes: to the rich, in courtesie, and to the poore,
for Gods sake. Wherefore, now marke; I ask'd you sixe crownes; and sixe
crownes, at other times, you have paid me; you shall not give me sixe crownes,
nor five, nor foure, nor three, nor two, nor one; nor halfe a duckat; no, nor a   180
muccinigo: sixe—pence it will cost you, or sixe hundred pound—expect
no lower price, for by the banner of my front, I will not bate a bagatine, that
I will have, only, a pledge of your loves, to carry something from amongst you,
to shew, I am not contemn'd by you. Therefore, now, tosse your handkerchiefes,
chearefully, chearefully; and be advertised, that the first heroique spirit, that
deignes to grace me, with a handkerchiefe, I will give it a little remembrance
of something, beside, shall please it better, then if I had presented it with a
double pistolet.   188

PEREGRINE   Will you be that heroique sparke, sir POL?   *CELIA at the*
O, see! the windore has prevented you.   *windo' throwes*
                                                                                          downe her
VOLPONE   *Lady, I kisse your bountie: and, for this timely grace, you have done*   *handkerchiefe.*
your poore SCOTO *of Mantua, I will returne you, over and above my oile,*
a secret, of that high, and inestimable nature, shall make you for ever enamour'd
on that minute, wherein your eye first descended on so meane, (yet not altogether
to be despis'd) an object. Here is a poulder, conceal'd in this paper, of which,
if I should speake to the worth, nine thousand volumes were but as one page,
that page as a line, that line as a word: so short is this pilgrimage of man
(which some call life) to the expressing of it. Would I reflect on the price? why,
the whole world were but as an empire, that empire as a province, that province
as a banke, that banke as a private purse, to the purchase of it. I will, onely,   200
tell you; It is the poulder, that made VENUS *a goddesse (given her by*
APOLLO) *that kept her perpetually yong, clear'd her wrincles, firm'd her*
gummes, fill'd her skin, colour'd her haire; from her, deriv'd to HELEN, *and*
at the sack of Troy *(unfortunately) lost: till now, in this our age, it was as*
happily recover'd, by a studious Antiquarie, out of some ruines of Asia, who
sent a moyetie of it, to the court of France *(but much sophisticated) wherewith*
the ladies there, now, colour their haire. The rest (at this present) remaines

with me; extracted, to a quintessence: so that, where ever it but touches, in
youth it perpetually preserves, in age restores the complexion; seat's your teeth,
210   did they dance like virginall jacks, firme as a wall; makes them white, as
ivory, that were black, as—

Act II. Scene 3

CORVINO, POLITIQUE, PEREGRINE.

[*Enter* CORVINO.]

He beates away   CORVINO Spight o' the devill, and my shame! come downe, here;
the monte-   Come downe: no house but mine to make your *scene*?
banke etc.   Signior FLAMINIO, will you downe, sir? downe?
     What is my wife your FRANCISCINA? sir?
     No windores on the whole *piazza*, here,
     To make your properties, but mine? but mine?
     Hart! ere to morrow, I shall be new christen'd,
     And cald the PANTALONE *di besogniosi*,
     About the towne.   [*Exit.*]

PEREGRINE   What should this meane, sir POL?

10   SIR POLITIQUE Some trick of state, beleeve it. I will home.

PEREGRINE It may be some designe, on you.

SIR POLITIQUE   I know not.
     I'le stand upon my guard.

PEREGRINE   It is your best, sir.

SIR POLITIQUE This three weekes, all my advises, all my letters,
     They have been intercepted.

PEREGRINE   Indeed, sir?
     Best have a care.

SIR POLITIQUE   Nay, so I will.

PEREGRINE   This knight,
     I may not lose him, for my mirth, till night.   [*Exeunt.*]

Act II. Scene 4

VOLPONE, MOSCA.

[*Enter* VOLPONE *and* MOSCA.]

VOLPONE O, I am wounded.

MOSCA   Where, sir?

VOLPONE   Not without;
Those blowes were nothing: I could beare them ever.
But angry CUPID, bolting from her eyes,
Hath shot himselfe into me, like a flame;
Where, now, he flings about his burning heat,
As in a fornace, an ambitious fire,
Whose vent is stopt. The fight is all within me.
I cannot live, except thou helpe me, MOSCA;
My liver melts, and I, without the hope
Of some soft aire, from her refreshing breath,   10
Am but a heape of cinders.

MOSCA   'Lasse, good sir!
Would you had never seene her.

VOLPONE   Nay, would thou
Had'st never told me of her.

MOSCA   Sir, 'tis true;
I doe confesse, I was unfortunate,
And you unhappy: but I'am bound in conscience,
No lesse then duty, to effect my best
To your release of torment, and I will, sir.

VOLPONE Deare MOSCA, shall I hope?

MOSCA   Sir, more then deare,
I will not bid you to despaire of ought,
Within a humane compasse.

VOLPONE   O, there spoke   20
My better Angell. MOSCA, take my keyes,
Gold, plate, and jewells, all's at thy devotion;
Employ them, how thou wilt; nay, coyne me, too:
So thou, in this, but crowne my longings. MOSCA?

MOSCA Use but your patience.

VOLPONE   So I have.

MOSCA   I doubt not

  To bring successe to your desires.

VOLPONE   Nay, then,

  I not repent me of my late disguise.

MOSCA If you can horne him, sir, you need not.

VOLPONE   True:

  Besides, I never meant him for my heire.

30   Is not the colour o' my beard, and eye-browes,

  To make me knowne?

MOSCA   No jot.

VOLPONE   I did it well.

MOSCA So well, would I could follow you in mine,

  With halfe the happinesse; and, yet, I would

  Escape your *epilogue*.

VOLPONE   But, were they gull'd

  With a beliefe, that I was SCOTO?

MOSCA   Sir,

  SCOTO himselfe could hardly have distinguish'd!

  I have not time to flatter you, now, wee'll part:

  And, as I prosper, so applaud my art.   [*Exeunt.*]

Act II. Scene 5

CORVINO, CELIA, SERVITORE.

[*Enter* CORVINO *and* CELIA.]

CORVINO Death of mine honour, with the cities foole?

  A juggling, tooth-drawing, prating mountebanke?

  And, at a publike windore? where whil'st he,

  With his strain'd action, and his dole of faces,

  To his drug-lecture drawes your itching eares,

  A crue of old, un-marri'd, noted lechers,

  Stood leering up, like *Satyres*: and you smile,

  Most graciously! and fan your favours forth,

  To give your hot spectators satisfaction!

10   What, was your mountebanke their call? their whistle?

Or were you'enamour'd on his copper rings?
His saffron jewell, with the toade-stone in't?
Or his imbroidred sute, with the cope-stitch,
Made of a herse-cloth? or his old tilt-feather?
Or his starch'd beard? well! you shall have him, yes.
He shall come home, and minister unto you
The fricace, for the moother. Or, let me see,
I thinke, you'had rather mount? would you not mount?
Why, if you'll mount, you may; yes truely, you may:
And so, you may be seene, downe to th' foot.   20
Get you a citterne, lady *vanitie*,
And be a dealer, with the vertuous man;
Make one: I'le but protest my selfe a cuckold,
And save your dowrie. I am a *Dutchman*, I!
For, if you thought me an *Italian*,
You would be damn'd, ere you did this, you whore:
Thou'ldst tremble, to imagine, that the murder
Of father, mother, brother, all thy race,
Should follow, as the subject of my justice!

CELIA Good sir, have patience!

CORVINO   What could'st thou propose   30
Lesse to thy selfe, then, in this heat of wrath,
And stung with my dishonour, I should strike
This steele into thee, with as many stabs,
As thou wert gaz'd upon with goatish eyes?

CELIA Alasse sir, be appeas'd! I could not thinke
My being at the windore should more, now,
Move your impatience, then at other times.

CORVINO No? not to seeke, and entertaine a parlee,
With a knowne knave? before a multitude?
You were an actor, with your handkerchiefe!   40
Which he, most sweetly, kist in the receipt,
And might (no doubt) returne it, with a letter,
And point the place, where you might meet: your sisters,
Your mothers, or your aunts might serve the turne.

CELIA Why, deare sir, when doe I make these excuses?
Or ever stirre, abroad, but to the church?
And that, so seldome—

CORVINO   Well, it shall be lesse;
                  And thy restraint, before, was libertie,
                  To what I now decree: and therefore, marke me.
50   First, I will have this bawdy light dam'd up;
                  And, til 't be done, some two, or three yards off,
                  I'le chalke a line: o're which, if thou but chance
                  To set thy desp'rate foot; more hell, more horror,
                  More wilde, remorcelesse rage shall seize on thee,
                  Then on a conjurer, that, had heedlesse left
                  His circles safetie, ere his devill was laid.
                  Then, here's a locke, which I will hang upon thee;
                  And, now I thinke on't, I will keepe thee backe-wards;
                  Thy lodging shall be backe-wards; thy walkes back-wards;
60   Thy prospect—all be backe-wards; and no pleasure,
                  That thou shalt know, but backe-wards: Nay, since you force
                  My honest nature, know, it is your owne
                  Being too open, makes me use you thus.
                  Since you will not containe your subtle nostrils
                  In a sweet roome, but they must snuffe the ayre
Knocke within. Of ranke, and sweatie passengers — One knockes.
                  Away, and be not seene, paine of thy life;
                  Not looke toward the windore: if thou dost—
                  (Nay stay, heare this) let me not prosper, whore,
70   But I will make thee an anatomie,
                  Dissect thee mine owne selfe, and read a lecture
                  Upon thee, to the citie, and in publique.
                  Away. [*Exit* CELIA.] Who's there?
                     [*Enter* SERVITORE.]
SERVITORE   'Tis signior MOSCA, sir.

Act II. Scene 6
CORVINO, MOSCA.

CORVINO Let him come in, [*Exit* SERVITORE.] his master's dead:
         There's yet
         Some good, to helpe the bad. [*Enter* MOSCA.] My MOSCA,
         welcome,

I ghesse your newes.

MOSCA   I feare you cannot, sir.

CORVINO Is't not his death?

MOSCA   Rather the contrarie.

CORVINO Not his recoverie?

MOSCA   Yes, sir.

CORVINO   I am curst,
I am bewitch'd, my crosses meet to vex me.
How? how? how? how?

MOSCA   Why, sir, with SCOTO's oyle!
CORBACCIO, and VOLTORE brought of it,
Whil'st I was busie in an inner roome—

CORVINO Death! that damn'd mountebanke! but, for the law,   10
Now, I could kill the raskall: 't cannot be,
His oyle should have that vertue. Ha' not I
Knowne him a common rogue, come fidling in
To th'*osteria*, with a tumbling whore,
And, when he ha's done all his forc'd trickes, beene glad
Of a poore spoonefull of dead wine, with flyes in't?
It cannot be. All his ingredients
Are a sheepes gall, a rosted bitches marrow,
Some few sod earewigs, pounded caterpillers,
A little capons grease, and fasting spittle: 20
I know 'hem, to a dram.

MOSCA   I know not, sir,
But some on't, there they powr'd into his eares,
Some in his nostrils, and recover'd him;
Applying but the fricace.

CORVINO   Pox o' that fricace.

MOSCA And since, to seeme the more officious,
And flatt'ring of his health, there, they have had
(At extreme fees) the colledge of physicians
Consulting on him, how they might restore him;
Where, one would have a cataplasme of spices,
Another, a flayd ape clapt to his brest,   30
A third would ha' it a dogge, a fourth an oyle
With wild cats skinnes: at last, they all resolv'd
That, to preserve him, was no other meanes,

But some yong woman must be streight sought out,
Lustie, and full of juice, to sleepe by him;
And, to this service (most unhappily,
And most unwillingly) am I now imploy'd,
Which, here, I thought to pre-acquaint you with,
For your advice, since it concernes you most,
40 Because, I would not doe that thing might crosse
Your ends, on whom I have my whole dependance, sir:
Yet, if I doe it not, they may delate
My slacknesse to my patron, worke me out
Of his opinion; and there, all your hopes,
Venters, or whatsoever, are all frustrate.
I doe but tell you, sir. Besides, they are all
Now striving, who shall first present him. Therefore—
I could intreat you, briefly, conclude some-what:
Prevent 'hem if you can.

CORVINO   Death to my hopes!
50 This is my villanous fortune! Best to hire
Some common curtezan?

MOSCA   I, I thought on that, sir.
But they are all so subtle, full of art,
And age againe doting, and flexible,
So as—I cannot tell—we may perchance
Light on a queane, may cheat us all.

CORVINO   'Tis true.

MOSCA No, no: it must be one, that ha's no trickes, sir,
Some simple thing, a creature, made unto it;
Some wench you may command. Ha' you no kinswoman?
Gods so— Thinke, thinke, thinke, thinke, thinke, thinke, thinke,
        sir.
60 One o' the Doctors offer'd, there, his daughter.

CORVINO How!

MOSCA   Yes, signior LUPO, the physician.

CORVINO His daughter?

MOSCA   And a virgin, sir. Why? Alasse
He knowes the state of 's bodie, what it is;
That nought can warme his bloud, sir, but a fever;
Nor any incantation rayse his spirit:

A long forgetfulnesse hath seiz'd that part.
Besides, sir, who shall know it? some one, or two—
CORVINO I pray thee give me leave. If any man
    But I had had this lucke— The thing in't selfe,
    I know, is nothing— Wherefore should not I   70
    As well command my bloud, and my affections,
    As this dull Doctor? In the point of honour,
    The cases are all one, of wife, and daughter.
MOSCA I heare him comming.
CORVINO   Shee shall doo't: 'Tis done.
    Slight, if this Doctor, who is not engag'd,
    Unlesse 't be for his counsell (which is nothing)
    Offer his daughter, what should I, that am
    So deeply in? I will prevent him: wretch!
    Covetous wretch! MOSCA, I have determin'd.
MOSCA How, sir?
CORVINO   We'll make all sure. The party, you wot of,   80
    Shall be mine owne wife, MOSCA.
MOSCA   Sir. The thing,
    (But that I would not seeme to counsell you)
    I should have motion'd to you, at the first:
    And, make your count, you have cut all their throtes.
    Why! 'tis directly taking a possession!
    And, in his next fit, we may let him goe.
    'Tis but to pull the pillow, from his head,
    And he is thratled: 't had beene done, before,
    But for your scrupulous doubts.
CORVINO   I, a plague on't,
    My conscience fooles my wit. Well, I'le be briefe,   90
    And so be thou, lest they should be before us;
    Goe home, prepare him, tell him, with what zeale,
    And willingnesse, I doe it: sweare it was,
    On the first hearing (as thou maist doe, truely)
    Mine owne free motion.
MOSCA   Sir, I warrant you,
    I'le so possesse him with it, that the rest
    Of his starv'd clients shall be banisht, all;
    And onely you receiv'd. But come not, sir,

Untill I send, for I have some-thing else

100   To ripen, for your good (you must not know't)

CORVINO But doe not you forget to send, now.

MOSCA   Feare not.   [*Exit.*]

Act II. Scene 7

CORVINO, CELIA.

CORVINO Where are you, wife? my CELIA? [*Enter* CELIA.] wife?
       what, blubbering?

    Come, drie those teares. I thinke, thou thought'st me in earnest?

    Ha? by this light, I talk'd so but to trie thee.

    Me thinkes, the lightnesse of the occasion

    Should ha' confirm'd thee. Come, I am not jealous.

CELIA No?

CORVINO   Faith, I am not, I, nor never was:

    It is a poore, unprofitable humour.

    Doe not I know, if women have a will,

    They'll doe 'gainst all the watches, o' the world?

10   And that the fiercest spies, are tam'd with gold?

    Tut, I am confident in thee, thou shalt see't:

    And see, I'le give thee cause too, to beleeve it.

    Come, kisse me. Goe, and make thee ready straight,

    In all thy best attire, thy choicest jewells,

    Put 'hem all on, and, with 'hem, thy best lookes:

    We are invited to a solemne feast,

    At old VOLPONE's, where it shall appeare

    How far I am free, from jealousie, or feare.   [*Exeunt.*]

Act III. Scene 1

MOSCA.

[*Enter* MOSCA.]

[MOSCA] I feare, I shall begin to grow in love

    With my deare selfe, and my most prosp'rous parts,

    They doe so spring, and burgeon; I can feele

A whimsey i' my bloud: (I know not how)
Successe hath made me wanton. I could skip
Out of my skin, now, like a subtill snake,
I am so limber. O! Your Parasite
Is a most precious thing, dropt from above,
Not bred 'mong'st clods, and clot-poules, here on earth.
I muse, the mysterie was not made a science,   10
It is so liberally profest! almost
All the wise world is little else, in nature,
But Parasites, or Sub-parasites. And, yet,
I meane not those, that have your bare towne-arte,
To know, who's fit to feede 'hem; have no house,
No family, no care, and therefore mould
Tales for mens eares, to bait that sense; or get
Kitchin-invention, and some stale receipts
To please the belly, and the groine; nor those,
With their court-dog-tricks, that can fawne, and fleere,   20
Make their revennue out of legs, and faces,
Eccho my-Lord, and lick away a moath:
But your fine, elegant rascall, that can rise,
And stoope (almost together) like an arrow;
Shoot through the aire, as nimbly as a starre;
Turne short, as doth a swallow; and be here,
And there, and here, and yonder, all at once;
Present to any humour, all occasion;
And change a visor, swifter, then a thought!
This is the creature, had the art borne with him;   30
Toiles not to learne it, but doth practise it
Out of most excellent nature: and such sparkes,
Are the true Parasites, others but their *Zani's*.

Act III. Scene 2

MOSCA, BONARIO.

[*Enter* BONARIO.]

MOSCA Who's this? BONARIO? old CORBACCIO's sonne?
   The person I was bound to seeke. Faire sir,

    You are happ'ly met.

BONARIO   That cannot be, by thee.

MOSCA Why, sir?

BONARIO   Nay, 'pray thee know thy way, & leave me:
    I would be loth to inter-change discourse,
    With such a mate, as thou art.

MOSCA   Courteous sir,
    Scorne not my povertie.

BONARIO   Not I, by heaven:
    But thou shalt give me leave to hate thy basenesse.

MOSCA Basenesse?

BONARIO   I, answere me, is not thy sloth
10   Sufficient argument? thy flatterie?
    Thy meanes of feeding?

MOSCA   Heaven, be good to me.
    These imputations are too common, sir,
    And eas'ly stuck on vertue, when shee's poore;
    You are unequall to me, and how ere
    Your sentence may be righteous, yet you are not,
    That ere you know me, thus, proceed in censure:
    St. MARKE beare witnesse 'gainst you, 'tis inhumane.

BONARIO What? do's he weepe? the signe is soft, and good!
    I doe repent me, that I was so harsh.

20 MOSCA 'Tis true, that, sway'd by strong necessitie,
    I am enforc'd to eate my carefull bread
    With too much obsequie; 'tis true, beside,
    That I am faine to spin mine owne poore rayment,
    Out of my mere observance, being not borne
    To a free fortune: but that I have done
    Base offices, in rending friends asunder,
    Dividing families, betraying counsells,
    Whispering false lyes, or mining men with praises,
    Train'd their credulitie with perjuries,
30   Corrupted chastitie, or am in love
    With mine owne tender ease, but would not rather
    Prove the most rugged, and laborious course,
    That might redeeme my present estimation;

Let me here perish, in all hope of goodnesse.
BONARIO This cannot be a personated passion!
    I was to blame, so to mistake thy nature;
    'Pray thee forgive me: and speake out thy bus'nesse.
MOSCA Sir, it concernes you; and though I may seeme,
    At first, to make a maine offence, in manners,
    And in my gratitude, unto my master,   40
    Yet, for the pure love, which I beare all right,
    And hatred of the wrong, I must reveale it.
    This verie houre, your father is in purpose
    To disinherit you—
BONARIO   How!
MOSCA   And thrust you forth,
    As a mere stranger to his bloud; 'tis true, sir:
    The worke no way ingageth me, but, as
    I claime an interest in the generall state
    Of goodnesse, and true vertue, which I heare
    T'abound in you: and, for which mere respect,
    Without a second ayme, sir, I have done it.   50
BONARIO This tale hath lost thee much of the late trust,
    Thou hadst with me; it is impossible:
    I know not how to lend it any thought,
    My father should be so unnaturall.
MOSCA It is a confidence, that well becomes
    Your pietie; and form'd (no doubt) it is,
    From your owne simple innocence: which makes
    Your wrong more monstrous, and abhor'd. But, sir,
    I now, will tell you more. This verie minute,
    It is, or will be doing: And, if you   60
    Shall be but pleas'd to goe with me, I'le bring you,
    (I dare not say where you shall see, but) where
    Your eare shall be a witnesse of the deed;
    Heare your selfe written bastard: and profest
    The common issue of the earth.
BONARIO   I'm maz'd!
MOSCA Sir, if I doe it not, draw your just sword,
    And score your vengeance, on my front, and face;

Marke me your villaine: You have too much wrong,
And I doe suffer for you, sir. My heart
Weepes bloud, in anguish——

70 BONARIO   Lead. I follow thee.   [*Exeunt.*]

Act III. Scene 3

VOLPONE, NANO, ANDROGYNO, CASTRONE.

[*Enter* VOLPONE, NANO, ANDROGYNO *and* CASTRONE.]

VOLPONE MOSCA stayes long, me thinkes. Bring forth your sports
And helpe, to make the wretched time more sweet.

NANO *Dwarfe, Foole, and Eunuch, well met here we be.*
A question it were now, whether of us three,
Being, all, the knowne delicates of a rich man,
In pleasing him, claime the precedencie can?

CASTRONE *I claime for my selfe.*

ANDROGYNO   *And, so doth the foole.*

NANO *'Tis foolish indeed: let me set you both to schoole.*
First, for your dwarfe, hee's little, and wittie,
10   *And every thing, as it is little, is prittie;*
Else, why doe men say to a creature of my shape,
So soone as they see him, it's a pritty little ape?
And, why a pritty ape? but for pleasing imitation
Of greater mens action, in a ridiculous fashion.
Beside, this feat body of mine doth not crave
Halfe the meat, drinke, and cloth, one of your bulkes will have.
Admit, your fooles face be the mother of laughter,
Yet, for his braine, it must alwaies come after:
And, though that doe feed him, it's a pittifull case,
20   *His body is beholding to such a bad face.*

One knocks. VOLPONE Who's there? my couch, away, looke, NANO, see:
                                      [*Exit* NANO.]
Give me my cappes, first—— go, enquire. [*Exeunt* ANDROGYNO
        and CASTRONE.] Now, CUPID
Send it be MOSCA, and with faire returne.
        [*Enter* NANO.]

NANO It is the beauteous madam—

VOLPONE   WOULD-BE—is it?

NANO The same.

VOLPONE   Now, torment on me; squire her in: [*Exit* NANO.]
　　For she will enter, or dwell here for ever.
　　Nay, quickely, that my fit were past. I feare
　　A second hell too, that my loathing this
　　Will quite expell my appetite to the other:
　　Would shee were taking, now, her tedious leave.   30
　　Lord, how it threates me, what I am to suffer!

Act III. Scene 4

LADY, VOLPONE, NANO, WOMEN. 2.

[*Enter* LADY WOULD-BEE *and* NANO.]

LADY WOULD-BEE I thanke you, good sir. 'Pray you signifie
　　Unto your patron, I am here. This band
　　Shewes not my neck inough (I trouble you, sir,
　　Let me request you, bid one of my women
　　Come hither to me) [*Exit* NANO.] in good faith, I, am drest
　　Most favourably, to day, it is no matter,
　　'Tis well inough. [*Enter* NANO *and* 1ST WOMAN.] Looke, see,
　　　　these petulant things!
　　How they have done this!

VOLPONE   I do feele the fever
　　Entring, in at mine eares; o, for a charme,
　　To fright it hence.

LADY WOULD-BEE   Come neerer: is this curle   10
　　In his right place? or this? why is this higher
　　Then all the rest? you ha' not wash'd your eies, yet?
　　Or do they not stand even i' your head?
　　Where's your fellow? call her.   [*Exit* 1ST WOMAN.]

NANO   Now, St. MARKE
　　Deliver us: anon, shee'll beate her women,
　　Because her nose is red.

　　　　[*Enter* 1ST *and* 2ND WOMEN.]

LADY WOULD-BEE   I pray you, view
   This tire, forsooth: are all things apt, or no?
2ND WOMAN One haire a little, here, sticks out, forsooth.
LADY WOULD-BEE Do's 't so forsooth? and where was your deare
   sight
20   When it did so, forsooth? what now? bird-ey'd?
   And you, too? 'pray you both approch, and mend it.
   Now (by that light) I muse, yo' are not asham'd!
   I, that have preach'd these things, so oft, unto you,
   Read you the principles, argu'd all the grounds,
   Disputed every fitnesse, every grace,
   Call'd you to counsell of so frequent dressings —
(NANO More carefully, then of your fame, or honour)
LADY WOULD-BEE Made you acquainted, what an ample dowrie
   The knowledge of these things would be unto you,
30   Able, alone, to get you noble husbands
   At your returne: and you, thus, to neglect it?
   Besides, you seeing what a curious nation
   Th' *Italians* are, what will they say of me?
   The *English* lady cannot dresse her selfe;
   Here's a fine imputation, to our countrie!
   Well, goe your wayes, and stay, i' the next roome.
   This *fucus* was too course too, it's no matter.
   Good-sir, you'll give 'hem entertaynement?
                [*Exeunt* NANO *and* WOMEN.]
VOLPONE The storme comes toward me.
LADY WOULD-BEE   How do's my VOLP?
40 VOLPONE Troubled with noise, I cannot sleepe; I dreamt
   That a strange *furie* entred, now, my house,
   And, with the dreadfull tempest of her breath,
   Did cleave my roofe asunder.
LADY WOULD-BEE   Beleeve me, and I
   Had the most fearefull dreame, could I remember 't —
VOLPONE Out on my fate; I ha' giv'n her the occasion
   How to torment me: shee will tell me hers.
LADY WOULD-BEE Me thought, the golden mediocritie
   Polite, and delicate —
VOLPONE   O, if you doe love me,

No more; I sweat, and suffer, at the mention
Of any dreame: feele, how I tremble yet.   50
LADY WOULD-BEE Alas, good soule! the passion of the heart.
Seed-pearle were good now, boild with syrrope of apples,
Tincture of gold, and corrall, citron-pills,
Your elicampane roote, mirobalanes—
VOLPONE Ay me, I have tane a grasse-hopper by the wing.
LADY WOULD-BEE Burnt silke, and amber, you have muscadell
Good i' the house—
VOLPONE   You will not drinke, and part?
LADY WOULD-BEE No, feare not that. I doubt, we shall not get
Some *english* saffron (halfe a dram would serve)
Your sixteene cloves, a little muske, dri'd mints,   60
Buglosse, and barley-meale—
VOLPONE   Shee's in againe,
Before I fayn'd diseases, now I have one.
LADY WOULD-BEE And these appli'd, with a right scarlet-cloth—
VOLPONE Another floud of wordes! a very torrent!
LADY WOULD-BEE Shall I, sir, make you a poultise?
VOLPONE   No, no, no;
I' am very well: you need prescribe no more.
LADY WOULD-BEE I have, a little, studied physick; but, now,
I' am all for musique: save, i' the fore-noones,
An houre, or two, for painting. I would have
A lady, indeed, t'have all, letters, and artes,   70
Be able to discourse, to write, to paint,
But principall (as PLATO holds) your musique
(And, so do's wise PYTHAGORAS, I take it)
Is your true rapture; when there is concent
In face, in voyce, and clothes: and is, indeed,
Our sexes chiefest ornament.
VOLPONE   The Poet,
As old in time, as PLATO, and as knowing,
Say's that your highest female grace is silence.
LADY WOULD-BEE Which o' your Poets? PETRARCH? or TASSO?
or DANTE?
GUERRINI? ARIOSTO? ARETINE?   80
CIECO *di Hadria*? I have read them all.

VOLPONE Is everything a cause, to my destruction?

LADY WOULD-BEE I thinke, I ha' two or three of 'hem, about me.

VOLPONE The sunne, the sea will sooner, both, stand still,
Then her eternall tongue! nothing can scape it.

LADY WOULD-BEE Here's PASTOR FIDO——

VOLPONE   Professe obstinate silence,
That's, now, my safest.

LADY WOULD-BEE   All our *English* writers,
I meane such, as are happy in th' *Italian*,
Will deigne to steale out of this author, mainely;

90   Almost as much, as from MONTAGNIE:
He has so moderne, and facile a veine,
Fitting the time, and catching the court-eare.
Your PETRARCH is more passionate, yet he,
In dayes of sonetting, trusted 'hem, with much:
DANTE is hard, and few can understand him.
But, for a desperate wit, there's ARETINE!
Onely, his pictures are a little obscene——
You marke me not?

VOLPONE   Alas, my mind's perturb'd.

LADY WOULD-BEE Why, in such cases, we must cure our selves,
Make use of our philosophie——

100   VOLPONE   O'y me.

LADY WOULD-BEE And, as we find our passions doe rebell,
Encounter 'hem with reason; or divert 'hem,
By giving scope unto some other humour
Of lesser danger: as, in politique bodies,
There's nothing, more, doth over-whelme the judgement,
And clouds the understanding, then too much
Settling, and fixing, and (as't were) subsiding
Upon one object. For the incorporating
Of these same outward things, into that part,

110   Which we call mentall, leaves some certaine *faeces*,
That stop the organs, and, as PLATO sayes,
Assassinates our knowledge.

VOLPONE   Now, the spirit
Of patience helpe me.

LADY WOULD-BEE   Come, in faith, I must

Visit you more, a dayes; and make you well:
Laugh, and be lusty.

VOLPONE   My good angell save me.

LADY WOULD-BEE There was but one sole man, in all the world,
With whom I ere could sympathize; and he
Would lie you often, three, foure houres together,
To heare me speake: and be (sometime) so rap't,
As he would answere me, quite from the purpose,   120
Like you, and you are like him, just. I'le discourse
(And't be but only, sir, to bring you a-sleepe)
How we did spend our time, and loves, together,
For some six yeeres.

VOLPONE   Oh, oh, oh, oh, oh, oh.

LADY WOULD-BEE For we were *coaetanei*, and brought up—

VOLPONE Some power, some fate, some fortune rescue me.

Act III. Scene 5

MOSCA, LADY, VOLPONE.

[*Enter* MOSCA.]

MOSCA God save you, Madam.

LADY WOULD-BEE   Good sir.

VOLPONE   MOSCA? welcom,
Welcome to my redemption.

MOSCA   Why, sir?

VOLPONE   Oh,
Rid me of this my torture, quickly, there;
My Madam, with the everlasting voyce:
The bells, in time of pestilence, ne're made
Like noise, or were in that perpetuall motion;
The cock-pit comes not neere it. All my house,
But now, steam'd like a bath, with her thicke breath.
A lawyer could not have beene heard; nor scarse
Another woman, such a hayle of wordes   10
Shee has let fall. For hells sake, rid her hence.

MOSCA Has shee presented?

VOLPONE   O, I doe not care,

I'le take her absence, upon any price,
With any losse.

MOSCA   Madam—

LADY WOULD-BEE   I ha' brought your patron
A toy, a cap here, of mine owne worke—

MOSCA   'Tis well
I had forgot to tell you, I saw your Knight,
Where you'ld little thinke it—

LADY WOULD-BEE   Where?

MOSCA   Mary,
Where yet, if you make haste, you may apprehend him,
Rowing upon the water in a *gondole*,
20   With the most cunning curtizan, of *Venice*.

LADY WOULD-BEE   Is't true?

MOSCA   Pursue 'hem, and beleeve your eyes:
Leave me, to make your gift. [*Exit* LADY WOULD-BEE.]
    I knew, 't would take.
For lightly, they that use themselves most licence,
Are still most jealous.

VOLPONE   MOSCA, hearty thankes,
For thy quicke fiction, and delivery of mee.
Now, to my hopes, what saist thou?
     [*Enter* LADY WOULD-BEE.]

LADY WOULD-BEE   But doe you heare, sir?—

VOLPONE   Againe; I feare a *paroxisme*.

LADY WOULD-BEE   Which way
Row'd they together?

MOSCA   Toward the *rialto*.

LADY WOULD-BEE   I pray you lend me your dwarfe.

MOSCA   I pray you, take
    him.   [*Exit* LADY WOULD-BEE.]
30   Your hopes, sir, are like happie blossomes, faire,
And promise timely fruit, if you will stay
But the maturing; keepe you, at your couch,
CORBACCIO will arrive straight, with the will:
When he is gone, ile tell you more.   [*Exit.*]

VOLPONE   My blood,
My spirits are return'd; I am alive:

And like your wanton gam'ster, at *primero*,
Whose thought had whisper'd to him, not goe lesse,
Methinkes I lie, and draw—for an encounter.

Act III. Scene 6
MOSCA, BONARIO.

[*Enter* MOSCA *and* BONARIO.]

MOSCA Sir, here conceald, you may heare all. But 'pray you
Have patience, sir; the same's your father, knocks: *One knockes.*
I am compeld, to leave you.
BONARIO   Do so. [*Exit* MOSCA.] Yet,
Cannot my thought imagine this a truth.

Act III. Scene 7
MOSCA, CORVINO, CELIA, BONARIO, VOLPONE.

[*Enter* MOSCA, CORVINO *and* CELIA.]

MOSCA Death on me! you are come too soone, what meant you?
Did not I say, I would send?
CORVINO   Yes, but I feard
You might forget it, and then they prevent us.
MOSCA Prevent? did ere man haste so, for his hornes?
A courtier would not ply it so, for a place.
Well, now there's no helping it, stay here;
Ile presently returne.
CORVINO   Where are you, CELIA?
You know not wherefore I have brought you hither?
CELIA Not well, except you told me.
CORVINO   Now, I will: 9
Harke hither.
MOSCA   Sir, your father hath sent word,   *To Bonario.*
It will be halfe an houre, ere he come;
And therefore, if you please to walke, the while,
Into that gallery—at the upper end,
There are some bookes, to entertaine the time:

And ile take care, no man shall come unto you, sir.

BONARIO Yes, I will stay there, I doe doubt this fellow.   [*Exit.*]

MOSCA There, he is farre enough; he can heare nothing:
And, for his father, I can keepe him off.

CORVINO Nay, now, there is no starting backe; and therefore,
20   Resolve upon it: I have so decree'd.
It must be done. Nor, would I move 't afore,
Because I would avoide all shifts and tricks,
That might denie me.

CELIA   Sir, let me beseech you,
Affect not these strange trials; if you doubt
My chastitie, why locke me up, for ever:
Make me the heyre of darkenesse. Let me live,
Where I may please your feares, if not your trust.

CORVINO Beleeve it, I have no such humor, I.
All that I speake, I meane; yet I am not mad:
30   Not horne-mad, see you? Go too, shew your selfe
Obedient, and a wife.

CELIA   O heaven!

CORVINO   I say it,
Do so.

CELIA   Was this the traine?

CORVINO   I' have told you reasons;
What the physitians have set downe; how much,
It may concerne me; what my engagements are;
My meanes; and the necessitie of those meanes,
For my recovery: wherefore, if you bee
Loyall, and mine, be wonne, respect my venture.

CELIA Before your honour?

CORVINO   Honour? tut, a breath;
There's no such thing, in nature: a meere terme
40   Invented to awe fooles. What is my gold
The worse, for touching? clothes, for being look'd on?
Why, this 's no more. An old, decrepit wretch,
That ha's no sense, no sinew; takes his meate
With others fingers; onely knowes to gape,
When you doe scald his gummes; a voice; a shadow;
And, what can this man hurt you?

CELIA   Lord! what spirit
  Is this hath entred him?

CORVINO   And for your fame,
  That's such a Jigge; as if I would goe tell it,
  Crie it, on the *piazza*! who shall know it?
  But hee, that cannot speake it; and this fellow,   50
  Whose lippes are i' my pocket: save your selfe,
  If you'll proclaime't, you may. I know no other,
  Should come to know it.

CELIA   Are heaven, and saints then nothing?
  Will they be blinde, or stupide?

CORVINO   How?

CELIA   Good Sir,
  Be jealous still, aemulate them; and thinke
  What hate they burne with, toward every sinne.

CORVINO I grant you: if I thought it were a sinne,
  I would not urge you. Should I offer this
  To some yong *Frenchman*, or hot *Tuscane* bloud,
  That had read ARETINE, conn'd all his printes,   60
  Knew every quirke within lusts laborinth,
  And were profest critique, in lechery;
  And I would looke upon him, and applaud him,
  This were a sinne: but here, 'tis contrary,
  A pious worke, mere charity, for physick,
  And honest politie, to assure mine owne.

CELIA O heaven! canst thou suffer such a change?

VOLPONE Thou art mine honor, MOSCA, and my pride,
  My joy, my tickling, my delight! goe, bring 'hem.

MOSCA Please you draw neere, sir.

CORVINO   Come on, what—   70
  You will not be rebellious? by that light—

MOSCA Sir, signior CORVINO, here, is come to see you.

VOLPONE Oh.

MOSCA   And hearing of the consultation had,
  So lately, for your health, is come to offer,
  Or rather, sir, to prostitute—

CORVINO   Thankes, sweet MOSCA.

MOSCA Freely, un-ask'd, or un-intreated—

CORVINO   Well.

MOSCA (As the true, fervent instance of his love)
>His owne most faire and proper wife; the beauty,
>Onely of price, in *Venice*—

CORVINO   'Tis well urg'd.

80   MOSCA To be your comfortresse, and to preserve you.

VOLPONE Alasse, I' am past already! 'pray you, thanke him,
>For his good care, and promptnesse, but for that,
>'Tis a vaine labour, eene to fight, 'gainst heaven;
>Applying fire to a stone: (uh, uh, uh, uh.)
>Making a dead leafe grow againe. I take
>His wishes gently, though; and, you may tell him,
>What I' have done for him: mary, my state is hopelesse!
>Will him, to pray for me; and t'use his fortune,
>With reverence, when he comes to't.

MOSCA   Do you heare, sir?
>Go to him, with your wife.

90   CORVINO   Heart of my father!
>Wilt thou persist thus? come, I pray thee, come.
>Thou seest 'tis nothing. CELIA. By this hand,
>I shall grow violent. Come, do't, I say.

CELIA Sir, kill me, rather: I will take downe poyson,
>Eate burning coales, doe any thing—

CORVINO   Be damn'd.
>(Heart) I will drag thee hence, home, by the haire;
>Cry thee a strumpet, through the streets; rip up
>Thy mouth, unto thine eares; and slit thy nose,
>Like a raw rotchet— Do not tempt me, come.

100   Yeld, I am loth— (Death) I will buy some slave,
>Whom I will kill, and binde thee to him, alive;
>And at my windore, hang you forth: devising
>Some monstrous crime, which I, in capitall letters,
>Will eate into thy flesh, with *aqua-fortis*,
>And burning cor'sives, on this stubborne brest.
>Now, by the bloud, thou hast incens'd, ile do't.

CELIA Sir, what you please, you may, I am your martyr.

CORVINO Be not thus obstinate, I ha' not deserv'd it:
>Thinke, who it is, intreats you. 'Pray thee, sweet;

(Good'faith) thou shalt have jewells, gownes, attires,   110
What thou wilt thinke, and aske. Do, but, go kisse him.
Or touch him, but. For my sake. At my sute.
This once. No? not? I shall remember this.
Will you disgrace me, thus? do'you thirst my'undoing?

MOSCA Nay, gentle lady, be advis'd.

CORVINO   No, no.
She has watch'd her time. God's precious, this is skirvy;
'Tis very skirvie: and you are—

MOSCA   Nay, good sir.

CORVINO An errant locust, by heaven, a locust. Whore,
Crocodile, that hast thy teares prepar'd,
Expecting, how thou'lt bid 'hem flow.

MOSCA   Nay, 'Pray you, sir,   120
Shee will consider.

CELIA   Would my life would serve
To satisfie.

CORVINO   (S'death) if shee would but speake to him,
And save my reputation, 'twere somewhat;
But, spightfully to affect my utter ruine.

MOSCA I, now you' have put your fortune, in her hands.
Why i' faith, it is her modesty, I must quit her;
If you were absent, shee would be more comming;
I know it: and dare undertake for her.
What woman can, before her husband? 'pray you,
Let us depart, and leave her, here.

CORVINO   Sweet CELIA,   130
Thou mayst redeeme all, yet; I'le say no more:
If not, esteeme your selfe as lost. Nay, stay there.

                    [*Exeunt* MOSCA *and* CORVINO.]

CELIA O god, and his good angels! whether, whether
Is shame fled humane brests? that with such ease,
Men dare put off your honours, and their owne?
Is that, which ever was a cause of life,
Now plac'd beneath the basest circumstance?
And modestie an exile made, for money?   138

VOLPONE I, in CORVINO, and such earth-fed mindes,   *He leapes off*
That never tasted the true heav'n of love.   *from his couch.*

Assure thee, CELIA, he that would sell thee,
Onely for hope of gaine, and that uncertaine,
He would have sold his part of paradise
For ready money, had he met a cope-man.
Why art thou maz'd, to see me thus reviv'd?
Rather applaud thy beauties miracle;
'Tis thy great worke: that hath, not now alone,
But sundry times, rays'd me, in severall shapes,
And, but this morning, like a mountebanke,
150 To see thee at thy windore. I, before
I would have left my practice, for thy love,
In varying figures, I would have contended
With the blue PROTEUS, or the horned *Floud.*
Now, art thou welcome.

CELIA   Sir!

VOLPONE   Nay, flie me not.
Nor, let thy false imagination
That I was bedrid, make thee thinke, I am so:
Thou shalt not find it. I am, now, as fresh,
As hot, as high, and in as joviall plight,
As when (in that so celebrated *scene,*
160 At recitation of our *comoedie,*
For entertainement of the great VALOYS)
I acted yong ANTINOUS; and attracted
The eyes, and eares of all the ladies, present,
T'admire each gracefull gesture, note, and footing.

                    SONG.
        Come, my CELIA, *let us prove,*
        While we can, the sports of love;
        Time will not be ours, for ever,
        He, at length, our good will sever;
170   *Spend not then his gifts, in vaine.*
        Sunnes, that set, may rise againe:
        But if, once, we lose this light,
        'Tis with us perpetuall night.
        Why should wee deferre our joyes?

> *Fame, and rumor are but toies.*
> *Cannot we delude the eyes*
> *Of a few poore houshold-spies?*
> *Or his easier eares beguile,*
> *Thus remooved, by our wile?*
> *'Tis no sinne, loves fruits to steale;* 180
> *But the sweet thefts to reveale:*
> *To be taken, to be seene,*
> *These have crimes accounted beene.*

CELIA Some *serene* blast me, or dire lightning strike
    This my offending face.

VOLPONE   Why droopes my CELIA?
    Thou hast in place of a base husband, found
    A worthy lover: use thy fortune well,
    With secrecie, and pleasure. See, behold,
    What thou art queene of; not in expectation,
    As I feed others: but possess'd, and crown'd. 190
    See, here, a rope of pearle; and each, more orient
    Then that the brave *Aegyptian* queene carrous'd:
    Dissolve, and drinke 'hem. See, a carbuncle,
    May put out both the eyes of our St. MARKE;
    A diamant, would have bought LOLLIA PAULINA,
    When she came in, like star-light hid with jewels,
    That were the spoiles of provinces; take these,
    And weare, and loose 'hem: yet remaines an eare-ring
    To purchase them againe, and this whole state.
    A gem, but worth a private patrimony, 200
    Is nothing: we will eate such at a meale.
    The heads of parrats, tongues of nightingales,
    The braines of peacoks, and of estriches
    Shall be our food: and, could we get the phoenix,
    (Though nature lost her kind) shee were our dish.

CELIA Good sir, these things might move a minde affected
    With such delights; but I, whose innocence
    Is all I can thinke wealthy, or worth th'enjoying,
    And which once lost, I have nought to loose beyond it,

210   Cannot be taken with these sensuall baites:
    If you have conscience——

VOLPONE   'Tis the beggers vertue,
    If thou hast wisdome, heare me, CELIA.
    Thy bathes shall be the juyce of july-flowres,
    Spirit of roses, and of violets,
    The milke of unicornes, and panthers breath
    Gather'd in bagges, and mixt with *cretan* wines.
    Our drinke shall be prepared gold, and amber;
    Which we will take, untill my roofe whirle round
    With the *vertigo*: and my dwarfe shall dance,
220   My eunuch sing, my foole make up the antique.
    Whil'st, we, in changed shapes, act OVIDS tales,
    Thou, like EUROPA now, and I like JOVE,
    Then I like MARS, and thou like ERYCINE,
    So, of the rest, till we have quite run through
    And weary'd all the fables of the gods.
    Then will I have thee in more moderne formes,
    Attired like some sprightly dame of *France*,
    Brave *Tuscan* lady, or proud *Spanish* beauty;
    Sometimes, unto the *Persian Sophies* wife;
230   Or the grand-*Signiors* mistresse; and, for change,
    To one of our most art-full courtizans,
    Or some quick *Negro*, or cold *Russian*;
    And I will meet thee, in as many shapes:
    Where we may, so, trans-fuse our wandring soules,
    Out at our lippes, and score up summes of pleasures,
          That the curious shall not know,
             How to tell them, as they flow;
          And the envious, when they find
             What their number is, be pind.
240 CELIA   If you have eares that will be pierc'd; or eyes,
    That can be open'd; a heart, may be touch'd;
    Or any part, that yet sounds man, about you:
    If you have touch of holy saints, or heaven,
    Do me the grace, to let me scape. If not,
    Be bountifull, and kill me. You doe know,
    I am a creature, hither ill betrayd,

By one, whose shame I would forget it were,
If you will daigne me neither of these graces,
Yet feed your wrath, sir, rather then your lust;
(It is a vice, comes neerer manlinesse)   250
And punish that unhappy crime of nature,
Which you miscal my beauty: flay my face,
Or poison it, with oyntments, for seducing
Your bloud to this rebellion. Rub these hands,
With what may cause an eating leprosie,
E'ene to my bones, and marrow: any thing,
That may disfavour me, save in my honour.
And I will kneele to you, pray for you, pay downe
A thousand hourely vowes, sir, for your health,
Report, and thinke you vertuous —

VOLPONE   Thinke me cold,   260
  Frosen, and impotent, and so report me?
  That I had NESTOR'S *hernia*, thou wouldst thinke.
  I doe degenerate, and abuse my nation,
  To play with oportunity, thus long:
  I should have done the act, and then have parlee'd.
  Yeeld, or Ile force thee.

CELIA   O! just God.

VOLPONE   In vaine —

BONARIO Forbeare, foule ravisher, libidinous swine,   *He leapes out*
  Free the forc'd lady, or thou dy'st, impostor.   *from where*
  But that I am loth to snatch thy punishment   *Mosca had*
  Out of the hand of justice, thou shouldst, yet,   *plac'd him.*
  Be made the timely sacrifice of vengeance,   270
  Before this altar, and this drosse, thy idoll.
  Lady, let's quit the place, it is the den
  Of villany; feare nought, you have a guard:
  And he, ere long, shall meet his just reward.

                              [*Exeunt* BONARIO *and* CELIA.]

VOLPONE Fall on me, roofe, and bury me in ruine,
  Become my grave, that wert my shelter. O!
  I am un-masqu'd, un-spirited, un-done,
  Betray'd to beggery, to infamy —

Act III. Scene 8

MOSCA, VOLPONE.

[*Enter* MOSCA.]

MOSCA Where shall I runne, most wretched shame of men,
　　To beate out my un-luckie braines?

VOLPONE　　　　　　　　　　Here, here.
　　What! dost thou bleed?

MOSCA　　　　　　　O, that his wel-driv'n sword
　　Had beene so courteous to have cleft me downe,
　　Unto the navill; ere I liv'd to see
　　My life, my hopes, my spirits, my patron, all
　　Thus desperately engaged, by my error.

VOLPONE Woe, on thy fortune.

MOSCA　　　　　　　　　　And my follies, sir.

VOLPONE Th'hast made me miserable.

MOSCA　　　　　　　　　　And my selfe, sir.

10　　Who would have thought, he would have harken'd, so?

VOLPONE What shall we do?

MOSCA　　　　　　　I know not, if my heart
　　Could expiate the mischance, I'ld pluck it out.
　　Will you be pleas'd to hang me? or cut my throate?
　　And i'le requite you, sir. Let's die like *Romanes*,

They knock　　Since wee have liv'd, like *Grecians*.
without.
VOLPONE　　　　　　　　　　　Harke, who's there?
　　I heare some footing, officers, the *Saffi*,
　　Come to apprehend us! I doe feele the brand
　　Hissing already, at my fore-head: now,
　　Mine eares are boring.

MOSCA　　　　　　　To your couch, sir, you
20　　Make that place good, how ever. Guilty men
　　Suspect, what they deserve still. Signior CORBACCIO!

Act III. Scene 9.

CORBACCIO, MOSCA, VOLTORE, VOLPONE.

[*Enter* CORBACCIO.]

CORBACCIO Why! how now? Mosca!

[*Enter* VOLTORE.]

MOSCA   O, undone, amaz'd, sir.
Your sonne (I know not, by what accident)
Acquainted with your purpose to my patron,
Touching your will, and making him your heire;
Entred our house with violence, his sword drawne,
Sought for you, call'd you wretch, unnaturall,
Vow'd he would kill you.

CORBACCIO   Me?

MOSCA   Yes, and my patron.

CORBACCIO This act, shall disinherit him indeed:
Here is the will.

MOSCA   'Tis well, sir.

CORBACCIO   Right and well.
Be you as carefull now, for me.

MOSCA   My life, sir,   10
Is not more tender'd, I am onely yours.

CORBACCIO How do's he? will he die shortly, think'st thou?

MOSCA   I feare,
He'll out-last *May*.

CORBACCIO   To day?

MOSCA   No, last-out *May*, sir.

CORBACCIO Couldst thou not gi' him a dram?

MOSCA   O, by no meanes, sir.

CORBACCIO Nay, I'le not bid you.

VOLTORE   This is a knave, I see.

MOSCA How, signior VOLTORE! did he heare me?

VOLTORE   Parasite.

MOSCA Who's that? O, sir, most timely welcome—

VOLTORE   Scarse,
To the discovery of your tricks, I feare.
You are his, onely? and mine, also? are you not?

MOSCA Who? I, sir!

20 VOLTORE   You, sir. What device is this
About a will?

MOSCA   A plot for you, sir.

VOLTORE   Come,
Put not your foist's upon me, I shall sent 'hem.

MOSCA Did you not heare it?

VOLTORE   Yes, I heare, CORBACCIO
Hath made your patron, there, his heire.

MOSCA   'Tis true,
By my device, drawne to it by my plot,
With hope——

VOLTORE   Your patron should reciprocate?
And, you have promis'd?

MOSCA   For your good, I did, sir.
Nay more, I told his sonne, brought, hid him here,
Where he might heare his father passe the deed;

30 Being perswaded to it, by this thought, sir,
That the unnaturalnesse, first, of the act,
And then, his fathers oft disclaiming in him,
(Which I did meane t'helpe on) would sure enrage him
To doe some violence upon his parent.
On which the law should take sufficient hold,
And you be stated in a double hope:
Truth be my comfort, and my conscience,
My onely ayme was, to dig you a fortune
Out of these two, old rotten sepulchers——

(VOLTORE I cry thee mercy, MOSCA.)

40 MOSCA   Worth your patience,
And your great merit, sir. And, see the change!

VOLTORE Why? what successe?

MOSCA   Most haplesse! you must helpe, sir.
Whilst we expected th' old raven, in comes
CORVINO's wife, sent hither, by her husband——

VOLTORE What, with a present?

MOSCA   No, sir, on visitation:
(I'le tell you how, anone) and, staying long,
The youth, he growes impatient, rushes forth,

Seizeth the lady, wound's me, makes her sweare
(Or he would murder her, that was his vow)
T'affirme my patron to have done her rape: 50
Which how unlike it is, you see! and, hence,
With that pretext, hee's gone, t'accuse his father;
Defame my patron; defeate you——

VOLTORE   Where's her husband?
Let him be sent for, streight.

MOSCA   Sir, I'le goe fetch him.

VOLTORE Bring him, to the *Scrutineo*.

MOSCA   Sir, I will.

VOLTORE This must be stopt.

MOSCA   O, you do nobly, sir.
Alasse, 'twas labor'd all, sir, for your good;
Nor, was there want of counsel, in the plot:
But fortune can, at any time, orethrow
The projects of a hundred learned *clearkes*, sir.   60

CORBACCIO What's that?

VOLTORE   Wilt please you sir, to goe along?
                    [*Exeunt* CORBACCIO *and* VOLTORE.]

MOSCA Patron, go in, and pray for our successe.

VOLPONE Neede makes devotion: heaven your labor blesse.
                                    [*Exeunt.*]

Act IV. Scene 1

POLITIQUE, PEREGRINE.

[*Enter* SIR POLITIQUE *and* PEREGRINE.]

SIR POLITIQUE I told you, sir, it was a plot: you see
What observation is. You mention'd mee,
For some instructions: I will tell you, sir,
(Since we are met, here in this height of *Venice*)
Some few particulars, I have set downe,
Onely for this *meridian*; fit to be knowne
Of your crude traveller, and they are these.
I will not touch, sir, at your phrase, or clothes,
For they are old.

PEREGRINE   Sir, I have better.

SIR POLITIQUE   Pardon,
   I meant, as they are *theames*.

10 PEREGRINE   O, sir, proceed:
   I'le slander you no more of wit, good sir.

SIR POLITIQUE First, for your garbe, it must be grave, and serious;
   Very reserv'd, and lock't; not tell a secret,
   On any termes, not to your father; scarse
   A fable, but with caution; make sure choise
   Both of your company, and discourse; beware,
   You never speake a truth—

PEREGRINE   How!

SIR POLITIQUE   Not to strangers,
   For those be they you must converse with, most;
   Others I would not know, sir, but, at distance,
20 So as I still might be a saver, in 'hem:
   You shall have tricks, else, past upon you, hourely.
   And then, for your religion, professe none;
   But wonder, at the diversitie of all;
   And, for your part, protest, were there no other
   But simply the lawes o' th' land, you could content you:
   NIC: MACHIAVEL, and monsieur BODINE, both,
   Were of this minde. Then, must you learne the use,
   And handling of your silver forke, at meales;
   The mettall of your glasse: (these are maine matters,
30 With your *Italian*) and to know the houre,
   When you must eat your melons, and your figges.

PEREGRINE Is that a point of state, too?

SIR POLITIQUE   Here it is.
   For your *Venetian*, if he see a man
   Preposterous, in the least, he has him straight;
   He has: he strippes him. I'le acquaint you, sir,
   I now have liv'd here ('tis some fourteene monthes)
   Within the first weeke, of my landing here,
   All tooke me for a citizen of *Venice*:
   I knew the formes, so well—

PEREGRINE   And nothing else.

40 SIR POLITIQUE I had read CONTARENE, tooke me a house,

Dealt with my *Jewes*, to furnish it with moveables—
Well, if I could but finde one man, one man,
To mine owne heart, whom I durst trust, I would—

PEREGRINE What? what, sir?

SIR POLITIQUE   Make him rich; make him a fortune:
He should not thinke, againe. I would command it.

PEREGRINE As how?

SIR POLITIQUE   With certaine projects, that I have:
Which, I may not discover.

PEREGRINE   If I had
But one to wager with, I would lay odds, now,
He tels me, instantly.

SIR POLITIQUE   One is, (and that
I care not greatly, who knowes) to serve the state   50
Of *Venice*, with red herrings, for three yeeres,
And at a certaine rate, from *Roterdam*,
Where I have correspondence. There's a letter,
Sent me from one o' th' States, and to that purpose;
He cannot write his name, but that's his marke.

PEREGRINE He is a chaundler?

SIR POLITIQUE   No, a cheesemonger.
There are some other too, with whom I treate,
About the same negotiation;
And, I will undertake it: For, 'tis thus,
I'le do't with ease, I'have cast it all. Your hoigh   60
Carries but three men in her, and a boy;
And she shall make me three returnes, a yeare:
So, if there come but one of three, I save,
If two, I can defalke. But, this is now,
If my mayne project faile.

PEREGRINE   Then, you have others?

SIR POLITIQUE I should be loath to draw the subtill ayre
Of such a place, without my thousand aymes.
Ile not dissemble, sir, where ere I come,
I love to be considerative; and, 'tis true,
I have, at my free houres, thought upon   70
Some certaine goods, unto the state of *Venice*,
Which I doe call my cautions: and, sir, which

        I meane (in hope of pension) to propound
        To the great councell, then unto the forty,
        So to the ten. My meanes are made already—
PEREGRINE By whom?
SIR POLITIQUE   Sir, one, that though his place b'obscure,
        Yet, he can sway, and they will heare him. H'is
        A *commandadore*.
PEREGRINE   What, a common sergeant?
SIR POLITIQUE Sir, such, as they are, put it in their mouthes,
80   What they should say, sometimes: as well as greater.
        I thinke I have my notes, to shew you—
PEREGRINE   Good, sir,
SIR POLITIQUE But, you shall sweare unto me, on your gentry,
        Not to anticipate—
PEREGRINE   I, sir?
SIR POLITIQUE   Nor reveale
        A circumstance— My paper is not with mee.
PEREGRINE O, but, you can remember, sir.
SIR POLITIQUE   My first is,
        Concerning tinder-boxes. You must know,
        No family is, here, without it's boxe.
        Now sir, it being so portable a thing,
        Put case, that you, or I were ill affected
90   Unto the state; sir, with it in our pockets,
        Might not I goe into the *arsenale*?
        Or you? come out againe? and none the wiser?
PEREGRINE Except your selfe, sir.
SIR POLITIQUE   Goe too, then. I, therefore,
        Advertise to the state, how fit it were,
        That none, but such as were knowne patriots,
        Sound lovers of their countrey, should be sufferd
        T'enjoy them in their houses: and, even those,
        Seal'd, at some office, and, at such a bignesse,
        As might not lurke in pockets.
PEREGRINE   Admirable!
100 SIR POLITIQUE My next is, how t'enquire, and be resolv'd,
        By present demonstration, whether a ship,
        Newly arrived from *Soría*, or from

Any suspected part of all the *levant*,
Be guilty of the plague: And, where they use,
To lie out fortie, fifty daies, sometimes,
About the *Lazaretto*, for their triall;
Ile save that charge, and losse unto the merchant,
And, in an houre, cleare the doubt.

PEREGRINE   Indeede, sir?

SIR POLITIQUE Or— I will loose my labour.

PEREGRINE   'My faith, that's much.

SIR POLITIQUE Nay, sir, conceive me. 'Twill cost me, in onions,   110
Some thirtie *liv'res*—

PEREGRINE   Which is one pound sterling.

SIR POLITIQUE Beside my water-workes: for this I doe, sir.
First, I bring in your ship, 'twixt two brickwalles;
(But those the state shall venter) on the one
I straine me a faire tarre-paulin; and, in that,
I stick my onions, cut in halfes: the other
Is full of loope-holes, out at which, I thrust
The noses of my bellowes; and, those bellowes
I keepe, with water-workes, in perpetuall motion,
(Which is the easi'st matter of a hundred)   120
Now, sir, your onion, which doth naturally
Attract th'infection, and your bellowes, blowing
The ayre upon him, will shew (instantly)
By his chang'd colour, if there be contagion,
Or else, remaine as faire, as at the first.
Now 'tis knowne, 'tis nothing.

PEREGRINE   You are right, sir.

SIR POLITIQUE I would, I had my note.

PEREGRINE   'Faith, so would I:
But, you ha' done well, for once, sir.

SIR POLITIQUE   Were I false,
Or would be made so, I could shew you reasons,
How I could sell this state, now, to the *Turke*;   130
Spight of their galleis, or their—

PEREGRINE   Pray you, sir POLL.

SIR POLITIQUE I have 'hem not, about me.

PEREGRINE   That I fear'd.

They'are there, sir?

SIR POLITIQUE   No, this is my *diary*,
Wherein I note my actions of the day.

PEREGRINE 'Pray you, let's see, sir. What is here? *notandum*,
A rat had gnawne my spurre-lethers; notwithstanding,
I put on new, and did goe forth: but, first,
I threw three beanes over the threshold. *Item*,
I went, and bought two tooth-pickes, whereof one

140   I burst, immediatly, in a discourse
With a *dutch* merchant, 'bout *ragion del stato*.
From him I went, and payd a *moccinigo*,
For peecing my silke stockings; by the way,
I cheapen'd sprats: and at St. MARKES, I urin'd.
'Faith, these are politique notes!

SIR POLITIQUE   Sir, I do slippe
No action of my life, thus, but I quote it.

PEREGRINE Beleeve me it is wise!

SIR POLITIQUE   Nay, sir, read forth.

Act IV. Scene 2

LADY, NANO, WOMEN, POLITIQUE, PEREGRINE.

[*Enter* LADY WOULD-BEE, NANO *and* 2 WOMEN.]

LADY WOULD-BEE Where should this loose knight be, trow? sure,
h'is hous'd.

NANO Why, then he's fast.

LADY WOULD-BEE   I, he plaies both, with me:
I pray you, stay. This heate will doe more harme
To my complexion, then his heart is worth.
(I do not care to hinder, but to take him)
How it comes of!

1ST WOMAN   My master's, yonder.

LADY WOULD-BEE   Where?

2ND WOMAN With a yong gentleman.

LADY WOULD-BEE   That same's the party!
In mans apparell. 'Pray you, sir, jog my knight:
I will be tender to his reputation,

How ever he demerit.

SIR POLITIQUE   My lady!

PEREGRINE   Where?   10

SIR POLITIQUE 'Tis shee indeed, sir, you shall know her. She is,

Were she not mine, a lady of that merit,

For fashion, and behaviour; and, for beauty

I durst compare——

PEREGRINE   It seemes, you are not jealous,

That dare commend her.

SIR POLITIQUE   Nay, and for discourse——

PEREGRINE Being your wife, she cannot misse that.

SIR POLITIQUE   Madame,

Here is a gentleman, 'pray you, use him, fairely,

He seemes a youth, but he is——

LADY WOULD-BEE   None?

SIR POLITIQUE   Yes, one

Has put his face, as soone, into the world——

LADY WOULD-BEE You meane, as earely? but to day?

SIR POLITIQUE   How's this!   20

LADY WOULD-BEE Why in this habit, sir, you apprehend me.

Well, master WOULD-BEE, this doth not become you;

I had thought, the odour, sir, of your good name,

Had beene more precious to you; that you would not

Have done this dire massacre, on your honour;

One of your gravity, and ranke, besides!

But, knights, I see, care little for the oath

They make to ladies: chiefely, their owne ladies.

SIR POLITIQUE Now, by my spurres (the symbole of my

knight-hood)

(PEREGRINE Lord! how his braine is humbled, for an oath).   30

SIR POLITIQUE I reach you not.

LADY WOULD-BEE   Right, sir, your politie

May beare it through, thus. Sir, a word with you.

I would be loth, to contest publikely,

With any gentlewoman; or to seeme

Froward, or violent (as the courtier sayes)

It comes too neere rusticity, in a lady,

Which I would shun, by all meanes: and, how-ever

I may deserve from master WOULD-BEE, yet,
T'have one faire gentlewoman, thus, be made
40 Th'unkind instrument, to wrong another,
And one she knowes not, I, and to persever;
In my poore judgement, is not warranted
From being a *soloecisme* in our sexe,
If not in manners.

PEREGRINE   How is this!

SIR POLITIQUE   Sweet madame,
Come neerer to your ayme.

LADY WOULD-BEE   Mary, and will, sir.
Since you provoke me, with your impudence,
And laughter of your light land-*siren*, here,
Your SPORUS, your *hermaphrodite*—

PEREGRINE   What's here?
Poetique fury, and historique stormes!

50 SIR POLITIQUE The gentleman, beleeve it, is of worth,
And of our nation.

LADY WOULD-BEE I, your *white-Friers* nation?
Come, I blush for you, master WOULD-BEE, I;
And am asham'd, you should ha' no more forehead,
Then, thus, to be the patron, or St. GEORGE
To a lewd harlot, a base fricatrice,
A female devill, in a male out-side.

SIR POLITIQUE   Nay,
And you be such a one! I must bid adieu
To your delights. The case appeares too liquide. [*Exit.*]

LADY WOULD-BEE I, you may carry 't cleare, with your state-face!
60 But, for your carnivale concupiscence,
Who here is fled for liberty of conscience,
From furious persecution of the Marshall,
Her will I disc'ple.

PEREGRINE   This is fine, i'faith!
And do you use this, often? is this part
Of your wits exercise, 'gainst you have occasion?
Madam—

LADY WOULD-BEE Go to, sir.

PEREGRINE   Do you heare me, lady?

Why, if your knight have set you to begge shirts,
Or to invite me home, you might have done it
A neerer way, by farre.

LADY WOULD-BEE   This cannot work you,
Out of my snare.

PEREGRINE   Why? am I in it, then?   70
Indeede, your husband told me, you were faire,
And so you are; onely your nose enclines
(That side, that's next the sunne) to the queene-apple.

LADY WOULD-BEE This cannot be endur'd, by any patience.

Act IV. Scene 3

MOSCA, LADY, PEREGRINE.

[*Enter* MOSCA.]

MOSCA What's the matter, madame?

LADY WOULD-BEE   If the *Senate*
Right not my quest, in this; I will protest 'hem,
To all the world, no *aristocracie*.

MOSCA What is the injurie, lady?

LADY WOULD-BEE   Why, the callet,
You told me of, here I have tane disguis'd.

MOSCA Who? this? what meanes your ladiship? the creature
I mention'd to you, is apprehended, now,
Before the *Senate*, you shall see her—

LADY WOULD-BEE   Where?

MOSCA I'le bring you to her. This yong gentleman
I saw him land, this morning, at the port.   10

LADY WOULD-BEE Is't possible! how has my judgement wander'd!
Sir, I must, blushing, say to you, I have err'd:
And plead your pardon.

PEREGRINE   What! more changes, yet?

LADY WOULD-BEE I hope, yo' ha' not the malice to remember
A gentlewomans passion. If you stay,
In *Venice*, here, please you to use me, sir—

MOSCA Will you go, madame?

LADY WOULD-BEE   'Pray you, sir, use mee. In faith,

The more you see me, the more I shall conceive,
You have forgot our quarrell.

     [*Exeunt* MOSCA, LADY WOULD-BEE *and* WOMEN.]

PEREGRINE   This is rare!
20 Sir POLITIQUE WOULD-BEE? no, sir POLITIQUE bawd!
To bring me, thus, acquainted with his wife!
Well, wise sir POL: since you have practis'd, thus,
Upon my freshman-ship, I'le trie your salt-head,
What proofe it is against a counter-plot.   [*Exit.*]

Act IV. Scene 4

VOLTORE, CORBACCIO, CORVINO, MOSCA.

[*Enter* VOLTORE, CORBACCIO, CORVINO *and* MOSCA.]

VOLTORE Well, now you know the carriage of the businesse,
Your constancy is all, that is requir'd
Unto the safety of it.

MOSCA   Is the lie
Safely convai'd amongst us? is that sure?
Knowes every man his burden?

CORVINO   Yes.

MOSCA   Then, shrink not.

CORVINO But, knowes the Advocate the truth?

MOSCA   O, sir,
By no meanes. I devis'd a formall tale,
That salv'd your reputation. But, be valiant, sir.

CORVINO I feare no one, but him; that, this his pleading
Should make him stand for a co-heire—

10 MOSCA   Co-halter.
Hang him: we will but use his tongue, his noise,
As we doe croakers, here.

CORVINO   I, what shall he do?

MOSCA When we ha' done, you meane?

CORVINO   Yes.

MOSCA   Why, we'll thinke,
Sell him for *mummia*, hee's halfe dust already.

To Voltore. Do not you smile, to see this *buffalo*,

How he doth sport it with his head?— I should
If all were well, and past. Sir, onely you   *To Corbaccio.*
Are he, that shall enjoy the crop of all,
And these not know for whom they toile.

CORBACCIO   I, peace.   19

MOSCA But you shall eate it. Much! Worshipfull sir,   *To Corvino,*
MERCURY sit upon your thundring tongue,   *then to Voltore*
Or the *French* HERCULES, and make your language   *againe.*
As conquering as his club, to beate along,
(As with a tempest) flat, our adversaries:
But, much more, yours, sir.

VOLTORE   Here they come, ha' done.

MOSCA I have another witnesse, if you neede, sir,
I can produce.

VOLTORE   Who is it?

MOSCA   Sir, I have her.

Act IV. Scene 5

AVOCATORI, 4, BONARIO, CELIA, VOLTORE, CORBACCIO,
CORVINO, MOSCA, NOTARIO, COMMANDADORI.

[*Enter* 4 AVOCATORI, BONARIO, CELIA, NOTARIO *and*
COMMANDADORI.]

IST AVOCATORE The like of this the *Senate* never heard of.

2ND AVOCATORE 'Twil come most strange to them, when we
report it.

4TH AVOCATORE The gentlewoman has beene ever held
Of un-reproved name.

3RD AVOCATORE   So, the yong man.

4TH AVOCATORE The more unnaturall part that of his father.

2ND AVOCATORE More of the husband.

IST AVOCATORE   I not know to give
His act a name, it is so monstrous!

4TH AVOCATORE But the impostor, he is a thing created
T'exceed example!

IST AVOCATORE   And all after times!

2ND AVOCATORE I never heard a true voluptuary   10

Describ'd, but him.

3RD AVOCATORE   Appeare yet those were cited?

NOTARIO All, but the old magnifico, VOLPONE.

1ST AVOCATORE Why is not hee here?

MOSCA   Please your father-hoods,
Here is his Advocate. Himselfe's, so weake,
So feeble—

4TH AVOCATORE What are you?

BONARIO   His parasite,
His knave, his pandar: I beseech the court,
He may be forc'd to come, that your grave eyes
May beare strong witnesse of his strange impostures.

VOLTORE Upon my faith, and credit, with your vertues,
20   He is not able to endure the ayre.

2ND AVOCATORE Bring him, how ever.

3RD AVOCATORE   We will see him.

4TH AVOCATORE   Fetch him.

VOLTORE Your father-hoods fit pleasures be obey'd,
But sure, the sight will rather moove your pitties,
Then indignation; may it please the court,
In the meane time, he may be heard in me:
I know this place most voide of prejudice,
And therefore crave it, since we have no reason
To feare our truth should hurt our cause.

3RD AVOCATORE   Speake free.

VOLTORE Then know, most honor'd fathers, I must now
30   Discover, to your strangely'abused eares,
The most prodigious, and most frontlesse piece
Of solid impudence, and trecherie,
That ever vicious nature yet brought foorth
To shame the state of *Venice*. This lewd woman
(That wants no artificiall lookes, or teares,
To helpe the visor, she has now put on)
Hath long beene knowne a close adulteresse,
To that lascivious youth there; not suspected,
I say, but knowne; and taken, in the act;
40   With him; and by this man, the easie husband,
Pardon'd: whose timelesse bounty makes him, now,

Stand here, the most unhappie, innocent person,
That ever mans owne goodnesse made accus'd.
For these, not knowing how to owe a gift
Of that deare grace, but with their shame; being plac'd
So'above all powers of their gratitude,
Began to hate the benefit: and, in place
Of thankes, devise t'extirpe the memorie
Of such an act. Wherein, I pray your father-hoods,
To observe the malice, yea, the rage of creatures   50
Discover'd in their evils; and what heart
Such take, even, from their crimes. But that, anone,
Will more appeare. This gentleman, the father,
Hearing of this foule fact, with many others,
Which dayly strooke at his too-tender eares,
And, griev'd in nothing more, then that he could not
Preserve him selfe a parent (his sonnes ills
Growing to that strange floud) at last decreed
To dis-inherit him.

1ST AVOCATORE   These be strange turnes!

2ND AVOCATORE The yong mans fame was ever faire, and honest.   60

VOLTORE So much more full of danger is his vice,
That can beguile so, under shade of vertue.
But as I said (my honour'd sires) his father
Having this setled purpose, (by what meanes
To him betray'd, we know not) and this day
Appointed for the deed; that parricide,
(I cannot stile him better) by confederacy
Preparing this his paramour to be there,
Entred VOLPONE's house (who was the man
Your father-hoods must understand, design'd   70
For the inheritance) there, sought his father:
But, with what purpose sought he him, my lords?
(I tremble to pronounce it, that a sonne
Unto a father, and to such a father
Should have so foule, felonious intent)
It was, to murder him. When, being prevented
By his more happy absence, what then did he?
Not check his wicked thoughts; no, now new deeds:

(Mischiefe doth ever end, where it begins)
80   An act of horror, fathers! he drag'd forth
The aged gentleman, that had there lien, bed-red,
Three yeeres, and more, out off his innocent couch,
Naked, upon the floore, there left him; wounded
His servant in the face; and, with this strumpet,
The stale to his forg'd practise, who was glad
To be so active, (I shall here desire
Your father-hoods to note but my collections,
As most remarkable) thought, at once, to stop
His fathers ends; discredit his free choice,
90   In the old gentleman; redeeme themselves,
By laying infamy upon this man,
To whom, with blushing, they should owe their lives.

1ST AVOCATORE What proofes have you of this?

BONARIO   Most honour'd fathers,
I humbly crave, there be no credit given
To this mans mercenary tongue.

2ND AVOCATORE   Forbeare.

BONARIO His soule moves in his fee.

3RD AVOCATORE   O, sir.

BONARIO   This fellow,
For six *sols* more, would pleade against his maker.

1ST AVOCATORE You do forget your selfe.

VOLTORE   Nay, nay, grave fathers,
Let him have scope: can any man imagine
100   That he will spare'his accuser, that would not
Have spar'd his parent?

1ST AVOCATORE   Well, produce your proofes.

CELIA I would I could forget, I were a creature.

VOLTORE Signior CORBACCIO.

4TH AVOCATORE   What is he?

VOLTORE   The father.

2ND AVOCATORE Has he had an oth?

NOTARIO   Yes.

CORBACCIO   What must I do now?

NOTARIO Your testimony's crav'd.

CORBACCIO   Speake to the knave?

I'le ha' my mouth, first, stopt with earth; my heart
Abhors his knowledge: I disclaime in him.

1ST AVOCATORE But, for what cause?

CORBACCIO   The meere portent of nature.
He is an utter stranger, to my loines.

BONARIO Have they made you to this!

CORBACCIO   I will not heare thee,   110
Monster of men, swine, goate, wolfe, parricide,
Speake not, thou viper.

BONARIO   Sir, I will sit downe,
And rather wish my innocence should suffer,
Then I resist the authority of a father.

VOLTORE Signior CORVINO.

2ND AVOCATORE   This is strange!

1ST AVOCATORE   Who's this?

NOTARIO The husband.

4TH AVOCATORE   Is he sworn?

NOTARIO   He is.

3RD AVOCATORE   Speak then.

CORVINO This woman (please your father-hoods) is a whore,
Of most hot exercise, more then a partrich,
Upon record—

1ST AVOCATORE No more.

CORVINO   Neighes, like a jennet.

NOTARIO Preserve the honour of the court.

CORVINO   I shall,   120
And modestie of your most reverend eares.
And, yet, I hope that I may say, these eyes
Have seene her glew'd unto that peece of cedar;
That fine well-timber'd gallant: and that, here,
The letters may be read, thorough the horne,
That make the story perfect.

MOSCA   Excellent! sir.

CORVINO There is no shame in this, now, is there?

MOSCA   None.

CORVINO Or if I said, I hop'd that she were onward
To her damnation, if there be a hell
Greater then whore, and woman; a good catholique   130

May make the doubt.

3RD AVOCATORE   His griefe hath made him frantique.

1ST AVOCATORE Remove him, hence.

2ND AVOCATORE   Looke to the woman.

She swownes.   CORVINO   Rare!

Prettily fain'd! againe!

4TH AVOCATORE   Stand from about her.

1ST AVOCATORE Give her the ayre.

3RD AVOCATORE   What can you say?

MOSCA   My wound
(May't please your wisdomes) speakes for me, receiv'd
In ayde of my good patron, when he mist
His sought-for father, when that well-taught dame
Had her cue given her, to cry out a rape.

BONARIO O, most lay'd impudence! Fathers—

3RD AVOCATORE   Sir, be silent,
140   You had your hearing free, so must they theirs.

2ND AVOCATORE I do begin to doubt th'imposture here.

4TH AVOCATORE This woman, has too many moodes.

VOLTORE   Grave fathers,
She is a creature, of a most profest,
And prostituted lewdnesse.

CORVINO   Most impetuous!
Unsatisfied, grave fathers!

VOLTORE   May her fainings
Not take your wisdomes: but, this day, she baited
A stranger, a grave knight, with her loose eyes,
And more lascivious kisses. This man saw 'hem
Together, on the water, in a *gondola*.

150   MOSCA Here is the lady her selfe, that saw 'hem too,
Without; who, then, had in the open streets
Pursu'd them, but for saving her knights honour.

1ST AVOCATORE Produce that lady.

2ND AVOCATORE   Let her come.   [*Exit* MOSCA.]

4TH AVOCATORE   These things,
They strike, with wonder!

3RD AVOCATORE   I am turn'd a stone!

Act IV. Scene 6

MOSCA, LADY, AVOCATORI, &C.

[*Enter* MOSCA *and* LADY WOULD-BEE.]

MOSCA Bee resolute, madame.

LADY WOULD-BEE   I, this same is shee.
  Out, thou *chameleon* harlot; now, thine eies
  Vie teares with the *hyaena*: dar'st thou looke
  Upon my wronged face? I cry your pardons.
  I feare, I have (forgettingly) transgrest
  Against the dignitie of the court—

2ND AVOCATORE   No, madame.

LADY WOULD-BEE And beene exorbitant—

3RD AVOCATORE   You have not, lady.

4TH AVOCATORE These proofes are strong.

LADY WOULD-BEE   Surely, I had no purpose:
  To scandalize your honours, or my sexes.

3RD AVOCATORE We do beleeve it.

LADY WOULD-BEE   Surely, you may beleeve it.   10

2ND AVOCATORE Madame, we do.

LADY WOULD-BEE   Indeede, you may; my breeding
  Is not so course—

4TH AVOCATORE   We know it.

LADY WOULD-BEE   To offend
  With pertinacy—

3RD AVOCATORE   Lady.

LADY WOULD-BEE   Such a presence:
  No, surely.

1ST AVOCATORE We well thinke it.

LADY WOULD-BEE   You may thinke it.

1ST AVOCATORE Let her o'recome. What witnesses have you,
  To make good your report?

BONARIO   Our consciences.

CELIA And heaven, that never failes the innocent.

4TH AVOCATORE These are no testimonies.

BONARIO   Not in your courts,
  Where multitude, and clamour overcomes.

1ST AVOCATORE Nay, then you do waxe insolent.

20 VOLTORE   Here, here,

Volpone is The testimonie comes, that will convince,
brought in, as And put to utter dumbnesse their bold tongues.
impotent. See here, grave fathers, here's the ravisher,
  The rider on mens wives, the great impostor,
  The grand voluptuary! do you not think,
  These limbes should affect *venery*? or these eyes
  Covet a concubine? 'pray you, marke these hands.
  Are they not fit to stroake a ladies brests?
  Perhaps, he doth dissemble?

BONARIO   So he do's.

VOLTORE Would you ha' him tortur'd?

30 BONARIO   I would have him prov'd.

VOLTORE Best try him, then, with goades, or burning Irons;
  Put him to the strappado: I have heard,
  The racke hath cur'd the gout, faith, give it him,
  And helpe him of a maladie, be courteous.
  I'le undertake, before these honour'd fathers,
  He shall have, yet, as many left diseases,
  As she has knowne adulterers, or thou strumpets.
  O, my most equall hearers, if these deedes,
  Acts, of this bold, and most exorbitant straine,
40 May passe with sufferance, what one citizen,
  But owes the forfeit of his life, yea fame,
  To him that dares traduce him? which of you
  Are safe, my honour'd fathers? I would aske
  (With leave of your grave father-hoods) if their plot
  Have any face, or colour like to truth?
  Or if, unto the dullest nostrill, here,
  It smell not rancke, and most abhorred slander?
  I crave your care of this good gentleman,
  Whose life is much indanger'd, by their fable;
50 And, as for them, I will conclude with this,
  That vicious persons when they are hot, and flesh'd
  In impious acts, their constancy abounds:
  Damn'd deeds are done with greatest confidence.

1ST AVOCATORE Take 'hem to custody, and sever them.

                  [*Exeunt* CELIA *and* BONARIO, *guarded.*]

2ND AVOCATORE 'Tis pittie, two such prodigies should live.

1ST AVOCATORE Let the old gentleman be return'd, with care:

    I'am sorry, our credulitie wrong'd him. [*Exit* VOLPONE, *attended.*]

4TH AVOCATORE These are two creatures!

3RD AVOCATORE   I have an earthquake in

    me!

2ND AVOCATORE Their shame (even in their cradles) fled their

    faces.

4TH AVOCATORE You'have done a worthy service to the state, sir,   60

    In their discoverie.

1ST AVOCATORE   You shall heare, ere night,

    What punishment the court decrees upon 'hem.

VOLTORE We thanke your fatherhoods. [*Exeunt* NOTARIO,

    AVOCATORI *and* COMMANDADORI.] How like you it?

MOSCA   Rare.

    I'ld ha' your tongue, sir, tipt with gold, for this;

    I'ld ha' you be the heire to the whole citie;

    The earth I'ld have want men, ere you want living:

    They'are bound to erect your statue, in St. MARKES.

    Signior CORVINO, I would have you goe,

    And shew your selfe, that you have conquer'd.

CORVINO   Yes.

MOSCA It was much better, that you should professe   70

    Your selfe a cuckold, thus, then that the other

    Should have beene prov'd.

CORVINO   Nay, I consider'd that:

    Now, it is her fault.

MOSCA   Then, it had beene yours.

CORVINO True, I doe doubt this Advocate, still.

MOSCA   I'faith,

    You need not, I dare ease you of that care.

CORVINO I trust thee, MOSCA.

MOSCA   As your owne soule, sir.

                               [*Exit* CORVINO.]

CORBACCIO   MOSCA.

MOSCA Now for your businesse, sir.

CORBACCIO   How? ha' you busines?

MOSCA Yes, yours, sir.

CORBACCIO   O, none else?

MOSCA   None else, not I.

CORBACCIO Be carefull then.

MOSCA   Rest you, with both your eyes, sir.

CORBACCIO Dispatch it.

MOSCA   Instantly.

80   CORBACCIO   And looke, that all,
        What-ever, be put in, jewels, plate, moneyes,
        Household-stuffe, bedding, cortines.

MOSCA   Cortine-rings, sir,
        Onely, the Advocates fee must be deducted.

CORBACCIO I'le pay him, now: you'll be too prodigall.

MOSCA Sir, I must tender it.

CORBACCIO   Two *cecchines* is well?

MOSCA No, six, sir.

CORBACCIO   'Tis too much.

MOSCA   He talk'd a great while,
        You must consider that, sir.

CORBACCIO   Well, there's three—

MOSCA I'le give it him.

CORBACCIO   Doe so, and there's for thee.   [*Exit.*]

MOSCA Bountifull bones! What horride strange offence

90   Did he commit 'gainst nature, in his youth,
        Worthy this age? you see, sir, how I worke
        Unto your ends; take you no notice.

VOLTORE   No,
        I'le leave you.

MOSCA   All, is yours; [*Exit* VOLTORE.] the devill, and all:
        Good Advocate. Madame, I'le bring you home.

LADY WOULD-BEE No, I'le goe see your patron.

MOSCA   That you shall not:
        I'le tell you, why. My purpose is, to urge
        My patron to reforme his will; and, for
        The zeale you' have shew'n to day, whereas before
        You were but third, or, fourth, you shall be now

Put in the first: which would appeare as beg'd, 100
If you were present. Therefore—

LADY WOULD-BEE You shall sway me. [*Exeunt.*]

Act V. Scene 1

VOLPONE.

[*Enter* VOLPONE.]

[VOLPONE] Well, I am here; and all this brunt is past:
I ne're was in dislike with my disguise,
Till this fled moment; here, 'twas good, in private,
But, in your publike, *Cave*, whil'st I breathe.
'Fore god, my left legge 'gan to have the crampe;
And I apprehended, straight, some power had strooke me
With a dead palsey: well, I must be merry,
And shake it off. A many of these feares
Would put me into some villanous disease,
Should they come thick upon me: I'le prevent 'hem. 10
Give me a boule of lustie wine, to fright
This humor from my heart; (hum, hum, hum) *He drinkes.*
'Tis almost gone, already: I shall conquer.
Any device, now, of rare, ingenious knavery,
That would possesse me with a violent laughter,
Would make me up, againe! So, so, so, so. *Drinkes againe.*
This heate is life; 'tis bloud, by this time: MOSCA!

Act V. Scene 2

MOSCA, VOLPONE, NANO, CASTRONE.

[*Enter* MOSCA.]

MOSCA How now, sir? do's the day looke cleare againe?
Are we recover'd? and wrought out of error,
Into our way? to see our path, before us?
Is our trade free, once more?

VOLPONE Exquisite MOSCA!

MOSCA Was it not carry'd learnedly?

VOLPONE   And stoutly.
    Good wits are greatest in extremities.

MOSCA It were a folly, beyond thought, to trust
    Any grand act unto a cowardly spirit:
    You are not taken with it, enough, me thinkes?

10 VOLPONE O, more, then if I had enjoy'd the wench:
    The pleasure of all woman-kind's not like it.

MOSCA Why, now you speake, sir. We must, here be fixt;
    Here, we must rest; this is our master-peece:
    We cannot thinke, to goe beyond this.

VOLPONE   True,
    Thou'hast playd thy prise, my precious MOSCA.

MOSCA   Nay, sir,
    To gull the court—

VOLPONE   And, quite divert the torrent,
    Upon the innocent.

MOSCA   Yes, and to make
    So rare a musique out of discordes—

VOLPONE   Right.
    That, yet, to me's the strangest! how th'hast borne it!

20   That these (being so divided 'mongst themselves)
    Should not sent some-what, or in me, or thee,
    Or doubt their owne side.

MOSCA   True, they will not see't.
    Too much light blinds 'hem, I thinke. Each of 'hem
    Is so possest, and stuft with his owne hopes,
    That any thing, unto the contrary,
    Never so true, or never so apparent,
    Never so palpable, they will resist it—

VOLPONE Like a temptation of the divell.

MOSCA   Right, sir.
    Merchants may talke of trade, and your great signiors

30   Of land, that yeelds well; but if *Italy*
    Have any glebe, more fruitfull, then these fellowes,
    I am deceiv'd. Did not your Advocate rare?

VOLPONE O (my most honor'd fathers, my grave fathers,
    Under correction of your father-hoods,
    What face of truth is here? If these strange deeds

May passe, most honour'd fathers——) I had much a doe
To forbeare laughing.

MOSCA   'T seem'd to mee, you sweat, sir.

VOLPONE In troth, I did a little.

MOSCA   But confesse, sir,
Were you not daunted?

VOLPONE   In good faith, I was
A little in a mist; but not dejected: 40
Never, but still my selfe.

MOSCA   I thinke it, sir.
Now (so truth helpe me) I must needes say this, sir,
And, out of conscience, for your advocate:
He' has taken paines, in faith, sir, and deserv'd,
(In my poore judgement, I speake it, under favour,
Not to contrary you, sir) very richly——
Well——to be cosen'd.

VOLPONE   'Troth, and I thinke so too,
By that I heard him, in the latter end.

MOSCA O, but before, sir; had you heard him, first,
Draw it to certaine heads, then aggravate,   50
Then use his vehement figures—— I look'd still,
When he would shift a shirt; and, doing this
Out of pure love, no hope of gaine——

VOLPONE   'Tis right.
I cannot answer him, MOSCA, as I would,
Not yet; but for thy sake, at thy intreaty,
I will beginne, ev'n now, to vexe 'hem all:
This very instant.

MOSCA   Good, sir.

VOLPONE   Call the dwarfe,
And eunuch, forth.

MOSCA   CASTRONE, NANO.

NANO   Here.

[Enter NANO and CASTRONE.]

VOLPONE Shal we have a jig, now?

MOSCA   What you please, sir.

VOLPONE   Go,
Streight, give out, about the streetes, you two,   60

That I am dead; doe it with constancy,
Sadly, doe you heare? impute it to the griefe
Of this late slander.   [*Exeunt* NANO *and* CASTRONE.]

MOSCA   What doe you meane, sir?

VOLPONE   O,
I shall have, instantly, my vulture, crow,
Raven, come flying hither (on the newes)
To peck for carrion, my shee-wolfe, and all,
Greedy, and full of expectation——

MOSCA And then to have it ravish'd from their mouthes?

VOLPONE 'Tis true, I will ha' thee put on a gowne,
70   And take upon thee, as thou wert mine heire;
Shew 'hem a will: open that chest, and reach
Forth one of those, that has the blankes. I'le straight
Put in thy name.

MOSCA   It will be rare, sir.

VOLPONE   I,
When they e'ene gape, and finde themselves deluded——

MOSCA Yes.

VOLPONE   And thou use them skirvily. Dispatch,
Get on thy gowne.

MOSCA   But, what, sir, if they aske
After the body?

VOLPONE   Say, it was corrupted.

MOSCA I'le say, it stunke, sir; and was faine t'have it
Coffin'd up instantly, and sent away.

80   VOLPONE Any thing, what thou wilt. Hold, here's my will.
Get thee a cap, a count-booke, pen and inke,
Papers afore thee; sit, as thou wert taking
An inventory of parcels: I'le get up,
Behind the cortine, on a stoole, and harken;
Sometime, peepe over; see, how they doe looke;
With what degrees, their bloud doth leave their faces!
O, 'twill afford me a rare meale of laughter.

MOSCA Your Advocate will turne stark dull, upon it.

VOLPONE It will take off his oratories edge.

90   MOSCA But your *Clarissimo*, old round-backe, he

Will crumpe you, like a hog-louse, with the touch.
VOLPONE And what CORVINO?
MOSCA   O, sir, looke for him,
To morrow morning, with a rope, and a dagger,
To visite all the streetes; he must runne mad.
My Lady too, that came into the court,
To beare false witnesse, for your worship—
VOLPONE   Yes,
And kist mee 'fore the fathers; when my face
Flow'd all with oyles.
MOSCA   And sweate, sir. Why, your gold
Is such another med'cine, it dries up
All those offensive savors! It transformes   100
The most deformed, and restores 'hem lovely,
As 't were the strange poeticall girdle. JOVE   *Cestus.*
Could not invent, t'himselfe, a shroud more subtile,
To passe ACRISIUS guardes. It is the thing
Makes all the world her grace, her youth, her beauty.
VOLPONE I thinke, she loves me.
MOSCA   Who? the lady, sir?
Shee's jealous of you.
VOLPONE   Do'st thou say so?
MOSCA   Harke,
There's some already.
VOLPONE   Looke.
MOSCA   It is the vulture:
He has the quickest sent.
VOLPONE   I'le to my place,
Thou, to thy posture.
MOSCA   I am set.
VOLPONE   But, MOSCA,   110
Play the artificer now, torture 'hem, rarely.

Act V. Scene 3

VOLTORE, MOSCA, CORBACCIO, CORVINO,

LADY, VOLPONE.

[*Enter* VOLTORE, *with* SERVANTS.]

VOLTORE How now, my MOSCA?

MOSCA   Turkie carpets, nine—

VOLTORE Taking an inventory? that is well.

MOSCA Two sutes of bedding, tissew—

VOLTORE   Where's the will?

Let me read that, the while.

[*Enter* CORBACCIO.]

CORBACCIO   So, set me downe:

And get you home.   [*Exit* SERVANTS.]

VOLTORE   Is he come, now, to trouble us?

MOSCA Of cloth of gold, two more—

CORBACCIO   Is it done, MOSCA?

MOSCA Of severall vellets, eight—

VOLTORE   I like his care.

CORBACCIO Dost thou not heare?

[*Enter* CORVINO.]

CORVINO   Ha? is the houre come, MOSCA?

VOLPONE I, now, they muster.

CORVINO   What do's the advocate here?

Or this CORBACCIO?

CORBACCIO   What do these here?

[*Enter* LADY WOULD-BEE.]

10 LADY WOULD-BEE   MOSCA?

Is his thred spunne?

MOSCA   Eight chests of linnen—

VOLPONE   O,

My fine dame WOULD-BEE, too!

CORVINO   MOSCA, the will,

That I may shew it these, and rid 'hem hence.

MOSCA Six chests of diaper, foure of damaske— There.

CORBACCIO Is that the will?

Volpone peepes from behinde a traverse.

MOSCA   Down-beds, and boulsters—

VOLPONE   Rare!

Be busie still. Now, they begin to flutter:
They never thinke of me. Looke, see, see, see!
How their swift eies runne over the long deed,
Unto the name, and to the legacies,
What is bequeath'd them, there—

MOSCA   Ten sutes of hangings—   20

VOLPONE I, i'their garters, MOSCA. Now, their hopes
Are at the gaspe.

VOLTORE   MOSCA the heire!

CORBACCIO   What's that?

VOLPONE My advocate is dumbe, looke to my merchant,
Hee has heard of some strange storme, a ship is lost,
He faints: my lady will swoune. Old glazen-eyes,
He hath not reach'd his dispaire, yet.

CORBACCIO   All these
Are out of hope, I'am sure the man.

CORVINO   But, MOSCA—

MOSCA Two cabenets—

CORVINO   Is this in earnest?

MOSCA   One
Of ebony.—

CORVINO   Or, do you but delude me?

MOSCA The other, mother of pearle—I am very busie.   30
Good faith, it is a fortune throwne upon me—
Item, one salt of agat—not my seeking.

LADY WOULD-BEE Do you heare, sir?

MOSCA   A perfum'd boxe—'pray you forebeare,
You see I am troubled—made of an _onyx_—

LADY WOULD-BEE   How!

MOSCA To morrow, or next day, I shall be at leasure,
To talke with you all.

CORVINO   Is this my large hopes issue?

LADY WOULD-BEE Sir, I must have a fayrer answer.

MOSCA   Madame!
Mary, and shall: 'pray you, fairely quit my house.

Nay, raise no tempest with your lookes; but, harke you:

40 Remember, what your ladiship offred me,
To put you in, an heire; goe to, thinke on't.
And what you said, eene your best madames did
For maintenance, and, why not you? inough.
Goe home, and use the poore sir POL, your knight, well;
For feare I tell some riddles: go, be melancholique.

[*Exit* LADY WOULD-BEE.]

VOLPONE O, my fine divell!

CORVINO   MOSCA, 'pray you a word.

MOSCA Lord! will not you take your dispatch hence, yet?
Me thinkes (of all) you should have beene th'example.
Why should you stay, here? with what thought? what promise?

50 Heare you, doe not you know, I know you an asse?
And, that you would, most faine, have beene a wittoll,
If fortune would have let you? that you are
A declar'd cuckold, on good termes? this pearle,
You'll say, was yours? right: this diamant?
I'le not deny't, but thanke you. Much here, else?
It may be so. Why, thinke that these good works
May helpe to hide your bad: I'le not betray you,
Although you be but extraordinary,
And have it onely in title, it sufficeth.

60 Go home, be melancholique too, or mad.   [*Exit* CORVINO.]

VOLPONE Rare, MOSCA! how his villany becomes him!

VOLTORE Certaine, he doth delude all these, for me.

CORBACCIO MOSCA, the heire?

VOLPONE   O, his foure eyes have found it!

CORBACCIO I'am cosen'd, cheated, by a parasite-slave;
Harlot, t'hast gul'd me.

MOSCA   Yes, sir. Stop your mouth,
Or I shall draw the onely tooth, is left.
Are not you he, that filthy covetous wretch,
With the three legges, that here, in hope of prey,
Have, any time this three yeere, snuft about,

70 With your most grov'ling nose; and would have hir'd
Me to the pois'ning of my patron? sir?
Are not you he, that have, to day, in court,

    Profess'd the dis-inheriting of your sonne?
    Perjur'd your selfe? Go home, and die, and stinke;
    If you but croake a sillable, all comes out:
    Away and call your porters, go, go, stinke.   [*Exit* CORBACCIO.]

VOLPONE Excellent varlet!

VOLTORE   Now, my faithfull MOSCA,
    I finde thy constancie.

MOSCA   Sir?

VOLTORE   Sincere.

MOSCA   A table
    Of porphyry— I mar'le, you'll be thus troublesome.

VOLTORE Nay, leave off now, they are gone.

MOSCA   Why? who are you?   80
    What? who did send for you? O 'cry you mercy,
    Reverend sir! good faith, I am greev'd for you,
    That any chance of mine should thus defeate
    Your (I must needs say) most deserving travels:
    But, I protest, sir, it was cast upon me,
    And I could, almost, wish to be without it,
    But, that the will o' th' dead, must be observ'd.
    Mary, my joy is, that you need it not,
    You have a gift, sir, (thanke your education)
    Will never let you want, while there are men,   90
    And malice, to breed causes. Would I had
    But halfe the like, for all my fortune, sir.
    If I have any suites (as I doe hope,
    Things being so easie, and direct, I shall not)
    I wil make bold with your obstreperous aide,
    (Conceive me) for your fee, sir. In meane time,
    You, that have so much law, I know ha' the conscience,
    Not to be covetous of what is mine.
    Good sir, I thanke you for my plate: 'twill helpe
    To set up a yong man. Good faith, you looke   100
    As you were costive; best go home, and purge, sir.
                            [*Exit* VOLTORE.]

VOLPONE Bid him, eat lettuce well: my wittie *mischiefe*,
    Let me embrace thee. O, that I could now
    Transforme thee to a VENUS— MOSCA, goe,

Streight, take my habit of *Clarissimo*;
And walke the streets; be seene, torment 'hem more:
We must pursew, as well as plot. Who would
Have lost this feast?

MOSCA   I doubt it will loose them.

VOLPONE O, my recovery shall recover all.

110   That I could now but thinke on some disguise,
To meet 'hem in: and aske 'hem questions.
How I would vexe 'hem still, at every turne?

MOSCA Sir, I can fit you.

VOLPONE   Canst thou?

MOSCA   Yes, I know
One o' the *Commandatori*, sir, so like you,
Him will I streight make drunke, and bring you his habit.

VOLPONE A rare disguise, and answering thy braine!
O, I will be a sharpe disease unto 'hem.

MOSCA Sir, you must looke for curses—

VOLPONE   Till they burst;
The *Foxe* fares ever best, when he is curst.   [*Exeunt.*]

Act V. Scene 4

PEREGRINE, MERCATORI. 3, WOMAN, POLITIQUE.

[*Enter* PEREGRINE *and* 3 MERCATORI.]

PEREGRINE Am I enough disguis'd?

1ST MERCATORE   I warrant you.

PEREGRINE All my ambition is to fright him, onely.

2ND MERCATORE If you could ship him away, 'twere excellent.

3RD MERCATORE To *Zant*, or to *Alepo*?

PEREGRINE   Yes, and ha' his
Adventures put i' th' *booke of voyages*,
And his guld story registred, for truth?
Well, gentlemen, when I am in, a while,
And that you thinke us warme in our discourse,
Know your approaches.

1ST MERCATORE   Trust it to our care.

                                        [*Exeunt* MERCATORI.]

[*Enter* WOMAN.]

PEREGRINE Save you, faire lady. Is sir POLL. within?   10

WOMAN I do not know, sir.

PEREGRINE   'Pray you, say unto him,
   Here is a merchant, upon earnest businesse,
   Desires to speake with him.

WOMAN   I will see, sir.

PEREGRINE   'Pray you.
                                    [*Exit* WOMAN.]

   I see, the family is all female, here.
       [*Enter* WOMAN.]

WOMAN He sai's, sir, he has waighty affaires of state,
   That now require him whole, some other time
   You may possesse him.

PEREGRINE   'Pray you say againe,
   If those require him whole, these will exact him,
   Whereof I bring him tidings. [*Exit* WOMAN.] What might be
   His grave affaire of state, now? how, to make   20
   Bolognian sauseges, here, in *Venice*, sparing
   One o' th' ingredients.
       [*Enter* WOMAN.]

WOMAN   Sir, he sai's, he knowes
   By your word, tidings, that you are no states-man,
   And therefore, wills you stay.

PEREGRINE   Sweet, 'pray you returne him,
   I have not read so many proclamations,
   And studied them, for words, as he has done,
   But— Here he deignes to come.   [*Exit* WOMAN.]
       [*Enter* SIR POLITIQUE.]

SIR POLITIQUE   Sir, I must crave
   Your courteous pardon. There hath chanc'd (to day)
   Unkinde disaster, 'twixt my lady, and mee:
   And I was penning my apologie   30
   To give her satisfaction, as you came, now.

PEREGRINE Sir, I am griev'd, I bring you worse disaster;
   The gentleman, you met at th' port, to day,
   That told you, he was newly arriv'd—

SIR POLITIQUE   I, was

  A fugitive punke?

PEREGRINE   No, sir, a spie, set on you:
  And, he has made relation to the Senate,
  That you profest to him, to have a plot,
  To sell the state of *Venice*, to the *Turke*.

SIR POLITIQUE O me!

PEREGRINE   For which, warrants are sign'd by this time,
40 To apprehend you, and to search your study,
  For papers—

SIR POLITIQUE Alasse, sir. I have none, but notes,
  Drawne out of play-bookes—

PEREGRINE   All the better, sir.

SIR POLITIQUE And some essayes. What shall I doe?

PEREGRINE   Sir, best
  Convay your selfe into a sugar-chest,
  Or, if you could lie round, a fraile were rare:
  And I could send you, aboard.

SIR POLITIQUE   Sir, I but talk'd so,
  For discourse sake, merely.

PEREGRINE   Harke, they are there.

SIR POLITIQUE I am a wretch, a wretch.

PEREGRINE   What, will you doe, sir?
  Ha' you ne're a curren-but to leape into?
50 They'll put you to the racke, you must be sudden.

SIR POLITIQUE Sir, I have an ingine—

(3RD MERCATORE   Sir POLITIQUE
  WOULD-BE?

2ND MERCATORE Where is he?)

SIR POLITIQUE   That I have thought upon, before time.

PEREGRINE What is it?

SIR POLITIQUE   (I shall ne're indure the torture.)
  Mary, it is, sir, of a tortoyse-shell,
  Fitted, for these extremities: 'pray you sir, helpe me.
  Here, I' have a place, sir, to put backe my leggs,
  (Please you to lay it on, sir) with this cap,
  And my blacke gloves, I'le lye, sir, like a tortoyse,
  Till they are gone.

PEREGRINE   And, call you this an ingine?

*They knocke
without.*

SIR POLITIQUE Mine owne device—good sir, bid my wives

    women   60

  To burne my papers.   *They rush in.*

    [*Enter* MERCATORI.]

1ST MERCATORE   Where's he hid?

3RD MERCATORE   We must,

  And will, sure, find him.

2ND MERCATORE   Which is his study?

1ST MERCATORE   What

  Are you, sir?

PEREGRINE   I'am a merchant, that came heere

  To looke upon this tortoyse.

3RD MERCATORE   How?

1ST MERCATORE   St. MARKE!

  What beast is this?

PEREGRINE   It is a fish.

2ND MERCATORE   Come out, here.

PEREGRINE Nay, you may strike him, sir, and tread upon him:

  Hee'll beare a cart.

1ST MERCATORE   What, to runne over him?

PEREGRINE   Yes.

3RD MERCATORE Let's jump, upon him.

2ND MERCATORE   Can he not go?

PEREGRINE   He creeps, sir.

1ST MERCATORE Let's see him creepe.

PEREGRINE   No, good sir, you will hurt him.

2ND MERCATORE (Heart) I'le see him creepe; or pricke his guts.   70

3RD MERCATORE Come out, here.

PEREGRINE   'Pray you sir, (creepe a little).

1ST MERCATORE   Foorth.

2ND MERCATORE Yet furder.

PEREGRINE   Good sir, (creep).

2ND MERCATORE   We'll see his legs.

3RD MERCATORE Gods'so, he has garters!   *They pull of the*

1ST MERCATORE   I, and gloves!   *shel and*

2ND MERCATORE   Is this   *discover him.*

  Your fearefull tortoyse?

PEREGRINE   Now, sir POLL. we are even;

For your next project, I shall be prepar'd:
I am sorry, for the funerall of your notes, sir.

1ST MERCATORE 'Twere a rare motion, to be seene in *Fleet-street*!

2ND MERCATORE I, i'the terme.

1ST MERCATORE   Or *Smithfield*, in the faire.

3RD MERCATORE Me thinkes, tis but a melancholique sight!

PEREGRINE Farewell, most politique tortoyse.

                [*Exeunt* PEREGRINE *and* MERCATORI.]

    [*Enter* WOMAN.]

80   SIR POLITIQUE   Where's my lady?
Knowes shee of this?

WOMAN   I know not, sir.

SIR POLITIQUE   Enquire. [*Exit* WOMAN.]
O, I shall be the fable of all feasts;
The freight of the *gazetti*; ship-boyes tale;
And, which is worst, even talke for ordinaries.

    [*Enter* WOMAN.]

WOMAN My lady's come most melancholique, home,
And say's, sir, she will straight to sea, for physick.

SIR POLITIQUE And I, to shunne, this place, and clime for ever;
Creeping, with house, on backe: and thinke it well,
To shrinke my poore head, in my politique shell.   [*Exeunt.*]

Act V. Scene 5

VOLPONE, MOSCA.

The first, in the habit of a Commandadore: the other, of a Clarissimo.

    [*Enter* VOLPONE *and* MOSCA.]

VOLPONE Am I then like him?

MOSCA   O, sir, you are he:
No man can sever you.

VOLPONE   Good.

MOSCA   But, what am I?

VOLPONE 'Fore heav'n, a brave *Clarissimo*, thou becom'st it!
Pitty, thou wert not borne one.

MOSCA   If I hold
My made one, 'twill be well.

VOLPONE   I'le goe, and see

What newes, first, at the court.   [*Exit.*]

MOSCA   Doe so. My FOXE
Is out on his hole, and, ere he shall re-enter,
I'le make him languish, in his borrow'd case,
Except he come to composition, with me:
ANDROGINO, CASTRONE, NANO.   10
    [*Enter* ANDROGYNO, CASTRONE *and* NANO.]
ALL   Here.
MOSCA Goe recreate your selves, abroad; goe, sport:
    [*Exeunt* ANDROGYNO, CASTRONE *and* NANO.]
So, now I have the keies, and am possest.
Since he will, needes, be dead, afore his time,
I'le burie him, or gaine by him. I'am his heire:
And so will keepe me, till he share at least.
To cosen him of all, were but a cheat
Well plac'd; no man would construe it a sinne:
Let his sport pay for't, this is call'd the FOXE-trap.   [*Exit.*]

Act V. Scene 6

CORBACCIO, CORVINO, VOLPONE.

    [*Enter* CORBACCIO *and* CORVINO.]
CORBACCIO They say, the court is set.
CORVINO   We must maintaine
Our first tale good, for both our reputations.
CORBACCIO Why? mine's no tale: my sonne would, there, have
    kild me.
CORVINO That's true, I had forgot: mine is, I am sure.
But, for your will, sir.
CORBACCIO   I, I'le come upon him,
For that, hereafter, now his Patron's dead.
    [*Enter* VOLPONE.]
VOLPONE Signior CORVINO! and CORBACCIO! sir,
Much joy unto you.
CORVINO   Of what?
VOLPONE   The sodaine good,
Dropt downe upon you—

CORBACCIO   Where?

VOLPONE   (And, none knowes how)
    From old VOLPONE, sir.

10   CORBACCIO   Out, errant knave.

VOLPONE Let not your too much wealth, sir, make you furious.

CORBACCIO Away, thou varlet.

VOLPONE   Why sir?

CORBACCIO   Do'st thou mocke me?

VOLPONE You mocke the world, sir, did you not change wills?

CORBACCIO Out, harlot.

VOLPONE   O! belike you are the man,
    Signior CORVINO? 'faith, you carry it well;
    You grow not mad withall: I love your spirit.
    You are not over-leaven'd, with your fortune.
    You should ha' some would swell, now, like a wine-fat,
    With such an *Autumne*— Did he gi' you all, sir?

CORVINO Avoid, you rascall.

20   VOLPONE   Troth, your wife has shew'ne
    Her selfe a very woman: but, you are well,
    You neede not care, you have a good estate,
    To beare it out, sir, better by this chance.
    Except CORBACCIO have a share?

CORBACCIO   Hence, varlet.

VOLPONE You will not be a'knowne, sir: why, 'tis wise.
    Thus doe all gam'sters, at all games, dissemble.
    No man will seeme to winne. [*Exeunt* CORBACCIO *and*
    CORVINO.] Here, comes my vulture,
    Heaving his beake up i' the ayre, and snuffing.

Act V. Scene 7

VOLTORE, VOLPONE.

[*Enter* VOLTORE.]

VOLTORE Out-stript thus, by a parasite? a slave?
    Would run on errands? and make legs, for crummes?
    Well, what I'le do—

VOLPONE   The court staies for your worship.

I eene rejoyce, sir, at your worships happinesse,
And that it fell into so learned hands,
That understand the fingering.——

VOLTORE   What doe you meane?

VOLPONE I meane to be a sutor to your worship,
For the small tenement, out of reparations;
That, at the end of your long row of houses,
By the *piscaria*: it was, in VOLPONE's time,   10
Your predecessor, ere he grew diseas'd,
A handsome, pretty, custom'd, bawdy-house,
As any was in *Venice* (none disprais'd)
But fell with him; his body, and that house
Decay'd, together.

VOLTORE   Come, sir, leave your prating.

VOLPONE Why, if your worship give me but your hand,
That I may ha' the refusall; I have done.
'Tis a meere toy, to you, sir; candle rents:
As your learn'd worship knowes——

VOLTORE   What doe I know?

VOLPONE Mary no end of your wealth, sir, god decrease it.   20

VOLTORE Mistaking knave! what, mock'st thou my misfortune?

VOLPONE His blessing on your heart, sir, would 'twere more.

                                    [*Exit* VOLTORE.]

(Now, to my first, againe; at the next corner.)

Act V. Scene 8

CORBACCIO, CORVINO, MOSCA, (*passant*) VOLPONE.

[*Enter* CORBACCIO *and* CORVINO; MOSCA *passes over the stage.*]

CORBACCIO See, in our habite! see the impudent varlet!

CORVINO That I could shoote mine eies at him, like gun-stones.

VOLPONE But, is this true, sir, of the parasite?

CORBACCIO Againe, t'afflict us? monster!

VOLPONE   In good faith, sir,
I'am hartily greev'd, a beard of your grave length
Should be so over-reach'd. I never brook'd
That parasites haire, me thought his nose should cosen:

There still was somewhat, in his looke, did promise
The bane of a *Clarissimo*.

CORBACCIO   Knave—

VOLPONE   Me thinkes,

10   Yet you, that are so traded i' the world,
A witty merchant, the fine bird, CORVINO,
That have such morall *emblemes* on your name,
Should not have sung your shame; and dropt your cheese:
To let the FOXE laugh at your emptinesse.

CORVINO   Sirrah, you thinke, the priviledge of the place,
And your red saucy cap, that seemes (to me)
Nayl'd to your jolt-head, with those two *cecchines*,
Can warrant your abuses; come you, hither:
You shall perceive, sir, I dare beate you. Approch.

20   VOLPONE   No haste, sir, I doe know your valure, well:
Since you durst publish what you are, sir.

CORVINO   Tarry,
I'ld speake, with you.

VOLPONE   Sir, sir, another time—

CORVINO   Nay, now.

VOLPONE   O god, sir! I were a wise man,
Would stand the fury of a distracted cuckold.

Mosca walkes by 'hem.

CORBACCIO   What! come againe?

VOLPONE   Upon 'hem, MOSCA; save me.

CORBACCIO   The ayre's infected, where he breathes.

CORVINO   Lets flye him.

[*Exeunt* CORVINO *and* CORBACCIO.]

VOLPONE   Excellent *Basiliske*! turne upon the *vulture*.

Act V. Scene 9

VOLTORE, MOSCA, VOLPONE.

[*Enter* VOLTORE.]

VOLTORE   Well, flesh-flie, it is sommer with you, now;
Your winter will come on.

MOSCA   Good Advocate,
'Pray thee, not raile, nor threaten out of place, thus;

Thou 'lt make a *soloecisme* (as madame sayes.)
Get you a biggen, more: your braine breakes loose.   [*Exit.*]
VOLTORE Well, sir.
VOLPONE   Would you ha' me beate the insolent slave?
Throw dirt, upon his first good cloathes?
VOLTORE   This same
Is, doubtlesse, some familiar!
VOLPONE   Sir, the court
In troth, stayes for you. I am mad, a mule,
That never read JUSTINIAN, should get up,   10
And ride an Advocate. Had you no quirke,
To avoide gullage, sir, by such a creature?
I hope you doe but jest; he has not done 't:
This's but confederacy, to blind the rest.
You are the heire?
VOLTORE   A strange, officious,
Trouble-some knave! thou dost torment me.
VOLPONE   I know—
It cannot be, sir, that you should be cosen'd;
'Tis not within the wit of man, to doe it:
You are so wise, so prudent, and, 'tis fit,
That wealth, and wisdome still, should goe together.   [*Exeunt.*]   20

Act V. Scene 10

AVOCATORI, 4, NOTARIO, COMMANDADORI,
BONARIO, CELIA, CORBACCIO, COR-
VINO, VOLTORE, VOLPONE.

[*Enter* 4 AVOCATORI, NOTARIO, COMMANDADORI,
BONARIO, CELIA, CORBACCIO *and* CORVINO.]
1ST AVOCATORE Are all the parties, here?
NOTARIO   All, but the Advocate.
2ND AVOCATORE And, here he comes.
          [*Enter* VOLTORE *and* VOLPONE.]
1ST AVOCATORE   Then bring 'hem foorth to sentence.
VOLTORE O, my most honour'd fathers, let your mercy
Once winne upon your justice, to forgive—

I am distracted——

(VOLPONE   What will he doe, now?)

VOLTORE   O,

I know not which t'addresse my selfe to, first,

Whether your father-hoods, or these innocents——

(CORVINO   Will he betray himselfe?)

VOLTORE   Whom, equally,

I have abus'd, out of most covetous endes——

(CORVINO   The man is mad!

CORBACCIO   What's that?

10   CORVINO   He is possest.)

VOLTORE   For which; now strooke in conscience, here I prostrate

My selfe, at your offended feet, for pardon.

1ST *and* 2ND AVOCATORI   Arise.

CELIA   O heav'n, how just thou art!

VOLPONE   I'am caught

I' mine owne noose——

CORVINO   Be constant, sir, nought now

Can helpe, but impudence.

1ST AVOCATORE   Speake forward.

COMMANDADORI   Silence.

VOLTORE   It is not passion in me, reverend fathers,

But onely conscience, conscience my good sires,

That makes me, now, tell truth. That parasite,

That knave hath been the instrument of all.

2ND AVOCATORE   Where is that knave? fetch him.

VOLPONE   I goe.   [*Exit.*]

20   CORVINO   Grave fathers,

This man's distracted; he confest it, now:

For, hoping to be old VOLPONE's heire,

Who now is dead——

3RD AVOCATORE   How?

2ND AVOCATORE   Is VOLPONE dead?

CORVINO   Dead since, grave fathers——

BONARIO   O, sure vengeance!

1ST AVOCATORE   Stay,

Then, he was no deceiver?

VOLTORE   O no, none:

The parasite, grave fathers.

CORVINO   He do's speake,
    Out of meere envie, 'cause the servant's made
    The thing, he gap't for; please your father-hoods,
    This is the truth: though, I'le not justifie
    The other, but he may be some-deale faulty.   30

VOLTORE I, to your hopes, as well as mine, CORVINO:
    But I'le use modesty. Pleaseth your wisdomes
    To viewe these certaine notes, and but conferre them;
    As I hope favour, they shall speake cleare truth.

CORVINO The devill ha's entred him!

BONARIO   Or bides in you.

4TH AVOCATORE We have done ill, by a publike officer,
    To send for him, if he be heire.

2ND AVOCATORE   For whom?

4TH AVOCATORE Him, that they call the parasite.

3RD AVOCATORE   'Tis true;
    He is a man, of great estate, now left.

4TH AVOCATORE Goe you, and learne his name; and say, the court   40
    Intreates his presence, here; but, to the clearing
    Of some few doubts.   [*Exit* NOTARIO.]

2ND AVOCATORE   This same's a labyrinth!

1ST AVOCATORE Stand you unto your first report?

CORVINO   My state,
    My life, my fame—

BONARIO   (Where is't?)

CORVINO   Are at the stake.

1ST AVOCATORE Is yours so too?

CORBACCIO   The Advocate's a knave:
    And has a forked tongue—

2ND AVOCATORE   (Speake to the point.)

CORBACCIO So is the parasite, too.

1ST AVOCATORE   This is confusion.

VOLTORE I doe beseech your father-hoods, read but those;

CORVINO And credit nothing, the false spirit hath writ:
    It cannot be, but he is possest, grave fathers.   [*Exeunt.*]   50

Act V. Scene 11

VOLPONE, NANO, ANDROGINO,
CASTRONE.

[*Enter* VOLPONE.]

VOLPONE To make a snare, for mine owne necke! and run
    My head into it, wilfully! with laughter!
    When I had newly scap't, was free, and cleare!
    Out of mere wantonnesse! o, the dull devill
    Was in this braine of mine, when I devis'd it;
    And MOSCA gave it second: he must now
    Helpe to seare up this veyne, or we bleed dead.
       [*Enter* NANO, ANDROGYNO *and* CASTRONE.]
    How now! who let you loose? whither goe you, now?
    What? to buy ginger-bread? or to drowne kitlings?

10 NANO Sir, master MOSCA call'd us out of doores,
    And bid us all goe play, and tooke the keies.

ANDROGYNO   Yes.

VOLPONE Did master MOSCA take the keyes? why, so!
    I am farder, in. These are my fine conceipts!
    I must be merry, with a mischiefe to me!
    What a vile wretch was I, that could not beare
    My fortune soberly? I must ha' my crotchets!
    And my *conundrums*! well, goe you, and seeke him:
    His meaning may be truer, then my feare.
    Bid him, he streight come to me, to the court;

20   Thither will I, and, if 't be possible,
    Un-screw my advocate, upon new hopes:
    When I provok'd him, then I lost my selfe.   [*Exeunt.*]

Act V. Scene 12

AVOCATORI, &C.

[*Enter* 4 AVOCATORI, NOTARIO, COMMANDADORI,
BONARIO, CELIA, CORBACCIO, CORVINO *and* VOLTORE.]

1ST AVOCATORE These things can nere be reconcil'd. He, here,

Professeth, that the gentleman was wrong'd;
And that the gentlewoman was brought thither,
Forc'd by her husband: and there left.

VOLTORE   Most true.

CELIA How ready is heav'n to those, that pray!

1ST AVOCATORE   But, that
Volpone would have ravish'd her, he holds
Utterly false; knowing his impotence.

CORVINO Grave fathers, he is possest; againe, I say,
Possest: nay, if there be possession,
And obsession, he has both.

3RD AVOCATORE   Here comes our officer.   10
   [*Enter* VOLPONE.]

VOLPONE The parasite will streight be here, grave fathers.

4TH AVOCATORE You might invent some other name, sir varlet.

3RD AVOCATORE Did not the notarie meet him?

VOLPONE   Not that I know.

4TH AVOCATORE His comming will cleare all.

2ND AVOCATORE   Yet it is mistie.

VOLTORE May't please your father hoods—

VOLPONE   Sir, the parasite   *Volpone*
Will'd me to tell you, that his master lives;   *whispers the*
That you are still the man; your hopes the same;   *Advocate.*
And this was, onely a jest—

VOLTORE   How?

VOLPONE   Sir, to trie
If you were firme, and how you stood affected.

VOLTORE Art' sure he lives?

VOLPONE   Doe I live, sir?

VOLTORE   O me!   20
I was to violent.

VOLPONE   Sir, you may redeeme it,
They said, you were possest; fall downe, and seeme so:
I'le helpe to make it good. God blesse the man!   *Voltore falls.*
(Stop your wind hard, and swell) see, see, see, see!
He vomits crooked pinnes! his eyes are set,
Like a dead hares, hung in a poulters shop!
His mouth's running away! doe you see, signior?

Now, 'tis in his belly.

(CORVINO   I, the devill!)

VOLPONE Now, in his throate.

(CORVINO   I, I perceive it plaine.)

30   VOLPONE 'Twill out, 'twill out; stand cleere. See, where it flies!

In shape of a blew toad, with a battes wings!

Doe not you see it, sir?

CORBACCIO   What? I thinke I doe.

CORVINO 'T is too manifest.

VOLPONE   Looke! he comes t'himselfe!

VOLTORE Where am I?

VOLPONE   Take good heart, the worst is past, sir.

You are dis-possest.

1ST AVOCATORE   What accident is this?

2ND AVOCATORE Sodaine, and full of wonder!

3RD AVOCATORE   If he were

Possest, as it appeares, all this is nothing.

CORVINO He has beene, often, subbject to these fits.

1ST AVOCATORE Shew him that writing, do you know it, sir?

40   VOLPONE Deny it, sir, forsweare it, know it not.

VOLTORE Yes, I doe know it well, it is my hand:

But all, that it containes, is false.

BONARIO   O practise!

2ND AVOCATORE What maze is this!

1ST AVOCATORE   Is he not guilty, then,

Whom you, there, name the parasite?

VOLTORE   Grave fathers,

No more then, his good patron, old VOLPONE.

4TH AVOCATORE Why, he is dead?

VOLTORE   O no, my honor'd fathers.

He lives—

1ST AVOCATORE How! lives?

VOLTORE   Lives.

2ND AVOCATORE   This is subtler, yet!

3RD AVOCATORE You said, he was dead?

VOLTORE   Never.

3RD AVOCATORE   You said so?

CORVINO   I heard so.

4TH AVOCATORE Here comes the gentleman, make him way.

    [*Enter* MOSCA.]

3RD AVOCATORE   A stoole.

4TH AVOCATORE A proper man! and were VOLPONE dead,   50

  A fit match for my daughter.

3RD AVOCATORE   Give him way.

VOLPONE Mosca, I was a'most lost, the Advocate

  Had betray'd all; but, now, it is recover'd:

  Al's o' the hinge againe—say, I am living.

MOSCA What busie knave is this! most reverend fathers,

  I sooner, had attended your grave pleasures,

  But that my order, for the funerall

  Of my deare patron did require me—

VOLPONE   (MOSCA!)

MOSCA Whom I intend to bury, like a gentleman.

VOLPONE I, quicke, and cosen me of all.

2ND AVOCATORE   Still stranger!   60

  More intricate!

1ST AVOCATORE And come about againe!

4TH AVOCATORE It is a match, my daughter is bestow'd.

MOSCA (Wil you gi' me halfe?

VOLPONE   First, I'le be hang'd.

MOSCA   I know,

  Your voice is good, cry not so lowd).

1ST AVOCATORE   Demand

  The Advocate. Sir, did not you affirme,

  VOLPONE was alive?

VOLPONE   Yes, and he is;

  This gent'man told me so, (thou shalt have halfe.)

MOSCA Whose drunkard is this same? speake some, that know

     him:

  I never saw his face. (I cannot now

  Affoord it you so cheape.

VOLPONE   No?)

1ST AVOCATORE   What say you?   70

VOLTORE The officer told mee.

VOLPONE   I did, grave fathers,

  And will maintaine, he lives, with mine owne life.

And, that this creature told me. (I was borne,
With all good starres my enemies.)
MOSCA   Most grave fathers,
    If such an insolence, as this, must passe
    Upon me, I am silent: 'twas not this,
    For which you sent, I hope.
2ND AVOCATORE   Take him away.
(VOLPONE MOSCA.)
3RD AVOCATORE   Let him be whipt.
(VOLPONE   Wilt thou betray me?
    Cosen me?)
3RD AVOCATORE   And taught to beare himselfe
    Toward a person of his ranke.
80 4TH AVOCATORE   Away.
MOSCA I humbly thank your father-hoods.
VOLPONE   Soft, soft: whipt?
    And loose all that I have? if I confesse,
    It cannot be much more.
4TH AVOCATORE   Sir, are you married?
He puts off his   VOLPONE They'll be ally'd, anon; I must be resolute:
disguise.   The FOXE shall, here, uncase.
(MOSCA   Patron.)
VOLPONE   Nay, now,
    My ruines shall not come alone; your match
    I'le hinder sure: my substance shall not glew you,
    Nor screw you, into a family.
(MOSCA   Why, patron!)
VOLPONE I am VOLPONE, and this is my knave;
90   This, his owne knave; this, avarices foole;
    This, a *Chimaera* of wittall, foole, and knave;
    And, reverend fathers, since we all can hope
    Nought, but a sentence, let's not now despaire it.
    You heare me briefe.
CORVINO   May it please your father-hoods—
COMMANDADORI   Silence.
1ST AVOCATORE The knot is now undone, by miracle!
2ND AVOCATORE Nothing can be more cleare.
3RD AVOCATORE   Or can more prove

These innocent.

1ST AVOCATORE Give 'hem their liberty.

BONARIO Heaven could not, long, let such grosse crimes be hid.

2ND AVOCATORE If this be held the high way to get riches,
    May I be poore.

3RD AVOCATORE This 's not the gaine, but torment.   100

1ST AVOCATORE These possesse wealth, as sicke men possesse
       fevers,
    Which, trulyer, may be said to possesse them.

2ND AVOCATORE Disroabe that parasite.

CORVINO *and* MOSCA   Most honor'd fathers.

1ST AVOCATORE Can you plead ought to stay the course of
      justice?
    If you can, speake.

CORVINO *and* VOLTORE We beg favor.

CELIA   And mercy.

1ST AVOCATORE You hurt your innocence, suing for the guilty.
    Stand forth; and, first, the parasite. You appeare
    T'have beene the chiefest minister, if not plotter,
    In all these lewd impostures; and now, lastly,
    Have, with your impudence, abus'd the court,   110
    And habit of a gentleman of *Venice*,
    Being a fellow of no birth, or bloud:
    For which, our sentence is, first thou be whipt;
    Then live perpetuall prisoner in our gallies.

VOLPONE I thanke you, for him.

MOSCA   Bane to thy woolvish nature.

1ST AVOCATORE Deliver him to the *Saffi*. [*Exit* MOSCA, *guarded*.]
      Thou, VOLPONE,
    By bloud, and ranke a gentleman, canst not fall
    Under like censure; but our judgement on thee
    Is, that thy substance all be straight confiscate
    To the hospitall, of the *Incurabili*:   120
    And, since the most was gotten by imposture,
    By faining lame, gout, palsey, and such diseases,
    Thou art to lie in prison, crampt with irons,
    Till thou bee'st sicke, and lame indeed. Remove him.

VOLPONE This is call'd mortifying of a FOXE.

[*Exit* VOLPONE, *guarded.*]

1ST AVOCATORE Thou VOLTORE, to take away the scandale
Thou hast giv'n all worthy men, of thy profession,
Art banish'd from their fellowship, and our state.
CORBACCIO, bring him neere. We here possesse
130   Thy sonne, of all thy state; and confine thee
To the monasterie of *San' Spirito*:
Where, since thou knew'st not how to live well here,
Thou shalt be learn'd to die well.

CORBACCIO   Ha! what said he?

COMMANDADORE You shall know anone, sir.

2ND AVOCATORE   Thou CORVINO,
shalt
Be straight imbarqu'd from thine owne house, and row'd
Round about *Venice*, through the *grand canale*,
Wearing a cap, with faire, long asses eares,
In stead of hornes: and, so to mount (a paper
Pin'd on thy brest) to the *berlino*—

CORVINO   Yes,
140   And, have mine eies beat out with stinking fish,
Bruis'd fruit, and rotten egges—'Tis well. I'am glad,
I shall not see my shame, yet.

1ST AVOCATORE   And to expiate
Thy wrongs done to thy wife, thou art to send her
Home, to her father, with her dowrie trebled:
And these are all your judgements.

(ALL   Honour'd fathers.)

1ST AVOCATORE Which may not be revok'd. Now, you begin,
When crimes are done, and past, and to be punish'd,
To thinke what your crimes are: away with them.
Let all, that see these vices thus rewarded,
150   Take heart, and love to study 'hem. Mischiefes feed
Like beasts, till they be fat, and then they bleed.   [*Exeunt.*]

VOLPONE.

[*Enter* VOLPONE.]

[VOLPONE] The seasoning of a play is the applause.
     Now, though the Fox be punish'd by the lawes,
     He, yet, doth hope there is no suffring due,
     For any fact, which he hath done 'gainst you;
     If there be, sensure him: here he, doubtfull, stands.
     If not, fare jovially, and clap your hands.   [*Exit.*]

THE END.

This Comoedie was first

acted, in the yeere

1605.

By the Kings Majesties
SERVANTS.

The principall Comoedians were,

RIC. BURBADGE.   JOH. HEMINGS.
HEN. CONDEL.   } {   JOH. LOWIN.
WILL. SLY.   ALEX. COOKE.

With the allowance of the Master of REVELLS.

Epicoene, or the Silent Woman

TO THE TRULY
NOBLE, BY ALL
TITLES.

Sir Francis Stuart:

SIR,

My hope is not so nourish'd by example, as it will conclude, this dumbe peece should please you, by cause it hath pleas'd others before: but by trust, that when you have read it, you will find it worthy to have dis-pleas'd none. This makes, that I now number you, not onely in the Names of favour, but the Names of justice, to what I write; and doe, presently, call you to the exercise of that noblest, 10 *and manlyest vertue: as coveting rather to be freed in my fame, by the authority of a Judge, then the credit of an Under-taker. Read therefore, I pray you, and censure. There is not a line, or syllable in it changed from the simplicity of the first Copy. And, when you shall consider, through the certaine hatred of some, how much a mans innocency may bee indanger'd by an un-certaine accusation; you will, I doubt not, so beginne to hate the iniquitie of such natures, as I shall love the contumely done me, whose end was so honorable, as to be wip'd off by your sentence.*

Your unprofitable, but true lover,

BEN. JONSON. 20

The Persons of the Play.

MOROSE. *A Gent. that loves no noise.*

DAUP. EUGENIE. *A Knight his nephew.*

CLERIMONT. *A Gent. his friend.*

TRUE-WIT. *Another friend.*

EPICOENE. *A yong Gent. suppos'd the silent Woman.*

JOH. DAW. *A Knight, her servant.*

AMOROUS LA FOOLE. *A Knight also.*

THOM: OTTER. *A land, and sea-Captaine.*

CUTBERD. *A Barber.*

10 MUTE. *One of* MOROSE *his servants.*

MAD. HAUGHTY.

MAD. CENTAURE. } *Ladies Collegiates.*

MRS. MAVIS.

MRS. TRUSTY. *The La.* HAUGHTIES *woman.*

MRS. OTTER. *The Captaines wife.* } *Pretenders.*

PARSON.

PAGES. [BOYS]

SERVANTS.

THE SCENE.

20 LONDON.

Epicoene, or the Silent Woman.

Prologue.

Truth sayes, of old, the art of making plaies
    Was to content the people; & their praise
    Was to the *Poet* money, wine, and bayes.
But in this age, a sect of writers are,
    That, onely, for particular likings care,
    And will taste nothing that is populare.
With such we mingle neither braines, nor brests;
    Our wishes, like to those (make publique feasts)
    Are not to please the cookes tastes, but the guests.
Yet, if those cunning palates hether come,   10
    They shall find guests entreaty, and good roome;
    And though all relish not, sure, there will be some,
That, when they leave their seates, shall make 'hem say,
    Who wrote that piece, could so have wrote a play:
    But that, he knew, this was the better way.
For, to present all custard, or all tart,
    And have no other meats, to beare a part,
    Or to want bread, and salt, were but course art.
The *Poet* prayes you then, with better thought
    To sit; and, when his cates are all in brought,   20
    Though there be none far fet, there will deare-bought
Be fit for ladies: some for lords, knights, squires,
    Some for your waiting wench, and citie-wires,
    Some for your men, and daughters of *white-Friars*.
Nor is it, onely, while you keepe your seate
    Here, that his feast will last; but you shall eate
    A weeke at ord'naries, on his broken meat:
          If his *Muse* be true,
          Who commends her to you.

Another.

The ends of all, who for the *Scene* doe write,
    Are, or should be, to profit, and delight.
And still 't hath beene the praise of all best times,
    So persons were not touch'd, to taxe the crimes.
Then, in this play, which we present to night,
    And make the object of your eare, and sight,
On forfeit of your selves, thinke nothing true:
    Lest so you make the maker to judge you.
For he knowes, *Poet* never credit gain'd
10   By writing truths, but things (like truths) well fain'd.
If any, yet, will (with particular slight
    Of application) wrest what he doth write;
And that he meant or him, or her, will say:
    They make a libell, which he made a play.

Act I. Scene 1

CLERIMONT, BOY, TRUE-WIT.

[*Enter* CLERIMONT *and* BOY.]

CLERIMONT Ha' you got the song yet perfect I ga' you, boy?

BOY Yes, sir.

CLERIMONT Let me heare it.

BOY You shall, sir, but i'faith let no body else.

CLERIMONT Why, I pray?

BOY It will get you the dangerous name of a *Poet* in towne, sir, besides me a perfect deale of ill will at the mansion you wot of, whose ladie is the argument of it: where now I am the welcom'st thing under a man that comes there.

10 CLERIMONT I thinke, and above a man too, if the truth were rack'd out of you.

BOY No faith, I'll confesse before, sir. The gentlewomen play with me, and throw me o' the bed; and carry me in to my lady; and shee kisses me with her oil'd face; and puts a perruke o' my head; and askes me an' I will weare her gowne; and I say, no: and then

she hits me a blow o' the eare, and calls me innocent, and lets me
goe.

CLERIMONT No marvell, if the dore bee kept shut against your
master, when the entrance is so easie to you——well sir, you shall
goe there no more, lest I bee faine to seeke your voyce in my   20
ladies rushes, a fortnight hence. Sing, sir.   *Boy sings.*

　　[*Enter* TRUE-WIT.]

TRUE-WIT Why, here's the man that can melt away his time, and
never feeles it! what, betweene his mistris abroad, and his engle at
home, high fare, soft lodging, fine clothes, and his fiddle; hee
thinkes the houres ha' no wings, or the day no post-horse. Well,
sir gallant, were you strooke with the plague this minute, or
condemn'd to any capitall punishment to morrow, you would
beginne then to thinke, and value every article o' your time, esteeme
it at the true rate, and give all for't.

CLERIMONT Why, what should a man doe?   30

TRUE-WIT Why, nothing: or that, which when 'tis done, is as idle.
Harken after the next horse-race, or hunting-match; lay wagers,
praise *Puppy*, or *Pepper-corne*, *White-foote*, *Franklin*; sweare upon   *Horses o' the*
White-maynes partie; spend aloud, that my lords may heare you;   *time.*
visite my ladies at night, and bee able to give 'hem the character
of every bowler, or better o' the greene. These be the things,
wherein your fashionable men exercise themselves, and I for
companie.

CLERIMONT Nay, if I have thy authoritie, I'le not leave yet. Come,
the other are considerations, when wee come to have gray heads,   40
and weake hammes, moist eyes, and shrunke members. Wee'll
thinke on 'hem then; then wee'll pray, and fast.

TRUE-WIT I, and destine onely that time of age to goodnesse, which
our want of abilitie will not let us employ in evill?

CLERIMONT Why, then 'tis time enough.

TRUE-WIT Yes: as if a man should sleepe all the terme, and thinke
to effect his businesse the last day. O, CLERIMONT, this time,
because it is an incorporeall thing, and not subject to sense, we
mocke our selves the fineliest out of it, with vanitie, and miserie
indeede: not seeking an end of wretchednesse, but onely changing   50
the matter still.

CLERIMONT Nay, thou'lt not leave now——

TRUE-WIT See but our common disease! with what justice can wee
complaine, that great men will not looke upon us, nor be at leisure
to give our affaires such dispatch, as wee expect, when wee will
never doe it to our selves: nor heare, nor regard our selves.

CLERIMONT Foh, thou hast read PLUTARCHS moralls, now, or some
such tedious fellow; and it showes so vilely with thee: 'Fore god,
'twill spoile thy wit utterly. Talke me of pinnes, and feathers, and
60   ladies, and rushes, and such things: and leave this *Stoicitie* alone,
till thou mak'st sermons.

TRUE-WIT Well, sir. If it will not take, I have learn'd to loose as little
of my kindnesse, as I can. I'le doe good to no man against his
will, certainely. When were you at the colledge?

CLERIMONT What colledge?

TRUE-WIT As if you knew not!

CLERIMONT No faith, I came but from court, yesterday.

TRUE-WIT Why, is it not arriv'd there yet, the newes? A new foundation, sir, here i' the towne, of ladies, that call themselves the
70   Collegiates, an order betweene courtiers, and country-madames,
that live from their husbands; and give entertainement to all the
Wits, and *Braveries* o' the time, as they call 'hem: crie downe, or
up, what they like, or dislike in a braine, or a fashion, with most
masculine, or rather *hermaphroditicall* authoritie: and, every day,
gaine to their colledge some new probationer.

CLERIMONT Who is the President?

TRUE-WIT The grave, and youthfull matron, the lady HAUGHTY.

CLERIMONT A poxe of her autumnall face, her peec'd beautie: there's
no man can bee admitted till shee be ready, now adaies, till shee
80   has painted, and perfum'd, and wash'd, and scour'd, but the boy
here; and him shee wipes her oil'd lips upon, like a sponge. I have
made a song, I pray thee heare it, o' the subject.

SONG.

[BOY]   *Still to be neat, still to be drest,*
                     As, you were going to a feast;
                     Still to be pou'dred, still perfum'd:
                     Lady, it is to be presum'd,
                     Though arts hid causes are not found,
                     All is not sweet, all is not sound.

Give me a looke, give me a face,
That makes simplicitie a grace;   90
Robes loosely flowing, haire as free:
Such sweet neglect more taketh me,
Then all th'adulteries of art.
They strike mine eyes, but not my heart.

TRUE-WIT And I am, clearely, o' the other side: I love a good dressing,
before any beautie o' the world. O, a woman is, then, like a delicate
garden; nor, is there one kind of it: she may varie, every houre;
take often counsell of her glasse, and choose the best. If shee have
good eares, shew 'hem; good haire, lay it out; good legs, weare
short cloathes; a good hand, discover it often; practise any art, to   100
mend breath, clense teeth, repaire eye-browes, paint, and professe
it.

CLERIMONT How? puqliquely?

TRUE-WIT The doing of it, not the manner: that must bee private.
Many things, that seeme foule, i' the doing, doe please, done. A
lady should, indeed, studie her face, when wee thinke shee sleepes:
nor, when the dores are shut, should men bee inquiring, all is
sacred within, then. Is it for us to see their perrukes put on, their
false teeth, their complexion, their eye-browes, their nailes? you
see guilders will not worke, but inclos'd. They must not discover,   110
how little serves, with the helpe of art, to adorne a great deale.
How long did the canvas hang afore *Ald-gate*? were the people
suffer'd to see the cities *Love*, and *Charitie*, while they were rude
stone, before they were painted, and burnish'd? No. No more
should servants approch their mistresses, but when they are compleat, and finish'd.

CLERIMONT Well said, my TRUE-WIT.

TRUE-WIT And a wise ladie will keepe a guard alwaies upon the
place, that shee may doe things securely. I once followed a rude
fellow into a chamber, where the poore madame, for haste, and   120
troubled, snatch'd at her perruke, to cover her baldnesse: and put
it on, the wrong way.

CLERIMONT O prodigie!

TRUE-WIT And the un-conscionable knave held her in complement an houre, with that reverst face, when I still look'd when shee should talke from the t'other side.

CLERIMONT Why, thou should'st ha' releev'd her.

TRUE-WIT No faith, I let her alone, as wee'l let this argument, if you please, and passe to another. When saw you DAUPHINE EUGENIE?

130 CLERIMONT Not these three daies. Shall we goe to him this morning? he is very melancholique, I heare.

TRUE-WIT Sicke o' the uncle? is hee? I met that stiffe peece of formalitie, his uncle, yesterday, with a huge turbant of night-caps on his head, buckled over his eares.

CLERIMONT O, that's his custome when he walkes abroad. Hee can endure no noise, man.

TRUE-WIT So I have heard. But is the disease so ridiculous in him, as it is made? they say, hee has beene upon divers treaties with the Fish-wives, and Orenge-women; and articles propounded

140 betweene them: mary, the Chimney-sweepers will not be drawne in.

CLERIMONT No, nor the Broome-men: they stand out stiffely. He cannot endure a Costard-monger, he swounes if he heare one.

TRUE-WIT Me thinkes, a Smith should be ominous.

CLERIMONT Or any Hammer-man. A Brasier is not suffer'd to dwel in the parish, nor an Armorer. He would have hang'd a Pewterers 'prentice once upon a shrove-tuesdaies riot, for being o' that trade, when the rest were quit.

TRUE-WIT A Trumpet should fright him terribly, or the Hau'-boyes?

150 CLERIMONT Out of his senses. The Waights of the citie have a pension of him, not to come neere that ward. This youth practis'd on him, one night, like the Bell-man; and never left till hee had brought him downe to the doore, with a long-sword: and there left him flourishing with the aire.

BOY Why, sir! hee hath chosen a street to lie in, so narrow at both ends, that it will receive no coaches, nor carts, nor any of these common noises: and therefore, we that love him, devise to bring him in such as we may, now and then, for his exercise, to breath him. Hee would grow resty else in his ease. His vertue would rust

160 without action. I entreated a Beare-ward, one day, to come downe with the dogs of some foure parishes that way, and I thanke him, he did; & cryed his games under master MOROSE's windore: till

he was sent crying away, with his head made a most bleeding spectacle to the multitude. And, another time, a Fencer, marching to his prize, had his drum most tragically run through, for taking that street in his way, at my request.

TRUE-WIT A good wag. How do's he for the bells?

CLERIMONT O, i' the Queenes time, he was wont to goe out of towne every satterday at ten a clock, or on holy-day-eves. But now, by reason of the sicknesse, the perpetuitie of ringing has made him devise a roome, with double walls, and treble seelings; the windores close shut, and calk'd: and there he lives by candle-light. He turn'd away a man, last weeke, for having a paire of new shooes that creak'd. And this fellow waits on him, now, in tennis-court socks, or slippers sol'd with wooll: and they talke each to other, in a trunke. See, who comes here.

170

Act I. Scene 2

DAUPHINE, TRUE-WIT, CLERIMONT.

[*Enter* DAUPHINE.]

DAUPHINE How now! what aile you sirs? dumbe?

TRUE-WIT Strooke into stone, almost, I am here, with tales o' thine uncle! There was never such a prodigie heard of.

DAUPHINE I would you would once loose this subject, my masters, for my sake. They are such as you are, that have brought mee into that predicament, I am, with him.

TRUE-WIT How is that?

DAUPHINE Mary, that he will dis-inherit me, no more. Hee thinks, I, and my companie are authors of all the ridiculous acts, and moniments are told of him.

10

TRUE-WIT S'lid, I would be the author of more, to vexe him, that purpose deserves it: it gives thee law of plaguing him. I'll tell thee what I would doe. I would make a false almanack; get it printed: and then ha' him drawne out on a coronation day to the *tower*-wharfe, and kill him with the noise of the ordinance. Dis-inherit thee! hee cannot, man. Art not thou next of bloud, and his sisters sonne?

DAUPHINE I, but he will thrust me out of it, he vowes, and marry.

TRUE-WIT How! that's a more portent. Can he endure no noise, and
will venter on a wife?

CLERIMONT Yes: why, thou art a stranger, it seemes, to his best trick,
yet. He has imploid a fellow this halfe yeere, all over *England*, to
harken him out a dumbe woman; bee shee of any forme, or any
qualitie, so shee bee able to beare children: her silence is dowrie
enough, he saies.

TRUE-WIT But, I trust to god, he has found none.

CLERIMONT No, but hee has heard of one that's lodg'd i' the next
street to him, who is exceedingly soft-spoken; thrifty of her speech;
that spends but six words a day. And her hee's about now, and
shall have her.

TRUE-WIT Is't possible! who is his agent i' the businesse?

CLERIMONT Mary, a Barber, one CUT-BERD: an honest fellow, one
that tells DAUPHINE all here.

TRUE-WIT Why, you oppresse mee with wonder! A woman, and a
barber, and love no noise!

CLERIMONT Yes faith. The fellow trims him silently, and has not the
knacke with his sheeres, or his fingers: and that continence in a
barber hee thinkes so eminent a vertue, as it has made him chiefe
of his counsell.

TRUE-WIT Is the barber to be seene? or the wench?

CLERIMONT Yes, that they are.

TRUE-WIT I pray thee, DAUPHINE, let's goe thether.

DAUPHINE I have some businesse now: I cannot i' faith.

TRUE-WIT You shall have no businesse shall make you neglect this,
sir, wee'll make her talke, beleeve it; or if shee will not, wee can
give out, at least so much as shall interrupt the treatie: wee will
breake it. Thou art bound in conscience, when hee suspects thee
without cause, to torment him.

DAUPHINE Not I, by any meanes. I'll give no suffrage to't. He shall
never ha' that plea against me, that I oppos'd the least phant'sie
of his. Let it lie upon my starres to be guiltie, I'll be innocent.

TRUE-WIT Yes, and be poore, and beg; doe, innocent: when some
groome of his has got him an heire, or this barber, if hee himselfe
cannot. Innocent! I pray thee, NED, where lyes shee? let him be
innocent, still.

CLERIMONT Why, right over against the barbers; in the house, where
sir JOHN DAW lyes.

TRUE-WIT You doe not meane to confound me!

CLERIMONT Why?

TRUE-WIT Do's he, that would marry her, know so much? 60

CLERIMONT I cannot tell.

TRUE-WIT 'Twere inough of imputation to her, with him.

CLERIMONT Why?

TRUE-WIT The onely talking sir i' th' towne! JACK DAW! And he
teach her not to speake—God b'w'you. I have some businesse
too.

CLERIMONT Will you not goe thether then?

TRUE-WIT Not with the danger to meet DAW, for mine eares.

CLERIMONT Why? I thought you two had beene upon very good
termes. 70

TRUE-WIT Yes, of keeping distance.

CLERIMONT They say he is a very good scholler.

TRUE-WIT I, and hee sayes it first. A poxe on him, a fellow that
pretends onely to learning, buyes titles, and nothing else of bookes
in him.

CLERIMONT The world reports him to be very learned.

TRUE-WIT I am sorry, the world should so conspire to belie him.

CLERIMONT Good faith, I have heard very good things come from
him.

TRUE-WIT You may. There's none so desperately ignorant to denie 80
that: would they were his owne. God b'w'you gentlemen. [*Exit.*]

CLERIMONT This is very abrupt!

Act I. Scene 3

DAUPHINE, CLERIMONT, BOY.

DAUPHINE Come, you are a strange open man, to tell every thing, thus.

CLERIMONT Why, beleeve it DAUPHINE, TRUE-WIT's a very honest
fellow.

DAUPHINE I thinke no other: but this franke nature of his is not for
secrets.

CLERIMONT Nay, then, you are mistaken DAUPHINE: I know where
he has beene well trusted, and discharg'd the trust very truely, and
heartily.

DAUPHINE I contend not, NED, but, with the fewer a businesse is
10   carried, it is ever the safer. Now we are alone, if you'll goe thether,
I am for you.

CLERIMONT When were you there?

DAUPHINE Last night: and such a *decameron* of sport fallen out!
BOCCACE never thought of the like. DAW do's nothing but court
her; and the wrong way. Hee would lie with her, and praises
her modestie; desires that shee would talke, and bee free, and
commends her silence in verses: which hee reades, and sweares,
are the best that ever man made. Then railes at his fortunes,
stamps, and mutines, why he is not made a counsellor, and call'd
20   to affaires of state.

CLERIMONT I pray thee let's goe. I would faine partake this. Some
water, Boy.   [*Exit* BOY.]

DAUPHINE Wee are invited to dinner together, he and I, by one that
came thether to him, sir LA-FOOLE.

CLERIMONT O, that's a precious mannikin!

DAUPHINE Doe you know him?

CLERIMONT I, and he will know you too, if ere he saw you but once,
though you should meet him at church in the midst of praiers.
Hee is one of the *Braveries*, though he be none o' the *Wits*. He will
30   salute a Judge upon the bench, and a Bishop in the pulpit, a Lawyer
when hee is pleading at the barre, and a Lady when shee is dauncing
in a masque, and put her out. He do's give playes, and suppers,
and invites his guests to 'hem, aloud, out of his windore, as they
ride by in coaches. He has a lodging in the *Strand* for the purpose.
Or to watch when ladies are gone to the *China* houses, or the
Exchange, that hee may meet 'hem by chance, and give 'hem
presents, some two or three hundred pounds-worth of toyes, to
be laught at. He is never without a spare banquet, or sweet-meats
in his chamber, for there women to alight at, and come up to, for
40   a bait.

DAUPHINE Excellent! He was a fine youth last night, but now he is
much finer! what is his christen-name? I ha' forgot.

[*Enter* BOY.]

CLERIMONT Sir AMOROUS LA-FOOLE.

BOY The gentleman is here below, that ownes that name.

CLERIMONT Hart, hee's come, to invite me to dinner, I hold my life.

DAUPHINE Like enough: pray thee, let's ha' him up.

CLERIMONT Boy, marshall him.

BOY With a truncheon, sir?

CLERIMONT Away, I beseech you. [*Exit* BOY.] I'le make him tell us
    his pedegree, now; and what meat he has to dinner; and, who are   50
    his guests; and, the whole course of his fortunes: with a breath.

Act I. Scene 4

LA-FOOLE, CLERIMONT, DAUPHINE.

[*Enter* LA-FOOLE.]

LA-FOOLE Save, deare sir DAUPHINE, honor'd master CLERIMONT.

CLERIMONT Sir AMOROUS! you have very much honested my lodg-
    ing, with your presence.

LA-FOOLE Good faith, it is a fine lodging! almost, as delicate a lodging,
    as mine.

CLERIMONT Not so, sir.

LA-FOOLE Excuse me, sir, if it were i' the *Strand*, I assure you. I am
    come, master CLERIMONT, to entreat you wait upon two or three
    ladies, to dinner, to day.

CLERIMONT How, sir! wait upon 'hem? did you ever see me carry   10
    dishes?

LA-FOOLE No, sir, dispence with me; I meant, to beare 'hem
    companie.

CLERIMONT O, that I will, sir. The doubtfulnesse o' your phrase,
    beleeve it, sir, would breed you a quarrell, once an houre, with the
    terrible boyes, if you should but keepe 'hem fellowship a day.

LA-FOOLE It should be extremely against my will, sir, if I contested
    with any man.

CLERIMONT I beleeve it, sir; where hold you your feast?

LA-FOOLE At TOM OTTERS, sir.   20

DAUPHINE TOM OTTER? what's he?

LA-FOOLE Captaine OTTER, sir; he is a kind of gamster: but he has
    had command, both by sea, and by land.

DAUPHINE O, then he is *animal amphibium*?

LA-FOOLE I, sir: his wife was the rich *China*-woman, that the courtiers
visited so often, that gave the rare entertainment. She commands
all at home.

CLERIMONT Then, she is Captaine OTTER?

LA-FOOLE You say very well, sir; she is my kins-woman, a LA-FOOLE
30   by the mother side, and will invite, any great ladies, for my sake.

DAUPHINE Not of the LA-FOOLES of *Essex*?

LA-FOOLE No, sir, the LA-FOOLES of *London*.

CLERIMONT Now, h'is in.

LA-FOOLE They all come out of our house, the LA-FOOLES o' the
north, the LA-FOOLES of the west, the LA-FOOLES of the east,
and south—we are as ancient a family, as any is in *Europe*—but I
my selfe am descended lineally of the *french* LA-FOOLES—and,
wee doe beare for our coate *Yellow*, or *Or*, checker'd *Azure*, and
Gules, and some three or foure colours more, which is a very noted
40   coate, and has, some-times, beene solemnely worne by divers
nobilitie of our house—but let that goe, antiquitie is not respected
now—I had a brace of fat Does sent me, gentlemen, & halfe a
dosen of phesants, a dosen or two of godwits, and some other
fowle, which I would have eaten, while they are good, and in good
company—there will be a great lady, or two, my lady HAUGHTY,
my lady CENTAURE, mistris DOL MAVIS—and they come a'
purpose, to see the silent gentlewoman, mistris EPICOENE, that
honest sir JOHN DAW has promis'd to bring thether—and then,
mistris TRUSTY, my ladies woman, will be there too, and this
50   honorable Knight, sir DAUPHINE, with your selfe, master CLERI-
MONT—and wee'll bee very merry, and have fidlers, and daunce—
I have beene a mad wag, in my time, and have spent some crownes
since I was a page in court, to my lord LOFTY, and after, my ladies
gentleman-usher, who got mee knighted in *Ireland*, since it pleas'd
my elder brother to die—I had as faire a gold jerkin on that day,
as any was worne in the *Iland*-voyage, or at *Caliz*, none disprais'd,
and I came over in it hither, show'd my selfe to my friends, in
court, and after went downe to my tenants, in the countrey, and
survai'd my lands, let new leases, tooke their money, spent it in
60   the eye o' the land here, upon ladies—and now I can take up at
my pleasure.

DAUPHINE Can you take up ladies, sir?

CLERIMONT O, let him breath, he has not recover'd.

DAUPHINE Would I were your halfe, in that commoditie—

LA-FOOLE No, sir, excuse mee: I meant money, which can take up
any thing. I have another guest, or two, to invite, and say as much
to, gentlemen. I'll take my leave abruptly, in hope you will not
faile—Your servant.   [*Exit.*]

DAUPHINE Wee will not faile you, sir precious LA-FOOLE; but shee
shall, that your ladies come to see: if I have credit, afore sir DAW. 70

CLERIMONT Did you ever heare such a wind-fucker, as this?

DAUPHINE Or, such a rooke, as the other! that will betray his mistris,
to be seene. Come, 'tis time, we prevented it.

CLERIMONT Goe.   [*Exeunt.*]

Act II. Scene 1

MOROSE, MUTE.

[*Enter* MOROSE *and* MUTE.]

MOROSE Cannot I, yet, find out a more compendious method, then
by this trunke, to save my servants the labour of speech, and mine
eares, the discord of sounds? Let mee see: all discourses, but mine
owne, afflict mee, they seeme harsh, impertinent, and irksome. Is
it not possible, that thou should'st answere me, by signes, and, I
apprehend thee, fellow? speake not, though I question you. You
have taken the ring, off from the street dore, as I bad you? answere
me not, by speech, but by silence; unlesse, it be otherwise (—)
very good. And, you have fastened on a thicke quilt, or flock-bed,
on the out-side of the dore; that if they knocke with their daggers,
or with bricke-bats, they can make no noise? but with your leg,
your answere, unlesse it be otherwise (—) very good. This is not,
onely, fit modestie in a servant, but good state, and discretion in
a master. And you have been with CUTBERD, the barber, to have
him come to me? (—) good. And, he will come presently? answere
me not but with your leg, unlesse it be otherwise: if it be otherwise,
shake your head, or shrug (—) so. Your *Italian*, and *Spaniard*, are
wise in these! and it is a frugall, and comely gravitie. How long
will it bee, ere CUTBERD come? stay, if an houre, hold up your

*At the breaches,
still the fellow
makes legs: or
signes.*

12

20 whole hand; if halfe an houre, two fingers; if a quarter, one; (—) good: halfe a quarter? 'tis well. And have you given him a key, to come in without knocking? (—) good. And, is the lock oild, and the hinges, to day? (—) good. And the quilting of the staires no where worne out, and bare? (—) very good. I see, by much doctrine, and impulsion, it may be effected: stand by. The *Turke*, in this divine discipline, is admirable, exceeding all the potentates of the earth; still waited on by mutes; and all his commands so executed; yea, even in the warre (as I have heard) and in his marches, most of his charges, and directions, given by signes, and

30 with silence: an exquisite art! and I am heartily asham'd, and angrie often-times, that the Princes of *Christendome*, should suffer a *Barbarian*, to transcend 'hem in so high a point of felicitie. I will

One windes a practise it, hereafter. How now? oh! oh! what villaine? what prodigie
horne without. of mankind is that? looke. [*Exit* MUTE.] Oh! cut his throat, cut his
Againe. throat: what murderer, hell-hound, devill can this be?

[*Enter* MUTE.]

MUTE It is a post from the court—

MOROSE Out rogue, and must thou blow thy horne, too?

MUTE Alas, it is a post from the court, sir, that sayes, hee must speake with you, paine of death—

40 MOROSE Paine of thy life, be silent.

Act II. Scene 2

TRUE-WIT, MOROSE, CUTBERD.

[*Enter* TRUE-WIT.]

TRUE-WIT By your leave, sir (I am a stranger here) is your name, master MOROSE? is your name, master MOROSE? fishes! *Pythagoreans* all! this is strange! What say you, sir, nothing? Has HARPO-CRATES beene here, with his club, among you? well sir, I will beleeve you to bee the man, at this time: I will venter upon you, sir. Your friends at court commend 'hem to you, sir—

(MOROSE O men! o manners! was there ever such an impudence?)

TRUE-WIT And are extremely sollicitous for you, sir.

MOROSE Whose knave are you!

10 TRUE-WIT Mine owne knave, and your compere, sir.

MOROSE Fetch me my sword—

TRUE-WIT You shall taste the one halfe of my dagger, if you do
(groome) and you, the other, if you stirre, sir: be patient, I charge
you, in the kings name, and heare mee without insurrection. They
say, you are to marry? to marry! doe you marke, sir?

MOROSE How then, rude companion!

TRUE-WIT Mary, your friends doe wonder, sir, the *Thames* being so
neere, wherein you may drowne so handsomely; or *London*-bridge,
at a low fall, with a fine leape, to hurry you downe the streame;
or, such a delicate steeple, i' the towne, as *Bow*, to vault from; or,   20
a braver height, as *Pauls*; or, if you affected to doe it neerer home,
and a shorter way, an excellent garret windore, into the street; or,
a beame, in the said garret, with this halter; which they have sent,   *He shewes him*
and desire, that you would sooner commit your grave head to this   *a halter.*
knot, then to the wed-lock nooze; or, take a little sublime, and
goe out of the world, like a rat; or a flie (as one said) with a straw
i' your arse: any way, rather, then to follow this goblin *matrimony*.
Alas, sir, doe you ever thinke to find a chaste wife, in these times?
now? when there are so many masques, plaies, puritane preachings,
mad-folkes, and other strange sights to be seene daily, private and   30
publique? if you had liv'd in king ETHELRED's time, sir, or
EDWARD the Confessors, you might, perhaps, have found in some
cold countrey-hamlet, then, a dull frostie wench, would have been
contented with one man: now, they will as soone be pleas'd with
one leg, or one eye. I'll tell you, sir, the monstrous hazards you
shall runne with a wife.

MOROSE Good sir! have I ever cosen'd any friends of yours of their
land? bought their possessions? taken forfeit of their morgage?
begg'd a reversion from 'hem? bastarded their issue? what have I
done, that may deserve this?   40

TRUE-WIT Nothing, sir, that I know, but your itch of marriage.

MOROSE Why? if I had made an assassinate upon your father; vitiated
your mother; ravished your sisters—

TRUE-WIT I would kill you, sir, I would kill you, if you had.

MOROSE Why? you doe more in this, sir: It were a vengeance centuple,
for all facinorous acts, that could be nam'd, to doe that you doe—

TRUE-WIT Alas, sir, I am but a messenger: I but tell you, what you
must heare. It seemes, your friends are carefull after your soules

health, sir, and would have you know the danger (but you may
doe your pleasure, for all them, I perswade not, sir). If, after you
are married, your wife doe run away with a vaulter, or the *Frenchman*
that walkes upon ropes, or him that daunces the jig, or a fencer
for his skill at his weapon, why it is not their fault; they have
discharged their consciences: when you know what may happen.
Nay, suffer valiantly, sir, for I must tell you, all the perills that you
are obnoxious too. If shee be faire, yong, and vegetous, no sweet
meats ever drew more flies; all the yellow doublets, and great roses
i' the towne will bee there. If foule, and crooked, shee'll bee with
them, and buy those doublets and roses, sir. If rich, and that you
marry her dowry, not her; shee'll raigne in your house, as imperious
as a widow. If noble, all her kindred will be your tyrannes. If
fruitfull, as proud as *May*, and humorous as *April*, she must have
her doctors, her midwives, her nurses, her longings every houre:
though it be for the dearest morsell of man. If learned, there was
never such a parrat; all your patrimony will be too little for the
guests, that must be invited, to heare her speake *Latine* and *Greeke*:
and you must lie with her in those languages too, if you will please
her. If precise, you must feast all the silenc'd brethren, once
in three daies; salute the sisters; entertaine the whole family, or
wood of 'hem; and heare long-winded exercises, singings, and
catechisings, which you are not given to, and yet must give for: to
please the zealous matron your wife, who, for the holy cause, will
cosen you, over and above. You beginne to sweat, sir? but this is
not halfe, i' faith: you may do your pleasure notwithstanding, as I
said before, I come not to perswade you. Upon my faith, master
servingman, if you doe stirre, I will beat you.

The Mute is
stealing away.

MOROSE O, what is my sinne! what is my sinne?

TRUE-WIT Then, if you love your wife, or rather, dote on her, sir: o,
how shee'll torture you! and take pleasure i' your torments! you
shall lye with her but when she lists; she will not hurt her beauty,
her complexion; or it must be for that jewell, or that pearle, when
she do's; every halfe houres pleasure must be bought anew: and
with the same paine, and charge, you woo'd her at first. Then, you
must keepe what servants shee please; what company shee will;
that friend must not visit you without her licence; and him shee
loves most shee will seeme to hate eagerliest, to decline your jel-

ousie; or, faigne to bee jealous of you first; and for that cause goe live
with her she-friend, or cosen at the colledge, that can instruct her
in all the mysteries, of writing letters, corrupting servants, taming
spies; where shee must have that rich goune for such a great day;   90
a new one for the next; a richer for the third; bee serv'd in silver;
have the chamber fill'd with a succession of groomes, foot-men,
ushers, and other messengers; besides embroyderers, jewellers,
tyre-women, sempsters, fether-men, perfumers; while shee feeles
not how the land drops away; nor the acres melt; nor forsees the
change, when the mercer has your woods for her velvets; never
weighes what her pride costs, sir: so shee may kisse a page, or a
smoth chinne, that has the despaire of a beard; bee a states-woman,
know all the newes, what was done at *Salisbury*, what at the *Bath*,
what at court, what in progresse; or, so shee may censure *poets*,   100
and authors, and stiles, and compare 'hem, DANIEL with SPENSER,
JONSON with the tother youth, and so foorth; or, be thought
cunning in controversies, or the very knots of divinitie; and have,
often in her mouth, the state of the question: and then skip to the
Mathematiques, and demonstration and answere, in religion to one;
in state, to another, in baud'ry to a third.

MOROSE O, o!

TRUE-WIT All this is very true, sir. And then her going in disguise
to that conjurer, and this cunning woman: where the first question
is, how soone you shall die? next, if her present servant love her?   110
next that, if she shall have a new servant? and how many? which
of her family would make the best baud, male, or female? what
precedence shee shall have by her next match? and sets downe
the answers, and beleeves 'hem above the scriptures. Nay, perhaps
she'll study the art.

MOROSE Gentle sir, ha' you done? ha' you had your pleasure o' me?
I'll thinke of these things.

TRUE-WIT Yes sir: and then comes reeking home of vapor and sweat,
with going afoot, and lies in, a moneth, of a new face, all oyle, and
birdlime; and rises in asses milke, and is clens'd with a new *fucus*:   120
god b'w'you, sir. One thing more (which I had almost forgot.) This
too, with whom you are to marry, may have made a convayance
of her virginity aforehand, as your wise widdowes doe of their
states, before they marry, in trust to some friend, sir: who can tell?

or if she have not done it yet, she may doe, upon the wedding
day, or the night before, and antidate you cuckold. The like has
beene heard of, in nature. 'Tis no devis'd impossible thing, sir.
God b'w'you: I'll be bold to leave this rope with you, sir, for a
remembrance. Farewell MUTE.   [*Exit.*]

MOROSE Come, ha' me to my chamber: but first shut the dore. O,
shut the dore, shut the dore: [*Enter* CUTBERD.] Is he come againe?

CUTBERD 'Tis I, sir, your barber.

MOROSE O, CUTBERD, CUTBERD, CUTBERD! here has bin a cut-
throate with me: helpe me in to my bed, and give me physicke
with thy counsell.   [*Exeunt.*]

Act II. Scene 3

DAW, CLERIMONT, DAUPHINE, EPICOENE.

[*Enter* DAW, CLERIMONT, DAUPHINE *and* EPICOENE.]

DAW Nay, and she will, let her refuse, at her owne charges: 'tis nothing
to me, gentlemen. But she will not bee invited to the like feasts,
or guests, every day.

CLERIMONT O, by no meanes, shee may not refuse—to stay at home,
if you love your reputation: 'Slight, you are invited thither o'
purpose to bee seene, and laught at by the lady of the colledge,
and her shadowes. This trumpeter hath proclaim'd you.

DAUPHINE You shall not goe; let him be laught at in your steade,
for not bringing you: and put him to his extemporall faculty of
fooling, and talking loud to satisfie the company.

CLERIMONT He will suspect us, talke aloud. 'Pray, mistris EPICOENE,
let's see your verses; we have sir JOHN DAW's leave: doe not
conceale your servants merit, and your owne glories.

EPICOENE They'll prove my servants glories, if you have his leave
so soone.

DAUPHINE His vaine glories, lady!

DAW Shew 'hem, shew 'hem, mistris, I dare owne 'hem.

EPICOENE Judge you, what glories?

DAW Nay, I'll read 'hem my selfe, too: an author must recite his
owne workes. It is a *madrigall* of modestie.

229
*The horne
againe.*

*They dissuade
her, privately.*

10

20

> *Modest, and faire, for faire and good are neere*
> > *Neighbours, how ere.——*

DAUPHINE Very good.

CLERIMONT I, is't not?

DAW *No noble vertue ever was alone,*
> > *But two in one.*

DAUPHINE Excellent!

CLERIMONT That againe, I pray sir JOHN.

DAUPHINE It has some thing in 't like rare wit, and sense.

CLERIMONT Peace. 30

DAW *No noble vertue ever was alone,*
> > *But two in one.*
> *Then, when I praise sweet modestie, I praise*
> > *Bright beauties raies:*
> *And having prais'd both beauty' and modestee,*
> > *I have prais'd thee.*

DAUPHINE Admirable!

CLERIMONT How it chimes, and cries tinke i' the close, divinely!

DAUPHINE I, 'tis SENECA.

CLERIMONT No, I thinke 'tis PLUTARCH. 40

DAW The *dor* on PLUTARCH, and SENECA, I hate it: they are mine owne imaginations, by that light. I wonder those fellowes have such credit with gentlemen!

CLERIMONT They are very grave authors.

DAW Grave asses! meere *Essaists*! a few loose sentences, and that's all. A man would talke so, his whole age, I doe utter as good things every houre, if they were collected, and observ'd, as either of 'hem.

DAUPHINE Indeede! sir JOHN?

CLERIMONT Hee must needs, living among the *Wits*, and *Braveries* too. 50

DAUPHINE I, and being president of 'hem, as he is.

DAW There's ARISTOTLE, a mere common-place fellow; PLATO, a discourser; THUCIDIDES, and LIVIE, tedious and drie; TACITUS, an entire knot: sometimes worth the untying, very seldome.

CLERIMONT What doe you think of the *Poets*, sir JOHN?

DAW Not worthy to be nam'd for authors. HOMER, an old tedious prolixe asse, talkes of curriers, and chines of beefe. VIRGIL, of dunging of land, and bees. HORACE, of I know not what.

CLERIMONT I thinke so.

60   DAW And so PINDARUS, LYCOPHRON, ANACREON, CATULLUS,
      SENECA the tragoedian, LUCAN, PROPERTIUS, TIBULLUS, MAR-
      TIAL, JUVENAL, AUSONIUS, STATIUS, POLITIAN, VALERIUS
      FLACCUS, and the rest—

CLERIMONT What a sacke full of their names he has got!

DAUPHINE And how he poures 'hem out! POLITIAN, with VALERIUS
      FLACCUS!

CLERIMONT Was not the character right, of him?

DAUPHINE As could be made, i' faith.

DAW And PERSIUS, a crabbed cockescombe, not to be endur'd.

70   DAUPHINE Why? whom do you account for authors, sir JOHN DAW?

DAW *Syntagma Juris civilis, Corpus Juris civilis, Corpus Juris canonici,* the
      King of *Spaines* bible.

DAUPHINE Is the King of *Spaines* bible an author?

CLERIMONT Yes, and *Syntagma.*

DAUPHINE What was that *Syntagma,* sir?

DAW A civill lawier, a *Spaniard.*

DAUPHINE Sure, *Corpus* was a *Dutch*-man.

CLERIMONT I, both the *Corpusses,* I knew 'hem: they were very
      corpulent authors.

80   DAW And, then there's VATABLUS, POMPONATIUS, SYMANCHA, the
      other are not to be receiv'd, within the thought of a scholler.

DAUPHINE Fore god, you have a simple learn'd servant, lady, in titles.

CLERIMONT I wonder that hee is not called to the helme, and made
      a councellor!

DAUPHINE He is one extraordinary.

CLERIMONT Nay, but in ordinarie! to say truth, the state wants such.

DAUPHINE Why, that will follow.

CLERIMONT I muse, a mistris can be so silent to the dotes of such
      a servant.

90   DAW 'Tis her vertue, sir. I have written somewhat of her silence too.

DAUPHINE In verse, sir JOHN?

CLERIMONT What else?

DAUPHINE Why? how can you justifie your owne being of a *Poet,*
      that so slight all the old *Poets*?

DAW Why? every man, that writes in verse, is not a *Poet*; you have of

the *Wits*, that write verses, and yet are no *Poets*: they are *Poets* that
live by it, the poore fellowes that live by it.

DAUPHINE Why? would not you live by your verses, sir JOHN?

CLERIMONT No, 'twere pittie he should. A knight live by his verses?
he did not make 'hem to that ende, I hope.   100

DAUPHINE And yet the noble SIDNEY lives by his, and the noble
family not asham'd.

CLERIMONT I, he profest himselfe; but sir JOHN DAW has more
caution: hee'll not hinder his owne rising i' the state so much! doe
you thinke hee will? Your verses, good sir JOHN, and no *poems*.

DAW   *Silence in woman, is like speech in man,*
                        Deny't who can.

DAUPHINE Not I, beleeve it: your reason, sir.

DAW   *Nor, is't a tale,*
                That female vice should be a vertue male,   110
                Or masculine vice, a female vertue be:
                        You shall it see
                        Prov'd with increase,
                I know to speake, and shee to hold her peace.

Do you conceive me, gentlemen?

DAUPHINE No faith, how meane you with increase, sir JOHN?

DAW Why, with increase is, when I court her for the comon cause
of mankind; and she says nothing, but *consentire videtur*: and in time
is *gravida*.

DAUPHINE Then, this is a ballad of procreation?   120

CLERIMONT A *madrigall* of procreation, you mistake.

EPICOENE 'Pray give me my verses againe, servant.

DAW If you'll aske 'hem aloud, you shal.

CLERIMONT See, here's TRUE-WIT againe!

Act II. Scene 4

CLERIMONT, TRUE-WIT, DAUPHINE, CUT-BERD,
DAW, EPICOENE.

[*Enter* TRUE-WIT.]

CLERIMONT Where hast thou beene, in the name of madnesse! thus
accoutred with thy horne?

TRUE-WIT Where the sound of it might have pierc'd your senses, with gladnes, had you beene in eare-reach of it. DAUPHINE, fall downe and worship me: I have forbid the banes, lad. I have been with thy vertuous uncle, and have broke the match.

DAUPHINE You ha' not, I hope.

TRUE-WIT Yes faith; and thou shouldst hope otherwise, I should repent me: this horne got me entrance, kisse it. I had no other way to get in, but by faining to be a post; but when I got in once, I prov'd none, but rather the contrary, turn'd him into a post, or a stone, or what is stiffer, with thundring into him the incommodities of a wife, and the miseries of marriage. If ever GORGON were seene in the shape of a woman, hee hath seene her in my description. I have put him off o' that sent, for ever. Why doe you not applaud, and adore me, sirs? why stand you mute? Are you stupid? you are not worthy o' the benefit.

DAUPHINE Did not I tell you? mischiefe!—

CLERIMONT I would you had plac'd this benefit somewhere else.

TRUE-WIT Why so?

CLERIMONT Slight, you have done the most inconsiderate, rash, weake thing, that ever man did to his friend.

DAUPHINE Friend! if the most malicious enemy I have, had studied to inflict an injury upon me, it could not bee a greater.

TRUE-WIT Wherein? for gods-sake! Gent: come to your selves againe.

DAUPHINE But I presag'd thus much afore, to you.

CLERIMONT Would my lips had beene soldred, when I spak on 't. Slight, what mov'd you to be thus impertinent?

TRUE-WIT My masters, doe not put on this strange face to pay my courtesie: off with this visor. Have good turnes done you, and thanke 'hem this way?

DAUPHINE Fore heav'n, you have undone me. That, which I have plotted for, and beene maturing now these foure moneths, you have blasted in a minute: now I am lost, I may speake. This gentlewoman was lodg'd here by me o' purpose, and, to be put upon my uncle, hath profest this obstinate silence for my sake, being my entire friend; and one, that for the requitall of such a fortune, as to marry him, would have made mee very ample conditions: where now, all my hopes are utterly miscarried by this unlucky accident.

CLERIMONT Thus 'tis, when a man will be ignorantly officious; doe services, and not know his why: I wonder what curteous itch possess'd you! you never did absurder part i' your life, nor a greater trespasse to friendship, to humanity.

DAUPHINE Faith, you may forgive it, best: 'twas your cause principally.

CLERIMONT I know it, would it had not.

[*Enter* CUTBERD.]

DAUPHINE How now CUTBERD? what newes?

CUTBERD The best, the happiest that ever was, sir. There has beene a mad gentleman with your uncle, this morning (I thinke this be the gentleman) that has almost talk'd him out of his wits, with threatning him from marriage— 50

DAUPHINE On, I pray thee.

CUTBERD And your unkle, sir, hee thinkes 'twas done by your procurement; therefore he will see the party, you wot of, presently: and if he like her, he sayes, and that she be so inclining to dombe, as I have told him, he sweares hee will marry her, to day, instantly, and not deferre it a minute longer.

DAUPHINE Excellent! beyond our expectation!

TRUE-WIT Beyond your expectation? by this light, I knewe it would bee thus. 60

DAUPHINE Nay, sweet TRUE-WIT, forgive me.

TRUE-WIT No, I was ignorantly officious, impertinent: this was the absurd, weake part.

CLERIMONT Wilt thou ascribe that to merit, now, was meere fortune?

TRUE-WIT Fortune? mere providence. Fortune had not a finger in 't. I saw it must necessarily in nature fall out so: my *genius* is never false to me in these things. Shew me, how it could be otherwise.

DAUPHINE Nay, gentlemen, contend not, 'tis well now.

TRUE-WIT Alasse, I let him goe on with inconsiderate, and rash, and what he pleas'd. 70

CLERIMONT Away thou strange justifier of thy selfe, to bee wiser then thou wert, by the event.

TRUE-WIT Event! By this light, thou shalt never perswade me, but I fore-saw it, aswell as the starres themselves.

DAUPHINE Nay, gentlemen, 'tis well now: doe you two entertaine sir JOHN DAW, with discourse, while I send her away with instructions.

TRUE-WIT I'll be acquainted with her, first, by your favour.

CLERIMONT Master TRUE-WIT, lady, a friend of ours.

TRUE-WIT I am sorry, I have not knowne you sooner, lady, to
celebrate this rare vertue of your silence.

CLERIMONT Faith, an' you had come sooner, you should ha' seene,
and heard her well celebrated in sir JOHN DAW's *madrigalls*.

[*Exeunt* DAUPHINE, EPICOENE *and* CUTBERD.]

TRUE-WIT JACK DAW, god save you, when saw you LA-FOOLE?

DAW Not since last night, master TRUE-WIT.

TRUE-WIT That's miracle! I thought you two had beene inseparable.

DAW Hee's gone to invite his guests.

TRUE-WIT Gods so! 'tis true! what a false memory have I towards
that man! I am one: I met him e'ne now, upon that he calls his
delicate fine blacke horse, rid into a foame, with poasting from
place to place, and person to person, to give 'hem the *cue*—

CLERIMONT Lest they should forget?

TRUE-WIT Yes: there was never poore captaine tooke more paines
at a muster to show men, then he, at this meale, to shew friends.

DAW It is his quarter-feast, sir.

CLERIMONT What! doe you say so, sir John?

TRUE-WIT Nay, JACK DAW will not be out, at the best friends hee
has, to the talent of his wit: where's his mistris, to heare and
applaud him? is she gone!

DAW Is mistris EPICOENE gone?

CLERIMONT Gone afore, with sir DAUPHINE, I warrant, to the place.

TRUE-WIT Gone afore! that were a manifest injurie; a disgrace and
a halfe: to refuse him at such a festivall time, as this, being a *Bravery*,
and a *Wit* too.

CLERIMONT Tut, hee'll swallow it like creame: hee's better read in
jure civili, then to esteeme any thing a disgrace is offer'd him from
a mistris.

DAW Nay, let her eene goe; she shall sit alone, and bee dumbe in her
chamber, a weeke together, for JOHN DAW, I warrant her: do's
she refuse me?

CLERIMONT No, sir, doe not take it so to heart: shee do's not refuse
you, but a little neglect you. Good faith, TRUE-WIT, you were too
blame to put it into his head, that shee do's refuse him.

TRUE-WIT She do's refuse him, sir, palpably: how ever you mince it.

An' I were as hee, I would sweare to speake ne're a word to her, to day, for't.

DAW By this light, no more I will not.

TRUE-WIT Nor to any body else, sir.

DAW Nay, I will not say so, gentlemen.

CLERIMONT It had beene an excellent happy condition for the company, if you could have drawne him to it.   120

DAW I'll be very melancholique, i' faith.

CLERIMONT As a dog, if I were as you, sir JOHN.

TRUE-WIT Or a snaile, or a hog-louse: I would roule my selfe up for this day, introth, they should not unwinde me.

DAW By this pick-tooth, so I will.

CLERIMONT 'Tis well done: he beginnes already to be angry with his teeth.

DAW Will you goe, gentlemen?

CLERIMONT Nay, you must walke alone, if you bee right melancholique, sir JOHN.   130

TRUE-WIT Yes sir, wee'll dog you, wee'll follow you a farre off.

[*Exit* DAW.]

CLERIMONT Was there ever such a two yards of knighthood, measur'd out by *Time*, to be sold to laughter?

TRUE-WIT A meere talking mole! hang him: no mushrome was ever so fresh. A fellow so utterly nothing, as he knowes not what he would be.

CLERIMONT Let's follow him: but first, let's goe to DAUPHINE, hee's hovering about the house, to heare what newes.

TRUE-WIT Content.   [*Exeunt.*]

Act II. Scene 5
MOROSE, EPICOENE, CUTBERD, MUTE.

[*Enter* MOROSE, EPICOENE, CUTBERD *and* MUTE.]

MOROSE Welcome CUTBERD; draw neere with your faire chardge: and, in her eare, softly intreat her to unmasque (—) So. Is the dore shut? (—) inough. Now, CUTBERD, with the same discipline I use to my family, I will question you. As I conceive, CUTBERD, this gentlewoman is shee, you have provided, and brought, in hope

shee will fit me in the place and person of a wife? Answer me not,
but with your leg, unlesse it be otherwise: (—) very well done
CUTBERD. I conceive, besides, CUTBERD, you have beene pre-
acquainted with her birth, education, and quallities, or else you

10 would not preferre her to my acceptance, in the waighty conse-
quence of marriage. (—) this I conceive, CUTBERD. Answer me
not but with your leg, unlesse it bee otherwise. (—) Very well
done CUTBERD. Give aside now a little, and leave me to examine

He goes about her condition, and aptitude to my affection. Shee is exceeding faire,
her, and viewes and of a speciall good favour; a sweet composition, or harmony
her. of limmes: her temper of beauty has the true height of my blood.
The knave hath exceedingly wel fitted me without: I will now trie
her within. Come neere, faire gentlewoman: let not my behaviour

19 seeme rude, though unto you, being rare, it may happely appeare
She curtsies. strange. (—) Nay, lady, you may speake, though CUTBERD, and
my man, might not: for, of all sounds, onely, the sweet voice of a
faire lady has the just length of mine eares. I beseech you, say lady,
out of the first fire of meeting eyes, (they say) love is stricken: doe
you feele any such motion, sodenly shot into you, from any part

Curt'sie. you see in me? ha, lady? (—) Alasse, lady, these answers by silent
curt'sies, from you, are too courtlesse, and simple. I have ever had
my breeding in court: and shee that shall bee my wife, must bee
accomplished with courtly, and audacious ornaments. Can you

29 speake lady?
She speakes EPICOENE Judge you, forsooth.
softly. MOROSE What say you, lady? speake out, I beseech you.
EPICOENE Judge you, forsooth.
MOROSE O' my judgement, a divine softnes! but can you naturally,
lady, as I enjoyne these by doctrine & industry, referre your self
to the search of my judgement, and (not taking pleasure in your
tongue, which is a womans chiefest pleasure) thinke it plausible,
to answer me by silent gestures, so long as my speeches jumpe
Curt'sie. right, with what you conceive? (—) Excellent! divine! if it were
possible she should hold out thus! Peace CUTBERD, thou art made
40 for ever, as thou hast made mee, if this felicitie have lasting: but
I will trie her further. Deare lady, I am courtly, I tell you, and I must
have mine eares banqueted with pleasant, and wittie conferences,
pretty girds, scoffes, and daliance in her, that I meane to choose

for my bedpheere. The ladies in court, thinke it a most desperate impaire to their quickenesse of wit, and good carriage, if they cannot give occasion for a man to court 'hem; and, when an amorous discourse is set on foot, minister as good matter to continue it, as himselfe: and doe you alone so much differ from all them, that, what they (with so much circumstance) affect, and toile for, to seeme learn'd, to seeme judicious, to seeme sharpe, 50 and conceited, you can bury in your selfe, with silence? and rather trust your graces to the faire conscience of vertue, then to the worlds, or your owne proclamation?

EPICOENE I should be sorry else.

MOROSE What say you, ladie? good ladie, speake out.

EPICOENE I should be sorrie, else.

MOROSE That sorrow doth fill me with gladnesse! O MOROSE! thou art happie above mankinde! pray that thou maiest containe thy selfe. I will onely put her to it once more, and it shall be with the utmost touch, and test of their sexe. But heare me, faire lady, I 60 doe also love to see her, whom I shall choose for my heicfar, to be the first and principall in all fashions; praecede all the dames at court, by a fortnight; have her counsell of taylors, linneners, lace-women, embroyderers, and sit with 'hem sometimes twise a day, upon *French* intelligences; and then come foorth, varied like Nature, or oftner then she, and better, by the helpe of Art, her aemulous servant. This doe I affect. And how will you be able, lady, with this frugalitie of speech, to give the manifold (but necessarie) instructions, for that bodies, these sleeves, those skirts, this cut, that stitch, this embroyderie, that lace, this wire, those 70 knots, that ruffe, those roses, this girdle, that fanne, the tother skarfe, these gloves? ha! what say you, ladie?

EPICOENE I'll leave it to you, sir.

MOROSE How lady? pray you, rise a note.

EPICOENE I leave it to wisdome, and you sir.

MOROSE Admirable creature! I will trouble you no more: I will not sinne against so sweet a simplicity. Let me now be bold to print, on those divine lips, the seale of being mine. CUTBERD, I give thee the lease of thy house free: thanke me not, but with thy leg (—) I know what thou wouldst say, shee's poore, and her friends 80 deceased; shee has brought a wealthy dowrie in her silence,

CUTBERD: and in respect of her poverty, CUTBERD, I shall have
her more loving, and obedient, CUTBERD. Goe thy waies, and get
me a minister presently, with a soft, low voice to marry us, and
pray him he will not be impertinent, but briefe as he can; away:
softly, CUTBERD. [*Exit* CUTBERD.] Sirrah, conduct your mistris
into the dining roome, your now-mistris. [*Exeunt* MUTE *and* EPICO-
ENE.] O my felicity! how I shall bee reveng'd on mine insolent
kinsman, and his plots, to fright me from marrying! This night I
90   wil get an heire, and thrust him out of my bloud like a stranger;
he would be knighted, forsooth, and thought by that meanes to
raigne over me, his title must doe it: no kinsman, I will now make
you bring mee the tenth lords, and the sixteenth ladies letter,
kinsman; and it shall doe you no good kinsman. Your knighthood
it selfe shall come on it's knees, and it shall be rejected; it shall
bee sued for it's fees to execution, and not bee redeem'd; it shall
cheat at the twelvepeny ordinary, it knighthood, for it's diet all the
terme time, and tell tales for it in the vacation, to the hostesse: or
it knighthood shall doe worse; take sanctuary in *Coleharbor*, and
100   fast. It shall fright all it friends, with borrowing letters; and when
one of the foure-score hath brought it knighthood ten shillings, it
knighthood shall go to the Cranes, or the Beare at the *Bridge*-foot,
and be drunk in feare: it shal not have money to discharge one
taverne reckoning, to invite the old creditors, to forbeare it knighthood; or the new, that should be, to trust it knighthood. It shall
be the tenth name in the bond, to take up the commoditie of
pipkins, and stone jugs; and the part thereof shall not furnish it
knighthood forth, for the attempting of a bakers widdow, a browne
bakers widdow. It shall give it knighthoods name, for a *stallion*, to
110   all gamesome citizens wives, and bee refus'd; when the master of
a dancing schoole, or (*How* do you call him) the worst reveller in
the towne is taken: it shall want clothes, and by reason of that,
wit, to foole to lawyers. It shall not have hope to repaire it selfe
by *Constantinople, Ireland,* or *Virginia*; but the best, and last fortune
to it knighthood shall be, to make DOL TEARE-SHEET, or KATE
COMMON, a lady: and so, it knighthood may eate.   [*Exit.*]

Act II. Scene 6

TRUE-WIT, DAUPHINE, CLERIMONT, CUTBERD.

[*Enter* TRUE-WIT, DAUPHINE *and* CLERIMONT.]

TRUE-WIT Are you sure he is not gone by?

DAUPHINE No, I staid in the shop ever since.

CLERIMONT But, he may take the other end of the lane.

DAUPHINE No, I told him I would be here at this end: I appointed him hether.

TRUE-WIT What a barbarian it is to stay then!

[*Enter* CUTBERD.]

DAUPHINE Yonder he comes.

CLERIMONT And his charge left behinde him, which is a very good signe, DAUPHINE.

DAUPHINE How now CUTBERD, succeedes it, or no?   10

CUTBERD Past imagination, sir, *omnia secunda*; you could not have pray'd, to have had it so wel: *Saltat senex*, as it is i' the proverbe, he do's triumph in his felicity; admires the party! he has given me the lease of my house too! and, I am now going for a silent minister to marry 'hem, and away.

TRUE-WIT Slight, get one o' the silenc'd ministers, a zealous brother would torment him purely.

CUTBERD *Cum privilegio*, sir.

DAUPHINE O, by no meanes, let's doe nothing to hinder it now; when 'tis done and finished, I am for you: for any devise of   20 vexation.

CUTBERD And that shall be, within this halfe houre, upon my dexterity, gentlemen. Contrive what you can, in the meane time, *bonis avibus*.   [*Exit.*]

CLERIMONT How the slave doth *latine* it!

TRUE-WIT It would be made a jest to posterity, sirs, this daies mirth, if yee will.

CLERIMONT Beshrew his heart that will not, I pronounce.

DAUPHINE And, for my part. What is't?

TRUE-WIT To translate all LA-FOOLES company, and his feast hether,   30 to day, to celebrate this bride-ale.

DAUPHINE I mary, but how will't be done?

TRUE-WIT I'll undertake the directing of all the ladie-guests thether, and then the meat must follow.

CLERIMONT For gods sake, let's effect it: it will be an excellent *comoedy* of affliction, so many severall noyses.

DAUPHINE But are they not at the other place already, thinke you?

TRUE-WIT I'll warrant you for the colledge-honors: one o' their faces has not the priming color laid on yet, nor the other her smocke sleek'd.

40

CLERIMONT O, but they'll rise earlier then ordinary, to a feast.

TRUE-WIT Best goe see, and assure our selves.

CLERIMONT Who knowes the house?

TRUE-WIT I'll lead you, were you never there yet?

DAUPHINE Not I.

CLERIMONT Nor I.

TRUE-WIT Where ha' you liv'd then? not know TOM OTTER!

CLERIMONT No: for gods sake, what is he?

TRUE-WIT An excellent animal, equall with your DAW, or LA-FOOLE, if not transcendent; and do's *latine* it as much as your barber: hee is his wifes Subject, he calls her Princesse, and at such times as these, followes her up and downe the house like a page, with his hat off, partly for heate, partly for reverence. At this instant, hee is marshalling of his bull, beare, and horse.

50

DAUPHINE What be those, in the name of *Sphinx*?

TRUE-WIT Why sir? hee has beene a great man at the beare-garden in his time: and from that subtle sport, has tane the witty denomination of his chiefe carousing cups. One he calls his bull, another his beare, another his horse. And then hee has his lesser glasses, that hee calls his deere, and his ape; and severall degrees of 'hem too: and never is well, nor thinkes any intertainement perfect, till these be brought out, and set o' the cupbord.

60

CLERIMONT For gods love! we should misse this, if we should not goe.

TRUE-WIT Nay, he has a thousand things as good, that will speake him all day. He will raile on his wife, with certaine common places, behind her backe; and to her face—

DAUPHINE No more of him. Let's goe see him, I petition you.

[*Exeunt.*]

Act III. Scene 1

OTTER, MRS. OTTER, TRUE-WIT, CLERIMONT,
DAUPHINE.

[*Enter* OTTER, MRS. OTTER, TRUE-WIT, CLERIMONT *and*
DAUPHINE, *unseen.*]

OTTER Nay, good Princesse, heare me *pauca verba*.

MRS. OTTER By that light, I'll ha' you chain'd up, with your bul-dogs,
and beare-dogges, if you be not civill the sooner. I'll send you to
kennell, i'faith. You were best baite me with your bull, beare, and
horse? Never a time, that the courtiers, or collegiates come to the
house, but you make it a *shrovetuesday*! I would have you get your
whitsontide-velvet-cap, and your staffe i' your hand, to intertaine
'hem: yes introth, doe.

OTTER Not so, Princesse, neither, but under correction, sweete Princesse, gi' me leave—these things I am knowne to the courtiers   10
by. It is reported to them for my humor, and they receive it so,
and doe expect it. TOM OTTERS bull, beare, and horse is knowne
all over *England*, in *rerum natura*.

MRS. OTTER Fore me, I wil *na-ture* 'hem over to *Paris*-garden, and
na-ture you thether too, if you pronounce 'hem againe. Is a beare
a fit beast, or a bull, to mixe in society with great ladies? thinke i'
your discretion, in any good politie.

OTTER The horse then, good Princesse.

MRS. OTTER Well, I am contented for the horse: they love to bee
well hors'd, I know. I love it my selfe.   20

OTTER And it is a delicate fine horse this. *Poetarum Pegasus*. Under
correction, Princesse, JUPITER did turne himselfe into a— *Taurus*,
or Bull, under correction, good Princesse.

MRS. OTTER By my integritie, I'll send you over to the banke-side,
I'll commit you to the Master of the garden, if I heare but a syllable
more. Must my house, or my roofe, be polluted with the sent of
beares, and buls, when it is perfum'd for great ladies? Is this
according to the instrument, when I married you? That I would
bee Princesse, and raigne in mine owne house: and you would be
my subject, and obay me? What did you bring me, should make   30

you thus peremptory? Do I allow you your halfe-crowne a day, to
spend, where you will, among your gamsters, to vexe and torment
me, at such times as these? Who gives you your maintenance, I
pray you? who allowes you your horse-meat, and mans-meat? your
three sutes of apparell a yeere? your foure paire of stockings, one
silke, three worsted? your cleane linnen, your bands, and cuffes
when I can get you to weare 'hem? 'Tis mar'l you ha' 'hem on
now. Who graces you with courtiers, or great personages, to speake
to you out of their coaches, and come home to your house? Were
you ever so much as look'd upon by a lord, or a lady, before I
married you: but on the Easter, or Whitson-holy-daies? and then
out at the banquetting-house windore, when NED WHITING, or
GEORGE STONE, were at the stake?

(TRUE-WIT For gods sake, let's goe stave her off him.)

MRS. OTTER Answere me to that. And did not I take you up from
thence, in an old greasie buffe-doublet, with points; and greene
vellet sleeves, out at the elbowes? you forget this.

(TRUE-WIT Shee'll worry him, if we helpe not in time.)

MRS. OTTER O, here are some o' the gallants! Goe to, behave your
selfe distinctly, and with good moralitie; Or, I protest, I'll take
away your exhibition.

Act III. Scene 2

TRUE-WIT, MRS. OTTER, CAP. OTTER, CLERIMONT,
DAUPHINE, CUTBERD.

TRUE-WIT By your leave, faire mistris OTTER, I'll be bold to enter
these gentlemen in your acquaintance.

MRS. OTTER It shall not be obnoxious, or difficill, sir.

TRUE-WIT How do's my noble Captaine? Is the bull, beare, and
horse, in *rerum natura* still?

OTTER Sir, *Sic visum superis.*

MRS. OTTER I would you would but intimate 'hem, doe. Goe your
waies in, and get tosts, and butter, made for the wood-cocks.
That's a fit province for you.   [*Exit* OTTER.]

CLERIMONT Alas, what a tyrannie, is this poore fellow married too.

TRUE-WIT O, but the sport will be anon, when we get him loose.

DAUPHINE Dares he ever speake?

TRUE-WIT No Anabaptist ever rail'd with the like licence: but marke
her language in the meane time, I beseech you.

MRS. OTTER Gentlemen, you are very aptly come. My cosin, sir
AMOROUS, will be here briefly.

TRUE-WIT In good time lady. Was not sir JOHN DAW here, to aske
for him, and the companie?

MRS. OTTER I cannot assure you, Mr. TRUE-WIT. Here was a very
melancholy knight in a ruffe, that demanded my subject for some   20
body, a gentleman, I thinke.

CLERIMONT I, that was he, lady.

MRS. OTTER But he departed straight, I can resolve you.

DAUPHINE What an excellent choice phrase, this lady expresses in!

TRUE-WIT O, sir! shee is the onely authenticall courtier, that is not
naturally bred one, in the citie.

MRS. OTTER You have taken that report upon trust, gentlemen.

TRUE-WIT No, I assure you, the court governes it so, lady, in your
behalfe.

MRS. OTTER I am the servant of the court, and courtiers, sir.   30

TRUE-WIT They are rather your idolaters.

MRS. OTTER Not so, sir.

[*Enter* CUTBERD.]

DAUPHINE How now, CUTBERD? Any crosse?

CUTBERD O, no, sir: *Omnia bene*. 'Twas never better o' the hinges,
all's sure. I have so pleas'd him with a curate, that hee's gone too't
almost with the delight he hopes for soone.

DAUPHINE What is he, for a vicar?

CUTBERD One that has catch'd a cold, sir, and can scarse bee heard
six inches off; as if he spoke out of a bull-rush, that were not
pickt, or his throat were full of pith: a fine quick fellow, and an   40
excellent barber of prayers. I came to tell you, sir, that you might
omnem movere lapidem (as they say) be readie with your vexation.

DAUPHINE Gramercy, honest CUTBERD, be there abouts with thy
key to let us in.

CUTBERD I will not faile you, sir: *Ad manum*.   [*Exit.*]

TRUE-WIT Well, I'll goe watch my coaches.

CLERIMONT Doe; and wee'll send DAW to you, if you meet him not.
[*Exit* TRUE-WIT.]

MRS. OTTER Is master TRUE-WIT gone?

DAUPHINE Yes, lady, there is some unfortunate businesse fallen out.

50   MRS. OTTER So I judg'd by the phisiognomy of the fellow, that came in; and I had a dreame last night too of the new pageant, and my lady Maioresse, which is alwaies very ominous to me. I told it my lady HAUGHTY t'other day; when her honour came hether to see some *China* stuffes: and shee expounded it, out of ARTEMIDORUS, and I have found it since very true. It has done me many affronts.

CLERIMONT Your dreame, lady?

MRS. OTTER Yes, sir, any thing I doe but dreame o' the city. It staynd me a damasque table-cloth, cost me eighteen pound at one time; and burnt me a blacke satten gowne, as I stood by the fire, at my
60   ladie CENTAURES chamber in the colledge, another time. A third time, at the Lords masque, it dropt all my wire, and my ruffe with waxe-candle, that I could not goe up to the banquet. A fourth time, as I was taking coach to goe to *Ware*, to meet a friend, it dash'd me a new sute all over (a crimson sattin doublet, and blacke velvet skirts) with a brewers horse, that I was faine to goe in and shift mee, and kept my chamber a leash of daies for the anguish of it.

DAUPHINE These were dire mischances, lady.

CLERIMONT I would not dwell in the citie, and 'twere so fatall to
70   mee.

MRS. OTTER Yes sir, but I doe take advise of my doctor, to dreame of it as little, as I can.

DAUPHINE You doe well, mistris OTTER.

[*Enter* DAW, *taken aside by* CLERIMONT.]

MRS. OTTER Will it please you to enter the house farther, gentlemen?

DAUPHINE And your favour, lady: but we stay to speake with a knight, sir JOHN DAW, who is here come. We shall follow you, lady.

MRS. OTTER At your owne time, sir. It is my cosen sir AMOROUS his feast.—

80   DAUPHINE I know it lady.

MRS. OTTER And mine together. But it is for his honour; and therefore I take no name of it, more then of the place.

DAUPHINE You are a bounteous kinswoman.

MRS. OTTER Your servant, sir.   [*Exit.*]

Act III. Scene 3

CLERIMONT, DAW, LA-FOOLE, DAUPHINE, OTTER.

CLERIMONT Why, doe not you know it, sir JOHN DAW?

DAW No, I am a rooke if I doe.

CLERIMONT I'll tell you then, shee's married by this time! And
whereas you were put i' the head, that shee was gone with sir
DAUPHINE, I assure you, sir DAUPHINE has beene the noblest,
honestest friend to you, that ever gentleman of your quality could
boast off. He has discover'd the whole plot, and made your mistris
so acknowledging, and indeed, so ashamed of her injurie to you,
that she desires you to forgive her, and but grace her wedding
with your presence to day—She is to be married to a very good   10
fortune, she saies, his unkle, old MOROSE: and she will'd me in
private to tell you, that she shall be able to doe you more favours,
and with more securitie now, then before.

DAW Did she say so, i' faith?

CLERIMONT Why, what doe you thinke of mee, sir JOHN! aske sir
DAUPHINE.

DAW Nay, I beleeve you. Good sir DAUPHINE, did shee desire mee
to forgive her?

DAUPHINE I assure you, sir JOHN, she did.

DAW Nay then, I doe with all my heart, and I'll be *joviall*.   20

CLERIMONT Yes, for looke you sir, this was the injury to you.
LA-FOOLE intended this feast to honour her bridale day, and made
you the propertie to invite the colledge ladies, and promise to
bring her: and then at the time, shee should have appear'd (as his
friend) to have given you the *dor*. Whereas now, sir DAUPHINE
has brought her to a feeling of it, with this kinde of satisfaction,
that you shall bring all the ladies to the place where shee is, and
be verie *joviall*; and there, she will have a dinner, which shall be in
your name: and so dis-appoint LA-FOOLE, to make you good
againe, and (as it were) a saver i' the main.   30

DAW As I am a knight, I honour her, and forgive her hartily.

CLERIMONT About it then presently, TRUE-WIT is gone before to
confront the coaches, and to acquaint you with so much, if hee
meet you. Joyne with him, and 'tis well. [*Enter* LA-FOOLE.] See,

here comes your *Antagonist*, but take you no notice, but be verie *joviall*.

LA-FOOLE Are the ladies come, sir JOHN DAW, and your mistris? sir DAUPHINE! you are exceeding welcome, and honest master CLERIMONT. Where's my cossen? did you see no collegiats, gentle-
40   men?   [*Exit* DAW.]

DAUPHINE Collegiats! Doe you not heare, sir AMOROUS, how you are abus'd?

LA-FOOLE How sir!

CLERIMONT Will you speake so kindly to sir JOHN DAW, that has done you such an affront?

LA-FOOLE Wherein, gentlemen? let me be a sutor to you to know, I beseech you!

CLERIMONT Why sir, his mistris is married to day, to sir DAUPHINES uncle, your cosens neighbour, and hee has diverted all the ladies,
50   and all your company thether, to frustrate your provision, and sticke a disgrace upon you. He was here, now, to have intic'd us away from you too: but we told him his owne, I thinke.

LA-FOOLE Has sir JOHN DAW wrong'd me so in-humanely?

DAUPHINE He has done it, sir AMOROUS, most maliciously, and trecherously: but if you'll be rul'd by us, you shall quit him i'faith.

LA-FOOLE Good gentlemen! I'll make one, beleeve it. How I pray?

DAUPHINE Mary sir, get me your phesants, and your godwits, and your best meat, and dish it in silver dishes of your cosens presently,
60   and say nothing, but clap mee a cleane towell about you, like a sewer; and bare-headed, march afore it with a good confidence ('tis but over the way, hard by) and we'll second you, where you shal set it o' the boord, and bid 'hem welcome to't, which shall show 'tis yours, and disgrace his preparation utterly: and, for your cosen, whereas shee should bee troubled here at home with care of making and giving welcome, shee shall transferre all that labour thether, and bee a principall guest her selfe, sit rank'd with the colledge-Honors, and bee honor'd, and have her health drunke as often, as bare, and as lowd as the best of 'hem.

70   LA-FOOLE I'll goe tell her presently. It shall be done, that's resolv'd.
                                         [*Exit.*]

CLERIMONT I thought he would not heare it out, but 'twould take him.

DAUPHINE Well, there be guests, & meat now; how shal we do for musique?

CLERIMONT The smell of the venison, going through the street, will invite one noyse of fidlers, or other.

DAUPHINE I would it would call the trumpeters thether.

CLERIMONT Faith, there is hope, they have intelligence of all feasts. There's good correspondence betwixt them, and the *London-cookes*. 'Tis twenty to one but we have 'hem.   80

DAUPHINE 'Twill be a most solemne day for my uncle, and an excellent fit of mirth for us.

CLERIMONT I, if we can hold up the aemulation betwixt FOOLE, and DAW, and never bring them to expostulate.

DAUPHINE Tut, flatter 'hem both (as TRUE-WIT sayes) and you may take their understandings in a purse-net. They'll beleeve themselves to be just such men as we make 'hem, neither more nor lesse. They have nothing, not the use of their senses, but by tradition.

    [*Enter* LA-FOOLE.]

CLERIMONT See! Sir AMOROUS has his towell on already. Have you perswaded your cossen?

He enters like a sewer.

LA-FOOLE Yes, 'tis verie faesible: shee'll do any thing she sayes, rather then the LA-FOOLES shall be disgrac'd.   91

DAUPHINE She is a noble kinswoman. It will be such a pest'ling device, sir AMOROUS! It will pound all your enemies practises to poulder, and blow him up with his owne mine, his owne traine.

LA-FOOLE Nay, wee'll give fire, I warrant you.

CLERIMONT But you must carry it privatly, without any noyse, and take no notice by any meanes—

    [*Enter* OTTER.]

OTTER Gentlemen, my Princesse sayes, you shall have all her silver dishes, *festinate*: and she's gone to alter her tyre a little, and go with you—   100

CLERIMONT And your selfe too, captaine OTTER.

DAUPHINE By any meanes, sir.

OTTER Yes, sir, I doe meane it: but I would entreate my cosen sir AMOROUS, and you gentlemen, to be sutors to my Princesse, that I may carry my bull, and my beare, as well as my horse.

CLERIMONT That you shall doe, captaine OTTER.

LA-FOOLE My cosen will never consent, gentlemen.

DAUPHINE She must consent, sir AMOROUS, to reason.

110 LA-FOOLE Why, she sayes they are no *decorum* among ladies.

OTTER But they are *decora*, and that's better, sir.

CLERIMONT I, shee must heare argument. Did not PASIPHAE, who was a queene, love a bull? and was not CALISTO, the mother of ARCAS, turn'd into a beare, and made a starre, mistris URSULA, i' the heavens?

OTTER O God! that I could ha' said as much! I will have these stories painted i' the beare-garden, *ex Ovidii metamorphosi*.

DAUPHINE Where is your Princesse, Captaine? pray' be our leader.

OTTER That I shall, sir.

120 CLERIMONT Make haste, good sir AMOROUS.   [*Exeunt.*]

Act III. Scene 4

MOROSE, EPICOENE, PARSON, CUTBERD.

[*Enter* MOROSE, EPICOENE, PARSON *and* CUTBERD.]

MOROSE Sir, there's an angel for your selfe, and a brace of angels for your cold. Muse not at this mannage of my bounty. It is fit wee should thanke fortune, double to nature, for any benefit she conferres upon us; besides, it is your imperfection, but my solace.

The parson speakes, as having a cold.

PARSON I thanke your worship, so is it mine, now.

MOROSE What sayes he, CUTBERD?

CUTBERD He saies, *Praesto*, sir, whensoever your worship needes him, hee can be ready with the like. He got this cold with sitting up late, and singing catches with cloth-workers.

10 MOROSE No more. I thanke him.

PARSON God keepe your worship, and give you much joy with your faire spouse. (Umh, umh.)

He coughes.

MOROSE O, o, stay CUTBERD! let him give me five shillings of my money backe. As it is bounty to reward benefits, so is it equity to mulct injuries. I will have it. What sayes he?

CUTBERD He cannot change it, sir.

MOROSE It must be chang'd.

CUTBERD Cough againe.

MOROSE What sayes he?

CUTBERD He will cough out the rest, sir.   20

PARSON (Umh, umh, umh.)   *Againe.*

MOROSE Away, away with him, stop his mouth, away, I forgive it.—

                    [*Exeunt* CUTBERD *and* PARSON.]

EPICOENE Fye, master MOROSE, that you will use this violence to a
    man of the church.

MOROSE How!

EPICOENE It do's not become your gravity, or breeding, (as you
    pretend in court) to have offered this outrage on a waterman, or
    any more boystrous creature, much lesse on a man of his civill
    coat.

MOROSE You can speake then!   30

EPICOENE Yes, sir.

MOROSE Speake out I meane.

EPICOENE I sir. Why, did you thinke you had married a statue? or a
    motion, onely? one of the *French* puppets, with the eyes turn'd
    with a wire? or some innocent out of the hospitall, that would
    stand with her hands thus, and a playse mouth, and looke upon
    you.

MOROSE O immodestie! a manifest woman! what CUTBERD?

EPICOENE Nay, never quarrell with CUTBERD, sir, it is too late now.
    I confesse, it doth bate somewhat of the modestie I had, when I   40
    writ simply maide: but I hope, I shall make it a stocke still
    competent, to the estate, and dignity of your wife.

MOROSE Shee can talke!

EPICOENE Yes indeed, sir.

MOROSE What, sirrah. None of my knaves, there? [*Enter* MUTE.]
    where is this impostor, CUTBERD?

EPICOENE Speake to him, fellow, speake to him. I'll have none of
    this coacted, unnaturall dumbnesse in my house, in a family where
    I governe.   [*Exit* MUTE.]

MOROSE She is my Regent already! I have married a PENTHESILEA,   50
    a SEMIRAMIS, sold my liberty to a distaffe!

Act III. Scene 5

TRUE-WIT, MOROSE, EPICOENE.

[*Enter* TRUE-WIT.]

TRUE-WIT Where's master MOROSE?

MOROSE Is he come againe! lord have mercy upon me.

TRUE-WIT I wish you all joy, mistris EPICOENE, with your grave
and honourable match.

EPICOENE I returne you the thankes, master TRUE-WIT, so friendly
a wish deserves.

MOROSE She has acquaintance, too!

TRUE-WIT God save you, sir, and give you all contentment in your
faire choise, here. Before I was the bird of night to you, the owle;
10 but now I am the messenger of peace, a dove, and bring you the
glad wishes of many friends, to the celebration of this good houre.

MOROSE What houre, sir?

TRUE-WIT Your marriage houre sir. I commend your resolution, that
(notwithstanding all the dangers I laid afore you, in the voice of a
night-crow) would yet goe on, and bee your selfe. It shewes you
are a man constant to your own ends, and upright to your purposes,
that would not be put off with left-handed cries.

MOROSE How should you arrive at the knowledge of so much!

TRUE-WIT Why, did you ever hope, sir, committing the secrecie of
20 it to a barber, that lesse then the whole towne should know it?
you might as wel ha' told it the conduit, or the bake-house, or the
infant'ry that follow the court, and with more securitie. Could your
gravitie forget so olde and noted a remnant, as, *lippis & tonsoribus
notum*? Well sir, forgive it your selfe now, the fault, and be communi-
cable with your friends. Here will bee three or foure fashionable
ladies, from the colledge, to visit you presently, and their traine of
minions, and followers.

MOROSE Barre my dores! barre my dores! where are all my eaters?
my mouthes now? [*Enter* SERVANTS.] barre up my dores, you
30 varlets.

EPICOENE He is a varlet, that stirres to such an office. Let 'hem stand
open. I would see him that dares moove his eyes toward it. Shal

I have a *barricado* made against my friends, to be barr'd of any
pleasure they can bring in to me with honorable visitation?

MOROSE O *Amazonian* impudence!

TRUE-WIT Nay faith, in this, sir, she speakes but reason: and me
thinkes is more continent then you. Would you goe to bed so
presently, sir, afore noone? a man of your head, and haire, should
owe more to that reverend ceremony, and not mount the marriage-
bed, like a towne-bul, or a mountaine-goate; but stay the due   40
season; and ascend it then with religion, and feare. Those delights
are to be steep'd in the humor, and silence of the night; and give
the day to other open pleasures, and jollities of feast, of musique,
of revells, of discourse: wee'll have all, sir, that may make your
Hymen high, and happy.

MOROSE O, my torment, my torment!

TRUE-WIT Nay, if you indure the first halfe houre, sir, so tediously,
and with this irksomnesse; what comfort, or hope, can this faire
gentlewoman make to her selfe hereafter, in the consideration of
so many yeeres as are to come—   50

MOROSE Of my affliction. Good sir, depart, and let her doe it alone.

TRUE-WIT I have done, sir.

MOROSE That cursed barber!

TRUE-WIT (Yes faith, a cursed wretch indeed, sir.)

MOROSE I have married his citterne, that's common to all men. Some
plague, above the plague—

TRUE-WIT (All *Egypts* ten plagues)

MOROSE Revenge me on him.

TRUE-WIT 'Tis very well, sir. If you laid on a curse or two, more, I'll
assure you hee'll beare 'hem. As, that he may get the poxe with   60
seeking to cure it, sir? Or, that while he is curling another mans
haire, his owne may drop off? Or, for burning some male-baudes
lock, he may have his braine beat out with the curling-iron?

MOROSE No, let the wretch live wretched. May he get the itch, and
his shop so lousie, as no man dare come at him, nor he come at
no man.

TRUE-WIT (I, and if he would swallow all his balles for pills, let not
them purge him)

MOROSE Let his warming pan be ever cold.

TRUE-WIT (A perpetuall frost underneath it, sir)   70

MOROSE Let him never hope to see fire againe.

TRUE-WIT (But in hell, sir)

MOROSE His chaires be alwaies empty, his scissors rust, and his combes mould in their cases.

TRUE-WIT Very dreadfull that! (And may hee loose the invention, sir, of carving lanternes in paper)

MOROSE Let there be no baud carted that yeare, to employ a bason of his: but let him be glad to eate his sponge, for bread.

TRUE-WIT And drinke *lotium* to it, and much good doe him.

80 MOROSE Or, for want of bread——

TRUE-WIT Eate eare-waxe, sir. I'll helpe you. Or, draw his owne teeth, and adde them to the lute-string.

MOROSE No, beate the old ones to poulder, and make bread of them.

TRUE-WIT (Yes, make meale o' the millstones.)

MOROSE May all the botches, and burnes, that he has cur'd on others, breake out upon him.

TRUE-WIT And he now forget the cure of 'hem in himselfe, sir: or, if he do remember it, let him ha' scrap'd all his linnen into lint for 't, and have not a rag left him, to set up with.

90 MOROSE Let him never set up againe, but have the gout in his hands for ever. Now, no more, sir.

TRUE-WIT O that last was too high set! you might goe lesse with him i' faith, and bee reveng'd enough: as, that he be never able to new-paint his pole——

MOROSE Good sir, no more. I forgot my selfe.

TRUE-WIT Or, want credit to take up with a combe-maker——

MOROSE No more, sir.

TRUE-WIT Or, having broken his glasse in a former despaire, fall now into a much greater, of ever getting another——

100 MOROSE I beseech you, no more.

TRUE-WIT Or, that he never be trusted with trimming of any but chimney-sweepers——

MOROSE Sir——

TRUE-WIT Or, may he cut a colliers throat with his rasor, by *chance-medlee*, and yet hang for't.

MOROSE I will forgive him, rather then heare any more. I beseech you, sir.

Act III. Scene 6

DAW, MOROSE, TRUE-WIT, HAUGHTY, CENTAURE,
MAVIS, TRUSTY.

[*Enter* DAW, HAUGHTY, CENTAURE, MAVIS *and* TRUSTY.]

DAW This way, madame.

MOROSE O, the sea breakes in upon me! another floud! an inundation!
I shall be orewhelm'd with noise. It beates already at my shores.
I feele an earthquake in my selfe, for't.

DAW 'Give you joy, mistresse.

MOROSE Has shee servants too!

DAW I have brought some ladies here to see, and know you. My
ladie HAUGHTY, this my lady CENTAURE, mistresse DOL MAVIS,
mistresse TRUSTIE my ladie HAUGHTIES woman. Where's your
husband? let's see him: can he endure no noise? let me come to
him.

She kisses them
severally as he
presents them.

10

MOROSE What *nomenclator* is this!

TRUE-WIT Sir JOHN DAW, sir, your wifes servant, this.

MOROSE A DAW, and her servant! O, 'tis decreed, 'tis decreed of
mee, and shee have such servants.

TRUE-WIT Nay sir, you must kisse the ladies, you must not goe away,
now; they come toward you, to seeke you out.

HAUGHTY I' faith, master MOROSE, would you steale a marriage
thus, in the midst of so many friends, and not acquaint us? Well,
I'll kisse you, notwithstanding the justice of my quarrell: you shall
give me leave, mistresse, to use a becomming familiarity with your
husband.

20

EPICOENE Your ladiship do's me an honour in it, to let me know
hee is so worthy your favour: as, you have done both him and me
grace, to visit so unprepar'd a paire to entertaine you.

MOROSE Complement! Complement!

EPICOENE But I must lay the burden of that, upon my servant, here.

HAUGHTY It shall not need, mistresse MOROSE, wee will all beare,
rather then one shall be opprest.

MOROSE I know it: and you will teach her the faculty, if shee bee to
learne it.

30

HAUGHTY Is this the silent woman?

CENTAURE Nay, shee has found her tongue since shee was married, master TRUE-WIT sayes.

HAUGHTY O, master TRUE-WIT! 'save you. What kinde of creature is your bride here? she speakes, me thinkes!

TRUE-WIT Yes madame, beleeve it, she is a gentlewoman of very absolute behaviour, and of a good race.

HAUGHTY And JACK DAW told us, she could not speake.

40 TRUE-WIT So it was carried in plot, madam, to put her upon this old fellow; by sir DAUPHINE, his nephew, and one or two more of us: but shee is a woman of an excellent assurance, and an extraordinarie happie wit, and tongue. You shall see her make rare sport with DAW, ere night.

HAUGHTY And he brought us to laugh at her!

TRUE-WIT That falls out often, madame, that he that thinkes himselfe the master-wit, is the master-foole. I assure your lady-ship, yee cannot laugh at her.

HAUGHTY No, wee'll have her to the colledge: and shee have wit,
50 she shall bee one of us! shall shee not CENTAURE? wee'll make her a collegiate.

CENTAURE Yes faith, madame, and MAVIS, and shee will set up a side.

TRUE-WIT Beleeve it madame, and mistris MAVIS, shee will sustaine her part.

MAVIS I'll tell you that, when I have talk'd with her, and try'd her.

HAUGHTY Use her very civilly, MAVIS.

MAVIS So I will, madame.

MOROSE Blessed minute, that they would whisper thus ever.

60 TRUE-WIT In the meane time, madame, would but your lady-ship helpe to vexe him a little: you know his disease, talke to him about the wedding ceremonies, or call for your gloves, or—

HAUGHTY Let me alone. CENTAURE, helpe me. Mr. bride-groome, where are you?

MOROSE O, it was too miraculously good to last!

HAUGHTY Wee see no ensignes of a wedding, here; no character of a brideale: where be our skarfes, and our gloves? I pray you, give 'hem us. Let's know your brides colours, and yours, at least.

CENTAURE Alas, madame, he has provided none.

70 MOROSE Had I knowne your ladiships painter, I would.

HAUGHTY He has given it you, CENTAURE, yfaith. But, doe you
    heare, M. MOROSE, a jest will not absolve you in this manner.
    You that have suck'd the milke of the court, and from thence have
    beene brought up to the very strong meates, and wine, of it; beene
    a courtier from the biggen, to the night-cap: (as we may say) and
    you, to offend in such a high point of ceremonie, as this! and let
    your nuptialls want all markes of solemnitie! How much plate have
    you lost to day (if you had but regarded your profit) what guifts,
    what friends, through your meere rusticitie?

MOROSE Madame—   80

HAUGHTY Pardon mee, sir, I must insinuate your errours to you. No
    gloves? no garters? no skarfes? no *epithalamium*? no masque?

DAW Yes, madame, I'll make an *epithalamium*, I promis'd my mistris,
    I have begunne it already: will your ladiship heare it?

HAUGHTY I, good JACK DAW.

MOROSE Will it please your ladiship command a chamber, and be
    private with your friend? you shall have your choice of roomes,
    to retire to after: my whole house is yours. I know, it hath beene
    your ladiships errand, into the city, at other times, how ever now
    you have beene unhappily diverted upon mee: but I shall be loth   90
    to breake any honorable custome of your ladiships. And therefore,
    good madame—

EPICOENE Come, you are a rude bride-groome, to entertayne ladies
    of honour in this fashion.

CENTAURE He is a rude groome, indeed.

TRUE-WIT By that light, you deserve to be grafted, and have your
    hornes reach from one side of the Iland, to the other. Doe not
    mistake me, sir, I but speake this, to give the ladies some heart
    againe, not for any malice to you.

MOROSE Is this your *Bravo*, ladies?   100

TRUE-WIT As god helpe me, if you utter such another word, I'll take
    mistris bride in, and beginne to you, in a very sad cup, doe you
    see? Goe too, know your friends, and such, as love you.

Act III. Scene 7

CLERIMONT, MOROSE, TRUE-WIT, DAUPHINE, LA-FOOLE,
OTTER, MRS. OTTER, &C.

[Enter CLERIMONT *and musicians.]*

CLERIMONT By your leave, ladies. Doe you want any musique? I
have brought you varietie of noyses. Play, sirs, all of you.

Musique of all sorts.

MOROSE O, a plot, a plot, a plot, a plot upon me! This day, I shall
be their anvile to worke on, they will grate me asunder. 'Tis worse
then the noyse of a saw.

CLERIMONT No, they are haire, rosin, and guts. I can give you the
receipt.

TRUE-WIT Peace, boyes.

CLERIMONT Play, I say.

10   TRUE-WIT Peace, rascalls. You see who's your friend now, sir? Take
courage, put on a martyrs resolution. Mocke downe all their
attemptings, with patience. 'Tis but a day, and I would suffer
heroically. Should an asse exceed me in fortitude? No. You betray
your infirmitie with your hanging dull eares, and make them insult:

La-Foole passes over sewing the meat.

beare up bravely, and constantly. Looke you here, sir, what honour
is done you unexpected, by your nephew; a wedding dinner come,
and a Knight sewer before it, for the more reputation: and fine
Mrs. OTTER, your neighbour, in the rump, or tayle of it.

MOROSE Is that *Gorgon*, that *Medusa* come? Hide me, hide me.

20   TRUE-WIT I warrant you, sir, shee will not transforme you. Looke
upon her with a good courage. Pray you entertayne her, and
conduct your guests in. No? Mistris bride, will you entreat in the
ladies? your bride-groome is so shame-fac'd, here——

EPICOENE Will it please your ladiship, madame?

HAUGHTY With the benefit of your companie, mistris.

EPICOENE Servant, pray you performe your duties.

DAW And glad to be commanded, mistris.

CENTAURE How like you her wit, MAVIS?

MAVIS Very prettily, absolutely well.

30   MRS. OTTER 'Tis my place.

MAVIS You shall pardon me, mistris OTTER.

MRS. OTTER Why I am a collegiate.

MAVIS But not in ordinary.

MRS. OTTER But I am.

MAVIS Wee'll dispute that within. [*Exeunt* LADIES.]

CLERIMONT Would this had lasted a little longer.

TRUE-WIT And that they had sent for the Heralds. [*Enter* OTTER.]
Captayne OTTER, what newes?

OTTER I have brought my bull, beare, and horse, in private, and
yonder are the trumpetters without, and the drum, gentlemen.   40

MOROSE O, o, o.

OTTER And we will have a rouse in each of 'hem, anon, for bold
Britons, yfaith.

MOROSE O, o, o.   [*Exit.*]

ALL Follow, follow, follow.   [*Exeunt.*]

*The Drum, and
Trumpets sound.*

Act IV. Scene 1

TRUE-WIT, CLERIMONT, DAUPHINE.

[*Enter* TRUE-WIT *and* CLERIMONT.]

TRUE-WIT Was there ever poore bride-groome so tormented? or
man indeed?

CLERIMONT I have not read of the like, in the *chronicles* of the land.

TRUE-WIT Sure, hee cannot but goe to a place of rest, after all this
purgatorie.

CLERIMONT He may presume it, I thinke.

TRUE-WIT The spitting, the coughing, the laughter, the neesing, the
farting, dauncing, noise of the musique, and her masculine, and
lowd commanding, and urging the whole family, makes him thinke
he has married a *furie*.   10

CLERIMONT And shee carries it up bravely.

TRUE-WIT I, shee takes any occasion to speake: that's the height
on't.

CLERIMONT And how soberly DAUPHINE labours to satisfie him,
that it was none of his plot!

TRUE-WIT And has almost brought him to the faith, i' the article.
[*Enter* DAUPHINE.] Here he comes. Where is he now? what's
become of him, DAUPHINE?

DAUPHINE O, hold me up a little, I shall goe away i' the jest else.

20 Hee has got on his whole nest of night-caps, and lock'd himselfe
up, i' the top o' the house, as high, as ever he can climbe from
the noise. I peep'd in at a crany, and saw him sitting over a
crosse-beame o' the roofe, like him o' the sadlers horse in *Fleetstreet*,
up-right: and he will sleepe there.

CLERIMONT But where are your collegiates?

DAUPHINE With-drawne with the bride in private.

TRUE-WIT O, they are instructing her i' the colledge-Grammar. If
shee have grace with them, shee knowes all their secrets instantly.

CLERIMONT Me thinks, the lady HAUGHTY lookes well to day, for
30 all my dispraise of her i' the morning. I thinke, I shall come about
to thee againe, TRUE-WIT.

TRUE-WIT Beleeve it, I told you right. Women ought to repaire the
losses, time and yeeres have made i' their features, with dressings.
And an intelligent woman, if shee know by her selfe the least
defect, will bee most curious, to hide it: and it becomes her. If
shee be short, let her sit much, lest when shee stands, shee be
thought to sit. If shee have an ill foot, let her weare her gowne
the longer, and her shoo the thinner. If a fat hand, and scald nailes,
let her carve the lesse, and act in gloves. If a sowre breath, let her
40 never discourse fasting: and alwaies talke at her distance. If shee
have black and rugged teeth, let her offer the lesse at laughter,
especially if shee laugh wide, and open.

CLERIMONT O, you shall have some women, when they laugh, you
would thinke they bray'd, it is so rude, and —

TRUE-WIT I, and others, that will stalke i' their gait like an *Estrich*,
and take huge strides. I cannot endure such a sight. I love measure
i' the feet, and number i' the voice: they are gentlenesses, that
oft-times draw no lesse then the face.

DAUPHINE How cam'st thou to studie these creatures so exactly? I
50 would thou would'st make me a proficient.

TRUE-WIT Yes, but you must leave to live i' your chamber then a
month together upon AMADIS *de Gaule*, or *Don* QUIXOTE, as you
are wont; and come abroad where the matter is frequent, to court,
to tiltings, publique showes, and feasts, to playes, and church
sometimes: thither they come to shew their new tyres too, to see,
and to be seene. In these places a man shall find whom to love,
whom to play with, whom to touch once, whom to hold ever. The

varietie arrests his judgement. A wench to please a man comes
not downe dropping from the seeling, as he lyes on his backe
droning a tobacco pipe. He must goe where shee is.   60

DAUPHINE Yes, and be never the neere.

TRUE-WIT Out heretique. That diffidence makes thee worthy it
should bee so.

CLERIMONT He sayes true to you, DAUPHINE.

DAUPHINE Why?

TRUE-WIT A man should not doubt to over-come any woman.
Thinke he can vanquish 'hem, and he shall: for though they denie,
their desire is to be tempted. PENELOPE her selfe cannot hold out
long. *Ostend*, you saw, was taken at last. You must persever, and
hold to your purpose. They would sollicite us, but that they are   70
afraid. Howsoever, they wish in their hearts we should sollicite-
them. Praise 'hem, flatter 'hem, you shal never want eloquence,
or trust: even the chastest delight to feele themselves that way
rub'd. With praises you must mixe kisses too. If they take them,
they'll take more. Though they strive, they would bee over-come.

CLERIMONT O, but a man must beware of force.

TRUE-WIT It is to them an acceptable violence, and has oft-times
the place of the greatest courtesie. Shee that might have beene
forc'd, and you let her goe free without touching, though shee
then seeme to thanke you, will ever hate you after: and glad i' the 80
face, is assuredly sad at the heart.

CLERIMONT But all women are not to be taken al waies.

TRUE-WIT 'Tis true. No more then all birds, or all fishes. If you
appeare learned to an ignorant wench, or jocund to a sad, or witty
to a foolish, why shee presently begins to mistrust her selfe. You
must approch them i' their owne height, their owne line: for the
contrary makes many that feare to commit themselves to noble
and worthy fellowes, run into the imbraces of a rascall. If shee
love wit, give verses, though you borrow 'hem of a friend, or buy
'hem, to have good. If valour, talke of your sword, and be frequent 90
in the mention of quarrels, though you be staunch in fighting. If
activitie, be seene o' your *barbary* often, or leaping over stooles,
for the credit of your back. If shee love good clothes or dressing,
have your learned counsell about you every morning, your *french*
taylor, barber, linnener, &c. Let your poulder, your glasse, and

your combe, be your dearest acquaintance. Take more care for the
ornament of your head, then the safetie: and wish the common-
wealth rather troubled, then a haire about you. That will take her.
Then if shee be covetous and craving, doe you promise any thing,
and performe sparingly: so shall you keepe her in appetite still.
Seeme as you would give, but be like a barren field that yeelds
little, or unlucky dice, to foolish, and hoping gamesters. Let your
gifts be slight, and daintie, rather then pretious. Let cunning be
above cost. Give cherries at time of yeere, or apricots; and say
they were sent you out o' the countrey, though you bought 'hem
in *Cheap-side*. Admire her tyres; like her in all fashions; compare
her in every habit to some deitie; invent excellent dreames to flatter
her, and riddles; or, if shee bee a great one, performe alwaies the
second parts to her: like what shee likes, praise whom she praises,
and faile not to make the houshold and servants yours, yea the
whole family, and salute 'hem by their names: ('tis but light cost
if you can purchase 'hem so) and make her physitian your pensioner,
and her chiefe woman. Nor will it bee out of your gaine to make
love to her too, so shee follow, not usher, her ladies pleasure. All
blabbing is taken away, when shee comes to be a part of the crime.

DAUPHINE On what courtly lap hast thou late slept, to come forth
so sudden and absolute a courtling?

TRUE-WIT Good faith, I should rather question you, that are so
harkning after these mysteries. I begin to suspect your diligence,
DAUPHINE. Speake, art thou in love in earnest?

DAUPHINE Yes by my troth am I: 'twere ill dissembling before thee.

TRUE-WIT With which of 'hem, I pray thee?

DAUPHINE With all the collegiates.

CLERIMONT Out on thee. Wee'll keepe you at home, beleeve it, i'
the stable, and you be such a stallion.

TRUE-WIT No. I like him well. Men should love wisely, and all
women: some one for the face, and let her please the eye; another
for the skin, and let her please the touch; a third for the voice,
and let her please the eare; and where the objects mixe, let the
senses so too. Thou wouldst thinke it strange, if I should make
'hem all in love with thee afore night!

DAUPHINE I would say thou had'st the best *philtre* i' the world, and
couldst doe more then madame MEDEA, or Doctor FOREMAN.

TRUE-WIT If I doe not, let me play the mounte-bank for my meate
    while I live, and the bawd for my drinke.

DAUPHINE So be it, I say.

Act IV. Scene 2

OTTER, CLERIMONT, DAW, DAUPHINE, MOROSE,
TRUE-WIT, LA-FOOLE, MRS. OTTER.

[*Enter* OTTER, DAW *and* LA-FOOLE.]

OTTER O Lord, gentlemen, how my knights and I have mist you
    here!

CLERIMONT Why, Captaine, what service? what service?

OTTER To see me bring up my bull, beare, and horse to fight.

DAW Yes faith, the Captaine saies we shall be his dogs to baite 'hem.

DAUPHINE A good imployment.

TRUE-WIT Come on, let's see a course then.

LA-FOOLE I am afraid my cousin will be offended if shee come.

OTTER Be afraid of nothing. Gentlemen, I have plac'd the drum and
    the trumpets, and one to give 'hem the signe when you are ready.   10
    Here's my bull for my selfe, and my beare for sir JOHN DAW, and
    my horse for sir AMOROUS. Now set your foot to mine, and yours
    to his, and—

LA-FOOLE Pray god my cousin come not.

OTTER Saint GEORGE, and saint ANDREW, feare no cousins. Come,
    sound, sound. *Et rauco strepuerunt cornua cantu.*

TRUE-WIT Well said, Captaine, yfaith: well fought at the bull.

CLERIMONT Well held at the beare.

TRUE-WIT Low, low, Captayne.

DAUPHINE O, the horse has kickt off his dog alreadie.   20

LA-FOOLE I cannot drinke it, as I am a Knight.

TRUE-WIT Gods so, off with his spurres, some-body.

LA-FOOLE It goes againe my conscience. My cousin will bee angrie
    with it.

DAW I ha' done mine.

TRUE-WIT You fought high and faire, sir JOHN.

CLERIMONT At the head.

DAUPHINE Like an excellent beare-dog.

CLERIMONT You take no notice of the businesse, I hope.

30 DAW Not a word, sir, you see we are *joviall*.

OTTER Sir AMOROUS, you must not aequivocate. It must bee pull'd
downe, for all my cousin.

CLERIMONT Sfoot, if you take not your drinke, they'll thinke you are
discontented with some thing: you'll betray all, if you take the least
notice.

LA-FOOLE Not I, I'll both drinke, and talke then.

OTTER You must pull the horse on his knees, sir AMOROUS: feare
no cousins. *Jacta est alea.*

TRUE-WIT O, now hee's in his vaine, and bold. The least hint given

40 him of his wife now, will make him raile desperately.

CLERIMONT Speake to him of her.

TRUE-WIT Doe you, and I'll fetch her to the hearing of it. [*Exit.*]

DAUPHINE Captaine hee-OTTER, your shee-OTTER is comming,
your wife.

OTTER Wife! Buz. *Titivilitium.* There's no such thing in nature. I
confesse, gentlemen, I have a cook, a laundresse, a house-drudge,
that serves my necessary turnes, and goes under that title: But
hee's an asse that will be so *uxorious*, to tie his affections to one
circle. Come, the name dulls appetite. Here, replenish againe:

50 another bout. Wives are nasty sluttish *animalls.*

DAUPHINE O, Captaine.

OTTER As ever the earth bare, *tribus verbis.* Where's master TRUE-WIT?

DAW Hee's slipt aside, sir.

CLERIMONT But you must drinke, and be *joviall*.

DAW Yes, give it me.

LA-FOOLE And me, too.

DAW Let's be *joviall*.

LA-FOOLE As *joviall* as you will.

OTTER Agreed. Now you shall ha' the beare, cousin, and sir JOHN

60 DAW the horse, and I'll ha' the bull still. Sound *Tritons* o' the
Thames. Nunc est bibendum, nunc pede libero—

Morose speakes MOROSE Villaines, murderers, sonnes of the earth, and traitors, what
from above: the doe you there?
trumpets
sounding. CLERIMONT O, now the trumpets have wak'd him, we shall have his
companie.

OTTER A wife is a scirvy *clogdogdo*; an unlucky thing, a very foresaid
beare-whelpe, without any good fashion or breeding: *mala bestia*.

DAUPHINE Why did you marry one then, Captaine?

*His wife is
brought out to
heare him.*

[*Enter* MRS. OTTER *and* TRUE-WIT, *unobserved.*]

OTTER A poxe— I married with sixe thousand pound, I. I was in
love with that. I ha' not kist my *furie*, these fortie weekes.

70

CLERIMONT The more to blame you, Captaine.

TRUE-WIT Nay, mistris OTTER, heare him a little first.

OTTER Shee has a breath worse then my grand-mothers, *profecto*.

MRS. OTTER O treacherous lyar. Kisse mee, sweet master TRUE-WIT,
and prove him a slaundering knave.

TRUE-WIT I'll rather beleeve you, lady.

OTTER And she has a perruke, that's like a pound of hempe, made
up in shoo-thrids.

MRS. OTTER O viper, mandrake!

OTTER A most vile face! and yet shee spends me fortie pound a
yeere in *mercury*, and hogs-bones. All her teeth were made i' the
Blacke-*Friers*: both her eye-browes i' the *Strand*, and her haire in
Silver-street. Every part o' the towne ownes a peece of her.

80

MRS. OTTER I cannot hold.

OTTER She takes her selfe asunder still when she goes to bed, into
some twentie boxes; and about next day noone is put together
againe, like a great *Germane* clocke: and so comes forth and rings
a tedious larum to the whole house, and then is quiet againe for
an houre, but for her quarters. Ha' you done me right, gentlemen?

89

MRS. OTTER No, sir, I'll do you right with my quarters, with my
quarters.

*She falls upon
him and beates
him.*

OTTER O, hold, good Princesse.

TRUE-WIT Sound, sound.

CLERIMONT A battell, a battell.

MRS. OTTER You notorious stinkardly beareward, do's my breath
smell?

OTTER Under correction, deare Princesse: looke to my beare, and
my horse, gentlemen.

MRS. OTTER Doe I want teeth, and eye-browes, thou bull-dog?

TRUE-WIT Sound, sound still.

100

OTTER No, I protest, under correction—

MRS. OTTER I, now you are under correction, you protest: but you did not protest before correction, sir. Thou JUDAS, to offer to betray thy Princesse! I'll make thee an example—

Morose descends
with a long
sword.

MOROSE I will have no such examples in my house, lady OTTER.

MRS. OTTER Ah—   [*Exeunt* MRS. OTTER, DAW *and* LA-FOOLE.]

MOROSE Mrs. MARY AMBREE, your examples are dangerous. Rogues, Hellhounds, *Stentors*, out of my dores, you sonnes of noise and tumult, begot on an ill *May*-day, or when the Gally-foist is

110

a-floate to *Westminster*! A trumpetter could not be conceiv'd, but then!

DAUPHINE What ailes you, sir?

MOROSE They have rent my roofe, walls, and all my windores asunder, with their brazen throates.   [*Exit.*]

TRUE-WIT Best follow him, DAUPHINE.

DAUPHINE So I will.   [*Exit.*]

CLERIMONT Where's DAW, and LA-FOOLE?

OTTER They are both run away, sir. Good gentlemen, helpe to pacifie my Princesse, and speake to the great ladies for me. Now must I

120

goe lie with the beares this fortnight, and keepe out o' the way, till my peace be made, for this scandale shee has taken. Did you not see my bull-head, gentlemen?

CLERIMONT Is 't not on, Captayne?

TRUE-WIT No: but he may make a new one, by that, is on.

OTTER O, here 'tis. And you come over, gentlemen, and aske for TOM OTTER, wee'll goe downe to *Ratcliffe*, and have a course yfaith: for all these disasters. There's *bona spes* left.

TRUE-WIT Away, Captaine, get off while you are well.

[*Exit* OTTER.]

CLERIMONT I am glad we are rid of him.

130

TRUE-WIT You had never beene, unlesse wee had put his wife upon him. His humour is as tedious at last, as it was ridiculous at first.

Act IV. Scene 3

HAUGHTY, MRS. OTTER, MAVIS, DAW, LA-FOOLE,
CENTAURE, EPICOENE, TRUE-WIT, CLERIMONT.

[*Enter* HAUGHTY, MRS. OTTER, MAVIS, DAW, LA-FOOLE,
CENTAURE *and* EPICOENE.]

HAUGHTY We wondred why you shreek'd so, Mrs. OTTER.

MRS. OTTER O god, madame, he came downe with a huge long naked
weapon in both his hands, and look'd so dreadfully! Sure, hee's
beside himselfe.

MAVIS Why what made you there, mistris OTTER?

MRS. OTTER Alas, mistris MAVIS, I was chastising my subject, and
thought nothing of him.

DAW Faith, mistris, you must doe so too. Learne to chastise. Mistris
OTTER corrects her husband so, hee dares not speake, but under
correction.   10

LA-FOOLE And with his hat off to her: 'twould doe you good to see.

HAUGHTY In sadnesse 'tis good, and mature counsell: practise it,
MOROSE. I'll call you MOROSE still now, as I call CENTAURE, and
MAVIS: we foure will be all one.

CENTAURE And you'll come to the colledge, and live with us?

HAUGHTY Make him give milke, and hony.

MAVIS Looke how you manage him at first, you shall have him ever
after.

CENTAURE Let him allow you your coach, and foure horses, your
woman, your chamber-maid, your page, your gentleman-usher,   20
your *french* cooke, and foure groomes.

HAUGHTY And goe with us, to *Bed'lem*, to the *China* houses, and to
the *Exchange*.

CENTAURE It will open the gate to your fame.

HAUGHTY Here's CENTAURE has immortaliz'd her selfe, with taming
of her wilde male.

MAVIS I, shee has done the miracle of the kingdome.

EPICOENE But ladies, doe you count it lawfull to have such pluralitie
of servants, and doe 'hem all graces?

HAUGHTY Why not? why should women denie their favours to men?   30

Are they the poorer, or the worse?

DAW Is the *Thames* the lesse for the *dyers* water, mistris?

LA-FOOLE Or a torch, for lighting many torches?

TRUE-WIT Well said, LA-FOOLE; what a new one he has got!

CENTAURE They are emptie losses, women feare, in this kind.

HAUGHTY Besides, ladies should be mindfull of the approach of age,
and let no time want his due use. The best of our daies passe first.

MAVIS We are rivers, that cannot be call'd backe, madame: shee that
now excludes her lovers, may live to lie a forsaken beldame, in a
40   frozen bed.

CENTAURE 'Tis true, MAVIS; and who will wait on us to coach then?
or write, or tell us the newes then? Make *anagrammes* of our names,
and invite us to the cock-pit, and kisse our hands all the play-time,
and draw their weapons for our honors?

HAUGHTY Not one.

DAW Nay, my mistris is not altogether un-intelligent of these things;
here be in presence have tasted of her favours.

CLERIMONT What a neighing hobby-horse is this!

EPICOENE But not with intent to boast 'hem againe, servant. And
50   have you those excellent receits, madame, to keepe your selves
from bearing of children?

HAUGHTY O yes, MOROSE. How should we maintayne our youth
and beautie, else? Many births of a woman make her old, as many
crops make the earth barren.

Act IV. Scene 4

MOROSE, DAUPHINE, TRUE-WIT, EPICOENE, CLERIMONT,
DAW, HAUGHTY, LA-FOOLE, CENTAURE, MAVIS, MRS.
OTTER, TRUSTY.

[*Enter* MOROSE *and* DAUPHINE.]

MOROSE O my cursed angell, that instructed me to this fate!

DAUPHINE Why, sir?

MOROSE That I should bee seduc'd by so foolish a devill, as a barber
will make!

DAUPHINE I would I had beene worthy, sir, to have partaken your
counsell, you should never have trusted it to such a minister.

MOROSE Would I could redeeme it with the losse of an eye (nephew) a hand, or any other member.

DAUPHINE Mary, god forbid, sir, that you should geld your selfe, to anger your wife. 10

MOROSE So it would rid me of her! and, that I did supererogatorie penance, in a bellfry, at *Westminster*-hall, i' the cock-pit, at the fall of a stagge; the tower-wharfe (what place is there else?) *London*-bridge, *Paris*-garden, *Belins*-gate, when the noises are at their height and lowdest. Nay, I would sit out a play, that were nothing but fights at sea, drum, trumpet, and target!

DAUPHINE I hope there shall be no such need, sir. Take patience, good uncle. This is but a day, and 'tis well worne too now.

MOROSE O, 'twill bee so for ever, nephew, I foresee it, for ever. Strife and tumult are the dowrie that comes with a wife. 20

TRUE-WIT I told you so, sir, and you would not beleeve me.

MOROSE Alas, doe not rub those wounds, master TRUE-WIT, to bloud againe: 'twas my negligence. Adde not affliction to affliction. I have perceiv'd the effect of it, too late, in madame OTTER.

EPICOENE How doe you, sir?

MOROSE Did you ever heare a more unnecessary question? as if she did not see! Why, I doe as you see, Empresse, Empresse.

EPICOENE You are not well, sir! you looke very ill! something has distempered you.

MOROSE O horrible, monstrous impertinencies! would not one of 30 these have serv'd? doe you thinke, sir? would not one of these have serv'd?

TRUE-WIT Yes, sir, but these are but notes of female kindnesse, sir: certaine tokens that shee has a voice, sir.

MOROSE O, is't so? come, and 't be no otherwise——what say you?

EPICOENE How doe you feele your selfe, sir?

MOROSE Againe, that!

TRUE-WIT Nay, looke you, sir: you would be friends with your wife upon un-conscionable termes, her silence——

EPICOENE They say you are run mad, sir. 40

MOROSE Not for love, I assure you, of you; doe you see?

EPICOENE O lord, gentlemen! Lay hold on him for gods sake: what shal I doe? who's his physitian (can you tel) that knowes the state

of his body best, that I might send for him? Good sir, speake.
I'll send for one of my doctors else.

MOROSE What, to poyson me, that I might die intestate, and leave
you possest of all?

EPICOENE Lord, how idly he talkes, and how his eyes sparkle! He
lookes greene about the temples! Doe you see what blue spots he
has?

CLERIMONT I, it's melancholy.

EPICOENE Gentlemen, for heavens sake counsell me. Ladies! Servant,
you have read PLINY, and PARACELSUS: Ne're a word now to
comfort a poore gentlewoman? Ay me! what fortune had I to
marry a distracted man?

DAW I'll tell you, mistris—

TRUE-WIT How rarely shee holds it up!

MOROSE What meane you, gentlemen?

EPICOENE What will you tell me, servant?

DAW The disease in *Greeke* is called Mανία, in *Latine, Insania, Furor,
vel Ecstasis melancholica*, that is, *Egressio*, when a man *ex melancholico,
evadit fanaticus*.

MOROSE Shall I have a lecture read upon me alive?

DAW But he may be but *Phreneticus*, yet, mistris? and *Phrenetis* is only
delirium, or so—

EPICOENE I, that is for the disease, servant: but what is this to the
cure? we are sure inough of the disease.

MOROSE Let me goe.

TRUE-WIT Why, wee'll intreat her to hold her peace, sir.

MOROSE O, no. Labour not to stop her. Shee is like a conduit-pipe,
that will gush out with more force, when shee opens againe.

HAUGHTY I'll tell you, MOROSE, you must talke divinitie to him
altogether, or morall philosophie.

LA-FOOLE I, and there's an excellent booke of morall philosophie,
madame, of RAYNARD the foxe, and all the beasts, call'd, DONES
philosophie.

CENTAURE There is, indeed, sir AMOROUS LA-FOOLE.

MOROSE O miserie!

LA-FOOLE I have read it, my lady CENTAURE, all over to my cousin,
here.

MRS. OTTER I, and 'tis a very good booke as any is, of the Modernes.

DAW Tut, hee must have SENECA read to him, and PLUTARCH, and
the Ancients; the Modernes are not for this disease.

CLERIMONT Why, you discommended them too, to day, sir JOHN.

DAW I, in some cases: but in these they are best, and ARISTOTLES
Ethicks.

MAVIS Say you so, sir JOHN? I thinke you are deceiv'd: you tooke it
upon trust.

HAUGHTY Where's TRUSTY, my woman? I'll end this difference. I
pr'ythee, OTTER, call her. Her father and mother were both mad,   90
when they put her to me.   [*Exit* MRS. OTTER.]

MOROSE I thinke so. Nay, gentlemen, I am tame. This is but an
exercise, I know, a marriage ceremonie, which I must endure.

HAUGHTY And one of 'hem (I know not which) was cur'd with the
Sick-mans salve; and the other with GREENES *groates-worth of wit*.

TRUE-WIT A very cheape cure, madame.

HAUGHTY I, it's very faesible.

> [*Enter* MRS. OTTER *and* TRUSTY.]

MRS. OTTER My lady call'd for you, mistris TRUSTY: you must decide
a controversie.

HAUGHTY O TRUSTY, which was it you said, your father, or your   100
mother, that was cur'd with the *Sicke-mans salve*?

TRUSTY My mother, madame, with the *salve*.

TRUE-WIT Then it was the *Sicke-womans salve*.

TRUSTY And my father with the *Groates-worth of wit*. But there was
other meanes us'd: we had a Preacher that would preach folke
asleepe still; and so they were prescrib'd to goe to church, by an
old woman that was their physitian, thrise a weeke—

EPICOENE To sleepe?

TRUSTY Yes forsooth: and every night they read themselves asleepe
on those bookes.   110

EPICOENE Good faith, it stands with great reason. I would I knew
where to procure those bookes.

MOROSE Oh.

LA-FOOLE I can helpe you with one of 'hem, mistris MOROSE, the
groats-worth of wit.

EPICOENE But I shall disfurnish you, sir AMOROUS: can you spare
it?

LA-FOOLE O, yes, for a weeke, or so; I'll reade it my selfe to him.

EPICOENE No, I must doe that, sir: that must be my office.

120   MOROSE Oh, oh!

EPICOENE Sure, he would doe well inough, if he could sleepe.

MOROSE No, I should doe well inough, if you could sleepe. Have I
no friend that will make her drunke? or give her a little *ladanum*?
or *opium*?

TRUE-WIT Why, sir, shee talkes ten times worse in her sleepe.

MOROSE How!

CLERIMONT Doe you not know that, sir? never ceases all night.

TRUE-WIT And snores like a *porcpisce*.

MOROSE O, redeeme me, fate, redeeme me, fate. For how many
130   causes may a man be divorc'd, nephew?

DAUPHINE I know not truely, sir.

TRUE-WIT Some Divine must resolve you in that, sir, or canon-
Lawyer.

MOROSE I will not rest, I will not thinke of any other hope or comfort,
till I know.   [*Exeunt* MOROSE *and* DAUPHINE.]

CLERIMONT Alas, poore man.

TRUE-WIT You'll make him mad indeed, ladies, if you pursue this.

HAUGHTY No, wee'll let him breathe, now, a quarter of an houre, or
so.

140   CLERIMONT By my faith, a large truce.

HAUGHTY Is that his keeper, that is gone with him?

DAW It is his nephew, madame.

LA-FOOLE Sir DAUPHINE EUGENIE.

CENTAURE He lookes like a very pittifull knight—

DAW As can be. This marriage, has put him out of all.

LA-FOOLE He has not a penny in his purse, madame—

DAW He is readie to crie all this day.

LA-FOOLE A very sharke, he set me i'the nicke t'other night at *primero*.

TRUE-WIT How these swabbers talke!

150   CLERIMONT I, OTTERS wine has swell'd their humours above a
spring-tide.

HAUGHTY Good MOROSE, let's goe in againe. I like your couches
exceeding well: we'll goe lie, and talke there.

EPICOENE I wait on you, madame.

                    [*Exeunt* LADIES, DAW *and* LA-FOOLE.]

TRUE-WIT 'Slight, I wil have 'hem as silent as Signes, & their posts

too, e're I ha' done. Doe you heare, lady-bride? I pray thee now,
as thou art a noble wench, continue this discourse of DAUPHINE
within: but praise him exceedingly. Magnifie him with all the height
of affection thou canst. (I have some purpose in't) and but beate
off these two rookes, JACK DAW, and his fellow, with any discon-   160
tentment hither, and I'll honour thee for ever.

EPICOENE I was about it, here. It angred mee to the soule, to heare
'hem beginne to talke so malepert.

TRUE-WIT Pray thee performe it, and thou win'st mee an idolater to
thee, everlasting.

EPICOENE Will you goe in, and heare me doe it?

TRUE-WIT No, I'll stay here. Drive 'hem out of your companie, 'tis
all I aske: which cannot bee any way better done, then by extolling
DAUPHINE, whom they have so slighted.

EPICOENE I warrant you: you shall expect one of 'hem presently.   170

[*Exit.*]

CLERIMONT What a cast of kastrils are these, to hawke after ladies,
thus?

TRUE-WIT I, and strike at such an eagle as DAUPHINE.

CLERIMONT He will be mad, when we tell him. Here he comes.

Act IV. Scene 5

CLERIMONT, TRUE-WIT, DAUPHINE, DAW, LA-FOOLE.

[*Enter* DAUPHINE.]

CLERIMONT O Sir, you are welcome.

TRUE-WIT Where's thine uncle?

DAUPHINE Run out o' dores in's night-caps, to talke with a *Casuist*
about his divorce. It workes admirably.

TRUE-WIT Thou would'st ha' said so, and thou had'st beene here!
The ladies have laught at thee, most *comically*, since thou wentst,
DAUPHINE.

CLERIMONT And askt, if thou wert thine uncles keeper?

TRUE-WIT And the brace of Babouns answer'd, yes; and said thou
wert a pittifull poore fellow, and did'st live upon posts: and had'st   10
nothing but three sutes of apparell, and some few benevolences
that lords ga' thee to foole to 'hem, and swagger.

DAUPHINE Let me not live, I'll beate 'hem. I'll binde 'hem both to grand Madames bed-postes, and have 'hem bayted with monkeyes.

TRUE-WIT Thou shalt not need, they shall be beaten to thy hand, DAUPHINE. I have an execution to serve upon 'hem, I warrant thee shall serve: trust my plot.

DAUPHINE I, you have many plots! So you had one, to make all the wenches in love with me.

20 TRUE-WIT Why, if I doe not yet afore night, as neere as 'tis; and that they doe not every one invite thee, and be ready to scratch for thee: take the morgage of my wit.

CLERIMONT 'Fore god, I'll be his witnesse; thou shalt have it, DAU-PHINE: thou shalt be his foole for ever, if thou doest not.

TRUE-WIT Agreed. Perhaps 'twill bee the better estate. Doe you observe this gallerie? or rather lobby, indeed? Here are a couple of studies, at each end one: here will I act such a *tragi-comoedy* betweene the *Guelphes*, and the *Ghibellines*, DAW and LA-FOOLE — which of 'hem comes out first, will I seize on: (you two shall be 30 the *chorus* behind the arras, and whip out betweene the *acts*, and speake.) If I doe not make 'hem keepe the peace, for this remnant of the day, if not of the yeere, I have faild once— I heare DAW comming: Hide, and doe not laugh, for gods sake.

[*Enter* DAW.]

DAW Which is the way into the garden, trow?

TRUE-WIT O, JACK DAW! I am glad I have met with you. In good faith, I must have this matter goe no furder betweene you. I must ha' it taken up.

DAW What matter, sir? Betweene whom?

TRUE-WIT Come, you disguise it—Sir AMOROUS and you. If you 40 love me, JACK, you shall make use of your philosophy now, for this once, and deliver me your sword. This is not the wedding the CENTAURES were at, though there be a shee-one here. The bride has entreated me I will see no bloud shed at her bridall, you saw her whisper me ere-while.

DAW As I hope to finish TACITUS, I intend no murder.

TRUE-WIT Doe you not wait for sir AMOROUS?

DAW Not I, by my knight-hood.

TRUE-WIT And your schollership too?

DAW And my schollership too.

TRUE-WIT Goe to, then I returne you your sword, and aske you   50
mercy; but put it not up, for you will be assaulted. I understood
that you had apprehended it, and walkt here to brave him: and
that you had held your life contemptible, in regard of your honor.

DAW No, no, no such thing I assure you. He and I parted now, as
good friends as could be.

TRUE-WIT Trust not you to that visor. I saw him since dinner with
another face: I have knowne many men in my time vex'd with
losses, with deaths, and with abuses, but so offended a wight as
sir AMOROUS, did I never see, or read of. For taking away his
guests, sir, to day, that's the cause: and hee declares it behind   60
your backe, with such threatnings and contempts— He said to
DAUPHINE, you were the errandst asse—

DAW I, he may say his pleasure.

TRUE-WIT And sweares, you are so protested a coward, that hee
knowes you will never doe him any manly or single right, and
therefore hee will take his course.

DAW I'll give him any satisfaction, sir—but fighting.

TRUE-WIT I, sir, but who knowes what satisfaction hee'll take? bloud
he thirsts for, and bloud he will have: and where-abouts on you
he will have it, who knowes, but himselfe?   70

DAW I pray you, master TRUE-WIT, be you a mediator.

TRUE-WIT Well, sir, conceale your selfe then in this studie, till I
returne. Nay, you must bee content to bee lock'd in: for, for mine
owne reputation I would not have you seene to receive a publique
disgrace, while I have the matter in managing. Gods so, here hee
comes: keepe your breath close, that hee doe not heare you sigh.
In good faith, sir AMOROUS, hee is not this way, I pray you bee
mercifull, doe not murder him; hee is a christian as good as you:
you are arm'd as if you sought a revenge on all his race. Good
DAUPHINE, get him away from this place. I never knew a mans   80
choller so high, but hee would speake to his friends, hee would
heare reason. JACK DAW. JACK DAW! a-sleepe?

DAW Is he gone, master TRUE-WIT?

TRUE-WIT I, did you heare him?

DAW O god, yes.

TRUE-WIT What a quick eare feare has?

DAW But is he so arm'd, as you say?

He puts him up.

TRUE-WIT Arm'd? did you ever see a fellow, set out to take possession?

90 DAW I, sir.

TRUE-WIT That may give you some light, to conceive of him: but
'tis nothing to the principall. Some false brother i' the house has
furnish'd him strangely. Or, if it were out o' the house, it was TOM
OTTER.

DAW Indeed, hee's a Captayne, and his wife is his kinswoman.

TRUE-WIT Hee has got some-bodies old two-hand-sword, to mow
you off at the knees. And that sword hath spawn'd such a dagger!—
but then he is so hung with pikes, halberds, peitronells, callivers,
and muskets, that he lookes like a Justice of peace's hall: a man

100 of two thousand a yeere, is not sess'd at so many weapons, as he
has on. There was never fencer challeng'd at so many severall
foiles. You would think hee meant to murder all Saint PULCHRES
parish. If hee could but victuall himselfe for halfe a yeere, in his
breeches, hee is sufficiently arm'd to over-runne a countrie.

DAW Good lord, what meanes he, sir! I pray you, master TRUE-WIT,
be you a mediator.

TRUE-WIT Well, I'll trie if he will be appeas'd with a leg or an arme,
if not, you must die once.

DAW I would be loth to loose my right arme, for writing *madrigalls*.

110 TRUE-WIT Why, if he will be satisfied with a thumb, or a little finger,
all's one to me. You must thinke, I'll doe my best.

He puts him up DAW Good sir, doe.
againe, and then
come forth. CLERIMONT What hast thou done?

TRUE-WIT He will let me doe nothing, man, he do's all afore me, he
offers his left arme.

CLERIMONT His left wing, for a JACK DAW.

DAUPHINE Take it, by all meanes.

TRUE-WIT How! Maime a man for ever, for a jest? what a conscience
hast thou?

120 DAUPHINE 'Tis no losse to him: he has no employment for his armes,
but to eate spoone-meat. Beside, as good maime his body as his
reputation.

TRUE-WIT He is a scholler, and a *Wit*, and yet he do's not thinke so.
But he looses no reputation with us, for we all resolv'd him an
asse before. To your places againe.

CLERIMONT I pray thee, let me be in at the other a little.

TRUE-WIT Looke, you'll spoile all: these be ever your tricks.

CLERIMONT No, but I could hit of some things that thou wilt misse,
and thou wilt say are good ones.

TRUE-WIT I warrant you. I pray forbeare, I'll leave it off, else.   130

DAUPHINE Come away, CLERIMONT.

> [*Enter* LA-FOOLE.]

TRUE-WIT Sir AMOROUS!

LA-FOOLE Master TRUE-WIT.

TRUE-WIT Whether were you going?

LA-FOOLE Downe into the court, to make water.

TRUE-WIT By no meanes, sir, you shall rather tempt your breeches.

LA-FOOLE Why, sir?

TRUE-WIT Enter here, if you love your life.

LA-FOOLE Why! why!

TRUE-WIT Question till your throat bee cut, doe: dally till the enraged   140
soule find you.

LA-FOOLE Who's that?

TRUE-WIT DAW it is: will you in?

LA-FOOLE I, I, I'll in: what's the matter?

TRUE-WIT Nay, if hee had beene coole inough to tell us that, there
had beene some hope to attone you, but he seemes so implacably
enrag'd.

LA-FOOLE 'Slight, let him rage. I'll hide my selfe.

TRUE-WIT Doe, good sir. But what have you done to him within,
that should provoke him thus? you have broke some jest upon   150
him, afore the ladies—

LA-FOOLE Not I, never in my life, broke jest upon any man. The
bride was praising sir DAUPHINE, and he went away in snuffe,
and I followed him, unlesse he took offence at me, in his drinke
ere while, that I would not pledge all the horse full.

TRUE-WIT By my faith, and that may bee, you remember well: but
hee walkes the round up and downe, through every roome o' the
house, with a towell in his hand, crying, where's LA-FOOLE? who
saw LA-FOOLE? and when DAUPHINE, and I, demanded the
cause, wee can force no answere from him, but (o revenge, how   160
sweet art thou! I will strangle him in this towell) which leads us

to conjecture, that the maine cause of his furie is for bringing your
meate to day, with a towell about you, to his discredit.

LA-FOOLE Like inough. Why, and he be angrie for that, I'll stay here,
till his anger be blowne over.

TRUE-WIT A good becomming resolution, sir. If you can put it on
o' the sudden.

LA-FOOLE Yes, I can put it on. Or, I'll away into the country presently.

TRUE-WIT How will you get out o' the house, sir? Hee knowes you
are i' the house, and hee'll watch you this se'n-night but hee'll have
you. Hee'll out-wait a sargeant for you.

LA-FOOLE Why, then I'll stay here.

TRUE-WIT You must thinke, how to victuall your selfe in time, then.

LA-FOOLE Why, sweet master TRUE-WIT, will you entreat my cousin
OTTER, to send me a cold venison pasty, a bottle or two of wine,
and a chamber pot?

TRUE-WIT A stoole were better, sir, of sir A-JAX his invention.

LA-FOOLE I, that will be better indeed: and a pallat to lie on.

TRUE-WIT O, I would not advise you to sleepe by any meanes.

LA-FOOLE Would you not, sir? why, then I will not.

TRUE-WIT Yet, there's another feare——

LA-FOOLE Is there, sir? What is't?

TRUE-WIT No, he cannot breake open this dore with his foot, sure.

LA-FOOLE I'll set my backe against it, sir. I have a good backe.

TRUE-WIT But, then if he should batter.

LA-FOOLE Batter! if he dare, I'll have an action of batt'ry, against
him.

TRUE-WIT Cast you the worst. He has sent for poulder alreadie, and
what he will doe with it, no man knowes: perhaps blow up the
corner o' the house, where he suspects you are. Here he comes,
in quickly. I protest, sir JOHN DAW, he is not this way: what will
you doe? before god, you shall hang no *petarde* here. I'll die rather.
Will you not take my word? I never knew one but would be
satisfied. Sir AMOROUS, there's no standing out. He has made a
petarde of an old brasse pot, to force your dore. Thinke upon some
satisfaction, or termes, to offer him.

LA-FOOLE Sir, I'll give him any satisfaction. I dare give any termes.

TRUE-WIT You'll leave it to me, then?

LA-FOOLE I, sir. I'll stand to any conditions.

He faines, as if one were present, to fright the other, who is run in to hide himselfe.

TRUE-WIT How now, what thinke you, sirs? wer't not a difficult thing to determine, which of these two fear'd most?

He calls forth Clerimont, and Dauphine.

CLERIMONT Yes, but this feares the bravest: the other a whiniling dastard, JACK DAW! but LA-FOOLE, a brave heroique coward! and is afraid in a great looke, and a stout accent. I like him rarely.

TRUE-WIT Had it not beene pitty, these two should ha' beene conceal'd?

CLERIMONT Shall I make a motion?

TRUE-WIT Briefly. For I must strike while 'tis hot.

CLERIMONT Shall I goe fetch the ladies to the *catastrophe*?

TRUE-WIT Umh? I, by my troth.   210

DAUPHINE By no mortall meanes. Let them continue in the state of ignorance, and erre still: thinke 'hem wits, and fine fellowes, as they have done. 'Twere sinne to reforme them.

TRUE-WIT Well, I will have 'hem fetch'd, now I thinke on't, for a private purpose of mine: doe, CLERIMONT, fetch 'hem, and discourse to 'hem all that's past, and bring 'hem into the gallery here.

DAUPHINE This is thy extreme vanitie, now: thou think'st thou wert undone, if every jest thou mak'st were not publish'd.

TRUE-WIT Thou shalt see, how unjust thou art, presently. CLERIMONT, say it was DAUPHINE's plot. [*Exit* CLERIMONT.] Trust me   220
not, if the whole drift be not for thy good. There's a carpet i' the next roome, put it on, with this scarfe over thy face, and a cushion o' thy head, and bee ready when I call AMOROUS. Away [*Exit* DAUPHINE.]—JOHN DAW.

DAW What good newes, sir?

TRUE-WIT Faith, I have followed, and argued with him hard for you. I told him, you were a knight, and a scholler; and that you knew fortitude did consist *magis patiendo quam faciendo, magis ferendo quam feriendo*.

DAW It doth so indeed, sir.   230

TRUE-WIT And that you would suffer, I told him: so, at first he demanded, by my troth, in my conceipt, too much.

DAW What was it, sir?

TRUE-WIT Your upper lip, and sixe o' your fore-teeth.

DAW 'Twas unreasonable.

TRUE-WIT Nay, I told him plainely, you could not spare 'hem all. So

after long argument (*pro & con*, as you know) I brought him downe
to your two butter-teeth, and them he would have.

DAW O, did you so? why, he shall have 'hem.

240 TRUE-WIT But he shall not, sir, by your leave. The conclusion is this,
sir, because you shall be very good friends hereafter, and this never
to bee remembred, or up-braided; besides, that he may not boast,
he has done any such thing to you in his owne person: hee is to
come here in disguise, give you five kicks in private, sir, take your
sword from you, and lock you up in that studie, during pleasure.
Which will be but a little while, wee'll get it releas'd presently.

DAW Five kicks? he shall have sixe, sir, to be friends.

TRUE-WIT Beleeve mee, you shall not over-shoot your selfe, to send
him that word by me.

250 DAW Deliver it, sir. He shall have it with all my heart, to be friends.

TRUE-WIT Friends? Nay, and he should not be so, and heartily too,
upon these termes, he shall have me to enemie while I live. Come,
sir, beare it bravely.

DAW O god, sir, 'tis nothing.

TRUE-WIT True. What's sixe kicks to a man, that reads SENECA?

DAW I have had a hundred, sir.

Dauphine comes TRUE-WIT Sir AMOROUS. No speaking one to another, or rehearsing
forth, and kicks old matters.
him.

DAW One, two, three, foure, five. I protest, sir AMOROUS, you shall
260 have sixe.

TRUE-WIT Nay, I told you, you should not talke. Come, give him
six, & he will needs. Your sword. Now returne to your safe custody:
you shall presently meet afore the ladies, and be the dearest friends
one to another—[*Exit* DAW.] Give me the scarfe, now, thou shalt
beat the other bare-fac'd. Stand by—sir AMOROUS.

LA-FOOLE What's here? A sword.

TRUE-WIT I cannot helpe it, without I should take the quarrell upon
my selfe: here he has sent you his sword—

LA-FOOLE I'll receive none on 't.

270 TRUE-WIT And he wills you to fasten it against a wall, and breake
your head in some few severall places against the hilts.

LA-FOOLE I will not: tell him roundly. I cannot endure to shed my
owne bloud.

TRUE-WIT Will you not?

LA-FOOLE No. I'll beat it against a faire flat wall, if that will satisfie him: If not, he shall beat it himselfe, for AMOROUS.

TRUE-WIT Why, this is strange starting off, when a man under-takes for you! I offered him another condition: Will you stand to that?

LA-FOOLE I, what is 't?

TRUE-WIT That you will be beaten, in private.   280

LA-FOOLE Yes. I am content, at the blunt.

[*Enter above* HAUGHTY, CENTAURE, MAVIS, MRS. OTTER, EPICOENE, TRUSTY *and* CLERIMONT.]

TRUE-WIT Then you must submit your selfe to bee hoodwink'd in this skarfe, and bee led to him, where hee will take your sword from you, and make you beare a blow, over the mouth, *gules*, and tweakes by the nose, *sans numbre*.

LA-FOOLE I am content. But why must I be blinded?

TRUE-WIT That's for your good, sir: because, if hee should grow insolent upon this, and publish it hereafter to your disgrace (which I hope he will not doe) you might sweare safely and protest, hee never beat you, to your knowledge.   290

LA-FOOLE O, I conceive.

TRUE-WIT I doe not doubt, but you'll be perfect good friends upon't, and not dare to utter an ill thought one of another, in future.

LA-FOOLE Not I, as god helpe me, of him.

TRUE-WIT Nor he of you, sir. If he should—Come, sir. All hid, sir JOHN.

LA-FOOLE Oh, sir JOHN, sir JOHN. Oh, o-o-o-o-o-Oh—   *Dauphine enters to tweake him.*

TRUE-WIT Good sir JOHN, leave tweaking, you'll blow his nose off. 'Tis sir JOHN's pleasure, you should retire into the studie. Why, now you are friends. All bitternesse betweene you, I hope, is   300 buried; you shall come forth by and by, DAMON & PYTHIAS upon 't: and embrace with all the ranknesse of friendship that can be. [*Exit* LA-FOOLE.] I trust, wee shall have 'hem tamer i' their language hereafter. DAUPHINE, I worship thee. Gods will, the ladies have surpris'd us!

Act IV. Scene 6

*Having
discovered part
of the past scene
above.*

HAUGHTY, CENTAURE, MAVIS, MRS. OTTER, EPICOENE,
TRUSTY, DAUPHINE, TRUE-WIT, &C.

[*Enter below* HAUGHTY, CENTAURE, MAVIS, MRS. OTTER,
EPICOENE, TRUSTY *and* CLERIMONT.]

HAUGHTY CENTAURE, how our judgements were impos'd on by
these adulterate knights!

CENTAURE Nay, madame, MAVIS was more deceiv'd then we, 'twas
her commendation utter'd 'hem in the colledge.

MAVIS I commended but their wits, madame, and their braveries. I
never look'd toward their valours.

HAUGHTY Sir DAUPHINE is valiant, and a wit too, it seemes?

MAVIS And a braverie too.

HAUGHTY Was this his project?

10   MRS. OTTER So master CLERIMONT intimates, madame.

HAUGHTY Good MOROSE, when you come to the colledge, will you
bring him with you? He seemes a very perfect gentleman.

EPICOENE He is so, madame, beleeve it.

CENTAURE But when will you come, MOROSE?

EPICOENE Three or foure dayes hence, madame, when I have got
mee a coach, and horses.

HAUGHTY No, to morrow, good MOROSE, CENTAURE shall send
you her coach.

MAVIS Yes faith, doe, and bring sir DAUPHINE with you.

20   HAUGHTY Shee has promis'd that, MAVIS.

MAVIS He is a very worthy gentleman, in his exteriors, madame.

HAUGHTY I, he showes he is judiciall in his clothes.

CENTAURE And yet not so superlatively neat as some, madame, that
have their faces set in a brake!

HAUGHTY I, and have every haire in forme!

MAVIS That weare purer linnen then our selves, and professe more
neatnesse, then the *french hermaphrodite*!

EPICOENE I ladies, they, what they tell one of us, have told a thousand,
and are the only theeves of our fame: that thinke to take us with

30   that perfume, or with that lace, and laugh at us un-conscionably
when they have done.

HAUGHTY But, sir DAUPHINES carelesnesse becomes him.

CENTAURE I could love a man, for such a nose!

MAVIS Or such a leg!

CENTAURE He has an exceeding good eye, madame!

MAVIS And a very good lock!

CENTAURE Good MOROSE, bring him to my chamber first.

MRS. OTTER Please your honors, to meet at my house, madame?

TRUE-WIT See, how they eye thee, man! they are taken, I warrant   40
thee.

HAUGHTY You have unbrac'd our brace of knights, here, master
TRUE-WIT.

TRUE-WIT Not I, madame, it was sir DAUPHINES ingine: who, if he
have disfurnish'd your ladiship of any guard, or service by it, is
able to make the place good againe, in himselfe.

HAUGHTY There's no suspition of that, sir.

CENTAURE God so, MAVIS, HAUGHTY is kissing.

MAVIS Let us goe too, and take part.

HAUGHTY But I am glad of the fortune (beside the discoverie of two
such emptie caskets) to gaine the knowledge of so rich a mine of   50
vertue, as sir DAUPHINE.

CENTAURE We would be al glad to stile him of our friendship, and
see him at the colledge.

MAVIS He cannot mixe with a sweeter societie, I'll prophesie, and I
hope he himselfe will thinke so.

DAUPHINE I should be rude to imagine otherwise, lady.

TRUE-WIT Did not I tell thee, DAUPHINE? Why, all their actions are
governed by crude opinion, without reason or cause; they know
not why they doe any thing: but as they are inform'd, beleeve,
judge, praise, condemne, love, hate, and in aemulation one of   60
another, doe all these things alike. Onely, they have a naturall
inclination swayes 'hem generally to the worst, when they are left
to themselves. But, pursue it, now thou hast 'hem.

HAUGHTY Shall we goe in againe, MOROSE?

EPICOENE Yes, madame.

CENTAURE Wee'll entreat sir DAUPHINES companie.

TRUE-WIT Stay, good madame, the inter-view of the two friends,
PYLADES and ORESTES: I'll fetch 'hem out to you straight.

HAUGHTY Will you, master TRUE-WIT?

70   DAUPHINE I, but noble ladies, doe not confesse in your countenance, or outward bearing to 'hem any discoverie of their follies, that wee may see, how they will beare up againe, with what assurance, and erection.

HAUGHTY We will not, sir DAUPHINE.

CENTAURE *and* MAVIS Upon our honors, sir DAUPHINE.

TRUE-WIT Sir AMOROUS, sir AMOROUS. The ladies are here.

LA-FOOLE Are they?

TRUE-WIT Yes, but slip out by and by, as their backs are turn'd, and meet sir JOHN here, as by chance, when I call you. JACK DAW.

80   DAW What say you, sir?

TRUE-WIT Whip out behind me suddenly: and no anger i' your lookes to your adversarie. Now, now.

    [*Enter* DAW *and* LA FOOLE.]

LA-FOOLE Noble sir JOHN DAW! where ha' you beene?

DAW To seeke you, sir AMOROUS.

LA-FOOLE Me! I honor you.

DAW I prevent you, sir.

CLERIMONT They have forgot their rapiers!

TRUE-WIT O, they meet in peace, man.

DAUPHINE Where's your sword, sir JOHN?

90   CLERIMONT And yours, sir AMOROUS?

DAW Mine! my boy had it forth, to mend the handle, eene now.

LA-FOOLE And my gold handle was broke, too, and my boy had it forth.

DAUPHINE Indeed, sir? How their excuses meet!

CLERIMONT What a consent there is, i' the handles?

TRUE-WIT Nay, there is so i' the points too, I warrant you.

MRS. OTTER O me! madame, he comes againe, the mad man, away.

    [*Exeunt* LADIES, DAW *and* LA-FOOLE.]

Act IV. Scene 7

MOROSE, TRUE-WIT, CLERIMONT, DAUPHINE.

He had found the two swords drawne within.

[*Enter* MOROSE.]

MOROSE What make these naked weapons here, gentlemen?

TRUE-WIT O, sir! here hath like to been murder since you went! A

couple of knights fallen out about the brides favours: wee were
faine to take away their weapons, your house had beene beg'd by
this time else——

MOROSE For what?

CLERIMONT For man-slaughter, sir, as being accessary.

MOROSE And, for her favours?

TRUE-WIT I, sir, heretofore, not present. CLERIMONT, carry 'hem
their swords, now. They have done all the hurt they will doe.   10

                              [*Exit* CLERIMONT.]

DAUPHINE Ha' you spoke with a lawyer, sir?

MOROSE O, no! there is such a noyse i' the court, that they have
frighted mee home, with more violence then I went! such speaking,
and counter-speaking, with their severall voyces of *citations, appella-
tions, allegations, certificates, attachments, intergatories, references, convictions,*
and *afflictions* indeed, among the Doctors and Proctors! that the
noise here is silence too 't! a kind of calme mid-night!

TRUE-WIT Why, sir, if you would be resolv'd indeed, I can bring you
hether a very sufficient Lawyer, and a learned Divine, that shall
inquire into every least scruple for you.   20

MOROSE Can you, master TRUE-WIT?

TRUE-WIT Yes, and are very sober grave persons, that will dispatch
it in a chamber, with a whisper, or two.

MOROSE Good sir, shall I hope this benefit from you, and trust my
selfe into your hands?

TRUE-WIT Alas, sir! your nephew, and I, have beene asham'd, and
oft-times mad since you went, to thinke how you are abus'd. Goe
in, good sir, and lock your selfe up till we call you, wee'll tell you
more anon, sir.

MOROSE Doe your pleasure with me, gentlemen; I beleeve in you: 30
and that deserves no delusion——   [*Exit.*]

TRUE-WIT You shall find none, sir: but heapt, heapt plentie of
vexation.

DAUPHINE What wilt thou doe now, WIT?

TRUE-WIT Recover me hether OTTER, and the Barber, if you can,
by any meanes, presently.

DAUPHINE Why? to what purpose?

TRUE-WIT O, I'll make the deepest Divine, and gravest Lawyer, out
o' them two, for him——

40   DAUPHINE   Thou canst not man, these are waking dreames.

TRUE-WIT   Doe not feare me. Clap but a civill gowne with a welt, o' the one; and a canonical cloake with sleeves, o' the other: and give 'hem a few termes i' their mouthes, if there come not forth as able a Doctor, and compleat a Parson, for this turne, as may be wish'd, trust not my election. And, I hope, without wronging the dignitie of either profession, since they are but persons put on, and for mirths sake, to torment him. The Barber smatters *latin*, I remember.

DAUPHINE   Yes, and OTTER too.

TRUE-WIT   Well then, if I make 'hem not wrangle out this case, to
50   his no comfort, let me be thought a JACK DAW, or LA-FOOLE, or any thing worse. Goe you to your ladies, but first send for them.

DAUPHINE   I will.   [*Exeunt.*]

Act V. Scene 1

LA-FOOLE, CLERIMONT, DAW, MAVIS.

[*Enter* LA-FOOLE, CLERIMONT *and* DAW.]

LA-FOOLE   Where had you our swords, master CLERIMONT?

CLERIMONT   Why, DAUPHINE tooke 'hem from the mad-man.

LA-FOOLE   And he tooke 'hem from our boyes, I warrant you?

CLERIMONT   Very like, sir.

LA-FOOLE   Thanke you, good master CLERIMONT. Sir JOHN DAW, and I are both beholden to you.

CLERIMONT   Would I knew how to make you so, gentlemen.

DAW   Sir AMOROUS, and I are your servants, sir.

[*Enter* MAVIS.]

MAVIS   Gentlemen, have any of you a pen-and-inke? I would faine
10   write out a riddle in *Italian*, for sir DAUPHINE, to translate.

CLERIMONT   Not I, in troth, lady, I am no scrivener.

DAW   I can furnish you, I thinke, lady.   [*Exeunt* DAW *and* MAVIS.]

CLERIMONT   He has it in the haft of a knife, I beleeve!

LA-FOOLE   No, he has his boxe of instruments.

CLERIMONT   Like a surgean!

LA-FOOLE   For the *mathematiques*: his squire, his compasses, his brasse pens, and black-lead, to draw maps of every place, and person, where he comes.

CLERIMONT How, maps of persons!

LA-FOOLE Yes, sir, of NOMENTACK, when he was here, and of the 20
Prince of *Moldavia*, and of his mistris, mistris EPICOENE.

CLERIMONT Away! he has not found out her latitude, I hope.

LA-FOOLE You are a pleasant gentleman, sir.

[*Enter* DAW.]

CLERIMONT Faith, now we are in private, let's wanton it a little, and
talke waggishly. Sir JOHN, I am telling sir AMOROUS here, that
you two governe the ladies, where e're you come, you carry the
feminine gender afore you.

DAW They shall rather carry us afore them, if they will, sir.

CLERIMONT Nay, I beleeve that they doe, withall—But, that you are
the prime-men in their affections, and direct all their actions— 30

DAW Not I: sir AMOROUS is.

LA-FOOLE I protest, sir JOHN is.

DAW As I hope to rise i' the state, sir AMOROUS, you ha' the person.

LA-FOOLE Sir JOHN, you ha' the person, and the discourse too.

DAW Not I, sir. I have no discourse—and then you have activitie
beside.

LA-FOOLE I protest, sir JOHN, you come as high from *Tripoly*, as I
doe every whit: and lift as many joyn'd stooles, and leape over
'hem, if you would use it—

CLERIMONT Well, agree on't together knights; for betweene you, you 40
divide the kingdome, or common-wealth of ladies affections: I see
it, and can perceive a little how they observe you, and feare you,
indeed. You could tell strange stories, my masters, if you would,
I know.

DAW Faith, we have seene somewhat, sir.

LA-FOOLE That we have—vellet petti-coates, & wrought smocks, or
so.

DAW I, and—

CLERIMONT Nay, out with it, sir JOHN: doe not envie your friend
the pleasure of hearing, when you have had the delight of tasting. 50

DAW Why—a—doe you speake, sir AMOROUS.

LA-FOOLE No, doe you, sir JOHN DAW.

DAW I' faith, you shall.

LA-FOOLE I' faith, you shall.

DAW Why, we have beene—

LA-FOOLE In the great bed at *Ware* together in our time. On, sir
   JOHN.

DAW Nay, doe you, sir AMOROUS.

CLERIMONT And these ladies with you, Knights?

60   LA-FOOLE No, excuse us, sir.

DAW We must not wound reputation.

LA-FOOLE No matter—they were these, or others. Our bath cost us
   fifteene pound, when we came home.

CLERIMONT Doe you heare, sir JOHN, you shall tell me but one thing
   truely, as you love me.

DAW If I can, I will, sir.

CLERIMONT You lay in the same house with the bride, here?

DAW Yes, and converst with her hourely, sir.

CLERIMONT And what humour is shee of? is shee comming, and
70   open, free?

DAW O, exceeding open, sir. I was her servant, and sir AMOROUS
   was to be.

CLERIMONT Come, you have both had favours from her? I know,
   and have heard so much.

DAW O, no, sir.

LA-FOOLE You shall excuse us, sir: we must not wound reputation.

CLERIMONT Tut, shee is married, now; and you cannot hurt her with
   any report, and therefore speake plainely: how many times, yfaith?
   which of you lead first? Ha?

80   LA-FOOLE Sir JOHN had her mayden-head, indeed.

DAW O, it pleases him to say so, sir, but sir AMOROUS knowes what's
   what, as well.

CLERIMONT Do'st thou yfaith, AMOROUS?

LA-FOOLE In a manner, sir.

CLERIMONT Why, I commend you lads. Little knowes *Don* Bride-
   groome of this. Nor shall he, for me.

DAW Hang him, mad oxe.

CLERIMONT Speake softly: here comes his nephew, with the lady
   HAUGHTY. Hee'll get the ladies from you, sirs, if you looke not
90   to him in time.

LA-FOOLE Why, if he doe, wee'll fetch 'hem home againe, I warrant
   you.   [*Exeunt.*]

Act V. Scene 2

HAUGHTY, DAUPHINE, CENTAURE, MAVIS, CLERIMONT.

[*Enter* HAUGHTY *and* DAUPHINE.]

HAUGHTY I assure you, sir DAUPHINE, it is the price and estimation
of your vertue onely, that hath embarqu'd me to this adventure,
and I could not but make out to tell you so; nor can I repent me
of the act, since it is alwayes an argument of some vertue in our
selves, that we love and affect it so in others.

DAUPHINE Your ladiship sets too high a price, on my weakenesse.

HAUGHTY Sir, I can distinguish gemmes from peebles —

DAUPHINE (Are you so skilfull in stones?)

HAUGHTY And, howsoever I may suffer in such a judgement as yours,
by admitting equality of ranke, or societie, with CENTAURE, or   10
MAVIS —

DAUPHINE You doe not, madame, I perceive they are your mere
foiles.

HAUGHTY Then are you a friend to truth, sir. It makes mee love you
the more. It is not the outward, but the inward man that I affect.
They are not apprehensive of an eminent perfection, but love flat,
and dully.

CENTAURE [*within*] Where are you, my lady HAUGHTY?

HAUGHTY I come presently, CENTAURE. My chamber, sir, my Page
shall show you; and TRUSTY, my woman, shall be ever awake for   20
you: you need not feare to communicate any thing with her, for
shee is a FIDELIA. I pray you weare this jewell for my sake, sir
DAUPHINE. [*Enter* CENTAURE.] Where's MAVIS, CENTAURE?

CENTAURE Within, madame, a writing. I'll follow you presently. I'll
but speake a word with sir DAUPHINE.   [*Exit* HAUGHTY.]

DAUPHINE With me, madame?

CENTAURE Good sir DAUPHINE, doe not trust HAUGHTY, nor make
any credit to her, what ever you doe besides. Sir DAUPHINE, I
give you this caution, shee is a perfect courtier, and loves no body,
but for her uses: and for her uses, shee loves all. Besides, her   30
physitians give her out to be none o' the clearest, whether she pay
'hem or no, heav'n knowes: and she's above fiftie too, and pargets!
See her in a fore-noone. Here comes MAVIS, a worse face then

shee! you would not like this, by candle-light. If you'll come to my
chamber one o' these mornings early, or late in an evening, I'll tell
you more. [*Enter* MAVIS.] Where's HAUGHTY, MAVIS?

MAVIS Within, CENTAURE.

CENTAURE What ha' you, there?

MAVIS An *Italian* riddle for sir DAUPHINE, (you shall not see it
40   yfaith, CENTAURE.) Good sir DAUPHINE, solve it for mee. I'll
call for it anon.   [*Exeunt* CENTAURE *and* MAVIS.]
    [*Enter* CLERIMONT.]

CLERIMONT How now, DAUPHINE? how do'st thou quit thy selfe
of these females?

DAUPHINE 'Slight, they haunt me like *fayries*, and give me jewells
here, I cannot be rid of 'hem.

CLERIMONT O, you must not tell, though.

DAUPHINE Masse, I forgot that: I was never so assaulted. One loves
for vertue, and bribes me with this. Another loves me with caution,
and so would possesse me. A third brings me a riddle here, and
50   all are jealous: and raile each at other.

He reades the   CLERIMONT A riddle? pray' le' me see't? *Sir* DAUPHINE, *I chose this*
paper.   *way of intimation for privacie. The ladies here, I know, have both hope, and*
purpose, to make a collegiate and servant of you. If I might be so honor'd, as
to appeare at any end of so noble a worke, I would enter into a fame of taking
physique to morrow, and continue it foure or five dayes, or longer, for your
visitation. MAVIS. By my faith, a subtle one! Call you this a riddle?
What's their plaine dealing, trow?

DAUPHINE We lack TRUE-WIT, to tell us that.

CLERIMONT We lack him for somewhat else too: his Knights*reformados*
60   are wound up as high, and insolent, as ever they were.

DAUPHINE You jest.

CLERIMONT No drunkards, either with wine or vanitie, ever confess'd
such stories of themselves. I would not give a flies leg, in ballance
against all the womens reputations here, if they could bee but
thought to speake truth: and for the bride, they have made their
affidavit against her directly—

DAUPHINE What, that they have lyen with her?

CLERIMONT Yes, and tell times, and circumstances, with the cause
why, and the place where. I had almost brought 'hem to affirme
70   that they had done it, to day.

DAUPHINE Not both of 'hem.

CLERIMONT Yes faith: with a sooth or two more I had effected it. They would ha' set it downe under their hands.

DAUPHINE Why, they will be our sport, I see, still! whether we will, or no.

Act V. Scene 3
TRUE-WIT, MOROSE, OTTER, CUTBERD,
CLERIMONT, DAUPHINE.

[*Enter* TRUE-WIT.]

TRUE-WIT O, are you here? Come DAUPHINE. Goe, call your uncle presently. I have fitted my Divine, & my Canonist, died their beards and all: the knaves doe not know themselves, they are so exalted, and alter'd. Preferment changes any man. Thou shalt keepe one dore, and I another, and then CLERIMONT in the midst, that he may have no meanes of escape from their cavilling, when they grow hot once. And then the women (as I have given the bride her instructions) to breake in upon him, i' the *l'envoy*. O, 'twill be full and twanging! Away, fetch him.   [*Exit* DAUPHINE.]

[*Enter* OTTER *and* CUTBERD.]

Come, master Doctor, and master Parson, looke to your parts   10
now, and discharge 'hem bravely: you are well set forth, performe it as well. If you chance to be out, doe not confesse it with standing still, or humming, or gaping one at another: but goe on, and talke alowd, and eagerly, use vehement action, and onely remember your termes, and you are safe. Let the matter goe where it will: you have many will doe so. But at first, bee very solemne, and grave like your garments, though you loose your selves after, and skip out like a brace of jugglers on a table. Here hee comes! set your faces, and looke superciliously, while I present you.

[*Enter* DAUPHINE *and* MOROSE.]

MOROSE Are these the two learned men?   20

TRUE-WIT Yes, sir, please you salute 'hem?

MOROSE Salute 'hem? I had rather doe any thing, then weare out time so unfruitfully, sir. I wonder, how these common formes, as *god save you*, and *you are well-come*, are come to be a habit in our lives!

or, *I am glad to see you*! when I cannot see, what the profit can bee
of these wordes, so long as it is no whit better with him, whose
affaires are sad, & grievous, that he heares this salutation.

TRUE-WIT 'Tis true, sir, wee'll goe to the matter then. Gentlemen,
master Doctor, and master Parson, I have acquainted you
30   sufficiently with the busines, for which you are come hether. And
you are now not to enforme your selves in the state of the question,
I know. This is the gentleman, who expects your resolution, and
therefore, when you please, beginne.

OTTER Please you, master Doctor.

CUTBERD Please you, good master Parson.

OTTER I would heare the Canon-law speake first.

CUTBERD It must give place to positive Divinitie, sir.

MOROSE Nay, good gentlemen, doe not throw me into circumstances.
Let your comforts arrive quickly at me, those that are. Be swift in
40   affoording me my peace, if so I shall hope any. I love not your
disputations, or your court-tumults. And that it be not strange to
you, I will tell you. My father, in my education, was wont to advise
mee, that I should alwayes collect, and contayne my mind, not
suffring it to flow loosely; that I should looke to what things were
necessary to the carriage of my life, and what not: embracing the
one and eschewing the other. In short, that I should endeare my
selfe to rest, and avoid turmoile: which now is growne to be
another nature to me. So that I come not to your publike pleadings,
or your places of noise; not that I neglect those things, that make
50   for the dignitie of the common-wealth: but for the meere avoiding
of clamors, & impertinencies of Orators, that know not how to
be silent. And for the cause of noise, am I now a sutor to you.
You doe not know in what a miserie I have beene exercis'd this
day, what a torrent of evill! My very house turnes round with the
tumult! I dwell in a wind-mill! The perpetuall motion is here, and
not at *Eltham*.

TRUE-WIT Well, good master Doctor, will you breake the ice? master
Parson will wade after.

CUTBERD Sir, though unworthy, and the weaker, I will presume.

60 OTTER 'Tis no presumption, *domine* Doctor.

MOROSE Yet againe!

CUTBERD Your question is, for how many causes a man may have *divortium legitimum*, a lawfull divorce. First, you must understand the nature of the word divorce, *à divertendo*——

MOROSE No excursions upon words, good Doctor, to the question briefly.

CUTBERD I answere then, the Canon-law affords divorce but in few cases, and the principall is in the common case, the adulterous case. But there are *duodecim impedimenta*, twelve impediments (as we call 'hem) all which doe not *dirimere contractum*, but *irritum reddere* 70 *matrimonium*, as wee say in the Canon-law, *not take away the bond, but cause a nullitie therein.*

MOROSE I understood you, before: good sir, avoid your impertinencie of translation.

OTTER He cannot open this too much, sir, by your favour.

MOROSE Yet more!

TRUE-WIT O, you must give the learned men leave, sir. To your impediments, master Doctor.

CUTBERD The first is *impedimentum erroris.*

OTTER Of which there are severall *species.* 80

CUTBERD I, as *error personae.*

OTTER If you contract your selfe to one person, thinking her another.

CUTBERD Then, *error fortunae.*

OTTER If shee be a beggar, and you thought her rich.

CUTBERD Then, *error qualitatis.*

OTTER If shee prove stubborne, or head-strong, that you thought obedient.

MOROSE How? is that, sir, a lawfull impediment? One at once, I pray you gentlemen.

OTTER I, *ante copulam*, but not *post copulam*, sir. 90

CUTBERD Mr. Parson saies right. *Nec post nuptiarum benedictionem.* It doth indeed but *irrita reddere sponsalia*, annull the contract: after marriage it is of no obstancy.

TRUE-WIT Alas, sir, what a hope are we fall'n from, by this time!

CUTBERD The next is *conditio*: if you thought her free borne, and shee prove a bond-woman, there is impediment of estate and condition.

OTTER I, but Mr. Doctor, those servitudes are *sublatae*, now, among us christians.

CUTBERD By your favour, master Parson——

100   OTTER   You shall give me leave, master Doctor.

MOROSE   Nay, gentlemen, quarrell not in that question; it concernes not my case: passe to the third.

CUTBERD   Well then, the third is *votum*. If either partie have made a vow of chastitie. But that practice, as master Parson said of the other, is taken away among us, thanks be to discipline. The fourth is *cognatio*: if the persons be of kinne, within the degrees.

OTTER   I: doe you know, what the degrees are, sir?

MOROSE   No, nor I care not, sir: they offer me no comfort in the question, I am sure.

110   CUTBERD   But, there is a branch of this impediment may, which is *cognatio spiritualis*. If you were her god-father, sir, then the marriage is incestuous.

OTTER   That *comment* is absurd, and superstitious, master Doctor. I cannot endure it. Are we not all brothers and sisters, and as much a kinne in that, as god-fathers, and god-daughters?

MOROSE   O me! to end the controversie, I never was a god-father, I never was a god-father in my life, sir. Passe to the next.

CUTBERD   The fift is *crimen adulterii*: the knowne case. The sixt, *cultus disparitas*, difference of religion: have you ever examin'd her what 120   religion shee is of?

MOROSE   No, I would rather shee were of none, then bee put to the trouble of it!

OTTER   You may have it done for you, sir.

MOROSE   By no meanes, good sir, on, to the rest: shall you ever come to an end, thinke you?

TRUE-WIT   Yes, hee has done halfe, sir. (On, to the rest) be patient, and expect, sir.

CUTBERD   The seventh is, *vis*: if it were upon compulsion, or force.

MOROSE   O no, it was too voluntarie, mine: too voluntarie.

130   CUTBERD   The eight is, *ordo*: if ever shee have taken holy orders.

OTTER   That's superstitious, too.

MOROSE   No matter, master Parson: would shee would go into a nunnerie yet.

CUTBERD   The ninth is, *ligamen*: if you were bound, sir, to any other before.

MOROSE   I thrust my selfe too soone into these fetters.

CUTBERD The tenth is, *publica honestas*: which is *inchoata quaedam affinitas.*

OTTER I, or *affinitas orta ex sponsalibus*: and is but *leve impedimentum.*

MOROSE I feele no aire of comfort blowing to me, in all this.   140

CUTBERD The eleventh is, *affinitas ex fornicatione.*

OTTER Which is no lesse *vera affinitas*, then the other, master Doctor.

CUTBERD True, *quae oritur ex legitimo matrimonio.*

OTTER You say right, venerable Doctor. And, *nascitur ex eo, quod per conjugium duae personae efficiuntur una caro—*

MOROSE Hey-day, now they beginne.

CUTBERD I conceive you, master Parson. *Ita per fornicationem aeque est verus pater, qui sic generat—*

OTTER *Et vere filius qui sic generatur—*

MOROSE What's all this to me?   150

CLERIMONT Now it growes warme.

CUTBERD The twelfth, and last is, *si forte coire nequibis.*

OTTER I, that is *impedimentum gravissimum*. It doth utterly annull, and annihilate, that. If you have *manifestam frigiditatem*, you are well, sir.

TRUE-WIT Why, there is comfort come at length, sir. Confesse your self but a man unable, and shee will sue to be divorc'd first.

OTTER I, or if there be *morbus perpetuus, & insanabilis*, as *Paralisis, Elephantiasis*, or so—

DAUPHINE O, but *frigiditas* is the fairer way, gentlemen.

OTTER You say troth, sir, and as it is in the *canon*, master Doctor.   160

CUTBERD I conceive you, sir.

CLERIMONT Before he speakes.

OTTER That *a boy, or child, under yeeres, is not fit for marriage, because he cannot reddere debitum*. So your *omnipotentes—*

TRUE-WIT Your *impotentes*, you whorson Lobster.

OTTER Your *impotentes*, I should say, are *minime apti ad contrahenda matrimonium.*

TRUE-WIT *Matrimonium*? Wee shall have most un-matrimoniall *latin*, with you: *matrimonia*, and be hang'd.

DAUPHINE You put 'hem out, man.   170

CUTBERD But then there will arise a doubt, master Parson, in our case, *post matrimonium*: that *frigiditate praeditus*, (doe you conceive me, sir?)

OTTER Very well, sir.

CUTBERD Who cannot *uti uxore pro uxore*, may *habere eam pro sorore.*

OTTER Absurd, absurd, absurd, and merely *apostaticall.*

CUTBERD You shall pardon me, master Parson, I can prove it.

OTTER You can prove a Will, master Doctor, you can prove nothing
    else. Do's not the verse of your owne *canon* say, *Haec socianda vetant*
180   *conubia, facta retractant*—

CUTBERD I grant you, but how doe they *retractare*, master Parson?

MOROSE (O, this was it, I fear'd.)

OTTER *In aeternum*, sir.

CUTBERD That's false in divinitie, by your favour.

OTTER 'Tis false in humanitie, to say so. Is hee not *prorsus inutilis ad*
    thorum? Can he *praestare fidem datam*? I would faine know.

CUTBERD Yes: how if he doe *convalere*?

OTTER He cannot *convalere*, it is impossible.

TRUE-WIT Nay, good sir, attend the learned men, they'll thinke you
190   neglect 'hem else.

CUTBERD Or, if he doe *simulare* himselfe *frigidum, odio uxoris*, or so?

OTTER I say, he is *adulter manifestus*, then.

DAUPHINE (They dispute it very learnedly, yfaith.)

OTTER And *prostitutor uxoris*, and this is positive.

MOROSE Good sir, let me escape.

TRUE-WIT You will not doe me that wrong, sir?

OTTER And therefore, if he bee *manifeste frigidus*, sir—

CUTBERD I, if he be *manifeste frigidus*, I grant you—

OTTER Why, that was my conclusion.

200 CUTBERD And mine too.

TRUE-WIT Nay, heare the conclusion, sir.

OTTER Then, *frigiditatis causa*—

CUTBERD Yes, *causa frigiditatis*—

MOROSE O, mine eares!

OTTER Shee may have *libellum divortii*, against you.

CUTBERD I, *divortii libellum* shee will sure have.

MOROSE Good *eccho's*, forbeare.

OTTER If you confesse it.

CUTBERD Which I would doe, sir—

210 MOROSE I will doe any thing—

OTTER And cleere my selfe in *foro conscientiae*—

CUTBERD Because you want indeed—

MOROSE Yet more?

OTTER *Exercendi potestate.*

Act V. Scene 4

EPICOENE, MOROSE, HAUGHTY, CENTAURE, MAVIS, MRS.
OTTER, DAW, TRUE-WIT, DAUPHINE, CLERIMONT,
LA-FOOLE, OTTER, CUTBERD.

[*Enter* EPICOENE, HAUGHTY, CENTAURE, MAVIS, MRS.
OTTER, DAW *and* LA-FOOLE.]

EPICOENE I will not endure it any longer. Ladies, I beseech you helpe
me. This is such a wrong, as never was offer'd to poore bride
before. Upon her marriage day, to have her husband conspire
against her, and a couple of mercinarie companions, to be brought
in for formes sake, to perswade a separation! If you had bloud, or
vertue in you, gentlemen, you would not suffer such eare-wigs
about a husband, or scorpions, to creep between man and wife—

MOROSE O, the varietie and changes of my torment!

HAUGHTY Let 'hem be cudgell'd out of dores, by our groomes.

CENTAURE I'll lend you my foot-man.   10

MAVIS Wee'll have our men blanket 'hem i' the hall.

MRS. OTTER As there was one, at our house, madame, for peeping
in at the dore.

DAW Content, yfaith.

TRUE-WIT Stay, ladies, and gentlemen, you'll heare, before you
proceed?

MAVIS I'lld ha' the bride-groome blanketted, too.

CENTAURE Beginne with him first.

HAUGHTY Yes, by my troth.

MOROSE O, mankind generation!   20

DAUPHINE Ladies, for my sake forbeare.

HAUGHTY Yes, for sir DAUPHINES sake.

CENTAURE He shall command us.

LA-FOOLE He is as fine a gentleman of his inches, madame, as any
is about the towne, and weares as good colours when he list.

TRUE-WIT Be brief, sir, and confesse your infirmitie, shee'll be a-fire to be quit of you, if shee but heare that nam'd once, you shall not entreat her to stay. Shee'll flie you, like one that had the marks upon him.

30 MOROSE Ladies, I must crave all your pardons—

TRUE-WIT Silence, ladies.

MOROSE For a wrong I have done to your whole sexe, in marrying this faire, and vertuous gentlewoman—

CLERIMONT Heare him, good ladies.

MOROSE Being guiltie of an infirmitie, which before I confer'd with these learned men, I thought I might have conceal'd—

TRUE-WIT But now being better inform'd in his conscience by them, hee is to declare it, & give satisfaction, by asking your publique forgivenesse.

40 MOROSE I am no man, ladies.

ALL How!

MOROSE Utterly un-abled in nature, by reason of *frigidity*, to performe the duties, or any the least office of a husband.

MAVIS Now, out upon him, prodigious creature!

CENTAURE Bride-groome uncarnate.

HAUGHTY And would you offer it, to a young gentlewoman?

MRS. OTTER A lady of her longings?

EPICOENE Tut, a device, a device, this, it smells rankly, ladies. A mere comment of his owne.

50 TRUE-WIT Why, if you suspect that, ladies, you may have him search'd.

DAW As the custome is, by a jurie of physitians.

LA-FOOLE Yes faith, 'twill be brave.

MOROSE O me, must I under-goe that!

MRS. OTTER No, let women search him, madame: we can doe it our selves.

MOROSE Out on me, worse!

EPICOENE No, ladies, you shall not need, I'll take him with all his faults.

60 MOROSE Worst of all!

CLERIMONT Why, then 'tis no divorce, Doctor, if shee consent not?

CUTBERD No, if the man be *frigidus*, it is *de parte uxoris*, that wee grant *libellum divortii*, in the law.

OTTER I, it is the same in *theologie*.

MOROSE Worse, worse then worst!

TRUE-WIT Nay, sir, bee not utterly dis-heartned, wee have yet a small relique of hope left, as neere as our comfort is blowne out. CLERIMONT, produce your brace of Knights. What was that, master Parson, you told me *in errore qualitatis*, e'ne now? DAUPHINE, whisper the bride, that shee carry it as if shee were guiltie, and asham'd.

OTTER Mary sir, *in errore qualitatis* (which master Doctor did forbeare to urge) if shee bee found *corrupta*, that is, vitiated or broken up, that was *pro virgine desponsa*, espous'd for a maid—

MOROSE What then, sir?

OTTER It doth *dirimere contractum*, and *irritum reddere* too.

TRUE-WIT If this be true, we are happy againe, sir, once more. Here are an honorable brace of Knights, that shall affirme so much.

DAW Pardon us, good master CLERIMONT.

LA-FOOLE You shall excuse us, master CLERIMONT.

CLERIMONT Nay, you must make it good now, Knights, there is no remedie, I'll eate no words for you, nor no men: you know you spoke it to me?

DAW Is this gentleman-like, sir?

TRUE-WIT JACK DAW, hee's worse then sir AMOROUS: fiercer a great deale. Sir AMOROUS, beware, there be ten DAWES in this CLERIMONT.

LA-FOOLE I'll confesse it, sir.

DAW Will you, sir AMOROUS? will you wound reputation?

LA-FOOLE I am resolv'd.

TRUE-WIT So should you be too, JACK DAW: what should keepe you off? shee is but a woman, and in disgrace. Hee'll be glad on 't.

DAW Will he? I thought he would ha' beene angrie.

CLERIMONT You will dispatch, Knights, it must be done, yfaith.

TRUE-WIT Why, an' it must it shall, sir, they say. They'll ne're goe backe. Doe not tempt his patience.

DAW It is true indeed, sir.

LA-FOOLE Yes, I assure you, sir.

MOROSE What is true gentlemen? what doe you assure me?

DAW That we have knowne your bride, sir—

LA-FOOLE In good fashion. Shee was our mistris, or so —

CLERIMONT Nay, you must be plaine, Knights, as you were to me.

OTTER I, the question is, if you have *carnaliter*, or no.

LA-FOOLE *Carnaliter?* what else, sir?

OTTER It is inough: a plaine *nullitie*.

EPICOENE I am un-done, I am un-done!

MOROSE O, let me worship and adore you, gentlemen!

EPICOENE I am un-done!

110 MOROSE Yes, to my hand, I thanke these Knights: master Parson, let me thanke you otherwise.

CENTAURE And, ha' they confess'd?

MAVIS Now out upon 'hem, informers!

TRUE-WIT You see, what creatures you may bestow your favours on, madames.

HAUGHTY I would except against 'hem as beaten Knights, wench, and not good witnesses in law.

MRS. OTTER Poore gentlewoman, how shee takes it!

HAUGHTY Be comforted, MOROSE, I love you the better for't.

120 CENTAURE So doe I, I protest.

CUTBERD But gentlemen, you have not knowne her, since *matrimonium*?

DAW Not to day, master Doctor.

LA-FOOLE No, sir, not to day.

CUTBERD Why, then I say, for any act before, the *matrimonium* is good and perfect: unlesse, the worshipfull Bride-groome did precisely, before witnesse demand, if shee were *virgo ante nuptias*.

EPICOENE No, that he did not, I assure you, master Doctor.

CUTBERD If he cannot prove that, it is *ratum conjugium*, notwithstand-
130 ing the premises. And they doe no way *impedire*. And this is my sentence, this I pronounce.

OTTER I am of master Doctors resolution too, sir: if you made not that demand, *ante nuptias*.

MOROSE O my heart! wilt thou breake? wilt thou breake? this is worst of all worst worsts! that hell could have devis'd! Marry a whore! and so much noise!

DAUPHINE Come, I see now plaine confederacie in this Doctor, and this Parson, to abuse a gentleman. You studie his affliction. I pray'

bee gone companions. And gentlemen, I begin to suspect you for
having parts with 'hem. Sir, will it please you heare me?   140

MOROSE O, doe not talke to me, take not from mee the pleasure of
dying in silence, nephew.

DAUPHINE Sir, I must speake to you. I have beene long your poore
despis'd kins-man, and many a hard thought has strength'ned you
against me: but now it shall appeare if either I love you or your
peace, and preferre them to all the world beside. I will not bee
long or grievous to you, sir. If I free you of this unhappy match
absolutely, and instantly after all this trouble, and almost in your
despaire, now—

MOROSE (It cannot be.)   150

DAUPHINE Sir, that you bee never troubled with a murmure of it
more, what shall I hope for, or deserve of you?

MOROSE O, what thou wilt, nephew! thou shalt deserve mee, and
have mee.

DAUPHINE Shall I have your favour perfect to me, and love hereafter?

MOROSE That, and any thing beside. Make thine owne conditions.
My whole estate is thine. Manage it, I will become thy Ward.

DAUPHINE Nay, sir, I will not be so un-reasonable.

EPICOENE Will sir DAUPHINE be mine enemie too?

DAUPHINE You know, I have beene long a suter to you, uncle, that   160
out of your estate, which is fifteen hundred a yeere, you would
allow me but five hundred during life, and assure the rest upon
me after: to which I have often, by my selfe and friends tendred
you a writing to signe, which you would never consent, or incline
too. If you please but to effect it now—

MOROSE Thou shalt have it, nephew. I will doe it, and more.

DAUPHINE If I quit you not presently, and for-ever of this cumber,
you shall have power instantly, afore all these, to revoke your act,
and I will become, whose slave you will give me to, for-ever.

MOROSE Where is the writing? I will seale to it, that, or to a blanke,   170
and write thine owne conditions.

EPICOENE O me, most unfortunate wretched gentlewoman!

HAUGHTY Will sir DAUPHINE doe this?

EPICOENE Good sir, have some compassion on me.

MOROSE O, my nephew knowes you belike: away *crocodile*.

CENTAURE He do's it not sure, without good ground.

DAUPHINE Here, sir.

MOROSE Come, nephew: give me the pen. I will subscribe to any thing, and seale to what thou wilt, for my deliverance. Thou art my restorer. Here, I deliver it thee as my deed. If there bee a word in it lacking, or writ with false orthographie, I protest before—I will not take the advantage.

He takes of Epicoenes perruke.

DAUPHINE Then here is your release, sir; you have married a boy: a gentlemans son, that I have brought up this halfe yeere, at my great charges, and for this composition, which I have now made with you. What say you, master Doctor? this is *justum impedimentum,* I hope, *error personae*?

OTTER Yes sir, *in primo gradu.*

CUTBERD *In primo gradu.*

He pulls of their beardes, and disguise.

DAUPHINE I thanke you, good Doctor CUTBERD, and Parson OTTER. You are beholden to 'hem, sir, that have taken this paines for you: and my friend, master TRUE-WIT, who enabled 'hem for the businesse. Now you may goe in and rest, be as private as you will, sir. I'll not trouble you, till you trouble me with your funerall, which I care not how soone it come. [*Exit* MOROSE.] CUTBERD, I'll make your lease good. Thanke mee not, but with your leg, CUTBERD. And TOM OTTER, your Princesse shall be reconcil'd to you. How now, gentlemen! doe you looke at me?

CLERIMONT A boy.

DAUPHINE Yes, mistris EPICOENE.

TRUE-WIT Well, DAUPHINE, you have lurch'd your friends of the better halfe of the garland, by concealing this part of the plot! but much good doe it thee, thou deserv'st it, lad. And CLERIMONT, for thy unexpected bringing in these two to confession, weare my part of it freely. Nay, sir DAW, and sir LA-FOOLE, you see the gentlewoman that has done you the favours! we are all thankefull to you, and so should the woman-kind here, specially for lying on her, though not with her! You meant so, I am sure? But, that we have stuck it upon you to day, in your own imagin'd persons, and so lately; this *Amazon*, the champion of the sexe, should beate you now thriftily, for the common slanders, which ladies receive from such cuckowes, as you are. You are they, that when no merit or fortune can make you hope to enjoy their bodies, will yet lie with their reputations, and make their fame suffer. Away you common moths of these, and all ladies honors. Goe, travaile to make legs and faces, and come home with some new matter to be laught at: you deserve to live in an aire as corrupted, as that wherewith you feed rumor. [*Exeunt* DAW *and* LA-FOOLE.] Madames, you are mute, upon this new *metamorphosis*! but here stands shee, that has vindicated your fames. Take heed of such *insectae* hereafter. And let it not trouble you that you have discover'd any mysteries to this yong gentleman. He is (a'most) of yeeres, & will make a good visitant within this twelve-month. In the meane time, wee'll all undertake for his secrecie, that can speake so well of his silence. Spectators, if you like this *comoedie*, rise cheerefully, and now MOROSE is gone in, clap your hands. It may be, that noyse will cure him, at least please him. [*Exeunt.*]

220

THE END.

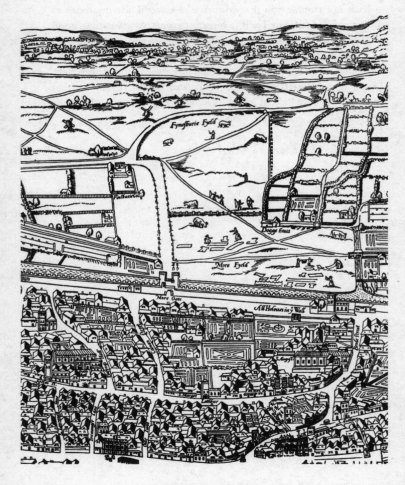

Agas' map of central London (c. 1570).

NOTES

ABBREVIATION

H&S Ben Jonson, ed. C. H. Herford, Percy and Evelyn Simpson, 11 vols. (Oxford: Clarendon Press, 1925–52)

Every Man in his Humour

As this Renaissance Dramatists volume offers a selection of Jonson's major drama in chronological sequence, the choice of the 1616 folio text (F) of *Every Man in his Humour* might seem to be illogical, since it represents what is, in effect, a revision of the earlier play. Yet it is a revision which, far from departing from the spirit of the earlier work, attempts to realize it more effectively. (See also Textual Procedure.) The change of scene from Italy to London gives point to the precision of the play's socio-linguistic observation, and, as the prologue in F makes clear, draws attention to Jonson's innovation among contemporary dramatists in choosing to make his comedy 'an Image of the times', exhibiting 'deedes, and language, such as men doe use'. Jonson's choice of *Every Man in his Humour* to open the 1616 edition, along with his decision to preface the revised play with a manifesto-like prologue and an unashamed dedication of this, the *'first'* of his educational *'fruits'* to his former schoolmaster, William Camden, testify to his retrospective estimation of the play as a worthy early representative of his continuing project of bringing a greater naturalism to English dramatic writing, a project evident in the London setting of *Epicoene*, and in the words of *The Alchemist*'s prologue: 'Our *Scene* is *London*, 'cause we would make knowne,/ No countries mirth is better than our owne' (*H&S*, V.294). There is, moreover, a strong argument for choosing the revised version of the play on the grounds of its subsequent influence. It was not the 1601 quarto (Q), but the 1616 folio version of *Every Man in his Humour* which impressed Dryden, which was subsequently revived to great acclaim in the eighteenth century by David Garrick, and which so captured the imagination of Charles Dickens that he himself revived it in 1845, 1847 and 1848, directing the production and taking a major role in the part of Bobadill (see *H&S*, IX.168–85).

While F represents a rational choice of text for this selection, however, it is worth considering how the earlier version, which has no dramatic afterlife beyond 1605, can, for that very reason, shed light on Jonson's original purpose in both texts of the play. The *London Magazine* of 1751 applauded Garrick for reviving *Every Man in his Humour*, and claimed to find the characters intelligible; 'The garb may alter, but the substance lives' it concluded (*Ben Jonson: The Critical Heritage*, ed. D. H. Craig (London: Routledge, 1990), p. 431). Yet Garrick had recognized that much in the play was obsolete, and had modernized it by adding an entire new scene in the fourth act between Kitely and Dame Kitely, effectively remoulding the play along Shakespearean lines by locating its centre of interest in the psychology of Kitely's jealous paranoia. For seventeenth-century readers, no such revision had been necessary: they found the interest of the play not in the psychology of any one character, but in its socio-linguistic drama, its concern with the question of eloquence in everyday language. Samuel Pepys in 1667 thus judged it to contain 'the greatest propriety of speech that ever I read in my life' (*Critical Heritage*, ed. Craig, p. 245). A brief consideration of the import of certain passages in Q which are dropped or revised in F may therefore help to reveal the urgency of the related issues of the state of the language and the devaluation of poetry, as Jonson originally conceived these in the context of the 1590s.

In Q, for example, Well-bred's letter to Edward Kno'well joked that Kno'well, being a poet, was nothing but a vagabond and a liar. These were the terms of abuse with which the humanist scholar Gabriel Harvey had responded to Thomas Nashe's important and innovative attempts to invent an authorial persona ('Pierce Penilesse') for his fiction in the 1590s. By 1616, it would seem, the respectability of poetry was more securely established, and the joking reminiscence of Harvey in the earlier version of the letter redundant. Another revision tells the same story: in F, Edward Kno'well explains to Well-bred that his father read the letter meant for him: 'my father had the full view o' your flourishing stile, some houre before I saw it' (III.1.41–2). In Q, however, the equivalent line reads: 'my father had the proving of your copy, some howre before I saw it'. The change is significant; the original indicates the seriousness of the sixteenth-century humanist belief that a person's moral worth could be ascertained by the reader's 'proving' or analysing the writer's rhetorical skill. It is no coincidence that a *letter* is in question here, since the best-selling humanist textbook on rhetorical amplification – Erasmus' *De Copia* – is directed at producing students who can write compellingly in a familiar, epistolary mode. That's why old Kno'well has such high moral expectations when reading a *familiar letter* by his son's esteemed friend, Well-bred; he assumes, after the manner of the humanist textbooks from which Jonson himself was taught, that skill in 'copia' or 'copy' is identifiable with moral fibre. And that's also why (though it's difficult for us to understand) he is so shocked by what he reads. Finally, in the last scene of Q, Jonson originally gave to Edward Kno'well a passionate speech in defence of the relevance of poetry to social and ethical life, a speech which he omitted in F, evidently concluding that the earlier version of the play had achieved its polemic purpose in helping to make this an orthodox view of poetry's refining powers.

Yet in spite of these revisions, Jonson evidently wanted the authoritative version of his play introducing his folio *Workes* to be a more faithful reproduction of 1590s

London culture than the original (with its fictive Italian setting) had been. Thus, for example, Bobadill, the most endearing braggart soldier ever composed by any drama-tist, is both a creature of his reading in popular Spanish chivalric romance (his name recalls the fall of Granada and the defeat of the Moors), and an evocation, along with the play's many references to military locations in London (the Artillery Yard, Finsbury Fields, Moorfields and Mile End), of the atmosphere of the 1590s, when fears of Spanish invasion increased the frequency of the general muster, and stepped up the training of the militia. As a 'humours' play, too, *Every Man in his Humour* retains distinctively turn-of-the-century characteristics. In 1597 Shakespeare's *1 & 2 Henry IV* interspersed the expected high-sounding blank verse and noble deeds of English chronicle history with whole scenes of compellingly decadent and inventive tavern conversation, and in the same year George Chapman's brittle comedy of manners, *An Humourous Days Mirth*, drew gallants and women into a tavern to bandy words, and pass judgement on each other's efforts. In 1586 George Pettie's translation of Stephano Guazzo's *Civile Conversation* advised readers it was not by solitary study, but by sociability – 'by the meanes of civil conversation' – that we gain 'the judgement that we have to knowe our selves' (*The Civile Conversation of M. Stephen Guazzo, written first in Italian, divided into four bookes, the first three translated out of French by G. Pettie* (London: Thomas East, 1586) sig. G4r, sig. H7r). While Jonson seeks on the one hand to bring the civilizing influence of poetry out of the hands of the humanist schoolmasters and into the sleazier realms of urban sociability, he also mocks the devourers of handy sixteenth-century conversation manuals, with their advice on how 'to get reputation with little charge' by copying out speeches from plays, and increasing one's vocabulary. So while Jonson's play agrees with Guazzo that 'the judgement that we have to know ourselves' comes from exposing ourselves to the opinions of others, it also sends up the 1590s fashion for 'civil conversation' in such moments as that when Bobadill, with exquisite ludicrousness, disparages Downe-right: 'Hang him, rooke, he! why, he has no more *judgement* then a malt-horse . . . He ha's not so much as a good phrase in his belly, but all old iron, and rustie proverbes!' (I.5.81 – 8; my italics). Utterances of this kind are the life of the play.

FURTHER READING

Barton, Anne, ' The *Case is Altered* and *Every Man in his Humour*', in *Ben Jonson: Dramatist* (Cambridge: Cambridge University Press, 1984), pp. 29 – 57

Dutton, Richard, ' The significance of Jonson's revision of *Every Man in his Humour*', *Modern Language Review* 49 (1974), 241 – 9

Maus, Katherine Eisaman, 'Horns of dilemma: jealousy, gender and spectatorship in English Renaissance drama', *Journal of English Literary History* 54 (1987), 561 – 83

Watson, Robert N., '*Every Man in his Humour*: the purging of monstrous conventions', in *Ben Jonson's Parodic Strategy* (Cambridge, Mass.: Harvard University Press, 1987), pp. 19 – 46

TEXTUAL NOTES

The base text for this edition is *The Workes of Benjamin Jonson* (First Folio, 1616) in the Bodleian Library, Oxford (shelfmark: AA 83 Art.). In these notes, the reading to the left of the bracket is that of this edition, and the second reading that of the base text. 'Q' represents readings incorporated into this edition from the Quarto of 1601; 'F2' represents readings taken from the Second Folio of 1640. If no source is given for a change, it is the text editor's. A caret (∧) is used for omitted punctuation.

Act I. Scene 2

53 BRAINE-WORME.] ~,
102 BRAYNE-WORME.] F2; ~,

Act I. Scene 3

0 *Scene misnumbered I.II in F*
20 he?] ~!
44 well.] ~,
52 *SD Kno'well*] F2; *Knowell*
58 be gelt] F2; be-gelt
75, 78 STEPHEN] F2; SERV.

Act I. Scene 5

82 you'ld] youl'd

Act II. Scene 3

2 for] For (*as if beginning verse line*)
14 Is't] F2; I'st
36 breakefast?] ~.
52 harme, in] F2; ~ ∧ ~,
55 DAME] F2; Dow.

Act II. Scene 5

41 affliction] affiction F affection
F2
49 still] *still*

Act III. Scene 1

65 you.] F2; ~ ∧
75 indeed, sir?] F2; ~. Sir?
76 melancholy.] F2] ~.
77 melancholy ∧] F2; ~,
134 blade?] F2; ~.

Act III. Scene 2

29 are ∧] ~,
29 right;] F2; ~?
32 though;] F2; ~?
38 shape?] F2; ~.

Act III. Scene 3

19 taste the] F2; the taste
107 no;] F2; no',

Act III. Scene 4

54 'hem] F2; ∧ ~

Act III. Scene 5

25 mar'le] F2; marl'e
33 sir.] F2; ~,
34, 37,
40 CASH] THO.
49 the] F2; *omitted in* F
61 sir;] F2; ~?
71 *Italy*)] ~ ∧

Act III. Scene 7

37 you: ha?] F2; ~? ~:

Act IV. Scene 1

11 'hem] F2; ∧ ~

Act IV. Scene 2

35 *Incipere*] *Insipere*

Act IV. Scene 3

40 within?] ~!

Act IV. Scene 5

2 and] And (*as if beginning verse
  line*)
2 for ever.] F2; for-ever,
3 But] F2; but

Act IV. Scene 6

30 they] F2; thy

Act IV. Scene 7

0.2 *To them.*] F2; *opposite* 0.1 *in* F
99 he.] ~?
132 'hem] F2; ∧ ~

Act IV. Scene 8

0.1 KIT.,] ~.
21 undiscover'd] F2; undiscour'd
30–1] *verse in* Q, *prose in* F

130–32] *printed as prose in* F

Act IV. Scene 9

0.1 BRAYNE-WORME.] ~,
  DOWNE-RIGHT.
23 sir.] F2; ~?
32 that, sir?] ~? ~.
60 jewell.] ~?
65 danger!] F2; ~?

Act IV. Scene 10

6 not,] Q; ~.
10 KNO'WEL] F2; KNO-WEL
22] *printed as prose in* F

Act IV. Scene 11

12 man?] F2; ~.
38 before ∧] F2; ~,
44–5] *one line in* F

Act V. Scene 1

7 and] And (*as if beginning verse
  line*)

Act V. Scene 3

18 sir.] F2; ~?
91 FORMALL?] ~.

Act V. Scene 5

74 some] Q, F2; *fame*

Variants from the early editions

It is customary in the Renaissance Dramatists series to conclude the Textual Notes with a selection of important variants between early texts of each play. With *Every Man in his Humour*, however, the revisions are so extensive that Q and F are effectively two different plays. Readers wishing to examine more closely the different stages of Jonson's compositional process are referred to the standard scholarly edition of Jonson's works, *H&S*, in which the two texts are printed consecutively, and with a full textual commentary. There is also a modern-spelling (and rather inaccurate) edition from the Regents Renaissance Drama series, in which the two texts are produced on facing pages for easy comparison: J. W. Lever, ed., *Every Man In His Humour: A Parallel Text* (University of Nebraska Press, 1971).

COMMENTARY

Dedication

5 *Mr. Cambden,* CLARENTIAUX: William Camden (1551–1623), historian, was Jonson's schoolmaster at Westminster; see *Epigrams*, 14 (*H&S*, VIII.31). 'Clarentiaux', the appellation of the second of the English Heraldic Kings-of-Arms, was conferred on Camden in 1597.

The Persons of the Play

16 *CAP[TAIN] BOBADILL*: Boabdill (Abu'Abd Allah); last king of the Moors in Spain, defeated when Granada fell in 1492. 'A Paules-man' was a frequenter of St Paul's, then a fashionable centre of business.

Prologue

10 *foot-and-halfe-foote words*: Thus Jonson renders 'sesquipedalia verba' in his translation of Horace's *Art of Poetry*, 139 (*H&S*, VIII.311).
11 *Yorke . . . jarres*: History plays (such as Shakespeare's) involving stage battles.

Act I. Scene 1

15–20 *My selfe . . . knowledge*: Adapted from Thomas Kyd, *The Spanish Tragedy* (1592), IV.1.71–4; see note to I.5.45 below.
32 *booke . . . hunting*: Hunting and hawking were aristocratic pastimes, and early humanist educationalists (Thomas Starkey, Sir Thomas Elyot) deprecated them by comparison with an education in ancient and modern languages. Note, however, that Stephen wants to know the 'languages' (I.1.40) of hunting and hawking.
45–7 *Because . . . ponds*: Archery in Finsbury Fields and ducking in Islington were

citizen pastimes; Hoxton was near to both, hence Stephen's snobbish anxiety to deny any association.

Act I. Scene 2

45–8 *remember . . . cover'd*: Reminding the servant to remote and replace his hat.

65–6 *old Jewrie . . . inhabit there, yet*: Old Jewry was originally named for its Jewish population; they had been expelled in 1291.

67 *change an olde shirt, for a whole smocke*: Exchange your father for a clean prostitute.

74–5 *Turkie . . . SIGNIOR*: The Turkey and subsequently Levant Companies made rich presents to the Sultan to promote trade.

76 *Poet-major . . . towne*: Q makes a disparaging reference to 'Poet Nuntius', i.e. 'Poet Announcer'. Both these references may glance at Anthony Munday, who composed City entertainments, and was satirized by Jonson as 'Antonio Balladino, Pageant Poet to the City of Millaine' in *The Case is Altered* (*c.* 1597).

80 *Guild-hall verdict*: London juries were known for their severity.

82 *wind-mill*: Tavern in the Old Jewry; originally the Jews' Synagogue.

84 *The Spittle . . . Pict-hatch*: Hospital, especially for sexual diseases, and haunt of prostitutes in Clerkenwell, respectively.

95 *Hesperian Dragon*: The Dragon Ladon, who watched the tree of golden apples in the Hesperides.

Act I. Scene 3

23 *scander-bag*: 'Scanderbag' (corruption of 'Iskander-bey', which apparently means 'Prince Alexander'); Turkish name of George Kastrioti (1403–68) who won Albania from the Turks. It is not clear why Stephen here uses the name pejoratively.

28 *wispe of hay, rould hard*: Rustic substitute for boots.

57 *our familiar Epistles*: Ironic allusion to practice of publishing letters to friends, famously employed by Cicero, Erasmus and others.

58–9 *Mr. JOHN TRUNDLE*: Publisher of the first Quarto of *Hamlet*, but otherwise specializing in ballads, 1603 to 1626.

87 *draw you into bond*: Make you security for a debt.

106–8 *shadow . . . cypresse*: Hide their glory, as the haberdasher's wife covers the embroidered front of her dress with a veil of fine linen, or black linen crêpe.

109 *DRAKES old ship, at Detford*: Drake's ship had been permanently laid up at Deptford.

111–14 *let . . . all one*: If appearance proclaims the inner nature, Stephen's appearance is like a fairground advertisement for a monster (clearly, '*miracle*' and '*monster*' are not 'all one').

120 *suburbe-humor*: Affectations typical of the suburbs, as opposed to the city. Stephen's pretentious suburbanism is most markedly demonstrated by his poor judgement of the qualities of weapons and of poetry, which judgement would define an urban gallant or a gentleman. See II.4.25–8 and III.1.143–61.

Act I. Scene 4

8–14 *ancient . . . Grand-father*: Cob's exaltation of the herring as 'King of fish' chimes with the theme of Thomas Nashe's *Lenten Stuffe, the praise of the red herring* (written in the spring of 1598, the year of *Every Man*'s first performance). *Lenten Stuffe* is an exuberant polemic against government censorship written in the wake of Nashe's and Jonson's troubles with the authorities over *The Isle of Dogs* (1597). Nashe celebrates the herring as the patron of Yarmouth and of poets (III.191), and satirizes the touchiness of aristocrats about allusions to their pedigrees ('if but a head or tayle of any beast he boasts of in his crest . . . be reckoned up by chance . . . he straight engageth himselfe by the honor of his house . . . to thresh down the hayry roof of that brayne that so seditiously mutined against hym', III, p. 214, ll. 20–26). Cob's ludicrous pedigree, therefore, may be a burlesque version of Jonson's broader concern with redefining the relationship between gentility, eloquence and the management of 'humours' (see Introduction and headnote).

13–14 *Harrots bookes*: Heralds' books, used for tracing noble pedigrees.

22–4 *ghost . . . coles*: Roger Bacon (*c.* 1214–92), famous necromancer, was not burned to death; perhaps his surname, carnival antithesis of 'herring', haunts Cob like the smell of meat on fasting days (see III.4).

46–7 *swallow'd a taverne-token*: Euphemism for getting drunk (tokens were issued at taverns instead of small change).

55 *Brasen-head*: According to popular legend, Roger Bacon planned to protect England from invasion by making a brazen head speak, so that he could wall England with brass; Robert Greene's romantic play *Frier Bacon, and Frier Bongay* (1594) dramatizes the legend, IV.1.

56 *Mo fooles yet*: In the legend, the words of the Brazen Head are 'Time is', 'Time was' and 'Time will be' (see *The Case is Altered*, IV.3.80); Cob's version both indicates his preferred reading, and suggests a certain scepticism.

58 *worshipfull fish-monger*: Member of the Company of Fishmongers; there's a proximity between Matthew's fishy pedigree and Cob's.

79–80 *Helter-skelter . . . hang-man*: '*Helter skelter*' is a nonsense phrase; 'hang sorrow' and 'care 'll kill a cat' are both proverbial expressions of the uselessness of anxiety, the latter referring to the fact that even a cat's nine lives can be worn away by worry; 'up-tailes all' is the refrain of an old song; a louse is proverbially worthless, so 'a louse for the hang-man' expresses contempt for the possible consequences of insolvency, since the penalty for petty theft was hanging. Cob is clearly anxious that Bobadill is a fake and won't pay his rent.

Act I. Scene 5

0 *Bobad. is discovered*: Jonson's stage direction suggests a curtain is drawn to reveal a space at the back of the stage.

5 *'ods so*: Abbreviated form of 'Godso', an exclamation of surprise. The disguising thus of blasphemous exclamations beginning with 'God' came into vogue in the 1600s (Q has 'Godso').

45 *Goe by, HIERONYMO*: Kyd's *Spanish Tragedy* (1601), phenomenally popular, here identified by a stock quotation. Jonson knew Kyd's play well: Dekker alleged that he had once taken 'mad Hieronimoes part' (*Satiromastix*) and in 1601–2 he was paid by the theatre manager Philip Henslowe to write 'new adicyons for Ieronymo' (*H&S*, XI.308).

60–5 *To thee . . . I conclude*: Parodic of 1590s sonnet sequences, such as Samuel Daniel's *Delia* (1592) and Michael Drayton's *Idea* (1593).

100–3 *The bastinado . . . ayre*: According to Jeronimo de Caranza, *De la filosofia de las armas* (1569), Matthew should now challenge Downe-right to a duel.

126 *passe upon me*: Matthew is confused by the phrase, which also meant 'impose on'.

Act II. Scene 1

6 *pieces of eight*: Spanish gold or silver *peso*.

10 *Exchange*: The Royal Exchange, established by Sir Thomas Gresham in 1567 as a financial centre on the Antwerp model to enable currency exchange in London.

15–17 *I tooke . . . Hospitall*: Sons of City freemen and foundlings were educated at Christ's Hospital.

75–7 *he has . . . assure him*: 'Rustie proverbes' (I.5.88) indicating Downe-right's indignation at the idea that Well-bred should seek financial help from him. '*claps his dish*': beggars carried wooden dishes and clapped the lids to beg for food.

86 *savour lesse of stomack*: Sound less angry.

105 *flat cap . . . shining shooes*: Citizens – as opposed to 'gentlemen' – were mockingly identified by their flat woollen hats and blackened shoes.

118–20 *penurious quack-salvers . . . upon my selfe*: Quack doctors, advertising their wares, made a mockery of themselves; Kitely suggests that admonishing Well-bred would similarly advertise his jealousy to scorn.

Act II. Scene 2

19 *Fleet-street*: Noted for brawls. (Stow, *The Survey of London*, records the proximity of Fleet Street to Fleet prison.)

26–7 *right hang-man cut*: Designed to be hanged.

Act II. Scene 3

1–4 *our maides . . . evening*: Kitely alludes to the proverb: 'the back of a herring, the belly of a wench, is best'; Cob's response suggests Kitely's 'maids' are in danger of getting pregnant.

31 *ejects*: It was believed that the eye physically emitted glances; Kitely's surveillance (like Corvino's in *Volpone*) is sexually charged.

46–52 *new disease . . . harme*: Any imperfectly diagnosed illness was referred to as 'the new disease'; Kitely detects a reference to his 'dis-ease' of suspected cuckoldry.

53 *shee has me i' the wind*: A hunting metaphor, to be on the scent of someone.

Act II. Scene 4

2 *a poore creature to a creator*: Transformed from servant into artist.

2–4 *now . . . coat*: Lying is expected of soldiers, but treacherous in servants.

16–17 *Veni . . . CAESAR*: Caesar's boast: 'I came, I saw, I conquered'.

52–7 *late warres . . . Vienna*: Brayne-worme's anachronisms betray him: the wars in Bohemia began in the 1540s, Aleppo was taken by Selim I in 1516 and Vienna freed in 1529.

81 *Higgin-Bottom*: Possibly Otwell Higginbottom, accused of sedition in 1579.

Act II. Scene 5

5–13 *When I was yong . . . good example*: Adapted from Juvenal, *Satires*, XIII.54–60.

14–37 *Nay, would . . . states*: Adapted from Quintilian, *Institutio Oratoria*, I.2.6–8.

40 *Baite . . . seale*: Bribe them, by a servant's sexual favours, to subscribe to a document conveying property.

45–6 *That travail'd . . . cortezans*: Thomas Coryat's *Crudities* (1611) praises Venetian courtesans.

51–6 *Neither have I . . . manners*: Juvenal, *Satires*, XIV.6–13.

139 *musters at Mile-end*: The citizens' militia regularly mustered and trained at Mile End Green; a certain festivity seems to have been associated with these military gatherings.

Act III. Scene 1

18 *quos . . . JUPITER*: Virgil, *Aeneid*, VI.129–30, 'whom impartial Jupiter has loved.'

31 *judgement . . . rogue*: The Statute 14 Eliz.c.5 (1572) enjoined burning through the right ear with a hot iron for rogues and vagabonds.

54–5 *the signe of the dumbe man*: As if Stephen were a tavern sign.

81 *utters . . . grosse*: With a pun on the commercial sense of 'utter': 'to put goods forth upon the market'.

101 *beleag'ring of Strigonium*: The siege of Graan in Hungary, retaken from the Turks in 1595.

105–6 *taking . . . Genowayes*: In Q, Tortosa (which was apparently taken by the Genoese in 1102) is specified.

137 *Morglay, Excalibur, Durindana*: Swords of heroes of chivalric romance; respectively, Bevis of Hampton, King Arthur and Orlando Furioso.

Act III. Scene 2

18–19 *by his leave . . . civilitie*: Mocking the etiquette by which Stephen avoids a duel.

47 *here, in Colman-street*: Continuation of Old Jewry, north of Lothbury Street.

63–4 *Thames-street . . . car-men*: The Custom-house quay was one of the quays in Thames Street, at which galleys bearing merchandise landed. 'Car-men' drove this merchandise in carts, while porters carried it; they were rivals for custom.

Act III. Scene 3

34–8 *Our . . . hornes ake*: Punningly identifies the rich ('three-pild') velvet on the fashionable 'acorn' caps worn by citizens' wives with the velvet on a stag's horns, suggesting that since wives started wearing these caps, their husbands have been cuckolds.

44 *Exchange time*: Q gives 'past ten'; time for making business deals.

61 *a chinke*: Q has 'rimarum plenus', 'full of cracks', from Terence, *Eunuchus*, I.105, spoken by a wily slave who subsequently arranges for his master to enter a heavily guarded house and rape a virgin.

88–90 *H'is . . . sweare*: Cash is neither a Puritan, with an aversion to oaths, nor a strict Roman Catholic. '*Fayles*' and '*Tick-tack*' were forms of backgammon, and Kitely has heard Cash swear in gambling.

Act III. Scene 4

1–4 *Fasting. . . burnt*: A statutory 'political lent' forbad meat consumption on numerous days, including Fridays, to boost the fishing industry.

13–14 *rewme . . . humour*: Though a somewhat fashionable term in the 1580s, 'rewme' was never metaphorically applied, as 'humour' was, to mood or disposition; it's as if Cob were trying to use the word 'catarrh' metaphorically.

30–31 *I doe stomack . . . horse*: Cob offers to defy ('stomack') fasting days by eating (stomacking) Bevis of Hampton's war-horse Arundel.

36–7 *Flemmish . . . butter*: The Dutch were proverbially fond of butter.

43–9 *A fasting-day . . . COPHETUA*: Continuing the joke begun at I.4.8 about Cob's herring ancestry; here he blames Lent for martyring his relatives (red herrings are smoked, like Saint Laurence who was tortured on a gridiron) and for forcing him into cannibalism. He muddles 'cannibal' with 'Hannibal', the Carthaginian general, and confuses King Cophetua, who married a beggar maid, with Croesus, the Lydian King whose wealth was proverbial.

57 *beaten like a stock-fish*: Dried cod was beaten before being boiled.

Act III. Scene 5

7 *seven wise masters*: The 'seven sages' – Bias, Pittacus, Cleobolus, Periander, Solon, Chilon and Thales – flourished on the threshold of Western philosophy, between 600 and 560 BC.

9 *gentlemen of the round*: Patrols of footsoldiers who often took to begging after being discharged.

10 *sit . . . citie*: Press hard upon, be a nuisance to the city.

26–7 *Hounds-ditch . . . broker*: Houndsditch, running north of the City wall into Bishopsgate, was a centre for brokers, or second-hand clothes dealers; the affinity of brokers and devils was often noted.

28–31 *a craftie . . . you'll say*: Demonstrating Brayne-worme's virtuosity: 'a crafty knave needs no broker' was a proverb; Well-bred uses it to deny belief in Brayne-worme's trip to Houndsditch, but Brayne-worme throws it back to prove the opposite.

32–3 *he ha's more . . . ha's ten, sir*: Play on 'shift', meaning both 'cunning trick' and 'change of clothes'.

50 *taking . . . horse*: To 'take the wall', away from the street's mud and traffic, was to claim social superiority.

51–2 *serving of god*: Perhaps comparable to Dogberry in *Much Ado about Nothing*, IV.2.18–23, who asks the accused criminals 'do you serve God?'

64–8 *I have been in the Indies . . . onely*: Hawkins's second voyage in Hakluyt, *Principall Navigations* (1589) gives an account of tobacco as a substitute for food.

72–4 *your greene . . . Nicotian*: Balsamum (balm) and St John's Wort were good for dressing open or 'green' wounds. 'Nicotian' (named of Jacques Nicot, who introduced it into France) is the tobacco plant.

121 SD *Master Stephen . . . the post*: Stephen is practising Bobadill's gentlemanly oaths to the 'post, in the middle of the ware-house' (see III.6.38).

129 *artillerie garden*: Training ground of the Artillery Company, near Bishopsgate. Praised by Jonson, *Under-wood* (1640) (*H&S*, VIII.213), but also often mocked for its citizen associations, and proximity to the pastimes in Finsbury Fields that Stephen was earlier anxious to deny (note to I.1.45–7).

Act III. Scene 6

22–4 *flowing . . . Cornu-copiae*: Associating the horn of plenty with the cuckold's horn, and the legend of Jupiter's pouring, as a shower of gold, into the lap of Danae (another reminiscence of Terence's *Eunuchus*, 584–92).

44 *egges on the spit*: Proverbial, to be very busy.

Act III. Scene 7

8–9 *greene lattice ... scot, and lot*: Inns had lattices across their windows, and parish rates, respectively.

26–7 *an' I die ... kill'd me*: A twelve month and a day was the legal period for determining the cause of death due to injury or wounds.

53 *Sweet OLIVER*: Stock epithet for Orlando's rival in *Orlando Furioso*; cf. *Under-wood* (*H&S*, VIII.206), 'All the madde *Rolands* and sweet *Oliveers*', and Nashe, *Lenten Stuffe*, 'if you be *boni socij* and sweete Olivers' (III.225).

Act IV. Scene 1

13 *no bodies fault, but yours*: Women were responsible for the sexual honour of the household.

Act IV. Scene 2

9–10 *odde ... withall*: Proverbial: 'a toy to mock an ape' meant something like 'taking candy from a baby', cheating the easily deceived.

32–5 *Incipere ... sense*: Playing on '*Incipere dulce*' ('it is sweet to begin') and '*insipere*' ('to be a fool').

38 *Benchers phrase: pauca verba*: Drunkards whose catchphrase was 'fewer words'.

39–42 *Rare ... thine*: These four lines and the four below are inaccurately quoted from Marlowe's *Hero and Leander* (written 1592–3, printed 1598), ll.199–204, 221–2.

56 *from the dead*: Marlowe was killed in 1593.

77–9 *perfections so transparent ... well of desire*: A joke: 'transparent' could mean beautiful, but Well-bred suggests, rather, that what is transparent is the poet's incompetence.

82–6 *Oh monster ... tricks*: Taken in a sexual sense.

91 *lampe of virginitie ... take it in snuffe*: Thomas Bentley's *The Monument of Matrons, conteining seven severall Lamps of Virginite* (London: 1582) was a well-known book of piety for women, and 'take it in snuffe' is to take offence. Well-bred first introduces sexual ambiguity, then suggests Bridget is being prim.

92–3 *you'll ... concealement*: Commissions for concealed monastery lands were begged as favours by courtiers; Well-bred suggests that Matthew may become ambitious of sexual favour.

101 *whose cow ha's calv'd*: Proverbial; Well-bred mocks Downe-right's rustic idiom.

114 *cut a whetstone*: Proverbially impossible.

Act IV. Scene 3

14–15 *BOB . . . Songs, and sonnets*: Alludes to Bobadill's baggy breeches, and the title of Tottel's Miscellany, *Songes and Sonettes* (1557).

Act IV. Scene 4

10 *How, the lye . . . stab'd*: Giving the lie was tantamount to challenging to a duel.

13–15 *O, must you . . . tickle him*: Cob takes 'stab'd' in a sexual sense. '*Burgullian*' is probably a reference to the Burgundian fencer John Barrose, who, having challenged all the fencers in England, was hanged for killing an officer who arrested him for debt in 1588.

19 *Trojan*: Alluding to the myth that London was founded by Aeneas' nephew, Brute, and that London is 'New Troy' or 'Troynovant'. Jonson elsewhere made fun of this standard resource of London's civic iconography.

Act IV. Scene 6

50–1 *travelling . . . aire*: As if expectation were pregnancy.

66 *reades in . . . Mile-end*: The sixteenth-century modernization of warfare relied on the scholarly study and promulgation of Roman military history; early English examples were Richard Morison's Frontinus, *Strategems* (1539) and Peter Whitehorn, *Caius Julius Caesar his Martiall Exploytes* (1565). Jonson owned Justus Lipsius' authoritative analysis of Polybius on the Punic Wars, by which Maurice of Nassau reformed his army. The joke here lies in Formall's equation of Roman military discipline with the citizens' manoeuvres at Mile End (see note to II.5.139).

Act IV. Scene 7

13 *hay*: Italian 'hai' ('you have it') when a thrust touches the opponent.

40–41 *skirts . . . Shore-ditch*: Disreputable areas, e.g. Turne-bull street was a haunt of prostitutes.

46 *doing . . . hill*: Raising anthills.

126–7 *strooke with a plannet*: Inexplicable ills were attributed to the malignant influence of planets.

Act IV. Scene 8

8 *Anger costs . . . nothing*: Ironic subversion of contemporary moral philosophy derived from Seneca and Plutarch.

62–3 *tower . . . service*: The couple could marry immediately at the Tower, as it was extra-parochial.

Act IV. Scene 9

10—11 *Nobilis . . . Gentelezza*: Latin adjective and Italian noun for 'nobility'.

37 *brace of angells*: The lawful fee was only ten groats. An angel was a gold coin worth 6—10s.; a groat was 4d.

Act IV. Scene 10

46 *When all thy powers in chastitie is spent*: Unclear; perhaps 'when you have spent your sexually active years chastely'.

55 *good-wife BA'D*: Pun on bawd; Kitely spells it out.

72 *Am I prefer'd thether*: 'Have I been promoted to brothel-keeper?'

79—80 *bundle o' hempe*: Hemp was beaten for ropemaking by prostitutes in Bridewell.

Act IV. Scene 11

2 *Serjeants gowne*: Uniform of the City serjeant, whose office was to arrest offenders, or summon them to appear before a court.

6 *mace*: City serjeant's badge of office, a pun on 'mace' as spice was common.

Act V. Scene 4

8 *doe penance . . . shirt*: Legal penalty in ecclesiastical courts.

Act V. Scene 5

10—13 *Mount . . . aloud*: Phlegon was one of the horses of the Sun; for *'Saturni podex'* (Saturn's anus) see Erasmus, *Adages*, III.3.58. No source for this poem has been traced.

19 *realme*: 'Realm' was written and pronounced 'ream'; the pun is quite common.

21—2 *Unto . . . eyes*: Burlesqued from the opening of Daniel's *Delia*: 'Unto the boundlesse Ocean of thy beautie,/ Runnes this poore River, charged with streams of zeale'.

31 *Sic . . . mundi*: 'So passes away the glory of this world'.

32 *embleme*: A picture with a short poem, expressing an abstract concept; collections of emblems were popular.

34—6 *They are not borne . . . Sheriffe*: The idea that sheriffs and aldermen are, unlike poets, annually created, is adapted from Florus, and used by Jonson elsewhere; cf. *Timber: or, Discoveries* (1640), 2430 (*H&S*, VIII.637).

39—40 *They cannot . . . fact*: Taken from Seneca, *On Anger*, III.26: 'the greatest punishment is to have done wrong.'

41 *Sir, you . . . defence*: Perhaps by 1616 Jonson no longer felt it necessary to spell out the defence of poetry implied by the plot, but in Q at this point, Edward Kno'well makes an impassioned speech to 'approve the state/ Of poesie' and affirm the importance of 'Sacred invention', over the 'stolne wares' of hack-writers and plagiarists whose words have 'currant passe' with 'the fat judgements of the multitude'.

Sejanus

This text of *Sejanus* is based on signatures Gg4ʳ–Oo3ʳ of William Stansby's 1616 folio edition of *The Workes of Benjamin Jonson* (F). The title-page and final page in F assert that the tragedy was first acted in 1603, by the King's Men; among the actors named are Richard Burbage and William Shakespeare. The theatres were closed at the death of Elizabeth on 24 March 1603, and plague appears to have kept them closed until 9 April 1604, so that the 1603 performance is likely to have been held at Court, perhaps in the autumn or winter. According to E. K. Chambers (*The Elizabethan Stage*, 4 vols. (Oxford: Clarendon Press, 1923), III.367, II.210) the most likely dates of performance are between 26 December 1603 and 19 February 1604. Jonson claims, in his dedication of F to Esmé, Lord Aubigny, that the play '*suffer'd no lesse violence from our people here, then the subject of it did from the rage of the people of* Rome', probably referring to a performance at the Globe, after the theatres reopened in 1604.

Sometime after the court or public performance of *Sejanus*, Jonson was summoned to appear before the Privy Council to answer charges of treason. Drummond of Hawthornden records Jonson's belief that the Earl of Northampton was behind this investigation: 'Northampton was his mortall enemie for brauling on a Sᴛ Georges day one of his attenders, he was called before *the* Couⁿcell for his Sejanus & accused both of popperie and treason by him' (*H&S*, I.141.325–7). If the brawl occurred on St George's Day 1605, when Northampton was made a Knight of the Garter, then Jonson would have been examined not long before the publication, in quarto, of *Sejanus*, printed by George Eld for Thomas Thorpe (Q). This printed text was, by Jonson's own account, 'not the same with that which was acted on the publike Stage, wherein a second Pen had good share' (To the Readers, 37–9). Jonson's revision of the stage version or versions (on which George Chapman may have been his collaborator) was clearly a radical one, and it may be that there existed, in performance, material which could have been construed as treasonous, and which he then excised from Q. Nevertheless, we know there was still room for malicious interpretation in the 1605 text; in Q, Silius, on trial for treason against Tiberius, accepts the charge and goes on to accuse the emperor of not being able to stomach being grateful to his military commander for his success: 'all best Turnes,/ with *Princes*, do convert to injuries', he says. In F, Jonson altered this to read, 'all best turnes,/ With doubtfull Princes, turne deepe injuries' (III.302–3). This later alteration gives us some indication of the kind of work Jonson may have already done to transform the acted version, for which he was accused of treason, into the carefully distanced and extensively annotated *Sejanus* of Q.

Critics have, on the basis of the printed texts of Q and F, conjectured reasons for the Council's action against Jonson. Some have argued that his treatment of the career of Sejanus, a royal favourite, offered unmistakable parallels with the rise and fall of the Earl of Essex, but Philip Ayres has, in his comprehensive Revels edition (Manchester, 1990), contended that the Essex rebellion would scarcely have been considered a burning issue in 1603–5, the Earl having been executed in 1601. He proposes instead that *Sejanus*, with its central double treason trial in Act III, may have been taken as a critical comment on the scandalous trial for treason of Sir Walter Ralegh in 1603; this theory gains plausibility from the fact that Northampton was, with Robert Cecil, Ralegh's chief enemy.

Treason is notoriously constituted as a crime of intention ('if it succeeds then none dare call it treason', as John Harington pointed out, in *The Epigrams of Sir John Harington*, ed. Norman McClure (Philadelphia: University of Pennsylvania Press, 1926), 4.259). Jonson's marginal annotations to Q (abandoned in F) seem accordingly to have been designed to disown liability for authorial intention by insisting on the text's fidelity to its historical sources, especially the *Annals* of Tacitus. The play itself, however, dramatizes the same process of disowning intention as a strategy of imperial power; Tiberius' masterful letter condemning Sejanus works not by admitting suspicion of his favourite's motives, but by attributing such suspicions to unnamed others: '*Some there bee, that* would interpret *this his publique severitie to bee particular ambition* . . . [*You*] *are able to examine, and censure these suggestions* . . . *we durst pronounce them* . . . *most malicious*' (V.580–1, 589–91, my emphasis). In the play, life or death depends on whether one is in the happy position of being able to attribute criminal malice to the words of others, or the unhappy position of being answerable for the malicious intentions inferred from one's own recorded words. Jonson's *Poetaster*, performed in 1601, and likewise concerned with the political hazards of authorship, brings on the poet Virgil to recite, from the fourth book of the *Aeneid*, the description of *Fama*, or Rumour. Rumour is the youngest of the Titans that piled up mountains in the hope of climbing to Olympus, 'last sister of that Giant race,/ That thought to scale JOVES court' (*Poetaster*, V.2.82–3, in *H&S*, IV.296). It can be no coincidence that Sejanus, whose power in Jonson's play derives from his ability to deploy the intelligence networks of the imperial court, is explicitly twinned with Virgil's Rumour. Arruntius, berating the Olympian Gods, calls Sejanus, 'this last of that proud Giant-race' who will 'Heave mountayne upon mountayne, 'gainst your state—' (IV.270–1). It may be less relevant, then, to consider Jonson's *Sejanus* as the tale of a political favourite, than as a comment on the conditions of historical and dramatic writing before the advent of the literary market-place as we know it, in a period when writing was still considered a form of service to a member of the political elite, and the ascription of authorship was consequently bound up with questions of political allegiance, and of liability arising from such service. 'Is he or *Drusian*? or *Germanican*?' (I.80) whispers one of Sejanus' clients to another, trying to determine the allegiance of the historian Cremutius

Cordus; such 'whispring fame (II.195)' will govern the uses subsequently made of his writings. These are the conditions under which, as Jonson shows, interpretation offers violence to meaning and to men; 'Nothing' as he memorably puts it, 'hath priviledge 'gainst the violent eare' (IV.311).

FURTHER READING

Archer, John Michael, ' "Lights of base stuff": Jonson's Roman plays', in *Sovereignty and Intelligence* (Stanford: Stanford University Press, 1993), pp. 97–109

Ayres, Philip, 'Jonson, Northampton and the "treason" in *Sejanus*', *Modern Philology* 80 (1983), 356–63

Dutton, A. R., 'The sources, texts and readers of *Sejanus*: Jonson's "integrity in the story" ', *Studies in Philology* 75 (1978), 181–98

Patterson, Annabel, 'Reading *Sejanus*: ciphers and forbidden books', in *Censorship and Interpretation: The Conditions of Writing and Reading in Early Modern England* (Madison: University of Wisconsin Press, 1984), pp. 49–58

Ricks, Christopher, '*Sejanus* and dismemberment', *Modern Language Notes* 76 (1961), 301–8

Worden, Blair, 'Ben Jonson among the historians', *Culture and Politics in Early Stuart England*, ed. Kevin Sharpe and Peter Lake (Basingstoke: Macmillan, 1994), pp. 67–89

TEXTUAL NOTES

The base text for this edition is *The Workes of Benjamin Jonson* (First Folio, 1616) in the Bodleian Library, Oxford (shelfmark: AA 83 Art.). In these notes, the reading to the left of the bracket is that of this edition and the second reading that of the base text. 'Q' represents readings incorporated into this edition from the Quarto of 1605; 'F2' represents readings taken from the Second Folio of 1640. (See also p. 434.)

To the Readers] *This passage is in Q only*

Act I

98 ashes,] Q; ~ ∧
111 me'] ~ ∧
122 know'] ~ ∧
152 temperance] temp'rance
167 seconds] F2; secon'ds
181 DRUSUS'] DRUSU'S
244 Emperour] Emp'rour
291 URGULANIA,] F2; ~.

366 need.] F2; ~,
534 flattering] F2; flatt'ring
559 emperour] emp'rour
561 I'] Q; ~ ∧

Act II

248 'hem.] ~,
259 both] Q; doth
267 them] *omitted in* F

330 'Εμο] F2; E'μου
330 Υαῖα] F2; Ŷᾶα
346 swell.] ~:
349 SD *Mutilia Prisca.] opposite l. 348 in* F
400 lets] Q; betts
434 vertu's] Q; vertuous
449 AGRIPPINA] F2; ARR.

307 May'] Q; ~ ∧
485 it is] F2; ~ 'tis
498 MINUTIUS] MAR.
514 LACO] MAC.
515 So'] Q; ~ ∧

Act III

11 take him] Q, F2; him take
123 'Gainst] Gain'st
149 prayers] F2; prayer's
222 more?] Q; mo (*faulty impression*)
374 CORDUS] CORD⁹
374 SECUNDUS] SECUND⁹
466 the ∧] F2; ~'
475 true,] Q; ~ ∧
526 and] F2; 'and
530 pietie,] ~ ∧
601 lusts,] F2; ~.
707 Saviour] Q, F2; savier
725 loose] Q; lose

Act IV

32 unhappy'] Q; ~ ∧
200 yond'] yon'd
251 SEJANUS'] SEJANU'S

Act V

96 Entred] F2; Entr'd
106 howre.] ~?
120 overtake] F2; over'take
212 I'] Q; ~ ∧
221 The'] Q; ~ ∧
255 alreadie'] Q; ~ ∧
335 happy',] Q; ~ ∧,
366 thou'] ~ ∧
420 SEJANUS] SEJAN⁹
427 Wil't] F2; Wilt
428 You'] Q; ~ ∧
459 thy'] Q; ~ ∧
460 They'] Q; ~ ∧
611 tempest.)] ~. ∧
631 *apprended*] F2; *apprênded*
656 downe,] Q; ~ ∧
668 *Phlegra*] P'*hlegra*
757 to] Q, F2; too
785 minute,] F2; ~ ∧
820 highly'] Q; ~ ∧

Variants from the early editions

The Folio text of *Sejanus* is typographically very different from the Quarto of 1605. The punctuation has been comprehensively reworked: it is generally much heavier, with semi-colons and colons replacing commas and full stops replacing colons. Conversely, Q's frequent deployment of 'gnomic pointing' (the use of inverted commas at the beginning and the end of lines to highlight them as *sententiae*) is abandoned; examples of lines which the Quarto designated as maxims in this way can be found, for instance, at Act II 195–201, 205–9 and 239–44. F also sporadically but intensively modernizes the Quarto's archaic forms; thus in just eight lines (III.275–82) there are six alterations of Q's 'thine', 'thy', and 'thee' or 'thou', to F's 'yours', 'your' and 'you'. The marginal stage directions are almost all found only in F, and this feature is connected to the biggest difference in the typographical appearance of the two texts, since the margins of Q are crammed with Jonson's citations from his Latin sources. Sometimes these consist of simple but precise references to the editions he has consulted, but often they include extensive quotations (in Latin) from the Roman historians. A translation of a passage from the *Annals* of Tacitus which Jonson quotes in the margins of the scene depicting the trial of Silius is offered as an example at the end of the selection of significant variants below. Finally, of the seven commendatory poems which prefaced the text of the play in Q, five, including John Marston's, are omitted altogether in F; George Chapman's poem is shortened, and, along with Hugh Holland's, relocated at the head of the volume.

The Argument

Q, *which prints* The Argument *in roman, has an additional final paragraph, set in larger type:*

This do we advance as a marke of Terror to all *Traytors, & Treason;* to shewe how just the *Heavens* are in powring and thundring downe a weighty vengeance on their unnatural intents, even to the worst *Princes* : Much more to those, for guard of whose Piety and Vertue, the *Angels* are in continuall watch, and *God* himself miraculously working.

Act III

62 sunnes (Q: springs)
62 drinke up (Q: exhaust)

303 With doubtfull Princes, turne deepe (Q: With *Princes*, do convert to)
384 hast (Q: last)
505 With . . . familiar (Q: To . . . inur'd)
529 master (Q: Prince)

Act IV

368 flesh (Q: traine)
503 troubled (Q: mated)

Act V

376 afford him (Q: bestow)
514–19 MEMMIUS . . . *not be taken*] Q *prints in capitals, with each word followed by a full stop, as if this were a Roman inscription*

An example of Q's marginalia

In the margin opposite Act III 197–208 Jonson cites (in Latin) Tacitus, *Annales,* IV.xix (trans. Michael Grant (Penguin, 1989), here and below):

> When accused, Silius requested a brief adjournment until the accuser's consulship should end. But Tiberius opposed this, arguing that officials often proceeded against private citizens, and that there must be no limitation of the rights of the consuls, on whose watchfulness it depended 'that the State takes no harm'. It was typical of Tiberius to use antique terms to veil new sorts of villainy.

COMMENTARY

Dedication

4–5 *Esmé L. Aubigny*: Esmé Stuart, Seigneur d'Aubigné (1574–1624), younger brother of the second Duke of Lennox, whom he succeeded in 1583. Jonson was grateful to him for support and hospitality over a period of years; see *Conversations with Drummond*, 254–5 (*H&S*, I.139) and Epigram 127 (*H&S*, VIII.80).

9 *violence . . . here*: Probably alluding to the play's unfavourable reception at the Globe in 1604; see p. 446 above.

To the Readers

6 *strict . . . Time*: See note to *Volpone*, Prologue, l. 31.

6–8 *a proper Chorus . . . the Auntients*: The Chorus, a defining feature of Greek and Roman tragedy, intrigued Jonson. He revived it in *Catiline* (1611).

14–15 *Observations . . . publish*: Jonson's translation of the *Art of Poetry* (in *Conversations with Drummond*, 82–8 (*H&S*, I.134), Jonson says he translated *Art of Poetry* while staying with Aubigné in 1604) survives, but the commentary was lost in the fire that destroyed his library; see *Under-wood*, 43 (*H&S*, VIII.202–16).

17 *Sentence*: Aphorism, or pithy, instructive saying (*sententia*).

22–3 *the Quotations . . . affected*: The marginal notes of Q might seem pretentious.

24 *integrity*: Both fidelity to the history ('*Story*') and political integrity; on the basis that the more faithful a modern author is to an ancient source, the less he can be accused of seditious intent with regard to the present; but see p. 446.

31 *save one*: The *Annals* of Tacitus had been translated by Richard Greneway in 1598.

34–5 *Tacit. Lips . . . Seneca. &c.*: For his marginal references in Q, Jonson specifies Justus Lipsius' edition of Tacitus, *Annals* (Antwerp, 1600) and Henri Estienne's edition of Dio Cassius, *Roman History* (Geneva, 1592); references to Suetonius, Seneca and others do not vary between editions.

38–9 *a second Pen*: Perhaps George Chapman (1559–1634), on the evidence of his commendatory verses prefaced to Q.

42–7 *I shall not . . . hate me for*: Cf. Persius, *Satires*, I.45–9: 'I'm not the man to shrink from applause; my skin's not that tough, But I do say that your "Bravo" and "Lovely" are not the final and ultimate test of what's good.' '*Neque . . . est*' (l. 51) is *Satires*, I.47: 'my entrails are not made of horn'.

49 *Quem . . . opimum*: Horace, *Epistles*, II.i.181: [for whom] 'a palm leaf, withheld or given, decides whether I'm haggard or fat!'

The Argument

2 *Vulsinium*: Volsinii (Bolsena) between Rome and Siena.

30 *people*: For the additional paragraph in Q, a declaration that the tragedy intends to admonish 'all *Traytors, & Treasons*', see Textual Notes, p. 450.

The Persons of the Play

TIBERIUS: Tiberius Claudius Nero, succeeded Augustus as emperor, AD 14.

DRUSUS se[nior]: Drusus Caesar, son of Tiberius; married to Livia (his first cousin); poisoned AD 23.

NERO: Julius Caesar Nero, eldest son of Germanicus and Agrippina, next in succession after Drusus senior; banished by Sejanus, and starved to death in AD 31.

DRUSUS ju[nior]: Julius Caesar Drusus, second son of Germanicus and Agrippina, next in succession after Nero; imprisoned and starved to death, AD 33.

CALIGULA: Caius Caesar, youngest son of Germanicus and Agrippina, next in succession after Drusus junior; succeeded Tiberius as emperor, AD 37.

ARRUNTIUS: Lucius Arruntius; according to Tacitus, a senator in high estimation with Augustus. In Jonson's play, the most outspoken of Tiberius' Germanican critics.

SILIUS: Caius Silius Caecina Largus, a general under Germanicus, defeated the Aedui at Sacrovir, AD 21; accused of treason, AD 24, and committed suicide.

SABINUS: Titius Sabinus, knight, friend to Germanicus; betrayed by Latiaris, and executed in AD 28.

LEPIDUS: Marcus Lepidus, consul, AD 6; Tacitus commends his cautious integrity, mitigating excesses of injustice without provoking imperial wrath.

CORDUS: Aulus Cremutius Cordus, historian. Seneca's *On Consolation* (which Jonson used for information about Cordus' life) is addressed to Cordus' daughter, Marcia.

GALLUS: Caius Asinius Gallus, arrested in AD 30, and died of starvation in AD 33.

REGULUS: Publius Memmius Regulus, opponent of Sejanus.

TERENTIUS: Marcus Terentius, faithful friend to Sejanus, even after his fall (Tacitus, *Annals*, VI.8).

LACO: Graecinus Laco, commander of the night watch, helped to overthrow Sejanus.

EUDEMUS: Physician to Livia, and collaborator in the murder of Drusus senior.

RUFUS: Petilius Rufus, helped Latiaris and Opsius betray Sabinus.

SEJANUS: Lucius Aelius Seianus, son of a Roman knight, rose, under Tiberius, to the highest eminence, and fell in AD 31.

LATIARIS: Latinius Latiaris, betrayer of Sabinus; fell with Sejanus.

VARRO: Lucius Visellius Varro, helped to denounce Caius Silius.

MACRO: Naevius Sertorius Macro, Guard prefect; selected by Tiberius to bring about the downfall of Sejanus.

COTTA: Marcus Aurelius Cotta Maximus Messalinus, participant in attacks against Silius and Cordus.

AFER: Cnaeus Domitius Afer, an ambitious orator; historically unconnected with the trial of Silius.

HATERIUS: Quintus Haterius, confused by Jonson with his son, Haterius Agrippa, whom Tacitus, *Annals*, VI.4 describes as 'a somnolent creature (and, when awake, depraved)' (see note on V.609–11).

SANQUINIUS: Accuser of Arruntius (Tacitus, *Annals*, VI.7).

POMPONIUS: Another of Sejanus' clients.

POSTHUMUS: Julius Postumus, lover of Mutilia Prisca, and used by Sejanus to exercise influence over Tiberius' mother, Augusta.

TRIO: Lucius Fulcinius Trio, supported Sejanus and committed suicide in AD 35.

MINUTIUS: Minucius Thermus, knight and friend of Sejanus; later denounced by Tiberius for his allegiance to Sejanus.

SATRIUS: Satrius Secundus, client of Sejanus, accused Cordus of publishing a treasonous history.

NATTA: Pinnarius Natta, also accuser of Cordus.

OPSIUS: Marcus Opsius, with Latiaris and Rufus, betrayed Sabinus.

TRIBUNI: Military tribunes of the Guard.

AGRIPPINA: Widow of Germanicus, granddaughter of Augustus; centre of the opposition to Tiberius and Sejanus. Exiled, and starved to death, AD 33.

LIVIA: Livia Julia, wife of Drusus senior and lover of Sejanus, with whom she murdered her husband; executed after the fall of Sejanus.

SOSIA: Sosia Galla, wife of Silius, and friend of Agrippina; fell with her husband in AD 24.

PRAECONES: Heralds.

FLAMEN: Priest.

TUBICINES: Trumpeters.

NUNTIUS: Messenger.

LICTORES: Attendants on magistrates, bearing the *fasces* (ensigns of authority).

MINISTRI: Attendants.

TIBICINES: Flautists.

SERVUS: Servant.

Act I

12 *then*: On that account.

14–15 *we owe . . . secrets*: Juvenal, *Satires*, I.75, III.49–57.

16 *deare*: Expensive (to keep quiet).

16–18 *Or live . . . subverting theirs*: 'Or live feared by them, as the objects of their restless suspicion that we are trying to build a fortune out of their ruin'.

23 *SEJANUS clients*: Protected by the patronage of Sejanus, and bound to render him service.

25–7 *it would . . . fit organs*: Open surgery on their hearts would reveal all but the paltriest sins harbouring there.

30–31 *cut . . . whisprings*: Juvenal, *Satires*, IV.109–10.

31–2 *sell . . . emptie smoake*: I.e. empty promises; cf. Nashe, *Lenten Stuffe*, in *The Works of Thomas Nashe*, ed. R. B. McKerrow, rev. by F. P. Wilson, 5 vols. (Oxford: Basil Blackwell, 1966), III.225.

33–40 *Laugh . . . breake winde well*: Juvenal, *Satires*, III.100–108.

59–60 *We, that . . . triumphed world*: I.e. before 50 BC, when Rome was still a republic (Julius Caesar's first dictatorship began in 49 BC).

64–6 *every . . . lives*: See Tacitus, *Annals*, I.74; III.37–8; Suetonius, III.61; Juvenal, *Satires*, X.87.

70–72 *Tyrannes . . . devoure*: Cf. Machiavelli, *The Prince*, ch. XIX, and Jonson, *Timber: or, Discoveries*, 1158–60 (*H&S*, VIII.599).

78 *so downe to these*: Suetonius, II.35 cites Cremutius Cordus on the reign of Augustus.

80 *Drusian? or Germanican*: Tacitus, *Annals*, II.43: 'For the court was disunited, split by unspoken partisanships for Drusus or Germanicus.'

104 *Brave . . . race*: Brutus' own words about Cassius, according to Plutarch, *Brutus*, 44.

114 *GERMANICUS*: Son of Tiberius' brother, Drusus, Germanicus had been the focus of Republican hopes after the death of his father. For his sons, Nero, Drusus and Caligula (I.248–9), see 'The Persons of the Play'.

122 *know' him*: Here and elsewhere Jonson's apostrophe is not an error, but an indication that two words are to be elided, and the first syllable of the word following the apostrophe is to be unstressed, to preserve the rhythm of the line.

131–6 *his funeralls . . . losses*: Germanicus died at Antioch, so the masks of his ancestors, kept in Rome, could not be worn at his funeral, as was customary.

139 *paralell'd . . . ALEXANDER*: Tacitus, *Annals*, II.72: 'Some felt that his [Germanicus'] appearance, short life and manner of death . . . recalled Alexander the Great.'

167 *seconds*: Gnaeus Calpurnius Piso made commander in Syria by Tiberius, when Germanicus went east in AD 18.

168 *damme*: Augusta, widow of Augustus and Tiberius' mother.

173 *a fine poyson*: Tacitus, *Annals*, II.69; Germanicus believed he had been poisoned by Piso.

183 *Fiftie sestertia*: 'Sestertia' is the plural of sestertium, a unit worth a thousand sesterces (the basic Roman coin, worth two-and-a-half asses, or a quarter of a denarius), so fifty sestertia is a very large sum. In Q, Jonson quoted from the French scholar Guillaume Bude's *De Asse* (*On the 'Asse'* – a Roman coin) (*Opera Omnia*, vol. I, Basel: 1557, p. 64), noting that this sum would be worth £375 in his own day.

217 *second face*: Juvenal, *Satires*, X.63.

235 *hard to court*: Possibly 'heard to court' (Xenophon's Cyrus was said to know the names of all his soldiers).

285 *feare no collours*: Pun on 'fear no rival' (military colours); cf. Shakespeare, *Twelfth Night*, I.v.6.

304–5 *doe not aske . . . violet*: Editors usually give explanations, none of which is convincing.

307–10 *Which . . . puts it*: Martial, *Epigrams*, X.xxxvii.3–5.

354 *whither I shall your lordship*: Q has 'whether I shall fetch your Lordship'.

396–7 *When power . . . intends*: Cf. Jonson, *Timber: or, Discoveries*, 1110–15 (*H&S*, VIII.597–8).

542–3 POMPEI'S *. . . statue*: Seneca, *To Marcia on Consolation*, 22.4–5, quotes Cordus saying this.

575 CASTOR: Famous gladiator of the time; see Dio Cassius, *Roman History*, LVII.xiv.9.

Act II

74–5 *that addition . . . expiate*: Sejanus' name will at least mitigate, if not absolve, the fault.

178–85 *The prince . . . list*: These lines translate Lucan, *The Civil War*, VIII.489–95; another translation can be found in Jonson's *Ungathered Verse*, 50.9–20 (*H&S*, VIII.422–3).

244–7 *We will . . . factions*: Suetonius, III.54 describes Tiberius' cruelty to the sons of Germanicus.

284 *clikt . . . thumb's*: 'Thumbs up' or 'thumbs down' decided the fate of gladiators; the former meant death.

313–16 *As if . . . by such*: Echoing Lucan, *Civil War*, III.138–40.

330 Ἐμοῦ .. πυρί: 'When I die let fire overwhelm the earth'; Dio, *Roman History*, LVIII.xxiii.4, reports this as a favourite saying of Tiberius.

342–3 *t' extoll . . . ladie*: Tacitus, *Annals*, IV.12, notes that Agrippina's close friends were persuaded by Sejanus to encourage her haughtiness.

349 *your kindest friend*: Mutilia Prisca; see Tacitus, *Annals*, IV.12.

369–70 *Our citi's . . . warre*: Cf. note on I.80.

383–4 *put . . . in bloud*: Invigorate.

406 *They . . . wind*: A hunting metaphor; cf. *Every Man in his Humour*, II.3.53.

Act III

0 *THE SENATE*: Three meetings of the Senate as recorded by Tacitus – in AD 23 after the death of Drusus, in AD 24 for the trial of Silius and in AD 25 for the trial of Cordus – are dramatically conflated in Act III.

4–5 *under colour . . . his*: Tacitus, *Annals*, IV.19: 'The consul Lucius Visellius Varro was set in motion, and with his father's feud against Silius as a pretext sacrificed his own honour to gratify Sejanus' enmity.' In Rome, where there was no class of professional advocates, the personal hostility of the prosecutor was played up as proof of sincerity.

12 *All under name of treason*: Tacitus, *Annals*, IV.19: 'in extortion they [Silius and his wife] were undoubtedly both involved. But the case was conducted as a treason trial.'

25 *so low*: The consuls are seated on lower benches, as a sign of mourning for Drusus.

28–9 *Fathers . . . Common-wealth*: For this formula Jonson cites, in Q, Barnabe Brisson, *De Formulis et Sollemnibus Populi Romani Verbis* (Paris, 1583), Bk. II.

113–18 *The burden . . . suspected*: Tacitus, *Annals*, IV.9: 'by reverting to empty discredited talk about restoring the Republic and handing the government to consuls or others, [Tiberius] undermined belief even in what he had said sincerely'.

123 *that charme*: Suetonius, III.69, says that Tiberius wore a laurel wreath to ward off lightning.

192–4 *If I . . . 'gainst him*: Jonson cites, in Q, Brisson, *De Formulis*, Bk. V.

197–208 *CAESAR . . . oblique course*: Tacitus, *Annals*, IV.19, notes that it was characteristic of Tiberius to veil his objections to Silius' request in old-fashioned, republican language about the dangers of limiting the rights of Senators.

245 *net of VULCANES filing*: Vulcan entrapped Venus and Mars in a net to expose their adultery.

252 *provoke*: Same subject and object as 'make', i.e. 'Shall, however they *provoke* me to accuse, not *make* me do so'.

257 *Romane Eagles*: Roman legionary standards.

261 *curl'd Sicambrians*: Martial, *Epigrams*, 'On the Spectacles', 3: 'Sygambrians have come with hair curled'. The Sicambrians or Sugambri were a tribe from the area between the rivers Sieg and Lahn (tributaries of the Ruhr) in Germany.

285 *Thy spie*: See II.417–18, where Afer is noted by Cordus and Arruntius as a spy.

324–5 *Shee . . . threats*: Lucan, *Civil War*, IX.569–70.

334–6 *The coward . . . dearest*: Lucan, *Civil War*, IX.583, 404.

339 *[Stabs himself]*: Tacitus does not say Silius killed himself in the Senate.

373–92 *For th'Annal's . . . Romanes*: Tacitus, *Annals*, IV.34: 'The year began with the prosecution of Aulus Cremutius Cordus on a new and previously unheard-of charge: praise of Brutus in his *History*, and the description of Cassius as "the last of the Romans".'

385 *vipers tooth*: Young vipers were thought to eat their way out of their mothers (Pliny, *Natural History*, X.lxxii.170).

407–60 *So innocent . . . of me*: The entire speech comes from Tacitus, *Annals*, IV.34–5; see *Conversations with Drummond*, 602 (*H&S*, I.149).

419 *SCIPIO, AFRANIUS*: Metellus Scipio, Pompey's father-in-law and colleague in the consulship. Lucius Afranius, consul in 60 BC, was Pompey's deputy in Spain.

424 *MESSALLA*: Marcus Valerius Messalla Corvinus fought with Cassius and Brutus at Philippi and later wrote a history of the Civil Wars.

428–9 *did CAESAR answere . . . oration*: Caesar's *Answers to Cato* is mentioned by Suetonius, I.56.

431 *ANTONIUS . . . pleadings*: Both lost.

453–4 *their images . . . defac'd*: Plutarch, *Dion and Brutus*, V, records that Augustus ordered the preservation of a statue of Brutus.

480 *an eternall name*: In Q Jonson notes that though Cordus' histories are lost, a fragment is preserved in the elder Seneca's *Suasoriae*, VI.19.

484–7 *AUGUSTUS . . . bruising*: The dying Augustus was rumoured to have said this after spending a day with Tiberius (Suetonius, III.21).

516 *his daughter*: Julia.

595 *charmes*: Seductive reasons for leaving Rome.

601 *thy lusts*: See Suetonius, III.43–4, for details of Tiberius' sexual habits.

639–40 *The injur'd . . . strike*: The injured and the favoured alike desire to harm their masters, but only the favourite has the means to do so.

651–4 *I' have . . . may live*: Pliny, *Natural History*, XXVII.ii.

689–92 *Wormes . . . int'themselves*: As worms and moths consume the material in which they breed, so favourites and court parasites eventually seek to ingest their very patrons and favourers.

Act IV

12–13 *At least . . . danger*: Made the excuse ('colour') if not the actual reason ('ground' – foundation for colour in painting) for every trumped-up danger.

21–2 *my niece. . . FURNIUS*: Tacitus, *Annals*, IV.53.

48 *Spelunca*: Now Sperlonga, where the 'Grotta di Tiberio' is a tourist attraction.

65 *In their offence*: Offensive to them.

110 *alli'd to him*: Jonson here follows Richard Greneway's *The Annales of Cornelius Tacitus* (London, 1598), IV.68: 'Latiaris, who was somewhat allied to Sabinus.' In Tacitus, the suggestion is merely that they were connected, not that they were kin. See *Sejanus*, ed. Philip Ayres, 15.

174 *ulcerous . . . face*: Tacitus, *Annals*, IV.57.

180–81 *Doe you . . . cut off*: Latiaris' oblique hints mimic the cautiously allusive conversational style of the Germanicans at II.479–500.

199 *straight . . . to CAESAR*: I.e. Sejanus reports back to Tiberius.

228–9 *The yeere . . . SEJANUS*: Sabinus is a New Year's sacrifice to Sejanus.

242–3 *subject . . . object*: The actual victim of his hatred, as opposed to its motive.

246–8 *since . . . armie*: Suetonius, III.53, says Tiberius accused Agrippina of flight.

268 *thy black-lidded eye*: Alluding to Jove's black brows.

270–1 *proud . . . upon mountayne*: As if Sejanus were one of the Titans, giants who heaped up mountains in an attempt to scale heaven, before being defeated by Jupiter.

285–7 *His faithfull dogge . . . with it*: Dio, *Roman History*, LVIII.i.3.

336–8 *Bolts. . . ALCIDES*: Arruntius exhorts the gods to arms: Vulcan, the blacksmith, is to forge thunderbolts for Jove, Apollo (a hunter) to take up his bow, Mars (God of war) his sword, Pallas Athene ('blue ey'd' in Homer) her spear and Hercules his club.

340 *I meant . . . dispatch*: Congratulating himself on avoiding a treasonous conclusion.

354–7 *Wee'll talke . . . be gone*: Cf. I.259–60, where Arruntius likewise openly defies lurking informers.

391–401 *Thither . . . name*: Suetonius, III.43; Tacitus, *Annals*, VI.VI.1; '*spintries*' and '*sellaries*' were newly invented names for the male and female prostitutes trained to gratify Tiberius' peculiar tastes.

410–22 *These letters . . . uncertayne*: See Dio, *Roman History*, LVIII.vi.3–5 on Tiberius' strategically confusing letters to the Senate.

426 *HELIOTROPE*: This plant always looks to the sun, even in cloudy weather, as Sejanus' clients here seek the expression of Tiberius, though obscured.

429–34 *New statues . . . more*: Dio, *Roman History*, LVIII.vi.2; Suetonius, III.65.

437 *forbid that last*: Dio, *Roman History*, LVIII.viii.4, 'because sacrifices were being made to Sejanus, he forbade such offerings to be made to any human being'.

438 *POLLUX . . . HERCULES*: Q, and the first state of F, have 'Castor' and 'Pollux'. Jonson then discovered that 'Castor' was a woman's oath, and corrected the text.

516 *he ha's a wife*: Historically, this liaison took place after the fall of Sejanus.

Act V

17–21 *Windes lose . . . opposites*: A version of Lucan, *Civil War*, III.362–6.

29–37 *they say . . . serpent*: Dio, *Roman History*, LVIII.vii.1.

39–40 *the hue . . . bosomes*: Presumably pale.

52–7 *the falling . . . prodigies*: Dio, *Roman History*, LVIII.v.5.

74 *a beeves fat*: The fat of an ox.

80 *lade poore ATLAS back*: Atlas, holding up the world, is unnecessarily burdened with the weight of useless Olympian gods.

91 *masculine odours*: Frankincense came in two varieties; the superior variety was called 'masculine'.

97 *The house of REGULUS*: Dio, *Roman History*, LVIII.ix.3, 'Macro entered Rome by night . . . and communicated [Tiberius'] instructions to Memmius Regulus, then consul, . . . and to Graecinus Laco, commander of the night watch.'

97 *opposite*: The other consul, Fulcinius Trio, sided with Sejanus.

129 *a veine . . . feet*: A pun: Mercury was the messenger god.

171–84 *Be all . . . great goddesse*: In Q Jonson cites, as authorities for the details of this scene, Brisson, *De Formulis* (see note on III.28–9); Joannes Rosinus, *Romanorum antiquatem libri decem* (Basel, 1583); Johann Wilhelm Stuck, *Sacrorum, sacrificiorumque gentilium descriptio* (Tiguri, 1598); and Onofrio Panvinio, *Reipublicae Romanorum commentariorum libri tres* (Venice, 1558).

171 *Be all profane farre hence*: A ritual expulsion; George Herbert opens his 'Temple' (1633) similarly: 'Avoid Profaneness'.

174–5 *pure hands . . . Garlands pure*: In Q Jonson notes the insistence on the cleanliness of all things in the sacred rituals of the ancients, citing Vergil, Plautus, Tibullus and Ovid.

253–64 *If you . . . my second*: Echoes, variously, Lucan, *Civil War*, V.659–60, III.108–12 and V.662.

363 *tribuniciall dignitie*: The holder of this had right of veto over Senatorial decrees, as well as the right to propose laws; Tiberius had held it under Augustus.

391–4 *Hang . . . henge*: Adapted from Seneca, *Thyestes*, 855–77.

514–22 *Consuls . . . common-wealth*: In Q Jonson gives as authorities Brisson, *De Formulis*, Bk. II and Justus Lipsius, *Satyra Menippea*.

515 *kalends of June*: 1 June AD 31. In fact, Sejanus was condemned on 18 October.

541–632 *TIBERIUS . . . exacts it*: For the substance and strategy of this letter, Jonson enlarges on the hints given in Suetonius, III.65; Juvenal, *Satires*, X.71–2; and especially, Dio, *Roman History*, LVIII.x.1–5.

559 *lapwing*: 'The lapwing cries most when farthest from her nest' was proverbial; cf. *Poetaster*, IV.7.53 (*H&S*, IV.284).

574–5 *no innocence . . . mercie*: From Seneca, *On Mercy*, I.i.8.

588 *your vultures*: See above, IV.446ff., in which Lepidus interpreted Tiberius' letters as portents of doom for Sejanus, as vultures are signs of carrion.

609–11 *Porcpisce . . . tempest*: Porpoises were said to dance before a storm. Haterius is 'constant' because his depravity has made him infirm; see 'The Persons of the Play'.

619–20 *it is not . . . your justice*: Compare Tiberius' language above, III.197–208 and n.

635–6 *now, you . . . Your propertie*: 'Now you have discharged your proper office'; cf. *Epigrams*, 59, where used-up spies are like burnt candle-ends.

661 *ingratefull viper*: See note on III.385.

668 *Phlegra*: Where the Titans were defeated; see note on IV.270–1.

695 *superstitious Moores*: Herodotus, IV.188, says that Lybians sacrifice to the sun and moon.

749 *POMPEI'S circke*: Pompey's theatre; see I.542.

771–87 *Enquire . . . emperour*: Imitates Juvenal, *Satires*, X.67–77.

797–815 *Old men . . . often buryed*: Jonson's source is Claudian, *Against Rufinus*, II.410–53.

822–40 *A sonne . . . Gemonies*: Tacitus, *Annals*, V.9.

842 *Th'expulsed APICATA*: See II.491.

862 *strangely open'd*: We, as audience, already knew the truth about Eudemus, Livia and Lygdus, but the Germanicans could only guess. Tacitus explains that at the time of the murder, rumour was rife, and 'The real story of the murder [of Drusus] was later divulged by Sejanus' wife, Apicata' (*Annals*, IV.11). Jonson dramatizes rumour: see II.479–500.

Volpone

The text is based on signatures Oo4^r–Xx4^r of William Stansby's 1616 folio edition of *The Workes of Benjamin Jonson* (F). The play had previously been published in a quarto (Q) dated 1607, printed by George Eld for Thomas Thorpe. The title-page and final page of F claim that the play was first performed in 1605, and according to his prologue, Jonson started to write it less than two months before it opened. Officially, the new year started on 25 March, so this means that the play must have been written between December 1604 and March 1606. It has in fact been usual to suppose that it was first performed by the King's Men at the Globe in early 1606, because Sir Politique Would-bee's hearing news of a whale at Woolwich (II.1.46–7) seems to refer to the whale mentioned by John Stow in his *Annales* (1615), p. 880, as being sighted in the Thames on 19 January 1606. After being performed in London, the play was taken to Oxford and Cambridge in 1606 or early 1607. How well the play was received in the universities is suggested by the dedication of Q to both of them 'FOR THEIR LOVE AND ACCEPTANCE' of it. It was revived twice in Jonson's lifetime by the King's Men, in 1624 for a performance at court, and again in 1630. The play appears to have been popular through the early seventeenth century and after the Restoration; on 14 January 1665 Pepys recorded that he went 'To the King's house, there to see "Vulpone", a most excellent play; the best I think I ever saw, and well acted' (*H&S*, IX.197).

Unlike recent criticism of *Sejanus*, approaches to *Volpone* have tended to eschew the study of sources and analogues, treating the play as an independent *tour de force* of Jonson's imagination. Nevertheless, paying some attention to its probable sources enables us to appreciate the quality of Jonson's imaginative daring. Behind *Volpone* (and perhaps accounting for its warm reception in the universities) lie such profoundly ironic humanist and classical texts as Erasmus' *Praise of Folly* (1509), Machiavelli's *Mandragola* (1518) ('Mandrake') and the Menippean dialogues of the Greek satirist Lucian, in which venerated and powerful persons and institutions naïvely confess their own nefarious activities. Thus, for example, in one of Lucian's *Dialogues of the Dead*, we find what is obviously the inspiration for Jonson's wild conception of the 'cunning purchase' (I.1.31) in which Volpone takes such pleasure. In Lucian's dialogue the old, rich and childless Polystratus braggingly describes how, in spite of his baldness, gummy eyes and snivelling rheum, beautiful and well-born lovers would flock to his bedside to court him, hoping to become his heir. Jonson's Volpone is a more perverse conception than Polystratus: because Volpone is young and virile, we can't imagine that he lacks lovers (as Polystratus would) and must suppose that he simply chooses to repudiate procreative love and familial ties, for the dubious pleasure of impersonating an old man and drawing 'new clients, daily, to my house,/ Women, and men, of every sexe, and age' (I.1.76–7). Jonson has obviously been attracted by Lucian's satire on the debased erotics of social aspiration (it's the wealth of the disgusting old lecher Polystratus that makes him so attractive to all his young lovers), and has twisted its cupidinous perversions further by identifying them with his hero's passion for *theatre*, a passion which naturally implicates the audience, as it becomes more and more absorbed in the improvised performances of Mosca and Volpone among their clients and the lawyers. Jonson, as John Creaser says in his definitive modern edition of the play (Hodder and Stoughton, 1978, p. 25), 'manages to walk a knife-edge between moral condemnation and existential pleasure' in his portrayal of Volpone. If this is so, it may be because, in Jonson's variant on the theme of legacy-hunting, the hunger after sexual and material novelty which, in classical versions, is an index of gold's power to corrupt, is partly identified with the illusionistic vitality of theatre itself.

Peter Womack has pointed out that where Shakespeare preserves the mystique of theatre, protecting the audience from a knowledge of the 'inert materiality' of costume and mask, Jonson insists harshly on the extent to which theatre is 'a matter of creaking contrivances, false whiskers, funny voices' ('Theatre', *Rereading Ben Jonson*, p. 112 – see Further Reading below). From this disenchanted viewpoint, theatre – the manufacture of illusion – becomes analogous to gold, as seen from the ironic perspective of Lucianic satire. As gold 'transformes / The most deformed, and restores 'hem lovely, / As 't were the strange poeticall girdle' (V.2.100–2), so theatre, in Volpone's materialistic world, is employed to sustain desire, and prevent it from waning, by offering the illusion of endless transformations of the object. Thus, as critics have often remarked, Volpone's attempted seduction of Celia is curiously caught up in fantasies of its own prolongation and multiplication through role-play and costume change, as Volpone declares he will 'have' Celia 'in more moderne formes, / Attired like some sprightly dame of *France*, / Brave *Tuscan* lady, or proud *Spanish* beauty' (III.7.226–8). And this scene, too, represents a further ironization of an already heavily ironized subtext. Volpone's plot to seduce the Venetian Celia inevitably recalls the successful seduction of the Florentine Lucrezia in Machiavelli's *Mandragola*, itself a cynical rewriting of the political iconography of virtuous republican-ism in Livy's account of the rape of Lucrece and the birth of the Roman state. While Machiavelli's Lucrezia succumbs to the overwhelming corruption of all about her, her adulterous lover is nevertheless integrated into the family, and her pregnancy suggests a rejuvenation of some kind in the civic community at large. In *Volpone*, by contrast (a play replete with *Mandragola*-style metaphors of generation and decay) even Machiavelli's hint of political rejuvenation is denied by the rape scene's being rewritten as a mere pretext for the relentlessly inventive narcissism and materialism of Volpone's private and expensive theatrical fantasies. Read in the context of such antecedent texts, Jonson's most daring innovation – the unprecedently harsh ending of *Volpone* – looks less like the aesthetic violation it has sometimes been said to be, and more like the logical conclusion of the play's Lucianic drive towards the ironic self-exposure of its apparently charismatic subject.

FURTHER READING

Barbour, Richmond, ' "When I acted young Antinous": boy actors and the erotics of Jonsonian theatre', *Publications of the Modern Language Association* 110 (1995), 1006–22

Barton, Anne, 'Sejanus and Volpone', in *Ben Jonson, Dramatist* (Cambridge: Cambridge University Press, 1984), pp. 92–119

Creaser, John, 'Volpone: the mortifying of a fox', *Essays in Criticism* 25 (1975), 329–56

Donaldson, Ian, 'Volpone: quick and dead', *Essays in Criticism* 21 (1971), 121–34

Parker, R. B., 'Volpone in performance, 1921–72', *Renaissance Drama* 9 (1978), 147–73

Womack, Peter, 'Theatre', in *Rereading Ben Jonson* (Oxford: Basil Blackwell, 1986), pp. 108–59

TEXTUAL NOTES

The base text for this edition is the copy of *The Workes of Benjamin Jonson* (the 1616 First Folio) in the Bodleian Library, Oxford (shelfmark: AA 83 Art.). The sheets of F incorporating *Volpone* underwent stringent correction as they went through the press, but uncorrected copies were still issued; this edition consistently follows corrected copy. In the notes which follow, the first readings are those of this edition and the second readings those of the base text. 'Q' represents readings incorporated into the edition from the Quarto of 1607; 'F2' represents readings taken from the Second Folio of 1640. (See also p. 434.)

Epistle

106 irritabile] iritabile

33 into] F2; unto
60 prospect—all] prospect-all
61 know,] Q; ~ ^

Act I. Scene 4

121 e'ene] 'eene

Act II. Scene 6

5 sir.] F2; ~,
61 physician.] ~,

Act I. Scene 5

12 He] '~
93 sir,] F2; ~.

Act III. Scene 2

4 Nay,] F2; ~ ^

Act II. Scene 1

33 sir,] ~ ^
41 and] and and

Act III. Scene 3

5 *Being, all,*] Q; ~ ^   ~ ^

Act II. Scene 2

164 i'th'] i'th

Act III. Scene 7

81 thanke him] ~'~
117 good] ~,
119 thy] thy thy
133–4 whether ^/] ~./
148 rays'd] F2; 'rays'd

Act II. Scene 5

20 to] ~'
30 could'st] coul'dst

Act III. Scene 8

12 I'ld] Il'd

Act III. Scene 9

12 feare,] ~.

Act IV. Scene 1

9 Pardon,] F2; ~ ʌ
17 speake] spake

Act IV. Scene 2

30 oath).] ~) ʌ

Act IV. Scene 4

16 I should] I'should

Act IV. Scene 6

7 3RD AVOCATORE] AVO. 4

Act V. Scene 2

42 sir,] Q; ~.

Act V. Scene 3

57 your] Q, F2; you

Act V. Scene 4

31 satisfaction] satifaction
49 Ha'] F2; ~ ʌ
71 little).] ~) ʌ
72 creep).] ~) ʌ

Act V. Scene 5

Misnumbered Act IV in F

Act V. Scene 6

18 now,] Q, F2; ~ ʌ
25 why,] Q; ~ ʌ

Act V. Scene 7

3 your] Q, F2; you
4 eene] eêne

Act V. Scene 8

13 your shame] Q, F2; you ~
25 me.] ~,

Act V. Scene 10

0.1 COMMANDADORI] Q;
COMMANDADORE
5 VOLTORE] VOLP.

Act V. Scene 12

11 be] F2; ~,
19 were] Q, F2; ~,
30 'twill] t'will
36 were] ~.
38 fits.] ~,
49 gentleman,] F2; ~ ʌ
64 lowd).] ~' ʌ
94 Silence] silence
102 trulyer,] Q; ~ ʌ
105 favor.] ~,
115 VOLPONE] VOLT.

Variants from the early editions

Lexical revision of the 1607 quarto is minimal and the only significant alterations are listed below. The bulk of Jonson's revisions are concerned with a comprehensive reworking of the text's punctuation, particularly the replacement of dashes by semi-colons or colons; F also makes far greater use of full stops to indicate the end of speeches and the completion of a thought within a speech. In addition, most of the marginal stage directions are only found in the Folio text.

Epistle

45 *ingenuously* (Q: ingeniously)
59 *severe* (Q: grave)

Act II. Scene 3

1 Spight (Q: Bloud)

Prologue

1 yet (Q: God)

COMMENTARY

Epistle

30 *abortive features*: Deformed births; bad plays.
38 *my yongest infant*: Possibly *Sejanus* or *Eastward Ho*.
42 *those . . . intirely mine*: The plays for which Jonson was imprisoned or under suspicion (*The Isle of Dogs*, *Sejanus* and *Eastward Ho*) were all collaborations.
49 *Application*: Looking for references to contemporary persons and events.
56–7 *whose living . . . stiles*: Whose living faces are carved by their angry pens.
64 *Sibi . . . odit*: Horace, *Satires*, II.i.23, which Jonson renders in *Poetaster* III.5.41–2 as 'In *satyres* each man (though untouch) complaines/ As he were hurt; and hates such biting straines.' The Latin means '[Satire] makes everyone, though untouched, fearful and hostile'. Jonson's translation is close, except for adding 'biting straines'.
65 *And men . . . sports*: And if anger aroused by a satire continues, men may then justly ascribe it to the licence of the author.
106 *genus irritabile*: Horace, *Epistles*, II.ii.102 calls poets 'an oversensitive species'.

The Persons of the Play

VOLPONE: 'An old fox, an old reinard, an old crafie, slie, subtle companion; sneaking lurking wily deceiver' (John Florio, *A Worlde of Wordes*, 1598). Jonson used Florio's Italian–English dictionary, *A Worlde of Wordes*, and gave Florio a copy of the quarto of *Volpone*, inscribed, 'To his loving father, and worthy friend . . . the aid of his Muses'.

MOSCA: 'Any kinde of flye' (Florio).

VOLTORE: 'A ravenous bird called a vultur' (Florio); Jonson calls lawyers 'gowned Vultures' (*Under-wood*, 33, *H&S*, VIII.187).

CORBACCIO: 'A filthie great raven' (Florio).

CORVINO: 'Of a raven's nature or colour' (Florio); a crow.

AVOCATORI: Judicial institution established, according to Gasparo Contarini, *The Commonwealth and Government of Venice*, tr. Lewis Lewkenor (London, 1599), sig. M3ʳ, 'to defend the lawes pure and inviolate'.

NOTARIO, the Register: Notary or clerk of court.

NANO: 'A dwarf or dandiprat' (i.e. tiny, insignificant man) (Florio).

GREGE: 'A troop or multitude' (Florio).

POLITIQUE WOULD-BEE: See Epistle, l. 39 '*supercilious politiques*', and Jonson's Epigram 92 (*H&S*, VIII.58).

PEREGRINE: *peregrinus* (Latin); foreign, a traveller.

BONARIO: 'Debonaire, honest, good, uncorrupt' (Florio).

MADAME WOULD-BEE: See Jonson's Epigram 62 (*H&S*, VIII.46).

CELIA: 'Heavenly, celestiall' (Florio).

Prologue

12 *a yeere about them*: Playwrights employed by professional companies collaborated on or wrote about a play a month.

21 *Nor . . . affrighted*: Alluding to the jester's leap into a giant custard in Lord Mayor's entertainments, and to the 'fierce teeth' of satire; see John Marston, *The Scourge of Villanie* (1598), sig. B8v.

31 *The lawes . . . observeth*: Glossing Aristotle and Horace, Italian Renaissance critics ruled plays should consist of a single action, taking place within a single day and location, and featuring consistent and appropriate characters.

Act I. Scene 1

3 *the worlds soule*: *Anima mundi*; in Neo-platonism, the love which animates the world.

10 *sonne of SOL*: In alchemy, gold is the offspring of the sun.

15 *that age . . . best*: The Golden Age; see note on ll.33–40.

24 *price of soules*: Blasphemous; the 'price' of Christian souls (1 Corinthians 6:20) is Jesus Christ.

24–7 *hell . . . wise*: Reversal of Christian and Stoic teaching; the Gospel (Mark 10:24) teaches the unattainability of heaven to those who trust riches, while Seneca, *Epistle*, cxv attacks the synonymity of gold and goodness.

33–40 *I use . . . usure private*: Volpone here claims that his perverse method of gain revives the classical Golden Age, in which there was no agriculture or commerce, and the Earth – 'unwounded' by the plough – poured forth her natural riches on innocent mankind. See Ovid, *Metamorphoses*, I.89–112.

37 *subtill glasse*: Venice was famed for intricate glass-blowing.

39 *I turne . . . banke*: Earliest recorded use of 'turn' for 'circulate money'; 'bank' meant 'money-changer's'.

Act I. Scene 2

6—59 *the Soule . . .* PYTHAGORAS: Based on *The Dream, or the Cock* by Lucian, a fantastic satire in which a cobbler, dreaming of riches, is wakened by a talking cockerel, who claims to possess the soul of Pythagoras by transmigration; he persuades the cobbler of the vexations of wealth.

8—13 APOLLO . . . *of Sparta*: Diogenes Laertes, *Lives of the Philosophers*, says Pythagoras' soul reached Euphorbus by way of Aethalides, son of Mercury. In Lucian 'goldy-lockt' Euphorbus is part of the satire against gold, while the '*Cuckold* of Sparta' is Menelaus, Helen's husband.

17 *Sophist of Greece*: Pythagoras.

26—8 *one, two . . . elements shift*: Pythagoras discovered the numerical basis of musical intervals, though the number Pythagoreans venerate and swear by is in fact *ten*, not four ('quater') as Jonson suggests. Pythagorus developed a theorem of the right-angled triangle ('*his* trigon'), and was reputed to have a golden thigh.

31—46 *Like . . . nativitie-pie*: Satirizing religious change through the variety of religious dietary practices: early attacks on the Catholic church targeted the Carthusians' strict observation of fish-eating in Lent; Pythagoras himself ruled against the eating of beans; the Puritan is carnivorous, but fastidious about names, and avoids an allusion to 'mass' by referring to 'Christmas' as 'nativitie'.

66—81 *Fooles . . . hee*: Cynical summary of Renaissance commonplaces on the virtues of folly, deriving especially from Erasmus' *Praise of Folly*.

87—8 *clients . . . visitation*: Referring to the Roman *salutatio*, the morning visit of clients to their patron, especially as satirized by Lucian in the nineteenth of the *Dialogues of the Dead*, where Polystratus, old, childless and rich, explains how clients flocked daily to him, bringing gifts.

94—6 *a foxe . . . crow*: Foxes were said to feign death to tempt the approach of carrion birds, such as the crow and the raven; see also Horace on legacy-hunters, *Satires*, II.v.55—7.

111 *reverend purple*: Worn by doctors of divinity.

Act I. Scene 3

35 *write . . . family*: 'Family' here means 'household'; servants' names were entered in household books.

58—9 *provoking . . . put it up*: Suggesting the lawyer humbly 'puts up' with provocation, but meaning that he pockets gold from both parties.

Act I. Scene 4

2 *Stand there, and multiply*: Blasphemous echo of Genesis 1:22: 'Be fruitful, and multiply'.

73 *aurum . . . potabile*: Varying *aurum potabile*, 'drinkable gold', a medicinal preparation of gold, to *aurum palpabile*, 'touchable gold', i.e. 'money'.

128 *gull . . . blessing*: Alluding to Jacob's cheating of Esau of their father's blessing, Genesis 27.

Act I. Scene 5

39 *blind harper*: Harpers were proverbially blind.

47–8 *Dwarfe . . . family*: He's their real father, not just the head of the household.

108–9 *a wench . . . yeere*: An unblemished yearling, an animal fit for sacrifice; cf. Leviticus 9:3.

Act II. Scene 1

10 *knowing . . . ULYSSES*: Alluding to *Odyssey* I.3, here 'stale' (l. 9) because much cited by travel writers; but Jonson's point is that, however often quoted, the project of 'knowing . . . minds' cannot 'stale', unlike the trivially fashionable project of following one's wife's 'humour'.

14 *with licence*: All except established merchants had to obtain special passports for travel.

17 *my lord Ambassador*: Sir Henry Wotton was at Venice from 1604 to 1612; Jonson appears to have admired Wotton's poetry: see *H&S*, I.135, 157.

22–3 *a raven . . . Kings*: Birds nesting in buildings or ships were read as omens; cf. the swallows in Cleopatra's sails (*Antony and Cleopatra*, IV.12.3).

30–1 *spider . . . flowre*: Proverbial that the bee sucks honey where the spider gathers poison; an infelicitous application.

34 *lyons . . . Tower*: Stow, *Annales* (1615), p. 844, records two whelps born in the Tower in 1604; both died.

36 *fires at Berwike*: An apparition of fighting men and fire was witnessed near Berwick in the New Year of 1604–5.

40–1 *porcpisces . . . sturgeon*: Stow, *Annales*, p. 880, records the sighting of a porpoise and a whale (see next note) near London in January 1606. Peregrine exaggerates, adding a sturgeon for good measure.

46–50 *a whale . . . Arch-dukes*: Whales were said to portend tempests (see also preceding note); 'Stode' or 'Stade' was a port near Hanover used by the English Merchant Adventurers. Sir Politique imagines the whale is a Catholic secret weapon against Dutch Protestant commerce.

51 *SPINOLA's whale*: Ambrogio Spinola (1569–1630), general-in-chief to the Catholic forces in the Netherlands from 1602.

53 *STONE, the foole*: Popular London fool, whipped in 1605 for licentious speech.

70–73 *cabages . . . pome-citrons:* Luxury produce; cabbages were imported from Holland.

88–91 *Bab'ouns . . . French plot:* Baboons were among the sights to be seen in London in 1603–5; the Mamelukes were the ruling class in Egypt (Sir Politique's geopolitical knowledge is patchy).

113 *that vulgar grammar:* A non-Latin grammar book; possibly John Florio's *Second Fruits* (1591).

Act II. Scene 2

2 *to mount a banke:* The Piazza San Marco in Venice was famous for 'mountebanks'; derived from the Italian *monta in banco,* 'mount on a bench'.

22 *SCOTO of Mantua:* Leader of Duke of Mantua's acting troupe who appeared before Elizabeth in 1576; famous for sleight-of-hand.

39–40 *Lombard . . . feet:* Contemporary Italian proverb, meaning 'forced by poverty (shoelessness) to sell cheap'.

42–4 *ALESSANDRO BUTTONE . . . BEMBO'S:* 'Buttone' means 'button', so the name is probably a joke; 'a 'Sforzato' means 'perforce'; the dash after 'Bembo's' indicates a bawdy innuendo comically at odds with the Florentine humanist Pietro Bembo's reputation as theorist of Platonic love.

48 *TABARINE:* Common name (meaning 'short cloak') for charlatan, or Italian travelling comedian.

80–85 *For . . . causes:* Contemporary medicine assumed man was composed of four *humours* or fluids (blood, phlegm, bile and black bile) corresponding to forms of temperament (sanguine, phlegmatic, choleric and melancholic) and associated with the elements (air, water, fire and earth). Illnesses were caused by imbalances in the humours; gold was said to blend the elements in harmony.

92 *retyred-nerves:* Shrunken sinews.

93 *hernia . . . passio:* Rupture; colic.

99 *ZAN FRITADA:* 'Zan' is Venetian dialect for 'Giovanni' or 'John'; 'frittata' is 'pancake'.

154–5 *Cardinals . . . Tuscany:* Names to conjure with: Cardinal di Montalto became Pope Sixtus V, Pope Paul III had been Cardinal Farnese and Cosimo di Medici was made 'Grand Duke of Tuscany'.

Act II. Scene 3

3–4 *FLAMINIO . . . FRANCISCINA:* Standard names for lover and serving maid in *commedia dell'arte.*

8 *PANTALONE di besogniosi:* 'Pantaloon of the beggars', old jealous dotard of the *commedia dell'arte.*

Act II. Scene 5

12 *saffron . . . toade-stone*: 'Saffron' was glazed tinfoil; stones thought to come from the heads of toads were worn as antidotes to poison.

58–61 *keepe thee . . . backe-wards*: Lewd, alluding to the supposed Italian preference for anal sex.

Act II. Scene 6

61 *signior LUPO*: 'Mr Wolf ', also ulcerous skin disease.

85 *directly . . . possession*: In legal transfers of estates, 'taking possession' might require armed entry, but not in this case.

Act III. Scene 1

21 *legs, and faces*: Bowing and smirking.

22 *lick . . . moath*: Flatterers were typically presented as picking threads and specks from the beards and clothes of their patrons.

Act III. Scene 2

65 *common . . . earth*: *terrae filius* (Latin), son of earth, i.e. of no one in particular.

Act III. Scene 4

0 *Scene 4*: This scene draws on *The Morose Man and his Talkative Wife* by Libanius (314–93), in which a man who hates noise pleads to a court of law to be allowed to die rather than listen to his wife's irrelevant chatter.

47 *golden mediocritie*: Aristotle's golden mean (hard to dream about).

51–4 *Alas . . . mirobalanes*: Diagnosing heart-burn; seed-pearl was supposed to be a cordial, 'citron-pills' or lemon rind good for digestion and elecampane against convulsions. Mirobalane was an Eastern plant, prescribed, according to Robert Burton, *Anatomy of Melancholy* (1632), p. 383, against melancholy.

59–61 *english saffron . . . barley-meale*: Saffron was grown in Saffron-Walden; the other remedies were anti-depressants, except barley-meal, used as a poultice.

76–8 *The Poet . . . silence*: Sophocles, *Ajax* 293; also cited by Aristotle, *Politics*, I.1260a20. See also *Epicoene*, II.3.106 and note.

79–81 *Which . . . all*: Medieval and Renaissance poets, examples of polite learning; the joke here derives from Libanius (see note on 0 above).

86–90 *PASTOR FIDO . . . MONTAGNIE*: Lady Would-bee mentions Guarini's pastoral 'The Faithful Shepherd' (*Il Pastor Fido* (1589)) and the essays of Montaigne as the latest in literary style. Montaigne's *Essays* (1588) had just been translated by John Florio into English (1603).

107 *Settling . . . subsiding:* Chemical terms for the separating, congealing and sedimenting of liquids.

Act III. Scene 5

36–8 *wanton . . . encounter:* Primero was a fashionable gambling card-game; 'goe lesse' is to wager less, 'lie' to place a wager, 'draw' to take another card from the pack and 'encounter' to pick a winner.

Act III. Scene 7

78–9 *beauty . . . price:* The only beauty worth mentioning.

152–3 *varying . . . Floud:* Proteus was a sea-god who could vary his shape; the epithet 'horned' for water recalls the river-god Achelous' ox-head.

159–64 *celebrated . . . footing:* In 1574 Venice entertained Henry of Valois, later Henry III of France, well known for his sexual preference for young men. Antinous was the boy-favourite of the emperor Hadrian.

166–83 *Come . . . beene:* An adaptation of the fifth song of Catullus, 'Vivamus, mea Lesbia' ('Let us live, my Lesbia'), reprinted by Jonson in *The Forest* (*H&S*, VIII.102–3). See also ll. 236–9 and note.

191–2 *See . . . carrous'd:* Pliny tells how Cleopatra dissolved a pearl in vinegar and drank it at a banquet.

215 *milke . . . breath:* Panthers were thought to have sweet breath; believers in the unicorn thought it exceptionally rare.

229–30 *Persian . . . grand-Signiors:* Shah of Persia and Sultan of Turkey respectively.

236–9 *That . . . pind:* See note on ll.166–83. Catullus' fifth song concludes with a plea for thousands of kisses, so many that no ill-wisher could count them, and blight the lovers. Jonson appends this quatrain to a second song, 'To Celia', in *The Forest*.

Act III. Scene 8

14–15 *Let's die . . . Grecians:* To die like a Roman was to commit suicide, while a 'Grecian' life style combined wit and voluptuousness; cf. the parasite 'Mathewe Merygreke' in Nicholas Udall's *Ralph Roister Doister* (published 1567).

Act IV. Scene 1

8–10 *I will . . . theames:* In his desire to avoid 'old' (hackneyed) topics, Sir Politique inadvertently suggests that Peregrine's clothes have seen better days.

50–2 *serve . . . Roterdam:* Comic variation on phenomenon of the economic project encouraged in the sixteenth century to improve English manufacture and commerce, but later subject, along with economic monopolies, to abuse. 'Red herrings' (see note on *Every Man in his Humour*, I.4.8 – 14) recall Nashe's *Lenten Stuffe*, and aptly characterize Sir Politique's 'intelligence'.

74 – 5 *great councell . . . ten*: Two thousand Venetian patricians sat on the 'Great Council', from which were drawn the Councils of Forty and the Council of Ten, the last consisting of the Doge and senior advisers.

91 *arsenale*: Headquarters of the Venetian defence navy, where a major outbreak of fire occurred in 1569.

110 *onions*: Peeled onions were supposed to attract plague infection.

135 – 45 *notandum . . . politique notes*: Humanist statesmen encouraged travellers to observe political institutions and military fortifications, but Sir Politique's notes liken him to the figure described in *The Superstitious Man* by Theophrastus (371 – 287 BC). The phrase *Ragion di stato*, 'reason of state', introduced in the 1520s by Guicciardini, became a key term in the political vocabulary of Europe.

Act IV. Scene 2

35 *as the courtier sayes*: Alluding to the ideal gentlewoman in Castiglione's *Book of the Courtier* (1528), Bk. III.

51 *white-Friers nation*: South of Fleet Street and east of the Temple, formerly a sanctuary, and so a haunt of beggars and prostitutes.

59 – 63 *you . . . disc'ple*: Your grave demeanour may absolve you, but I'll punish your sexual partner, who has evidently escaped from English laws to enjoy Catholic Venetian liberty. 'Carnival' for 'carnal' is appropriate for Venice, famous for carnivals.

Act IV. Scene 3

17 – 21 *'Pray you . . . with his wife*: Lady Would-bee's friendly overtures sound like a sexual invitation; Peregrine puns lewdly on 'quaint', then a common version of 'cunt'.

Act IV. Scene 4

21 – 2 MERCURY *. . . French* HERCULES: Mercury was the god of eloquence, thieves and merchants; the 'French Hercules' was depicted leading men by chains of gold from his tongue, a common Renaissance icon of eloquence.

Act IV. Scene 6

2 – 3 *chameleon . . . hyaena*: The chameleon could change colour; the hyena was said to be able to change the colour of its eyes, and to counterfeit the voice of men, but not to cry.

13 *pertinacy*: I.e. 'obstinacy'.

Act V. Scene 2

50 *Draw . . . aggravate*: Arrange the evidence under headings, then bring in charges.

90—1 *he . . . hog-louse*: He will curl up like a wood-louse.

93 *rope . . . dagger*: Signs of suicidal despair.

98—102 *Why . . . poeticall girdle*: Lucian's *The Dream* likened gold to the girdle (*cestus*) of Venus described in the *Iliad*, XIV.214ff., which made the wearer irresistible.

Act V. Scene 4

4—5 *Zant . . . voyages*: The island of Zante in Greece and the city of Aleppo in Syria were centres of Venice's oriental trade; collections of exploring and mercantile voyages, such as Hakluyt's *Principle Navigations, Voyages, Traffics and Discoveries of the English Nation* (1598—1600), were in vogue.

54—60 *tortoyse-shell . . . device*: The tortoise emblematized the virtues of staying at home, apt advice for Sir Politique.

77—8 *'Twere . . . faire*: Puppet shows, held in Fleet-Street and in Smithfield, during Bartholomew Fair.

Act V. Scene 8

11—14 *fine bird . . . emptinesse*: Alluding to Aesop's fable in which the fox flatters the crow into song, causing it to drop the cheese held in its beak.

15 *priviledge of the place*: Immunity of the Scrutineo, near ducal palace.

Act V. Scene 12

9—10 *nay . . . both*: In possession, the evil spirit entered the body; in obsession, it worked on the body from outside.

120 *hospitall, of the Incurabili*: Founded in 1522 to house diseased beggars and prostitutes.

125 *mortifying of a FOXE*: Pun on 'mortifying' as killing and as religious chastisement ('mortifying the flesh').

Epicoene

Unlike the other plays in this volume, Jonson's *Epicoene, or the Silent Woman* appears not to have been printed in a separate quarto edition before being published as part of William Stansby's 1616 Folio *Workes* (F). While entries exist in the Stationers' Register for the right to publish 'A booke called, Epicoene or the silent woman by Ben: Johnson' in the years 1610 and 1612 (see *H&S*, V.141), no such publication has been found. The present text is necessarily, therefore, based on F, signatures Xx5v–Ddd6r.

Both the title-page of F, and Jonson's note at the end of the text, give 1609 as the date of the play's first performance, 'By the Children of her Maiesties REVELLS' (*H&S*, V.153). The theatre was the Whitefriars, as specified in the Prologue (l. 24), and the time likely to have been not long after 9 December, when the theatres opened again after being closed for eighteen months because of plague; at I.1.170, Clerimont refers to the 'perpetuitie of ringing' in London, 'now, by reason of the sicknesse'. However, Jonson's reference to the 'Children of her Majesty's Revels' may indicate that the first performance actually took place in 1610, because the Children of the Chapel Royal who acted the play were not permitted to call themselves the Children of the Queen's Revels before confirmation of their patent of 4 January 1610 (*H&S*, IX.208). Whether performed in December 1609 or January 1610, however, *Epicoene* was clearly Jonson's first play since *Volpone*, and was written shortly after *The Key Keeper*, his masque to celebrate the opening of the New Exchange on 11 April 1609.

By February 1610, *Epicoene* had, it seems, been banned by the authorities. In dedicating the play to Sir Francis Stuart, Jonson refers to an 'un-certaine accusation' motivated by the 'certaine hatred of some' that brought his 'innocency' into danger (ll. 14–15). In the play's second prologue he objects that people tend to 'make a libell, which he made a play' (l. 14). The passage that appears to have caused the trouble occurs at V.1.19–22, when La-Foole describes Sir John Daw as drawing maps of places and persons:

> CLERIMONT How, maps of persons!
> LA-FOOLE Yes, sir, of NOMENTACK, when he was here, and of the Prince of
>   *Moldavia*, and of his mistris, mistris EPICOENE.
> CLERIMONT Away! he has not found out her latitude, I hope.

Although the apposition of 'mistris EPICOENE' to the words 'his mistris' makes it probable that it is Daw's mistress that is being referred to, the syntax permits a less innocuous reading, the topicality of which could hardly have been ignored in 1609/10. Jonson's Prince of Moldavia would have been recognized as one Stephano Janiculo, an imposter who came to England in 1601 to beg for help from Queen Elizabeth, and returned, asking for more assistance, in 1607. King James gave him financial support, after which Janiculo went around saying that he was going to marry Arbella Stuart, James's cousin. As a claimant to the throne, Arbella Stuart suffered from being under constant suspicion of contracting such dangerous liaisons, though she appears not to have encouraged Janiculo. On 8 February 1610 the Venetian Ambassador reported that

> Lady Arbella is seldom seen outside her rooms and lives in greater dejection than ever. She complains that in a certain comedy the play-wright introduced an allusion to her person and the part played by the Prince of Moldavia. The play was suppressed. Her Excellency is very ill-pleased and shows a determination

in this coming Parliament to secure the punishment of certain persons, we don't
know who.   (*H&S*, V.146)

While Jonson protested his innocence of defamatory intention, it is not easy to
understand why he should have felt it necessary to include so contentious a possible
reference to the 'mistress' of the Prince of Moldavia at all. Some critics, however,
have proposed that the allusion to Janiculo fits in with the play's more general concern
with the theme of transvestism and gender ambiguity, since Janiculo had, in 1606,
made a famous escape from a prison in Constantinople, disguised as a woman (*H&S*,
V.144).

Jonson's *Epicoene* is a play which curiously anticipates contemporary conceptions
of the way in which language and social practice are constitutive of the so-called
'natural' differences between the sexes. Jonson was the first person in English to use
the word 'epicoene' (a Greek adjective used of nouns that have one form for either
gender) in a sexual as opposed to purely grammatical sense. In blending a Greek
declamation against the loquacity of women spoken by an absurdly anti-social man
(called, in the Latin translation Jonson used, 'Morosus'[1]) with a sadistic Italian farce
about the torments suffered by a homosexual stable master on learning that he must
take a wife, Jonson has contrived a play revolving around implied norms of masculine
and feminine linguistic and sexual behaviour. Yet these sexual and linguistic norms,
in spite of being constantly invoked by the energetically satirical dramatic dialogue,
are nevertheless ostentatiously transgressed by all of the characters. It would be
misleading, however, to give the impression that the play is some kind of free-floating
celebration of gender indeterminacy. Jonson was affected by a classical rhetorical and
ethical tradition which linked virility to an eloquence that was neither loquaciously
redundant nor ineffectually at a loss for words. According to this tradition, an
inadequate style was characterized as 'womanish' in the terms used to describe the
pathic or 'passive' man who had immoderate sexual relations with other men.[2] Such
an ideal homology of manly eloquence and manly social and sexual conduct is
represented, in *Epicoene*, as being under assault by the relentlessly 'effeminizing' effects
of an emergent consumer culture in which the older forms of economic and social
interdependence (such as the reciprocally beneficial relationship that Sir Amorous
should have had with his tenants, or the socially generative alliance that Morose's
marriage should have been) are giving way to newer, more commercialized forms
which are at once more aggressive and more sycophantic. Thus, whether men are,
like Morose and Dauphine, reluctant to engage in the redundancies of conversational
exchange or, like Sir Amorous and Sir John Daw, lavishly indiscriminate in their
linguistic engagements, they are alike represented as responding to the grotesquely
feminized phenomenon of West London's emergent leisure economy, in which all

---

[1] *Libanii Sophistae Clariss. Declamatio Lepedissima de moroso qui cum uxorem loquacem duxisset, seipsum accusat*, ed. Federigo Morello (Paris, 1597).

[2] See Patricia Parker, 'Virile Style', in *Premodern Sexualities*, ed. by Louise Fradenburg and Carla Freccero (London: Routledge, 1996), pp. 201–22.

relations are relentlessly commercialized. 'How much plate have you lost to day', Lady Haughty berates Morose on learning he intended to keep his wedding secret from his women friends, 'what guifts, what friends, through your meere rusticitie?' (III.6.77–9), while Sir Amorous's indiscriminate sociability towards these same ladies of fashion tends to reduce him to the ingratiating seeker of favour that Lady Haughty would like Morose to have been: Sir Amorous attends his guests at the wedding feast '*like a sewer*' (a waiter), with a towel round his waist (III.3.89). Jonson's representation of sexual and linguistic deviants is inseparable, in this unforgettable farce, from his prophetic adumbration of what was to become the stock setting of Restoration comedy: London's leisured West End.

FURTHER READING

Brown, Steve, 'The boyhood of Shakespeare's heroines: notes on gender ambiguity in the sixteenth century', *Studies in English Literature* 30 (1990), 243–59.

Campbell, Oscar J., 'The relation of *Epicoene* to Aretino's *Il Marescalco*', *Publications of the Modern Language Association* 46 (1931), 752–62

Jones, Emrys, 'The first West End comedy', *Proceedings of the British Academy* 68 (1982), 215–58

Newman, Karen, 'City talk: women and commodification. *Epicoene* 1609', *Journal of English Literary History* 57 (1989), 503–18

Salingar, Leo, 'Farce and fashion in the Silent Woman', *Essays and Studies* (1967), 29–46

TEXTUAL NOTES

The base text for this edition is the copy of *The Workes of Benjamin Jonson* (the 1616 First Folio) in the Bodleian Library, Oxford (shelfmark: AA 83 Art.). In the notes which follow, the first readings are those of this edition and the second readings those of the base text. 'Q' represents readings incorporated into the edition from the Quarto of 1620; F2 represents readings taken from the Second Folio of 1640. The Folio (F) text underwent 'correction' as it was being printed; unless otherwise stated this edition follows the corrected copy, but occasionally the corrections were misguided, and uncorrected readings have been retained; in the notes, C represents the 'corrected' copies, and U the uncorrected. (See also p. 434.)

The Persons of the Play

1 no] U; *omitted in* C
12 *Collegiates*] U; *Collegiate in* C
14 MRS. TRUSTY] U; Mʳˢ. MAVIS *in* C
14–15 F *has a vertical line against the names of Mrs. Trusty and Mrs. Otter, and the*

bracketed 'Pretenders' is opposite the latter's name only.

Act I. Scene 1

94 They] U; *Thy in* C
147 upon] Q; up on

Act II. Scene 2

50 sir).] ~) ∧

Act II. Scene 3

11 'Pray,] Q; 'Pray'
24 is't] Is't
28 pray ∧] F2; ~'
52 common-place fellow] F2;
   common place-fellow
76 lawier] Q; lawer
98 JOHN?] ~.
109 DAW] MS *corrected* F; DAV.
109 *is't*] F2; *i'st*
121 procreation] proceation
123 you'll] MS *corrected* F; you you'll

Act II. Scene 5

1 your] Q; you
55 else.] ~ ∧
71 ladie?] ~.
79 wouldst] woulst

Act II. Scene 6

19 now;] F2; ~ ∧

Act III. Scene 1

37 ha' 'hem] ha'hem

Act III. Scene 3

1 Why,] ~ ∧
17 DAW] MS *corrected* F; DAVP.
30 main] man

Act III. Scene 5

9 owle;] F2; ~ ∧
24 *notum?*] F2; ~.

34 visitation?] F2; ~.
39 reverend] MS *corrected* F;
   reveverend

Act III. Scene 6

49 wee'll] weell

Act III. Scene 7

28 MAVIS?] F2; ~.

Act IV. Scene 1

82 al waies] alwaies

Act IV. Scene 5

87 But] F2; And
112 (*marginal direction*) come] came
176 pot?] ~.
201 most?] ~.
216 to 'hem] to ∧ hem
225 sir?] ~.
233 sir?] F2; ~.
261 you, you] F3; you ∧
265 by—] ~,
279 is't?] F2; ~.
298 Good ∧] Q; ~,

Act V. Scene 1

9 -inke?] ~.

Act V. Scene 3

3 themselves,] F2; ~ ∧
179 say,] Q; ~.
183 *In*] In
188 cannot] C; can not

Act V. Scene 4

167 presently,] F2; ~?

Variants from the early editions

Unlike the other texts in this volume the First Folio text of *Epicoene* is not a revision of any known earlier text. The quarto edition of 1620 is not only later but it is also rather carelessly printed; it shows no signs of Jonson's involvement in its preparation, and thus has no textual authority. Perhaps of most interest is the copy of the First Folio in the Folger Shakespeare Library (shelfmark: V. a. 162), which contains manuscript alterations in an early seventeenth-century hand. The way in which the annotator rewrote the song in the opening scene can be examined in the notes which follow.

Act I. Scene 1

34 spend (F2: speak)
87 *causes* (MS Folger: secrets)
88 *sweet* (MS Folger: well)
89 *looke* (MS Folger: form)
91 *flowing* (MS Folger: hanging)
92 *Such sweet neglect more taketh me* (MS Folger: Those sweet neglects more please me)
94 *They strike ... my heart* (MS Folger: Those eyes delight, but these the heart)

Act I. Scene 4

72 mistris (F2: master)

Act II. Scene 3

109 DAW (Q: *Daup.*)

Act IV. Scene 4

167 TRUE-WIT (Q: *Cle.*)

Act IV. Scene 5

117 DAUPHINE (Q: *Daw.*)

COMMENTARY

Dedication

4 *Sir Francis Stuart*: Second son of James Stuart; husband of Elizabeth, Countess of Moray; made a Knight of the Bath on 2 June 1614.
6 *dumbe peece*: Pun on silent or suppressed play (see p. 473) and silent woman ('peece' being sexual slang for 'woman').
13–14 *There ... first Copy*: See p. 477.

The Persons of the Play

MOROSE: From Libanius, *The Morose Man* (see *Volpone,* note on III.4.0 and Headnote); Jonson used an edition of 1597, with a Latin translation of the Greek, which refers to the husband as '*morosus*' (Morose).

DAUP. EUGENIE: 'Dauphin' is the French Royal heir, and 'Eugene' is Greek (εὐγενής) meaning, 'of noble race'.

EPICOENE: From Greek, ἐπίκοινος, 'common to many', used of nouns which have one form to denote either gender. Hence Jonson's use, meaning: 'having the characteristics of both genders'. See *Under-wood*, 49 (*H&S*, VIII.222).

JOH. DAW: Suggesting 'jackdaw', a bird known as a chatterbox and a thief.

THOM: OTTER: Otters are amphibious (see I.4.24), hence transgressive of the usual classificatory boundaries between mammal and fish.

MAD. CENTAURE: Centaurs, half-man, half-horse, represented wild, animal sexuality; female centaurs do not exist in classical mythology.

Ladies Collegiates: See below, I.1.68–75 and note.

MRS. MAVIS: 'Song-thrush'; also 'Maviso, for Malviso, and an ill face' (John Florio, *A Worlde of Wordes*, 1598).

Prologue

2 *to content the people*: Cf. Terence, *Andria*, Prologue.

21–2 *far fet . . . ladies*: Proverbial, 'dear bought and far-fetched is good for ladies'.

24 *men . . . white-Friars*: Both the audience of the Whitefriars theatre, where *Epicoene* was performed, and prostitutes; see *Volpone*, note to IV.2.51.

Another [Prologue]

0 *Occasion'd . . . exception*: See pp. 473–4.

2 *profit, and delight*: Horace, *Art of Poetry*, 343–4; frequently cited by Jonson.

9–10 *Poet . . . fain'd*: Horace, *Art of Poetry*, 338.

Act I. Scene 1

6–8 *dangerous . . . argument of it*: Being named a poet is dangerous because personal references (intended or not) are easily construed in one's writings.

8–10 *welcom'st thing . . . above a man*: A sexual pun; 'under a man', i.e. 'passive' partner in sodomy, 'above a man', i.e. sexually preferred over men.

57 *PLUTARCHS moralls*: Plutarch's moral essays on such topics as marriage, anger, education, modesty, etc., were greatly influential in the sixteenth century. Philemon Holland's complete translation appeared in 1603.

60 *rushes*: Proverbially trifling, i.e. 'Not worth a rush' (see also Glossary).

68 – 75 *A new foundation . . . probationer*: Possibly a reference to a contemporary society, but no record of it exists.

72 *Wits, and Braveries*: Trend-setters in speech and clothes; cf. *Under-wood*, 42, 33 – 6 (*H&S*, VIII.200).

83 – 94 *Still to be . . . heart*: Modelled on an anonymous Latin poem, first published by Joseph Justus Scaliger in *Publii Virgilii Maronis Appendix* (Lyons, 1572), p. 208.

97 – 100 *nor, is there . . . discover it often*: From Ovid, *Art of Love*, III.135 – 40.

105 – 16 *Many things . . . finish'd*: From Ovid, *Art of Love*, III.217 – 18, 225 – 34.

112 – 14 *How . . . burnish'd*: Aldgate was demolished in 1606; the new gate, completed in 1609, was adorned with two female statues representing 'Peace' and 'Charity'.

119 – 22 *I once . . . wrong way*: From Ovid, *Art of Love*, III.243 – 6.

132 *Sicke o' the uncle*: Adapting 'sick of the mother' (hysteria).

133 *turbant of night-caps*: Nightcaps were exclusively worn by men; 'turbant' was the usual spelling until the nineteenth century.

138 – 46 *they say . . . Armorer*: Libanius, *Morose Man*, 8: 'I take to my heels to get away from all the workshops that have hammers and anvils and noise.' Jonson's adaptation draws on the cries of London, preserved in popular rhymes and ballads.

142 *Broome-men . . . stiffely*: Playing on 'to stand out', meaning to defy, and the bristles of the broom.

146 – 7 *Pewterers . . . riot*: Apprentices traditionally rioted on Shrove Tuesday.

150 *Waights of the citie*: Official city musicians.

164 – 5 *Fencer . . . drum*: Fencers were drummed through the streets before a prize-fight.

169 – 70 *now . . . sicknesse*: Plague was virulent in 1609.

Act I. Scene 2

9 – 10 *acts, and moniments*: Play on John Foxe's *History of the Acts and Monuments of the Church*, popularly known as the *Book of Martyrs*, first published in English, 1563.

14 – 15 *coronation . . . ordinance*: Guns fired a salute on 24 March, the anniversary of James I's coronation.

34 – 5 *A woman . . . noise*: Barbers were proverbially talkative (compare hairdressers nowadays); women are still so considered.

Act I. Scene 3

13 – 14 *decameron . . . like*: Giovanni Boccaccio's *Decameron* (1358), a byword for ribaldry.

35 – 6 *China . . . Exchange*: The Earl of Salisbury's shopping centre, the New Exchange, was opened on 11 April 1609, containing milliners, haberdashers, booksellers and china houses.

Act I. Scene 4

12 *dispence with me*: Excuse me (pretentious).

16 *terrible boyes*: Thugs, usually called 'roarers' or 'roaring boys'.

38–9 *Or . . . Gules*: Yellow and red in heraldry.

54–61 *knighted . . . pleasure*: Amorous benefited from the Earl of Essex's notorious inflation of knighthoods in Ireland in 1599; Essex's expeditions to Cadiz ('*Caliz*') in 1596 and the Azores in 1597 were characterized by a consciousness of rank and fashion; Nashe (*Lenten Stuffe*, III.147) speaks of 'Bravamente seignors, with *Cales* beards as broade as scullers maples'. In surveying his lands, Amorous follows new and controversial practices of landlordly efficiency, so that he can afford to join the increasing numbers of gentry engaging in conspicuous consumption in London.

60–64 *take up . . . commoditie*: 'Taking up commodities' meant contracting interest-bearing loans which were paid in goods, rather than money (see also II.5.105–6); Dauphine deliberately misunderstands Amorous to mean contracting sex.

Act II. Scene 1

25–30 *The Turke . . . with silence*: The Ottoman Empire was renowned throughout Christendom for military discipline and for observing silence at courtly ceremonies; Morose improbably conflates the two.

Act II. Scene 2

2–3 *Pythagoreans*: Pythagoras' religious order imposed silence on novitiates; see *Poetaster* IV.3.132 (*H&S*, IV.270).

19 *low fall*: ebb-tide.

26–7 *flie . . . arse*: Obscure; editors offer unsubstantiated explanations.

30 *mad-folkes*: Inmates of the asylum Bedlam were a tourist attraction.

31–5 *if you had . . . one eye*: Adapted from Juvenal, *Satires*, VI.1ff.

50–53 *If, after . . . weapon*: Adapted from Juvenal, *Satires*, VI.60–94; the French tightrope walker was seen by Queen Elizabeth in 1600.

68 *silenc'd brethren*: Puritan clergymen who refused to conform, and so lost their licences to preach.

78–98 *Then, if . . . states-woman*: Juvenal, *Satires*, VI.206–10, 352–4, 366–7, 402–3.

99 *Salisbury . . . Bath*: Fashionable resorts for racing and for medicinal bathing, respectively.

101–2 *DANIEL . . . youth*: Juvenal, *Satires*, VI.434–7. Contemporaries compared Daniel and Spenser; 'tother youth' is probably a joke about Jonson's age.

108–10 *her going . . . love her*: Juvenal, *Satires*, VI.565–8.

Act II. Scene 3

52–41 *ARISTOTLE . . . entire knot*: 'Commonplace' or 'locus communis' was a term in logic designating where arguments might be found (appropriate for Aristotle); Plato wrote more discursively, in dialogues. Livy, however, was praised for the liveliness of his descriptions, while Tacitus was praised for aphoristic concision.

56–8 *HOMER . . . know not what*: Horses and oxen figure prominently in Homer's *Iliad* and Virgil's *Georgics* discuss farming. Daw is at a loss to describe Horace, a favourite poet of Jonson's.

60–63 *PINDARUS . . . FLACCUS*: A catalogue of major, minor and obscure classical poets, with an Italian humanist, Politian (Angelo Poliziano), thrown in.

71 *Syntagma . . . canonici*: Titles Daw has seen. 'Syntagma' is Greek for 'Corpus', so the books are complete collections of civil and of canon law.

95 *every man . . . not a Poet*: Usually meant the other way around: not every versifier qualifies as a poet.

101 *SIDNEY lives by his*: Refutation, by a pun, of Daw's assumption that to profess oneself a poet, and to publish, is to be a hack; Sidney, though not a professional poet in his lifetime, 'lives' by his writings, which had been published in the 1590s, after his untimely death in 1586.

106 *Silence . . . in man*: Cf. *Volpone*, III.4.76–8 and note. Aristotle, *Politics*, I.1260a, quotes Sophocles on silence as a female virtue even as he defines man as a 'political animal' because 'man alone of all the animals possesses speech' (I.1253a). Daw's lyric equates the male virtue of speech with sexual potency.

118–19 *consentire videtur . . . gravida*: 'Seems to consent' and 'pregnant'.

Act II. Scene 4

92–3 *paines at a muster*: Captains were regularly ordered by lord-lieutenants to muster men and arms.

94 *quarter-feast*: Sarcastic coinage from 'quarter-day', day when rents fall due.

134–5 *mushrome . . . fresh*: Insipid, but also newly sprouted; a social climber.

Act II. Scene 5

65 *French intelligences*: News of French fashions.

97 *it knighthood*: Archaic form of possessive, used derisively as baby-talk; cf. *Lear*, I.iv.214–15.

99 *Coleharbor*: Disreputable tenement on Upper Thames Street, sanctuary for debtors and vagrants.

102 *Cranes . . . Bridge-foot*: The Three Cranes on Upper Thames Street, and the Bear at the south end of London Bridge, well-known taverns.

106 *take up . . . stone jugs*: See above, note on I.4.60–64.

108 *attempting . . . browne bakers widdow*: Seducing a (brown) baker's widow, as brown bread was inferior to white.

111 *How do you call him*: A personal reference seems to be intended; cf. Nashe, 'Epistle of the Author to the Printer' in *Pierce Pennilesse*.

113–14 *Constantinople . . . Virginia*: Places where younger brothers or impoverished gentlemen might repair their fortunes.

115 *DOL TEARE-SHEET*: Prostitute at the Boar's Head Tavern in Shakespeare's *1 & 2 Henry IV*; possibly a generic name.

Act II. Scene 6

11–12 *omnia secunda . . . Saltat senex*: Latin proverb: 'all's well, the old man is leaping about'.

18 *Cum privilegio*: With authority.

24 *bonis avibus*: If the omens are good.

56 *beare-garden*: On the Bankside, centre of bull- and bear-baiting.

Act III. Scene 1

1 *pauca verba*: In few words.

13 *in rerum natura*: In the physical world, anywhere.

14 *Paris-garden*: See note on II.6.56.

21 *Poetarum Pegasus*: The poets' pegasus.

22–3 *JUPITER . . . Bull*: When he seduced Europa.

35 *three sutes . . . a yeere*: A servant's allowance.

42–3 *NED . . . STONE*: Champion bears, the latter was killed at Court in 1606.

Act III. Scene 2

3 *obnoxious, or difficill*: Offensive or troublesome (pretentious).

6 *Sic visum superis*: As decreed by those above.

7 *intimate*: Get intimate with (neologism).

8 *tosts . . . wood-cocks*: Woodcock (also slang for a fool) was served with toast and butter.

13 *Anabaptist*: Puritan sect from Germany, Switzerland, etc., which rejected infant baptism.

34 *Omnia bene*: All's well.

34 *o' the hinges*: Running smoothly.

42 *omnem movere lapidem*: Leave no stone unturned.

45 *Ad manum*: At hand.

57 *new pageant*: City entertainment for the installation of the Lord Mayor.

63 *Ware*: Twenty miles north of London, favoured for assignations.

78–9 *sir AMOROUS his feast*: Pretentious form of genitive.

Act III. Scene 3

30 *i' the main*: From the old game of Hazard; to throw the 'main' was to throw the dice and have the number that had been called come up.

76–80 *fidlers . . . London-cookes*: Indicative of the 'service economy' growing up in response to the influx of gentry to London.

83–4 *if we can . . . expostulate*: If we can continue to make Daw and Amorous compete for honour, without explicitly confronting one another.

95 *traine*: Line of gunpowder.

110–11 *decorum . . . decora*: 'Decora' is more decorous or fitting than 'decorum' because it is in plural form, to agree with the plurality of animals.

117 *ex Ovidii metamorphosi*: Out of Ovid's *Metamorphoses*.

Act III. Scene 4

27 *waterman*: Thames boatmen were known for their vociferousness.

Act III. Scene 5

21 *conduit . . . bake-house*: Centres of gossip, as people gather to fetch water and bake their bread.

23–4 *lippis & tonsoribus notum*: 'Known . . . to every barber in town and everyone with sore eyes' (Horace, *Satires*, I.vii.2–3), i.e. known to everybody.

28–9 *eaters . . . mouthes*: I.e. servants.

45 *Hymen*: Wedding.

67 *balles*: Of soap.

76 *lanternes in paper*: Commonly found in barbers' shops.

77–8 *no baud . . . bason of his*: Bawds were punished by being carted through the streets to the sound of a basin being beaten.

81–2 *eare-waxe . . . lute-string*: Barbers cleaned ears and pulled teeth; the teeth were apparently hung on strings.

96 *credit . . . combe-maker*: See above, note on I.4.60–64.

Act III. Scene 6

67–2 *skarfes . . . gloves*: Presented to guests at weddings.

102 *beginne . . . cup*: Begin to drink your health (cuckold you).

Act IV. Scene 1

23 *sadlers . . . Fleetstreet*: Like the sign of a horse-rider, outside a saddler's shop.

32–42 *Women . . . open*: Ovid, *Art of Love*, II.677–8, II.261–80.

43–8 *when they laugh . . . the face*: Ovid, *Art of Love*, II.287–90, 299–304.

52 *AMADIS . . . QUIXOTE*: Montalvo's *Amadís de Gaula* (1508) was the first and most popular of numerous printed Spanish chivalric romances, satirized by Cervantes in *Don Quixote* (1605). Jonson, while deprecating these, knew them well.

68–9 *PENELOPE . . . Ostend*: From Ovid, *Art of Love*, I.477–86; note the comic juxtaposition of Penelope and Ostend (which fell, after long siege, to the Spanish in 1604).

72–81 *Praise 'hem . . . the heart*: Ovid, *Art of Love*, I.623–4, 663–6, 673–8.

83–8 *No more . . . rascall*: Ovid, *Art of Love*, I.755–6, 763–70.

99–106 *doe you promise . . . Cheap-side*: From Ovid, *Art of Love*, I.443–4, 449–52, II.261–6.

110–13 *the houshold . . . chiefe woman*: Ovid, *Art of Love*, II.251–4, I.351–3, 383–6, 389–90.

Act IV. Scene 2

16 *Et rauco . . . cantu*: 'The horns blared out a hoarse note' (Virgil, *Aeneid*, VIII.2).

38 *Jacta est alea*: 'The die is cast', Caesar's words on crossing the Rubicon.

52 *tribus verbis*: In three words.

61 *Nunc . . . libero*: 'Now is the time to drink, now tread the earth . . .' from Horace, *Odes*, I.37, on the downfall of Cleopatra.

66 *clogdogdo*: Incomprehensible.

66–7 *foresaid beare-whelpe*: Bear-cubs were supposed to be lumps without shape; 'foresaid' means here 'forbidden'.

67 *mala bestia*: Evil beast.

73 *profecto*: Truly.

81 *mercury, and hogs-bones*: Ingredients of perfume.

81–3 *teeth . . . Silver-street*: See Martial, *Epigrams*, IX.xxxvii.1–6; the street names pun on decaying body parts: black teeth, moulting brows, grey hair.

87 *Germane clocke*: Sixteenth-century 'lantern' clocks, manufactured in Italy and South Germany, had no pendulum, and so kept time poorly in spite of their complex clockwork (they had only hour and quarter-hour hands). See *Love's Labour's Lost*, III.i.180–84: 'A woman, that is like a German clock'.

108 *Stentors*: Stentor was the 'brazen voiced' herald of the Greeks at Troy (*Iliad*, V.785–6).

109 *ill May-day*: All May-days involved festivity, but this refers to 1517, when Londoners viciously attacked foreign merchants.

109 *Gally-foist*: State barge on which the Lord Mayor travelled to Westminster to be sworn in.

126 *Ratcliffe*: Resort of seafarers, in Stepney.

127 *bona spes*: Good hope.

Act IV. Scene 3

48 *What . . . hobby-horse*: Clerimont is disgusted that Daw should boast thus.

Act IV. Scene 4

11–15 *supererogatorie . . . lowdest*: Noisy places: Westminster Hall contained law courts; cock-pits hosted cock-fights; hounds bayed at the fall of a stag; London Bridge's piers made the water roar, '*Belins*-gate' or Billingsgate was a clamorous fish market.

15–16 *play . . . target*: The sort of play Jonson despised; cf. *Every Man in his Humour*, Prologue, 11.

60–62 *Mavía . . . fanaticus*: madness . . . insanity, frenzy, or melancholic ecstasy . . . a going out of one's senses, when a man, out of melancholy, goes mad.

64–5 *Phreneticus . . . Phrenetis . . . delirium*: Frantic, frenzy, delirium.

70–71 *Shee . . . opens againe*: Libanius, *Morose Man*, 42.

75–6 *DONES philosophie*: *The Moral Philosophy of Doni*, a collection of beast fables, translated by Thomas North (1570).

95 *Sick-mans . . . wit*: Popular literature; Robert Greene, a hack writer, wrote the admonitory *Groatsworth* on his deathbed; *The Sickman's Salve* was a popular religious treatise by Thomas Becon, published seventeen times between 1561 and 1632.

122–8 *Have I . . . porcpisce*: See Libanius, *Morose Man*, 32: 'My wife is not a drunkard. That's the trouble; if she drank, she would have slept, and if she slept she might perhaps have been silent.'

148 *set me i'the nicke*: Cleaned me out.

Act IV. Scene 5

10 *upon posts*: By running errands.

28 *Guelphes . . . Ghibellines*: Papal and imperial factions feuding in Italy in the twelfth and thirteenth centuries.

41–2 *wedding . . . CENTAURES*: Famous drunken battle of the Lapiths and the Centaurs at the wedding of Pirithous (Ovid, *Metamorphoses*, XII.210ff.).

88–9 *take possession*: See *Volpone*, note to II.6.85.

96 *two-hand-sword*: Antiquated, fearsome weapon.

102 *Saint PULCHRES*: St Sepulchre's, a highly populated parish in north-west London.

153 *in snuffe*: See *Every Man in his Humour*, note to IV.2.91.

177 *A-JAX his invention*: Alluding to Harington's advocacy of the flushing water closet, *A New Discourse of a Stale Subject, called the Metamorphosis of Ajax* (1596); a 'jakes' (i.e. Ajax) was a close-stool.

209 *catastrophe*: Technical term for dramatic denouement, used by Jonson in *Magnetic Lady* (*H&S*, VI.527).

228–9 *magis . . . feriendo*: More in suffering than in doing, more in enduring than striking.

285 *sans numbre*: Without number.

302 *DAMON & PYTHIAS*: Classical exemplars of friendship.

Act IV. Scene 6

24 *set in a brake*: In an immovable facial expression; the image comes from horse-breaking.

27 *french hermaphrodite*: Possibly a general term, or a reference to Henry III of France, a notorious transvestite satirized in Thomas Arthus's *Isle des Hermaphrodites* (1605).

59–63 *but as . . . themselves*: In other words, just like the male courtiers who lack learning; the difference is, of course, that women are *supposed* to lack learning, and hence there can be no positive feminine standard.

68 *PYLADES and ORESTES*: As in IV.5.302, classical exemplars of friendship.

Act IV. Scene 7

12–16 *such a noyse . . . Proctors*: See Libanius, *Morose Man*, 6.

Act V. Scene 1

21 *Prince of Moldavia*: Stephano Janiculo, who made a bid for the hand of Lady Arbella Stuart. The passage caused trouble; see pp. 473–4.

37 *come . . . Tripoly*: Perform acrobatics; see *Epigrammes*, 115.11.

56 *great bed at Ware*: Famous bed of the Saracen's Head, Ware, made about 1580, held twelve people. See *Twelfth Night*, III.ii.47–8.

77–8 *you cannot . . . report*: Alluding to the common law judgement that sexual defamation was only materially damaging to women when they were negotiating marriage; see 'Davis v. Gardiner' (1593) *The Reports of Sir Edward Coke, knt*, 6 vols. (London: Butterworth, 1826), vol. III, p. 302.

Act V. Scene 2

22 *FIDELIA*: 'Trusty', common name for female servant in romantic fiction.

54–6 *a fame . . . visitation*: Pretend to be ill, so you can visit me.

56–7 *riddle . . . dealing*: The objection is that Mavis is too obvious, but it is hard to imagine that subtlety would be better received.

Act V. Scene 3

23–5 *these . . . glad to see you*: Libanius, *Morose Man*, 7: 'a practice, that has somehow come into our lives, of greeting people by saying, "have a happy day". I don't for the life of me see any advantage in this.'

36 *Canon-law*: Ecclesiastical law.

42–4 *My father . . . loosely*: Libanius, *Morose Man*, 6: 'My father, Members of Council, advised me always to collect and control my thoughts, and not to allow them to wander.'

55–6 *perpetuall . . . Eltham*: Famous perpetual motion machine invented by Dutchman Cornelius Drebbel on display at Eltham Palace.

64 *à divertendo*: It is derived.

91 *Nec post nuptiarum benedictionem*: Nor after the blessing of the nuptials.

95 *conditio*: Stipulation, condition.

97 *sublatae*: Annulled.

111 *cognatio spiritualis*: Spiritual kinship.

118 *crimen adulterii*: Accusation of adultery.

137 *publica honestas*: Public reputation.

137–8 *inchoata . . . affinitas*: Previous, unfinished relationship.

139 *affinitas . . . sponsalibus*: Relationship arising from betrothal.

141 *affinitas ex fornicatione*: Sexual liaison.

142 *vera affinitas*: True relationship.

143 *quae . . . matrimonio*: Than that which arises from legal marriage.

144–5 *nascitur . . . caro*: It springs from this, that through physical union two people become one flesh.

147–8 *Ita . . . generat*: Thus he is equally a true father who begets through fornication.

149 *Et vere . . . generatur*: And he truly a son who is thus begotten.

152 *si forte coire nequibis*: If you are unable to copulate.

153 *gravissimum*: Most serious.

154 *manifestam frigiditatem*: Evident frigidity.

157 *morbus . . . insanabilis*: Continuous, incurable disease.

164 *reddere debitum*: Pay his debt.

166–7 *minime apti . . . matrimonium*: Least suited to contracting marriages.

169 *matrimonia*: True-wit objects to Otter's ungrammatical 'matrimonium' (marriage) and substitutes 'matrimonia', the correct accusative plural form, i.e. 'marriages'.

172 *frigiditate praeditus*: Endowed with frigidity.

175 *uti . . . sorore*: Use a wife as a wife, may have her as a sister.

179–80 *Haec . . . retractant*: These things forbid joining in marriage, and annul marriages once made.

185–6 *prorsus . . . datam*: Utterly useless for the marriage bed . . . fulfil the promise given.

187 *convalere*: Recover.

191 *simulare . . . uxoris*: Pretend to be frigid out of hatred of his wife.

192 *adulter manifestus*: Manifest adulterer.

194 *prostitutor uxoris*: A prostitutor of his wife.

205 *libellum divortii*: Petition of divorce.

211 *in foro conscientiae*: At the bar of conscience.

214 *Exercendi potestate*: The power of putting into effect.

Act V. Scene 4

62 *de parte uxoris*: On behalf of the wife.

76 *dirimere . . . reddere*: Dissolve the contract . . . render it null and void.

104 *carnaliter*: Carnally.

116 *except . . . Knights*: A Knight proved by wager of battle to be recreant was no longer admitted on juries, or as a witness in law.

127 *virgo ante nuptias*: Virgin before marriage.

129 *ratum conjugium*: Valid marriage.

183 *He takes of Epicoenes perruke*: Jonson is here indebted to Pietro Aretino's *Il Marescalco* (1533), Act V, scene 10, in which the stablemaster's bride is revealed to be his page, Carlo, in disguise. See Introduction, p. 31.

188 *in primo gradu*: In the highest degree.

GLOSSARY

absolving acquitting

accompt account

aconite poisonous herb

activitie acrobatics

addition honorific title

adjection addition

admit allow

adscribe sign

adulterate counterfeit

advance erect

advertisement information

Aediles Roman officials charged with execution of senatorial decrees

affect wish for

affections passions

affie trust

afflicting affecting

against in preparation for

aire airing, revelation of news

alembeks vessels used in alchemical distilling

Almanacks books combining astrological charts with lists of feast and fasting days

ambuscado ambush

ampulla test-tube

amus'd puzzled

an if

angells coins worth about half of a pound

annointed covered with oils (used in the treatment of sexually transmitted diseases)

answer'd repaid

antique (a) grotesque dance; (b) grotesquely grimacing

apozemes infusions

apple-squire pimp

apprehend feel, understand

aqua-fortis nitric acid, used in etching

argue accuse, condemn

artificer artist

assassinate murderous attack

atomi atoms

bable fool's bauble (and common slang for penis)

baggatine tiny Venetian coin

ballance scales of justice

balloo Venetian ball game

band (a) hat-band; (b) collar, ruff

barbary horse

bare bareheaded

Basiliske mythical reptile with the ability to kill with a look or a breath

bastinado beating

bate abate, terminate

bayes laurel wreath awarded to honoured poets

Beare-ward trainer of bears for the baiting shows

bedpheere bedfellow

bed-staffe stick used for smoothing sheets

Bell-man night watchman, crying the hours

berlino pillory

Beshrew curse

Bet'lem Bedlam, the London asylum

biggen (a) lawyer's cap; (b) baby's bonnet

blanket toss in a blanket

blew-waiters servingmen (who wore blue coats)

bond legally binding financial transaction, often a loan

borrowed affected, assumed

bottom of pack-thred coil of rope

braverie finery

Bravo hired thug

breaches pauses

breath exercise

bride-ale wedding feast

Bride-well workhouse, later a prison

brock badger

browne bill halberd or spear, bronzed

brunt crisis

buffon buffoon

Burdello brothel

butter-teeth front teeth

by-occasion marginal matter

cabinets repositories

callet whore

callivers light muskets

canaglia scum, rascals

Candian Cretan

candle rents rents from deteriorating property

cankers sores

cannes wooden or metal drinking vessels

caract carat (of gold)

carefull gained with care, hard-earned

carpet tablecloth

carthusian austere monastic order who ate little but fish

carve make affected gestures

cassock soldier's greatcoat

cast (a) throw a dice; (b) vomit

Casuist theologian engaged with cases of conscience; often pejorative

cataplasme poultice

catch attention

cates choice foods

cautions financial safeguards

Cave beware (Latin)

cecchine Venetian coin worth a little under half a pound

censur'd judged

ceruse white cosmetic

Chaldee's astrologers (the Chaldaeans, the ruling caste in Babylon, were famed for it)

chance-medlee legal jargon for manslaughter

change reiterate

character (a) code, cipher; (b) description of a person

chartel challenge

cheapen'd haggled over

Ciarlitani charlatans

circke theatre

circumstance (a) manner of speech; (b) formality, ceremony

citie pounds, the Counters debtors' prisons

citie-wires aspiring citizens' wives who wore the wires that supported the fashionable ruff

citterne guitar, so identified with courtesans that 'citterne' became a word for one

Clarissimo Venetian patrician

clients lackeys bound by ties of patronage

climate clime, region

clot-poules leaden simpletons

clouts cloths

coacted enforced

co-adjutor fellow-writer

coaetanei of the same age

cob (a) a great (mighty) man; (b) the head of a (red) herring

cocker pamper

cock-pit exclusive theatre, the Cockpit-in-Court in Whitehall

cocted boiled

codd'ling stewing (with pun on 'cuddling')

collections conclusions

colour pretext, explanation

commented devised

compere equal

comprehends encompasses

concave vault of heaven

conceipted jesting

concent concert, harmony

confer compare

conger eels

connie-catching slang for performing a con[fidence] trick

considerative prudent

construction interpretation

Consuls annually elected magistrates, two of whom exercised supreme authority in the Roman republic

Controll rebuke

cope-man dealer

cope-stitch stitching on the edge of a cloak

coppresse green vitriol

Costar-monger apple seller

costive constipated

counter-point very opposite

Counters debtors' prisons

course (a) way of behaving; (b) round of drinks

courtings flatteries

covetously enthusiastically

coyle fuss

coystrill knave; literally, groom

crest (a) reputation (with heraldic implications); (b) head

crisped curly

crosse coin of small value

crotchets perverse whims

crude sour

cullion knave (but still bearing original sense, 'testicle')

culvering cannon

cumber burden

curious fastidious, careful

curren-but currant basket

cutis skin

cypresse thin piece of (Cyprus) linen

decline turn away, deflect

decoction boiling down to extract essences

decreed sentenced, doomed

defalke allow a reduction in prices

degenerous degenerate

degrees steps

delate report

delude make a mockery of

demeanes conducts

demi-culverings cannon

dentifrice tooth powder or paste

dependance pretext for a duel

deserts obligation

detect reveal

diaper costly fabric

dilate extensive

discernes distinguishes

disc'ple discipline

dispris'd disparaged

dissolv'd disordered

dole limited repertoire

donative gift, customarily an emperor's reward to successful troops

dors makes a fool of

doubtfull (a) indecisive, apprehensive; (b) dreaded, giving cause for apprehension

draught cesspool

drawers servers of drink

drie foot by scent and leaving no footprints

drifts schemes

droning sucking

ducking duck-hunting with spaniels

during enduring

election discrimination

encomions verses of praise

enforst instigated

engle ingle, young male prostitute

ensigns signs

entertainment (a) service; (b) gains at the state's expense

epithalamium nuptial song, or poem

erection (a) mental vigour; (b) high spirits (with sexual pun)

Ergo therefore (Latin)

errant arrant

estate greatness

even equal

event (a) outcome; (b) fate

Exchange Royal Exchange, hub of London's mercantile community

execution action of legal enforcement

exhibition allowance of money

expected speculated about

expulsed divorced, rejected

extraordinary supernumerary

faces about military command: 'about turn'

facinorous criminal

fackins rustic form of 'faith'

fact criminality

factions rebellions

faeces sediment

farder farther

far fet outlandish, imported

fasces ceremonial symbols (axes, rods) carried before senior judges

fascinated bewitched

fasting spittle saliva of a starving man

Fautors adherents

feat dainty

female copes-mate mistress

festinate quickly, promptly

fico (a) fig; (b) insulting hand gesture

fit moment, short period

Flag'd flapped

flash fop

fleering sneering

Fleming notoriously cheap and unreliable sword

flesh-flie blow-fly, which lays eggs in dead flesh

flesht encouraged by success, normally used of hunting dogs

fluxe morbid discharge

foist cheat, thief

folded embracing

fond foolish, doting

foot-clothes rich draperies for horses, sign of conspicuous wealth

footing footsteps

forced (a) obligatory; (b) clumsy, inept

fore-head countenance

foresaid predictable

foundre disable

fraile rush basket for carrying fruit

free confiding

free of admitted to a City Company

frequently in full number

fricace massage

fricatrice whore

fripperie used clothes shop

front confront

frontlesse shameless

fruition possession

fucus make-up

garb bearing, demeanour

gazets Venetian coins, worth less than a penny

gazetti news-sheets

gelt gelded

Gemonies the Gemonian steps, a dumping ground for the bodies of the condemned

Genius attendant spirit

gigglot wanton woman

ging gang

girds taunts

glebe soil

godwits marsh birds, a delicacy

gor-crow carrion crow

gorget armour for the throat

gossip godfather

grace favour

graces degrees

grafted with foreign stock, i.e. cuckolded

gravida pregnant (Latin)

griefe illness

gripe grasp

grist strong beer, literally crushed malt

grogran's fabrics of mohair and wool mixed with silk

ground source

guacum drug extracted from the guaiacum tree

guilder (a) Dutch coin worth only a few pence; (b) those who disguised base metal as gold; (c) one who gilds (for adornment)

halberdeirs officers carrying halberds (spears)

hammes thighs

hang-by's hangers-on

hanger loop in a belt from which a sword hung

hang-man cut of an appearance that merits hanging

HANNIBAL malapropism for 'cannibal'

hants haunts

harpyies avaricious birds with the faces of women

Harrots bookes books of heraldry and illustrious genealogies

Hau'-boyes early type of oboe

havings accomplishments

hecatombes public sacrifices to the gods

heicfar heffer (abusive term for a wife)

height geographical latitude

HELIOTROPE a plant which turns constantly towards the sun

Hight called

hoddie-doddie cuckold

hoigh small trading vessel

honested honoured

horne (a) cuckold; (b) horn-book, a spelling primer

Hospitall Christ's Hospital, a school for foundlings

hough intentionally archaic form of 'ho!'

huishers ushers

hum-drum mediocrity

humorous capricious

huswife hussy

Imbroccata a thrust over an opponent's weapon (Spanish)

impaire injury

impeach damage

impertinent irrelevant, prolix

industrie deliberation, intent

inforce emphasize, stress

ingag'd irretrievably committed

ingine (a) intelligence (from the Latin '*ingenium*'); (b) contrivance, scheme

inlarge exaggerate, embellish

In sadnesse seriously

insinuate ingratiate oneself

instructed invested

instrument legal contract

interess'd concerned, affected by

intergatories interrogatories, written legal questions

intrench mark, disfigure

jarres conflicts

jealous suspicious

jennet fiery Spanish horse

jolt-head blockhead

joviall (a) merry; (b) Jove-like (lustful)

joyn'd patten become a shareholder

julebes medicinal drinks

july-flowres gillyflowers (clove-scented pinks)

kind nature

knacke sharp crack

Lance-knights mercenaries armed with lances

lawne fine linen

Lazaretto plague or quarantine hospital

leagure siege

leape jump on (sexually)

leash set of three

left-handed sinister, ill omened

lets obstacles

levin yeast

leystalls dung-heaps

liberall generous

liburnian Croatians, renowned for their stature

lift raise an arm threateningly

light window

lightly usually

limber supple

linstock forked stick holding the flame by which a cannon was fired

liv'res predecessor of the French franc, and worth almost the same

lose loose

lotium stale urine, used as a setting gel by barbers

mack By the mass (oath)

Madge-howlet owl

magazines storehouses

Magistrall of a special formula

mal-caduco falling sickness, epilepsy

malepert impudently

mallowes medicinal herbs, supposed to relieve hunger

mandrake poisonous plant of anthropomorphic shape

manhood existence

mankind human feeling

mannage management, exercise

mannikin diminutive person, puppet-like

marie indeed

marke reputation

marks (a) plague or pox marks; (b) coins worth ⅔ of an English pound

marle marvel, wonder

MASS' master

meant perceived

mere absolute

meretrix prostitute (Latin)

messe meal for four persons

mettall glass in its molten state

mimick burlesque actor

mince make light of

minion lover, invariably illicit

misc'line miscellaneous, jumbled (from Latin, *ludi miscelli*)

mithridate antidote to poison

moccinigo, muccinigo Venetian coin

moile mule

Montanto upward sword thrust

moother hysteria

more greater

moscadelli muscatel wine

motion puppet show

motives passions

motley the apparel of fools

motte motto (French)

moyetie a half, or a portion

moyle mule

mulct fine

mummia medicine made from mummified flesh

MUSSE mouse, term of endearment

nation sect

naturall uncontrived

neere nearer

neesing sneezing

nere never

nomenclator announcer of guests (Latin), with pun on 'clatter'

nonage youth

nones nonce, occasion

notes marks of infamy

nothing meaningless chatter

now current

noyse band of musicians

nupson simpleton

oblique malicious

obnoxious liable, prone

observe treat with obsequious reverence

obstancy legal opposition

obstreperous clamorous
office performance
officious zealous, dutiful
Once at some time
oppilations obstructions
ordinarie tavern offering fixed-price
    meals
orient rare, fine
ostería inn
over walk all over
painter cosmetician
painted pretended
parcels items
pargets plasters (literally) with make-up
parted separately given
partiall gratuitously unjust
parting sharing
pash dash
passada forward thrust
passengers passers-by
pathick 'passive' partner in acts of
    sodomy (from Latin *patior*, 'to
    suffer')
peculiar private
Pedarii senators of inferior rank
peec'd mended, patched up
pensioner hireling
perboyl'd thoroughly boiled
period end
perplex'd intricate
person physical appearance
pest'ling crushing
petarde bomb
petrionel pistol
phant'sie imagination
philtre aphrodisiac
pick-tooth toothpick
pind tormented
piscaria fish market
pismier ant
pistolet valuable Spanish coin, regarded
    as good currency anywhere,
    especially Italy

playse puckered
podex rump
poesie posy, verse inscribed on a ring
Poetasters paltry poets
Point (a) appoint; (b) conclusion
politie (a) society; (b) policy
politiques schemers
poll'd plundered
pomatum skin cream
pome-citrons limes
porcpisces porpoises
portico colonnade
portion dowry
post messenger
posts running errands
potlings drinking companions
pottle half a gallon
poulder powder
poulters poulterers
poynard dagger
practice intrigue
Praesto ready
Praetors Consuls as leaders of the army
precise puritanical
precisian puritan
presage portents
present immediate
prest conscripted
prevent anticipate
pride of bloud sexual appetite
primero card game resembling poker
private personal interest
prize fencing match
procuratia residence of the Procurators
    (governing oligarchy) of Venice
prodigie ominous portent
produc't extended
profecto truly
prolepse's anachronisms
Promptly readily
proper handsome
propertie (a) instrument, tool;
    (b) function

protested avowed

provant of standard issue, literally 'provender'

prove endure, pit oneself against, test

providing anticipating

punke whore

punto (a) sword thrust; (b) instant (Italian)

purse-net net for catching rabbits

pyed gawdy, vulgar

quarter-feast meal celebrating each of the four legal terms in the calendar

quarter-looke sidelong glance

quarters (a) quarter chimes of a clock; (b) quarter-blows (fencing)

queasie hazardous

queene-apple the queening, a red apple

quit requite, repay

rack'd extracted by force (from the torture)

ragion di stato reasons of state

ranknesse exuberance

rapt carried forcefully

reaching striving to apply to

rector governor

Rectresse governor (female)

Reformados disbanded soldiers

resolve melt, evaporate

resolved slackened

respects considerations

rests arrests

retricato possibly a garbled version of the Italian *rintricato*, entangled

reversion inheritance

Romagnia sweet wine

rosaker a poison

roses fashionable adornments on shoes

rotchet red gurnet fish

rounds rungs of a ladder

rouse alcoholic toast

rout rabble

rushes rush leaves, used as floor coverings

sacke sweet wine

saffi low-ranking policemen

salt (a) wanton, lecherous; (b) seasoned; (c) salt-cellar

sanitâ Venetian health authority

sassafras dried bark, recently introduced for medicinal purposes

saver one who avoids losses (from gambling)

scald scabby

scartoccios wrapping paper for spices

scotomy dizziness, with poor vision

scroyles scoundrels

Scrutineo important Venetian law-court

'Sdeynes 'God's deynes' (dignesse, i.e. dignity)

sear cauterize, stem bleeding

second (a) assistant; (b) second choice; (c) reinforcement

Senators members of the Senate, the legal and administrative assembly of Rome, consisting originally of representatives elected by patricians, and later of former holders of high office

sensive (a) of the senses; (b) capable of feeling

seige excrement

serene mist, once believed poisonous

sess'd assessed (for the provision of soldiers for the nation's army)

sewer head waiter at aristocratic banquets

Sforzato galley slave

shambles slaughterhouse

shape (a) costume; (b) appearance

shifts (a) subterfuges; (b) shirts

shittles shuttles (weaving)

shoo-thrids shoelaces

shove-groat shilling coin used for the game of shove-ha'penny

side rival

signe inn-sign

silly simple

simple herb

S'lid 'By God's lid', a common oath

S'light 'By God's light', a common oath

slight sleight (of hand)

slip pass over, omit

S'lud 'By God's blood', a common oath

snuff a huff, sulk

sod boiled

soldados soldiers (Spanish)

sols French coins of little value

sophisticated adulterated

Soria Syria

sort pack, pejorative word for company

sound measure of depth or profundity

spiced precise, fastidious

Spittle hospital, associated with the treatment of venereal disease

spoile purse

squibbe exploding firework

squire square

staine disgrace

stale cheap prostitute, used as a decoy by thieves

start flinch

state (a) dignity of bearing; (b) needs of state

staunch restrained

stewes brothels

stoccata thrust (Spanish)

stock-fish cod

stomach anger

stomacher garment worn over the breast

stopple plug for water jug

store remainder

strappado Venetian torture involving the hoisting up of the victim by a rope, with hands bound behind

sublimate mercuric chloride, a strong poison

subtle delicate, cunning

suffering humble, submissive

sulphure lightning

suspect suspicion

swabbers louts

swinge beat

take undertake

take up borrow, purchase

target shield

tell count

Temper equanimity

terme period when the law courts were in session

terra-ferma Venetian possessions on the Italian mainland

teston sixpence

tightly soon

tilt-feather plume in a jousting helmet

Titivilitium a worthless object (Latin)

Toledo renowned Spanish sword

tonnells nostrils

touch'd slandered or libelled

translated transformed

travaile in undertake

treasure treasury

tremor-cordia palpitations

trencher plate

Tritons sea gods who sounded conch shells

triumph formal celebration to honour a conqueror

triumphed conquered

trunke speaking tube

tumbrell-slop breeches, as wide as a tumbrel (cart)

turkise turquoise, a precious stone thought to change colour according to the health of the wearer

twice sod twice boiled, tasteless

tyres attire, fashions

tyring-house actors' dressing room

unbrac'd i.e. disgraced, exposed

uncarnate bodiless, a perversion of 'incarnate'

uncouth strange, unfamiliar

Under-taker patron, guarantor, sponsor

under-worketh contrives secretly

unequal unjust

unkind unnatural

unperfect suspended

unquento ointment

unquit undischarged

untrain'd unready, unused

upsolve resolve, explain

use practice

utter offer for sale

vegetous vigorous

vellets velvet hangings

venne archaic (French) term for thrust

venter speculative financial enterprise

vents issues out of, is published of

vernaculous scurrilous, low-bred

vertigine dizziness

vervin branches used to decorate Roman altars

viaticum expenses for the journey

visor mask

vitiated (a) violated; (b) corrupted

want lack

warn'd summoned

water-bearer professional water carriers fetched water to prosperous households in London

weale state

welkin sky

whimsey whirling

whiniling whimpering

wind-fucker kestrel

winke close

wittoll willing or acquiescent cuckold

wood crowd, forest

wood-cocks fools (easily caught)

worry injure or kill (from bear-baiting)

wreake vengeance

wrest (a) distort; (b) in adequately represent

writhen contorted

wusse of course (variant of *iwis*, 'certainly')

Zany comic assistant

LIST OF HISTORICAL AND MYTHOLOGICAL NAMES

ACRISIUS Father of Danae; he was unable to prevent the seduction of his daughter, when Jove assumed the form of a shower of gold.

AESCULAPIUS God of healing; killed by Zeus for his presumption in attempting to revive a dead patient.

AESON Jason's father, whose youth was restored by Medea's magic arts.

AETHALIDES Son of Mercury, herald to the Argonauts, and possessed of perfect and everlasting memory.

ANTONIUS Mark Antony, a distinguished cavalry officer and aide to Julius Caesar, who formed a ruling triumvirate with Lepidus and Octavian after the emperor's assassination. Suetonius appears to quote from Antony's published writings, but these 'letters' are lost.

APICATA Wife of Sejanus; bore him three children, was divorced and took her own life after his murder.

APICIUS Marcus Gavius Apicius, writer of a treatise on extravagant cooking; so notorious was his self-indulgence that his name became proverbial for gluttony.

APOLLO Phoebus Apollo, god of the sun, youth and the arts.

ARCUS Son of Calisto, eponymous king of Arcadia; he almost killed his mother when she had been turned into a bear, and it was as hunted and hunter that both were represented in the star forms they eventually became.

ARETINE Pietro Aretino (1492–1556), Italian poet whose works, especially the 'Sonnets of Lust' he issued to accompany the designs of Giulio Romano in 1524, became the most notorious erotic publications of the century.

ARTEMIDORUS Second-century AD Ephesian who wrote a massive work on how the future is revealed in dreams.

ASPASIA Mistress of the great Athenian statesman Pericles; neither an Athenian herself nor legally married, she was unsuccessfully slandered as a prostitute.

ATLAS Perseus transformed Atlas into an African mountain whose summit supported the heavens; made to bear the weight of the universe on his shoulders as a punishment for assisting a Giants' rebellion against the gods.

BIBACULUS First-century BC Roman poet, who attracted the derision of both Horace and Quintilian.

BODINE Jean Bodin (1530–96), French political theorist, advocate of religious toleration; his *Six Books of the Commonwealth* was much admired in English intellectual circles at the end of the sixteenth century.

BROUGHTON Rabbinical scholar and puritan, author of voluminous, learned but obscure theological works.

BRUTUS Marcus Junius Brutus (85–42 BC), most principled of Julius Caesar's assassins who committed suicide after his defeat by Antony and Octavius at Philippi.

CALISTO Seduced by Jupiter, thus provoking the jealousy of Juno, who turned her first into a bear, and then into the constellation Ursa Major.

CASSIUS Cassius Longinus (d. 42 BC), Epicurean and irascible assassin of Julius Caesar, who committed suicide after his and Brutus' defeat at Philippi.

CATO Marcus Porcius Cato Uticensis (95–46 BC), republican opponent of Julius Caesar, ally of Pompey, and a Stoic whose theatrical suicide became the archetypical act of integrity in the face of tyranny.

CATULLUS First-century BC Roman poet, celebrated for his innovative love poetry but also a persistent if witty detractor of Julius Caesar.

CICERO Marcus Tullius Cicero (106–43BC), Athenian-educated Roman statesman and orator. He approved but did not participate in the assassination of Julius Caesar; and wrote a republican defence of Cato, to which the emperor replied with a two-volume denunciation; both works are lost. He was strongly opposed to the rule of Mark Antony, who had him proscribed and eventually killed.

CIECO *di Hadria* Luigi Groto (1541–85), prolific dramatist whose works include an early version of the Romeo and Juliet story.

CINNAMUS A surgeon-barber praised by Martial (*Epigrams*, VI.lxiv.24–6) for his skill in removing brands (stigmata).

CONTARENE Cardinal Contarini, whose treatise on the Venetian constitution had been translated into English by Lewis Lewkenor in 1599.

CORIDON Generic name for (invariably stupid) shepherd.

CRATES Fourth-century BC Greek philosopher, of the school of Diogenes, whose rejection of civilization earned him the title Cynic (Greek = dog).

ERYCINE Venus, so-called after her temple at Eryx, Sicily; she deceived her husband Vulcan with Mars, god of war.

EUPHORBUS Courageous Trojan who wounded the Greek Patroclus but was subsequently killed by Menelaus; Pythagoras claimed to have been Euphorbus in a past life.

EUROPA Jupiter seduced her by adopting the guise of a playful bull, and then carried her on his back to Crete.

FOREMAN, Doctor Astrologer and quack, alleged to have supplied aristocratic women (including Lady Essex) with potions which either aroused or quenched the sexual ardour of their partners.

FURNIUS Member of the Agrippina faction, condemned for adultery with one of her relations.

GALEN Second century AD physician, who expounded the theory of 'humours', and whose dominance of medical doctrine was only beginning to be challenged in Jonson's time.

GARAGANTUA Larger than life hero of Rabelais' comic masterpiece *Gargantua and Pantagruel*.

GONSWART Probably Cornelius Hamsfort, chief physician at the Danish court from whence James's new queen, Anne, had recently arrived.

GORGON One of the three female monsters of classical mythology whose gaze turned onlookers to stone.

GUERRINI Giovanni Battista Guarini, sixteenth-century Italian dramatist and influential author of the first theoretical defence of tragicomedy.

HARPOCRATES Egyptian sun god, often represented with his finger in his mouth and thus mistakenly taken for the god of silence; also supposed to have inherited the club of Hercules.

HERMOTIMUS Ancient Greek philosopher whose soul, separated from his body, was reputed to have both travelled widely and prophesied.

HIPPOCRATES Fifth-century BC Greek physician who invented the theory of 'humours'; widely and long regarded as the paragon of medical integrity; works (often dubiously) attributed to him were still of the utmost importance in Jonson's day.

HOLOFERNES Archetypal tyrant of the apocryphal book of Judith.

JUSTINIAN The Emperor Justinian I of Constantinople organized the first codification of Roman law; the resultant legal texts consequently bear his name.

LINCEUS One of the Argonauts, famed for his keen sight.

LIVIUS, TITUS Livy, Roman and republican historian (*c.* 60 BC–*c.* 12 AD); of his massive history of Rome, roughly three-quarters (including the books concerning the Civil War involving Pompey and Caesar) did not survive into the Renaissance.

LOLLIA PAULINA Wife (briefly) to the Emperor Caligula, heiress to a vast fortune which her grandfather accumulated through extortion in Rome's eastern provinces.

LULLY Raymond Lull, thirteenth-century Spanish mystic, to whom influential alchemical treatises were attributed in the Renaissance.

LYGDUS According to Tacitus, a eunuch who poisoned Drusus; it is Jonson's addition that he should have been Drusus' 'cup-bearer', or sexual slave.

MACHIAVEL Niccolo Machiavelli (1469–1527), political theorist and historian; enduring bogeyman on the English stage because of his alleged ruthlessness and atheism.

MARY AMBREE Heroine of a popular ballad, reputed to have disguised herself as a man to take part in the siege of Ghent in 1584.

MEDEA Sometime wife of Jason, who magically restored her husband's aged father to youthfulness.

MEDUSA The gorgon (see above) who was slayed by Perseus; her hair consisted of snakes and anyone who looked at her would turn to stone.

MONTAGNIE Michel de Montaigne (1533–92), French philosopher whose hugely influential *Essayes* had received their first English translation (by John Florio) in 1603.

NESTOR Oldest and wisest of the Greeks who besieged Troy; Juvenal (*Satires*, VI. 326) renders him as made impotent by a hernia.

NOMENTACK Indian chief from Virginia, brought to England as a hostage between 1608 and 1609.

OEDIPUS Legendary king of Thebes, who was disgraced for his incestuous relationship with his mother, Jocasta, and the unwitting murder of his father, Laius. The story was famously dramatized by Sophocles and later adapted by Seneca. Also known for solving the riddle of the Sphinx and thereby ridding Thebes of a devastating plague.

PAGONIANUS Sextus Paconianus, a one-time praetor; a notorious spy for Sejanus who later turned informer but was eventually strangled in prison for writing verses against Tiberius.

PALLAS Motherless, she sprang fully armed from the head of her father Zeus to become the goddess of wisdom, war, justice, the liberal arts and handicrafts; she carried a shield which reflected the snaky head of the gorgon, Medusa; also known as Minerva and Athene.

PARACELSUS Flamboyant Swiss medical researcher of the sixteenth century, alleged to have kept his experimental medicines in the hollow pommel of his sword.

PASIPHAE Made to fall in love with a bull by Poseidon, a union from which the Minotaur was born.

PENELOPE Wife to Odysseus and archetype of marital fidelity who frustrated her many suitors by insisting that she would not remarry until she had completed a woven shroud. During the ten-year period of her husband's return voyage, she would spend each night unravelling the shroud, ensuring that it would never be finished.

PENTHESILEA Amazon queen, famed for her slaying of Greeks in the Trojan War; she was eventually killed by Achilles, who nonetheless fell in love with her corpse.

PERSIUS Roman satirist and Stoic.

PHLEGON A horse of the sun who drew Apollo's chariot.

PHOEBUS Alternative name for Apollo in his manifestation as sun god.

PLINIE Pliny the younger, first-century AD Roman intellectual, famed for the ten books of his letters.

PLUTARCH Greek philosopher and historian (AD 45–120), renowned for both his essays (*Moralia*) and his *Lives*.

POLLIO, ASINIUS Addressee of Virgil's 'Messianic' *Eclogue* IV, friend of Augustus and of the poets Catullus and Horace, and founder of Rome's first public library; both Suetonius and Plutarch were indebted to his (now lost) history of the Civil Wars.

POMPEI Pompey (106–48 BC), Roman general, administrator and consul; tarnished Republican hero who became involved in conspiracies against Julius Caesar and whose eventual defeat at Pharsalia was taken by many, including the poet Lucan, to herald the collapse of political freedom.

POMPONATIUS Minor sixteenth-century scholar.

PRISCA Mutilia Prisca, mistress of Sejanus' lackey Julius Postumus; she had great influence over the Augusta, whose jealousy she used against Agrippina (her granddaughter by marriage).

CLAUDIA PULCHRA A cousin of Agrippina, condemned for adultery with Furnius, and for casting spells against and attempting to poison Tiberius. Her accuser, Afer, also prosecuted her son, Quinctilian Varus.

PYRRHUS Early Greek philospher said (in *The Lives of the Eminent Philosophers* of Diogenes Laertius) to be a fisherman.

PYTHAGORAS Sixth-century BC ascetic, mathematician, philosopher, who originated the doctrine of metempsychosis, or transmigration of souls.

RHADAMANTH Son of Zeus and Europa, whose just life was posthumously acknowledged by his being made a judge of the dead.

SACROVIR Leader of a serious rebellion against Rome amongst the Aedui and other tribes in southern Gaul; defeated by Silius in 21 AD, he committed suicide.

SEMIRAMIS Beautiful warrior queen of Assyria, famous for promiscuity; she may have murdered her husband, and in order to retain power she impersonated her son, for whom she also developed an incestuous and ultimately fatal attraction. She was also supposed to have built the hanging gardens of Babylon.

SILANUS Governor of Asia, accused (probably rightly) of extortion. Tacitus (*Annals*, iii.65–9) cited him as a typical victim of Senatorial persecution orchestrated by Tiberius, but also as the recipient of a rare gesture of mercy; Silanus was banished to the relatively pleasant island of Cythnos (not Cithera, the reading of the sixteenth-century texts of Tacitus Jonson followed), instead of the uninhabited Gyaros.

SINON He persuaded the Trojans to accept as a gift the wooden horse from which the Greeks emerged to destroy the city; his name became a byword for treachery.

SPINOLA Contemporary commander of the Catholic forces in the Netherlands.

SPORUS A minion who was castrated, dressed in women's clothing and even publicly married by the Emperor Nero.

SYMANCHA Minor sixteenth-century scholar.

SYMMACHUS Fourth-century AD scholar, noted for the letters he exchanged with the emperors he served.

TYPHOEUS A monster with a hundred serpentine heads whose revolt against the gods frightened them into assuming the forms of birds and animals; but he was eventually crushed by Jupiter.

URGULANIA A highly influential favourite of the Augusta.

VATABLUS Minor sixteenth-century scholar.

VERTUMNUS God of natural growth and fecundity, capable of metamorphosing himself at will; the Romans came to associate him with all forms of change, including the seasons.

READ MORE IN PENGUIN

RENAISSANCE DRAMATISTS

The *Renaissance Dramatists* series provides scrupulously prepared texts with original spelling and punctuation, edited by leading scholars with extensive explanatory notes. The General Editor is John Pitcher.

Published or forthcoming:

The Spanish Tragedie by Thomas Kyd, ed. Emma Smith
includes the anonymous *The First Part of Jeronimo*

Plays and Poems by George Chapman, ed. Jonathan Hudston
includes *All Fooles, Bussy D'Ambois, The Widdowes Teares* and a selection of poems

Three Tragedies by Renaissance Women, ed. Diane Purkiss
includes *The Tragedie of Iphigeneia*, by Jane, Lady Lumley; *The Tragedie of Antonie*, by Mary, Countess of Pembroke; and *The Tragedie of Mariam*, by Elizabeth Cary

Volpone and Other Plays by Ben Jonson, ed. Lorna Hutson
includes *Every Man in his Humour*; *Sejanus, His Fall*; *Volpone, or the Foxe*; and *Epicoene, or the Silent Woman*

The Malcontent and Other Plays by John Marston, ed. David Pascoe
includes *The History of Antonio and Mellida*; *Antonios Revenge*; *The Malcontent*; *The Dutch Courtezan*; and *Parasitaster, or the Fawne*

A New Way to Pay Old Debts and Other Plays by Philip Massinger, ed. Richard Rowland
includes *The Roman Actor, Believe as you List, The Maid of Honour* and *A New Way to Pay Old Debts*

The Complete Plays by Christopher Marlowe, ed. Frank Romany